# DID YOU KNOW?

***Resting place*** *A parrotfish, found in tropical seas, lies in its 'sleeping bag' – a protective cocoon it constructs out of mucus before retiring for the night.*

# DID YOU KNOW?

New insights into a world that is full of
astonishing stories and astounding facts

Reader's Digest

Published by The Reader's Digest Association Limited
London · New York · Montreal · Sydney · Cape Town

# DID YOU KNOW?

Originally published by
The Reader's Digest Association Limited, London

**DID YOU KNOW?** was conceived by Reader's Digest
and was edited and designed by Dorling Kindersley Limited in conjunction with
The Reader's Digest Association Limited.

| | |
|---|---|
| *Project Editor* | **Douglas Amrine** |
| *Senior Art Editor* | **Arthur Torr-Brown** |
| *Senior Editors* | **Reg Grant** |
| | **James Harrison** |
| | **W. McDonald** |
| | **Lesley Riley** |
| *Art Editor* | **Kevin Williams** |
| *Assistant Editors* | **Susie Behar** |
| | **Monika Cunnington** |
| | **Sean Moore** |
| *Editorial Research* | **Rupert Thomas** |
| *Picture Research* | **Frances Vargo** |
| *Editorial Director* | **Jackie Douglas** |
| *Contributors* | **Christopher Cooper** |
| | **Jonathan Elphick** |
| | **Brian Innes** |
| *Editorial Consultants* | **Peter Brookesmith** |
| | **John May** |

ISBN 0-276-42014-4

Printed in the United States of America

# Contents

Chapter 4:

# THE WONDERS OF WILDLIFE

Chapter 5:

# MIND AND BODY

Chapter 6:

# SIGNS, WONDERS AND WORDS

Chapter 9:

# TRAVELLING WAYS

Chapter 10:

# MASTERS OF THEIR ART

# chapter one

# The
# FRONTIERS
## *of*
# KNOWLEDGE

HOW COLD is cold? In human experience, temperature has no bounds: today may be bitterly cold, but tomorrow could be even colder – there seems to be no limit to how cold it can get. But scientists now know that a lower limit to temperature does exist: -273°C (-460°F) (*page 34*). Temperature is a measure of the speed at which molecules are moving, and at that temperature all motion stops. This is just one of the basic principles that dictate the workings of our Universe. The discovery and codifying of such principles underpins all scientific progress.

# MASTER MINDS

### Science began – and continued – with the strangest ideas

ARISTOTLE – a Macedonian logician and philosopher who worked in Athens in the 4th century BC – is known today as the 'father of science'. His interests ranged over the entire natural and human world, including art, metaphysics and ethics, and he created a system for classifying living things similar to that in use today. Yet some of his theories were often wildly inaccurate.

He described more than 500 species of animal, and dissected over 50, yet believed that the brain was a device for cooling the blood. He also thought that meat would spontaneously generate maggots; that a heavy body falls faster than a light one; and that earthquakes were caused by air trying to escape from the Earth. All these errors were based on logic and observation – and also on a profound misunderstanding of the properties governing the physical world.

Aristotle's theory about earthquakes, for instance, was a result of the belief that all matter was made up of a combination of earth, water, air and fire. He could see for himself that 'earthen' matter sank in water and other liquids; air bubbled up through liquids; fire rose up into the air.

Aristotle reasoned that each element had its particular quality of greater or lesser 'gravity' or 'levity'. Fire, which leaps up through the air, had the most levity. Earth, the heaviest

***Tutor of royalty*** *About 343 BC, Aristotle (right), then the leading philosopher and scientist in Greece, was commissioned to prepare the young Alexander the Great for his future role as king of Macedonia.*

element, had the most gravity; and gravity was greatest at the centre of the planet, which was also the centre of the cosmos. To explain how the stars floated above the Earth, Aristotle proposed a fifth element, the ether, which had no gravity. He was so sure that his theories were correct that he made his biggest mistake of all. He scorned the idea of Democritus that the whole cosmos was made up of tiny particles, called atoms.

### Putting theory to the test

Aristotle could reach such conclusions, which seem so odd to us, because it never occurred to him – or any other ancient Greek, for that matter – to test a theory by experiment. It was not until the 17th century, when Francis Bacon introduced the idea, that scientists began to accept a theory only after experiments had proved it to be true.

But Aristotle is rightly called the 'father of science' because he established the principle that a theory was valid only if derived logically from observations of the real world. And that is the foundation of all science.

***Prolific writer*** *Aristotle wrote several hundred books covering every branch of learning – from drama to biology. Regrettably, very few have survived.*

# THE OTHER SIDE OF ALCHEMY
*Was it a search for gold – or something more startling?*

THROUGH the centuries, the dream of the medieval alchemists was to discover how to turn lead and other 'base' metals into gold. If that seems an ambitious aim, it pales beside the prize the alchemists hoped to win as a result – immortality itself.

Their initial quest for gold was based on the ancient idea that everything consists of different proportions of just four basic substances – earth, water, air and fire. The alchemists believed that it ought to be possible to adjust the proportions of the elements that made up lead by chemical means so that it turned into gold. Their experiments were concerned with finding the substance – which they dubbed the 'philosophers' stone' – that, when added to lead, would cause this astonishing transmutation to take place.

### Levels of meaning

However, descriptions of these experiments are so laden with obscure metaphors that it is easy to interpret them on more than one level. One text, for example, says: 'Ascend with the greatest sagacity from Earth to Heaven, and then descend again to the Earth, and unite together the power of things superior and things inferior . . ..'

This could be understood as a reference to combining certain chemicals. But it was also understood to be describing a parallel process of spiritual self-purification. As they worked through their experiments, alchemists believed that they would gradually refine 'base' materials to their purest essence – which would be the philosophers' stone. At the same time, they would liberate the soul from the 'base' body. The substance that could create gold from lead would therefore confer

spiritual perfection and immortality on the alchemist himself. And in achieving this godlike condition, the alchemist would become a hermaphrodite.

*Reading the signs* Two alchemists study the contents of a glass vial used to distil chemical substances during their constant search for the philosophers' stone.

## DID YOU KNOW..?

*THE LAST OCCASION on which professional scientists took any serious notice of an alchemist's claim to have turned lead into gold occurred in 1783. The Royal Society in London called on one of its Fellows, James Price, to show how he had achieved the alchemists' dream. But Price failed to repeat his successful experiment and, before the eyes of three colleagues, drank prussic acid and died.*

## ECCENTRIC GENIUSES

BOTH ISAAC NEWTON and Albert Einstein were complex and contradictory characters. Despite his powerfully analytical mind and his astonishing mathematical genius, Newton held many strange beliefs. To the end of his life, he studied alchemy and the transmutation of metals, that is, how to turn lead into gold. He wrote many curious manuscripts concerning the end of the world and the prophecies of Daniel, which so embarrassed his friends when they discovered them after his death that these writings remained hidden for years.

As a child, Albert Einstein had a poor memory and spent much of his time building card towers or solving jigsaw puzzles. Einstein stopped going to school when he was 15; the next year, he failed the entrance examination to the Zurich Polytechnic. When he finally entered the Polytechnic, he hated learning so much that, he later claimed, he lost all interest in science for 12 months. Scraping through his final examinations, he worked as a tutor and then as an examiner of patents in Bern.

It was not a promising start for the greatest scientist of the 20th century. Yet, only three years after taking up his job in Bern, Einstein's now famous Special Theory of Relativity was published.

# A WEIGHT OFF THE MIND

*The geniuses who put the planets in their places*

TWO SCIENTISTS have had a greater influence on our understanding of the Universe than any other: Isaac Newton and Albert Einstein. Both were brilliant mathematicians, and both became fascinated by the problem of gravity.

In 1687, Newton published his great work, *Principia Mathematica*. He showed, for the first time, that gravity was a force – and that the laws governing gravity both caused apples to fall from trees, and dictated the paths of the Moon around the Earth and of the planets around the Sun. To do this he virtually invented a new mathematics: differential calculus.

### Primacy of Newton

For more than two centuries, no one questioned Newton's laws of motion. Scientists saw the Universe as a great machine, rather like clockwork, in which the movement of every part was directly connected to the movement of every other part, even down to the motions of individual atoms. The whole machine itself seemed to be like a ship floating down a smoothly flowing river of time. And then came Einstein.

In 1905, Einstein's Special Theory of Relativity proposed concepts that were totally different from Newton's. They seemed, indeed, to defy common sense and everyday experience.

### It's all relative

Using extremely sophisticated mathematics, Einstein showed that the Universe is not like clockwork at all. The dimensions of things are not fixed, and even time can move at different rates. The appearance of an event or object will change entirely if the circumstances in which it is observed are altered radically enough.

For example, Einstein's theory says that, if a person on Earth could measure and weigh a rocket passing by at half the speed of light, it would seem to be about half as long and twice as heavy as it did to an astronaut inside it. To the astronaut, the Earth would seem to be passing *him* by, and to be shaped like an egg – and would also seem to be twice as heavy as it seems to us.

*Simple at heart A scientist of international renown, Albert Einstein, here shown in his study shortly before his death in 1955, preferred to lead a quiet, unglamorous life.*

And to each observer, the other's clocks would seem to be greatly speeded up.

In everyday situations, however, these differences are not detectable, and Newton's laws remain accurate enough. But Einstein's theories hold true for the behaviour of the tiny particles inside atoms, as well as on the astronomical scale.

From his discoveries that neither time nor space is an absolute quantity, and that they are intimately connected, Einstein devised his General Theory of Relativity. This, published in 1916, contained his most radical departure from Newton. He suggested that gravity results from the 'bending' of both space and time that occurs near large bodies (such as stars and planets) as a result of their mass. Before he was 37 years old, Einstein had swept aside the Newtonian concept of the Universe as a simple piece of machinery and introduced ideas that made it possible to unravel the secrets of both astronomy and the atom.

# IMPOSSIBLE QUESTIONS
*What is the sound of one hand clapping?*

ONE DAY, a master of Zen Buddhism was strolling by the riverside. There he saw what should have been an astonishing, miraculous sight. One of his disciples was walking on the water.

'What are you doing?' cried the master. 'Crossing the river,' called back his disciple. 'Come with me,' ordered the Zen master, and together they walked a great distance in the heat of the day until they found a ferryman. As they climbed into the boat, the master said pointedly: 'This is the way to cross a river.'

This brief tale is typical of the apparent nonsensicality that permeates Zen Buddhism, which was introduced into China by the Indian monk Bodhidharma in the year AD 520. Of all mankind's means of investigating what really lies beneath the surface of the everyday world, Zen seems the least logical and the least like science. The object of the Zen school of Buddhism is to go beyond words and ideas in order that the original insight of the Buddha may be brought back to life and true enlightenment, as distinct from doctrine, experienced.

### Learning by example

A Zen master does not teach his disciples. They simply attend him, hoping to discover the secret of his serenity and the spontaneity with which he acts. That moment of enlightenment is known as *satori*. There is no set way to achieve it, but when *satori* is attained the disciple knows and – not in his reason but in his intuition – understands.

### Conundrum

Perhaps the most bewildering aspect of Zen is the *koan*: a problem with no intellectual solution. If there is an answer, it has no logical connection with the question. 'What is the Buddha?' asks one *koan*, and the answer that Zen masters have appreciated most is: 'Three pounds of flax.' Asked where all the Buddhas came from, one master somewhat mysteriously replied: 'The East Mountain walks over the water.'

Some *koans* involve logical impossibilities: 'What is the sound of one hand clapping?', for example, or 'When the many are reduced to the one, to what is the one to be reduced?' or even 'Walk while riding on a donkey.'

### Underlying philosophy

But behind Zen's mask of unreason lies a profoundly sane philosophy. One of the underlying purposes of such baffling riddles is to teach the hopelessness of using logic or language to achieve something so inexpressible as spiritual enlightenment. Another is to encourage totally spontaneous, unhesitating reactions to events and problems, so that the adept instantly and intuitively responds in the way most appropriate to the circumstances without getting ensnared in abstract thought. (It was this aspect of Zen that led the samurai, the warrior class of Japan, to adopt its discipline, with devastating effect on its enemies.) But to ask why walking on water is not evidence of enormous spiritual powers might be to invite a thoroughly confusing reply.

---

# THE WAYWARD PROPHET
*How one early scientist failed to prove a point*

THE ANCIENT Greeks believed that everything in the cosmos was made up of four elements: earth, water, air and fire. But Empedocles, the 5th-century BC philosopher who first proposed this theory, had other ideas that sound far more modern.

The four basic elements, said Empedocles, were governed by two fundamental forces: love and strife. The first produced a combination of elements, the second separated them. Such combinations were temporary, but the elements and the two forces were indestructible. This fundamental indestructibility of matter is a principle with which modern scientists would agree.

Empedocles believed that the history of the Universe was a series of cycles in which love and strife dominated in turn. Initially, love was dominant and earth, water, air and fire intermingled. Strife then entered to separate these elements, which eventually became rearranged in partial combinations in certain places. Volcanoes and springs, for example, show the presence of both fire and water in the Earth.

### How it all began

Empedocles's idea has a parallel in the modern theory that the Universe began with a tremendous explosion or Big Bang, will expand as far as it can, and then contract again until its concentrated energy explodes in a rebirth.

According to Empedocles, the first life forms on Earth were trees. This was when love was dominant. In his newly created world, trees were followed by the earliest animal forms, which were a jumble of bodily parts – headless torsos, creatures composed of innumerable hands, or the bodies of cattle and the heads of men. Some were simply single limbs on their own. These bizarre forms combined as best they could and, eventually, only the most efficient forms survived. Thus, this aspect of Empedocles's theory anticipated Charles Darwin's doctrine of the 'survival of the fittest'.

### The final reckoning

Empedocles was a curiously contrary character. When the people of Agrigento, a Greek colony in Sicily, where he was born early in the 5th century BC, offered him the crown, he established a democracy. Yet, apparently, he was sure that he was a god.

To prove he was no ordinary mortal, Empedocles decided to vanish without trace, as a god might, rather than be seen to die an ordinary death. So he slipped away one night and threw himself into the crater of the volcano Mount Etna. The mountain duly swallowed him up, but would not allow him to be taken as divine: it threw out one of his sandals. His friends found it, on the crater's rim, the next morning.

---

## DID YOU KNOW..?

*NOT EVERYONE regards a Nobel prize as an honour. In 1958, Boris Pasternak was forced by the Soviet authorities to refuse the literature prize. They objected again when it was offered to Alexandr Solzhenitsyn in 1970. He accepted – and four years later was exiled from the Soviet Union.*

# GLITTERING PRIZES

*The strange background to the world's greatest honour*

IT IS IRONIC that the man who probably brought more destruction to the world than any other should have dedicated the fortune he thus made to the promotion of peace. This man was Alfred Nobel, inventor of dynamite and founder of the Nobel prize.

Nobel was born in Stockholm in 1833, and as a young man travelled around the world. When he returned to Sweden in 1863, he began to experiment with the manufacture of nitroglycerin, a notoriously unstable liquid explosive. After his laboratory blew up, killing his younger brother and four workers, Nobel took to a raft to work beyond police jurisdiction. Eventually, he found that nitroglycerin could be handled safely by absorbing it into a form of silica and moulding that into sticks.

### Worldwide success

Nobel's invention – which he named dynamite – was a phenomenal commercial success. He built 93 factories throughout the world, which were manufacturing 66 500 tonnes of dynamite a year by the time he died in 1896.

### DID YOU KNOW..?

*ONE FAMILY has won a hat trick of Nobel prizes. Marie and Pierre Curie shared the physics prize in 1903, and Marie Curie also won the chemistry prize in 1911. Then their daughter Irène, with her husband Frédéric Joliot-Curie, won the chemistry prize in 1935.*

Nobel was preoccupied with the problems of maintaining peace between nations, and his will stipulated that the major part of his fortune should provide an income to be 'distributed annually in the form of prizes to those who during the preceding year had conferred the greatest benefit on mankind'.

It took four years of bitter wrangling over the interpretation of the will before the Nobel Foundation was finally set up. Five prizes were to be awarded each year (a sixth, for economics, was added in 1969) on the recommendations of four institutions: the Royal Swedish Academy of Sciences (for physics, chemistry

*Medallion for excellence Along with a cash award (about US $400 000 in 1992), winners of the Nobel prize receive a medal – designed by Erik Lindberg in 1902 – bearing Nobel's portrait on one side and personifications of Nature and Science on the other.*

and economics), the Royal Caroline Medico-Chirurgical Institute (for physiology or medicine), the Swedish Academy (for literature) and the Norwegian Nobel Committee (for peace).

### Unintended results

Despite its intention to promote peace, however, the Nobel prize has provoked much bitterness, envy and competition. Scientists have been known to delay, or speed up, publication of their work in order to be eligible for a prize in a particular year. From the very beginning, the literature and science prizes have been awarded for genuinely original achievements that have certainly contributed to international understanding – but how far they have promoted peace between nations is questionable.

Most ironic of all, the general public seems to take far more interest in these awards – and the controversy that frequently surrounds them – than it does in the prize for peace. Like others before him, Alfred Nobel has found it all but impossible to change the ways of the world.

## A SACRIFICE FOR SCIENCE

FRANCIS BACON, who called himself 'the trumpeter of a new age', was the first man to insist that scientific ideas should be verified by practical experiment.

One wintry day early in 1626, when he was 65, Bacon was travelling in a coach up Highgate Hill on the outskirts of London with a Dr Witherborne. The two friends were discussing how food could be preserved by ice. Seeing the upper parts of the hill covered in snow, Bacon proposed an experiment. He bought a chicken from a woman living

nearby, and got her to kill and gut it; Bacon helped her to stuff it with snow.

All this took time, and the snow so chilled Bacon that he was soon shivering violently. Before long, he was too ill to make the journey home. He was taken to a house nearby, which belonged to his friend the Earl of Arundel.

There, he had the misfortune to be given a damp bed. The chill turned to bronchitis, and on April 9 he died. 'As for the experiment itself,' he wrote in his last letter, 'it succeeded excellently well.'

# SMALL BEGINNINGS

## Mysteries in miniature at the extremes of life

WHAT MAKES a living thing alive? What is the driving force that animates a frog or even a potato, but is absent from a stone?

Typical living things breathe, feed, convert food to energy, excrete, grow, reproduce and react to various kinds of stimulus – all in their own way. Using this definition, however, an alien from outer space might, at first sight, think that the principal form of life on Earth is the motor car. Cars do not seem to grow. But they do, after a fashion, breathe, feed, convert fuel to energy, excrete, move and respond to the stimulus provided by a driver. And they are well adapted to their environment.

Nevertheless, everyone agrees that machines are not alive. Cars cannot reproduce – they have no way of making copies of themselves – in the way that all plants and animals can. Without human beings to make them, they would immediately become extinct.

Where does the boundary between life and non-life really lie? One organism that seems to exist on the very borderline is the virus. Viruses lack the cell nucleus that is the regulator and source of reproduction and

***Obvious signs of life*** *Moving at high speed, and creating their own light to allow them to travel in darkness, cars are arguably the most conspicuously mobile objects on the face of the Earth.*

growth in other, more complex living things. To make copies of themselves, they depend on other forms of life. They proliferate by invading living cells, taking them over, and using the nucleic acids of their hosts to reproduce. Ultimately, when the new viruses leave to infect new cells, they destroy the host cell completely.

Many parasitic organisms depend on a host body in order to live and reproduce. In the case of viruses, however, this dependency is absolute, for, when removed from living tissue, they show no signs of life at all. They simply become inert molecules arranged in a crystalline pattern. Scientists at Stanford University in California have created viral material artificially by assembling the appropriate chemicals in the laboratory. When introduced to living cells the material sprang to life, using the cells to grow and reproduce itself.

The chemicals themselves were molecules of protein and nucleic acid – the basic constituents of living things. But no one can explain exactly what happens to make these chemicals come to life. The nature and the source of the 'life force' itself remain a mystery.

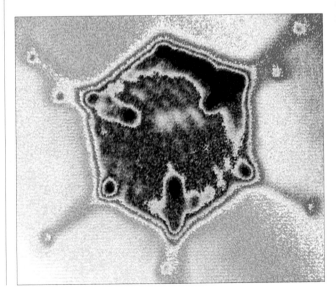

***Life at its most basic*** *This computer graphic shows an influenza virus, consisting of a core of nucleic acid with a protein coat inside a flexible membrane like the wall of a cell. Other kinds of virus are even simpler in design, lacking the protection of an outer envelope.*

15

# SMALLEST BIG, BIGGEST SMALL
## *How animals measure up*

**T**HE SMALLEST mammal living today is the Etruscan shrew; the smallest bird is the bee humming bird. Each weighs about 2 g (0.07 oz) – less than a bumble bee. These creatures are at the limit of miniaturisation for warm-blooded animals. This is because warm-blooded animals lose heat from the surface of their bodies, and at this size their skin area is so large in proportion to their volume that virtually all the heat the animals generate is lost.

Cold-blooded animals can be much smaller, because their body temperature varies with the environment and they do not need to retain heat. The smallest vertebrate (creature with a spinal column) is the pygmy goby, a fish just 8 mm (0.3 in) long – about the width of a pencil. It tips the scales at 4 mg (0.0014 oz), not a catch a fisherman would boast about. Insects may be even tinier – the smallest of all being the fairy fly, at 0.4 mm (0.016 in) long.

These creatures are made up of a vast number of individual cells. Early forms of life, the protozoa, consisted of a single cell. Since the average human body contains 50 000 million cells, you might expect all protozoa to be microscopic in size. But some extinct species were almost 25 mm (1 in) across. Living forms reach 15 mm (0.6 in) in diameter.

Eggs, too, whatever their size, are just single cells. Those of some extinct birds and reptiles were enormous. The largest yet discovered is the egg of the *aepyornis*, or elephant bird, which lived on the island of Madagascar between 2 000 000 and 10 000 BC. This laid an egg 375 mm (15 in) long.

*Fifteen dozen in one* One aepyornis egg would have provided 180 people with the equivalent of a hen's egg each.

---

## INVISIBLE ANIMALS

**M**ICROBIOLOGY, the study of life forms invisible to the naked eye, became a possibility in the second half of the 17th century, when the Dutch lens-grinder, Anton van Leeuwenhoek, constructed a microscope that could magnify 280 times, allowing people to see single-celled protozoans, yeasts, human blood cells and bacteria, all for the first time. Nobody knew what to make of many of these wonderful 'animalcules'; bacteria, for example, remained an unexplained curiosity for almost 200 years.

Bacteria are the smallest animal forms capable of an independent existence. Even the largest are less than a tenth the size of a human red blood corpuscle, which itself is a mere 0.08 mm (0.003 in) across. The smallest bacteria of all are a minuscule one-fourteen-thousandth the size of the blood cell.

### *Slipping through*
Yet these minute organisms are giants compared to viruses, organisms that require a host cell in which to live and reproduce. At the beginning of this century, viruses were known as 'filterable agents' because they passed through filters fine enough to trap any bacteria. The influenza virus, for example, is about one-sixth the size of the smallest bacterium. The tobacco mosaic virus, which discolours the leaves of the tobacco plant, is 100 times smaller than the smallest bacterium, and the smallest known virus of all, one that causes spindle tuber disease in potatoes, is 2500 times smaller. They are only 'visible' through powerful electron microscopes.

Somewhere between bacteria and viruses, both in size and complexity, is a third group of microorganisms, known as rickettsia, which includes the agents of diseases like typhus. Rickettsiae are classified with viruses because they use the cells of other living things in order to reproduce. Their discoverer, Howard T. Ricketts, was studying typhus in Mexico City in 1907, when he contracted the disease and died. The larger rickettsiae can be seen under an optical microscope, and are ten times bigger than the smallest bacteria. This hardly makes them monsters – they measure only about 0.00006 mm (0.0000022 in) across, small enough to pack 9500 of them within a hair's breadth.

***We're no angels*** *Rod-shaped bacteria (not shown in their true colour) reveal their relative size on the head of a pin.*

# THE COSMIC SOUP

*How did life on Earth begin?*

ACCORDING to the book of Genesis, 'God saw every thing that he had made, and, behold, it was very good.' People with strong religious beliefs have never had any problem with the origin of life on Earth. Although most scientists reject scriptural accounts of the Creation, a convincing alternative explanation of how life began still eludes them.

If, as many theories suggest, life began spontaneously, the process of creation could still be going on. The simplest form of life we know is the virus. New kinds are continually being discovered, but, since viruses are probably rogue pieces of genetic material that escaped from the cells of other living things, they may not be the best candidates as the ultimate be-getters of life.

Another theory says that life and matter have al-ways existed to-gether, that life was present in some form even before the 'big bang', the enormous explosion of energy with which, astronomers believe, the Universe was born. This idea, too, is hard to support, for most scientists agree that before the 'big bang', all matter was condensed into a minute space. In the unbelievably high temperatures and pressures created by this densely concentrated matter, no known form of life could have survived.

## Chance combinations

Finally, life may be an accident, created on Earth (and perhaps on the planets of other solar systems) by chance chemical reactions. There is some experimental evidence to support this notion. Amino acids, which make up the proteins on which all life is based, can be made in the laboratory by passing electrical discharges – artificial lightning – through a mixture of methane, hydrogen, ammonia and water vapour. In the 1950s, scientists at Florida State University obtained 13 different amino acids from similar mixtures of gases, using heat – at temperatures around 1000°C (1830°F) – rather than electricity as their source of energy.

Scientists used to be confident that methane and ammonia were important constituents of the Earth's primitive atmosphere, but many now think that it consisted largely of carbon dioxide, nitrogen and water, with smaller quantities of hydrogen and carbon monoxide. Researchers in Japan have recently bombarded a mixture of carbon monoxide, water and nitrogen with high energy atomic particles called protons. This simulated the radiation emitted by solar flares, periodic surges of intense energy at points on the surface of the Sun. Large quantities of amino acids were produced, and also a number of nucleic acids, the chemicals that enable a living cell to reproduce itself.

Thus the basic organic ingredients for life could well have been generated in the thick, soupy fog of gases surrounding the primeval Earth. But we are still far from discovering how those ingredients, if God did not provide 'the breath of life', could have organised themselves into living creatures.

*The forces of creation* Lightning, cosmic radiation and meteorites may all have played a part in creating the organic molecules that combined to form the first living creatures on Earth.

## LIFE FROM ELSEWHERE

IS LIFE ON EARTH nearly as old as the planet itself? The Earth is about 4500 million years old, and the oldest fossils found by geologists are only 3100 million years old. But these fossils have been identified as the remains of bacteria and blue-green algae – quite complicated microorganisms that must have taken hundreds of millions of years to evolve. That means that their evolutionary ancestors would have had to survive the incredible heat of the newborn planet in an atmosphere that lacked oxygen. Did they in fact evolve on Earth, or is there another explanation?

In the last 20 years, astronomers have discovered that among the matter thinly scattered through interstellar space there are many organic molecules. The British astronomer Sir Fred Hoyle has suggested that amino acids, which make up the protein in living cells, and even viruses are carried through space by comets and meteorites. Should they reach a planet where the conditions are right, they may slowly evolve into new forms. The origin of Earth's earliest fossils may lie elsewhere in the cosmos.

**Seeds of life** *Amino acids, like these highly magnified arginine crystals, may have fallen to Earth aboard a comet or meteorite.*

# LIVING ROUGH
### *Life goes on as usual in the most astonishing conditions*

LIVING ORGANISMS survive in the most unexpected places. Bacteria are found in pools of near-boiling water in Yellowstone National Park, Wyoming, USA. Others can live and reproduce at temperatures several degrees over the boiling point of water. And one species of alga actually thrives in hot, concentrated sulphuric acid.

At the other end of the scale, there are microorganisms that are unaffected by temperatures lower than those in a deepfreeze. Tiny invertebrates known as water bears show remarkable tolerance to cold. Fired into space, they were subjected to temperatures as low as -272°C (-522°F), only one degree above absolute zero, the lowest possible temperature. Once thawed out, they returned to life undamaged. Scientists have also immersed the creatures, which are just 1 mm (0.04 in) long, in carbonic acid, pure hydrogen, nitrogen, helium and hydrogen sulphide. In each case the creatures appeared quite dead, but revived with a few drops of water.

There are even bacteria that survive the intense neutron beams at the heart of nuclear reactors. Yet, strangely, most microorganisms are vulnerable to ultraviolet light, a far milder form of radiation. Some are killed even by sunlight.

Bacteria and fungal spores also live in the almost airless, freezing cold stratosphere. Even birds fly at heights up to 9000 m (30 000 ft), and jumping spiders have been found 6700 m (22 000 ft) up the sides of Mt Everest. In the deepest trenches of the ocean bed, fish, crustaceans and other creatures live in total darkness. Built to withstand pressures hundreds of times that at sea level, they explode if brought to the surface.

### Alternative forms of life

Given the adaptability of these organisms, there is no reason why life should not exist on other planets. Life on Earth depends on compounds of carbon. But silicon, a far tougher element, can replace carbon in many molecules, and some scientists suggest that organisms based on silicon rather than carbon would be better suited to the extreme heat or cold of other planets.

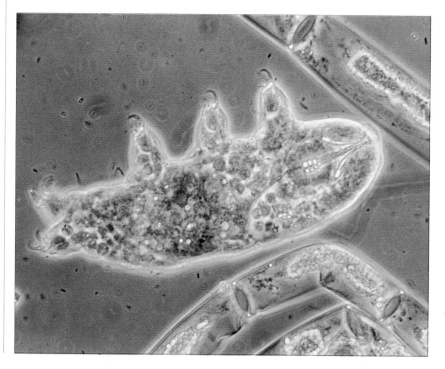

**Almost indestructible** *Scientists have sent the minuscule water bear into outer space, deep-frozen it, dried it out and soaked it in chemicals. In all cases, it survived.*

# THE REAL EVE

### *Scientists trace the mother of all mankind*

JUST AS the Book of Genesis says, human beings may well all be descended from a single female ancestor. That is the conclusion of a team of geneticists at the University of California at Berkeley. They say that the mother of mankind was not, however, the only woman on Earth at the time. But it is from her that all of modern humanity – the species *Homo sapiens* – is descended.

The key to the team's claim lies in DNA, one of the complex acids in the nucleus of every cell in any living thing. DNA controls the chromosomes that, scientists believe, determine the physical characteristics that we inherit. When the reproductive cells divide to produce human eggs and sperm, half of each parent's DNA is lost; the other half is recombined in a single set of chromosomes. This accounts for the normal physical variation between generations. Sometimes, however, a mistake in the copying – a mutation – causes a totally new characteristic to appear in a family.

### *A pure maternal line*

But the nucleus is not the only part of an animal or human cell that contains DNA. The mitochondria, small free-swimming bodies that control aspects of our metabolism – the means by which food is converted into energy and living tissue – are inherited through their own DNA independently of the chromosomes in the nucleus. For the researchers at Berkeley, the crucial fact was that we inherit mitochondria only from our mothers – it is not combined with male mitochondria during reproduction. A child's mitochondria will therefore be identical to that of his or her mother, unless there is a chance mutation in the DNA.

The University of California team tabulated all the known differences in the mitochondrial DNA of five main racial and geographical groups,

**African Eden** *The story of Genesis is partly borne out by genetics. Every human being alive may be descended from a single African female, although it is not suggested that she was the first woman.*

from Africa, Asia, Europe, Australia and New Guinea. By tracing the mutations shared by two or more groups and those found only in a single group, the scientists drew up a family tree of modern man. Biochemists have a rough idea of the rate at which mutations occur, so they could estimate not only where, but also when each one took place. The tree they constructed led back to one woman, who lived in Africa between 140 000 and 290 000 years ago – an unknown African Eve.

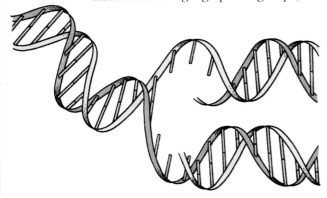

**The tangle of heredity** *The double helix structure of DNA allows coded instructions for a living organism to be copied as the nucleus of each cell divides. The code itself is contained in the sequence of the four chemicals that make up the 'rungs' of the DNA spiral.*

19

# THE TOAD THAT CAUSED A SUICIDE

*How a controversial biologist was driven to despair*

TOADS HAVE interesting mating habits. Most species mate in water, and to ensure success the male will cling onto the female, for weeks if necessary, until she produces her spawn, which he then fertilises. To help him to hang onto her slippery skin in the water, the male develops a dark pad, bristling with spines, on each of his hands during the mating season.

The midwife toad is different: it mates on dry land. And, as a result, the male never develops the so-called 'nuptial pads'. But, in 1909, the Austrian biologist Paul Kammerer claimed to have bred several generations of midwife toad that did develop nuptial pads.

Kammerer had kept his midwife toads in surroundings that forced them to mate in water. The male offspring of these toads adapted to the new conditions by growing crude versions of nuptial pads. But in the next generation, the pads appeared fully developed.

Kammerer's work created a furore among his fellow biologists. It seemed

to confirm the long-abandoned theory, put forth by the naturalist Jean Baptiste Lamarck 100 years earlier, that the physical adaptations that animals acquired in response to their environment could be passed to their offspring. If this were so, the calluses a carpenter gets in a lifetime's work would appear on his children's hands. But modern geneticists can find no physical mechanism that will transmit such adaptations. Kammerer's midwife toads seemed to have achieved the impossible.

### Inky evidence

Some members of the scientific establishment were outraged by Kammerer's claims and began a bitter attack that lasted for years. Finally, in 1926, one of his American critics visited Vienna and dissected one of the controversial toads. The spiny bristles on the preserved specimen – the only one remaining, as the others had been lost during the First World War – had broken down from repeated handling, but worse was to come: he found that the darkness of the toad's skin was the result of an injection of Indian ink. There was no sign that the toad ever had nuptial pads.

Kammerer sadly acknowledged the presence of the ink, but denied any knowledge of the fraud. Several years previously, the same preserved toad had been examined by two

***Odd ones out*** *Unlike most other toads, midwife toads, found in Western Europe, mate on land rather than in water, and do not normally grow 'nuptial pads'.*

independent teams of scientists. Both had seen the pads, and neither had noticed any signs of an ink injection.

About six weeks after news of the tampering was published, Kammerer killed himself, at the age of 46. Had he faked his results? Certainly no other biologist has repeated his experiments successfully. But he himself did not attach the importance to his toads that others did. He suggested that the nuptial pads his toads developed were the result of a genetic 'throwback' to a time before midwife toads had evolved to mate on land instead of in water like other toads.

Today no one knows who injected ink into the toad's skin. Kammerer had a strong reputation for honesty. The culprit may have been an assistant eager to improve the appearance of the badly-preserved toad, or even one of Kammerer's critics intent on sabotaging the remaining evidence of his experiments.

At the time of his death, Kammerer was penniless and involved in a tortured love affair. The thought that someone may have felt so threatened by his work that they tampered with his specimens to discredit him could simply have been the final straw.

## DID YOU KNOW..?

*THE MIDWIFE toad takes its name from the way in which the male ensures the safe delivery of its young into the world. The male fertilises the strings of eggs laid by the female and then wraps them around his hind legs. For the next few weeks, he carries them with him wherever he goes, keeping them moist and protecting them from predators. When they are ready to hatch, the toad dips his legs into a pond and 'delivers' the tadpoles into the water.*

## HOW FIT IS THE FRIGATE BIRD?

**D**ARWIN'S THEORY of 'natural selection' predicts that, over long periods of time, species will evolve specialised adaptations to their environment. But the natural world contains many apparent exceptions to this tendency. Frigate birds, for example, are tropical sea birds, but their feathers, feet and wings are completely unsuited to an aquatic way of life.

Frigate birds' feathers are not waterproof, so they cannot swim, or dive for food, without getting waterlogged. As their feet are only partially webbed, they would be unable to paddle far if they were to land on the sea. And for their long slender wings to function – the span may be as great as 2.3 m (7 ft 6 in) – they need a draught of air under them. If the birds tried to take off again after landing on the ocean, they would smash their wings uselessly into the waves.

On land, too, frigate birds' wings are a hindrance, but their nests are built on high rocks or in treetops, from which they can launch themselves into their true element, the air. There they are capable of hanging on the wind for hours at a time. They live by harassing other sea birds and forcing them to regurgitate food – then, with astonishing skill, catching what the other birds drop before it hits the water. They can also snatch fish – flying fish in particular – from near the surface of the sea.

There are many ways of making a living from the sea, and the frigate bird pursues one very familiar to human mariners – piracy. When food is difficult to catch, it makes good sense to let others catch it for you. In many respects, the frigate bird may seem poorly adapted, compared with other sea birds. But as a pirate it is without rival, living on fish without ever having to get its feet or feathers wet.

*Buccaneer A magnificent frigate bird launches out on a voyage of aerial piracy. Males use their red throat pouches in courtship display.*

# LOOK OUT FOR THE PATENT MOUSE
### A future of tailor-made animals and plants

**I**N APRIL 1988, the US Patent and Trademark Office granted a patent, number 4 736 866, for a mouse. Harvard University and two of its scientists had applied for the patent because the mouse carried a gene responsible for breast cancer. No research animal had ever been patented before – in deciding to set this precedent, the examiners at the Patent Office took more than four years to study Harvard's application.

Previous attempts to patent genetically altered animals had failed on the grounds that the techniques employed were not new. But soon after the news of Harvard's patent, the University of Adelaide announced that they had applied for an Australian patent on a fast-growing pig.

These are just two products of the new science of genetic engineering, which could bring huge benefits to scientific and medical research and has enormous commercial potential for agriculture. But how does the way genetic engineers alter the nature of plants and animals differ from traditional selective breeding?

The form and functions of all living things are ultimately controlled by the complex acid DNA. It operates through genes, sections of the chromosomes in the nuclei of cells. Genes, singly or in

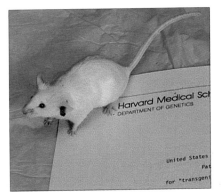

*Our own design This genetically engineered mouse has been patented by scientists at Harvard University.*

concert with other genes, determine, for example, whether an animal has blue eyes or a plant has a red flower. This characteristic passes from one generation to the next. The genetic engineer's task is to identify which genes produce the characteristic they are seeking to reproduce, copy them, and then transplant them into living tissue.

This is a daunting task. Each pair of chromosomes in a cell may contain between 10 000 and 90 000 genes. Their exact role in controlling an organism's growth, biochemistry and behaviour is still barely understood, and each individual plant and animal has its own unique set. Only where there is already a large fund of information about an organism is the genetic engineer's job relatively easy.

There is then the problem of transferring the genes once they have been identified. One way is to modify certain bacteria so that when they attack the cells of a target organism they leave new genes behind. Another way is to shoot tiny tungsten 'bullets' coated with new genes into cells, or use electricity to punch holes in cells, through which biologists then feed the genes. And even after all this, there is no guarantee that the new genes will 'take' as part of the cell, or that they will have precisely the effect that is sought.

But there have been some fascinating successes in genetic engineering. For example, a flock of sheep near Edinburgh, Scotland, now produces milk that contains blood-clotting substances previously found only in human blood. These can be extracted from the milk and used to treat haemophiliacs, whose blood fails to clot.

'Designer' plants, too, are beginning to appear. Botanists are talking of producing coffee beans without caffeine, and even tobacco without nicotine.

21

# THE TALL AND THE SHORT OF IT
### How the giraffe got its long neck

**W**HY DO GIRAFFES have long necks? Sooner or later, almost every argument about evolution will fix on the giraffe's neck as the specific example on which to concentrate the debate. It has been a favourite subject of biological controversy ever since the beginning of the 19th century. It still causes confusion, because many people find the Darwinian explanation given by today's textbooks more difficult to accept than the version put forward by the French natural scientist, Jean Baptiste Lamarck.

### Lucky chance

Modern biologists, combining Charles Darwin's theory of natural selection with 20th-century genetics, say that evolutionary change is the result of minute, random variations in DNA, the sequence of chemicals that contains coded instructions for the development of any living organism. A giraffe, because of a chance mutation in its genetic material, might be born with an especially long neck. It would thus be better equipped than its shorter-necked relatives for eating leaves growing high up on trees. Having greater success in finding food, it would live longer than other giraffes and therefore produce more offspring, many of which would inherit a similarly long neck. Short-necked giraffes, lacking this crucial advantage, would eventually die out.

What many people find unacceptable in this account is its reliance on pure chance. In Lamarck's theory of 'transformism', first proposed in detail in 1809, 50 years before Darwin published *The Origin of Species*, evolution was directed by a vaguely-defined force which impelled creatures to improve their own design in order to cope with their environment.

### Self-improvement

In the case of the giraffe, his view was that short-necked giraffes began reaching higher into the trees because competing species had eaten the leaves lower down. In doing so, they stretched their necks. The next generation of giraffes inherited these slightly longer necks. Succeeding generations continued the process, inheriting increasingly long necks, and stretching them, until giraffes were born with necks so long that they did not need to strain for food. In short, the physical

*A long way down* As the giraffe evolved its long legs, its neck must have grown longer at more or less the same rate, so that it could still lower its head in order to drink.

attributes acquired by the parents could be passed on to the succeeding generation.

Lamarck is now remembered chiefly for suggesting that this 'inheritance of acquired characters' was the mechanism of evolutionary change, a theory which is anathema to all today's orthodox Darwinians.

In Darwin's time, biologists had no inkling of the true nature of genes and the processes that cause variation between individuals. The chemistry of heredity was still completely misunderstood. Darwin himself considered use and disuse of limbs and organs as one of many possible sources of variation within a population of plants or animals. Although he saw natural selection as the ultimate agent of evolutionary change, he did not dismiss Lamarck's theory as an unacceptable heresy, as today's biologists do.

The reason giraffes have evolved long necks may in fact have less to do with feeding and more to do with drinking. Giraffes have difficulty in bending their long legs. They need their long necks, because without them they would have to kneel down in order to reach water.

*High-level browsers* The giraffe feeds on leaves beyond the reach of competitors. Lower down the tree, the gerenuk gains a similar advantage by standing on its hind legs.

# THE CLOAK OF LIFE

*What keeps our atmosphere down to Earth?*

ITHOUT AIR, this would be a lifeless world. The very least, apart from sunlight, that plants and animals need to survive – and to have evolved in the first place – is a supply of oxygen and water. Both are part of the atmosphere. And for the continued existence of the atmosphere, we have gravity to thank.

The air consists of gas molecules moving at high speed. The Earth's gravity is so strong that nothing moving slower than 40 000 km/h (25 000 mph) – 17 times the top speed of Concorde – can escape it. Fortunately, the air's molecules move at nothing like this speed, and so the atmosphere remains held in the embrace of the Earth's gravitational field. Some astronomers believe that the Moon may once have had an atmosphere, too. But, because its gravity is only one-sixth as strong as the Earth's, the Moon's atmosphere dispersed into space.

## A place in the Sun

The Earth is also uniquely placed in the solar system to nurture the development of life as we know it. The first complex living things on Earth were plants, which depend on having sufficient sunlight to live and reproduce.

Plants also give out oxygen. Land animals, particularly mammals, could have developed in the forms we know them only in an atmosphere containing oxygen. If the Earth were nearer the Sun, the rise in temperature would make the oxygen molecules move faster, and they could leak away. If it were further away, it would be too cold for life to have evolved.

***Layers of the blanket*** *Only recently have scientists begun to understand the nature of the various layers of the atmosphere. At the end of the 19th century, they began to send unmanned balloons equipped with barometers and thermometers into the lower atmosphere, and discovered that while pressure decreases steadily with altitude, temperature variations are more complex. Scientists have divided the atmosphere into layers based on these temperature variations. In the troposphere and mesosphere, temperature decreases with height, while in the stratosphere and thermosphere, it actually increases. Since the advent of rocket and satellite technology in the 1940s, scientists have been able to gather detailed information about the upper atmosphere.*

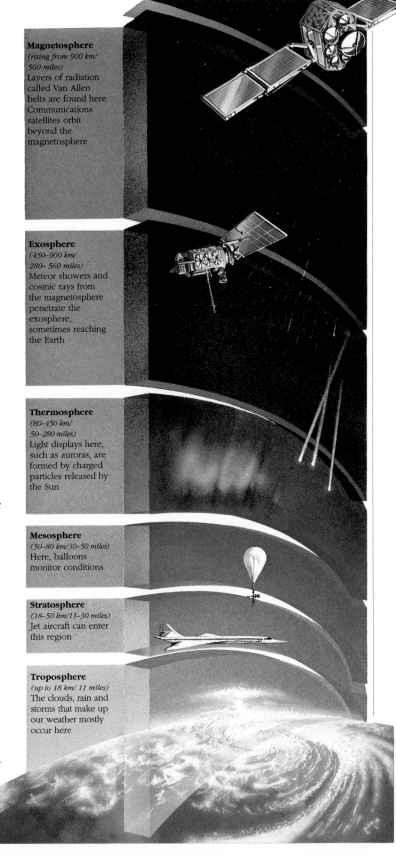

**Magnetosphere**
*(rising from 900 km/ 560 miles)*
Layers of radiation called Van Allen belts are found here. Communications satellites orbit beyond the magnetosphere

**Exosphere**
*(450–900 km/ 280– 560 miles)*
Meteor showers and cosmic rays from the magnetosphere penetrate the exosphere, sometimes reaching the Earth

**Thermosphere**
*(80–450 km/ 50–280 miles)*
Light displays here, such as auroras, are formed by charged particles released by the Sun

**Mesosphere**
*(50–80 km/30–50 miles)*
Here, balloons monitor conditions

**Stratosphere**
*(18–50 km/11–30 miles)*
Jet aircraft can enter this region

**Troposphere**
*(up to 18 km/ 11 miles)*
The clouds, rain and storms that make up our weather mostly occur here

## REACHING THE HEIGHTS

IN THE 1860s, the British meteorologist James Glaisher made a series of balloon ascents, at the request of the British Association, to explore the stratosphere. On September 5, 1862, with his pilot Henry Coxwell, he recorded an ascent of 8840 m (29 000 ft) – very nearly the height of Mount Everest. But the balloon continued rising, until Glaisher was unconscious from lack of oxygen in the thin atmosphere.

Coxwell was so weak that he could bring the balloon down only by opening the control valve with his teeth. The two balloonists subsequently estimated their maximum height at 11 300 m (37 000 ft). This was certainly the greatest altitude any person had ever reached at that time.

Their record was broken in 1931, when a Swiss physicist, Professor Auguste Piccard, reached 16 201 m (53 153 ft) in a balloon carrying a sealed cabin – the first to be used in flight. The current record for ascent in a balloon is held by Commander Malcolm D. Ross

***Height of folly*** *Glaisher was saved by his pilot, Coxwell, after he passed out while ascending 11 km (7 miles) in 1862.*

and the late Lieutenant Commander Victor Prather of the US Navy, who reached 34 668 m (113 740 ft) over the Gulf of Mexico in 1961.

# THE SECRET OF LIFE
*How lightning helps plants to grow – and more*

A SINGLE FLASH of lightning can discharge sufficient electrical energy to make the oxygen and nitrogen gases in the air combine. Together they form nitric oxide, which dissolves in rainwater and reaches the ground as nitric acid.

All growing plants need nitrogen, but few can obtain it directly from the air. At least some of their supply is provided by the electro-chemical action of lightning.

Lightning may once have had an even more profound influence on the processes of life. In the early 1950s, chemist Harold Urey and his students at the University of Chicago simulated the effect of lightning on a mixture of the gases thought to have made up the early atmosphere of Earth. Products of the experiment included amino acids, the chemicals which form the protein molecules of all animal and vegetable life. Perhaps, many millions of years ago, the first life on Earth developed from the products of a lightning flash.

***Spark of life*** *Lightning bolts are well known for their destructive power. Yet it is thought that some of the essential building blocks of living matter were originally formed by the electrical energy of lightning.*

# THE HEAT THAT FREEZES

## Hot is cold on the edge of space

**A**S YOU ascend through the Earth's atmosphere, the temperature does not drop off steadily as you approach outer space. At first it does, at a rate of about 1˚C (1.8˚F) every 150 m (500 ft) to reach an average of -65˚C (-85˚F) at 18 km (11 miles). But there, where the stratosphere and the ozone layer begin, ultraviolet light from the Sun turns oxygen into ozone. That chemical reaction produces heat, and so the temperature begins to rise again steadily, reaching -3˚C (-27˚F) at 50 km (30 miles) from the Earth's surface.

This is where the stratosphere and ozone layer end. Beyond this, the air is so thin that the effect of ultraviolet heating is insignificant, and it gets steadily colder out to about 80 km (50 miles). At this point the temperature has dropped to -90˚C (-130˚F).

But in the ionosphere, which begins here, and stretches out for 300 km (185 miles), a very strange effect occurs. Short wavelength ultraviolet light and X-rays from the Sun penetrate the gas molecules and strip their atoms of electrons. The molecules that are left, called ions, move very fast and as a result are extremely hot.

The temperature of individual ions may be as high as 5000 or 10 000˚C (9000 or 18 000˚F). But these incredibly hot particles are so few and far between that an astronaut would freeze instantly if he stepped out into this 'heat' without his suit.

---

### DID YOU KNOW..?

*THE COLDEST place in the Earth's lower atmosphere is usually not over the North or South Poles, as you might expect, but over the Equator. The tropopause (the boundary between the two lowest layers of the atmosphere) varies in height from an average of only 9 km (6 miles) above the two poles to 18 km (11 miles) over the Equator. Air temperature steadily decreases right up to the top of the tropopause. Thus, temperatures often fall as low as -80˚C (-110˚F) high above the Equator, whereas over the North and South Poles they rarely fall below -55˚C (-65˚F).*

---

# THE MAGICAL MAYOR

## A showman who harnessed the power of the atmosphere

**I**N 1654, Otto von Guericke acquired a reputation as a magician among the people of Magdeburg, Germany, where he was mayor.

Von Guericke, an engineer, was intrigued by current investigations into the nature of the atmosphere. He decided to demonstrate the power of atmospheric pressure by showing its effect on a container that he had emptied of air – in other words, one that contained a vacuum. And so he built a vacuum pump, rather like a water pump except that instead of removing water it removed air.

Von Guericke had a strong streak of the showman in him, and he demonstrated the powers of his pump, and of the atmosphere too, with some spectacular stunts. The one that gave him his reputation as a magician was mounted at Magdeburg before Emperor Ferdinand III and his court.

Von Guericke had built two copper hemispheres, 510 mm (20 in) in diameter, each with a flange so accurately finished that, when the two were greased and fitted together they formed a single, airtight sphere. He pumped the air out of this, and then harnessed a team of eight horses to each hemisphere to try to pull them apart – without success. As soon as he let the air into the sphere again, the two halves separated easily.

In another demonstration, he pumped the air out of a large vertical cylinder fitted with a piston. Fifty men held ropes attached via pulleys to the piston and, as the air left the cylinder, the piston sank – until the 50 men were dangling in the air.

Twenty years later, the people of Magdeburg were astonished again by von Guericke's magical powers, when he built a water barometer attached to the side of his house. It was a brass tube over 9 m (30 ft) high, with a sealed glass section at the top. Passers-by would see a tiny figure of a man floating high in the glass when the weather was fine, and sinking out of sight as storms approached.

---

### DID YOU KNOW..?

*IN THE 1640s, Evangelista Torricelli, a pupil of Galileo, found that the pressure of the atmosphere would raise a column of mercury about 760 mm (30 in) in a glass tube. When Blaise Pascal repeated the experiments shortly afterwards he, being French, used red wine – but because wine is much less dense than mercury, he had to build a tube 14 m (46 ft) high to accommodate the effect.*

---

**Piston power** *In 1654, Otto von Guericke was able to lift 50 men with his newly invented air pump as it created an unbreakable vacuum. Many people believed that von Guericke must have been a magician to produce such showmanlike feats.*

# THE EVERLASTING DREAM

*The fruitless search for perpetual motion*

EVERY MACHINE, whatever its size or use, needs a source of energy to make it run. Whether that source is fuel for burning, electric power from the mains, the Sun's light, or any other form of energy, when it is cut off, the machine will stop. But inventors have tried for centuries to develop a machine that, once started, recycles its own energy in order to power itself. Waterwheels that always turn, windmills that forever rotate, clocks that never stop ticking – all have been built in the quest for a perpetual motion machine.

This quest is, however, doomed to fail, for, were such a machine to work, it would defy the very workings of the Universe. According to the laws of thermodynamics,

when one form of energy (such as running water) is converted into another form (such as a moving wheel), some of that energy is always lost in the form of heat or friction. Any machine that is not fed some form of energy will sooner or later grind to a halt as its energy dissipates.

Man has nearly achieved perpetual motion by launching probes into a stable orbit around the Sun. In the frictionless conditions of space they orbit indefinitely without ever needing a push. But even their motion is not perpetual – eventually our Sun will burn up its fuel and the entire solar system will be destroyed.

*Self-blowing windmill* In the early 1500s, the Italian philosopher Marco Zimara devised a machine that recycled the energy of an initial gust of wind. As the sails of the windmill turned, they operated a set of bellows that in turn provided enough wind to drive the sails. The machine never worked, for the force needed to compress the bellows was far more than could ever be produced by the windmill.

*Doing a good turn* Since ancient times, the screw has been known to be an efficient device for lifting objects. In 1618, a British physician, Robert Fludd, used it in his plans for a watermill that would revolve forever. The screw lifted the water (or, in the variation above, ballbearings) up to the top of the wheel. The rotation of the wheel was meant to drive the screw, but too much of its energy was lost through friction.

**Weather machine** *During the 1760s, a London clockmaker, James Cox, produced a clock that appeared at first glance to be a perpetual motion machine. Inside the clock was a column of mercury, just as in a barometer. The column rose and fell with changes in atmospheric pressure, and these movements pushed a lever that wound up the weights that drove the pendulum mechanism. Today the clock, which is no longer in working order, sits in London's Victoria and Albert Museum. It cannot be considered a true perpetual motion machine, for instead of recycling its own energy, it depended on energy from outside – the forces of weather that continually change the atmospheric pressure.*

mercury column

## FRAUDULENT MOTION

I N THE 1850s, a Connecticut engineer developed a machine that purported to show perpetual motion. As the larger wheel turned, weights on its spokes shifted position, resulting in an imbalance that kept the wheel in motion and turned the flywheel. In fact, a hidden source of compressed air turned both wheels.

lodestone

**Constant attraction** *The use of a lodestone – a natural magnet of iron ore – to produce perpetual motion was proposed in 1648 by the Bishop of Chester in England. A powerful lodestone placed on top of a pillar attracted a metal ball up a slope. Near the top, the ball was meant to drop through a hole and fall back to begin its journey again. However, the force of the magnet required to pull the ball was so great that the ball did not drop through the hole but continued towards the magnet.*

metal ball

weights

dry sponges

wet sponges

**Squeeze effect** *In British inventor William Congreve's machine from 1827, the force of gravity on heavy wet sponges was meant to pull dry sponges up an incline. Dry sponges (left) absorbed water by capillary action as they met the surface of a tank, and sank, causing the entire triangular band to move. As wet sponges left the tank (right), their water was squeezed out by the pressure of weights, making them light enough to be pulled up the incline. The machine failed to move – the friction of the rollers and the water was too great.*

# SECRETS OF THE CRYSTAL

*What do a diamond, a pencil and a snowflake have in common?*

THE HIDDEN LINK between a diamond, a pencil and a snowflake is the crystal – one of nature's most fascinating methods of building. The word 'crystal' comes from the Greek word *krystallos*, meaning 'cold' – it was once believed that a certain variety of quartz crystal was ice that had been frozen so deeply that it would never melt.

We tend to think of crystals as the regular, often beautiful shapes that certain solids take – such as ice in the form of a snowflake, or the glittering faces of a diamond. But graphite – the 'lead' in a pencil – is a crystal too. To a scientist, a crystal is any solid substance whose molecular structure follows a regular pattern.

Crystals can form in virtually any shape or size and from a huge range of substances. The Giant's Causeway in Ireland consists of basalt rock crystals that tower as high as a four-storey building, while the individual crystals in graphite are almost invisible. And a single element can produce crystals that are startlingly unlike each other. Water may crystallise into a lump of ice, or into the delicate form of a snowflake.

pure quartz or rock crystal

Diamonds, graphite and coal are all crystals of carbon. But why is diamond so hard, and graphite so soft that it is used not only in pencil leads but also as a lubricant?

In scientific terms, there are two distinct kinds of crystal: those, like diamond, built up in a three-dimensional framework and those, like graphite, made up in layers.

Every carbon atom in a diamond is attached to its nearest neighbour on each side, and above and below it, in a regular pattern in the tightest chemical bond possible. In graphite, the bonds from side to side are also numerous – and just as regular – but there are only a few above and below. The thin, weakly linked layers of carbon shear off easily; it is this 'soft' quality that makes it possible to write or draw with a pencil, as layers of graphite break away and stick to the page. And graphite's layered bonding means the atoms can slide over one another, enabling it to be used as a solid lubricant.

***Giant's Causeway*** *Thousands of basalt rock crystals make up this promontory on the coast of Antrim, Northern Ireland.*

Some crystals, such as quartz, become electrically charged when pressure is applied. Conversely, electricity makes quartz expand or contract. In a quartz clock, the alternating electric current makes the crystal vibrate, and these vibrations are so regular that they allow the clock to keep time within one second a year.

## FIT FOR A QUEEN

THE MASSIVE CULLINAN diamond that was discovered in the Premier mine in Transvaal, South Africa, on January 25, 1905, weighed 3106 carats – more than a third as much as this book. It was more than three times the size of the previous record holder, the 995-carat Excelsior diamond. South Africa was then part of the British Empire, and in 1907 the Transvaal government gave the stone to King Edward VII of England for his 66th birthday.

Amsterdam jeweller Isaac Asscher had the task of cutting the stone. He cut it into 9 large gems and more than 100 smaller ones. The largest, the size and shape of a hen's egg, weighs 530 carats. It is known as the Star of Africa, and is set in the British Royal Sceptre. The next largest gem, the Cullinan II, was set in the British Imperial State Crown. It weighs 317 carats and has the diameter of the face of a man's watch.

***A rare glimpse*** *The Star of Africa sits atop Queen Elizabeth II's Royal Sceptre. The Cullinan II is set below the large ruby in the Imperial State Crown.*

# THE FLYING DETECTIVE

## *The airborne crystal that monitors the effects of the Chernobyl disaster*

IN THE WINTER of 1988, a helicopter took a remarkable piece of equipment into the air above the bleak landscape of Cumbria in northern England. It was a large crystal of sodium iodide, encased in a stainless steel tank, and its purpose was to detect radioactivity still remaining after the disastrous nuclear accident at Chernobyl, in the USSR, in 1986.

To Dr David Sanderson, leader of the team at the Scottish Universities Research and Reactor Centre who developed the detector, a crystal was the natural candidate for the device. Radioactive substances produce gamma rays; these can penetrate most materials, but a dense crystal like sodium iodide can stop them. When the rays strike the crystal, it absorbs energy and vibrates.

The crystal was coated with thallium, an element that reacts to the energy of each gamma ray by producing a pulse of ultraviolet light. The strength of the light is like a signature that identifies each radioactive substance that hits the crystal. The team was looking for caesium 134 which, because it is man-made, would be a sure indicator that radiation from Chernobyl was present.

A series of devices connected to the tank analysed the pulses of ultraviolet light and found caesium 134 in various strengths. In this way, the vibrating crystal produced the most detailed map yet of the remaining effects of the Chernobyl disaster on Britain.

## DID YOU KNOW..?

*ICE CRYSTALS, as everyone knows, will melt as soon as their temperature rises above 0°C (32°F). But Nobel prize-winning scientist Percy Bridgman made one form of ice, called ice-VII, that will not melt even at temperatures over 100°C (212°F) – the boiling point of water. He achieved this while investigating the effects of phenomenally high pressure on different substances. By putting ice under ultra-high pressures, he crammed its atoms and molecules so close together that even this amount of heat could not force them apart.*

## THE SOLID LIQUID

LEAD CRYSTAL glass is valued all over the world for its clarity, purity and brilliance. It was invented in 1674 in England by George Ravenscroft, who discovered that by adding red lead oxide to his glass formula he was able to make a tougher, clearer glass than anyone else. But neither this, nor any other glass, is a crystal. The glass of Ravenscroft's time was not colourless, but a dull red or green, from the colour of the sand used in its manufacture. He was simply looking for a way to make glass as clear as natural rock crystal. He succeeded, and the name stuck.

Not only is glass not a crystal, it is scarcely even a solid. In most solid materials the atoms and molecules – the building blocks that give any substance its unique nature – are joined in a regular pattern. If you melt a solid, the molecules lose this regular arrangement. If you then cool it to the point where it becomes solid again, the regularity will reappear. When the delicate form of a snowflake melts into water, its molecules become jumbled up; but when the water freezes again into a snowflake, it once more assumes an intricate pattern. Glass, however, solidifies or 'freezes' very quickly and unevenly, with the result that when it is completely solid its molecules are still in a highly irregular arrangement.

Oddly enough, this also makes glass astonishingly tough. In theory, if it were possible to make perfect glass it would be five times as strong as the toughest steel. However, with today's technology such glass cannot be made – tiny flaws formed in the manufacturing process create weak points. The toughest glass made today is as strong as, but no stronger than, steel.

# THE LUMINOUS LURE OF A FIREFLY
## *How crystals may help the firefly to survive*

IN PARTS of tropical Asia, you can see trees glowing in the dark – single trees where waves of light ripple from top to bottom and back again, and rows of trees where the light leaps from one tree to another.

This extraordinary effect is caused not by the trees themselves, but by the synchronised flashing of thousands of fireflies that have gathered in the branches. Look closely and you will find that each tree harbours a different species of these luminescent insects.

Why these mass displays occur is not fully understood. But biologists do know why fireflies flash when flying alone, and how they produce light.

Fireflies glow in order to find a mate. The male of one common species of North American firefly, *Photinus pyralis*, flashes regularly while flying. The female, watching from the ground, flashes back in a rhythm unique to its own species. The male recognises this signal and drops towards a new mate.

It is possible that the flashing light also serves as a warning mechanism, reminding would-be predators of the firefly's bitter taste. But it does not always work – certain frogs eat so many fireflies that they themselves glow.

Firefly 'lanterns' contain oxygen and a substance called luciferin. The chemical reaction between the two produces light. An enzyme called luciferase helps to speed up the process, and this in turn intensifies the light.

Where do crystals come into all of this? In the lantern is a layer of ammonium urate crystals, behind the light-emitting luciferin. These crystals help to scatter the light and increase the effectiveness of this remarkable natural signalling system.

***Crystal light*** *Fireflies light up a tree with synchronised signals reflected by crystals in the insects' bodies.*

# MEASURE FOR MEASURE

### *How long is a piece of string?*

THE WIDTH of a man's thumb, the length of a girdle, the weight of a wheat seed, the volume of a handful of flour – all these measures are over a thousand years old. And, although we may not realise it, they are still used by many of us today. The inch (25 mm) is based on the width of a man's thumb: as a rough measure it is surprisingly accurate. The Romans introduced the inch (they called it the *uncia*), and had 12 of them to their foot, which was almost the same as the imperial foot (300 mm) still used in Britain and the United States today. The ancient Greek foot was the same length as the modern foot, but it was made up of 16 *finger* widths.

### *Waists and measures*

The Anglo-Saxons took the length of a man's girdle to be a yard (900 mm/36 in). The system had obvious disadvantages, and early in the 12th century the English King Henry I is said to have standardised the yard by stretching out his arm and measuring the distance from his nose to the end of his thumb. The oldest surviving measure of the yard is a silver rod made in 1445, belonging to the Merchant Taylors' Company in London.

From seeds came a measure of weight: the 'grain' is still part of the imperial system, and once represented

**Small change** *Shown at actual size, ancient Greek drachmas (the larger coins) and obols bear images of gods and kings. Six obols equalled one drachma.*

the weight of a single seed. As different kinds of seed weigh different amounts, this was a source of some confusion. Even so, 7000 'grains' were held to be equivalent to one pound (450 g), a proportion still in use today. In ancient Babylon, seeds were used to establish a unit of area: land was measured by the number of seeds needed it sow it.

### *Cash in hand*

The handful is still with us today, and in more than one form. In ancient Greece, six tiny iron weights called obols made one drachma, which means 'handful'. This was both a coin – the drachma remains the unit of Greek currency to this day – and a weight, which still survives in the imperial system as the drachm, which equals one-sixteenth of an ounce (1.8 g).

**Ancient measure** *A Roman mosaic in Algeria shows a farmer and his oxen. The Roman ager (field), from which the modern term 'acre' comes, was related to the size of a piece of land that a pair of oxen could plough in a day.*

---

### DID YOU KNOW..?

*IN OLD TESTAMENT times, two measures of weight were used in the Middle East – the 'common measure' and the 'royal measure'. The royal measure was the larger. When a king demanded taxes in kind, these had to be paid in the royal measure. When a king paid out, he used the common measure. And so the royal coffers always made a profit.*

# RIGHT AND WRONG

## *The entire metric system is based on a miscalculation*

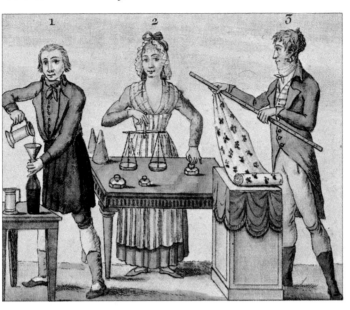

N THE tumultuous years following the 1789 revolution, the French Academy of Sciences was at last allowed to carry through a reform that it had been urging for many years: the establishment of a simple, logical system of measures. This was desperately needed to simplify international trade – but even within France itself measures varied widely from one locality to another.

A committee which included two esteemed scientists, chemist Antoine Laurent de Lavoisier and mathematician Joseph-Louis Lagrange, agreed that, to make calculations easier, the new system should be based on the number ten – and that the basic unit would be one ten-millionth of the length of the line running through Paris from the North Pole to the Equator. This measure would be known as the metre, while the distance itself would be

***Revolutionary system*** *A French newspaper illustration from 1800 helps explain metric values: the litre (figure 1), the gram (figure 2) and the metre (figure 3).*

reckoned as 10 000 kilometres. It took eight years to complete the surveys and calculations involved, and in 1799 the young Republic of France formally adopted its new metric system of weights and measures.

Every unit of measurement was based on the length of the metre. The unit of weight, the gram, was the weight of a cubic centimetre of distilled water at 4°C (39.2°F). The unit of volume, the litre, was 1000 cubic centimetres. We rarely hear of some of the original basic measures today. The 'are', for example, which is an area of 10 metres square, has been superseded by the hectare, which is 100 times larger.

As the revolution in France gave way to the era of Napoleon's conquests, the

metric system spread throughout Europe with the French Army. Its simplicity and logic made it the international language of science during the 19th century. But it was based on a falsehood.

By 1960, data from artificial satellites had confirmed suspicions that the original calculation of the distance between the North Pole and the Equator had been incorrect. The actual distance is not 10 000 km but 10 002 km – wrong by only one part in 5000, but an error nonetheless. There was no need to alter the metre, of course, but it was necessary to define it in different terms. Since 1983, the metre has been officially described as the distance 'travelled by light in a vacuum during a time interval of 1/299 792 458 of a second'. This makes little difference to anybody who simply wants to measure a piece of wood or fabric, but it is as accurate as science can make it.

***Esoteric term*** *The 'stere', which measures volume, is another obscure metric unit.*

***Out of fashion*** *The 'are' is a metric measure of surface area little used today.*

# WEIGHING THE EARTH
## *An ingenious experiment cracks gravity's code*

TWO CENTURIES ago, the English scientist Sir Henry Cavendish became the first man to measure the mass of the Earth – a task he accomplished from the privacy of his home.

Cavendish knew from Sir Isaac Newton's work that all objects exert the force of gravity, and that the gravitational attraction between two objects depends both on their mass (the greater their mass, the greater the pull of gravity between them) and on their distance from each other. This distance is measured from the centres of the objects concerned, not their surfaces. So you will weigh less on the top of a high mountain than in a valley, because at a high altitude you are further from the source of gravity at the centre of the Earth.

Newton expressed his law of gravity as a mathematical equation consisting of five quantities: the masses of the two objects ($M_1$ and $M_2$); the distance ($D$) between their centres; the force of gravity ($F$) between them; and an abstract term ($G$) that stood for a number – the 'gravitational constant' – that never changed, whatever masses and distances were involved. Newton's formula was:

$$F = \frac{M_1 \times M_2 \times G}{D^2}$$

But as Newton was concerned purely with the *principles* of gravity, he had no need to discover the numerical value of $G$. In fact, no one knew what it was.

If any four of the quantities of Newton's equation were known, the fifth could be calculated, and Cavendish therefore realised he could use Newton's formula to measure the mass of the Earth. For $M_1$, he would choose a small object whose mass he knew. $M_2$ would be his unknown quantity, the mass of the Earth. As the approximate distance to the centre of the Earth was known at the time, he would therefore also know the distance ($D$) between his two objects. A simple weighing scale would show the force of gravity ($F$) between his object and the Earth. But he would still need to have a fourth known value – the value of $G$ – in order to work out Newton's equation.

The problem in defining $G$ was that the sheer weakness of the force of gravity made this 'gravitational constant' extremely difficult to measure – between ordinary man-made objects, even those as big as a house, it is negligible.

Cavendish's achievement was to build an apparatus, enclosed in a mahogany case to shield it from any air currents, that magnified the effect of gravity and made it detectable.

Inside the case he placed two small spheres, 50 mm (2 in) in diameter, whose weight he knew precisely. He attached them to either end of a long rod suspended horizontally from a slender wire. He then hung two much larger spheres, 300 mm (12 in) in diameter, from another horizontal rod, pivoted directly above the centre of the first rod.

Cavendish brought the large spheres gradually closer to the small spheres by turning the pivot. The large spheres' gravitational field pulled the small ones toward them, causing the rod suspended from the wire to move a tiny, but measurable, amount.

He then measured the force needed, without the gravitational influence of the large spheres, to move the small spheres and their rod by the same amount. This gave him all the figures needed to work out the value of Newton's 'gravitational constant': the masses of his two sets of spheres ($M_1$ and $M_2$); the distance between their centres ($D$); and the force ($F$) that gravity had exerted on them. Inserting these known quantities into Newton's equation, he discovered a precise figure for $G$.

After that, calculating the mass of the Earth was easy. But because the distance to the centre of the Earth was misjudged at the time, Cavendish's calculation of its mass was not, in fact, entirely accurate. But his method was used in 1895 to give a true figure. The Earth is now known to weigh 5976 million million million tonnes.

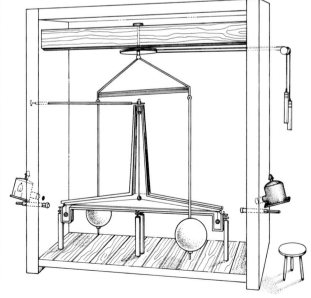

**Observation box** *To measure the gravity exerted by two large spheres on two small spheres, Cavendish built an apparatus inside a protective mahogany case. Candles provided light through holes, and Cavendish took his measurements using telescopes that penetrated the sides.*

# HOT AND COLD

## *Once, water boiled at zero degrees*

COMPARATIVELY few people feel absolutely at home with both Fahrenheit and Celsius ('centigrade') temperature scales. Most of us, hearing a temperature expressed in the scale that is less familiar to us, will mentally convert the figure into the one we know better. But imagine how confusing things must have been early in the 18th century – when at least 35 different measures of temperature were in use.

It was not until 1714, when the German-Dutch instrument maker Gabriel Daniel Fahrenheit made the first really efficient thermometer using mercury in a sealed tube, and created his own scale, that a single measure of temperature came into common use.

### *Warm-blooded science*

Fahrenheit started with the coldest thing he knew of – a mixture of ice and salt. This he marked on his thermometer as 0°. Next, he measured the temperature of the healthy human body. He had originally intended to divide his scale between this point and his zero into only 12 degrees, but the mercury in his thermometer

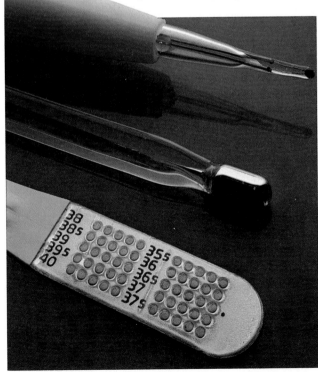

**Health check** *These three types of thermometer (electrical, mercury and disposable) are used today to monitor body temperature.*

moved much further up the tube than he had expected. To avoid such large, unwieldy units he decided his scale needed eight times as many divisions. So, instead of assigning a value of 12° to body temperature, as he had first intended, Fahrenheit called body temperature 96° (8 x 12). The precise figure is 98.6° on Fahrenheit's scale (37°C) – but small variations in the bore of the tube caused his thermometer to show a lower reading.

Fahrenheit next measured the freezing and boiling points of pure water, which came to 32° and 212° respectively. A scale based on the freezing and boiling temperatures of water had been proposed as long ago as the 2nd century AD, by Galen, a Greek physician. Fahrenheit realised that these two temperatures are ideal reference points, because they are constant at a given pressure. His scale of temperature quickly became popular, particularly in English–speaking countries.

But it was soon followed by a rival. In 1742, the Swedish astronomer Anders Celsius proposed a scale on which water boiled at 0° and froze at 100°. (This system was reversed after his death in 1744.)

When, at the end of the 18th century, France introduced the decimal metric system of measures, Celsius's 'centigrade' scale found a natural home within it. It soon became the standard temperature scale for all scientific work, and is used in countries that have adopted the metric system. Fahrenheit, however, is still used in many English-speaking countries.

**Weather gauge** *This 18th-century French mercury thermometer is calibrated on the Celsius scale. Heat waves and extreme cold spells of previous years are marked on the inside of the case.*

## REACHING THE VANISHING POINT

EARLY in the 19th century, the French chemist J.L. Gay-Lussac came to a bizarre but entirely logical conclusion concerning the effect of temperature on gases. He started from the observation that gases, like all other substances, contract as they become colder. His calculations showed that at about -270˚C (-454˚F), any gas would vanish, since it would shrink so far that it would occupy no space at all. The impossible would happen: matter would disappear.

### Stopped cold

The Scottish physicist William Thomson (who later became Lord Kelvin) found the answer to this conundrum half a century later. He first showed that the temperature of a substance was in fact a measure of how fast its molecules were moving about. This movement requires space: and as a gas cools, its molecules need less room to move about. Thomson used this more refined theory to calculate that any gas molecule would come to a complete standstill at -273.15˚C (-459.67˚F). It followed that nothing could reach a lower temperature than this, and so it is known as 'absolute zero', or zero Kelvin (0˚K).

It also followed that, because Kelvin had shown how temperature depends on the movement of molecules, Gay-Lussac's conclusion had to be reconsidered. A gas does not contract into apparent nothingness at this temperature. It will liquefy first – and some gases will even turn solid. After that, they contract hardly at all. And it is then virtually impossible to extract the remaining energy that keeps the molecules in motion. In reality the impossible state was not that of the 'vanishing' gas, but a temperature as low as absolute zero.

### Lowest of the low

However, scientists cannot resist a challenge, and keep trying to reach that elusive limit. The lowest temperature so far obtained involved a sophisticated technique of reducing the magnetic energy in a compound called cerium ethyl sulphate and so reducing its heat. This brought its temperature down to an astonishing 0.00002˚K – that is, within one fifty-thousandth of a degree of absolute zero.

# COLD CURRENTS
## *Total electrical efficiency proves irresistible*

IN 1987, K. Alex Müller of Switzerland and J. Georg Bednorz of West Germany broke a speed record: they were awarded a Nobel prize (for physics) less than two years after making a scientific breakthrough.

The alacrity with which they were awarded the highest honour in science reflected the importance attached to their discovery of 'high temperature' superconductors – materials that have no electrical resistance. This means that electricity will pass through the material without losing any of its energy. All everyday electrical equipment has some resistance, sapping the energy flow just as a piece of cheese slows down the knife that slices through it.

The term 'high temperature', when applied to superconductors, is a little misleading. The Dutch physicist Kamerlingh Onnes discovered in 1911 that mercury lost its electrical resistance at an extremely low temperature: 4.12˚K (-269.03˚C). Nobel winners Müller and Bednorz had, early in 1986, succeeded in finding a ceramic compound that superconducted at 35˚K (-238˚C). A so-called 'high temperature' superconductor, then, is nonetheless very cold.

Why are superconductors so important? The first reason is economic. The electricity industry loses about 2 per cent of what it generates to resistance in transformers and power lines. That is a waste of about £500 (US $800) million of electricity each year in the UK alone.

A vast array of vital electrical equipment would dramatically increase in effectiveness if it were to function at 100 per cent efficiency. Computers would function more quickly. The huge power consumption of new friction-free trains that use magnetic levitation would be enormously reduced. Medical scanning systems that exploit magnetism would be cheaper, and thus available to more people in need.

In 1989, researchers found a ceramic compound of thallium, barium, calcium and copper oxides that became superconductive at 128˚K (-145˚C). The ideal superconductor would, of course, work at ordinary room temperatures, disposing of the need for cooling it at all.

The obstacle to this dream is that no one has discovered precisely why superconductors lose their electrical resistance. But even if the room-temperature superconductor remains a dream, super-cooled superconductors may still have a place in the technology of the future – in factories in space, where maintaining low temperatures is no problem.

***Art of levitation*** *Magnetic fields cannot pass through most superconductors. This small magnet is therefore repelled by the superconducting ceramic below it.*

# A ROCKET'S LIQUID LUNCH

### Super-cooled gases power the space shuttle

**G**ETTING a rocket into space is a difficult business. The rocket has to be able to lift its own weight fast enough to escape from the Earth's gravity, and to do this it needs a constant steady thrust. All combustion engines work by controlled explosion, but a rocket engine has to provide a massive explosion that goes on and on.

In all large rockets, fuel flows constantly into a combustion chamber, where it burns, while the exhaust gases are forced out of a nozzle. But the fuel requires oxygen to burn, and there is no oxygen in space. So a space rocket has to carry not only fuel, such as hydrogen, but its own supply of oxygen.

### Double advantage

Space rockets carry hydrogen and oxygen in a super-cooled liquid state for two reasons. In their liquid form, these substances – like all gases – take up far less room than they would at warmer temperatures. And the mixture of hydrogen and oxygen can be much more accurately metered – and their explosion more exactly controlled – as a liquid.

*Liquid power A US space shuttle waits to be coupled to its enormous external fuel tank (flanked by its twin rocket boosters). The tank contains liquid hydrogen and oxygen.*

## CHAOS OUT OF ORDER

**I**F YOU put a layer of coffee grounds into a jar and add a layer of sugar, then screw the lid on the jar and shake it, you will see that the more you shake, the more

*Heat image The friction of a saw as it cuts causes an energy loss through heat. This infrared image shows warm areas (along the handgrip and where the blade touches wood) as red and yellow.*

the substances are mixed. What were two ordered layers become totally disordered.

This illustrates the second law of thermodynamics: 'within a closed system, entropy increases'. In terms of the coffee and sugar mixture, maintaining a 'closed system' simply means keeping the lid on the jar – otherwise it would be possible to separate the sugar grains from the coffee. 'Entropy' is a measure of the degree of disorder.

No matter how efficiently one form of energy is converted into another – for example, electricity into light – some energy is always lost as heat in the process. Heat is matter that is agitated – hot air is simply air in a state of extremely disordered motion. So an increase in heat is the same as an increase in disorder – in other words, an increase in entropy.

In the Universe, energy is constantly being converted from one form to another. If the Universe is a closed system (and astronomers are still arguing over whether or not it is), then the amount of disorder – entropy – in it is constantly increasing as lost energy warms it up. Eventually – although not before millions upon millions of years have passed – the Universe may run out of useful energy, literally warming itself to death.

The Greeks coined the word chaos to describe the state of complete disorder that they believed existed before the creation of the ordered cosmos. But if entropy is always increasing, then what the Greeks believed was chaos must, according to the laws of thermodynamics, have been a state of complete order.

# WATER, WATER, EVERYWHERE
### *The commonest – and most unusual – substance on Earth*

WATER IS the most common chemical compound on Earth. There is so much of it that if the Earth's crust were made absolutely smooth, the oceans would cover the entire planet to a uniform depth of almost 2.5 km (1.5 miles). It is unique in that it occurs naturally in all three possible states of matter – as a solid, as a liquid and as a gas (water vapour). And it has other remarkable properties, too.

More substances will dissolve into water than into any other liquid. This is because water molecules have an unusual arrangement of atoms that turns them into miniature 'magnets', with a positive electrical charge on one side and a negative one on the other. Since opposite electrical charges attract, this means that one or the other side of the water molecule will attach itself to molecules of other substances, whatever their charge. For example, compounds as different as salt, sugar and alcohol all dissolve easily in water. Water is

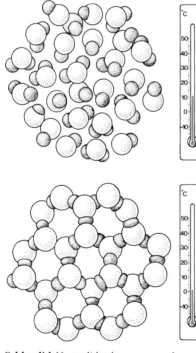

***Odd solid*** *Most solid substances are denser than their liquid form. To form a solid, molecules come close to each other and link up. But when water molecules (top) link to form the regular pattern of an ice crystal (bottom), their odd shape creates a gap between them, increasing the amount of space they take up. Ice is therefore less dense than water – which is why ice cubes float.*

***Cold welcome*** *Having cut a square out of the ice sheet, a British Antarctic Survey diver plunges below.*

extremely 'sticky', in this sense, and it dissolves other materials by tearing their molecules away from one another.

Because of their unusual electrical properties, water molecules stick to one another, too, with extraordinary tenacity. It requires an enormous amount of energy to pull them apart and so change the water's state from, say, solid to liquid. This is the reason why, unlike many other simple compounds containing hydrogen, water melts and boils at such high temperatures. The boiling temperature of methane, for instance, is -161°C (-258°F), far below the freezing point of water.

Water is unusual, too, in the way it freezes. Most liquids freeze from the bottom up: as they are cooled, their density increases steadily. This means that warmer layers, being lighter, will always rise, and the coolest liquid will gather at the bottom.

### *Stopping point*

But ice forms first on the surface of a body of water. For example, the temperature of a lake may be 10°C (50°F) in autumn. As the cold air of winter begins to cool the lake, the top layer of water will become denser and sink to the bottom. Unlike other liquids, though, water reaches its maximum density at 4°C (39°F) – well above freezing point. So at this temperature the movement of water in the lake will stop.

The top layer will cool further, becoming less dense, but will not sink because the water below it is denser. If the air is cold enough, the water at the surface will then approach 0°C (32°F) and become ice. This layer of ice will, unless the winter is extremely severe, shield the lake from the cold atmosphere and thus prevent it from freezing solid.

## DID YOU KNOW..?

*WHEN sea water freezes, most of the salt is contained in pockets of liquid that do not freeze. Sea ice thus contains between a tenth and a hundredth as much salt as sea water, and it can be melted and drunk like fresh water.*

\* \* \*

*ONLY 2.8 per cent of the Earth's water is fresh, and of that small proportion only 6 per cent is liquid – well over 90 per cent is locked up in the polar ice-caps, and the remainder is water vapour in the atmosphere. And about 98 per cent of the Earth's liquid fresh water is underground.*

\* \* \*

*THE AMOUNT of water on Earth has remained the same since the planet was created some 4600 million years ago.*

# SOUND AND SILENCE

## *The high and low and long and short of what we hear*

THE BIGGEST drum in the world, some 2.4 m (8 ft) in diameter, used to stand under a glass roof in the factory yard of the English musical instrument makers Boosey & Hawkes, in Edgware near London. When struck, the huge drum made very little sound – but the clothing of bystanders flapped as if in a breeze.

The skin of the drum vibrated and made waves in the air, but the length of most of these waves was so great, and therefore the pitch of the sound generated was so low, that the human ear could not register them.

The ear hears sound in exactly the same way as a drum makes it – the waves of sound make the stretched membrane of the eardrum vibrate. If the waves come very slowly – at a rate of less than 20 a second – the human eardrum does not respond. As the pitch of the sound rises, the waves become more rapid, and the ear can react to them. If the pitch rises above the point where the air is vibrating more than about 20 000 times a second, the waves arrive too rapidly for our ears to respond, and we cannot hear this sound either.

Sound needs a material medium to carry its vibrations. Unlike light, it will not pass through a vacuum, because there is nothing in the vacuum to

*Big boom The 2.4 m (8 ft) drum was used for thunder effects in London theatres.*

carry the sound waves. So there would be no point in shouting for help in outer space.

Air, however, is not a very efficient way of transmitting sound. It travels at about 1200 km/h (750 mph) through air, but more than four times faster than that through sea water, ten times faster through wood or cast iron, and 16 times faster through glass. Some very hard metals, such as carboloy, can transmit sound at speeds as high as 43 000 km/h (27 000 mph).

Longwave sound, low in pitch, travels furthest because small obstacles do not affect the basic structure of the wave, just as ocean waves pass undisturbed over small rocks. This is why ships' foghorns are pitched so low, to carry their warning as far as possible.

When low-pitched sound meets a surface, however, it is absorbed, whereas faster vibrations bounce off. Sonar detectors are an example of this phenomenon. They locate objects by bouncing a high-pitched 'ping' sound off them.

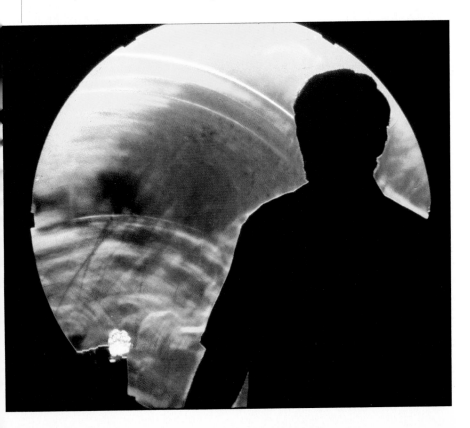

***Schlieren technique*** *This special type of photography can reveal the motion of air itself. The image here shows the sound waves emitted by an electric spark.*

## DEAF AS A BLUE-EYED WHITE

**D**EAFNESS in animals often goes undetected because so few people are on the look-out for it. Cat-breeders, however – more specifically, breeders of British short- and long-haired whites – are only too familiar with the condition.

The gene that makes a cat white all over has other effects besides determining the colour of its coat. It is also responsible, in combination with other genes, for the colour of a cat's eyes and for the formation of its ears. Many white cats are born with a congenital hearing defect – sometimes just in one ear, sometimes in both. The eye-colour of white cats is also unpredictable: some have orange eyes, some blue; a few even have odd-coloured eyes, one orange and one blue.

Unfortunately the cats most frequently found to be deaf are those with blue eyes, the variety that appeals most to the tastes of buyers. However, a recently-created breed, the blue-eyed Foreign White, which has added Siamese blood, is able to hear perfectly well.

# HE THAT HATH EARS
### Some animals have odd ways of hearing

**T**WO HUNDRED years ago, the Italian scientist Lazzaro Spallanzani decided to investigate how bats could find their way in the dark. First, he blinded some bats, and found that they could navigate just as well as before. Then he plugged their ears with wax – and the bats became helpless. Why were their ears so important?

Only a very few people have hearing sharp enough to hear a bat's squeak, and for 150 years nobody solved the problem. It was only in 1938, after highly sensitive microphones had been developed, that two Harvard scientists, Donald Griffin and G.W. Pierce, were able to detect the pulses of high-frequency sound (normally between 20 000 and 130 000 vibrations per second) that bats produce. They use these pulses as a sort of radar, picking up the echo reflected from obstacles in their path.

Recent experiments show that bats also use the sound to locate their food. Some insect-eating bats can 'home in' on their prey by increasing the rate of the pulses. A rapid series of squeaks and echoes gives the bat a constant fix on its fast-moving target. Fish-eating bats detect the disturbances that fish make on the surface of the water. Fruit-eating bats, however, generally use their big eyes to find their food.

Bats are mammals, and have ears similar to humans. But living things hear in many different ways, and some of their 'ears' are quite unlike human ones. Insects have a bundle of nerves attached directly to a thin spot of cuticle, which vibrates when sound strikes it. Crickets have these spots on their front 'knees', bugs have them on their 'chests', and other insects have them on their abdomens.

Hairs on the bodies of caterpillars can detect the sounds made by wasps flying near them. Male mosquitoes and midges can 'hear' the hum of flying females by means of their antennae.

***Excellent listeners*** *Bats make high-pitched sounds whose echoes help them to locate fast-moving prey. But some species of hawkmoth can hear these sounds and take avoiding action.*

# BEWARE OF SILENT NOISE
### *Inaudible sound can ruin your health*

**S**OUNDS whose vibrations are fewer than about 20 per second are too low for the human ear to hear. But such 'infrasound' does have effects on the human body, and if it occurs at high energy levels – so that it would be extremely loud if it were audible – the effects can be devastating.

Some machinery can produce infrasound at unpleasant levels. Recent research has shown that heavy machinery, air intakes on jet engines, even enormous organ pipes, can generate high enough levels of low-frequency noise to produce dizziness and nausea.

In the 1970s, Vladimir Gavreau, of the French National Scientific Research Centre, built a number of what he called 'giant police whistles' to discover if the effects of low-frequency sound could be used in fighting crime. Criminals and terrorists who took hostages, for instance, might be disabled by infrasound at a distance – relieving security forces of the need to enter besieged premises and so lessening the risk that hostages would be killed in a shoot-out.

#### *Demolition pitch*
One of Gavreau's first 'whistles' was 1.5 m (5 ft) in diameter and was embedded in concrete. It has never been run at full blast – a shattering 160 decibels – but Gavreau estimates that another of his machines, which is somewhat less powerful, is probably capable of knocking down walls. As an anti-terrorist device, however, these devices proved useless at any power, as the operators could not direct the sound efficiently and were themselves affected. Gavreau has designed a 'whistle' that produces sound at 3.5 vibrations per second, which can be directed, but this has never been built.

More positive in its effects is 'white noise'. This is constant sound produced over the whole range of audible frequencies. Dentists have used white sound to help to relax their patients.

Because it blankets the mid-range pitch of the human voice, white sound can also render bugging devices ineffective. This effect explains why running a shower masks conversation from a microphone – the water produces sound over a wide range of frequencies and drowns out the human voice.

# HOLDING THE WORLD TOGETHER

### *Compared to other natural forces, gravity is a featherweight*

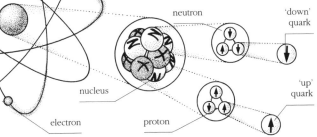

Gravity keeps our feet on the ground, the planets in their places, and entire galaxies together. Yet of the four fundamental forces in the Universe, gravity is the weakest. The other three forces – electromagnetism and the 'strong' and 'weak' nuclear forces – act on the minute particles that make up atoms.

Electromagnetism – the same energy that runs the electric appliances in our homes and carries radio and television signals – keeps electrons in orbit around the nucleus of an atom; the electrical charge they carry also creates a magnetic field that holds them in place.

The nucleus itself consists of protons and neutrons, bound tightly together by the so-called 'strong' nuclear force. If a nucleus breaks down – as it does in a nuclear explosion – it fires out particles and produces radioactivity. The 'weak' nuclear force determines the

***Inside an atom*** *This beryllium atom has four electrons orbiting a nucleus of four protons (+) and five neutrons (N). A neutron consists of two 'down' quarks and one 'up', a proton of two 'up' and one 'down'.*

neutron

'down' quark

nucleus

electron      proton

'up' quark

***Nuclear fission*** *The energy of an atomic bomb is released by bombarding a uranium atom with neutrons until it splits. The split atom releases more neutrons, which in turn split more atoms. This self-perpetuating process is known as a chain reaction.*

### DID YOU KNOW..?

*LORD RUTHERFORD, the New Zealand-born physicist who discovered the protons inside the nucleus of the atom, and so opened the way to nuclear weapons and power stations, said in 1933: 'The energy produced by the breaking down of the atom is a very poor kind of thing. Anyone who looks for a source of power in the transformation of the atom is talking moonshine.'*

behaviour of some of the particles involved in the decay of a neutron. It also controls the enormous thermonuclear explosion that fuels our Sun.

The difference in the strengths of these various forces is extraordinary. A 50 000 tonne ship is big enough to exert a noticeable amount of gravity. Two ships of such size lying side by side in harbour will be pulled together by their own gravity – yet this is still so feeble that they can be kept apart by mooring each of the ships with a single piece of string.

### *Defying gravity*

The electromagnetic force is 100 million million million million million million times stronger than gravity. A small horseshoe magnet defeats the Earth's gravity every time it picks up a pin. The human body has a neutral electrical charge, but if two people standing at arm's length each had one-millionth of their body weight negatively charged with electricity, they would be hurled apart violently like repellent magnets.

More powerful still is the 'strong' nuclear force. This is 100 times stronger than electromagnetism – and yet it is effective only over distances of the same order of magnitude as the width of the nucleus of an atom. And even the so-called 'weak' force is 100 000 million million million million million times stronger than gravity. Yet gravity acts on a cosmic scale, holding whole galaxies together, whereas the 'weak' force acts only on particles so tiny that their dimensions are meaningless when measured in everyday terms.

# WHERE EVEN SCIENTISTS FALL DOWN

### The most mysterious force in the Universe

LONG BEFORE a falling apple is said to have inspired Isaac Newton to investigate the effects of gravity, anyone who fell downstairs or dropped a stone into a pond was aware that some kind of force makes things fall to Earth. We take gravity for granted – yet, of all natural forces, it is the one scientists know least about.

Physicists can describe the other three basic forces in the Universe. These are electromagnetism and the 'strong' and 'weak' nuclear forces. All three operate inside atoms, and each force governs a particular kind of activity within the atom.

One mathematical theory covers how these three forces operate. But that theory does not describe gravity, and scientists cannot say what gravity is 'made of' in the way that they can describe what happens inside an atom. However, they have noticed that, in some respects, the behaviour of gravity parallels the behaviour of light, and the similarities may help to reveal gravity's true nature.

### Waves and packets

Light consists of basic 'packets' of energy called photons. These will, in certain circumstances, behave as if they were separate material objects. In other circumstances, light behaves as if it were a single continuous wave of energy. Another characteristic of light is that if you double your distance from a lamp, you will receive not half but only a quarter of the light you did before. This is because light radiates in a circle from its source. At double the distance, the light is having to cover four times the area.

Gravity, too, loses its force at this rate. And scientists have proposed that gravity, too, travels either as particles or as waves, or both. But no one has yet detected either. So we are left with the paradox that we know exactly what gravity does, and can predict its effects with extreme accuracy. But we cannot be certain what it is. The most familiar of the forces governing the Universe remains the most mysterious.

# PHOTOGRAPHS OF THE INVISIBLE

### Tracing the path of a particle

**Leaving a wake** *This artificially coloured photograph shows the courses followed by subatomic particles passing through a 'bubble chamber' of liquid hydrogen.*

THE PARTICLES that make up an atom cannot be seen and weigh hardly anything. A 1 kg (2.2 lb) bag of protons, for example, would contain 1673 million million million million million of them. But many photographs exist of these particles in flight. If they are so small, how do physicists manage to photograph them?

The pictures are, in fact, of the tracks the particles make as they rocket through a container full of something else. Scientists first saw subatomic particles in a device called a 'cloud chamber', for which the Scottish physicist Charles Wilson won a Nobel prize in 1927. This is a container in which water vapour is allowed to expand and therefore cool, so that it becomes supersaturated – that is, the vapour reaches a temperature at which it normally condenses into water droplets. For supersaturation to occur, there must be no particles of dust, on which water vapour normally forms, in the chamber.

But when an electron or a proton passes through the vapour, it heats it up, and the vapour does condense, forming a miniature track behind the particle like the contrail of a high-flying jet. It is possible, too, to measure the mass of the particle, by applying an electric or magnetic field to make it curve off course; from the amount of energy this takes, physicists can calculate the particle's mass.

### Beer bubbles

In 1952, the American scientist Donald Glaser refined the technique with the 'bubble chamber'. This contains liquid hydrogen heated to a point at which the slightest amount of additional energy will turn it to vapour. A particle fired through the chamber vaporises the liquid, leaving a trail of tiny bubbles in its wake. Scientists can even photograph particles as they collide and scatter. The idea came to Glaser while he was watching the fine lines of bubbles rising from the bottom of a glass of beer.

---

## DID YOU KNOW..?

AMERICAN physicist Murray Gell-Mann won the 1969 Nobel prize for physics for predicting the existence of quarks, the subatomic particles that are the fundamental basis of physical matter. He believed that the particles were of three kinds, and named them after a quotation from James Joyce's Finnegans Wake: 'Three quarks for Muster Mark.' Scientists now believe there are more than three kinds, but that quarks move in groups of three. Quarks have such odd qualities that physicists have coined equally odd terms for them. They come in six 'flavours' – up, down, charmed, strange, top and bottom. (The last two used to be called truth and beauty.) And they have six 'colours': red, green, blue, cyan, magenta and yellow.

*chapter two*

# SKYWATCH

IS THERE ANY connection between the extinction of the dinosaurs 65 million years ago and a giant swarm of comets orbiting the Sun beyond Pluto? Some scientists think so. They say that there may be an undiscovered star travelling round the Sun in an elliptical orbit (*page 58*). Every 30 million years, this star's approach would send millions of comets towards the Sun, and some would strike the Earth, disturbing our climate and causing mass extinctions. Such a 'death star' may yet be discovered – today's astronomers are detecting fascinating celestial bodies and events that, despite their enormous distance from the Earth, subtly influence our solar system.

# INSIDE THE TURBULENT SUN

### *The power of the hydrogen bomb creates the sunlight we depend on*

TO THE non-astronomer, the Sun is a model of constancy – a featureless white globe that has shone steadily throughout human history. But astronomers know the Sun to be a nuclear powerhouse in constant turmoil, and it may be far less reliable than we think.

The Sun is a vast ball of hot gas, principally hydrogen, big enough to swallow up 1.3 million Earths. To express its weight in tonnes you would need to write a 2 followed by 27 noughts. This weight, some 300 000 times that of the Earth, crushes the Sun's core to a pressure of over 300 million times that of our atmosphere.

The temperature at the centre of the Sun is 15 000 000°C (27 000 000°F). In this furnace rages the nuclear reaction that creates the Sun's light and heat. It is the same reaction that powers the H-bomb – the nuclear 'burning' of hydrogen into helium. As in all nuclear reactions, matter is converted into energy. The amount of helium produced in the reaction is only 92.3 per cent of the amount of hydrogen used up. The difference has been converted into light, heat, X-rays

*Loops of fire These dramatic solar 'prominences' are clouds of hydrogen many times the size of the Earth.*

and other forms of energy. Four million tonnes of the Sun's matter vanish in this way each second.

At the surface, the Sun's temperature is a mere 5800°C (10 400°F). The visible surface is mottled – bright where hot gas has just risen from the depths, darker where a cooled area is about to descend. Invisible, looping magnetic fields occasionally break through the surface from the depths beneath. The magnetic fields block the flow of energy, so the areas of the surface where the loops emerge and re-enter become relatively cool and appear as dark sunspots. Prominences – spectacular clouds of glowing red hydrogen many times the size of the Earth – climb into the solar sky and fall back again.

Can a body as violent as the Sun be relied upon not to change its behaviour in the future – not to scorch us or let us freeze to death?

Constant monitoring shows many irregularities. It appears, for example, that since 1979 the Sun has cooled by one-tenth of 1 per cent. This minor fluctuation will probably reverse, staying in step with regular ups and downs in general solar activity, such as the number of sunspots. All theorists agree that the Sun will continue to support life on Earth for about another 5000 million years.

---

## BOMBARDMENT FROM THE SUN

ON JULY 7, 1988, 3000 homing pigeons fluttered from cages in northern France, circled a few times and set off on their annual race for their homes in southern England. But events on the distant Sun were to doom the race.

Two days before, a solar flare – a colossal explosion on the surface of the Sun – had fired clouds of electrically-charged protons and other subatomic particles into space, some of which had disrupted the Earth's magnetic field. When bad weather prevents them from steering by the Sun or the stars, homing pigeons use internal magnetic 'compasses' to guide them. Misled by the celestial

disturbances, the pigeons flew way off course. Few made it to their homes.

Pigeons are not the only creatures at risk from solar flares. The high-energy particles they fire out pose a serious risk of radiation sickness and even cancer to space travellers. Space shuttle flights are postponed whenever astronomers observe a flare. If astronauts one day build bases on the Moon or Mars they may need to cover them with rocks as protection against the radiation emitted by solar flares. And long-distance manned spacecraft will have to be equipped with 'storm shelters' for the crew to retreat into when flares occur.

---

### DID YOU KNOW..?

*IF THE REACTIONS in the Sun's core were to be 'switched off' now, it would be 10 million years before the solar surface started to cool – and before the Earth felt the effects.*

# SHADOWS IN THE SKY
## *How the motions of the Earth and Moon cause eclipses*

IN MANY adventure stories, the hero has been able to get the better of superstitious tribal people by means of his superior understanding of eclipses. A classic example is in Hergé's *Prisoners of the Sun*, when boy reporter Tintin terrifies his captors with his apparent power to blot out the Sun.

One of the first writers to use this convenient plot device was H. Rider Haggard in *King Solomon's Mines*. But when Haggard first published his story, his understanding of eclipses was, unfortunately, far from perfect. Until corrected in a later edition, the story implied that the Moon is full on the nights before and after eclipses of the Sun. But these occur when the Moon passes between the Sun and the Earth, while the Moon is full when it is on the opposite side of the Earth to the Sun. There is always a gap of two weeks between an eclipse of the Sun and the full Moon preceding or following.

Eclipses of the Moon, however, take place only at full Moon (though not at every full Moon). They occur when the Moon enters the Earth's shadow.

During an eclipse of the Sun, the centre of the Moon's shadow passes along a band on the Earth's surface up to 272 km (169 miles) wide. Within this band all sunlight is cut off for a few minutes, the sky darkens and the stars come out. By pure chance, the Moon and the Sun appear to be almost exactly the same size when viewed from the Earth, so the Moon effectively covers the Sun during an eclipse of the Sun. Features of the Sun normally blotted out by its own intense light become visible around the dark edge of the Moon. Fiery red prominences – clouds of hydrogen – and a pearly white corona, the Sun's 'atmosphere', can be seen.

The Earth's shadow is large enough to cover the Moon completely in an eclipse of the Moon. Sometimes the Moon passes through the edge of the shadow and it merely seems to fade a little. In order for there to be a total eclipse of the Moon, it must enter the central part of the shadow.

But even then the Moon is not wholly obscured – some rays of sunlight, bent by the Earth's atmosphere, still fall on it. Since only light at the red end of the spectrum bends at just the right angle to illuminate the Moon, our familiar silver satellite then takes on a beautiful deep copper hue.

---

### DID YOU KNOW..?

*FRENCH astronomers studying old records of eclipses recently reported that the Sun must have been slightly bigger a few centuries ago. But a group of British astronomers claim their French colleagues were probably misled by air pollution, which over the last 300 years has dimmed the Sun's image. They point out that the size of the Sun as measured in unpolluted parts of America has always been greater than that measured at Greenwich, near smoky London.*

---

# JOURNEY TO THE NEAREST STAR
## *A fleet of space probes will take a fresh look at the Sun*

A SERIES of space probes, built by the European Space Agency and launched by the United States, will increase our knowledge of the Sun in the 1990s and beyond.

*Ulysses* was launched from the US space shuttle in 1990. It was the first probe to fly over the Sun's poles. First *Ulysses* was headed away from the Sun, towards Jupiter, the largest planet in the solar system. It was sucked in by the giant planet's powerful gravity, whirled around like a stone in a sling, and flung out of the ecliptic – the imaginary plane in which the orbits of the planets lie.

*Ulysses* will fly high over one pole of the Sun in 1994; the following year, its orbit will carry it over the other. The data it collects and transmits will give scientists a new understanding of the Sun's polar regions, solar wind, the Sun's magnetic field, and cosmic dust.

### *Monitoring 'sunquakes'*

In 1995, a second satellite will be launched, called *SOHO*, which stands for Solar Heliospheric Observatory. The heliosphere is the vast region around the Sun, where the effect of solar wind – the steady stream of atomic particles emanating from the Sun – can be detected. *SOHO* will follow a more conventional orbit than *Ulysses*, but its observations will be far from conventional.

By analysing variations in sunlight, *SOHO* will provide information on 'sunquakes' – vibrations of the Sun's surface as sound waves roll back and forth through the interior. A rise and fall of the Sun's surface by as little as 10 km (6 miles) will be detectable.

Farther in the future is *Vulcan*, for which no launch date has been set. Whereas *SOHO* will follow an orbit much closer to the Earth than to the Sun, *Vulcan* will be a 'sun-grazer', flying to within the orbit of Mercury, the innermost planet. On Mercury itself, which moves at an average distance of 58 million km (36 million miles) from the Sun, the noon temperature on the Equator is over 300°C (570°F) – hot enough to melt lead. *Vulcan*, flying as close as 2.4 million km (1.5 million miles) to the Sun, will have to withstand temperatures of 2200°C (4000°F).

*Vulcan* will be equipped with a heat-resistant shield. The shield will glow white hot and will very slowly vaporise, but not before the instruments on board have had a chance to study the gases of the Sun's 'atmosphere'.

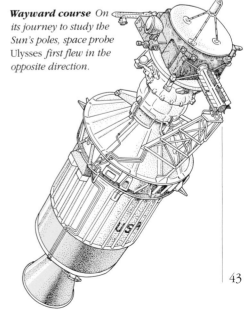

***Wayward course*** *On its journey to study the Sun's poles, space probe Ulysses first flew in the opposite direction.*

# FRONTIERS IN SPACE

## *Why go to the trouble of manufacturing something on a space ship?*

THE FIRST industrial products to be labelled 'made in space' were thousands of millions of minute spheres, made from a liquid plastic in the American space shuttle during several missions in the early 1980s. When such spheres are manufactured on Earth, the pull of gravity on the materials and equipment causes minute imperfections. But, thanks to the weightless conditions of space, spheres made there are geometrically perfect.

The spheres, about as big as a pin point, have many uses, such as providing an accurate size reference when placed alongside specimens on a microscope slide, and testing filters with superfine pores. They were made in batches of 15 g (0.5 oz) – but businesses and universities were prepared to pay for their perfection at a rate of $23 million per 1 kg (2.2 lb), making the plastic worth 2000 times its weight in gold.

### *Growth industry*

Another process that is best carried out under conditions of weightlessness is the growth of crystals from a chemical solution as it is cooled. Scientists trying to work out the composition of a substance sometimes turn it into crystal form, because X-ray analysis of crystals can reveal their precise chemical structure. On Earth, convection – currents of rising warm liquid and descending cool liquid – interferes with the composition of a solution as it crystallises. In weightless conditions, convection does not occur.

### *Medicines, metals and microchips*

Because of the cost of sending materials and special equipment into space, only products that can show a profit despite being made in small quantities are suitable for manufacture there. These include drugs of unprecedented purity, alloys of metals that will not mix well under gravity, and near-perfect microchips made from crystalline materials.

An American aerospace company has teamed up with a pharmaceutical firm to make purer versions of drugs, such as interferon, a protein used to fight cancer, and Factor 8, a blood-clotting agent used by haemophiliacs. Both of these drugs are purified by a process called electrophoresis. This can be carried out far more efficiently in space than on Earth, producing extremely pure versions of these invaluable drugs.

# SPOTTED FROM AFAR

## *Observation satellites can provide images of any place on Earth*

SATELLITE photography used to be confined to military 'spies in the sky', but now you can buy pictures of your own back yard taken from civilian satellites belonging to France and the United States.

The most advanced of these spacecraft are the French satellites called *SPOT* (*Satellite Pour l'Observation de la Terre*). These satellites circle the Earth from pole to pole, at a height of 830 km (520 miles), photographing strips of the Earth's surface up to 80 km (50 miles) wide. In the course of 26 days, each satellite's telescopes and cameras view every place on Earth.

Each *SPOT* satellite observes the ground through two telescopes. These point in different directions, so that, as the satellite passes overhead on successive and slightly different orbits, pictures of a given region can be taken from two angles. A computer can then use these pictures to build up a relief map or a three-dimensional picture of the terrain. Customers for *SPOT*'s images include mining companies prospecting for minerals, government departments building up pictures of their nation's natural resources, and pipeline constructors surveying vast tracts of land. A European national TV authority even used *SPOT* pictures to work out the best position for new transmitters.

Due to be launched in the late 90s, *SPOT 4* will be even more advanced than its predecessors. It will observe four specific wavelengths of light reflected from the Earth – one green, one red and two infrared (heat) wavelengths. Comparison of each area of the Earth at these wavelengths will reveal such features as the type and health of vegetation, soil moisture, types of rock, and the extent of built-up areas.

*SPOT 4* will be able to distinguish objects as small as 10 m (33 ft) in diameter – the spread of an average tree.

***In the picture*** *By analysing* SPOT *images, such as this photograph of a mountainous region of Algeria, scientists can survey a nation's natural resources.*

# BEYOND THE WILD BLUE YONDER

*Drawing up blueprints for craft that are both spaceships and aeroplanes*

I N THE PAST, ordinary air passengers have seen little benefit from the technological advances made in space travel. But this may be about to change – airliners are on the drawing board that will whisk the tourist or businessman from Europe to Japan in just three hours, compared to the 12 hours taken by today's jets.

The next breakthrough in spaceflight is likely to be the spaceplane – a craft able to take off from a normal runway, climb to the upper atmosphere and then either continue into space, or fly on at hypersonic speeds (many times the speed of sound) to a destination on Earth.

In the lower atmosphere, the spaceplane will be powered by an air-breathing jet engine, like the turbojets used on today's large commercial aircraft. At high altitudes, more advanced ramjets will take over. (Turbojets have fast-spinning turbines to compress the intake air and make the fuel burn well. Ramjets have no moving parts – the aircraft's high forward speed rams air into the engine and compresses it.)

Higher up still, where there is very little oxygen to burn fuel, the spaceplane

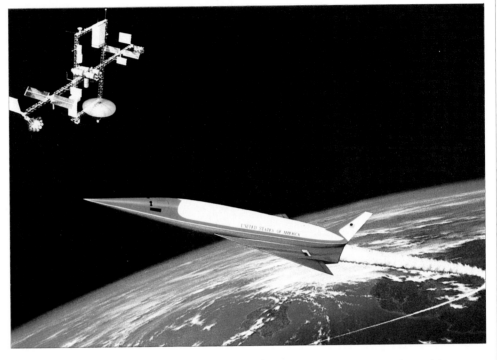

**Space traveller** *NASA's National Aerospace Plane would be capable of making a rendezvous with an orbiting satellite as well as serving as a hypersonic passenger plane.*

will switch to rocket engines, which rely on liquid oxygen carried by the craft's tanks. Here, where air resistance is minimal, the spaceplane will build up speeds it could never reach at lower altitudes.

Since a spaceplane will consume oxygen from the air for much of its flight, it will not need to carry as much oxygen as a conventional rocket. For example, a spaceplane would need only about half the oxygen used by the space shuttle's engines, and would therefore not have to carry, as the shuttle does, a huge oxygen tank which is discarded soon after launch. These savings could cut the costs of launching a satellite into low Earth orbit – say, 300 km (190 miles) high, roughly the same altitude at which the shuttle orbits – to a fifth of what they are today.

### Robot plane

This technology would also lend itself to airliners capable of flying at hypersonic speeds in the thin air of high altitudes. Several nations are now developing spaceplanes.

The main British proposal is called HOTOL (Horizontal Take-off and Landing). The first model would be an unmanned robot plane capable of carrying a 7 tonne satellite into orbit. But it could also be developed into a liner carrying up to 80 people between

continents, even though much of its 52 m (170 ft) body (about the length of Concorde) would be taken up by a liquid-hydrogen fuel tank.

### Three engines

NASA is pressing ahead with a research aircraft called NASP, the National Aerospace Plane. This may have three engines: two types of jet – a turbojet and a hydrogen-burning 'scramjet' (supersonic-combustion ramjet) – plus a rocket engine.

The German Sänger II vehicle would be powered by 'turboramjets', which function as turbojets at speeds up to two to three times that of sound and convert to ramjets to reach six times the speed of sound. As a means of global transport, it could carry 250 passengers 15 000 km (9300 miles) – say, from London to Hong Kong in three hours. Alternatively, it could give another craft – for example, a winged orbiter, like the space shuttle, capable of flying back to Earth – a piggy-back ride up to an altitude of 35 km (22 miles), where the orbiter would separate and continue under rocket power into space.

---

## DID YOU KNOW..?

*BENOIT LEBON, a French scientist, has suggested building a 'monorail' transport system around the Earth. A hollow ring would be constructed outside the atmosphere, possibly 100 km (60 miles) up, from sections brought from the ground by rocket. A vast rotating loop, consisting of wire or a stream of metallic grains, would circulate within the ring, propelled by electromagnetic motors. The centrifugal force of the loop's motion would support not only the loop itself, but also the stationary ring enclosing it. Cables hanging from the ring to the Earth's surface could haul up cargoes, which would be whisked around the ring on transporter units and lowered to the ground in some other part of the globe.*

# THE BURDEN OF WEIGHTLESSNESS

## Lack of gravity can harm long-distance space travellers

SPACE scientists and engineers foresee manned flights to Mars taking 18 months each way – and voyages to the outer planets taking many years. So people may one day spend large parts of their lives on space stations – children may even be born and raised on them. But, before these dreams can become reality, scientists must first solve the physiological problems caused by prolonged weightlessness.

### Weight off one's shoulders

Before the age of space flight, science-fiction writers and visionary scientists thought weightlessness would be an exhilarating experience, humanity's release from the bonds of gravity. Astronauts have found that this is true – but only for a short while. They have also found associated discomforts and dangers that threaten to limit the prospects for long-distance space travel.

One of the immediate effects of weightlessness is a sudden rush of blood to the head. The body's main arteries are equipped with organs, called baroreceptors, that ensure that the heart pumps the right amount of blood to the head. In conditions of weightlessness, the baroreceptors think there is not enough blood in the upper body, and allow extra blood to move upwards from the legs. This makes the face puff out and causes nasal stuffiness.

Furthermore, the brain thinks the extra blood in the head means there is too much fluid in the body. It therefore releases hormones that tell the kidneys

### HURLED INTO ORBIT

LIFTING a satellite into orbit is a very expensive business – and the higher the orbit, the greater the cost. But substantial savings could one day be achieved simply by exploiting the curious physical effects of tethering two spacecraft together with a cable.

Imagine that a satellite is launched from an orbiting spacecraft, such as the space shuttle, and a long cable links the two. If the satellite is gently pushed from the shuttle's cargo bay in the direction of outer space, the cable will – thanks to the laws of physics – end up in a straight, taut line extending vertically above the shuttle away from the Earth.

Normally, an object orbiting freely moves more slowly the farther its orbit is from the Earth. But a satellite 'hanging' above a shuttle would be dragged along at the shuttle's own speed. If the satellite were then released, it would be moving too fast for its orbit. The excess speed would send it into a higher orbit.

For example, suppose a shuttle orbiting at a height of 400 km (250 miles) pays out a 100 km (60 mile) cable with a satellite attached. Once the satellite is released, its speed will cause it to climb 10 km (6 miles) higher. The satellite has received a 110 km (68 mile) boost free of charge. The energy it gains will, in fact, be 'paid for' by a corresponding energy loss by the shuttle. This loss will drive the shuttle into a lower orbit. But since the shuttle eventually needs to return to Earth anyway, the exchange would profit both spacecraft.

Such a cable could be useful in another way, provided it was an electrical conductor: an electric current would develop along it as it swept through the Earth's magnetic field. The wire would generate enough power to top up batteries or power onboard computers.

An Italian experiment involving a satellite tethered to a space shuttle by a cable took place in 1992.

to discharge more urine, causing dehydration, and to lower the number of red cells in the blood, resulting in anaemia.

### A feeling in the bones

At the same time, muscles, freed from the need to combat gravity, become very weak. On long flights, the most important muscle of all, the heart, can shrink by as much as 10 per cent. Bones, too, react to a release from gravity. On Earth, bones regulate their uptake of calcium from the blood according to the stresses of bearing weight.

In the absence of these habitual stresses, the bones lose calcium, most of which is discharged in the urine. Unless countermeasures are taken, the bones could become dangerously brittle and painful kidney stones could form from the discharged calcium.

Russian cosmonauts, some of whom have remained in orbit for more than a year, perform exercises that simulate the normal effects of gravity on the body. But exercises take up a lot of their time – they devote several hours a day to them – and do not solve all the problems of

weightlessness. So the Russians have also experimented with a device that stimulates the muscles with electrical pulses and a special garment, known as a 'penguin suit', which demands constant muscular exertion from the wearer, even to stand upright.

**No up, no down** *During the short flights of the space shuttle, weightlessness can be a nuisance but it does not harm the body.*

### DID YOU KNOW..?

*PERHAPS the most bizarre idea for the commercial exploitation of space was proposed by Space Services of America, Inc., run by a former astronaut, Deke Slayton, in association with a consortium of Florida morticians. As the ultimate funeral service, they planned to place the ashes of the departed in capsules aboard a satellite. The satellite would have been covered with a reflective material, so that at night it would appear as bright as a star as it orbited the Earth. Interest in this novel form of immortality was not sufficient to get the idea off the ground.*

# THE EMPIRE OF THE SUN

*Why is Venus too hot for life, Mars too cold and Earth just right?*

EARTH'S neighbouring planets, Venus and Mars, once seemed the most promising places in our solar system to find conditions suitable for life. But space probes have discovered that Venus is far too hot, with an average temperature of 460°C (860°F) and a crushing atmospheric pressure 93 times as great as our own. And Mars is a chilly planet, with temperatures averaging -60°C (-75°F) and a thin carbon dioxide atmosphere. Neither planet would be suitable for life even of a very primitive kind.

The Earth, however, has always had a relatively balmy climate: there has always been liquid water here, even a few thousand million years ago, when the Sun was only 70 per cent as bright as it is now. The explanation appears to lie in the way the Sun's heat is trapped by carbon dioxide in our atmosphere. Over the aeons, the levels of carbon dioxide have adjusted to keep the Earth at the right temperature. On Venus, there is always too much carbon dioxide; on Mars, never enough.

### Give and take

The Earth's planetary thermostat is controlled by a constant exchange of carbon dioxide between its atmosphere and its rocks. Some of the carbon dioxide is continually dissolving in rainwater, and being chemically absorbed by rocks as they weather. On the other hand, volcanic eruptions discharge carbon dioxide. (A cycle independent of this one also controls carbon dioxide. Plants consume carbon dioxide and manufacture oxygen, which is in turn converted by animals into carbon dioxide.)

If the Earth's average temperature should fall for any reason, less surface water would evaporate, so there would be less rainfall and less weathering of rocks, while the amount of carbon dioxide discharged by volcanoes would be unchanged. Atmospheric carbon dioxide levels would increase, so more of the Sun's energy would be trapped in the atmosphere, causing the temperature to rise again. The opposite would

happen should the Earth's average temperature rise above its normal average level.

On Venus, the carbon dioxide 'thermostat' does not function because there is no water and hence no rainfall. The planet's orbit is slightly too close to the Sun; there was originally as much water as there is on the Earth, but it escaped from the atmosphere into space. The carbon dioxide that might have been washed into the rocks has instead stayed in the Venusian atmosphere.

Mars probably once had a benign climate – valleys carved by running water are still visible. But, because of the planet's small size, its internal heat has faded, and the crust is not in constant turmoil like the Earth's. Carbon dioxide has remained trapped in the rocks, leaving a thin atmosphere that can no longer trap heat.

***Peaceful landscape*** *Mars has volcanoes, as shown by the three on the left of this photograph, and some of them may be active. But because the planet has lost much of its internal heat, eruptions are rare.*

# COLLISION WITH A COMET

*Millions once feared an encounter with
the tail of a celestial beast*

**Long tail** *Comet West passes
across the sky, leaving a
trail of gas (coloured blue)
and dust (white).*

IN 1910, a panic swept round the
world. In Lexington, Kentucky,
prayer meetings were held by the
faithful preparing to meet their doom.
In Rome, citizens hoarded oxygen
cylinders. In Chicago, householders
stuffed rags into the chinks under the
doors of their homes. In Istanbul, people kept vigil on their rooftops. The
world was preparing to pass through
the tail of Halley's comet.

William Huggins, a British astronomer, had just announced the discovery
of cyanogen gas in several comets,
including Halley's. Cyanogen gas readily forms the deadly poison potassium
cyanide, and many people believed our
atmosphere would be poisoned.

### Dirty snowball

The nucleus of a comet is a ball of
dusty ice, sometimes as large as 10 km
(6 miles) across. If, during its orbit, the
comet comes close to the Sun – that is,
within three times the distance of the
Earth from the Sun – some of this ice
will melt and then vaporise, and the
released gases and dust will form a
'head' spreading for 100 000 km
(60 000 miles) or more. Some of this

matter will also be
pushed by solar radiation
into a tail. The longest
comet tail ever recorded
was that of the Great
comet of 1843. It
stretched 330 million km
(205 million miles) – over
twice the distance from
the Earth to the Sun.

But the fears of 1910
were unfounded – the
gases of a comet's tail are
so rarefied that when the
Earth does pass through
them, the contamination
is unmeasurable.

The distinction of the
closest recorded ap-
proach by the nucleus of a comet
belongs to Lexell's comet of 1770,
which came to within 1 200 000 km
(750 000 miles) of the Earth – fully
three times the distance of the Earth
from the Moon. There is no need to

worry about another approach by
Lexell's comet. It was subsequently
swung into a new orbit by the gravitational pull of Jupiter, and has been lost
to astronomers ever since.

Roughly every million years, the
Earth does collide with a comet nucleus
or asteroid of 1 km (3300 ft) or more in
diameter. But no comet has ever come
close to a collision with the Earth during recorded history.

### A brighter Sun

However, in August 1979 a comet hit
the Sun. The event was recorded by a
video camera linked to a telescope on
a US Air Force satellite. The collision
did not become known until the tapes
were studied over two years later. The
comet had never been seen before, and
its debris caused the corona, the Sun's
outer 'atmosphere', to shine more
brightly for hours. The collisions of
other comets with the Sun have since
been observed.

---

## THE CANTELOUPE WORLD

VOYAGER 2, the unmanned explorer
launched in 1977, sent back spectacular views of the largest of Neptune's
moons, Triton. Its highly textured surface shows great variety, in some places
resembling tripe, in others the skin of a
canteloupe melon. This terrain is in low
relief: hills and crater walls are less than
500 m (1500 ft) high. Scientists believe
this is because the surface is a soft,
slushy mixture of rock fragments and
frozen nitrogen and methane. There are
also vast frozen lakes, probably of water
ice. At -236°C (-393°F), the satellite is the
coldest world yet observed.

Triton's southern hemisphere is covered by 'snow' of nitrogen and methane,
made slightly pinkish by chemical
changes caused by cosmic radiation. It is
one of the three moons in the solar system that have atmospheres. (The others
are Jupiter's Io and Saturn's Titan.) This
atmosphere is extraordinarily thin – its
surface pressure is only a ten-millionth

that of the Earth's – but it is composed
of nitrogen, which is also the main com-
ponent of our atmosphere.

There are intriguing smudges of dark
material showing up against Triton's
snow. These may be patches of dusty
material thrown up by the activity of
volcanoes – the result of liquid nitrogen
gathering in pockets beneath the surface, being warmed by subterranean
heat, and vaporising in an explosion.

There are auroras in Triton's thin nitrogen atmosphere, fed by particles that
are shed from the particle belts girdling
the parent planet. But these auroras
would be invisible to our eyes, as they
give out ultraviolet light.

*Voyager* also discovered six new
moons as it flew past Neptune. Previously, only Triton and one other moon,
Nereid, were known. Remarkably, one
of *Voyager*'s new discoveries was larger
than Nereid; but because it was darker,
it had gone unseen by Earth telescopes.

---

## DID YOU KNOW..?

*REPORTS of comet sightings have come
down to us from ancient times. The word
'comet' comes from the Greek word*
kometes, *meaning 'long-haired' – a
reference to the comet's tail trailing
across the sky.*

# THE BLUE PLANET

*Voyager's last mission yielded many surprises about the farthest world in the solar system*

I N AUGUST 1989, the indefatigable solar system explorer *Voyager 2* swept past the distant world of Neptune. As with every other flyby that it has carried out since its launch in 1977, *Voyager* transformed astronomers' view of its target. But it raised as many questions as it answered about this giant blue planet.

Neptune is currently the outermost world of the Sun's family. Tiny Pluto usually holds this position, but it is now at the closest point in its orbit to the Sun, which brings it just within Neptune's distance from the Sun.

At that distance, never less than 4347 million km (2702 million miles) from Earth, sunlight is only a nine-hundredth as bright as it is to us. In this gloom, each picture taken by *Voyager* needed a three-second exposure before it was transmitted to Earth.

### Poisonous atmosphere

From Earth, Neptune is a tiny, feature-less bluish disc. *Voyager* found a world with a thick blue atmosphere of poisonous methane. Painstaking observations with Earth-based telescopes had led astronomers to believe that Neptune's day lasted for 18 hours and 12 minutes. This estimate was over two hours wrong; radio waves from within the planet revealed to *Voyager* that the rotation period is 16 hours 3 minutes.

*Voyager* discerned intricate detail in the planet's face. There was a permanent storm, christened the Great Dark Spot and reminiscent of Jupiter's Great Red Spot. Close to the planet's south pole was a smaller spot. The Great Dark Spot is being blown westwards at 1100 km/h (685 mph), while the more southerly storm is roughly at rest in relation to the unseen surface of the planet. Approximately midway between the two storms was another long-lived patch of cloud dubbed 'the Scooter' because of its rapid motion.

### Violent storms a puzzle

This violent atmospheric activity is even more intense than that of Jupiter, whose swirling cloud patterns made such striking images when *Voyager* passed by. Neptune's atmosphere is powered by an energy supply, from sunlight and internal heat, that is only one-twentieth that which powers Jupiter's atmosphere. Atmospheric scientists

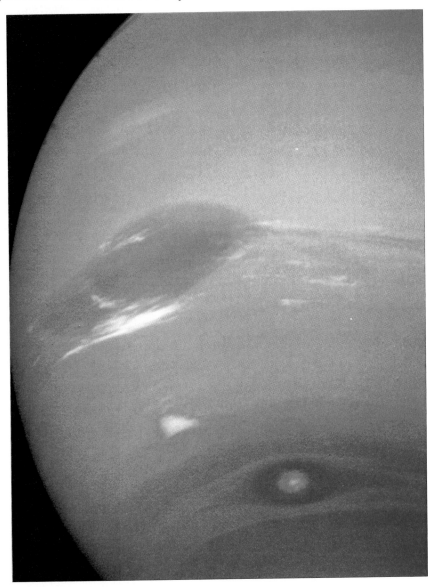

are now seeking an explanation of how Neptune's atmosphere can move so vigorously on so little energy.

The orientation of Neptune's magnetic field was another surprise. Scientists had assumed that, as on the Earth, the planet's magnetic poles would lie close to its geographical poles. They aimed the probe to fly over Neptune's north geographical pole. It turned out that the magnetic poles are tilted fully 50 degrees away from the axis of rotation; because scientists had not expected this, *Voyager* had been programmed to fly through a region of the magnetic field that was less interesting than had been hoped.

*Face of Neptune* Voyager's photos show a storm called the Great Dark Spot (centre left), a smaller storm (bottom) and a cloud patch, 'the Scooter' (halfway between the storms).

Five years before *Voyager* reached Neptune, astronomers announced the discovery of arcs that seemed to be parts of rings around Neptune. *Voyager* confirmed that Neptune does indeed have several thin rings. In the outermost of these are the arcs – bright patches, each with a tiny moonlet at its centre. The arcs, and other details of the rings that bedeck the outer planets, are mysteries waiting to be explained.

49

# THE DOUBLE PLANET

*Astronomers can tell a lot about Pluto by the company it keeps*

ASTRONOMERS often describe the Earth and Moon as making up a 'double planet' because the Moon is so large – its diameter is about a quarter that of the Earth's. But, in 1978, it was found that distant, tiny Pluto has an even better claim to that description, with a partner that is half its diameter.

No one suspected the existence of Pluto's companion until an American astronomer, James Christy, re-examined old photos of the planet. The pictures had been rejected because the image of Pluto was slightly elongated into an oval shape. Christy realised that this was no defect – the pictures showed a companion to Pluto that the camera had been unable to separate from the primary body.

The newly discovered body was christened Charon, after the mythological boatman who ferried souls to Hades across the River Styx – and in tribute to Christy's wife, Charlene. Charon circles Pluto at a distance of 20 000 km (12 500 miles), taking about a week to do so.

### Measuring the mass

Observation of Charon immediately provided a wealth of information about the obscure world of Pluto, which is only seen as a pinpoint of light in even the largest telescopes. Previously, astronomers had not known its size or mass. By applying the laws of gravity to the movement of Charon, astronomers worked out that the combined mass of the system is a five-hundredth that of the Earth's. Most of this belongs to Pluto.

This means that the density of Pluto is about twice that of water, which suggests that it is made mostly of rock, with some ice – probably water ice. Many astronomers once thought that Pluto was a satellite of Neptune gone astray. But since the moons of the outer solar system, such as those of Neptune, are largely made of water ice or frozen gases, this theory now seems unlikely.

At present the orbit of Charon is so positioned that, as seen from the Earth, Charon passes first in front of and then behind Pluto, so that the brightness of each body is obscured in turn. This fortunate alignment makes it possible to measure the size of the two bodies very accurately: astronomers know the speed at which the two bodies are travelling, and can time how long one obscures the brightness of the other. We now know that Pluto is 2284 km (1419 miles) across; Charon is 1192 km (741 miles) across.

### Bright spots

Astronomers have also analysed moments when, for example, the brightness of Pluto has dropped particularly sharply as Charon passes in front of it. This happens when a light area of Pluto's surface is being obscured by Charon, and astronomers have identified these light areas as being Pluto's bright ice caps. There are no similar drops of brightness when Pluto passes in front of Charon, however, so it is likely that Charon has no ice caps.

Astronomers will have to content themselves with this low-definition view of Pluto and Charon for years to come. There are no plans to send any more probes to the farthest reaches of the solar system.

# VERMIN OF THE SKIES

*Asteroids swarm in a region where a planet was expected*

THE CELESTIAL POLICE were on the lookout for a fugitive. They believed that a member of the solar system was missing. They had no description, but thought they knew where to look: near the ecliptic, the band in which the orbits of the planets lie. There was a conspicuously large gap between Mars and Jupiter – surely some undiscovered planet must lurk there.

This scenario comes not from some futuristic science fiction epic, but from the past. The Celestial Police were a group of 24 astronomers called together in 1800 by the German Johann Schröter at his observatory in Lilienthal. Maddeningly, it was an astronomer outside the group, Giuseppe Piazzi, who reported the discovery of a faint new planet, on January 1, 1801. He named it Ceres, after the patron goddess of Sicily, Piazzi's home.

### Police success

By 1807, the Celestial Police had found three more faint objects circling between Mars and Jupiter. These minor planets are known as asteroids, and, by the end of the century, more than 450 had been found.

In 1891, an asteroid appeared in a photograph of the sky for the first time. In long exposures taken with telescopes that follow the motion of the sky as the Earth revolves, the fixed stars show up as points. But, because of their motion in relation to the stars, asteroids show up as streaks. They are so numerous that they have earned the name 'Vermin of the Skies'.

### A satellite of Saturn?

Today astronomers have named and numbered more than 2000 asteroids and established their orbits. The largest is Ceres, 1003 km (623 miles) in diameter, followed by Pallas at 608 km (378 miles) and Vesta at 538 km (334 miles). Only Vesta occasionally comes close enough to Earth to become visible – if only just – to the naked eye.

Perhaps the most mysterious asteroid is Chiron, because it may in fact be an escaped satellite of Saturn rather than an asteroid. Its orbit mostly lies between that of Saturn and Uranus – one sixth of it comes within Saturn's orbit.

The first theory of the asteroids' origin was that they were the remains of a planet that had exploded. Today it seems certain that they formed from material that never succeeded in forming a planet. Added together, their mass is less than that of the Moon.

---

## DID YOU KNOW..?

*ASTEROIDS were originally given classical names, but as more have been discovered, more inventive names have been devised. Asteroid number 694 is called 'Ekard' – its orbit was computed by students of Drake University, Iowa, and Ekard is Drake reversed. Asteroid 1625 is called 'The NORC', after an early electronic computer, the Naval Ordnance Research Calculator. 'Hapag' is named after a German shipping line, the Hamburg-Amerika Packetfahrt Aktien Gesellschaft. 'Bettina' is named after the wife of Baron Albert von Rothschild, who bought the right to name the asteroid. Four asteroids discovered in the 1980s have been named after the members of the Beatles.*

## JUPITER RULES THE ASTEROIDS

THE SPEED with which an object orbits the Sun is determined by its distance from the Sun: the farther out an object's orbit, the slower it travels. Therefore, an asteroid in an orbit that lies closer to the Sun than that of Jupiter regularly overtakes the giant planet. Each time the asteroid does so, its motion is disturbed by Jupiter's powerful gravitational pull. In some orbits these disturbances are cumulative, and eventually force the asteroid into another orbit.

For example, suppose that, forced by some disturbance, an asteroid wanders into an orbit where it takes four years to circle the Sun. Jupiter's orbit takes 12 years, so the asteroid will overtake Jupiter every six years, during which time the asteroid will complete one and a half orbits, while Jupiter completes half an orbit. The two bodies will pass at a point 180 degrees away from their previous encounter. After another six years, the asteroid will overtake Jupiter again, in the same part of its orbit as it did originally.

Jupiter's gravitational field will repeatedly tug at this asteroid at the same two points in its orbit, and send it into a new orbit, either farther from or closer to the Sun. There are indeed no asteroids to be found in the four-year orbit – or in any other of a large number of 'forbidden' orbits. These forbidden zones are called Kirkwood gaps, after the American astronomer Daniel Kirkwood who, in 1857, predicted their existence.

There is a more dramatic example of the influence of Jupiter's orbit: dozens of asteroids have actually been 'captured' by Jupiter and are compelled to share the giant planet's orbit.

These 'prisoner' asteroids are in two groups. One is centred on a point 60 degrees ahead of Jupiter, the other 60 degrees behind, but individual members of the groups wander far from these positions. Members of these groups have been named after the heros of the Trojan Wars.

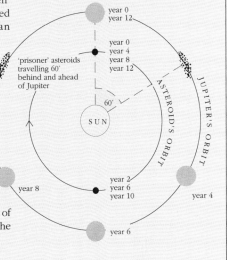

**Forbidden orbit** *An asteroid that takes four years to orbit the Sun will overtake Jupiter, which takes 12 years, every six years. Jupiter's gravity makes such a four-year orbit impossible. 'Prisoner' asteroids are caught in Jupiter's orbit itself.*

# THE POWER OF THE SHRINKING GIANT
*The largest planet of the solar system is heated by the movement of gases*

JUPITER IS the monster of the planets, 1300 times the volume of the Earth. It is predominantly a great ball of hydrogen, mostly gaseous but possibly crushed by the huge gravitational pressures at the centre of the planet into a strange metallic state.

What appears from Earth to be Jupiter's surface, with its yellow and brown bands, is the top level of deep clouds of ammonia and sulphur compounds. Lighter, higher clouds probably consist of ammonia crystals, which exist in a solid state because the temperatures here are -167°C (-269°F) and below.

Jupiter seethes with energy. This is revealed by bursts of radio waves which come from storms raging in its atmosphere and from vast auroras. Our reception of these bursts is disturbed by the movements of Io, the innermost of Jupiter's four largest moons. Io is 3630 km (2256 miles) in diameter, slightly larger than the Earth's Moon.

Particles whirling in Jupiter's intense magnetic field – 20 times stronger at its surface than the Earth's magnetic field is to us – give rise to another, steadier stream of radio waves. The magnetic field is the opposite way round to the Earth's (in relation to its axis of rotation), so a magnetic compass from Earth would point south, not north, on Jupiter.

### Danger to space probes

This powerful field traps deadly, fast-moving subatomic particles that are a hazard to spacecraft. They nearly disabled the instruments on NASA's *Pioneer 1* when it flew by Jupiter late in 1973. The probe encountered radiation 500 times more intense than would be needed to kill a human being. Io moves within these radiation belts, which blast material from its surface to form a doughnut-shaped trail of gas all along its orbit.

There is a third type of radio emission from Jupiter. This comes from some internal source of heat. Astronomers think that Jupiter is continuing to shrink as it did when it was first formed from a primordial gas cloud, and this shrinkage releases energy. The gas molecules pick up speed as they fall inwards; when they collide with the dense matter found closer to the centre of the planet, the energy of their motion is converted into heat energy, which warms the giant planet.

**Moon dwarfed by a planet**
*Voyager spotted Io (bottom centre) casting its shadow (lower left) onto Jupiter.*

# A HOME AWAY FROM HOME

## *The technology needed to establish a colony on Mars*

**I**T IS ONE THING to land scientific instruments on Mars – Russia has a mission planned for 1994 that will carry scientific instruments and surface probes – but quite another to establish a base for men to explore the planet. Daytime temperatures can rise above freezing, but, because of the extremely thin atmosphere, the Sun's heat radiates back into space. Even at the equator, the temperature drops to -50˚C (-60˚F) at night. In addition, there is no ozone layer to keep out the Sun's lethal ultraviolet radiation and the atmosphere consists almost entirely of carbon dioxide, with hardly any oxygen for breathing or burning conventional fuels. Undaunted by these problems, scientists are devising transport and clothing appropriate for Mars and an artificial environment in which colonists could live.

*Mars Ball This ingenious two-wheeled 'surface rover' (below) exists in prototype at the University of Arizona. Each wheel is made of eight gas-filled bags. As the bags are deflated and re-inflated in turn, the machine rolls forwards. The gas cylinder that controls the motion is carried on the hub that links the two wheels, along with scientific instruments for collecting data on the rover's journeys.*

## THE GREENING OF MARS

**T**HE SURFACE of Mars is a desert, coloured rusty red by iron oxides. Scientists have conceived an ambitious plan to turn it into a planet like ours – to 'terraform' it. We would have to transport vast quantities of gas there to give it a denser atmosphere that would trap more of the Sun's heat. If we could engineer a 'greenhouse effect' that stopped heat reflected from the planet's surface escaping into space, the Martian ice caps (*left*), might melt to create a polar ocean (*right*). Once enough ice had melted, suitable plants could be introduced that would slowly build up the level of oxygen in the atmosphere, so that, in time, the planet would be able to support animal life as well. But the process would take tens of thousands of years and the cost makes the idea, for the moment, just a fantastic dream.

*Walking dress A Mars suit (right) must be lighter than those worn by astronauts on the Moon, because of the planet's stronger gravity. The backpack contains food, drink, oxygen and batteries to power the array of instruments that regulate the environment inside the suit. To prevent the wearer from becoming uncomfortably warm, water is pumped along narrow tubes sewn into the astronaut's underwear.*

**Pilotless plane** *Atmospheric pressure on the surface of Mars is 100 times less than the pressure at sea level on Earth. An aeroplane depends on the uplift it receives as it moves through the air, so a Marsplane (below and left) would need to be extremely light and fast to become and remain airborne. American researchers have proposed this unmanned craft weighing only 300 kg (660 lb), launched by vertical takeoff rocket or by catapult and powered by hydrazine, a liquid rocket fuel.*

**Dual balloon** *Unmanned balloons may be used for surveys of the planet's surface. The Sun's heat would warm the air inside the balloon (left) and make it rise during the day; then, as the air inside the balloon cooled at night, it would fall to the surface again. A smaller helium balloon would be attached to the main balloon to give it some initial buoyancy, with survey equipment carried on the heavy 'tail'.*

**Small world** *Biosphere 2 (below), a "self-contained" environment of the kind scientists hope to build on Mars, became operational in the Arizona desert late in 1991. Eight researchers, along with thousands of species of plants and animals, were sealed in the 3-acre structure for two years. Despite the last-minute installation of a carbon dioxide recycling system, officials have defended the validity of the experiment.*

# THE CRADLE OF LIFE

*A telescope in space may have seen other solar systems being born*

I F LIFE LIKE that on Earth exists anywhere else in the Galaxy, it needs planets to live on. Astronomers think they have seen stars and planetary systems like the Sun and its family being born in the depths of space.

No ordinary telescope could witness these events. Star birth takes place in the heart of interstellar clouds of gas and dust, from which visible light cannot escape. But infrared (heat) radiation can. So the unmanned satellite *IRAS* (Infrared Astronomy Satellite) was put into orbit in January 1983 to look for such regions, as well as many other infrared sources that are never seen from beneath the Earth's obscuring atmosphere. The telescope on board *IRAS* had to be cooled with liquid helium to just 2.4°C (4.3°F) above absolute zero to prevent it from being 'dazzled' by its *own* heat radiation.

*New stars* NASA technicians check the IRAS *satellite (below) before its launch in 1983. It is helping scientists study the three stages of star formation (right). First, clouds of dust are disturbed by the shock wave of an exploding star (top); the clouds contract, creating reddish hot spots that become protostars (centre); finally, at 10 million°C (18 million°F), nuclear reactions begin and new stars appear (bottom).*

Stars may begin to form when an interstellar gas cloud is disturbed – by the gravitational pull of passing stars, for example, or by a shock wave from an exploding star. The cloud begins to break up into globules, each perhaps hundreds of times as massive as our Sun. Each begins to collapse into a dense knot of matter. At its core a 'protostar' is formed. This is not yet a true star, since it does not shine by the release of nuclear energy. It is heated entirely by the energy released by the infalling matter.

When the core of the protostar reaches a temperature of 10 million°C (18 million°F), nuclear reactions begin and a new star shines out. It may be seen by Earth astronomers as a 'variable' star, fluctuating in apparent brightness as the last wraiths of the mother cloud swirl round it.

Astronomers are less sure of what happens next. Solid matter in the form of dust particles and stones may be left orbiting the new star. *IRAS* found evidence of gravel-sized particles circling two young stars. These may be the building material of future planets, or the debris left over from the formation of existing planets.

# CANDIDATES FOR LIFE OUT IN SPACE

*When stars wobble they reveal their unseen companions*

**A**S SEEN through present-day telescopes, any planet beyond our solar system would be lost in the glare from its parent star. But there are indirect ways of finding such a planet if it exists. And there are quite a few candidates.

As a planet orbits its parent star, its gravitational field tugs on the star and makes it 'wobble'. The effect of an Earth-sized planet is imperceptible, but that of a planet the size of Jupiter, which has 318 times the mass of the Earth, is substantial.

Such a wobble has been claimed for several stars. Some of these observations have been discredited – they were probably due to a wobble in the telescope itself. Others still require independent confirmation.

But the observations seem to show that two bodies, one with 70 per cent of the mass of Jupiter and another with half Jupiter's mass, are orbiting a faint nearby star called Barnard's star. In infrared observations of another star, an object with a mass 60 times that of Jupiter seemed to show up. This may be a small star rather than a large planet.

Another way of detecting unseen companions of stars is to analyse the wavelength of light from the star. If the star is wobbling, the wavelength changes: reduced while the star is moving towards the Earth, lengthened while the star is moving away. This method has revealed, for example, an apparent companion 1.6 times as massive as Jupiter circling the star Gamma Cephei.

A planet large enough to be detected by us today would be a giant ball of gas, so far from the parent star that it

| 0 | 5 | 10 | 15 | 20 | 25 | 30 | 35 | 40 | 45 | 50 | 55 | 60 | 65 | 70 | 75 |

**Slow pull** *Over 75 years, the path a star traces across the sky may 'wobble' because of the influence of an unseen planet or star.*

**YEAR 10** **YEAR 15** **YEAR 20**

centre of gravity of star and its companion — unseen companion — orbital path of unseen companion — orbital path of visible star — gravitational pull — visible star — path of star as seen from Earth

**Star system** *A star and its companion – a large planet in its system or another star – travel through space orbiting a common centre of gravity. The 'wobble' in the star's path reveals the presence of the companion.*

would be freezing cold. It could not be the home of life anything like that which we know.

But where there are Jupiter-like planets, there may also be others like Earth.

The Hubble Space Telescope, launched in April 1990 from the American space shuttle, has an unprecedented view of the skies: it orbits at 600 km (373 miles), high above our hazy, shifting atmosphere. In the light from a star it may be able to detect the characteristic signs of an oxygen-rich planetary atmosphere. That would be an almost certain indicator of the conditions necessary for sustaining life.

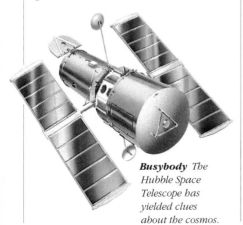

**Busybody** *The Hubble Space Telescope has yielded clues about the cosmos.*

# ROBOT EXPLORERS

*Swarms of self-reproducing robots could colonise the Galaxy*

**L**IGHT TRAVELS at 300 000 km (186 000 miles) per second. Yet even at this speed, light takes over four years to reach us from the nearest star, Proxima Centauri. Even if we assume that one day it will be possible to travel at a tenth of the speed of light, it would still take up to 50 years for us to travel to nearby stars. But exploration of the Galaxy could be speeded up if we used self-reproducing robots.

NASA scientists have seriously discussed the possibility of sending a robotic probe to some nearby star system that the advanced science of the future had shown to have planets. It would take, say, 40 years to get there.

When it arrived, it would mine materials from a convenient asteroid and build two replicas of itself. Then, while the original probe settled down to make observations about the new system and transmit them back to Earth, the two daughter probes would launch themselves towards two further stars, where they would repeat the performance.

Roughly every 40 years the number of probes would double. In about 160 years there would be 16 probes in flight, not to mention those at work studying planetary systems. After another 160 years there would be 256, and after 1000 years there would be over 30 million spreading across the Galaxy.

# A UNIVERSE MADE FOR US

*The Universe seems tailormade to nurture life*

IN THE 1950s, Fred Hoyle, a distinguished British cosmologist, pointed out a curious fact about the creation of the elements: they were in the right proportions for life to emerge. Most of the elements that make up the Earth were created thousands of millions of years ago in the interior of a star. (Hydrogen and helium are the exceptions.

They were formed much earlier, in the 'big bang' in which the Universe was born.) The star exploded and mingled them with the gas and dust of interstellar space. The Earth was later formed from the interstellar material and incorporated these elements.

There are approximately equal numbers of carbon and oxygen atoms in living things. Familiar materials such as rock and soil – which contain much oxygen – could not have existed if there had been too little oxygen on Earth; and the giant molecules of which living things are made could not have formed if there had been too much oxygen around.

Carbon and oxygen were formed from other types of atom in the stellar 'pressure cooker'. Hoyle pointed out that if the strengths of the nuclear forces were only very slightly different, the balance of carbon and oxygen would have been quite wrong. The Earth could not have harboured life.

*Science and fiction This 1939 magazine is wrong – Venus has no green men – but in many ways our Universe seems designed for life.*

Such 'coincidences', which are numerous, suggest the 'cosmological anthropic principle': that the Universe has been designed as a place suitable for the emergence of life – especially intelligent life (anthropic means 'relating to human beings').

The force of gravity also appears to be 'fine-tuned' in relation to electromagnetism and atomic forces. If gravity had been slightly stronger than it is, the 'big bang' would not have been so big. The expanding primordial hydrogen and helium would have slowed, stopped and begun to collapse. The total lifetime of the Universe could have been measured in centuries – far too short a time for stars to evolve.

If, on the other hand, the force of gravity had been weaker, the gas would have thinned out too quickly for stars to appear. Again, the starting conditions of the Universe seem somehow to have been 'fine-tuned'.

### Random creation

Some sceptical scientists have put forward an explanation that does not involve intelligent design of the Universe. The cosmos we can see, they suggest, is only one of countless 'parallel' universes created in the 'big bang'. The initial conditions in these varied randomly from one to the next – only in a tiny number were natural laws just right for the emergence of life. We think the Universe miraculously 'fine-tuned' because we cannot see all the other, 'unsuccessful' universes.

---

## RIDING A MICROWAVE BEAM TO THE STARS

WE MAY be able to get a close look at a neighbouring star in a matter of decades. The *Starwisp* project is already on the drawing board. It calls for a giant 'cobweb', 1 km (3000 ft) across, to be constructed in space.

The probe would be made of wire mesh so fine that it would weigh only 20 g (0.7 oz), and would be pushed into interstellar space by a powerful micro-wave beam from a solar-powered satellite orbiting the Earth.

The microwave beam would be focused by a lens 50 000 km (31 000 miles) wide – four times the diameter of the Earth – floating in space. With an

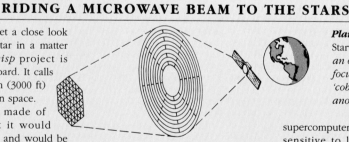

*Planet spotter In the Starwisp project, power from an orbiting satellite would be focused by a huge lens onto a 'cobweb' to propel it towards another star.*

acceleration of 155 times the Earth's gravity, the probe would be boosted to 60 000 km (37 300 miles) per second – one-fifth the speed of light – in a week. *Starwisp* would be covered with ultra-sensitive microchips, making it a giant

supercomputer. The chips would also be sensitive to light. Jointly they could assemble an image of the probe's surroundings. *Starwisp* could reach Proxima Centauri, the nearest star, after a journey of 21 years. During the 40 hours in which the probe was speeding past the star, it could send back images of any orbiting planets.

# A CITY OF STARS

*Our Galaxy resembles a whirlpool of stars*

THE PALE BAND of light running around the sky and called the Milky Way gives only the merest hint of the great assemblage of stars, gas and dust that it represents. The Galaxy is in the shape of a great disc, and the Milky Way is the effect that arises from looking across the diameter of the disc, where multitudes of stars seem to fuse into a mass of faint light.

Viewed from outside, the Galaxy would be seen to have a spiral structure, as do 30 per cent of all galaxies. The spiral's arms, marked out by lanes of stars, gas and dust, are really ripples sweeping through the disc. Their bluish colour shows they are relatively hot – just as the bluish colour of an arc lamp shows it is hotter than, say, an electric bulb. Where gas clouds are squeezed together by the passing of a ripple, the birth of stars is triggered. As a result, each arm is studded with young stars.

The core of the Galaxy is thicker than the rest of the disc. It is relatively free of gas and dust, and consists of

**Starry sky** *This photograph shows the Milky Way from the constellation of Sagittarius (on the left) to Centaurus (right). Sagittarius's bright clouds of stars and dark dust clouds obscure the Galaxy's centre.*

older stars. These are reddish, showing that they are cooler than stars in the prime of life, just as a red-hot piece of iron is cooler than a white-hot piece.

The centre of the Galaxy is a strong source of radio waves, and this suggests that there is some kind of commotion going on. But dark clouds of gas and dust in the constellation of Sagittarius obscure the source, which may be a black hole, swallowing millions of tonnes of matter every second. (A black hole is the extremely dense remnant of a supernova – a massive star that has exploded.)

### 200-million-year cycle

The Galaxy is 100 000 light-years across and our solar system is two-thirds of the way out from the centre. It takes the solar system, moving round the Galaxy at 250 km (155 miles) per second, over 200 million years to orbit the Galaxy once. As it does so, it bobs up and down through the central plane of the disc, passing through it every 30 million years.

This immense celestial pinwheel was once thought to comprise the whole Universe. Now we know of millions upon millions of other galaxies – and we are certain that others fill space beyond the reach of our greatest telescopes.

**Spiral of stars** *An artist's impression of our Galaxy shows cooler stars in the core, and younger, bluish stars in the spiral's arms. The orange spots are clusters of thousands of stars.*

## WHITE DWARFS AND NEUTRON STARS

THE EVENTUAL fate of all stars about the size of our Sun is to become the kind of star known as a white dwarf. When the hydrogen fuel in the Sun's core has run out, the Sun will shrink to a ball of hot gas somewhat smaller than the Earth. It will be so tightly packed that if one thimbleful were brought to Earth it would weigh a tonne.

However, any star with a mass more than 40 per cent greater than the Sun's will end its days as a supernova. The remnant of this explosion is thought to be a neutron star, which is even denser than a white dwarf. A neutron star is not made of atoms, but is a solid ball of a single type of subatomic particle, the neutron.

A neutron star packs a mass equal to that of the Sun into a volume only 20 km (12 miles) across. The force of gravity at its surface is so great that a 'mountain' on

a neutron star would only be about half as high as a sugar cube – but it would take more energy to scale that 'mountain' than a human being's body generates in a lifetime.

*Old star* Geminga, the large orange spot in this gamma-ray image, is thought to be a neutron star, the densest matter we can observe. When matter is more tightly crushed, which happens in the centre of the largest supernova explosions, its gravity becomes so intense that it vanishes into a black hole.

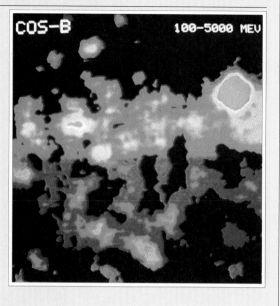

# THE DEATH STAR

*Extinctions in the distant past may be a clue that the Sun has a companion*

THE FOSSIL record shows, time and again, sudden disappearances of thousands of plant and animal species occurring in a matter of a few thousand years. The disappearance of the dinosaurs at the end of the Cretaceous period, about 65 million years ago, is the most famous example.

Yet not only the dinosaurs, but all the flying and swimming reptiles – in fact,

### DID YOU KNOW..?

*THE ORION nebula is an immense cloud of gas and dust visible to the naked eye in the 'sword' of the constellation Orion. It is about 30 light-years (290 million million km or 180 million million miles) across. Like all interstellar nebulae, it is incredibly rarefied. A sample 25 mm (1 in) in diameter taken right across the entire nebula would yield only as much matter as is contained in a small coin.*

✳ ✳ ✳

*THE FASTEST-moving star across the night sky is Barnard's star. This faint object – too dim to be seen with the naked eye – takes 180 years to move across the sky by an amount equal to the diameter of the full Moon. In the year 11 800 it will pass the Sun at a distance of 3.85 light-years – closer than the present nearest star, Proxima Centauri.*

some 75 per cent of all species – died out with them. An extinction about 245 million years ago was even more devastating. Over 90 per cent of species are believed to have died out. Comparable, though less drastic, events punctuate the fossil record.

One hotly debated explanation for these holocausts was proposed by Luis Alvarez and his son Walter, both professors at the University of California at Berkeley. In samples from Gubbio in Italy, they discovered a thin layer of the metal iridium at the boundary between the rocks of the Cretaceous period and the following Tertiary period. Similar discoveries have been made at sites around the globe.

Iridium is rare on Earth, but common in meteorites. Luis and Walter Alvarez suggested that the iridium layer was deposited when a comet collided with the Earth. Such a collision, they said, raised enormous dust clouds that veiled the Sun for years, disturbed the climate and caused the mass extinction.

### Finding the pattern

But then David M. Raup and J. John Sepkoski Jr, palaeontologists at the University of Chicago, discovered that the extinctions seem to occur roughly every 30 million years. And geologists, following this lead, have found what seems to be a similar regularity in the dates at which impact craters – signs of

comet collisions – were formed on the Earth. All this is very uncertain, because the data are patchy.

But if these regularities exist, why should comets collide with the Earth so reliably? Comets are believed to originate in a giant swarm orbiting the Sun far beyond the orbit of Pluto. Some are occasionally deflected towards the Sun by the random disturbances of passing stars. What additional regular disturbance could affect them on cue every 30 million years?

### Faint neighbour

Perhaps the cause is an undiscovered companion to the Sun, a star so faint that it has not been noticed. If so, the star would travel round the Sun in a highly elliptical orbit. Its average distance from the Sun would be 1.4 light-years, but every 30 million years it would come to within a quarter of this distance. Its approach would send about a thousand million comets inwards towards the Sun over a period of a few million years – and some would collide with the Earth.

Because of its disastrous consequences for life on Earth, the hypothetical companion star has been dubbed Nemesis, after the Greek goddess of retribution. Happily, its next assault on the solar system is not expected soon: we seem to be halfway between cometary bombardments.

# DOWNFALL OF A SUPERGIANT

*Celestial fireworks in a neighbouring galaxy have dazzled the world's astronomers*

I N FEBRUARY 1987, astronomers saw an obscure star in a nearby galaxy, the Large Magellanic Cloud, tear itself apart. For the first ten seconds of its death agony, it poured out more energy than the rest of the visible Universe combined. Only four times before had such violent events – called supernovas – been recorded so relatively close to the Sun. And all of these had occurred before the invention of the telescope.

The new arrival was dubbed Supernova 1987A. The star from which it was born had been known only by a catalogue number, Sanduleak -69° 202. From past records and astrophysical theory its history was reconstructed.

### The big die young

Massive stars burn fast and furiously, and their lives are brief. The Sun, at about 4500 million years old, is in early middle age. Sanduleak -69° 202, which became what is known as a Type II supernova, had been about 20 times as massive as the Sun, and consequently its life was run in a mere 11 million years. For the first ten million years it

*Large Magellanic Cloud Supernova 1987A is the bright object in the lower right corner of this telescope photograph. In the opposite corner is the Tarantula nebula, an immense cloud of dust and gas.*

'burned' hydrogen into helium in nuclear reactions, as the Sun does. When hydrogen ran low, the helium in turn began to burn and was transformed into other elements, including carbon and oxygen. The outer parts of the star swelled, turning it into a red supergiant – a star so huge that, if it replaced our Sun, it would extend as far as the Earth.

When the helium had been burned, the star grew hotter, turning bluish. It shrank somewhat, but was still large enough to be called a supergiant. The star successively burned carbon and a chain of further elements.

During the last week of its life, its core was

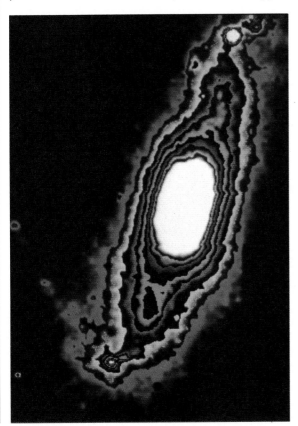

*Exploding star A false-colour image taken with an infrared camera shows spiral galaxy M66. The white spot in the top right corner is Supernova 1989B. This is a Type I supernova, which occurs when gas from one star flows onto a nearby white dwarf star. The increased mass causes the white dwarf to explode.*

transformed into a ball of iron the size of Mars, surrounded by layers of partly consumed elements. The doomed star was now 80 000 times as bright as the Sun.

Then came the cataclysm. The chain of reactions had to end here, for iron is not a fuel for nuclear fusion. The core of the star now collapsed, releasing a burst of subatomic particles known as neutrinos. These tore the star asunder, throwing off its outer layers as an expanding cloud of gas and releasing particles and radiation.

### News flash

Signals from this event travelled across space for 170 000 years before they reached the Earth. On February 23, 1987, neutrino detectors in Ohio and Japan registered the first sign of the death of Sanduleak -69° 202. News spread quickly – within hours, every available telescope in the world had been turned towards the Large Magellanic Cloud. At its peak luminosity, in May 1987, Supernova 1987A was 250 million times as bright as the Sun.

Early in 1990, astronomers found traces of a recent supernova in our own Galaxy. It apparently exploded sometime this century, but was not noticed because of interstellar dust and fog.

# GALAXIES IN COLLISION

*Computer simulations may help scientists explain the shape of some galaxies*

ASTRONOMERS today can 'play God' by making simulated galaxies collide on their computer screens. These simulations are not simply video games to while away the time – they mimic real events. During its lifetime of thousands of millions of years, each member of a large cluster of galaxies has a better than even chance of a near miss with one of its neighbours.

In a near miss, each galaxy is deformed by the gravitational pull of the other. Even if the encounter is an actual collision, individual stars do not hit each other – they are much too thinly scattered through space for that. The swarms of stars penetrate each other like two swarms of gnats. But the interstellar gas clouds in the galaxies collide, are heated by the energy of the collision, and give out light, heat and radio waves.

### Football-shaped galaxies

Such collisions may explain the origin of the elliptical galaxies. These show no sign of the spiral structure of galaxies like our own. They range in shape from spherical to a 'flattened globe' like an American football. They have little of the gas and dust from which new stars are born, and their star populations therefore lack younger members. At their heart they often contain powerful sources of light and radio energy.

In simulations performed by Joshua E. Barnes and Lars Hernquist of Princeton University's Institute for Advanced Study in New Jersey, spiral galaxies

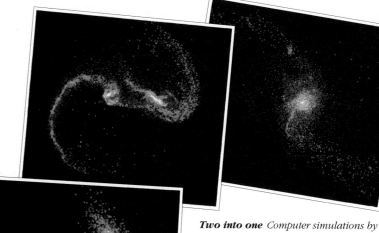

***Two into one*** *Computer simulations by Professors Barnes and Hernquist at Princeton University show two spiral galaxies of equal mass colliding. As they approach each other (bottom), most of their gases (here coloured blue and white) are pushed towards the centre of each galaxy. When the galaxies meet (top left), the gases begin to combine into one centre. Finally (top right), the stars (here coloured red) of the new galaxy form an elliptical shape.*

approached, 'caught' each other, and merged to form an elliptical galaxy. The force of the collision squashed huge quantities of gas together at the centre of the newly formed galaxy, forming a black hole that soon swallowed the gas. Heated by its inward fall, the matter pumped out radiation energy just before it vanished into the black hole.

Barnes and Hernquist had apparently created an elliptical galaxy on their computer screens. Additional computer simulations have created images that look strikingly like other actual galaxies of unusual appearance. These suggest that some of the objects we can see through telescopes are indeed the remnants of cosmic highway accidents.

## THE BRILLIANT GRAVEYARD OF STARS

THE FARTHEST outposts of the Universe are marked by the fantastically violent outpourings of energy called quasars. A quasar is brighter than the galaxy that houses it, and it keeps up this brightness constantly. (Supernovas can be brighter, but only for a matter of seconds.) Yet these cosmic powerhouses are so remote that they look like stars, as their name – short for quasi-stellar object – suggests.

### Ever more distant

Analysis of quasars' light shows that some of them are moving away from us at close to the speed of light. Speed of recession seems to go hand in hand with distance – at least, this holds true for

galaxies. On this assumption, the farthest quasar is so distant that its light has been travelling 14 000 million years to reach us. This is about three times the age of the Earth. The light left the quasar when the Universe itself was probably only a few thousand million years old.

Paradoxically, the cause of this outpouring of energy is something invisible – a black hole at the heart of the quasar. A black hole is a 'sink' in the Universe from which no energy can escape. It appears around matter that has become so compressed that neither matter nor light nor any other form of energy can escape from its intensely powerful gravitational field. Some black holes are formed as the

remnants of very massive stars when they explode at the end of their lives.

A black hole is surrounded by orbiting matter that it is about to swallow, and it is this incandescent matter that constitutes a quasar. It is a maelstrom in which stars, gas and dust vanish from our Universe.

### Death throes of a star

We can follow this death of matter in almost gruesome detail. Some quasars show a slight jump in brightness from time to time. Astronomers believe that this pulse of extra energy is the death cry of a star vanishing into the maw of the quasar: before a star is pulled into the black hole, it absorbs heat and releases radiation.

# GLIMPSING AN INFINITE UNIVERSE

## *Whole galaxies can act like huge natural telescopes*

N 1979, astronomers in Hawaii found themselves 'seeing double'. In the constellation of Ursa Major, the Great Bear, they observed two of the brilliant objects known as quasars, lying hundreds of millions of light-years beyond our Galaxy. They were only a six-hundredth of a degree apart, and it seemed unlikely that such a close conjunction could be pure chance. When they analysed the light from the two objects, they found they were uncannily alike.

The astronomers realised they were not dealing with heavenly twins – they were seeing one quasar twice. They deduced that some massive object lay between the Earth and the quasar. The quasar's light was being bent as it passed through that object's gravitational field, and was being split to form a double image. Scrutiny with more sensitive instruments revealed this natural gravitational 'lens' to be a massive, but previously unknown, galaxy.

More gravitational lenses have been found since. Sometimes the body responsible for the effect is so far away that it is too dim to be seen, but often it has been identified as a galaxy or a cluster of galaxies.

Some of these gravitational lenses cause visual effects of a different kind, according to the strength of their gravity and their precise position in relation to the quasar beyond. One quasar, in the constellation of Leo, appears to us in the shape of a ring.

Other quasars appear as arcs of several images, some of which appear larger or brighter than they would otherwise – the gravitational lens is acting as a cosmic 'telescope'.

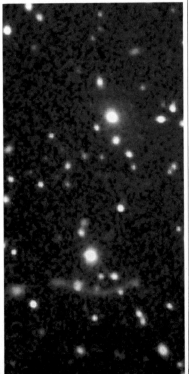

**Trick of the light** *Because of the gravitational influence of a cluster of galaxies, a quasar can appear as an arc of light (three-quarters down in this image, left) rather than as a single point.*

**Two for one** *Quasar 0957+561 (far left in diagram, below) was, in 1979, the first 'double quasar' to be discovered. Light from the quasar is split by the gravitational field of a galaxy (orange spot). From Earth (far right), we see a double image of the quasar (on green panel).*

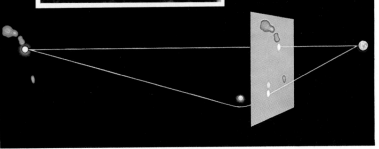

---

## STRINGS IN SPACE

AMONG THE latest exotic brainchildren of cosmological theorists are cosmic strings. If these strange entities exist, they were formed in the first fraction of a second of the 'big bang' in which, most scientists agree, the Universe was born.

Modern physicists view 'empty space' as far from being a mere void. It is actually a turmoil of energy and particles coming into existence, living briefly, and vanishing again. The cosmos in the early moments of the 'big bang' was even more dynamic – a maelstrom of energy at enormous temperatures and pressures. The hypothetical strings are essentially samples of that primeval space, living on into the less frenzied Universe of today.

A cosmic string would have no ends: it would either be infinite, stretching across the entire observable Universe and into the regions beyond – or else it would be a loop, light-years in circumference.

### Thin yet heavy

The thickness of each string is reckoned to be only about five times that of the diameter of an atom. Its mass would be colossal – typically 1 million million tonnes per millimetre (25 million million tons per inch). Thus a string with a length equal to the Earth's diameter would have twice the Earth's mass.

Scientists liken cosmic strings to elastic bands under enormous tension, losing energy as they quiver and squirm in space. Strings would curl and cross over themselves from time to time and form loops that break off. These would gradually radiate energy and finally vanish.

Threadlike radio sources in the centre of our Galaxy have been detected by radio telescopes. These radio sources may come from hot gas around cosmic strings – if so, they are the first sign that the strings exist outside the theorists' imaginations.

# THE END OF ALL THINGS
*What kind of death will claim the Universe?*

**M**ODERN SCIENCE cannot say with certainty what eventually will become of the Universe. The greatest uncertainty concerns the ongoing expansion of the Universe. Will the clusters of galaxies making up the Universe continue to fly apart from each other, or will they at some stage start to come together again under the force of their mutual gravity?

### Invisible matter

This depends on a simple question, to which no scientist knows the answer: how much matter is there in the Universe? The matter we can observe – stars, gas, dust and so on – amounts to only a hundredth of what would be required to halt the expansion that has been going on since the 'big bang' created the Universe some 15 thousand million years ago.

But the motions of some galaxies show that the gravitational force of matter we cannot see is pulling on them, too. This invisible matter, known as 'dark matter', exists within and between the galaxies, and may comprise most of the matter in the Universe. But even the combination of these unseen substances with the stars and other visible matter still adds up to only a tenth of the mass

that would be needed to turn the expansion into a contraction.

Therefore, cosmologists think that the Universe will continue to expand, and look ahead to developments at truly staggering distances in the future. In 100 million million years, the longest-lived stars will have used their fuel and faded out. On a timescale that is much longer yet, the galaxies will disappear. Even in the vastness of space, stars sometimes come close enough to be affected by each other's gravitational fields and, if the time scale is long enough, chance near misses among dead stars will cause at least 90 per cent of them to be ejected into intergalactic space. The rest will settle at the galaxies' centres, forming enormous black holes.

While the clusters of galaxies continue to move apart, each cluster will begin to

**Down the drain** *A black hole's massive gravitational force pulls in material from a nearby star (shown in blue). Before entering, the material releases radiation (reddish glow).*

collapse upon itself. The black holes – the remnants of the galaxies – and the stray dead stars in intergalactic space will spiral in towards each other. As they merge, even greater black holes will grow. This will all take place over a period of 10 million million million years.

### Sea of particles

Far beyond even this horizon lies the death of matter. Most physicists believe that the seemingly stable matter around us today will eventually 'decay' into a sea of lighter particles and radiation. Even a body the size of a star will vanish in this way – but taking a number of years written as 1 followed by 32 zeros.

Although for all practical purposes neither matter nor radiation can escape from a black hole, on the truly cosmic timescale black holes will slowly 'evaporate', giving out a slow stream of radiation. The number of years required for the decay of the black hole formed from the collapse of a galaxy cluster is written as 1 followed by 117 zeros.

This is the farthest horizon that physicists can currently discern. They believe that the Universe at this distant epoch will be a featureless mass of subatomic particles, bathed in a sea of radiation, close to the absolute zero of temperature: -273°C (-460°F).

---

## DID YOU KNOW..?

*ABOUT 9000 stars in the sky are visible to the naked eye. At any one time and place only half the sky can be seen, and haze reduces the number of stars that are seen near the horizon, so a keen-sighted person can see no more than 3000 stars even on a very dark, clear night.*

---

## THE GREAT ATTRACTOR

**I**N 1986, an international group of astronomers announced the discovery of the largest object ever found by science. But they don't know what it is.

The mystery object lies in the direction of the stars of the Southern Cross, but far beyond it. Its mass is equivalent to tens of thousands of galaxies. Though invisible to us, it reveals its existence by its pull on galaxies within 200 million light-years of the Earth. These galaxies are rushing

apart from each other at speeds up to about 4500 km (2800 miles) per second, sharing in the general expansion of the Universe. But on top of this motion is an extra movement of 700 km (435 miles) per second towards the unseen object.

The Great Attractor, as it has been called, is believed to lie about 500 million light-years away from us. About 300 million light-years across, it may be a giant cluster of galaxies too faint to be seen.

# *The* RESTLESS EARTH

NOTHING SEEMS more stable than the ground beneath our feet, and nothing more unchanging than the seasons. But we now know that the Earth's internal heat keeps the tectonic plates that make up its surface in constant motion – Antarctica, for example, once lay on the Equator (*page 70*). Even man may be causing structural change on a global scale as pollution threatens a dramatic and irreversible warming of the atmosphere (*page 69*). Nothing on Earth is truly permanent; over the years, air, land and sea alter, and living things adapt as best they can.

# TO FREEZE OR TO BURN

*Where the world's weather goes to extremes*

ALTHOUGH we may complain about bad weather from time to time, most of us live in reasonable comfort as far as the climate is concerned. But there are parts of the world where human existence borders on the impossible.

One of the least hospitable areas of the globe is the Arctic. Parts of Alaska, Canada, Scandinavia and the Soviet Union lie within the Arctic Circle, where temperatures remain below freezing for about nine months of the year, and may drop to -57°C (-70°F). Even in summer, the thermometer rarely rises above 7°C (45°F). So it is no wonder that these areas are only sparsely populated.

Just as such persistent discomfort has discouraged most people from populating the freezing Arctic, the baking heat of the Sahara, where ground temperatures have been known to reach 84°C (183°F), keeps people away. In parts of Chad and Libya there may be no rain for years at a time, and occasionally the air may even become too dry for people to breathe safely.

No one at all lives in the driest place on Earth: the Atacama desert in Chile. Cold ocean currents and

***Parched sands*** *The Sun rises over the Sahara, where only 150–180 mm (6–7 in) of rain falls a year, on average. Only a fifth of the world's largest desert is sand – the rest is smooth rock or rubble.*

coastal mountains form a barrier to rain clouds, and in some sections of the Atacama no rain has ever been recorded. Yet it is not particularly hot: average summer temperatures are around 19°C (66°F).

This is totally unlike conditions further north in South America, where the vast tropical rain forests of Brazil are home to numerous peoples. They cope with an annual rainfall of up to 3500 mm (140 in) and temperatures that remain much the same throughout the year, averaging 27°C (81°F).

## No man's land

No human beings, apart from the most intrepid scientists, live in Antarctica, the coldest and windiest of all the world's continents. Here the air temperature rises above freezing for only 20 days of the year, and has dropped as low as -89°C (-129°F). Constant winds do nothing to make life easier: in the region known as Adélie Land, they have been known to blow for months at a time at an average of about 70 km/h (45 mph).

***Coldest continent*** *Antarctica receives roughly the same number of hours of sunlight each year as regions around the Equator. But because the continent lies at one of the Earth's two polar extremities, sunlight reaches it at an oblique angle and has little warming effect.*

# TWISTING IN THE WIND

*Tornadoes concentrate enormous power in little time and space*

TORNADOES can rip trees out by the roots, derail trains, and sweep people, animals and even small buildings into the air. In April 1880, an entire house in Missouri, USA was carried 19 km (12 miles) from 'home'.

Although tornadoes can wreak terrible damage, the area they devastate at any one time is quite small. The path of greatest destruction is seldom more than 100 m (330 ft) wide. As a result, a tornado can demolish a house on one side of a street while a house opposite escapes unscathed.

### Short and sharp

It is difficult to measure the exact speed of the wind at the centre of a tornado, because monitoring equipment has never survived the onslaught. But the wind is estimated to reach 400 km/h (250 mph). Tornadoes are usually shortlived, though, petering out within an hour or two.

By far the most devastating tornadoes occur in the Midwestern states of the United States. 'Tornado Alley', a stretch of land running from northern Texas across Oklahoma, Kansas and Nebraska, suffers an average of 300 – and sometimes as

*Narrow path of destruction A tornado in Maryland uprooted a large tree, yet it removed only a few roof tiles from a house.*

*Turn of events The characteristic funnel-shaped column of a tornado can be spotted from a great distance. Sometimes smaller columns break off and go their own way.*

many as 1000 – tornadoes a year, usually during spring and early summer.

A tornado is the result of a layer of high, cold air flowing in one direction and meeting moist, warm air flowing the other way. As the warmer air rises and meets the cold, the water in it condenses into rain – releasing heat. The warm, dry air is sucked up in a spiral. Colder air on top is drawn down through the centre of the storm, and is warmed up. It then rises again rapidly, adding impetus to the already violent updraughts. The spinning air gradually tightens into a funnel-shaped column, the speed of spin increasing as its diameter narrows. Within this funnel, the air pressure is extremely low, so that the difference in pressure inside and outside can make a building explode as the tornado passes over.

Tornadoes may explain the falls of fish, frogs and other animals from the sky that have been recorded over centuries. At any rate, tornadoes are the best explanation scientists can offer for such odd events as that which occurred in Cerney Wick, England, in 1987, when a shower of tiny pink frogs fell on the village.

## DID YOU KNOW..?

*ON MAY 29, 1986, twelve schoolchildren in west China were sucked up by a tornado. It put them down again on some sand dunes 20 km (12 miles) away – completely unharmed.*

\* \* \*

*TORNADOES usually spin anticlockwise in the Northern Hemisphere, clockwise in the Southern Hemisphere.*

\* \* \*

*A TORNADO that struck the town of Sweetwater, Texas, in April 1986 blew a car off the road and smashed its rear window. As a police officer helped the driver out of the vehicle, he noticed a drenched kitten on the back seat – although it had not been a passenger before the tornado struck. The kitten's owner came on the scene a few minutes later, and claimed his missing pet.*

\* \* \*

*AN AVERAGE of 708 tornadoes strike the United States each year. In April 1974, 148 tornadoes savaged 13 states in just 24 hours, leaving 315 people dead.*

# A TIDE OF MISERY

## *A wave of snow, ice and rock can overwhelm a village without warning*

ON MAY 31, 1970, a vast slab of ice and rock, about 800 m (2600 ft) wide and weighing millions of tonnes, broke away from the north peak of the Huascarán, at 6768 m (22 205 ft) the highest mountain in Peru. It fell down a sheer face for nearly 1000 m (3250 ft) before crashing into the mountainside and pouring down

***Preventive step*** *In the French Alps, a controlled explosion sets off a minor avalanche. Releasing small masses of snow reduces the chances of a major avalanche.*

the valley, hurling boulders and chunks of ice as big as houses into the air as it raced along at up to 480 km/h (300 mph). By the time it came to rest in the Santa valley, the avalanche had virtually obliterated the town of Yungay and engulfed 11 nearby villages. Estimates of the number of people killed ranged from 18 000 to 25 000.

This was by far the most destructive avalanche on record. It was started by an earthquake, but an avalanche can be triggered by the slightest imbalance of snow, ice or rock. A single crystal

slipping out of place can set an 'airborne' snow avalanche in motion, building up into a massive, swirling snowball that can weigh millions of tonnes and reach speeds of up to 400 km/h (250 mph). (There are no confirmed accounts, however, of an avalanche being set off by shouting.)

'Slab' avalanches begin differently. They are the result of an entire layer of snow slipping, and the more snow there is on top, the greater the devastation.

Avalanches have astonishing power: they have stripped forests, thrown trains from their tracks, and torn houses from their foundations. Such destruction is not always caused directly by the sheer volume of material involved. A great wave of air can build up in front of an avalanche, blasting anything in its path. In 1900, one forestry worker from Glarus, Switzerland, found himself hurled through the air 'like a leaf driven by a storm'. He landed in deep snow 670 m (2200 ft) further down the mountain. In 1952, a bus was flung off a bridge near Langen, Austria by the blast of air from an avalanche – 24 people were killed.

### *Holding back the tide*

It is nearly impossible to predict an avalanche, but much can be done to prevent them. Steel barriers can hold the snow in place and prevent slippage; in less accessible places, explosives can be used to set off minor, harmless avalanches before a mass of snow grows to dangerous proportions.

---

### DID YOU KNOW..?

*AVALANCHES claim, on average, 150 lives a year. Most of the victims are skiers who themselves set off the snowslip that kills them.*

✳ ✳ ✳

*IN AUGUST 1820, an avalanche on Mont Blanc swept a nine-man team of mountaineers into a glacial crevasse on the mountainside. Local people who knew the rate at which the glacier was moving calculated that in 40 years the bodies would appear at the foot of the mountain in the Chamonix valley, some 8 km (5 miles) from where they had died. The bodies appeared in 1861 – a year later than expected – but they still looked, some reports said, 'in the bloom of youth'.*

# HISTORY IN A ROD

*A picture of the past frozen in time*

I N A SLIM rod of ice 2083 m (6835 ft) long lies the history of the Earth's atmosphere over the last 160 000 years. This record of the past has been extracted from the Antarctic by Russian scientists who spent five years from 1980 drilling deep into the ice sheet, and it holds secrets reaching back to the ice age before last. The Antarctic ice reveals the past so clearly because each year's snowfall contains minute traces of the dust and chemicals currently in the atmosphere. And the recent discovery of fossil air – air bubbles trapped in the ice – has enabled scientists to measure the proportions of different gases in the atmosphere itself.

With these clues, scientists can work out how warm, or how cold, the Earth was in the past. They can thus date ice ages accurately – and have already learned that the last one developed over only a few decades.

Analytic techniques are now sensitive enough to detect one part of lead (which may have come from vehicle exhausts) in a thousand million parts of ice, as well as dust from the

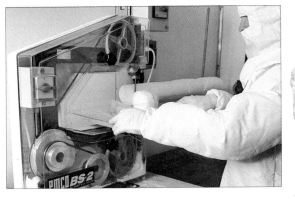

***Drilling for data*** *Two scientists remove a rod of ice (right) for chemical analysis. Back in the laboratory (above), they saw through the rod, wearing special garments to protect it from contamination.*

Sahara, sulphuric acid that contributes to acid rain, and radioactive fallout. Dating the ice is easy, as succeeding annual falls of snow form distinct layers, rather as tree rings show each year's growth.

By building up a picture of cause and effect in these changes in the atmosphere, scientists hope to predict the likely results of the 'greenhouse effect' – the gradual but potentially disastrous warming of the Earth's atmosphere that has been increasing since the Industrial Revolution – and so plan to contain or control it. Looking into the Earth's past through the polar ice in this way may help us to ensure a bearable future for humanity.

---

## MYSTERIOUS WHIRLWINDS

H AVE FLYING SAUCERS landed on Earth? Besides the hundreds of reports of weird lights in the night sky and bizarre flying machines seen by day, people convinced that creatures from outer space are constantly visiting our planet have pointed to one incontrovertibly objective piece of evidence for their claim: the curious round, flattened areas found in fields of crops all over the world.

### Secret visitors

Discoveries of 'crop circles' have often coincided with reports of unidentified flying objects (UFOs). And the circles usually seem to be made at night. So some believers in UFOs say the circles are the traces of secret landings by alien spacecraft. This is a more plausible explanation than another theory put

forward in Britain: that vast herds of hedgehogs had tramped out the circles.

Meteorologists have noted that crop circles bear the classic marks of minor tornadoes: they show clear signs of a circular motion in whatever made them, and a sharp cut-off point between affected and untouched areas. But tornadoes are extremely destructive, and the crops, although flattened, are left undamaged. And tornadoes move along the ground – whatever causes this phenomenon leaves no other trace of its passing.

Nonetheless, scientists from Britain's Tornado and Storm Research Organisation believe that some form of atmospheric vortex or whirlwind is at work. But it is an odd whirlwind, for it seems to consume all its energy as it strikes the ground. They say that it may take decades to work out exactly what makes the circles.

---

### DID YOU KNOW..?

*THE WEIGHT of ice on Antarctica has depressed the continent's land so far that most of it lies below sea level. The Bentley Trench, the lowest point, is 2538 m (8325 ft) below sea level. Yet Antarctica is also reckoned to be the world's highest continent. The ice surface averages 2050 m (6700 ft) above sea level. In contrast, the polar ice cap covering the Arctic Ocean is only 2–3 m (7–10 ft) thick, and average temperatures there are 15˚C (27˚F) warmer than in Antarctica.*

✳ ✳ ✳

*ONLY TWO flowering plants grow in Antarctica. One is a grass, the other a relative of the carnation.*

# WHITHER THE WEATHER
*Meteorologists keep track of the rain in Spain – and everywhere else*

THE ANCIENT Greeks regarded a rainbow as a sign of approaching rain, and the same advice was still being offered by English sages in Elizabethan times. At least there was a chance that this omen would prove to be true, but other, equally long-held beliefs about the weather seem plainly ridiculous: shooting stars presaged high winds, tempests would follow if asses shook their ears, and an owl hooting at night was a sign of fair weather.

Today, weather forecasters are still struggling to make their business into an exact science. The world's weather is one huge, interconnected system: to predict the weather in Sydney 24 hours ahead calls for detailed information from the Antarctic, the western Pacific and Indonesia. A forecast for four days ahead requires intimate knowledge of conditions all over the globe.

### By land, by sea, by air
Meteorologists do know an astonishing amount about the world's weather, if not as much as they would like. Some 12 000 pieces of weather data arrive every hour at the World Meteorological Organisation's two World Area Forecasting Centres – one in Washington, DC and the other in Bracknell, England. This information comes from the 7000 weather stations around the globe, from ships at sea, aircraft, readings from the 1000 balloons that the weather stations launch daily into the air, and from satellites in space.

It includes surface readings of atmospheric pressure, rainfall, wind speed and direction, and temperature, as well as airborne readings from near ground level to the stratosphere 50 km (30 miles) up. Computers process the 5 million numbers that represent this array of information to give a worldwide,

**Weather report** *On Canada's Ellesmere Island, northwest of Greenland, climatologists set up equipment to measure temperature, humidity and wind speed.*

three-dimensional picture of what is happening. They divide the Earth's surface into units 150 km (95 miles) square, with 15 levels from the ground to the stratosphere, to show the atmosphere in the form of some 350 000 cubes. For North America, Europe and the Atlantic, a picture four times more detailed is produced.

Using extremely sophisticated mathematical models, the computer then predicts how the current state of the weather should change over periods ranging from one to 140 hours ahead.

### A more detailed picture
Computers eight times more powerful than these are now on trial. They divide the atmosphere into 19 levels, and the surface areas used for calculations are only one-third as large as those currently in use.

With this level of refinement and extra computer capacity at their disposal, forecasters are well prepared for even more comprehensive data. But some areas of the globe, such as the Pacific Ocean and the great deserts, are so empty of people that data about the weather there cannot be collected and reported daily.

---

## DID YOU KNOW..?

*THE STUDY and forecasting of weather is called meteorology because it was once precisely that – the study of meteors. The idea that meteors were formed in the sky from various combinations of earth, water, air and fire, and that they contributed to weather conditions, goes back to Aristotle in the 4th century BC. It was believed in Europe until late in the 17th century.*

\* \* \*

*IN AD 582, it rained 'blood' on Paris. The terrified populace saw this as a sign from Heaven, and responded by indulging in an agony of repentance for their sins. The true cause of this weird event was the sirocco, the wind that sometimes blows from the Sahara across the Mediterranean into Europe. It is laden with a fine red dust from the desert interior, and this had dyed the rain that fell on Paris.*

---

## THE DREADED CALM OF THE SEA

FEW THINGS look as unnatural as a square-rigged ship crowded with sail and completely becalmed. Canvas flaps idly, masts creak, and the ship makes barely enough way to steer. But this was what faced every sailing ship that made the long voyage from Europe to the West Indies across the Atlantic. Once south of the stormy stretch of ocean known as the 'roaring forties', at around 30° to 35° latitude north – on a line, roughly, between the Canary Islands and the Florida coast – they encountered the calm of the 'horse latitudes'.

It was a calm of the weather only. Ships' masters fretted over lost time, which meant lost money. All sailors would be aware that fresh water could run dangerously short. And a few may have spared a thought for the horses, for the name of those regions is said to have a grim origin.

As Europeans colonised the New World, they shipped huge numbers of horses west across the Atlantic. But as ships were becalmed and supplies, especially water, ran short, the horses were thrown overboard. So frequently did this happen that, legend has it, ships in these latitudes occasionally came across floating graveyards of the discarded creatures.

Today this stretch of ocean and its counterpart in the Southern Hemisphere have a more prosaic name: 'subtropical high pressure areas'.

## AN ILL WIND

LATE WINTER in the Swiss Alps can see a strange rapid change among the snow-laden mountains. It begins with the sudden appearance of columns of discuss-shaped clouds along the mountain tops.

In a few minutes, the day alters from bright and cold to dark and hot, as a warm, extremely dry wind, called the föhn, sweeps down from the peaks – and within hours the crisp piles of snow on the mountains will have melted into

torrents of water. This is one effect of the föhn. Another is stranger yet, for it seems to involve the human mind.

People exposed to prolonged bouts of the föhn complain of headache and depression; heart attacks and even suicides have been blamed on it. The effects are real enough, but research has so far failed to identify their cause.

A föhn forms as moist winds pass up the windward side of a mountain range.

At the higher altitude, the wind cools and its moisture condenses, creating clouds and releasing heat. The wind is now cold and extremely dry, and races down the other side of the mountain range. As it descends, the increasing atmospheric pressure compresses it, warming it up. Once the föhn arrives, the valley below experiences a dramatic increase in temperature, sometimes from below freezing to as high as 20°C (70°F).

# THE HEAT IS ON
### *Is the greenhouse effect speeding out of control?*

AS WINTER sets in over northern Canada, the polar bears travel south after spending the summer foraging in the Arctic. They cross one section of Hudson's Bay on the ice. But, in November 1988, they came to an unprecedented halt there. The water had not yet frozen. The stranded bears had to wait six weeks before they were able to continue their journey to their hibernation grounds. This, many experts say, is one of a growing number of signs that the 'greenhouse effect', the general warming of the Earth's atmosphere, is already with us.

### Growing blanket of gas

The greenhouse effect is caused by increasing levels of certain gases in the atmosphere. Among them are methane and nitrous oxide, but the worst offender is carbon dioxide, which comes mainly from burning fossil fuels – coal, oil and gas – and forests.

Man releases about 400 thousand million tonnes of carbon dioxide every year into the air. Without any carbon dioxide in the atmosphere, the Sun's heat would radiate back into space and the Earth would freeze. But as this carbon dioxide blanket becomes thicker, too much heat is trapped.

Between 1968 and 1989, the world's average temperature seemed to rise by 0.8°C (1.45°F). Some scientists say that this variation is normal. Others believe that the increase was caused by the greenhouse effect – and say their computers predict an additional rise in temperature of 2 to 5°C (3.6 to 9°F) by 2050.

### Time for action

This rate of increase allows some time, at least, to organise counter-measures – such as a considerable reduction in the burning of fossil fuels – to prevent any

drastic shifts in climatic and agricultural patterns. These include the likelihood that rainfall would increase in some parts of the world, hurricanes would be more intense, and the fertile prairies of the American Midwest and the steppes of the Ukraine would become desert.

But a few experts believe that global warming could be occurring much faster than this, and that its catastrophic results could be irreversible by the end of this century. They say that the computers have not been programmed to consider 'feedback mechanisms' – the way that warming in one part of the world's weather systems will speed up the warming process in others.

The increase in carbon dioxide in the atmosphere, for example, will not come solely from burning fossil fuels. As temperatures rise, the tundra – the vast frozen peat bog that runs from Canada to Siberia – will warm, releasing carbon dioxide that now lies trapped by the ice. This additional carbon dioxide will intensify the greenhouse effect.

### Swelling oceans

The effects of global warming are extremely complex and difficult to predict. For example, many scientists agree that warmer temperatures would cause sea levels to rise – as the oceans warmed up, they would occupy more space. The glaciers and the polar ice caps would also begin to melt. But since the humidity of the atmosphere increases with temperature, more snow would fall at the Earth's extremes, somewhat balancing the melting.

So no one can predict by exactly how much the sea will rise. A conservative estimate generally accepted today is 150 to 300 mm (6 to 12 in) by the year 2030. This could endanger coastal towns and cities round the world.

The world's oceans and the polar ice-caps also contain half the world's carbon dioxide. With both significantly warmer, yet more of the blanketing gas would be released. These effects would build up like compound interest in a bank, bringing forward the date of possible catastrophe by several decades.

## DID YOU KNOW..?

*THE AUSTRALIAN Southerly Buster, a cool wind that blows in from the sea to the south coast of the island continent, can reduce temperatures by up to 20°C (36°F) in just a few minutes.*

✳ ✳ ✳

*THE HIGHEST wind speeds ever officially recorded have occurred atop Mount Washington in New Hampshire, USA, where gusts have reached 370 km/h (230 mph).*

✳ ✳ ✳

*A TERRIFYING forecast known as the 'Toledo letter' circulated in western Europe in 1185. Johannes, a Spanish astronomer, predicted dire weather when all the known planets came into conjunction (aligned with each other) in September the following year. Ferocious winds would destroy most buildings, he said, and famine and other disasters would follow. Many people took precautions against the calamity, some even building shelters underground – but the cataclysm failed to materialise.*

✳ ✳ ✳

*NINETY-NINE per cent of Antarctica's land mass is covered in ice, and that represents nine-tenths of all the ice on Earth.*

# MIRACLE IN THE DESERT

*After years of drought, flowers bloom in the wilderness*

THE ATACAMA desert in Chile is the driest place in the world. The average annual rainfall there is nil. But, perhaps once in five years, sometimes longer, it does rain – and then something like a miracle occurs.

'It was like stepping into Paradise,' wrote one British visitor, Gill Ross, who saw what the rains of 1988 brought to the Atacama. She went on to describe 'beautiful fragile flowers of brilliant colours growing in giant sweeps as though God had scattered handfuls of seed into the wind'.

The following year, another of the world's least fertile places burst into bloom: dried-out Lake Eyre in central Australia, where summer temperatures can reach 54°C (130°F). Torrential rains in April and May filled the lake, and the drab surrounding desert burst into colour as plants sprang seemingly from nowhere and blossomed.

The flowers grow from the millions of seeds left lying in the sand since the time of the desert's last blooming. How do they cope with the extraordinarily harsh conditions that greet them? The answer lies in the speed with which the

*Bone dry The Mojave Desert, near Los Angeles, usually receives less than 270 mm (5 in) of rain a year, yet flowering plants survive.*

plants go through their life cycle, and the nature of their seeds. Whereas plants in more temperate climates may take months to mature, flower and produce seeds, these desert 'ephemerals' may take only two weeks. The seeds themselves will not germinate unless they are saturated with water, which will happen only after especially heavy rains. Otherwise, they lie dormant inside tough shells that will protect them from drought for as long as 25 years. When the rains do come, they bring colour to the desert for just a few brief weeks.

The seeds of some plants in these uniquely arid regions react to different amounts of water, so ensuring that they do not all germinate at once: some are always kept in reserve for the future. And almost all of these seemingly magical plants have huge, brilliant flowers to attract as many pollinating insects as possible. Short-lived as they are, they thus have good chances of being fertilised and giving rise to another generation.

# SWELTERING IN ANTARCTICA

*The icy continent has warmed and cooled more than once*

GEOLOGISTS and archaeologists have long known that the frozen desert of Antarctica was once a semi-tropical paradise. The coldest continent on Earth has, like the world's other major land masses, drifted round the globe over the last 600 million years due to continual shifts in the tectonic plates making up the Earth's crust.

Five hundred million years ago, Antarctica was actually on the Equator. By about 350 million years ago, it had moved further south, but not far enough to prevent the growth of lush vegetation – whose remains are still visible as rich seams of coal. The continent continued to drift, first south – 280 million years ago it was over the South Pole – then north, until roughly 135 million years ago it was warm enough to support vegetation again. And that, in turn, fed dinosaurs. Some 60 million years ago, Antarctica settled over the South Pole once more. Thirty-five million years ago, the huge ice sheet that now covers it – at heights of 3650 m (12 000 ft) in places – began to form.

Antarctica's ice, and its inhospitable nature, have been increasing uniformly ever since. Or so experts once believed. But in 1982, American scientists found the fossilised remains of a small marsupial, 40 to 45 million years old. Apart from suggesting that the ancestors of Australia's kangaroos came from Antarctica, the discovery raised the question of how warm the continent must then have been for such heat-loving creatures to live there.

### Unexpected remains

Fossils of dolphins, a crocodile jaw and the skeleton of a flightless bird, as well as fossils of wood and plants, have since been discovered. All are between only 2 and 5 million years old. These have led experts to the conclusion that Antarctica's ice sheet has fluctuated wildly in size since the continent came to rest in the far south. The sea, they say, may at one time have flowed through the interior of Antarctica, and the temperature may have been 10–20°C (18–36°F) warmer than it is today. But they cannot yet explain these fluctuations.

# THE EARTH BEGAN TO SHAKE

*Does anyone notice the million earthquakes that occur each year?*

## DID YOU KNOW..?

*DURING the San Francisco earthquake of 1906, a cow fell headlong into a fissure that opened suddenly in the ground. It closed just as quickly, leaving only the cow's tail visible. In Fukui, Japan, in 1948, a fissure opened and closed again, crushing a woman to death.*

M ENTION of earthquakes conjures images of appalling destruction, horrifying death tolls and people made homeless in their thousands. An earthquake can, indeed, wreak terrible havoc if it strikes a heavily populated area. But of the million or so earthquakes that seismologists record each year, most are so tiny that hardly anyone is aware of them. Some may go as low as -2 on the Richter scale, which measures the strength of earthquakes – such an earthquake would represent about as much energy as a brick falling from your hand onto the ground. While earthquakes with the energy of 200 tonnes of TNT occur about once a fortnight, most of these happen far from human habitation, under the world's oceans.

All this activity is due to the constant movement of the tectonic plates that make up the Earth's crust. Stresses build up deep underground as the movement of the plates pushes or pulls rock, until eventually it gives way – with sometimes cataclysmic results.

*Fault line A suburban street in Los Angeles shows damage from one of the 18 000 earthquakes of magnitude 3 or more that have occurred since 1808 along the San Andreas Fault and its subfaults.*

A truly major earthquake involves phenomenal amounts of energy. The one that struck Tangshan, China, in 1976, killing 300 000 people, registered 8.3 on the Richter scale. It generated as much energy as a 100-megatonne hydrogen bomb – the equivalent of 5000 Hiroshima explosions, or 100 million tonnes of TNT. The greatest known earthquakes since the invention of modern seismographs struck near Quito, Ecuador, in 1906 and at Honshu, Japan, in 1933. Both reached 8.9 on the Richter scale, equalling an explosion of almost 300 million tonnes of TNT.

Scientists consider a more powerful earthquake than this to be impossible. There is a limit to the stress that any rock can withstand as it is compressed or pulled by the forces within the Earth's crust – even the toughest rock will shatter under the strain that builds up to create an earthquake of magnitude 8.9 on the Richter scale.

71

# PICTURES FROM THE CENTRE OF THE EARTH
### Oceans and mountains lie at the Earth's core

SCIENTISTS long believed the core of the Earth to be a smooth, spherical mass of iron, molten on the outside and solid, but still astonishingly hot, within. However, research techniques developed during the 1980s suggest a very different picture. The Earth's core is not smooth at all, but features 'valleys' deeper than the Grand Canyon and 'peaks' higher than Mount Everest. These 'valleys' are not filled by air, but by 'oceans' of molten rock.

This latest view of the Earth's interior was developed by scientists at Harvard University and the California Institute of Technology, using a process called seismic tomography. This is a computer technique that produces three-dimensional pictures of the Earth, using information from seismological recorders at sites all over the globe.

### Timing the waves
The seismologists were trying to analyse the paths of earthquake pressure waves through the Earth. If, as they believed, the crust, the mantle – a 3200 km (2000 mile) thick layer of viscous, molten rock

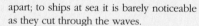

## DID YOU KNOW..?

*THE ALGONQUIN Indians of North America believed that the Earth lay on the back of a giant tortoise, and when it shuffled its feet the Earth would quake. One ancient Japanese legend held that the movement of a vast underground spider caused earthquakes; a later account ascribed them to a monster catfish. The ancient Greeks blamed huge giants wrestling underground.*

that lies beneath the crust – and the core were all regularly shaped, it should have been possible to predict the time it would take an earthquake wave to travel to a particular monitoring station. However, in practice, the waves arrived sooner or later than predicted.

The seismologists knew that the pressure waves slow down as they encounter denser or hotter material within the Earth (as at the core) and speed up again through less dense or cooler

areas (as in the mantle). But they were changing speeds in totally unexpected places. The scientists concluded that the core and the mantle were not as smooth or as even in temperature as had been thought.

### Peaks and troughs
Beneath the Gulf of Alaska, for example, a 'mountain' at least 10 km (6 miles) high rises from the core into the mantle. And beneath southeast Asia is a 'valley' in the core that is equally deep. Such 'mountains' are created by movements of extra-hot masses of molten rock within the mantle, rising as they are heated by the core and thereby pulling the core's surface out of shape. The molten rock of the mantle then cools and sinks, forming 'valleys' in the core. This constant motion creates 'oceans' of liquid rock of lower density between the core and the mantle.

Where molten rock of different temperatures meets, a 'rain' of iron particles falls down to the core – just as, in the Earth's atmosphere, rain can form where air fronts of different temperatures meet.

## WAVES OF DESTRUCTION

ONE OF the most destructive side effects of an earthquake is a tsunami – often called a 'tidal wave' but frequently caused by disturbances on the ocean floor. In the open ocean, where the water may be 3000 m (10 000 ft) deep, a tsunami may rise only 1 m (3 ft) above the surface, with its crests as far as 950 km (600 miles)

***Quick thinking*** *Thanks to an alert captain, the Royal Mail's* La Plata *survived a tsunami in the Virgin Islands in 1867.*

apart; to ships at sea it is barely noticeable as they cut through the waves.

But the tsunami can be racing along at 800 km/h (500 mph), and when it reaches shallow coastal water it can be truly devastating. The front of the wave is slowed down considerably as it approaches a beach or coastal shelf – but the rear of the wave is still travelling at enormous speed. As a result, the whole mass of water piles up on itself, creating a much higher wave, which breaks with overwhelming force on the shore.

One of the highest such waves ever recorded broke on Cape Lopatka, Siberia, in 1737. It left a watermark on the cliff face 64 m (210 ft) above normal sea level. A 23 m (75 ft) high tsunami crashed into Sanriku, Japan, in 1896 and drowned 27 120 people. In

1960, at least 10 000 people died at Agadir, Morocco, from the combined effects of earthquake, tsunami and fire. Tsunamis from the great Alaskan earthquake of 1964 caused damage and death in Crescent City, California, 2500 km (1600 miles) away from the earthquake's epicentre at Prince William Sound. And a tsunami resulting from the explosion of the volcano Krakatoa in 1883 killed 36 000 people in Java and Sumatra.

### Powerful lift
In 1868, an earthquake off the coast of Chile generated a series of giant waves that came thundering into the harbour of Arica. Their force carried a US Navy steamship 5 km (3 miles) up the coast and 3 km (2 miles) inland. The crew found themselves at the foot of a cliff; from a mark on the rock they could tell that the wave had broken against it 14 m (47 ft) from the ground. Nearby lay a British three-masted sailing ship. Its anchor chain was wrapped time and again about its hull from being spun over and over by the mighty sea, and its crew had perished.

# HIDDEN BENEATH THE WAVES
## *The unseen landscape of the ocean floor*

TWO-THIRDS of the surface of the Earth we never see, for the simple reason that it is covered by water. If, to satisfy our curiosity, we could temporarily drain the ocean, some of the landscapes revealed would seem vaguely familiar. Like the landmasses, the ocean floor has its mountain ranges, its active and extinct volcanoes, its canyons, plateaus and plains.

However, in the middle of a waterless Atlantic, we would find a symmetrical landscape quite unlike anything seen on land. A range of mountains, the Mid Atlantic Ridge, runs the length of the ocean, from Iceland to the Antarctic. On average, the Ridge rises to a height of about 3000 m (9800 ft) above the level of the ocean floor. It is flanked on both sides by scores of smaller, parallel ranges and broken at right angles

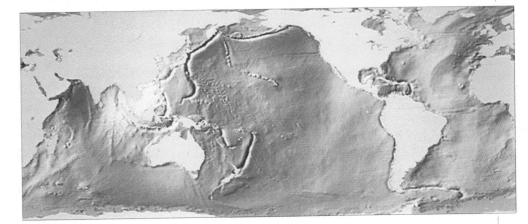

*Heights and depths* *The lighter areas on this relief map of the world's oceans show mountains under the sea; the dark depressions are the trenches where one tectonic plate slides beneath another.*

along its length by dramatic fractures. Its central crest is divided by a wide rift valley.

This landscape holds the key to the formation of the ocean floor. According to the theory of plate tectonics developed over the last 30 years, the Earth's crust is made up of a series of interlocking, slowly shifting plates. Over millions of years the plates have moved, diverging from, colliding with or grinding against each other, and in the process moving and changing the outline of the continents, creating new areas of the seabed, building mountains and volcanoes and bringing about earthquakes.

When the plates move apart, molten rock from below the Earth's crust rises, cools and solidifies, extending the edges of the plates. The Mid Atlantic Ridge is the result of such movement, and is just one of the mid-ocean ridges that run for over 60 000 km (40 000 miles) through all the oceans of the globe.

Other areas of the ocean floor are undisturbed by cataclysmic rock-formation. 'Abyssal plains', for example, are among the flattest parts of the Earth's surface. These are featureless expanses, covered by sedimentary deposits, which can stretch for 250 km (150 miles) on either side of a mid-ocean ridge.

*Fractured ridge* *In this ocean ridge west of Central America, a huge fracture has divided the northern segment (which runs horizontally in the foreground) from the southern (flanked by mountains at the top).*

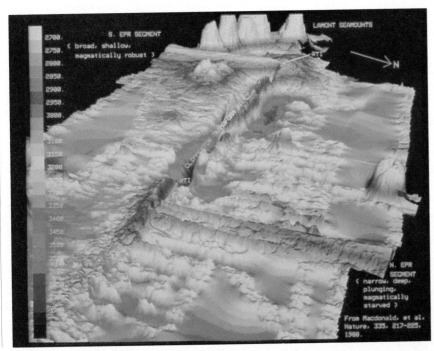

# NEW LAND FOR OLD

*How the Earth's crust is continuously recycled at the bottom of the ocean*

THE OLDEST continental rocks were formed between 3000 and 4000 million years ago, which makes them almost as ancient as the Earth itself. On the ocean bed, however, the oldest known rocks date back a mere 190 million years.

The theory of 'sea floor spreading' could explain this difference in age: when the plates of the Earth's crust move apart, mid-ocean ridges are created. The molten rock beneath the crust reaches the surface and spreads out. It then cools and sinks. Thus a new sea floor spreads over the Earth's crust.

### Going under

In other areas, rock is being reabsorbed into the 'mantle' below the crust. This process, known as subduction, takes place over millions of years at points where plates collide, forcing one down beneath the other. Plates of 'continental' crust (those that form the continents) are made largely of granite and sedimentary rock. 'Oceanic' crust (which forms the seabed) is made of basaltic rock. When the two collide, oceanic crust, being heavier, is subducted. So, while at the mid-

ocean ridges new crust is constantly being created, in other parts of the oceans it is simultaneously being destroyed. The process of subduction normally takes place along the coastline of continents or chains of offshore islands, giving rise to violent earthquakes and forming the deepest parts of the oceans.

If this account of sea floor spreading is correct, the islands that lie close to mid-ocean ridges should be formed of young rock. As one travels away from the ridge, the rock of which islands are

**Land from the seabed** *São Miguel is the largest of the Azores. The young rock of these volcanic islands in the Atlantic is consistent with the theory of sea floor spreading.*

made should become older. Geological dating of islands in the Atlantic confirms the theory. The Azores, which rise from the ocean bed just west of the Mid Atlantic Ridge, came into existence only 15 million years ago, whereas the Cape Verde Islands, close to the coast of Africa, are 150 million years old.

---

## DID YOU KNOW..?

*THE DEEPEST point in the oceans is 11 022 m (36 160 ft) below sea level. It lies in the Marianas Trench, southwest of Guam in the Pacific Ocean.*

---

## THERE'S GOLD IN THEM THERE OCEANS

IN 1921, it was decided that Germany should pay the sum of 132 000 million marks in gold (at that time worth about US $1900 million) as reparation for the losses sustained by the Allies in the First World War. At first the German government tried desperately to keep up with the impossible schedule of payments, but the resulting hyperinflation plunged the country into economic chaos. At this point, a patriotic chemist, Fritz Haber, Nobel prize winner of 1918, determined to rescue Germany from bankruptcy by extracting gold from sea water.

Along with the familiar salt, sodium chloride, the sea holds a whole range of metals and mineral compounds.

Scientists had known that there was gold in the sea since the middle of the last century, but had always found it difficult to estimate the quantities involved. It is now thought that the world's oceans may contain as much as 10 000 million tonnes. Untapped wealth indeed, but it is dissolved in an immeasurably greater volume of water.

The average concentration of gold in sea water is of the order of 0.004 mg (0.00000014 oz) per tonne. The highest concentration Haber managed to find was in the South Atlantic, where he calculated there might be 0.044 mg (0.0000015 oz) per tonne. But such tiny amounts would never pay off the

German war indemnity, so in 1926 he abandoned his quest.

Since then, the only serious attempt made to harvest gold from the sea has been by the US Dow Chemical Company. Since a Dow plant in North Carolina was profitably extracting bromine (used in dyes and photographic materials) from the Atlantic, company scientists thought it would be interesting to see how much gold they could find at the same time. To their great disappointment, all they succeeded in collecting, after laboriously processing 15 tonnes of sea water, was 0.09 mg (0.000003 oz), worth about a hundredth of a US cent at the time.

# MORE THAN A PINCH OF SALT

*The unusual geology and ecology of the Dead Sea and the Great Salt Lake*

HOLIDAYMAKERS on a first visit to the Dead Sea are invariably in for a surprise: those who enjoy swimming underwater in town pools at home have great difficulty in just staying below the surface. This is because the Dead Sea contains 25 to 30 per cent salt, compared to 4 to 6 per cent in ocean water. Similar readings have been recorded at Utah's Great Salt Lake in the United States, where it is equally difficult to sink.

### Lying low

The two salt lakes have very different histories. The spectacular trench occupied by the Dead Sea and the Jordan River, which flows into it, was created some 26 million years ago by an upheaval on the seabed at a time when the Mediterranean covered the Holy Land. At 400 m (1300 ft) below sea level, the Dead Sea is the lowest body of water on Earth.

The Great Salt Lake is of more recent origin, being the remnant of the glacial Lake Bonneville which came into existence 18 000 to 25 000 years ago. Having shrunk, through evaporation, to one-twentieth of its original size, it

now, like the Dead Sea, has no outlet. But rivers still feed the lake, bearing minerals dissolved from surrounding rocks. As the water evaporates, the minerals remain – 60 million tonnes of them, including magnesium, lithium, boron and potash.

Salt lakes are conventionally seen as barren, because they support no fish, but the Dead Sea is not completely

*A walk on the briny The vast level expanses of the Bonneville Salt Flats mark the former extent of a lake created when the glaciers melted at the end of the last Ice Age.*

*Pillar of salt Ever since the time of the story of Lot's wife, the most plentiful and profitable of the minerals found around the shores of the Dead Sea has been common table salt.*

dead: certain algae and bacteria are adapted to its salt-rich environment. The Great Salt Lake, too, has its single-cell organisms, most noticeably the algae that colour the northern part of the lake pink. There are also larger life forms: brine shrimps and flies, whose larvae develop in the water. The shrimps are eaten by gulls, and shrimp eggs are harvested for sale as tropical fish food.

This business is minuscule compared to trade in the lake's great mineral wealth, such as the valuable potash used for fertiliser. The Dead Sea also yields potash, and the Israelis run health spas where tourists can coat themselves in rich, black mineral mud.

## DID YOU KNOW..?

*THERE IS enough salt in the oceans to cover all the continents with a layer 150 m (490 ft) thick.*

✴ ✴ ✴

*OF THE 92 natural elements, scientists have found around 70 dissolved in sea water. They expect to find all the remaining elements one day as well.*

# TURNING ON ALL THE TAPS

### *The astonishing truth about how much water we use*

THE AVERAGE home (that is, one containing two to three people) in the United States uses 486 000 litres (107 000 gal) of water every year, the equivalent of running eight baths a day. In the course of a day, at home and at work, the average American will consume 770 litres (170 gal) of water. But in many developing countries, people make do with far less. In rural Ghana, for example, a family of four uses on average only 20 litres (4 gal) a day, or less than the water it takes to flush a toilet.

Cleaning your teeth with the tap on consumes a surprising 9 litres (2 gal) of water. An average-sized dishwashing machine uses about 35 litres (8 gal) of water, while washing and rinsing dishes by hand usually takes about 90 litres (20 gal).

But these figures pale beside the amounts of water that industry uses. An oil refinery consumes 8 litres (or gal) of water in producing 1 litre (or gal) of petrol, and 180 000 litres (40 000 gal) of water goes into cleaning and milling a tonne of raw wool to make it into cloth.

Farming, too, is thirsty work, demanding enormous quantities of water (in the form of rainfall or irrigation) not only for the actual growth of the plants, but also for applying fertilisers and pesticides. For example,

*Unusual drought* In the hot, dry summer of 1989, English farmers – accustomed to worrying about the ill effects of too much rain – had to rely on irrigation to save their crops and grazing fields.

growing 1 kg (2 lb) of cherries takes 3580 litres (715 gal) of water, and about 2800 litres (570 gal) goes into growing 1 kg (2 lb) of rice. In Western countries, an average day's meals for one person require 19 800 litres (4400 gal) of water simply in growing the foodstuffs (that is, not including any processing, cleaning, storing, transport or cooking) – 900 litres (200 gal) for breakfast, 6300 litres (1400 gal) for lunch, and 12 600 litres (2800 gal) for dinner.

*Cooling off* As newly formed strips of red-hot steel leave the finishing mill, they are cooled by a water spray. A steelworks consumes at least 4500 litres (990 gal) of water for each tonne of steel it produces.

## DID YOU KNOW..?

*THE HIGHEST waterfall in the world is the Angel Fall, in Venezuela, which drops 979 m (3212 ft). The Fall was known only to Indians until 1910. Its name has nothing to do with its dramatic descent from the heavens: an American pilot called Jimmy Angel survived a crash-landing not far from the Fall in 1937, while travelling across the high plateaus of the area in search of gold.*

* ✳ ✳ ✳ *

*THERE IS no living thing that does not contain some water. Plants need water to carry out photosynthesis, and animals need water for digesting food, excreting waste and, in the more complex species, circulating the blood. A lettuce leaf is 94 per cent water, a human being 60 to 70 per cent, and a pine tree 55 per cent.*

# NIAGARA'S DISAPPEARING ACT

*A waterfall that appears timeless is under threat from its own awesome power*

LITTLE BY LITTLE, the world's waterfalls are eating themselves away, eroding the cliffs over which they tumble. They gradually retreat upstream, and will finally destroy themselves completely, allowing the rivers that once fed them to flow gently down to the sea. For example, Zimbabwe's magnificent Victoria Falls have retreated at least 130 km (80 m) along the Zambezi river during the few thousand years of their existence. In the case of the Niagara Falls, on the border between the United States and Canada, the Niagara River will eventually meet up with Lake Erie, and partially drain it.

### Where hard meets soft

Not all waterfalls are the products of the same set of geological circumstances, but a very common factor in their formation is the change in the rate of erosion when the course of a river leaves a bed of hard, resistant rock to enter an area of softer rock. The latter wears away more quickly, leaving behind a precipice over which the river pours.

In most geographical formations, sloping layers of softer rock underlie the hard rock of the upper river bed. As the height of the falls grows, these

*Erosive power Jets of spray shooting up from the plunge pool of the Niagara Falls wear away soft layers of sandstone and shale, leaving a 'cornice' of harder dolomite.*

will also be exposed. The force of the falling water hollows out 'plunge pools' at the base of the falls, and turbulence and splashback from these pools eat away at the less resistant underlying rocks. Eventually, the overhanging 'cornice' of hard rock that remains crashes down into the river below.

This is what is happening to Niagara Falls, where a very hard limestone called dolomite overlies softer shale and sandstone. Over a period of 12 000 years, the falls have retreated 11 km (7 miles), leaving behind a massive gorge.

The great tourist attraction at Niagara is the 'horseshoe' falls on the Canadian side. The curving shape of the cliff is not a permanent characteristic. In the course of history, different patterns of erosion have changed the falls' shape many times – sometimes producing narrow 'V' shapes, which erode more quickly. The neighbouring 'American' falls have a much straighter, more stable shape.

Even though the process of erosion at Niagara has been reduced by the diversion of water to generate hydroelectric power, scientists are trying to work out how to slow it down even further. However, there is still time to plan your visit: experts predict that the Niagara Falls will not disappear for at least another 25 000 years.

# A MIGHTY RIVER SEA

*The Amazon is in a class of its own*

WHEN Portuguese explorers first sailed along – and across – the Amazon in the 16th century, the scale of the river was so unlike anything they had experienced before that they called it *O Rio Mar* (The River Sea).

The Amazon is indeed a mighty river. At its mouth, it is 300 km (200 miles) wide, and even 1600 km (1000 miles) inland the main branch measures up to 11 km (7 miles) across. For over half of its length of 6448 km (4007 miles), it is deep and wide enough to accommodate an ocean-going liner, and 22 500 km (14 000 miles) of its tributaries are navigable by river steamer.

The water that pours from the mouth of the Amazon represents a fifth of all the river water in the world, and ten times more than the Mississippi discharges. The world's second largest river, in terms of volume of water discharged each year, is the Zaire (Congo), but even its output is less than a quarter that of the Amazon. A Londoner would have to stand on the embankment of the River Thames for a whole year to witness the passage of as much water as the Amazon discharges in a single day. So powerful is the outrush of water that it pushes back the salt waters of the Atlantic for a full 160 km (100 miles).

### River of silt

On its way to the sea, the Amazon collects huge amounts of sand and silt, which it rolls along the river bottom in huge dune-like ripples. Much of this is deposited over the flood plain of the Middle and Lower Amazon, when the river reaches peak flow in May. The total land flooded each year is roughly equal in area to the Republic of Ireland. Even more sediment is simply washed into the ocean. A German hydrologist once estimated that the silt the Amazon empties into the Atlantic each day would fill 9000 goods trains, each with 30 ten-tonne trucks.

The Amazon is a murky cocktail mixed from the waters of 1100 tributaries. From the west come brownish-white waters that carry eroded minerals from the Andes; from the north, waters turned reddish-black by decaying rainforest vegetation; and from the south, translucent, blue-green waters that have flowed over the weathered rocks of the highlands of central Brazil.

Seventeen of the Amazon's tributaries are longer than the Rhine (which is 1320 km/820 miles long), and two – the Negro and the Madeira – each discharge as much water as the Zaire. If you were to unravel the maze of tributaries and creeks and put them all end to end, they would measure 80 000 km (50 000 miles) – enough to take you twice round the Earth at its Equator.

# IN THE HEAT OF THE EARTH

*Making use of the power beneath our feet*

THE WORLD'S RESERVES of coal and oil will sooner or later be exhausted, but there is another virtually unlimited source of energy directly beneath our feet. This is geothermal energy, the heat of the Earth's core. The outer part of the core, directly below the Earth's crust, consists of magma, the red-hot molten rock familiar as lava from erupting volcanoes. In many volcanic areas of the world, geothermal energy reaches the surface as hot water or steam, which can be used to drive turbines to generate electricity. A power station running on geothermal energy was opened in the Italian town of Larderello as long ago as 1904, but the electricity produced is only enough to satisfy local needs. Today, in places like Cornwall in England and Los Alamos, New Mexico, scientists are working on ways of tapping the energy that lies buried in hot dry rock deeper underground.

***Mining for heat*** *Near Los Alamos in the New Mexico desert, scientists have drilled pairs of parallel boreholes, the deepest pair reaching 4400 m (14 440 ft) underground, where the temperature of the rock is 327°C (620°F). Water is pumped down at extremely high pressure to crack the rock and form fractures linking the two wells. Then water forced down one of the bores turns to steam, which escapes through the fractures to the other bore, where it is pumped back up to the surface. If this 'hot dry rock' technology can be perfected, water heated in this way can be used to generate electricity on an enormous scale, with no pollution of the environment.*

**Hothouse bananas**
*Icelandic farmers living near the Arctic Circle manage to grow tropical fruits by using water from the island's hot springs to heat their greenhouses.*

Hot water or steam is pumped up the recovery well

Cold water is forced down the injection well

Layers of hot granite are fractured artificially to enable water to pass from one borehole to the other

mud pool

geyser

jet of steam

hot spring

geyser
chamber

porous rock

magma

***Letting off steam*** *In
various parts of the world, most
notably Iceland, Italy and Japan,
geothermal energy is released from beneath the
Earth's crust by natural means. Rain water (shown by the
blue arrows) trickles down from the surface and collects in layers of
porous rock, where it is heated by the underlying magma. The hot
water (marked in red) rises back to the surface through fissures in the
rock, emerging in the form of hot springs, mud pools, jets of steam or
geysers. People can benefit from this natural energy supply with the
help of relatively simple technology. More than 80 per cent of Iceland's
houses are centrally heated by piped geothermal hot water.*

## SCULPTED FROM THE ROCK

**V**OLCANIC ACTIVITY can provide the most unexpected benefits to man. In one area of central Turkey it
has furnished generations of local residents with cool
homes of solid rock. Volcanic eruptions in the distant
past poured out layer upon layer of ash and lava to
cover the surrounding countryside. Over the
millennia, these layers solidified into a soft stone,
known as tufa. Rain, wind and sand gradually
eroded the tufa into a landscape of extraordinary spiked cones, varying in colour from brick
red to tawny to snowy white. Since the 4th
century AD, and possibly before, people
have hollowed out these cones to make
cave-like apartments. The early Christians
of Cappadocia, as the region was then
called, turned many of the larger cones
into richly decorated churches.

***Magical dwelling place*** *Isolated
cones in the volcanic landscape of
Cappadocia are
known locally as
'fairy chimneys'.*

***The simplest of ovens*** *In São
Miguel in the Azores, islanders cook
their meat and vegetables in holes
in the warm ground. The food has
to be sealed in metal containers to
keep out sulphur fumes that would
ruin it.*

# THE GREENING OF THE EARTH

## *How plant life led the colonisation of the land from the sea*

IMAGINE A DESOLATE landscape, covered in ash from countless volcanic eruptions. Here and there are sulphurous pools, more mud than water. Nothing in this terrain can support life as we know it, for the atmosphere is unbreathable: it is almost devoid of oxygen.

This was the picture that land on Earth presented until about 500 million years ago. In the water, however, life had been slowly evolving for at least 2500 million years, and the oceans now supported an abundance of varied plant and animal forms. Much of the plant life was concentrated in shallow coastal waters and estuaries, where it could absorb the Sun's energy. Algae, exposed to the atmosphere by retreating tides, began to adapt to life out of water.

A further 100 million years passed before plants appeared that could survive out of the sea altogether, with stems that drew up water from the ground, and waxy skins to prevent drying out. Most were leafless and less than 55 mm (2 in) high, but the colonies they formed in coastal swamps marked the beginning of the greening of the land.

In the course of their long evolution, plants had also been working a gradual transformation of the atmosphere, by absorbing carbon dioxide and emitting oxygen. The increased oxygen in the atmosphere allowed sea

*Carboniferous Age* Three hundred million years ago, swamp forests and bogs developed. These were inhabited by giant winged insects, such as dragonflies with wingspans of up to 600 mm (24 in).

creatures to evolve into air-breathing animals that could live on dry land, and the coastal swamps became their home. Among the first land-dwellers were forebears of modern millipedes – one species grew up to 2 m (6 ft 6 in) long – and wingless insects. These animals, which fed on the vegetation, were followed – and preyed on – by the first land carnivores, spider-like creatures, scorpions and centipedes. A complex, interdependent web of life was now firmly established on land.

### *Putting down roots*

Another 50 million years later – 350 million years ago – plants had spread over the land and evolved to include primitive forms of mosses, liverworts and ferns. As countless generations of plants and animals died and decayed, mixing with dust as weather eroded the landscape, layers of soil built up on the land, enabling plants to develop more substantial roots and grow to ever greater heights. By the beginning of the Carboniferous Age, some 300 million years ago, the soils were able to support vast forests of tree ferns with a canopy over 10 m (33 ft) high.

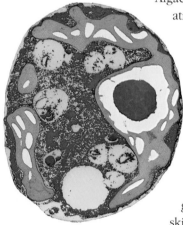

A false-colour microscope image of a one-celled alga. Photosynthesis takes place in the chloroplasts (in green).

---

**DID YOU KNOW..?**

*THE TALLEST tree alive today is believed to be a coast redwood growing in northern California. It stands 112 m (367 ft) high – taller than a 35-storey skyscraper. The record for the tallest-ever tree goes to an Australian eucalyptus, which reached 114 m (374 ft).*

## THE BREATH OF LIFE

**A**LL FORMS of life on Earth need food, and, apart from a few types of bacteria, they must have oxygen to convert that food into energy. Without plants, there would be no food and only tiny quantities of breathable oxygen. The planet is provided with both through photosynthesis, the process by which plants manufacture their own food from sunlight.

The key agent in photosynthesis is chlorophyll, the pigment that gives leaves and stems their green colour. Chlorophyll captures the Sun's energy and uses it to make sugars out of carbon dioxide (from the air) and water. The sugars fuel the growth of roots, stems, leaves and seeds. In a supreme example of nature's providence, the oxygen needed to consume this

wealth of food is given out as a by-product of the chemical reaction that creates it.

And the story of plants' vital role in maintaining the balance of life on Earth does not end here. The quantities of carbon dioxide they absorb from the air are equally important. High in the atmosphere, carbon dioxide and other gases act as a 'greenhouse' over the Earth, trapping heat from the Sun reflected from the Earth's surface, which would otherwise escape back into space.

### The worth of a forest

Today, however, more and more carbon dioxide is being released into the atmosphere by the burning of fossil fuels – coal, oil and gas – and forests. At the

same time, the destruction of the world's forests means there are not enough plants to absorb the carbon dioxide. The resulting build-up of 'greenhouse gases' may cause the Earth to become too warm, with disastrous consequences for its climate and ecology.

One way to lessen the 'greenhouse effect' would be to reduce the burning of fossil fuels through energy conservation. Some ecologists have suggested another solution: planting an area the size of the United States with trees. When mature, these would consume as much carbon dioxide as is currently released by the world's industries. Having originally created the environment we live in, plants may be called on once more to save it.

# TREES THAT BUILD ISLANDS

*Mangroves slowly extend their habitat by pushing back the sea*

**M**ANGROVE trees grow in the tropics along the shores of estuaries and muddy seacoasts, places where any other tree would perish as a seedling beneath the daily tides. The various species of mangrove belong to different families, but are united by one essential common property: their tolerance of salt.

Some mangroves take in sea water, extract the salt with special glands, then secrete it from their leaves. Others have roots that filter out much of the salt as it enters the tree. The remaining salt is

stored in the trees' oldest leaves which, in any case, are just about to fall, so the salt does very little harm.

Shorelines, their sand continually shifted by waves, normally offer little opportunity for trees to take hold. Faced with a shortage of land, mangroves build their own. Most kinds grow a forest of long 'stilt' or 'prop' roots, which support the trunk in mid-air, so that, except at high tide, it is safely above the level of the water. The tangled roots below trap silt and floating debris from the sea, as well as

the tree's own fallen leaves. This collection of detritus not only helps to feed the growing tree, but in time will support its seedlings, too. The newly-created habitat is colonised by other salt-resistant plants, whose own roots help consolidate the structure of the expanding island.

The muddy water of the mangrove swamp contains very little oxygen, but mangroves have an ingenious solution to this problem, too: the trees send out a second, air-breathing root system – not downwards, but poking up above the mud like divers' snorkels.

The offspring of mangrove trees are as remarkable as their parents. The seeds of most mangroves germinate on the tree, producing a pointed stem about 300 mm (12 in) long, with roots and leaves just formed.

### Stick in the mud

If the juvenile plant drops into the water at low tide, the stem plunges into the mud below, like a throwing knife, and is ready to take root immediately. Otherwise, the young plants are washed out to sea, where some may eventually strike land, for example, on a sandbar that has formed on top of a coral reef. If conditions are right, the pioneer mangrove and its progeny can trap sufficient debris in their roots to convert the sandbar into a densely planted island of mud.

***Out of danger*** *The 'prop' roots of this mangrove in Thailand keep its trunk safely above water level.*

# HOLDING ON TO LIFE
## *Tracing the visible and invisible work of roots*

PLANTS DEPEND on their roots to draw the water they need out of the soil. Such enormous quantities of water are involved – a single wheat plant needs 2.5 litres (4 pints) each day to survive, while a mature oak tree may consume more than 910 litres (200 gal) – that many plants ceaselessly extend their roots in the desperate search for moisture.

The roots of some plants grow at a prodigious rate. In one study, scientists found that a four-month-old rye plant had put out a total of 620 km (385 miles) of roots – an average of 5 km (3 miles) every day. If the root hairs, which help the root to grip the soil as well as to take in water, had been laid out end to end, they would have stretched for 10 600 km (6600 miles).

### Keeping a grip

Besides being the plant's vital link with water, roots also anchor it to the soil. Where the soil is thin, very large plants may need more support than underground roots can provide. Many tropical trees, for example, have such dense, heavy foliage that they produce widespreading 'buttress' roots that grow out from the trunk to hold it upright.

In wet soils and habitats subject to flooding, some trees grow supports known as 'stilt' roots. In the pandanus, or screw pine, a number of thin, branchlike roots grow down at an angle from the trunk, forming a structure that looks

like an untidy wigwam. These roots provide such effective support that sometimes the base of the original trunk will wither away completely.

The banyan tree of tropical Asia grows so many supporting roots that it looks more like a dense thicket than a single plant. As the banyan's branches spread outwards, fine vertical roots grow from them down to the ground.

Once they take root in the soil, they thicken up to form a cluster of 'pillars' supporting the tree's massive canopy. In time, the pillars themselves produce branches, which in turn drop

### Underground quest
*Tree roots have penetrated this cave in Tunnel Creek National Park, Australia, in their search for water.*

***Mighty umbrella*** *The numerous roots that emerge from the branches of a banyan eventually reach the soil and grow into 'pillars' supporting the tree. Thanks to this stability, the crown of a banyan can grow to be bigger than that of any other tree in the world.*

roots to the ground. In this way, the banyan is able to spread to enormous size: one near Poona in India has 320 pillars. It measures an astonishing 600 m (2000 ft) in circumference, and it is said that its crown could shelter some 20 000 people.

---

### DID YOU KNOW..?

*THE AFRICAN baobab tree may have a circumference as great as 30 m (100 ft). One baobab in eastern Zimbabwe is so wide that its hollowed-out trunk has been used as a bus shelter, holding as many as 40 people.*

✳ ✳ ✳

*THE LEAVES of the Raphia palm, found in tropical forests in the Americas and Africa, can be 22 m (72 ft) long.*

# SEEDS OF SUCCESS

*Plants go to amazing lengths to continue the family line*

I N TROPICAL forests, competition for growing space is intense. Tall trees have the added difficulty that, if their seeds are to reach the ground, they must not get caught up in the dense foliage of the canopy as they fall.

*Allexis cauliflora*, a tree that grows in the rain forests of West Africa, ensures that its seeds reach the ground by the simple expedient of producing its flowers and fruit on its trunk rather than its branches. When the fruit dries, it explodes, shooting its seeds up to 5 m (16 ft) through the undergrowth.

### Riotous send-off

This distance is impressive, but is still a long way short of the record for dispersing seeds by means of bursting pods. The hard, woody fruit of the Central American sandbox tree bursts with a loud bang, firing its seeds into the air to land up to 14 m (46 ft) away.

*Natural parachutes The fine hairs on dandelion seeds help them to travel far in even a light breeze.*

And the dwarf mistletoe of the western United States, a parasitic plant that feeds on conifers, blasts its sticky seeds over a similar distance. When the seeds land on a conifer branch, they germinate and quickly penetrate their host.

These plants are simply doing what all seed-bearing plants have to do: distributing their seeds as far as they can, to give them the best chance of survival. Other plants use less spectacular, but no less effective methods.

Orchids produce such tiny seeds that they can be carried in their millions on the wind; the seeds of some plants, such as dandelions and cotton, are heavier, and need wings, parachutes or plumes of very fine hairs to help disperse them through the air.

In the case of the tumbleweeds of desert or plains areas, the whole plant dries out when it produces seeds; it is then uprooted by the wind and tumbles along the ground, scattering seeds as it goes.

### A lift to a new home

Some seeds are equipped with hooks, bristles, barbs or spines to hitch a ride to a new area on the fur or feathers of a passing bird or animal. The burrs that get tangled in children's hair are simply seeds looking for a new place to grow.

A more common strategy is for seeds to make the journey inside an animal. The purpose of producing a tasty fruit is that it should be eaten and the undigested seeds dispersed along with a ready supply of fertiliser.

In some cases, such as the small hard seeds of the guava, the action of the digestive system contributes to the seed's success. The seed's outer skin is softened, making it easier for it to germinate once it has been deposited far from its parent tree.

## ALMOST AS DEAD AS THE DODO

T HE ISLAND of Mauritius in the Indian Ocean is the home of the tambalacoque tree, which, until the 17th century, flourished in the hot and humid climate. Then, all of a sudden, the tree seemed to lose the ability to grow from seed. Existing trees continued to grow, but not one of the seeds they shed would germinate. No answer was found to this botanical mystery, with the result

that, by the 1970s, there were only 13 tambalacoque trees left in the world.

It was then that an American ecologist, Stanley Temple, noticed that the tambalacoque had stopped growing from seed at precisely the time when the island's most celebrated former resident, the dodo, became extinct. The dodo, a large, flightless pigeon, had been killed for its meat by sailors and the first settlers on the island. Were the two events connected?

Many seeds will germinate only after they have been eaten by a particular animal and passed through its digestive system. If this were the case with the tambalacoque and the dodo, the tree would be doomed, unless a bird with a similar gizzard and gut could be found to act as a substitute. As an experiment, Temple fed tambalacoque seeds to turkeys and gathered the seeds up from their droppings. Happily, some of these seeds did germinate, and there is hope that the tambalacoque tree will survive.

*Surviving partner The tambalacoque tree is threatened by extinction, possibly because the dodo became extinct 300 years ago: it seems that the tree's seeds only germinate if they have passed through the digestive system of a dodo.*

### DID YOU KNOW..?

*THE COCO DE MER, or double coconut palm, of the Seychelles bears the biggest seed in the plant kingdom, weighing up to 27 kg (60 lb).*

## FLOWERS OF DESTRUCTION

WHEN THE atomic bomb was dropped on Hiroshima in August 1945, it devastated the plant life of the area. Over a radius of 8 km (5 miles) from the centre of the explosion, trees were broken or burned and all other vegetation disappeared. The first reports on the damage predicted that nothing would grow there for 70 years.

As it turned out, within a few weeks of the blast the ruins of the city were covered by a carpet of greenery and wildflowers. The heat of the explosion had actually caused seeds buried underground to germinate.

Even stranger was the fact that plants that had previously been difficult to grow in Hiroshima, such as tomatoes, flourished as never before. Wheat and soybean harvests were also unexpectedly plentiful. The reason was that the fungal blights and insect pests that had hindered their growth had been killed off by the flames and the nuclear radiation.

Other effects of the radiation were far more sinister. Strange mutations began to

*Scorched earth The nuclear explosion at Hiroshima devastated life above ground.*

appear in local plants: deformed flowers, whitened leaves and retarded growth were all reported. Thankfully, these mutant strains died out within three or four years, although the long-term genetic effects of the radiation are largely unknown.

Since the explosion of the nuclear reactor at Chernobyl in April 1986, Soviet scientists have studied the effects on the plant life in the area. Many of the abnormal growths appear to be only temporary phenomena, but the persistence of radioactive particles in the soil will contaminate subsequent generations of plants and the animals and people that eat them. For example, local people are forbidden to gather and eat forest mushrooms. Forty years earlier, no one knew to give a similar warning to the hungry survivors of Hiroshima.

# DRINKING IN THE DESERT
*The cactus has ingenious ways of living with drought*

THE ARIZONA desert is harsh, hot, and extremely dry, yet row upon row of giant saguaro cacti, up to 18 m (60 ft) tall, grow there, all well-supplied with water. How do the saguaro and the many smaller cacti survive in a land that hardly ever sees rain?

Nature has provided cactus plants with a highly specialised architecture that enables them to gather and retain

*Kidnapped cacti Despite being up to 18 m (60 ft) tall, many saguaros have been stolen from the Arizona desert and now grace California gardens.*

water in desert conditions. Unlike conventional plants, whose roots delve deep underground for moisture, cacti have very shallow, finely branching roots. These take in water very quickly, almost as soon as rain, dew or mist touches the ground. On a large cactus like the saguaro, the roots cover a vast area, radiating outwards 50 to 100 m (165 to 330 ft) from the stem.

The characteristic spines of the cactus also help in gathering water. In many species they point downward, so that tiny drops of water collect on the tips when there is a light rain or a morning mist. Eventually these droplets fall to the ground and are soaked up by the roots.

Since months may pass between falls of rain, the cactus has other features designed to retain as much water as possible. Other plants store water in their leaves, but a cactus has none – water would evaporate from them far too easily. Instead, the cactus stores all its water in the pulp in its stem, which has a waxy skin to reduce evaporation. Furthermore, cacti breathe only in the

cool of the desert night, so that as little water as possible escapes from their pores. These stay firmly closed in the blistering temperatures of the day.

The ribbed structure of many cacti also has a role in water-retention. Like the pleats in an accordion, the ribs allow the plant to swell or shrink as it collects or consumes water.

### Defence strategy

As the desert's most efficient reservoirs of water, cacti must protect themselves from the predations of thirsty animals. The greatest threat comes from rodents, but the spines keep them away from most of the plant's moist pulp. Cactus flowers would also make a juicy meal, so many small cacti open them only in the hottest part of the day – when rodents are hiding in the shade and the only visitors are insect pollinators.

Other species employ a different strategy, producing particularly fragrant flowers that they open at night to be pollinated by moths or nectar-feeding bats. Once they have served their purpose, most cactus flowers wilt on the very same day that they open. Only the giant saguaro and a few particularly spiny species can afford to put out flowers that bloom for any length of time.

# THE ODD COUPLE

## *A pair of plants make a unique partnership*

LICHENS ARE ONE of the most successful examples of a partnership between two life forms. To the naked eye, a lichen appears to be a single living unit, but the microscope reveals that it is in fact two different forms of plant life, a fungus and an alga, so closely intertwined that they appear as one.

The body, or thallus, of the lichen is composed of millions of cells of algae held in a web of fungal strands. The algal cells are sensitive to light, and provide the fungus with food by producing carbohydrates (mainly sugars) through photosynthesis; the fungus absorbs water vapour from the air for the alga and protects it from strong light. Carbohydrate production by the alga decreases rapidly if it is separated from the fungus.

### *Adaptable in the extreme*

Together the two organisms are far better equipped to cope with life than either partner by itself. Lichens can exist in extreme conditions where no other plants are to be found. Their choice of habitat reflects their differing needs for moisture. There are three main forms of lichen. The *Crustose* type are prominent in

**Mountain-topper** *The shrub-like* Cladonia *lichen grows on banks, rocks and mountain summits. Like other* Fruticose *lichens, it thrives in a humid atmosphere.*

bleak landscapes; they have adapted to the dry climates of deserts and to Arctic and Antarctic regions. *Foliose* lichens flourish in rainforests, whereas *Fruticose* lichens prefer the humid air of seacoasts and mountainous tropical regions.

Most lichens will not, however, grow happily in industrial towns and cities. Their highly sensitive mechanism for absorption of water vapour and other gases cannot bear the extreme dryness and pollution of such areas. Yet some forms have adapted to foul air: for example, in Britain the lichen *Lecanora conizaeoides* only thrives in cities.

So close is the relationship between a lichen's fungus and alga that they reproduce together. The lichen produces little blisters that contain tissues of both partners; the blisters readily break away from the main body, and the tissues gradually develop into the lichen. The fungus and alga work in unison so successfully that a lichen can live for hundreds, or even thousands, of years.

---

## A MATTER OF GIVE AND TAKE

MOST FLOWERING plants produce seeds that have a built-in food supply to help the young seedling in the early stages of its life. But the orchid *Dactylorchis purpurella* is an exception. Its seeds are so tiny that there is no room for a food store. The seed of this flower survives only because of its relationship with a particular kind of fungus, which feeds it and helps it to germinate.

The fungus, a species of the *Rhizoctonia* family, penetrates the seed and provides it with nutrients from the soil until it has grown leaves that can produce their own food through photosynthesis. As the orchid develops, the fungus takes nourishment from the orchid's roots. The two plants live side by side, in what at first appears to be a mutually beneficial relationship.

But as the orchid takes the nutrients it needs, it actually eats away at the fungus. Eventually, when the orchid can depend on its leaves to provide enough food, it devours its life-giving partner completely.

# THE SEEDS OF DECEPTION
## Some master mimics of the plant world

MANY PLANT species need insects to act as couriers for their pollen, so that flowers can be fertilised and a new generation be born. A few species have devious strategies to entice insects to collect their pollen. For example, the *Ophrys* group of orchids, found mainly in Mediterranean countries, uses impersonation. Their flowers mimic the female fly, wasp or bee, developing features that resemble the wings, eyes and antennae of these insects. Some flowers, such as that of the fly orchid, even produce an odour similar to the one the female insect gives out when ready to mate. The deception works so well that male insects try to mate with the flowers. In the process, pollen sticks to their bodies, and is deposited in the next orchids they visit.

### Sweet surprise

The bucket orchid, *Coryanthes speciosa*, of Central America, drugs the bees that visit it, intoxicating them with a sweet-smelling nectar which they find irresistible. The sluggish bee slips and, guided by the shape of the flower, falls into a well of liquid. Having fallen, the only way out is through a narrow tunnel containing pollen; as it struggles to get out, the pollen sticks to the bee's wet body. Once free, it will fly off to the next bucket orchid and unwittingly transfer the pollen.

*Sticky situation The bucket orchid drugs bees with a sweet-smelling nectar. The bees fall into a well of liquid, and their only escape is through a pollen-lined tunnel.*

*Phoney female The flower of the yellow bee orchid resembles a female bee. This attracts males, who collect pollen while trying to mate.*

Odour also aids the pollination of the carrion flower, of southern Africa. Dung beetles and carrion flies normally lay their eggs on decomposing meat, so the carrion flower attracts these insects by both smelling and looking like rotting meat. The carrion flower is so convincing that the insects lay their eggs on the flower, as they would do in a carcass – and inadvertently pick up pollen in the process. This is later transferred to another carrion flower. When the eggs hatch, however, they find themselves on an inhospitable, inedible petal, and inevitably die of starvation.

Sometimes plant and insect depend on each other for survival. The creamy white flowers of the Central American yucca, for example, develop a scent at night to attract the yucca moth. This moth's proboscis is specially curved to collect the yucca's pollen, which it moulds into a ball for easy carriage. The moth then flies to another yucca where it lays its eggs in the flower and deposits the pollen ball. The plant is thus pollinated, and eventually about one-fifth of its growing seeds become food for the moth larvae hatching from the eggs. The adult moths emerge when yuccas are next in bloom – and so the cycle begins again.

Neither plant nor insect can multiply without the other's help: if one of them were to become extinct, the other, too, would be lost.

---

## DID YOU KNOW..?

*HONEY BEES may collect pollen from as many as 500 flowers – all of the same species – in a single trip. And the hummingbird hawkmoth has been seen to visit 106 viola flowers in four minutes.*

✳ ✳ ✳

*SOME PLANTS rely on the wind to carry their pollen from one individual to another, and produce pollen in great quantities to increase the chances of success. Just one catkin, or flower cluster, of a birch tree can produce up to 5.5 million grains of pollen.*

✳ ✳ ✳

*A VENEZUELAN orchid, Cycnoches chlorochilon, has been known to carry 3.7 million seeds in a single seed pod, which is about the size of a short fat pea pod. There is a real need for this abundance – many of the seeds will die before they germinate.*

# A SENSE OF TIMING

*How plants keep in rhythm with the seasons and the hours of the day*

MANY PLANTS possess a very sensitive 'biological clock' that regulates their activity through the day. It makes sure, for example, that flowers are open at the time of day when the greatest number of pollinating insects are on the wing. It also triggers enzyme activity for growth, the production of nectar, and, during the hours of darkness, rest.

Plants can tell not only what time of day it is but also what time of year. They measure the lengths of day and night to know when to flower. The temperature of the atmosphere and moisture of the soil are other important elements – in the right combination they stimulate germination. But while temperature and humidity may fluctuate from year to year, day-length at a specific time in the year is constant, and thus a more reliable signal.

Day-length is also critical for stimulating flowering. But, surprisingly, experiments on plants that, in natural conditions, flower at just one time of year show that a plant's sense of the moment to begin flowering is more disturbed by flashing lights at it in the middle of the night, than by covering it during the day.

## Chemical cues

Phytochrome, the light-sensitive chemical that is found in the leaves of all plants and that activates their timing devices, is a protein combined with a bluish pigment. Each species makes a slightly different use of the chemical messages it receives from its phytochrome, but, from their responses to day-length, plants have been classified in three broad groups.

'Short-day plants', like the chrysanthemum or poinsettia, flower when the night exceeds a certain length in autumn or winter, or, in the case of some tropical plants, in summer. 'Long-day plants', such as carnations and spinach, flower in spring or summer when the day has reached a certain length. For both these categories, the critical day or night length varies from species to species. 'Day-neutral plants', which include the dandelion and tomato, can flower as soon as they are mature, whatever the length of the day.

**Now's the time** *Having received a message from a light-sensitive chemical known as phytochrome, a bud on an* Achimenes *('hot-water plant') blossoms.* Achimenes *is native to Mexico, Jamaica and Central America, and is a 'short-day plant': its buds begin to open in July as the hours of daylight decrease.*

# DROPPING THE MASK
*The cover-up behind the brilliant colours of autumn*

**P**HOTOSYNTHESIS, the process by which plants capture the energy of sunlight to convert water and carbon dioxide into sugars to fuel their growth, cannot occur without chlorophyll. As chlorophyll is so essential for plant life, it forms almost instantly in seedlings as they come into contact with light. It is a green pigment, and is responsible for the colour of all green plants. But what turns the leaves of deciduous trees brilliant red and gold in autumn?

### Overpowering green

Trees do not manufacture new pigments specially for the season. Orange, red, yellow, purple, blue and brown pigments are present in their leaves throughout the spring and summer – but they are masked by a far greater quantity of chlorophyll. These lesser pigments help to absorb light of different wavelengths and pass this energy on to the chlorophyll.

When the days become shorter and temperatures start to fall, deciduous trees sense the onset of autumn and prepare to drop their leaves. They form an 'abscission layer' – a gelatinous

corklike barrier of tissue – at the base of each leaf stalk. Thus no nourishment reaches the leaf; conversely, some of the sugar created through photosynthesis cannot reach the rest of the tree. The sugar builds up in the leaf, and the chlorophyll begins to break down and its green to fade. The orange and red carotenoids, yellow xanthophylls, and purple and blue anthocyanins now come into their own, giving the leaves their vibrant colour.

The splendour of autumnal foliage varies considerably with soil and climate. Also, because a dying leaf converts sugar into pigment, the more

*Festival of colour The spectacular autumn leaves in North Carolina and other parts of America are a major tourist attraction.*

sugar left trapped in the leaves, the more colourful the display. This is most apparent in the magnificent scarlet leaves of the red and sugar maples of the New England states.

The cycle of leaf-fall holds an enigma: scientists are not sure what happens to the chlorophyll once it has started to decay. They believe that it is broken down into colourless remains, but the greater part disappears, almost without trace.

---

### DID YOU KNOW..?

*SOME PLANTS have changed from evergreen to deciduous, or vice versa, to suit a new environment. For example, Chinese rhododendrons, evergreen in their normal habitat, became deciduous after being transplanted to regions of Europe and North America.*

---

## THE WEARING OF THE GREEN

**O**VER WIDE areas of the Northern Hemisphere, trees as different in character and appearance as maples and firs can thrive side by side in the same soils. The differences become most apparent in the autumn, when the deciduous maples drop all their leaves, while evergreen firs retain their dark foliage, shedding needles gradually throughout the year. These contrasting strategies are both solutions to the same problem: how to survive seasonal changes in temperature and rainfall.

In a deciduous, broad-leaved tree, like the maple, beech or oak, vast quantities of water evaporate each day from the large surface area of the leaves. In cold weather, when the soil may freeze, the roots may not be able to absorb enough water to compensate for this loss.

### Closing down for the season

So, in response to a signal (the lengthening nights of autumn or, in the tropics, the start of the dry season), deciduous trees make their leaves fall, shutting down most

of their normal biochemical processes. The leaves do not simply die of old age.

Evergreen trees, on the other hand, have adapted their leaves to minimise evaporation, and can therefore keep them through the cold winter. Conifers, the most familiar evergreens, have small, thick-skinned leaves shaped like needles or scales, whose relatively small surface area prevents great loss of moisture. The broad-leaved conifers – like the various hollies found around the world – have a waxy coating that locks moisture in.

# THIEVES AND KILLERS

## *The deadly traps laid by carnivorous plants*

THE USUAL ORDER of events in nature is that plants manufacture their own food through photosynthesis, while animals either eat plants or other animals. But more than 500 plant species are exceptions to this order: they eat animals. All grow in soil or water that contains little or no nitrogen, an element vital for plant growth, and animals provide that missing nourishment.

Pitcher plants, for example, a family of climbing vines found throughout the tropics of the Old World, grow pitcher- or urn-shaped traps, some large enough to capture a rat. Although they occasionally digest small mammals or reptiles, they are designed for eating insects, which enter the trap under the illusion that it is a flower, attracted by its scent or by a supply of false nectar. Once over the pitcher's rim, they slither helplessly down to the bottom, where downward-pointing spikes prevent escape. The plant then secretes an acid and

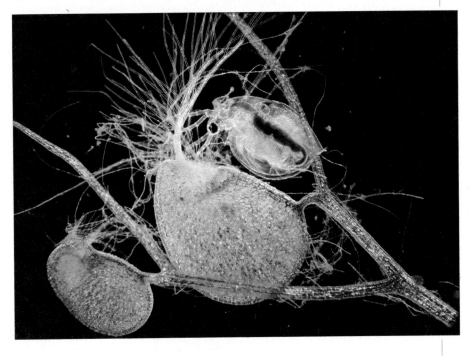

**Watery grave** *A daphnia, a common variety of water flea, has been sucked into one of the bladders of this bladderwort. The insect will die either of suffocation or starvation before being digested by the plant.*

digestive enzymes to break down the body of its victim. The pitcher plant's distinctive lid serves as a lure to flying insects and as an umbrella to prevent the pitcher from filling up with rainwater. Some species, however, do let rainwater enter their pitchers, thus drowning their prey, instead of killing it with acid.

### Trigger hairs

In mechanical terms, the most sophisticated traps of all are those of the bladderworts, a successful and varied group established throughout the world. They are mainly water plants, which, depending on their size, feed on anything from single-celled protozoans to small fish. Among their branching underwater leaves grow tiny bladders, each fitted with an inward-opening trap door. Sticking out from the entrance are hairs, and any creature brushing against these makes the trap fly open. As water rushes in to fill the bladder, it sucks the hapless animal in with it. The bladder then uses special glands to extract the water, allowing the door to close again, and leaving the animal trapped.

**Plant food** *The trapped insects in this cutaway of a pitcher plant have been drowned by rainwater. When rotted, they will be absorbed into the plant for the sake of the valuable nitrogen they contain.*

89

# THE BOA CONSTRICTOR TREE

*The strangler fig envelops its host in a deadly embrace*

CERTAIN FIG trees known as 'stranglers' are parasites with a difference. Of the many species found throughout the tropics, there are some that can germinate and grow just like an ordinary tree, but normally, to gain a start in life, they rely on a host tree, growing in such a way that eventually they can dispense with the host's services and live quite independently. On the way to achieving this independence, the parasitic fig gradually strangles its unfortunate host to death.

### Seed carriers

The process starts when monkeys, birds, squirrels and bats eat the fruit of an existing strangler fig and drop the seeds among the upper branches of other trees – the dense crowns of palm trees are particularly vulnerable, but a strangler can live on any tree.

There, the seedlings take root in the debris and leaf mould that collects in nooks and crannies in the bark, sending out further roots that penetrate and feed on the trunk and branches of the tree. As they proliferate, the roots often intertwine, wrapping the host in what looks like basketwork. Once they have taken firm hold, the young plants send more roots down to the ground, in order to begin an independent life.

This is the beginning of the end for the host, for the additional nutrients the fig takes directly from the soil give it extra energy and strength. It sends down yet more roots, enveloping the host tree in a maze of miniature trunks.

These trunk-like roots grow bigger and bigger, until eventually – the process may take as long as a century – the pressure of the tightly clinging growths literally strangles the original tree. The host's trunk can no longer expand as it grows, while the fig saps all the available nutrients from the soil.

The final bizarre spectacle, after the original tree has died and decayed, is

*Fatal hold This strangler fig is firmly established on a mopane tree in the Namibian bush. When the host eventually dies, the parasitic fig will live on in its place.*

of a sturdy, mature tree with myriad 'trunks' forming a hollow cylinder around the space formerly occupied by the host. Thanks to their flying start in life, many become veritable giants.

---

## TWO MOVES AND YOU'RE DEAD

TO MAKE sure that it traps only what it can eat, Venus's-flytrap has evolved a primitive nervous system that gives it both a sense of 'taste' and a rudimentary memory. A native of the damp soils of North and South Carolina in the United States, the flytrap is a popular houseplant on account of its carnivorous diet. But the people who keep it as a 'pet' may not be aware of just how sophisticated its trapping mechanism is.

Each leaf ends in a pair of spiky hinged lobes, and on the inner surface of each lobe there are three tiny hairs. When any object touches one of the hairs, the flytrap waits to see whether the first hair is touched again or a second hair is disturbed – a sign that whatever is there is probably alive.

### Waiting for a cue

When there is no second touch within 30 to 40 seconds, the plant 'forgets' the original stimulus – its memory is not very long. If the flytrap does sense a second touch within this time, the lobes snap shut, their interlocking spikes forming a kind of cage. The plant only feeds on larger prey, such as flies attracted by the scent of nectar, so the 'bars' of its cage are far enough apart to allow an ant or other small insect to escape.

As a further check, special glands 'taste' the intruder to see whether or not it is worth eating; if it is, the lobes close completely and crush it, and the flytrap releases its digestive enzymes. If the captured object is of no nutritional value – a wind-blown leaf, for example – the 'jaws' slowly open again, a process that takes some 24 hours to complete.

Each of the traps on a Venus's-flytrap eats only about three fly-sized insects before it dies. This is what makes the plant so choosy about what it digests – the process takes so long (about ten days), and consumes so much energy, that the flytrap dare not risk missing a real meal.

# SNIFFING OUT A SMALL FORTUNE
*The highly specialised art of hunting for truffles*

A SMALL, WARTY subterranean fungus is one of the world's most sought-after and expensive delicacies. The rarity in question is the French Périgord truffle, whose exquisite aroma and delicate, musky flavour were prized by gourmets even in Roman times. The traditional Périgord truffle, tiny slices of which are mixed into pâté de foie gras, is black, but there is an even rarer white variety.

Finding truffles is an art in itself. The elusive fungi grow about a spade's depth underground, usually among the roots of an oak tree. Above ground there are very few clues to guide the truffle-hunter – perhaps a crack in the soil made by a particularly large specimen, or a cloud of the small, yellow truffle flies, which lay their eggs on the fungus and help propagate it by dispersing its spores.

But the truffle is best located by smell. The best sniffers-out are pigs, although specially trained dogs run them a close second. The truffle hounds of the northern Italian province of Piedmont, where a fine white truffle is found, are especially talented. In Russia, goats and even bear cubs are enlisted in the hunt.

**On the scent** *A trained pig uses his well developed sense of smell to track down truffles in the Périgord region of France.*

Unfortunately, the fungi, which take about seven years to mature, remain in peak edible condition for only about a week. They can be bottled in oil, and even frozen, but preserved truffles lose much of their wonderful aroma. Prices vary, but typical prices are US $220/kg ($100/lb) for black Périgord truffles and up to $1,760/kg ($800/lb) for the still rarer white variety. To serve truffles baked in pastry, for example, would cost around $11 per portion for the black variety, and $84 per portion for the white.

---

## A MUSHROOM FOR CHRISTMAS

YOU WOULD never suspect that a hallucinogenic fungus could have anything to do with the jolly, smiling figure of Santa Claus. But speculation as to the origins of his white beard, sleigh and team of reindeer has thrown up a plausible connection.

Santa Claus – an abbreviated name for St Nicholas, the patron saint of children – has long been associated with Christmas, particularly in Holland. Dutch settlers took the tradition with them to America in the 17th century. But Santa Claus was not known to fly, to drive a team of reindeer through the sky or, indeed, to come down chimneys, until Clement Moore described this unconventional method of delivering gifts in his poem 'A Visit from Saint Nicholas', published in New York in 1823. So where did Moore get his inspiration? The presence of the reindeer gives us the first clue.

The Koryak, Kamchadal and Chukchi peoples of northeastern Siberia worship the 'great reindeer spirit'. They believe that the only person who can communicate with this spirit is the tribal shaman, or witch doctor. This he does by eating the fly agaric mushroom, which induces an ecstatic trance. He then 'flies' to the spirit world, to collect messages and 'gifts' in the shape of new songs, dances and stories for the tribe. The shaman enters the realm of the spirits through the smoke hole in the roof of his hut.

The obvious parallels with the Santa Claus legend are intriguing, to say the least. But how did the obscure rituals of Siberian tribesmen find their way into Clement Moore's poem? The answer may lie in the fact that Moore was a professor of Oriental languages. The rituals of the Siberian peoples had been known to scholars in the West for at least a century before Moore wrote his poem. It is possible that he used that knowledge to give the legend of St Nicholas an additional, magical spice.

---

# A MONSTROUS BEAUTY
*The fleshy flower with a revolting scent*

IN A FEW remote sites on the island of Sumatra, you may find, draped over the tangled roots and vines that cover the jungle floor, the bright rust-red flower of *Rafflesia arnoldi*. It can measure more than 1 m (3 ft) across and weigh nearly 7 kg (15 lb). Its beauty is not matched by its smell, for it gives off a stink of rotting meat.

This smell, in itself, is not unusual; many plants use a similar deception to attract pollinating insects. What is really odd about *Rafflesia arnoldi* is that it has no green stem or leaves; its initial growth, as in other smaller members of its family, resembles a fungus, rather than a plant. Two species of wild grape vine are its only known hosts.

### Shrews and elephants

Rafflesia is not only one of the rarest plants in the world, it is also one of the least understood. How its seeds are dispersed is not known for certain: it is believed that squirrels and shrews may eat the fruit, then deposit the seeds at the foot of a host vine as they gnaw at its roots and bark. Wild pigs, deer and elephants may also help in seed dispersal, by trampling the flower and picking up seeds on their feet.

When the seeds germinate, thin threads spread throughout the host vine. These develop into tightly packed buds, which, after about 18 months, burst through the vine bark. The buds take another nine months to grow into the huge, fleshy, five-lobed flowers.

**Brief glory** *Rafflesia flowers wilt within seven days of reaching maturity, allowing just enough time for pollination.*

# THE BODY SNATCHERS

*Fungi attack and feed on live animals as well as plants*

FUNGI ARE not fussy. In order to live, they need carbohydrates; but, unlike green plants, they cannot use the energy of sunlight to manufacture their own. Instead, they absorb carbohydrates directly from plants or animals. If there is any way of getting to a source of nourishment, be it dead or alive, a fungus will usually find it.

A fungus feeds by spreading a network of fine filaments, known as the mycelium, through the matter on which it is growing. Enzymes are secreted to digest any food the filaments meet, and the nutrients are then absorbed directly through the filament walls.

The most macabre of all fungi are those that use their mycelium to make traps to capture and kill their prey. The usual victims are eelworms – creatures only as big as a pinhead, which are found in soil and on the roots of plants. The mycelium traps can be nets, sticky knobs or even nooses, which tighten round the eelworm's body and kill it.

Other fungi invade and gradually eat away the bodies of living animals, such as stinkbugs, looper caterpillars and wheatbulb flies. Some fungi use their incredibly fine filaments to drill their way through an insect's hard exterior. Still others produce a sticky substance and literally glue themselves to caterpillars and other larvae before penetrating their flesh. Once the fungi's filaments reach an animal's soft, moist interior, they spread rapidly throughout the muscle tissues, feeding off the living creature until it dies.

Of more concern to man are the fungi that invade living plants. Each year, hundreds of millions of dollars' worth of cereals, fruit and timber are destroyed by fungi worldwide. Huge forests of sweet chestnut that once grew in eastern North America have been wiped out by them, and in recent times millions of elm trees in Europe and North America have suffered a slow, lingering death through infection with Dutch elm disease, a fungus first noticed in the Netherlands in 1921. The blight that ruined the Irish potato crops in the 1840s, provoking a famine that led to the deaths of at least one million people, was also a fungus.

Not all fungi are so destructive; many species feed exclusively off dead organic matter and release valuable nutrients into the soil, playing a vital role in maintaining the Earth's ecological balance.

***Look, but don't eat*** *The fungi of Europe range in shape from the familiar mushrooms that we eat to the strange forms shown here. Many species of fungus are, however, poisonous.*

*Myriostoma coliformis* (inedible)

basket fungus (inedible)

yellow fairy clubs (inedible)

common morel (edible and tasty)

collared earth star (inedible)

chicken of the woods (edible when young; not very tasty)

birch bracket (inedible)

# chapter four

# The
# WONDERS
## of
# WILDLIFE

THE WOODPECKER finch of the Galapagos
Islands can pick up a cactus spine in its bill
to dig out grubs from under the bark of trees
(*page 112*). Only a few animals have evolved
the ability to use tools, but all animals, from
microscopic bacteria to the great whales,
have adapted to their environment in unexpected ways. As we learn more about animals' feeding, courtship and migrations, we
discover a complex world of mutual dependence, involving mysterious means of
communication, extraordinarily acute senses
and prodigious feats of endurance.

# THE FALLEN MIGHTY

### Was it volcanoes that killed off the dinosaurs?

*ABOUT 65 MILLION years ago, all the dinosaurs perished over a comparatively short period of time, along with a large proportion of the other animal species existing at the time. What caused this puzzling extinction? Was there a major change in the weather, or were the plant-eating dinosaurs poisoned by new kinds of flowering plant, leaving the flesh-eaters deprived of their major source of food?*

In the early 1980s, some geologists thought they had the explanation for this global catastrophe. They had found a strong concentration of iridium in rocks laid down almost exactly 65 million years ago. Iridium is an element that is more abundant in meteorites than on Earth. So they argued that a large extraterrestrial body, either a giant meteorite or a comet, must have struck the Earth, causing, among other dramatic results, the extinction of the dinosaurs.

It is now widely accepted that some major impact from outer space did indeed happen in this way, but

*Carefree days* *Apart from each other, dinosaurs had no enemies. Scientists, such as this team uncovering fossil remains of these huge creatures (upper right), still wonder how they became extinct.*

does it account for the death of the dinosaurs? Not entirely, many scientists believe. Some argue that the impact from space may have been only the trigger that set off a far more destructive force – volcanic eruptions.

If the impact of a comet split the Earth's crust, it could have released a chain reaction of volcanoes, spewing out vast quantities of ash and lava for many years afterwards. Ash from these eruptions would have circled the Earth, blotting out the Sun. Without sunlight, plants would have died, followed by plant-eaters and then the meat-eaters that preyed on them.

Some dinosaurs would have been killed by the initial impact from outer space; many would have been buried by volcanic material; the rest would soon have been frozen to death or died of starvation in a dark world lit only by the glow of molten lava.

## MULTICOLOURED MONSTERS

**T**HINK OF a dinosaur and the first colour that comes to mind is probably grey. But some palaeontologists are now working to brighten up the dinosaur's image. Instead of drab greys, greens and browns, they imagine the prehistoric creatures in a riot of bright colours and bold markings, just like present-day mammals and birds.

No one can know for certain what colour dinosaurs were, because no skin has survived. But it is a reasonable guess, for instance, that dinosaurs that lived by hunting would have had camouflage to conceal them from their prey. Like leopards and tigers today, they may have had stripes or spots to make them harder to see in the shadows under trees.

Some dinosaurs may have made use of bright colours in their sexual behaviour. Hadrosaurs, for example, were a group of dinosaurs with strange protuberances – crests, lumps and bumps – on their heads. If these protuberances were used for sexual display, they may have shone in splendid shades of red, blue, orange or green, especially in the mating season.

# LITTLE AND LARGE

*A dinosaur could be as small as a bird or bigger than a house*

**C**ONTRARY to popular belief, not all dinosaurs were massive giants. Compsognathus, the smallest adult dinosaur yet found, measured only 600 mm (2 ft) in length and weighed around 3 kg (6.6 lb) – little more than a large chicken. It was a strange two-legged creature with small grasping forearms and a long tail and neck, living off a diet of insects and lizards.

A small dinosaur that probably fed on plants was the lesothosaur, which measured 900 mm (3 ft) in length. It had flat, leaf-shaped teeth, a 'beak' at the front of its mouth, and thin legs and tail.

By contrast, the largest complete dinosaur skeleton in a museum collection, a brachiosaur, measures some 12.5 m (40 ft) from the soles of its feet to the top of its head. But we know that other dinosaurs – nicknamed supersaurs – were much bigger still. These were the classic sauropods, very slow-moving, small-brained vegetarians, with trunk-like legs and a long serpentine neck.

Calculating on the basis of a 2.5 m (8 ft) long shoulder blade they have dug up, scientists estimate that these dinosaurs must have measured 15 m (50 ft) in height – tall enough to have looked into the top windows of a five-storey

building – and 33 m (110 ft) from nose to tip of tail. The most recent bone findings, in New Mexico, suggest that even the supersaur was dwarfed by the seismosaur, or 'earth shaker', whose

height was more than 40 m (130 ft). It weighed at least 40 tonnes – about five times as much as the largest African bull elephant, the heaviest land animal living today.

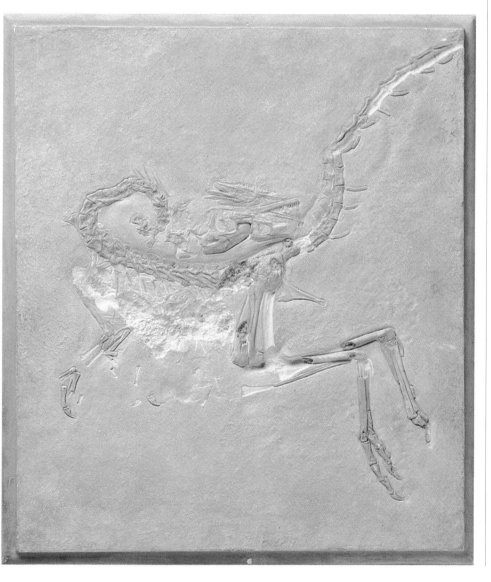

***Small fry*** *This cockerel-sized compsognathus (pretty jaw) lived 140 million years ago.*

# FOOTPRINTS IN TIME

*Dinosaurs have left their mark on the Earth*

**A** STORM LINGERED on the horizon as a herd of apatosaurs – huge plant-eating dinosaurs with long flexible necks – followed the shore line of a lake in what is now Colorado, USA. The largest dinosaur led the animals, the smallest were protected in the centre of the herd. As they walked, they crushed freshwater clams underfoot and left a trail of deep footprints in the mud.

The herd moved on; its members died; eventually the whole species became extinct. But, buried by layer on layer of fresh mud, the footprints remained, very slowly turning to stone. Frozen in time, the tracks waited to be uncovered in the 20th century, when they would enable palaeontologists to reconstruct the passage of the dinosaur herd 100 million years after it had happened.

### Signs of life

Footprints have been vital to our new understanding of dinosaurs. Whereas bones allow scientists to reconstruct the dinosaurs' physical appearance, footprints offer clues to their behaviour – how fast

***Heavy legacy*** *From fossilised footprints, an expert may be able to tell whether a creature was walking or running and at what speed.*

they ran, whether they lived alone or in groups, how they cared for their young, and how they fared in the desperate survival game as hunters or hunted.

Sometimes, patterns of footprints offer 'snapshots' of dramatic encounters. In Texas, one set of tracks seems to show a single giant plant-eating sauropod being pursued by a pack of carnivorous dinosaurs – the sauropod's

broad heavy prints are surrounded by the imprint of lighter three-toed hunters. In Queensland, Australia, large numbers of hypsilophontids, small plant-eating dinosaurs, left a chaotic jumble of footprints as they fled in panic from flesh-eating theropods.

### Mass migration

Elsewhere, it is the density of the dinosaur tracks that astonishes, revealing the extraordinary numbers of the creatures that once roamed the planet. There are so many dinosaur footprints on the eastern slopes of the Rocky Mountains, in Colorado and New Mexico, that the area has been dubbed a 'dinosaur motorway'. Geologist Martin Lockley believes the millions of tracks record an annual mass migration of dinosaurs, similar to the great movements of wildebeest across the Serengeti Plain in modern-day Africa.

Reconstructing the life of the dinosaurs will always be a work of the imagination. But their footprints are the closest we can come to the living reality of the dinosaurs' world.

---

## ENCOUNTERS WITH A LIVING FOSSIL

**H** AVE YOU ever wondered what might happen if a small group of dinosaurs was found to have survived on a remote part of the planet in some 'land that time forgot'? The story of the coelacanth may provide an answer.

The coelacanth is a fish that was common throughout the world's oceans at the time of the dinosaurs. Until 1938, it was known to science only as a fossil and was thought to have been extinct for up to 90 million years. Then, by chance, a fisherman noticed a strange steel-blue fish in his catch from the Indian Ocean – and it was identified by local museum staff as a coelacanth, a true living fossil.

Although not extinct, the coelacanth was very rare, apparently existing only around the Comoro Islands, north of Madagascar. And since it was identified, numbers appear to have fallen. Apart

***Unplumbed depths*** *Discovered millions of years after its supposed extinction, the coelacanth has made scientists wonder whether the sea might be a repository for other prehistoric life forms.*

from the toll taken by modern fishing methods, there has been a strong demand for the fish from curio-hunters and scientific establishments. It is illegal to trade in such a rare species, but this has not deterred poachers.

Now that the coelacanth is known to man, there is a strong chance of its becoming extinct after all. So if there is any other living fossil, such as a dinosaur, surviving somewhere in the world, it would be safer if it remained undiscovered.

# THE DANCING DINOSAUR

*Animals that flourished for 135 million years must have been doing something right*

DINOSAURS are above all famous for being extinct. They have traditionally been portrayed as nature's failures – sluggish, cold-blooded reptiles that, despite their enormous size, were too clumsy and too slow to survive in a rapidly changing world.

But this picture of dinosaurs as dimwitted, lumbering giants is on the way out. Modern research suggests that many of the dinosaurs were in reality dynamic creatures, powerful but at the same time fast-moving. Meat-eaters like deinonychus hunted in packs, stalking larger vegetarian dinosaurs across open country. The spectacular triple-horned triceratops, which was as much as 8 m (26 ft) long, could charge faster than a rhinoceros. And the plant-eating hypsilophodons roamed in herds, stampeding when attacked by predators, just as antelopes do if threatened by a lion.

### Balancing act

Some dinosaurs were not only fast, but agile too. The two-legged deinonychus, for instance, was probably able to stand on one foot (using its long tail for balance) and, at the same time, strike at its prey with the 120 mm (5 in) claw on its other foot.

There is, however, a major problem in understanding the primeval speed and agility of what one scientist has nicknamed 'the dancing dinosaurs'. It has always been assumed that dinosaurs were cold-blooded, as all reptiles are today – depending on the Sun for warmth, instead of generating their own internal heat as mammals do. But no cold-blooded animal is capable of sustaining a high level of activity for long periods of time. It has to stop continually to recharge its batteries, so to speak, between short bursts of action. So were the dinosaurs warm-blooded after all? It looks quite possible that they were not only lively, but warm-hearted as well.

One traditional belief about dinosaurs really is true, however: they did have very small brains.

For instance, the stegosaur, a creature weighing 1.5 tonnes, had a brain the size of a walnut. Yet this does not seem to have damaged the dinosaurs' prospects in life. They flourished in all parts of the world for about 135 million years – from 200 million to 65 million years ago. By comparison, *Homo sapiens* – modern man – has been in existence for a mere 35 000 years. The dinosaurs may have become extinct in the end, but they were great survivors.

*Protective instinct A herd of triceratops form a circle to shield their young from two tyrannosaurs. The three sharp horns of the triceratops were an effective defence against predators, and may also have been used for territorial fighting between males.*

# LIVING TOGETHER

## The kinder side of wild animals

**A**HAWK HOVERS above a lark at her nest, ready to dive for the kill. Far from staying to protect her chicks, the mother lark runs away from the nest, dragging one wing along the ground as if it were broken. She is doing this to make herself appear an easy prey, drawing the hawk's attention away from her chicks. She does protect them – but only by putting herself at risk.

The instinct that drives a mother to sacrifice herself for her offspring has an obvious logic, but in many species of bird and mammal, similar sacrifices are made by aunts, brothers and sisters. Can animals that behave in this way be considered selfless or altruistic?

Among red foxes, sisters live together in a group, but only one vixen breeds. The others help to rear the cubs, feeding and grooming them, and making sure they do not stray from their earth or den. The Florida scrub jay enlists the help of up to six other jays in caring for her young. The helpers, usually the elder brothers or sisters of the hatchlings, bring food and chase away predators. Grey meerkats, too, care for younger members of the extended family group and teach them how to forage. Mongooses, African hunting dogs and jackals do the same.

Many zoologists used to explain such behaviour by saying that the animals did it for the good of the species – that the survival of the species as a whole is more important than the survival of the individual. Most modern biologists, however, reject this view as hopelessly sentimental. They suggest that animals only behave altruistically when it helps to preserve or pass on genes they have in common with other members of their family. By protecting their nephews and nieces or brothers and sisters, they are preserving a certain amount of their own genetic material – not as much as they would pass on by breeding themselves, but enough to make their sacrifices worthwhile.

*Baby sitter* Meerkats live in large family groups that rely on cooperative effort for their survival. Tasks such as caring for youngsters are shared by older members of the group.

---

# SWEET REASON

## The unlikely partnership of the honey guide and the honey badger

**Y**OU MIGHT not expect a bird and a badger to have much in common, but in tropical Africa an unusual collaboration between the two assists both creatures to obtain one of their favourite foods: honey.

The small bird known as the honey guide is remarkably adept at finding the nests of wild bees, but it cannot get into them and is wary of being stung. Its 'accomplice', the ratel, or honey badger, on the other hand, has powerful claws that easily break the nest open, and it is well protected from the bees' stings by a tough hide and a thick layer of fat.

Bees are less active in the cooler parts of the day, and it is then that the honey guide sets out on its search. When the bird finds a nest, it flies off in search of a ratel, attracting its attention with a distinctive song. Then, fluttering and singing, it leads the ratel through the forest, making shorter and shorter flights as it nears the nest site.

The bird waits while the ratel plunders the nest and devours the honey. Then it takes its turn, feasting on the larval bees and the wax of the honeycomb that is left behind.

Unfortunately, perhaps, for the ratel, the honey guide will provide the same service for any honey-fancier capable of breaking into a hive. People, too, have learned the significance of the bird's distinctive call, and have used it to lead them to nests, where they gather the honey that might have gone to the bird's traditional partner, the ratel. In recognition of this service, scientists have given the bird the Latin name of *Indicator*.

**Pointing the way**
*Rather than climb every tree in search of honey, the ratel (right) relies on the honey guide (far left) to lead it to a bees' nest.*

# THE ANT AND THE BUTTERFLY

*A tragic end to an extraordinary partnership*

IN 1979, the large blue butterfly was declared extinct in Britain. It had always been rare, but wildlife experts did not understand what had caused it to die out – until they studied the butterfly's strange lifestyle in other countries. For ten months of its life as a caterpillar, the large blue lives below ground inside a red ants' nest, tricking its hosts into believing it is an ant grub.

The butterfly, *Maculinea arion*, lays its eggs on the leaves of wild thyme. When the eggs hatch, the newborn caterpillars feed on the plants for about three weeks, but then fall to the ground and wait to be found by a passing red ant.

When stroked by the ants' antennae, the caterpillar releases pheromones – chemical smells – that convince the ants that it is one of their own, and it exudes a sugary substance that the ants like to eat. So they carry the caterpillar back to their nest. There it stays for ten months, gorging itself on the ant grubs in the nest. Then, in late May or June, the butterfly emerges, spreads its wings and flies away.

Scientists looked at the sites in Britain previously occupied by the butterfly. More than half had been ploughed up or built over, yet others seemed hardly to have changed. Thyme was still abundant and there were plenty of red ants on the ground. There was no clue as to what had caused the large blue to become extinct.

Butterfly expert Jeremy Thomas then discovered that the butterfly was more specialised than had previously been thought. It depends on one specific red ant, *Myrmica sabuleti*, and in all the sites investigated this species had died out.

*Myrmica sabuleti* builds its nest in short-cropped grass on warm, south-facing slopes, where the Sun's heat bakes the ground. If the grass is too long, the ant

*Choosy insect The life cycle of the large blue butterfly (above) depends on the cooperation of one species of ant (below left), seen carrying a young caterpillar to its nest.*

freezes to death. Cattle and rabbits had once grazed the land, but there were now fewer cattle and myxomatosis had killed most of the rabbits. The grass grew long, and *Myrmica sabuleti* perished. Other species of ant, which could survive the cold, took over the territory – but they were of no use to the large blue, and it was doomed to extinction.

# LIFEGUARDS OF THE DEEP

*People owe their lives to the dolphin patrol*

WHEN ADAM MAGUIRE and his two friends Jason Moloney and Bradley Thompson went surfing in Halftide Bay, in New South Wales, early in January 1989, they found themselves in exhilarating company. For an hour or more, a school of dolphins played with them in the surf, riding in on the waves towards the beach.

But then the dolphins became agitated, splashing and turning in the water, and making loud clicking and whistling noises. It was then that Adam saw the fin of a shark speeding towards him through the waves.

Before he knew it, the shark had attacked, biting a large chunk out of his surfboard and knocking him into the water. He hit out at the shark with his fists, but it bit him in the stomach and side. Adam thought the end had come. Then the dolphins came to his rescue. They surrounded the shark and drove it out to sea by ramming it with their beaks.

### A friendly push

The dolphin has a reputation for being friendly to humans, and there have been many other reports of dolphins rescuing people in distress – chasing off attacking sharks, pulling drowning sailors to the surface, even guiding them to dry land. In 1945, a woman swimming off a beach in Florida was pulled under by a strong current. As she struggled to get her head above water, something pushed her violently from behind and she landed on the beach, face down. When she looked around, no one was near – but a dolphin was leaping through the waves, 6 m (20 ft) from the shore. More recently, in 1983, a Dutch helicopter pilot was helped by a dolphin after he

had crashed into the Java Sea: for nine days the dolphin swam beside his rubber life raft, nudging it along until it at last reached the coast.

It is tempting to believe that we do have a special affinity with these gentle, intelligent creatures. But would an animal really take the trouble to save a human being, in some cases risking its own life in the process?

### Blind instinct

Dolphin expert Dr Margaret Klinowska, of Cambridge University, believes not. She says that when attacking sharks, dolphins are only following a natural instinct to defend themselves; indeed, the presence of humans is probably coincidental. As for pulling people to the surface or pushing stranded boats along in the water, these too are probably instinctive reactions useful for the survival of the species: a dolphin is born underwater, but its mother immediately nudges it to the surface so that it can start to breathe. Perhaps the Dutch helicopter pilot's dinghy seemed to be no more than a struggling baby to the dolphin that guided it to safety.

---

## DID YOU KNOW..?

*A BOTTLE-NOSED dolphin served as a marine escort for 24 years between 1888 and 1912. Named Pelorus Jack, he used to meet ships as they entered New Zealand's Pelorus Sound and accompany them up a narrow channel for about 10 km (6 miles). Sailors believed that he was seeing the vessels safely into harbour.*

# ANIMAL OLYMPICS

## *The fastest, the slowest, the highest birds*

I N THE SAME WAY that human speed and endurance records are constantly being broken, so too the animal world's fastest, slowest and highest continues to change as naturalists discover previously unknown facts. For instance, it was widely accepted among naturalists that the white-throated spinetail swift of northeast Asia and Japan was the world's fastest bird, reaching speeds of up to 150 km/h (95 mph). But researchers have fitted speedometers to the legs of the peregrine falcon and discovered that when hunting its main prey of ducks, pigeons and other birds, it makes a 'stoop' or power dive at 160 km/h (100 mph). Sometimes this falcon knocks the head clean off its victim as it strikes it in midair with its strong talons.

By contrast, the slowest flying (rather than hovering) bird is the American woodcock. The male's display flight has been measured at only 8 km/h (5 mph). It circles high above its woodland territory at dusk, giving twittering calls before zigzagging down to Earth on whistling wings. The combination of the slow, circling flight and the sudden descent seem to impress the females waiting on the ground.

Although birds such as kestrels and buzzards can remain stationary in midair by flying into the wind, very few birds can truly hover. Only the hummingbirds have mastered the art. They have the fastest wingbeats of any bird – up to 78 beats per second – and can fly backwards as well as hover. Their short 'arm' bones, stiff wing joints and flexible shoulder joints allow them to rotate their wings in a figure of eight, and thus achieve their feats.

Other birds flap their wings very slowly – some large vultures do so only once per second. Albatrosses, using wind currents to their best advantage, are able to soar over the waves for days on end with scarcely a flap of their great wings, which, with a span of up to almost 4 m (12 ft), are the longest of any living bird.

*Power diver The peregrine falcon can dive for prey at 160 km/h (100 mph).*

*High-flier A Rüppell's griffon vulture broke bird altitude records when it collided with an aircraft at 11 250 m (36 900 ft).*

### Soaring to new heights

Some animals fly fast, others fly high. The great majority of birds remain below 150 m (500 ft) for much of their lives, perhaps reaching 1500 m (5000 ft) when migrating. But bar-headed geese have been seen by mountaineers flying over the Himalayas at a height of almost 9000 m (30 000 ft). The undisputed holder of the bird altitude record is the Rüppell's griffon vulture that collided with an aircraft at 11 250 m (36 900 ft) over western Africa in 1973.

Birds can survive in the thin atmosphere of such heights, where humans would need oxygen masks, because their circulatory system is far more efficient at extracting oxygen than our own. The high-fliers can also cope with very low temperatures: whooper swans, for instance, have been recorded at heights where the temperature was as low as -48°C (-54°F).

---

### DID YOU KNOW..?

THE BASILISK lizard of Central America can literally run over the water on its hindlegs, should danger threaten while it is near a river or lake. It does not sink because of its high speed, up to 12 km/h (7½ mph), and its fringed toes that spread its weight. A basilisk has been seen to cross a 400 m (1300 ft) wide lake without sinking. Should this fail to shake off a predator, it can swim strongly and is also able to dive, remaining underwater for long periods, until the danger is past.

\* \* \*

INSECTS do not fly nearly as fast as birds: the fastest insect is the deer botfly, which can reach 58 km/h (36 mph) in a sustained burst of speed.

# FURRY FLIERS

*Mammals that have conquered the air on sails of skin*

THE ONLY mammals that are capable of powered flight are bats. They have proper wings that they can flap like a bird's. But a select band of other animals has evolved the ability to glide through the air. These are the flying possums, flying squirrels and colugos.

All three are tree-dwellers that launch themselves into the air from the upper branches of a high tree. Their fall to Earth, or to a tree-trunk or lower branch, is slowed down by a thin flap of skin running along either side of their bodies and generally attached to their front and hind limbs. When the animals are roaming through the trees, this skin flap is tucked out of the way to prevent it

**Night flight** *The sugar glider, a small, nocturnal possum, glides from tree to tree in the woodlands of Australia.*

becoming caught or torn on twigs. When it is time to take to the air, the animal extends its limbs and the flap forms a taut, fur-covered gliding membrane that acts like a parachute.

All three groups have developed this bizarre method of travel for the same reasons: to escape predators and to find food. Surprisingly, the three groups of gliding mammals are not related; they have all evolved the same method of travel independently.

The flying possums (more correctly known as gliders) of the Australian forests are marsupials, like kangaroos and koalas. They carry their young in a pouch even when they glide. Their head and body length ranges from 130 to 480 mm (5 to 19 in) and the tail is about the same length again. The largest of the nine species can travel over 100 m (330 ft) in a single glide.

There are 35 species of flying squirrel, all forest-dwellers, ranging in length from 70 to 600 mm (3 to 24 in), again with the tail equalling that length. The larger ones can glide for 100 m (330 ft). While most live in the tropical forests of Asia, one species is found in Finland and Russia and another two live in North and Central America.

### Farthest glide

Colugos, once known as flying lemurs, range in size from 360 to 420 mm (14 to 16$\frac{1}{2}$ in) with tails 180 to 280 mm (7 to 11 in) long, and have even larger gliding membranes than the flying possums and flying squirrels. These membranes run all the way from the animal's neck via its wrists and ankles to the tip of its tail, and enable it to make its record-breaking glides of 135 m (445 ft) or more.

There are two species of colugo: one is found in the Philippines, the other in southeast Asia. Both species live in tropical forests, rubber plantations and coconut groves.

## CHAMPIONS OF THE WATER

THE FASTEST fish in the ocean is the sailfish. By flattening its large sail-like dorsal fin to its back, and thus streamlining its body, it is capable of swimming at speeds of 100 km/h (60 mph) over 90 m (300 ft) – faster than a sprinting cheetah. By comparison, the fastest human swimmer can manage only about 8 km/h (5 mph).

The fastest swimming mammal is the common dolphin, which can reach speeds of 55 km/h (35 mph). This great speed is achieved with minimal muscular effort and can, in part, be attributed to the dolphin's silky-smooth skin, which is lubricated with oil. (Artificial skin similar to that of the dolphin has been produced for torpedoes to reduce turbulence and achieve greater speed.)

As with swimming, the diving abilities of animals put humans to shame. The

deepest possible human breath-held dive, without artificial aids, is about 100 m (330 ft). Emperor penguins can reach depths of more than 260 m (850 ft) and remain underwater for 18 minutes.

But even this remarkable feat pales into insignificance when set beside the achievements of the world's champion diver, the sperm whale. A signalling device was attached to a sperm whale and recorded a dive of 2250 m (7380 ft ), a depth equivalent to five times the height of the Empire State Building and half the height of Mont Blanc. By contrast, humans have only reached depths of 686 m (2263 ft), using gas cylinders and pressurised suits.

**Full sail** *These baby sailfish might have grown up to 3.4 m (11 ft) long and reached swimming speeds of 100 km/h (60 mph).*

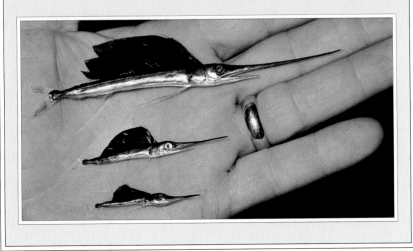

## DID YOU KNOW..?

*SQUIRRELS can fall prodigious distances without coming to harm. One squirrel was observed plummeting 180 m (600 ft) from a tree to the ground yet was unhurt, thanks to the long fur on its limbs and tail, which when spread out helped slow down the animal's descent.*

# LIKE FISH OUT OF WATER

*Some fish have evolved fins that can be used as wings, and can take to the air to escape danger*

ABOUT 50 species of flying fish, ranging from 100 to 450 mm (4 to 18 in) in length, are found in warm seas worldwide. If chased by a barracuda, dolphinfish or other large, swift predatory fish, flying fish sail through the air by using their oversized pectoral fins on either side of the front of their body.

When swimming underwater, flying fish hold these fins flush with their sleek bodies. After building up speed to about 50 km/h (30 mph) in the water, they leave the sea at an angle of about 15°. Then they spread their pectoral fins out wide so that the air rushing past lifts them up, allowing them to glide along up to a height 1 m (3.3 ft) above the waves. To increase their speed on takeoff, they thrash the water with their tail fins, which are equipped with an extra-long lower lobe. A typical flight lasts four to ten seconds and may cover up to 45 m (150 ft). Some species of flying fish can manage up to 90 m (300 ft) at

heights of 1.5 m (5 ft) or more above the ocean surface for about ten seconds.

Flying fish can make several consecutive glides: each time they sink back to the surface, their beating tails propel them back up again. Flying into the wind also helps them travel further. The lift it provides may carry them to considerable heights: flying fish have landed on decks of ships 11 m (36 ft) above the ocean surface.

*All in a flap  The marbled hatchetfish, found in South American rivers, achieves real flight (rather than gliding) by flapping its large pectoral fins.*

Although flying fish are the best known of the fish that take to the air, there is another group that does so – the freshwater hatchetfish of South America, which are distant relatives of carp and electric eels.

Unlike the flying fish, these little fish, measuring only 70 mm (3 in) long, have mastered powered flight – the only fish to have done so. Their very deep chests house huge muscles for powering their long pectoral fins. The fins beat very fast, making a buzzing noise, as they escape predators by making flights up to 900 mm (3 ft) above the rivers in which they live. The flights are very brief – about 1.5 m (5 ft) – compared with the distance required to achieve takeoff, which may be as much as 12 m (40 ft).

## OUTPERFORMING THE HUMAN RACE

THE FASTEST animal on land is the cheetah, which sprints over the open plains of southern Africa for short distances in pursuit of its prey at about 90 km/h (55 mph) – twice the top speed human sprinters can momentarily achieve. The cheetah also has the acceleration of a high-performance sports car, reaching its top speed from a standing start in only 3 seconds. The cheetah can keep up this pace for only 15 seconds or

so, however, and should its intended victim, such as a gazelle, manage to evade it for more than about 400 m (1300 ft), it generally abandons the chase.

A snail's pace, by contrast, is around 10 m (33 ft) per hour, or 0.01 km/h (0.006 mph). The slowest mammal is the three-toed sloth of tropical South America, which clambers through the trees, during the 2½ hours of the day it is awake, at a leisurely pace of 4 m (13 ft) per minute. And on ground it is even slower, moving on average 2 m (7 ft) per minute.

Although the black-tailed prairie dogs of the United States build the animal world's largest colonies – inhabited by millions of animals – the world's champion burrowers are the blind mole-rats of southern Russia, the Balkans, and north Africa. A colony of just 80 are able to create a burrow system of up to 4 km (2½ miles). They tunnel their way through the soil using their giant incisor teeth like the blade of a bulldozer.

***Slowly does it**  The three-toed sloth is the world's slowest mammal. At its fastest it takes 15 seconds to travel 1 m (3 ft).*

## DID YOU KNOW..?

*POLAR BEARS are surprisingly fast and agile. They can outrun a reindeer, achieving a top speed of 40 km/h (25 mph) for short stretches, and are also capable of jumping at least 3.7 m (12 ft) horizontally and leaping mounds of snow up to 2 m (6½ ft) high.*

\* \* \*

*INSECTS BEAT their wings at an amazing rate – the record-holder is a tiny midge called Forcipomyia that manages 62 670 beats per minute. Even the slowest rate, that of the swallowtail butterfly, is still a speedy 300 beats per minute.*

# GRACEFUL GLOBETROTTERS

## *How birds find their way over enormous distances*

THE RUBY-THROATED hummingbird tips the scales at a mere 3 g (0.1 oz) – the weight of 60 small postage stamps. Yet each autumn, this tiny creature flies up to 3200 km (2000 miles) from the eastern USA to spend the winter in Central America. This epic voyage includes a 1000 km (600 mile) nonstop crossing of the Gulf of Mexico. It is an amazing feat that requires the bird to store relatively huge nectar reserves for its travels. But the hummingbird is not unique, for countless other birds crisscross the globe in their annual migrations. How do they know where to fly?

Biologists unravelling the mysteries of migration have discovered that birds do not use just one

**Pigeon post** *Homing pigeons were used for communication by this cavalry division of the French Army, seen here on manoeuvres near Soissons, Aisne, in 1897.*

method to find their way, but call on many navigational aids; for example, they follow features such as rivers, mountain chains and coastlines.

Birds also have built-in directional finders that work in conjunction with the direction of the Sun in daylight, and that rely on their observations of the stars at night. These 'compasses' are probably activated by internal clocks, which are set using the birds' perception of day and night, not just through their eyes but also directly through their skulls.

### *Magnetic pull*

Birds also have an ability to sense changes in the Earth's magnetic field. The magnetic compass seems to be located between a bird's skull and its brain, for this is where a tiny chain of magnetite crystals is found in pigeons. Tiny electric currents are set up within the bird's nervous system as it moves its head in relation to the Earth's magnetic field. The currents are then turned into flight directions by the pigeon's brain. Other birds are thought to use similar magnetic compasses.

Other methods of navigation that may be used by birds include detecting changes in barometric pressure, interpreting patterns of ocean waves, and possibly even detecting variations in the Earth's gravity. Some seabirds have well-developed senses of smell and taste, and may use these to scent or taste the water and thus recognise their whereabouts.

### DID YOU KNOW..?

*ORNITHOLOGISTS sometimes stay up all night watching the Moon through binoculars or a telescope – they can count migrating birds as they pass in front of the Moon's disk. But this method of tracking migration has been largely superseded: modern radar sets are so sensitive that it is possible to identify bird species and track individual birds from their radar 'pictures'. Some radar sets even pick up a bird's heartbeat.*

# AVIAN MOTORWAYS
## *Tracing the routes followed by migrating birds*

THE BASIC pattern of bird migration in the Northern Hemisphere is between northern breeding grounds and southern wintering grounds, although some species make oblique, lateral or even opposite movements in the course of their journeys. Most migrating birds fly in a general direction across a broad 'front', but some follow a very specific route each time they migrate.

These major bird routes are known as flyways. A flyway may be as little as 100 m (30 ft) wide along a narrow mountain pass, but they are usually much broader and follow the features of the landscape, such as rivers or mountain ranges. Migrating bats and butterflies, too, have been found to follow similar aerial highways. The most clearly defined, and best-studied, bird flyway systems are those of wildfowl migrating in autumn from North America to as far south as northern South America.

Many larger migrants, such as eagles and buzzards, rely mainly on soaring flight to reach their destination. They need the updraughts of warm air or thermals to soar, ascending each one as though walking up a great spiral staircase, then gliding down again to the next one before starting the process all over again. Such thermals are found only on warm days over land, so the migrants follow isthmuses, or land bridges, and avoid crossing long stretches of open ocean.

One famous site where soaring migrant birds of prey, including the black kite, buzzard and honey buzzard,

**Central flyway**
**Atlantic flyway**
**Mississippi flyway**
**Pacific flyway**

PACIFIC OCEAN

ATLANTIC OCEAN

***Favourite routes*** *Ducks, geese (such as Canada geese above) and swans follow four major flyways (right) when migrating from North to Central and South America.*

can be seen is the Strait of Gibraltar, where their numbers combine with those of storks, which also migrate by soaring. Nearly a quarter of a million of

these two groups of bird pass south over the Strait each autumn, providing an unforgetable spectacle for bird-watchers. Another mecca for soaring birds of prey and their human watchers is Hawk Mountain in Pennsylvania, USA, where, on one record-breaking day, more than 10 000 birds of prey were observed.

Not all birds of prey are soarers, however. Falcons and harriers, for example, travel long distances by flapping their wings in powered flight. They do not rely on thermals, so their migration is on a much broader front.

## THE SUN-WORSHIPPER WITH WINGS

THE ARCTIC TERN a slender, graceful relative of the gull, makes possibly the most spectacular migration of any bird on Earth. Each autumn, the bird, which is only about 350 mm (14 in) long, leaves its breeding grounds in northern Europe, North America and Greenland to fly halfway round the world to the Antarctic Circle for the southern summer.

Because Arctic terns do not fly the shortest route, but take a path that takes

***Long haul*** *The Arctic tern migrates some 35 000 km (22 000 miles) each year.*

advantage of following winds, they make a round trip of over 35 000 km (22 000 miles). As a consequence, these birds probably see more daylight than any other creature: at their breeding grounds, they experience the almost 24-hour days of the Arctic summer, and, at the opposite end of their journey, they enjoy the equally long days of the Antarctic summer.

Ornithologists fitted one newly born Arctic tern with a lightweight ring and monitored its 26-year lifetime: flying virtually from pole to pole twice a year, the bird travelled almost 1 million km (565 000 miles).

# THE ULTIMATE RETURN TICKET

*The European eel has the longest journey before breeding*

THE EEL undertakes one of the most daunting return journeys in the natural world. During March and April, adult European eels spawn in the deep, warm waters of the Sargasso sea, an area of the western Atlantic Ocean. Their eggs, none of which have ever been found, hatch into tiny transparent larvae, some 7 mm (1/4 in) long. As the larvae begin to grow, they assume a leaflike shape.

### Older, yet smaller

For the next three years, the larvae drift with the currents for some 4000–5000 km (2500–3000 miles) until they reach the coasts of Europe, by which time they are about 80 mm (3 in) long. Close to the coast, the larvae shrink in size and change into transparent eels, or elvers, about 65 mm (2¹/₂ in) long. In winter and early spring, these mass together in their thousands near estuaries of Britain and northern Europe.

Then, as the elvers encounter the brackish waters of the estuaries, their behaviour begins to change. Instead of

*Eel migration By the time they have arrived in European estuaries (right), eel larvae have matured into elvers (below). They then develop narrow gill slits and thick skins (below right) that prevent them drying out, and so allow overland migration.*

## DID YOU KNOW..?

*EELS HAVE acute senses of smell and taste: they can detect as little as a thimbleful of a chemical in 4 cu km (1 cu mile) of water*

✳ ✳ ✳

*BECAUSE EELS can close up their narrow gill openings, and obtain up to 60 per cent of the oxygen they need for respiration through their slimy skins, they can migrate overland through wet grass during the cool of the night.*

drifting along passively, the elvers start swimming vigorously upriver. If they encounter strong currents, they wriggle through pebbles or rock crevices or burrow into the sandy riverbed rather than struggle against the currents or succumb to the seaward drag of an outgoing tide.

Some eels stay in the lower reaches of the river, in estuaries and coastal waters, but others swim to the freshwater of upper rivers and streams. Some even migrate overland to ditches, ponds and lakes.

Eventually, in late summer, when they are between four and ten years old, the eels feel the urge to move towards the coast. They stop feeding and their stomachs shrink to make way for their developing sex organs.

### Last journey

The eels then set out on the great return journey to the Sargasso Sea, possibly navigating by detecting the increasing saltiness and temperature of the water. Once they reach their goal they mate and then, exhausted by their efforts, die. No mature eels have ever been known to return to the European rivers.

European eels share their Sargasso breeding grounds with a close relative, the American eel. This eel makes a much shorter journey – about 1600 km (1000 miles) – to the rivers of the eastern seaboard of North America: a mere day's outing compared with the odyssey of its European cousin.

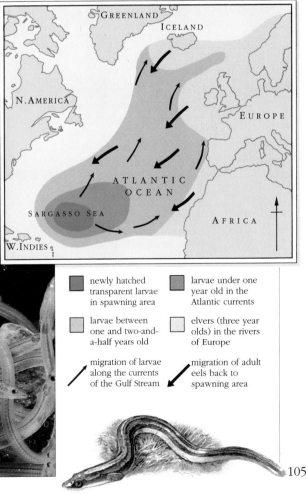

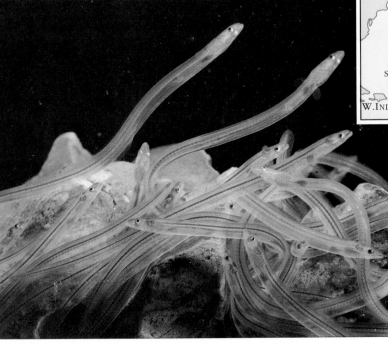

| | | |
|---|---|---|
| ■ newly hatched transparent larvae in spawning area | ■ larvae under one year old in the Atlantic currents | |
| ☐ larvae between one and two-and-a-half years old | ☐ elvers (three year olds) in the rivers of Europe | |
| ╱ migration of larvae along the currents of the Gulf Stream | ↙ migration of adult eels back to spawning area | |

# UNPARALLELED VARIETY

## The animals of the tropical rain forest

**A** SECTION OF tropical rain forest just three times the size of New York's Central Park can contain 750 species of tree, 1500 other plant species, 125 species of mammal, 400 of bird and 100 of reptile. The animals of the Amazon rain forest shown here give an impression of this diversity of life. The diversity of insects is equally astonishing – single trees have yielded as many as 800 species.

A vast complex web of life manages to thrive on the poor, acidic soils of the rain forest, because nutrients are constantly recycled. At different levels, the forest provides a series of quite distinct habitats, from the canopy of the giant trees, festooned with lianas, to the leaf litter of the forest floor. Although canopy-dwellers, living at a height of 30 to 40 m (100 to 130 ft), seldom interact with creatures of the sunless understorey, they are all part of a finely balanced system. Destroy this balance and the forest will revert to infertile scrubland, condemning unique plants and animals to extinction.

**Keeping in touch** The booming calls of a troop of wandering howler monkeys can carry up to 1.6 km (1 mile) through the dense foliage of the canopy.

**Climbing for ants** The tamandua's prehensile tail allows it to hang from a branch while feeding on tree ants or raiding a termites' nest.

**Versatile hunter** The jaguar, the only big cat of the South American jungles, usually drops on its prey from a tree. It also feeds on fish, attracting them to the surface by hitting the water with its tail, then scooping them up or stunning them with its paw.

**Roaming bandits** Travelling in groups of up to 40 individuals, coatis hold their ringed tails in the air as signals to keep the group together.

**Terror of the forest floor** The lethal bushmaster, the largest poisonous snake of the Amazon region, can reach lengths of 1.8 m (6 ft) or more.

**Aerial strike** The fierce harpy eagle preys on creatures that inhabit the upper canopy, such as monkeys, sloths and large birds.

**Startling effect** Toucans' brightly-coloured bills are used to gather fruit, but also serve to frighten off hawks and other predators.

**Living like pigs** Herds of white-lipped peccaries sniff out roots, shoots seeds, fungi and small dead animals on the forest floor.

**Voracious vegetarians** Piranhas are notorious for the speed with which a shoal can devour an animal carcass. Many species, however, are harmless plant-eaters. Some of these lie in wait for ripe fruit to drop from the trees into the water.

**Marsupial frog** The females of many rainforest frogs have pouches on their bodies, where the young develop from eggs to tadpoles to fully-formed froglets.

**Bright and deadly** The vivid colours of arrow-poison frogs warn birds and animals not to eat them, but Indians collect their poison for hunting.

# WAYS OF THE FAMILY

### Courtship is by no means solely a human preoccupation

THROUGHOUT the animal world, males and females signal their amorous intentions to one another in a remarkable variety of ways. Giraffes rub their noses together during courtship, many lizards bob their heads or bodies up and down, and some fish, such as the stickleback, display bright colours to their prospective partners. Female glow-worms shine to attract males with a light so intense that, given sufficient numbers of these small beetles, one can read a book by it.

Birds of paradise, found in Australia, New Guinea and neighbouring islands, have evolved the most elaborate decoration to attract a mate and deter rivals. The males of most of the 43 species are adorned with fantastic feathers. These are held erect or vibrated in their extraordinary dances, and may be lacy, velvety or glittering with a metallic iridescence.

### Seduction by sound

Visual signals are not the only ones used in courtship, however. The birdsong that rings through our gardens, fields and woodlands in spring has two functions: it warns rival males that the singer has staked a claim to his territory, and it attracts females. Some birds even sing duets: the timing of some African boubou shrikes is so perfect that it is hard to believe the *boo-boo* note (from which it gets its name), followed by a *whee-ooo*, come from two separate birds.

Other animals, too, sing to attract their mates. Grasshoppers rub a 'file' on one leg against a 'scraper' on

***Feathery attraction*** *A bird of paradise hangs upside down at the climax of his courtship display, ostentatiously showing his magnificent plumage to a potential mate.*

a wing to produce their familiar chirping sounds. Mole crickets even go so far as to dig out a specially shaped burrow that greatly amplifies the sound they produce: humans can hear it 600 m (2000 ft) away.

### The architecture of love

Perhaps the most remarkable of all bird courtship behaviour is that of the 18 species of bowerbird found in Australia and New Guinea. Male bowerbirds build remarkable structures that are not used as nests, but are built solely to attract mates. Some are relatively simple, while others are more elaborate, consisting of a tower of twigs surrounding a central sapling, or even a miniature 'house', complete with entrance and thatched roof, and can reach up to 2.7 m (9 ft) high. The floor is strewn with layers of fresh leaves.

The birds decorate their bowers with a variety of items, including moss, flowers, fruit, snail shells and human artefacts, from buttons to discarded children's toys. Several species even paint their bowers with crushed berries, charcoal or other natural pigments mixed with saliva and applied with a 'brush' of bark fibre or a wad of leaves held in the bill.

Despite their amazing architectural skills, male bowerbirds play no part in nest-building – or in the incubation of the eggs and care of the young – this being entirely the responsibility of the female.

***Courtship lights*** *Glow-worms illuminate a cave on the shore of Lake Te Ana, on New Zealand's South Island.*

## THE WORLD'S BIGGEST TOWNS

ALTHOUGH many animals lead relatively isolated lives as families, couples or even solitary individuals, some live in large, complex groups.

The prairie dogs of western USA and northern Mexico – which are not dogs at all, but a type of ground squirrel named for their barking calls – live in burrows they dig in the ground. The difference between their burrows and those of other ground squirrels is in the impressive scale of their engineering.

The 'towns' of prairie dogs were once immense: one found in 1901 covered an area of 380 by 160 km (240 by 100 miles) and may have been home to as many as 400 million of the little animals.

### Not man's best friend

Because prairie dogs are considered a pest – they compete with livestock for grass and damage crops, and horses stumble in their burrows – man has greatly reduced the size of the towns by laying poison. An average

town now covers less than 2 hectares (5 acres) and contains about 1000 individuals.

Prairie dogs have a complex social structure, based on elaborate rituals. For example, individuals greet each other by spending a long time rubbing noses. The populations are organised into units called coteries, wards and towns. Each coterie contains an adult male, two to four adult females and several young. Several coteries make up a ward, and two or more wards make up a town.

# LORD OF THE LODGE

*Architect, lumberjack and engineer, the beaver is master of its environment*

BEAVERS are the most accomplished engineers of all the mammals, apart from man. They live in a lodge half-submerged in the centre or on the banks of a lake – and if no lake is at hand, they create one by building a dam across a stream or river. These dams can be made entirely of

mud, but are usually felled trees and branches weighed down with stones and plastered with mud.

An adult beaver can fell a tree 120 mm (5 in) in diameter in less than half an hour, using its strong incisor teeth as chisels. The beavers cut tall trees into shorter lengths and float them down canals that they have dug specially for that purpose.

Water provides a good refuge for the beaver from its predators (such as wolves) – if alarmed, a beaver will slap the water with its tail as a signal and its family will immediately enter the water. As the lodge can only be entered from underwater, it makes a safe home. It is dome-shaped, with the top of the dome above water. The interior can be as high as 1.8 m (6 ft), and it is made of sticks and stones packed with mud.

Gradually the pond or lake that the beavers have created will silt up, raising the water level, and the height and width of the dam will need to be increased. New dams are built on top of old ones, and some are now 1000 years old. They can be as long as 1000 m (3300 ft) – the

length of a beaver dam on the Jefferson River in the American state of Montana.

Beaver dams also serve as a larder during the hard winter months when the lake is frozen. Beavers feed largely on woody maple, aspen and willow stems, and cut extra branches to store underwater, anchored in the mud. The water acts as a refrigerator, keeping the wood at a temperature just above 0°C (32°F) and preserving its nutritional value. These underwater larders allow beavers to stay away from land – and their predators – for long stretches.

Beavers are sociable animals who often work together cooperatively. They live in colonies of up to four lodges per pond or lake, and each lodge may contain more than one family. A family generally consists of a parent pair, who mate for life, and two sets of offspring – their annual litter of two to eight kits, and the yearlings from the previous season.

***Impregnable fortress*** *A beaver lodge is well insulated so the family can keep snug and warm throughout the year. Underwater entrances make it safe from predators.*

## DID YOU KNOW..?

*THE BEAVER'S front teeth are so sharp that ancient Europeans and North American Indians used them as knife blades. Beavers have long been trapped for their fur and meat, and for a secretion from their musk glands used in perfumes. European beavers, now extinct in many areas, are being reintroduced to parks and reserves. American beavers, though reduced in numbers, are far more numerous, especially in the north.*

\* \* \*

*IN 1899, a beaver dam made solely of coal was found in North Dakota, USA.*

# SOCIAL WORKERS

*Termites have organised themselves against the Sun and rain*

**T**ERMITES have changed little in the last 200 million years. They were probably among the world's first social insects, with an elaborate caste system of workers and different types of soldier ruled by a large queen.

Because termites have soft skins and dry out easily, most live hidden in nests underground or inside dead wood, which may house millions of individuals. Some termites cultivate fungus in their colonies. The fungus grows on 'combs' made of wood, and only the queen, king and young termites are allowed to eat it.

In the hot, dry conditions of the African savannahs, where temperatures can reach 50°C (120°F), some termites build hollow towers up to 8 m (26 ft) high to prevent the underground nest from overheating during the day or losing too much heat at night; the towers also prevent loss of moisture, for termites thrive at high humidities.

These impressive structures are painstakingly constructed by the worker termites from grains of soil cemented together with their saliva and baked by the Sun. And species found in African rain forests build 'roofs' of chewed-up plants over their nests as protection from heavy rain.

**High rise** *This tower (above) in Turkana, Kenya, was built by fungus-growing termites, which are extremely destructive wood-eating pests. While the queen lays her eggs in the royal cell, the workers tend the food stores and larval galleries (below).*

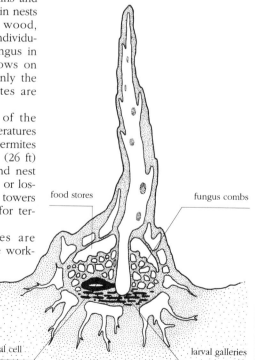

food stores

fungus combs

royal cell

larval galleries

# LEARNING THE ROPES

*Even some of the simplest animals have an ability to learn*

**A** SPIDER SPINS a web of amazing intricacy using delicate silk with the strength of high-tensile nylon. Yet it performs this feat of engineering without ever having a single lesson. The lives of spiders and other invertebrates (animals without backbones) are controlled largely by instinct, involving behaviour patterns handed down in the animals' genes from one generation to the next.

### Back to their digs

Even so, invertebrates are capable of learning. For example, digger wasps, found in southern and central Europe, find their way back to eggs they have laid in the ground by recognising pebbles and twigs around the site.

Although vertebrates (animals with backbones) also inherit instinctive behaviour patterns, such as a bird's ability to build a complex nest, they generally have a much greater potential for learning. Coupled with this goes a greater degree of parental care and teaching of the young by adults. Many young songbirds, for example, cannot produce a proper song until they have learned it from their parents.

### Practice makes perfect

Such learning is equally important for young predators – if they do not discover the secrets of hunting for themselves, they starve. So a tigress brings back wounded or young live prey for her cubs to practise on. The cubs remain with their mother for about 18 months, watching her hunt and perfecting their own technique, before starting to fend for themselves.

---

**DID YOU KNOW..?**

*A SWEDISH researcher has found that female grey partridges look for a vigilant father when choosing a mate. He separated his partridges into two aviaries, one shielded from the outside world and the other open to it. The females were allowed to choose between males from both groups. Males from the open enclosure, who were more alert, were preferred, as they would do a better job protecting the young chicks.*

# MOTHER LOVE IN THE WILD
## *How animals protect their young from predators*

HISSING and grunting loudly, a mute swan belies its name in defence of its young against an intruder. Should a suspected foe approach too closely, this great white bird can deliver a knockout blow with its powerful wings, capable of breaking a man's arm.

Many animals protect their young, though not all so aggressively. Some birds, such as plovers, try instead to outwit a predator. Either parent may feign injury, careering across the ground with one wing held out as if broken, or run off like a small rodent, to lure the predator, such as a fox or stoat, away from their young. Some birds fly off with their chicks from the danger area: a rail will carry them, one at a time, in its bill, while a woodcock carries them between its feet.

Mother crocodiles, too, carry their young. After hatching from the eggs laid on the river bank, the young crocodiles are vulnerable to predators such as marabou storks and hornbills. The mother picks her young up with remarkable tenderness in her great toothed jaws, and takes them down to a safe stretch of quiet water. Few other reptiles show such gentle care.

Fish generally leave their eggs and young to fend for themselves. The

*Toothy tenderness A female crocodile from the Nile holds her baby in her mouth while moving away from a predator.*

mouthbrooders are an exception. The female or male, or both, depending on the species, take the eggs into their mouths. Protected from predatory fish and from fungi and bacteria, the eggs hatch in the mouth and the baby fish swim out, though they will rush back in should danger threaten.

Even some insects show a surprising degree of parental care. Earwigs remain with their eggs until they have hatched. Among bees, wasps, ants and termites, a queen does all the laying of eggs, and then the workers (sterile females) care for the eggs and the larvae until they turn into adults.

## FISHY SLEEPING BAG

ALTHOUGH FISH have no eyelids and cannot shut their eyes, they still rest and sleep. Some sleep buried in the sand, others seek out a crevice or tangle of seaweed safe from marauding night-time predators, while the little clown fish found in tropical coral reefs is covered with a special mucus that allows it to hide among the poisonous tentacles of a sea anemone.

Yet no sleeping place is stranger than that of some species of parrotfish, which spend the night in a sleeping bag. These members of the perch order of fishes are robust and blunt-headed, and measure up to 1.2 m (4 ft) long.

Often coloured in bright shades of blue, green, yellow, orange and red, they are found in tropical and subtropical coral reefs worldwide. As they settle down for the night among the corals, they secrete from their bodies a transparent cocoon of sticky mucus that surrounds them. This process takes up to half an hour, and a similar amount of time is needed for the fish to free themselves in the morning.

The parrotfish do not produce their sleeping bags every night, and the bags' function is still a mystery, though it is possible they prevent predators, such as moray eels, from detecting the parrotfish's scent.

*Night-time security A parrotfish sleeps in its protective cocoon.*

## DID YOU KNOW..?

*THE LONGEST gestation period of any animal is that of the Alpine salamander, which takes up to 38 months to give birth at altitudes over 1400 m (4600 ft) in the Swiss Alps, though this drops to about 25 months at lower altitudes. The gestation period of the Virginia opossum, by contrast, may be as little as eight days. The longest pregnancy of any mammal is that of the Asiatic elephant, with an average of 609 days (over 20 months) and a maximum of 760 days – over two and a half times that of a human mother.*

✳ ✳ ✳

*SOME MALE birds and insects offer their mates 'nuptial gifts' of food. For example, female scorpion flies will only accept a mate if presented with a large dead insect. The females do little hunting themselves.*

# HUNTING HIGH AND LOW

*Some animals use tools when a source of food is hard to reach*

PEOPLE SEEKING confirmation of mankind's superior intelligence sometimes claim that we are the only animals to use tools. In fact we are not alone in this ability; a select band of other animals, including birds and mammals, employ simple tools.

The Egyptian vulture is a rather scruffy-looking, white and brown bird, about the size of a chicken, found in parts of Europe, Africa and Asia. It may not be as impressive to look at as some of its larger relatives, but it has a remarkable trick for getting at the rich food inside an ostrich egg: standing erect above the egg, the vulture can pick up a large stone in its bill and repeatedly hurl it until the thick shell smashes. The technique is not used by all Egyptian vultures; it is found only in isolated local populations. It seems, therefore, to be something learned by imitation, rather than an innate ability.

### Poker, spear or goad

An even more ingenious tool-user is the woodpecker finch, found only on certain of the Galapagos Islands, which lie some 1100 km (680 miles) off the coast of Ecuador. This sparrow-sized bird searches for insects on trees, prising off the bark like a woodpecker. When

**Dexterous feeder** *A woodpecker finch, native to the Galapagos Islands, probes the bark of a tree with a twig in its search for food.*

**Cunning trick** *A young chimpanzee patiently holds a stick in an insect nest until it is covered with live food.*

it fails to find food in this way, it collects a cactus spine or small twig. If the twig has any awkwardly projecting stems, it will remove them.

On returning to the tree, the finch holds its chosen tool in its bill and uses it in one of three ways. It may employ it as a poker to push or drag an insect from a hole; as a spear to impale a grub or other slow-moving insect; or as a goad to harass and drive out a particularly active or reluctant quarry. When it has forced its prey out onto the surface, it transfers the spine or twig to one of its feet and quickly snaps up the insect in its bill.

### Backscratchers and fishing rods

A few mammals also use tools. Horses have been seen to use sticks to scratch otherwise inaccessible areas of their backs, and chimpanzees select small branches to probe into crevices or termite nests as a kind of fishing rod. When enough insects are clinging to the branch, the chimp withdraws it and licks them off. Like the woodpecker finch, the chimpanzee may trim off inconvenient stems from its chosen branch. Animals not only use tools; in their own rudimentary but very effective way some also make them.

# A WELL-STOCKED LARDER
### *The gory housekeeping of the 'butcher bird'*

A SMALL, HANDSOME chestnut and grey bird, with a tail that twitches constantly from side to side, scans the ground from its vantage point atop a gorse bush. Suddenly, it flies down to pounce on a smaller bird, killing it with its strong, sharply hooked bill. Its prize clasped firmly by its strong feet and sharp claws, it flies off to a thorn bush, where it impales its victim securely on a thorn.

The predator in question is a male red-backed shrike – one of a family of 70 species. Three-quarters of the

**Handsome killer**
*The male red-backed shrike has strong feet and sharp claws with which to grip its prey.*

species live in Africa, and the rest are distributed throughout Europe, Asia and North America.

These fierce predators, which are only 15 to 38 cm (6 to 15 in) long, hunt for a wide variety of prey. The largest species may pursue mice and other small mammals, lizards, small and young birds, while the smaller shrikes eat small birds, worms and insects. As well as pouncing from observation perches, shrikes also hunt on the wing, sometimes hovering above the ground or hawking for insects in mid air.

Shrikes eat much of their prey, or feed it to their young immediately after catching it, but most species in the Northern Hemisphere also store some of their food on thorns or barbed wire fences, known as 'larders'. This habit, reminiscent of a butcher hanging meat on a hook, has earned them the popular name of 'butcher birds'. Other local names for shrikes include 'murdering bird' and 'nine killer', the latter because of an old superstition that the shrike

**Aerial store** *A shrike sometimes hangs up its victim, such as this lizard, on a thorn or barbed wire fence.*

killed nine creatures before it started to feed. The word 'shrike' itself is an Old English form of the word 'shriek', although not all species make the harsh, grating cries that gave rise to the name; some African ones are quite tuneful.

Shrikes create their food stores principally during the breeding season, when extra food is needed for the young. Often, though, a shrike will abandon its larder, perhaps because there is a food surplus or because the hoarded titbits are too dried out.

## FEEDING WITH YOUR STOMACH INSIDE OUT

MANY STARFISH have evolved a remarkable method of feeding: they extrude their stomachs out of their mouths and begin the process of digesting their prey outside the body. Some species are able to open the tightly clamped shells of double-valved molluscs, such as mussels, oysters and scallops.

After locating its prey by sensing chemicals that the mollusc releases into the water, the starfish wraps its arms around the tightly closed shell. The arms are equipped with rows of little tube feet, sticking out through the starfish's armour plating. Each tube foot bears a tiny but powerful sucker at its tip. When the starfish has a secure grip on its victim, it anchors the ends of its arms firmly to the seabed. It then retracts its tube feet, a manoeuvre that exerts sufficient force to prise the shell gradually open. This forced entry may take some time to succeed, as molluscs' shell muscles are very strong.

Then the starfish can extrude its stomach into the body cavity of the mollusc and begin to digest its victim with enzymes released from its intestine. Once the food is partly digested, tiny hairs on the surface of the stomach create a current that carries the food into the starfish's body, where digestion is completed.

**Mealtime contortions** *Having prised open a mussel, a common starfish pushes its stomach through its mouth and into the shell. There it surrounds the soft mollusc body with digestive enzymes.*

# A HIGH-ENERGY DIET

*Why the tiny hummingbird has to work so hard for a living*

**D**ARTING HITHER and thither, beating their wings up to 78 times a second, hummingbirds live life at fever pitch. Weight for weight, they have the greatest energy output of any warm-blooded animal. They burn up so much energy partly because their small size demands a hectic lifestyle. The smaller an animal, the greater surface area it exposes for each gram it weighs. Hummingbirds are found only in the Americas, where there are some 320 different species. With their tiny bodies – most are only 60 to 130 mm (2½ to 5 in) long – hummingbirds have exceedingly little mass

*Floral feast A violet-cheeked hummingbird prepares to feed from a flower using its tongue to search for nectar and small insects. Its tongue may be longer than its body and can be rolled into a sucking tube.*

for producing heat to make up the loss from their relatively large surface area. They therefore require a great deal of fuel to maintain their high rate of metabolism, a normal body temperature of 39° to 42°C (102° to 108°F) and a heartbeat rate of about 500 per minute while resting and up to 1000 or more per minute when very active.

The energy for this comes partly from eating insects but chiefly from the high-calorie nectar of flowers. A hummingbird generally needs to eat over half its weight in food every day. If we had to expend the equivalent amount of energy, we would have to consume 60 kg (130 lb) of bread or 170 kg (370 lb) of boiled potatoes every day to obtain sufficient calories.

To save energy during cool weather, hummingbirds may become torpid, falling into a deep sleep for several hours, their body temperature dropping to within a few degrees of the air temperature. At 15°C (60°F), the slumbering hummingbird may consume as little as one-fiftieth of the fuel it uses when active.

## DID YOU KNOW..?

*A VAMPIRE bat may drink so much blood at one sitting that it cannot fly off until it has digested and excreted some of its meal.*

✳ ✳ ✳

*THE SMALLEST hummingbird is the bee hummingbird of Cuba, which is only 57 mm (2¼ in) long – and half of this is bill and tail. It weighs less than 2 g (¹/₁₅ oz) and is the smallest warm-blooded animal in the world.*

# THE REAL VAMPIRES

*Bats that require a nightly feast of blood*

**T**HE ONLY mammal to live solely on a diet of blood, the vampire bat is found in Central and South America. Its name is slightly misleading, in that it does not suck blood from its victim after puncturing the skin with Dracula-style fangs. Instead, it painlessly cuts out a thin sliver of skin, about the diameter of a drinking straw, using its razor-sharp incisor teeth. It then laps up the blood that oozes from the wound. Its saliva contains an anticoagulant that prevents the victim's blood from clotting while the bat feeds.

## Fond of birds or big prey

Despite popular stories and films, vampire bats rarely attack people. There are three species, two of which, the white-winged vampire and the hairy-legged vampire, are thought to prey chiefly on birds. The habits of the third species, the common vampire, are much better known. Before the advent of settlers, they fed on the blood of large wild animals, but over the past 400 years, with the replacement of much of their natural prey by domesticated animals, they have switched their attention to cattle, horses, pigs and other livestock.

Flying close to the ground, they are thought to search for their prey using a combination of sight, smell and echolocation. They land near a sleeping animal, then hop and scuttle to reach it, using the wrists of their wingbones to support themselves.

*Disease carrier Vampire bats take relatively little blood from livestock, but they can transmit rabies and other diseases.*

114

# PODS OF SUBMARINE KILLERS
### The formidable hunting techniques of the killer whale

ALTHOUGH they never attack people, and kill only when they are hungry, from the point of view of other marine creatures, killer whales certainly live up to their name. They hunt down a huge variety of prey, ranging in size from small salmon to the blue whale, which is, at nearly 30 m (100 ft) in length, the largest creature that has ever lived on Earth.

Other important items in their diet are penguins, sharks, squid, dolphins and porpoises, seals and sea lions, and turtles. And their appetites are prodigious. A large killer whale can easily swallow a porpoise or seal whole. The stomach of one was found to contain the remains of 14 seals and 13 porpoises, while another revealed 30 seals.

### Team workers
Measuring up to 9.4 m (31 ft) long – and armed with 40 to 50 large conical teeth, each 5 cm (2 in) in diameter – killer whales, or orcas, are the largest member of the dolphin family. They can weigh between 7 and 10 tonnes. Widely distributed throughout the world's oceans, they are highly efficient cooperative hunters, living in packs, or 'pods', of a few to 50 individuals.

> ### DID YOU KNOW..?
>
> TAILOR ANTS, found in the tropics of Africa, use their own larvae as tools. The larvae spin sticky silk, so the ants pick them up in their jaws and use them to glue leaves together to form a protective shelter for their nest cavities. The larvae are then placed in the home they have helped to build, where they eventually hatch.

Scientists believe that the members of a pod are probably related to one another. They remain together for life. A pod may combine with other pods, but only if they are members of the same local 'community'. Each pod has its own 'dialect' of whistles, clicks and pulsed calls, which help the whales to communicate with one another and find prey by natural 'sonar'. A pod often swims in rows or a single line.

Killer whales can visually detect prey by 'spy hopping', resting vertically in the water with their heads in the air.

*Waiting game Sea lions watch warily as a pod of killer whales – one of the most intelligent of marine animals – tries to frighten them into the sea to certain death.*

*Fearsome predators Killer whales hunt in packs, known as 'pods', and attack a wide range of sea creatures, including the blue whale, which can be three times its own size.*

The methods they employ in the hunt itself are cunning and ruthless. A pod will methodically herd a shoal of salmon or other fish, cornering them into bays and posting sentries to cut off their escape. When they attack a great whale, they surround and harry it, and finally drown it by throwing themselves over the whale's blowhole to prevent it breathing. To devour such large prey, they tear off great strips of flesh with their sharp teeth by shaking their heads from side to side. A delicacy of which they are reported to be particularly fond is the blue whale's tongue.

Even when their prey is out of the water, killer whales have devised ingenious ways of getting at it. When they spot penguins or seals on surface ice, killer whales will dive deep below them, then swim upwards at great speed, smashing through ice as thick as 1 m (3 ft) and tipping their unwary prey into the water. If they spot a seal breeding ground on a beach, they sometimes move close inshore and cruise up and down in the shallow water, until the panic-stricken seals attempt to escape through the surf, where they can be snapped up by their resourceful tormentors.

# DEFENCE AND ATTACK

## *Hunter and hunted maintain an uneasy balance*

EVOLUTION can be seen as a kind of neverending arms race. Whenever times have been hard for a predatory animal, the individuals that survived to breed were invariably the strongest or the fastest, or those with the sharpest teeth, the keenest sense of smell or the greatest cunning. Natural selection made the species more efficient at hunting. Similarly, creatures preyed upon by carnivores have evolved an impressive variety of defences: greater strength or speed, keener eyesight or smell, protective camouflage or poison.

Between episodes of evolutionary change, there are periods of relative stability between the hunter and the hunted as the daily battle goes on: lions stalk zebra and antelope in the African savannah, sharks and dolphins catch flying fish in the open ocean, and bats hawk for moths in the moonlight.

Neither side can be said to win the battle; provided the environment remains the same and the balance is not disturbed by any foreign species, the population ratio between predator and prey will remain more or less the same. Temporary catastrophes, such as drought, may alter the balance for a time, but, when the rains return, the pattern of predation will be restored.

Take, for example, the case of the lion and the springbok, a species of antelope on which lions commonly prey. The contest is far from unequal. The lion is indeed a formidable hunter: lionesses, well camouflaged by their tawny coats, often cooperate in stalking their prey with immense patience, before one makes the final attack in a short, powerful run.

Yet the springboks have evolved a ready defence against the lions' stealth and strength. To escape from predators, springboks flee in a series of high, bouncing leaps on all four feet at once, a manoeuvre known as 'pronking'. As they leap into the air, their white rumps act as warning flags that, together with their short barks, alert other members of the herd to the danger and, at the same time, confuse their foes.

Hunting is not easy, even for the mighty lion. But for every few fruitless hunts, the lion will catch one of the weaker members of a springbok herd. In a stable ecosystem, no matter how efficient the hunter, its prey will have developed sufficient defences to maintain the status quo. The evolutionary arms race is inevitably a stalemate – unless, of course, man interferes with it.

---

### DID YOU KNOW..?

*IN THE WARM, shallow waters of the Indian and Pacific Ocean reefs lurks the stonefish. It is a grotesque-looking creature, about 30 cm (1 ft) long, with rough, wrinkled, warty skin, drably mottled in grey and brown – perfect camouflage for the coral nooks and crannies it inhabits. Should any predator manage to spot and attack a stonefish, it has a second line of defence: it erects its spiny dorsal fin and injects a lethal poison. Unlucky swimmers occasionally tread on a stonefish; at first the pain is extreme, then numbness sets in. If the wound is not treated quickly, it can result in death.*

---

## A PAIR OF DEADLY SPURS

WE USUALLY think of poison as a weapon used by cold-blooded creatures like snakes and scorpions, rather than by warm, furry mammals. Of the few mammals that do include it in their armoury, the strangest is undoubtedly the duck-billed platypus of Australia – it does not have a poisonous bite, but a poisonous kick to ward off predators pursuing it through the water.

Only adult males are equipped with this means of defence. The poison is produced by a gland in the thigh, and is released via a hollow, horny spur behind the ankle of each hind foot. One scratch from a spur can kill a dog and can cause a human excruciating pain.

With its mallard-like bill, mole-like body and beaver-like tail, everything about the platypus is so odd that zoologists were hardly surprised to discover it possessed yet another anatomical curiosity. When the first skin was sent to Europe at the end of the 18th century, the creature was thought to be a hoax stitched together by a mischievous practical joker.

Adult male echidnas (sometimes called spiny anteaters) of Australia and New Guinea also possess spurs on their rear ankles, but these lack a functional venom gland. Whatever predator these spurs were meant for probably no longer exists, and, in any case, echidnas are well-defended by their porcupine-like quills.

The platypus and the echidna are classed as monotremes, animals that both lay eggs and suckle their young.

### Nasty bite

The only other poisonous mammals are found among insectivores that bite into their prey. A number of species of shrew have toxic saliva to help them subdue their prey, as do their larger relatives, the rare solenodons found only on the Caribbean islands of Hispaniola and Cuba. Shrews' and solenodons' usual victims are insects and worms, but the American short-tailed shrew can kill quite sizable frogs which would otherwise be too large to overcome.

# SLOW AND STEADY

*Changing colour is only one of the chameleon's many tricks*

SMALL LIZARDS normally rely on speed and agility both for defence and attack. The chameleon, however, lies in wait on a branch, perfectly motionless except for its protruding, scale-covered eyeballs, each of which swivels independently searching for food. All the chameleon's speed and agility is in its coiled-up tongue, which it flicks out to capture insects on the sticky tip. In some of the smaller species – chameleons range from 17 to 60 cm (7 in to 2 ft) in length – the extended tongue is almost as long as the lizard's body.

The chameleon's well-known ability to change colour to match its surroundings is, in reality, rather less impressive than most people think, and many of the chameleon's colour changes are associated with the time of day and angry displays to rivals rather than its background. Some species are not equipped with red pigment, and others are unable to turn green. The nerve impulses that alter the concentration of pigments in the chameleon's skin cells appear to be triggered by changes in light, temperature and the creature's own hormones.

Nevertheless, a chameleon on a branch is often impossible to spot. Chameleons stalking their prey climb so slowly through the trees that often they seem to be barely moving at all. Their feet are curiously jointed so that three toes point one way and two the other, allowing them to encircle the twigs they walk on in a tight grasp. And for extra grip and balance, they use their tail as a fifth limb.

A chameleon's camouflage relies on another factor besides its coloration and lack of movement: it can also alter its shape, making its body appear as thin and flat as a large leaf.

### Scare tactics

In defence, far from relying on camouflage, chameleons employ tactics that make them extremely conspicuous. They can puff themselves up to enormous size and into monstrous shapes, and frighten predators by hissing like snakes and revealing the brightly-coloured interiors of their mouths. And when attacked by, for example, a tree snake advancing along the branch they are on, they have another handy defence mechanism: they simply let go of the branch and tumble to a lower one or to the ground.

# SECOND-HAND POISON

*Some sea slugs find their weaponry ready-made*

LIKE THEIR terrestrial namesakes, sea slugs have no shell, but there the similarity in appearance ends, for these carnivorous slugs are among the most conspicuous and beautiful creatures in the world's shallow ocean waters. Their soft, gently undulating bodies may be orange, pale yellow, bright red, deep purple, dark green or vivid blue – or a dramatic pattern of several bright colours, depending on the species. Just as startling as these brilliant colours are the bizarre growths, shaped like petals or branching stalks, that decorate the backs of some species. The growths are thought to serve as a kind of breathing apparatus.

*Chemical warfare The bright patches on this* Phyllidia *sea slug are glands that secrete poison. Other sea slugs arm themselves with stinging cells taken from creatures they eat.*

A sea slug can afford to advertise its presence because it is protected by stinging poisons. But instead of manufacturing stinging chemicals themselves, some species find them ready-made in the sea anemones and jellyfish that they eat. The stinging cells of their prey are not digested or expelled; these sea slugs transfer them intact through their digestive system to special sacs on the surface of their skin, where they act as a powerful deterrent to predators.

# NOT SO DUMB

## *Breaking the code of animals' systems of communication*

A MALE CRAB stands near the entrance to his burrow in the tidal mud on the shore of the Indian Ocean. One of his pair of brightly-coloured claws is much larger than the other, and he starts to wave it in the air; he is a fiddler crab and he is attempting to attract a mate. At first he waves quite gently, but when a female becomes interested and starts to approach him, the motion becomes increasingly frantic, the crab's whole body vibrating with excitement. The female joins him, and follows him to his burrow; his courtship has been successful.

All around us animals are engaged in a constant exchange of information through sounds, smells and visual signals. The amount and nature of the information varies from one kind of animal to another, but all need to communicate in some way. The prime concern of creatures that do not live in social groups is to find a mate of the same species. The death-watch beetle, a pest that burrows into the woodwork of houses, does this by tapping its head on the roof of its

*Attracting a mate The brilliant colours and patterns that appear on the skins of a pair of mating cuttlefish are a form of silent communication. Every colour change has a specific meaning.*

tunnel. The noise, said to recall the ominous ticking of a clock, gave the insect its sinister name.

Social animals, on the other hand, require a far greater range of signals. Living together in a group creates problems of status and dominance, quarrels have to be resolved and the group has to act in unison when hunting, travelling or confronting an enemy. The sounds and gestures made, for example, by troops of monkeys and packs of wolves have been studied in some detail. Four clearly distinguishable alarm signals have been identified in the 'language' of the African vervet monkey. These warn chiefly against leopards, large snakes, birds of prey and fellow primates, the signal for a man being the same as that for a baboon. Attempts are also being made to interpret the songs of whales and the whistles and clicks of dolphins.

### *Colourful language*

Another underwater signalling system has started to intrigue zoologists: the language of body colour used by the cephalopods – octopus, squid and cuttlefish. The rapid changes in the bright patterns of colour on cephalopod skins are not merely for camouflage – they seem to indicate a wide range of emotions including aggression, readiness to mate and alarm. Even a creature as apparently silent as a squid is very far from dumb.

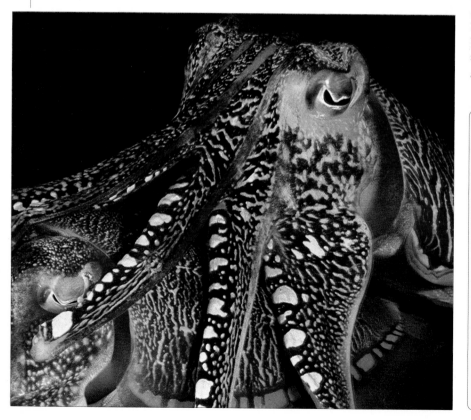

### DID YOU KNOW..?

*THE MARSH warbler, an accomplished mimic which migrates between Africa and Europe, picks up a truly international repertoire of songs from other species. Scientists have analysed the song of a single bird and identified phrases borrowed from over 200 different birds. Half of the phrases were picked up from species in Africa, the other half were from species in Europe.*

✳ ✳ ✳

*THE BUZZING noise made by female mosquitoes in flight serves as a signal to attract a mate. The males' antennae act as a kind of radio receiver tuned in to the high pitched whine of the females' wingbeats.*

# A NEW SONG FOR A NEW SEASON

*Humpback whales continually rearrange their underwater music*

THE SONGS of the humpback whale are beautiful, haunting sequences of chirps, moans and sighs. These sounds can be recorded by an underwater microphone, and an expert listening to an unlabelled recording of a humpback song can tell you the year in which it was sung and whether, for example, it belonged to a whale that used the central Pacific breeding grounds off Hawaii or the western Atlantic ones off Bermuda.

### Solitary singers

The whales do most of their singing during the winter breeding season, after they have migrated south from their summer and autumn feeding grounds in the Arctic. It is always the young males who set off first on the annual migrations to the tropical breeding areas, and the songs are performed by solitary animals, whom scientists assume to be males in search of a mate.

An important part of the songs' function is to maintain an appropriate distance between individuals, but when a mother with a young calf comes near a singer, he oftens stops singing and joins the pair as an 'escort'. Scientists who

---

## DID YOU KNOW..?

*THE VOLUME of humpback whale singing has been measured at over 100 decibels, comparable to the sound of a pneumatic drill, and the vibrations can be unbearable to people swimming nearby. At 188 decibels, the whistle of the blue whale is probably the loudest sound produced by any living animal.*

✳ ✳ ✳

*KILLER WHALES live in 'pods' of a few to 50 individuals. All members of a pod use the same calls. Unlike the songs of humpback whales, these do not change over time, but there are subtle differences between the calls of one pod and those of its nearest neighbour. By comparing the calls of two pods, scientists can tell how closely related the two groups of whales are.*

---

## THE SOPHISTICATED LANGUAGE OF CHICKENS

A FLOCK OF CHICKENS is scratching around peacefully in a farmyard. As the birds cluck away to themselves, a fox stealthily creeps up on them. Fortunately a rooster sees the interloper and calls loudly; all the chickens run for shelter. The commotion attracts the farmer and the fox quietly slinks away.

If a hawk then flies over the farmyard, a member of the flock again gives the alarm – but a different alarm from the one provoked by the fox. The alarm given for the hawk is a 'raaay!' noise, alerting the flock to danger in the air. It is quite different from the 'danger on the ground' alarm, which is a 'gogogogock!'. By having different alarms, the chickens can communicate not only the presence of a threat, but also give some idea of its direction of approach.

### Knowing your place

Chickens have an entirely different means of communication for maintaining the social structure of their flock. We use the phrase 'pecking-order' to describe a hierarchy in human society. The term comes originally from observations of the behaviour of chickens. In a flock there is a well-defined social order, which determines, among other things, which chickens get to eat first. There is a dominant bird that has first go at the food. Secondary birds are subordinate to the top bird, but dominate the rest, and so on down the flock.

### Ruffled feathers

The hierarchy is maintained by pecking; the top bird can peck at any of the others, and thus assert its dominance; the second tier birds can peck at any but the top bird, and so on. Similar systems of dominance are common in many species of animal in the wild, but some students of animal behaviour think that the pecking order in chickens is a result of the artificial conditions and confined space of the farmyard. Whether or not the system would function in the wild, it maintains social stability in small domestic flocks of a few dozen birds – at the price of a few ruffled feathers.

For a pecking order to work, the chickens have to recognise one another. Flocks on modern farms can contain tens of thousands of chickens, making recognition impossible, so, for their own protection, the birds have to be caged, singly or in small groups. Otherwise, all the chickens would peck at all the others, resulting in horrifying carnage.

---

have analysed the structure of the songs say that each consists of a very definite sequence of themes, and that each theme contains a number of 'phrases' made up of similar series of notes. Whales from the Atlantic include more themes in a song than those of the Pacific. A song may last for as long as 30 minutes and be repeated over and over for the best part of a day.

Most curious of all is the way in which the songs change over time. At the beginning of the breeding season, the songs are usually the same as at the end of the previous season. But over the next few months themes may be altered, abbreviated, added or dropped altogether. The pitch of a theme is often lowered, but the order of the themes is never re-arranged. There seem to be certain rules of composition that must not be broken. After about eight years, all the themes will have changed completely.

### Changing fashions

Within a breeding region (of which there are three in the northern Pacific, for example) all whales always sing the most up-to-date version of the song.

How the changes are communicated through the population remains a mystery. As it is thought that only males are responsible for the singing, one dominant male may be the trendsetter, and the others all copy him. But it appears more likely that the song is evolving as human language does, with spontaneous creative contributions from many members of the population.

### Distant voices

The study of humpback whale song was still in its infancy, when in 1979 it was discovered that whales off Hawaii and whales off Baja California – separated by 4800 km (3000 miles) of open ocean – were singing an identical song. How this is possible is still a mystery, although whales from the two breeding areas are found in the same Arctic feeding grounds before they migrate south in the winter. This would explain the basic similarity of their song, but changes in the new season's song can hardly be relayed from whale to whale halfway across the Pacific. The greatest distance over which the sound of a humpback whale singing has been measured is 32 km (20 miles).

# CHATTING WITH CHIMPS
## *The apes who talk with their hands*

NATURALISTS have long known that the apes, our nearest relatives in the animal kingdom, communicate with one another through gestures, sounds and facial expressions. But it was long believed that only human beings could use words and sentences. In the 1960s, however, determined researchers set themselves the task of teaching chimpanzees and other apes to talk in English.

### Poor speakers
At first the scientists tried to make the animals speak. But no chimp ever managed to acquire a vocabulary of more than four words, and these were spoken with great difficulty as their vocal tracts are not well adapted for producing the highly nuanced sounds of human speech.

The breakthrough came when Trixie and Allen Gardner, a husband-and-wife team of scientists at the University of Nevada, decided to try American Sign Language (ASL), a system of gestures used by the deaf. After four years of dedicated effort, they had taught their first chimpanzee, Washoe, to use 132 ASL signs correctly to communicate her wants and needs.

Washoe clearly 'understood' words – asked in sign language to fetch an

*Language of gesture The Gardners and their staff taught their chimps to use well over 100 signs, including verbs and names for objects and animals.*

*Clever chimp Using American Sign Language, one of the Gardners' researchers asks Washoe: 'What that?' The chimpanzee replies: 'lollipop'.*

apple, she would bring that fruit rather than, say, a banana. But her linguistic abilities went much further. She would not only produce simple combinations like 'give apple' or 'please, hurry' to get what she wanted from her keepers, but also talked to herself in sign language when she thought no one was watching: she was often observed making the sign for 'quiet' for her own benefit alone as she crept stealthily across the yard towards an area that she had been forbidden to enter. Washoe even learned to

swear, applying the word for 'dirty' to anything or anyone she disliked.

The Gardners went on to assemble a small community of baby chimps that were constantly in the presence of adults who used sign language among themselves as well as with the animals. The researchers reported that the chimps grew accustomed to talking to one another in sign language. They even started inventing their own words by combining signs they knew – for instance, 'water bird' for a swan.

### Word order
Apart from sign language, apes have been taught by other scientists to communicate using plastic tokens on a board, having learned that each token represented an object, action, colour or concept. Some researchers have noticed that the apes prefer to use symbols in a particular order, and see this as evidence of a primitive grammar. For example, they will request something to drink by signing 'more drink' rather than 'drink more'.

Yet other scientists still doubt whether the apes are using language in a truly human sense. They point out that the apes rarely put together more than two words in a sentence, and they spend most of their time exactly mimicking the series of signs made by their teachers. But the Gardners at least are in no doubt that their chimps really can talk with their hands.

| listen | ball | toothbrush | bird | eat | drink |

# SOMETHING TO SING ABOUT

### *The purpose and meaning of the songs and calls of birds*

SONG IS the language of birds. Whether it is the raucous trumpeting of a crane or the delicate melody of a warbler, birdsong is as vital to birds as language is to us.

The sounds birds make can be divided into songs and calls. A call is usually no more than one or two notes, with a precise purpose, such as recognition or alarm. By contrast, a song is a structured sequence of notes, and it is normally used by males to court females and to assert territorial boundaries.

Each species has its own distinct song; this helps individuals to recognise members of their own species. It is particularly useful in habitats such as woodland and forest, where the vegetation may prevent birds from seeing each other. In some species that inhabit particularly dense forest, the male and female sing together to proclaim their territory to other pairs. The duet of the Australian whipbird is so well coordinated that it sounds to human listeners like the song of a single bird.

#### *Keep out*

If, as scientists think, a male bird is merely proclaiming its presence to unmated females and to rival males that might invade its territory, it is difficult to understand why the songs of some species are so much more elaborate than those of others.

For birds that sing on exposed perches, such as song thrushes, the reason appears to be straightforward competition for females: the male with the finest voice is the first to win a mate. In

## THE PURRING CAT

ONE OF THE most familiar animal sounds in many people's lives is the purring of domestic cats, yet, strangely, nobody knows for sure how cats produce the sound. What is certain is that purring does not come from a cat's vocal cords. These are used for the less agreeable sounds in its repertoire – meows and wails.

When cats emit the characteristic soft buzzing sound of a contented purr, their throats can be felt to vibrate. Inside their throats, along with their vocal cords, cats possess a pair of structures known as vestibular folds, or false vocal cords. Some scientists think that these false vocal cords vibrate as the cat breathes in and out. Purring clearly uses up very little energy, and the cat can keep it up for minute after minute.

Another theory, however, is that the false vocal cords have nothing to do with purring, and that the experience of pleasure may increase turbulence in the cat's bloodstream. This turbulence, some scientists suggest, is greatest where the blood flows through an unusually large vein in the cat's chest. When the muscles around this vein contract, the vibrations produced by the resulting turbulence are amplified by the diaphragm before being passed up the windpipe and resonating in the cat's sinuses. For new-born kittens, which cannot hear well, the reassuring feel of the vibrations in their mother's body is probably a more important signal than the actual purring sound.

It is not only the family pet that purrs; many of the smaller wild cats, including the lynx, bobcat and ocelot, can also communicate pleasure in this way. The big cats, such as lions, tigers and jaguars, however, cannot.

other species that sing under cover of woodland foliage, there may be another advantage. It seems that the greater a male bird's repertoire, the larger the territory he can control. His range of songs may deceive rivals into thinking that his territory is defended by more than one bird. The most versatile singers of all are those species, like mockingbirds, that mimic the phrases of other birds – and other sounds, including pianos on occasion – incorporating them in short snatches in the complex structure of their songs.

A call is a shorter note that is used for rapid, urgent communication between members of a flock or between a pair that has mated. It gives the alarm when predators approach, for example, or keeps birds in contact with each other when they are flying or feeding.

Among small birds that feed together there are often alarm calls that can be understood by several different species. In Britain, birds such as sparrows, blackbirds, tits and finches have a simple common language of alarms: a reedy, high-pitched call will alert a flock of birds to danger overhead from a passing hawk or falcon, while a short, sharp 'chat' indicates the approach of a prowling cat or other ground-level hunter.

#### *Noisy neighbours*

In species that nest communally, birds need to recognise individual 'voices' above the hubbub of their noisy neighbours. When a gannet comes in to land at its nest, it gives a call that identifies it to its mate sitting on the nest. If it did not do so, the bird on the nest might treat it as an intruder and try to drive it off. Emperor penguins have an even more urgent need for recognition calls, because the adult birds carry the eggs around on their feet. Whenever one member of a pair returns from the sea, it has to summon its mate out from the midst of a shuffling mass of penguins.

*Meaningful variations The male great reed warbler warns off rivals with a short series of clicking notes. To attract females, he uses a longer, more melodious version of the song.*

# A VENTRILOQUIST IN THE GRASS

*Why it is so difficult to pounce on a chirping cricket*

ANYONE WHO has walked in the country on a summer's day or evening will have heard the seemingly endless chirping of grasshoppers and crickets. Grasshoppers call mainly during the day, crickets at dusk. Children attempting to capture a cricket are often thwarted by the insect's ingenious ability to 'throw its voice' like a ventriloquist. If it senses danger nearby, a cricket can alter the pitch of its calls, giving the impression that the sound is coming not from the insect itself, but from a spot some distance away.

Crickets' chirping comes entirely from males competing among themselves and advertising their presence to potential mates. In many species of grasshopper, however, the male's song is answered by the female.

There are two basic methods of producing these penetrating chirps. Both are forms of stridulation, rubbing parts of the body together to produce a sound. Short-horned grasshoppers rub a row of tiny pegs on the inside of their hind legs against veins on their front wings, like someone playing a washboard in a jazz band. The same rough and ready technique is used by their close relatives, the locusts.

### Volume control

Crickets have superior musical equipment, located on their two front wings, which they shuffle rapidly together.

Each wing has a vein bearing a row of teeth, which are rasped across a kind of scraper or plectrum on the edge of the other wing, producing a very pure, high-pitched pulse. Each 'chirp' is made up of a rapid succession of these pulses. A smoothly polished part of the wing membrane is used to amplify the sound. When the wings are raised during stridulation, the space between them and the body serves as a resonating chamber. It is by varying the size of this space that these insects are able to make their chirps appear to come from nearer or farther away.

*Musical vein On each of a cricket's wings, part of the front edge acts as a plectrum for plucking the row of tiny bristling teeth along a vein on the underside of the other wing.*

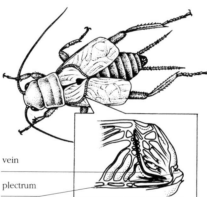

vein

plectrum

*Sound knees Crickets hear through membranes on their front legs, as seen on the bush cricket (below).*

hearing membrane

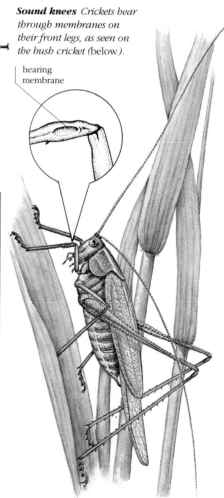

## A ONE-BIRD QUARTET

WHEN WE speak, the sound comes from vibrations of the vocal cords in the larynx. The sound produced is then modified by the tongue and the shape of the mouth. The human larynx, the voice box that we see as the Adam's apple, is situated at the point where the throat meets the windpipe.

In birds, the sound-producing chamber is lower down, where the windpipe branches into the two bronchi, the tubes that lead to the lungs. The chamber, called the syrinx after the pipes of the Greek god, Pan, contains thin, elastic membranes which vibrate as air passes over them. The tension in the membranes is altered by special muscles to regulate the nature and pitch of the sound. The structure of the syrinx varies enormously from one group of birds to another. The American turkey vulture and its relatives have no syrinx at all, and can only produce grunts and hisses.

The organ reaches its greatest complexity in the so-called 'songbirds', where it is controlled by as many as six pairs of tiny muscles. A remarkable feature of birdsong is that the two halves of the syrinx, each receiving air from one of the lungs, can act independently. This allows many species of songbird to produce two notes, and even two tunes, simultaneously. Recordings of the North American brown thrasher, a member of the mockingbird family, have revealed that the bird somehow manages to produce no less than four different sounds at the same time.

# BEYOND HUMAN PERCEPTION

*How things appear to animals with different sensory organs from our own*

O N A SUNNY DAY in the scrubland of the Californian Chapparal, a bee approaches what appears to us a plain yellow flower. As it lands it follows brightly marked runways on the petals. A short distance away, a hunting rattlesnake homes in on a gopher or other small rodent, to our eyes completely hidden among the vegetation. Evening falls. Under kitchen floorboards nearby, a nest of baby house mice have been left for a few minutes by their mother. They feel cold, and start calling for her – a cacophony of ultrasonic distress calls which we cannot hear, but which bring the mother scurrying back to the nest. In the next room, someone changes the TV channel. A goldfish, swimming peacefully around its bowl, sees a beam of red light shoot across from the remote control to the TV set. Outside, a moth stops dead in its flight and tumbles steeply to the ground, just avoiding being caught by a bat.

Human beings are simply not equipped to pick up any of the stimuli that provoked these responses. Many insects, for example, can see ultraviolet light. The runways followed by bees as they land on flowers are ultraviolet patterns that lead them to nectar. Rattlesnakes, on the other hand, can sense infrared radiation, or warmth. They belong to a group of snakes that are known as 'pit vipers' because they have additional sensory 'pits' situated between the eyes and the nostrils. The pits enable them to locate prey by the warmth it gives off. Goldfish, like many freshwater fish, can see light far into the red end of the spectrum. This is because they live in rivers and streams that turn a rusty red from the presence of fallen leaves. They cannot, however, detect the infrared radiation 'seen' by pit vipers.

### A world apart

The mouse and the moth – which takes evasive action from the echo-locating squeaks of the bat – hear ultrasonic sound, as do dogs responding to dog whistles. At the other end of the sound spectrum, below the range of human hearing, elephants hear and communicate with very low frequency sound – infrasound. The extremes of animals' sensory abilities reveal to them aspects of the world of which we remain completely unaware.

---

# SEEN THROUGH DIFFERENT EYES

*Animals' eyes range from a few cells to structures with thousands of lenses*

A JUMPING SPIDER pounces nimbly onto an insect. A dragonfly twists in the air to take a tiny fly. An eagle searches for prey from high on the wing. For all these animals, keen vision is essential to their particular way of life, and they have eyes of different designs – and abilities – to help them cope with their particular problems of navigation, recognising objects and finding food.

The most primitive form of 'eye' in the animal kingdom is found in some single-celled animals. Their minute light-sensitive eye spots can only tell them the direction from which light is coming. The simplest 'true eyes' – that is, eyes that form images – are found in various kinds of worm. These eyes are just pits, without lenses, but lined with light-sensitive pigment, giving a crude picture of the world, sufficient to detect the approach of a predator, but little more.

Insects have compound eyes, which consist of a large number of tiny hexagonal units. Each unit has a lens that focuses light onto light-sensitive cells behind it. This gives a much more sophisticated view of the world than the worm gets. Dragonflies, for example, have up to 30 000 lenses, and obtain an image that is probably rather like a grainy photograph.

Crabs, too, have compound eyes. They carry them on stalks, which can be drawn back into the shell if a dangerous predator approaches.

Spiders have as many as eight eyes capable of varying degrees of resolution. In their principal pair of eyes, jumping spiders have a single lens for each eye, which means that they perceive the world much as we do. Even so, the larger size of our eyes makes our vision six times clearer than theirs.

### Spotting a meal

Many birds, however, are much sharper-eyed than we are. Eagles and other birds of prey depend on their eyes, which slightly magnify the centre of the field of view, to spot prey from afar. Their ability to distinguish a distant object is reckoned to be two to three times as good as ours.

### DID YOU KNOW..?

*A FEW nocturnal birds employ echolocation to find their way in the dark, but their equipment is not nearly as sophisticated as that found in bats. For example, the cave-dwelling oilbird of South America emits echolocating clicks that are audible to human ears, unlike the high-frequency sounds used by bats. The relatively long wavelength of the oilbird's signals means that the sound is not reflected back by small objects. Oilbirds can use echolocation to negotiate the caves where they nest and roost, but to find fruit at night they rely on their sense of smell and eyesight.*

## WHY BIRDS NEED GOOD COLOUR VISION, BUT CATS CAN DO WITHOUT

THE FIELDS of eastern England can be silent and cold in winter, and food is thin on the ground for the birds. But the thrushes, redwings and fieldfares that patrol the hedges unerringly pick out the fallen hawthorn berries from among the tangle of vegetation at the bottom of the bank – to them the half-hidden fruits shine out like beacons.

Birds have the best-developed colour vision of all animals. Their eyes, like ours, contain light-sensitive pigments, each of which reacts to a slightly different range of colours. When the eye sees an object, the brain analyses the responses of each of the pigments and combines the information to interpret the colour of the object. But while we have three different pigments, birds have five, and can therefore distinguish subtle differences in hue to which we are blind. This ability helps

them recognise both suitable food and, in species such as birds of paradise, colourful plumage displays during courtship.

### Night stalkers

But some animals experience a much less colourful world. Colour-sensitive visual pigments function best in bright light, and nocturnal animals have little use for them. Cats, for example, can distinguish between colours to a limited extent, but they are night-time hunters, and their eyes are much more efficient at making the best of poor light than at seeing in colour. The important thing for a hunting cat is to detect the slightest movement that might indicate the presence of a mouse or vole.

Cats' eyes are large and are well-supplied with rods – light-sensitive cells that function efficiently in dim light – and

their pupils can open very wide to let in the maximum amount of available light.

These adaptations alone are not enough to guarantee good night vision, and cats' eyes have one more important feature to help them see in the dark. In the back of their eyes is a layer of reflective cells called the tapetum. Any light that is not absorbed by the rod cells on its way into the eye is reflected by the tapetum, giving the rods a chance to pick it up on its way out.

When a headlight's beam strikes a cat's eyes, not all the light is absorbed by the rods. It is the light reflected back out by the tapetum that gives cat's eyes their golden night-time glow.

But even a cat cannot hunt in utter darkness, and to back up its superb vision it has excellent senses of smell and hearing – and its highly sensitive whiskers.

# FOLLOWING A FALSE SCENT
## Man-made chemicals confuse insect pests

THE COMBS or antennae on the heads of male moths are designed to pick up the scent of a potential mate. In response to this chemical signal, males fly off to the source of the smell to compete for the favours of a female. Imagine how confused the male becomes when the air is so saturated with the scent that it appears to be coming from all directions.

For many insects, the only guarantees that males and females of the same species will meet and mate are the chemical attractants known as pheromones. Females need only produce and release a tiny quantity to arouse the interest of a distant male, despite the thousands of competing scents – such as those of other insects and

flowers – filling the atmosphere. But by synthesising insect pheromones in the laboratory, scientists have acquired a powerful means of interfering with the normal course of nature.

For example, a particularly destructive pest of cottonfields is the caterpillar known as the pink boll worm, the larva of a greyish-brown moth with fringed wings. Each spring, the adult moths emerge from their cocoons, and, guided by the females' pheromone, the males soon succeed in mating. The females then lay their eggs among the buds and bolls of the cotton plants. When the caterpillars emerge from the eggs, they eat into the bolls, seriously damaging the crop.

Instead of attacking the caterpillars with insecticide, some American farmers have adopted a new tactic: they prevent the larvae from being born in the first place. Just before the moths emerge from the cocoons where they have spent the winter, the farmers strew their fields with plastic fibres impregnated with artificial pheromone.

### Seeking in vain

As the pheromone steadily evaporates into the air, the males are bewildered by this unnatural abundance of sexual attractant, cannot find the females, and fail to mate. A generation of boll worms is lost, and a small battle has been won against this pest of the cottonfields.

### DID YOU KNOW..?

*THE SENSE of smell possessed by male emperor moths and some other members of the silk moth family is reckoned to be one of the most acute in the animal kingdom. Males have a pair of large, feathery antennae. These are not general-purpose organs of smell, like a human nose; they are sensitive only to the pheromone released by the female, and can detect this at a distance of 500 m (1600 ft). On each antenna there may be up to 40 000 sex-odour reception cells.*

# STILL KILLING AFTER 200 MILLION YEARS
## The tried and tested efficiency of the crocodile's senses

CROCODILES make full use of their senses in finding and catching prey. Scientists believe they have a good sense of smell out of the water, and their eyesight is excellent. With their eyes located on top of their heads, they can swim along nearly submerged and still see around them. Many species hunt at dusk or night, and the pupils of their eyes, like those of cats, appear in bright light as vertical slits, but can be widened at night to admit more light.

But crocodiles cannot adjust their eyes very well to underwater conditions, and when fully submerged they are long-sighted. While underwater, they are believed to use sound to detect their prey. They have the most sophisticated ears of any present-day reptile, with external flaps that can be closed to protect them in the water.

Crocodiles' senses have stood them in good stead – they have been hunting in much the same way for over 200 million years, and have changed little in that time. They have been fortunate in the environment in which they hunt – birds and animals must come to the water to drink, and the rivers have always been stocked with fish.

# STEREO EQUIPMENT

*The array of senses that make owls supreme night hunters*

**Hearing its way** *A tawny owl sweeps from a branch. The packed feathers around its eyes channel sounds into its ears, enabling the owl to orientate itself in relation to prey.*

THE CIRCLES of feathers around an owl's eyes do not, as you might expect, help it to see; they help it to hear. Known as facial discs, the circles have tightly packed feathers around their rims. The feathers channel high-frequency sounds, such as the squeak of a mouse, into the owl's ears, which lie behind the discs. They perform essentially the same function as the fleshy external ears of mammals such as rabbits and cats.

With their enormous eyes, owls are particularly well-equipped for hunting in dim light. But their remarkable vision cannot help them in the complete darkness they encounter under trees at night. They then have to rely on their extremely acute hearing.

Owls locate sounds much as we do; a sound from the right reaches the right ear fractionally before it reaches the left, and their brains analyse this tiny difference to give the direction of the sound. In the same way, some species of owl can sense the exact height a sound is coming from, as one of their ears is higher than the other. Owls turn their heads to balance a sound in both ears – this gives them the precise direction of a sound, and allows them to pinpoint their prey with complete accuracy in total darkness.

As if all this was not enough, owls have extremely soft plumage, allowing them to make their final gliding assault in almost complete silence. A mouse scuttling through the undergrowth has very little chance of escape.

## DID YOU KNOW..?

*LIKE MOST desert creatures, the North American kangaroo rat has extremely keen hearing. Its huge eardrums amplify sound so effectively that it can hear the air moving over a swooping owl's wings.*

# BUILT-IN HEADLIGHTS

*Fish that live in darkness produce their own light to attract prey*

ON THE BOTTOM of the ocean, at depths of around 3000 m (10 000 ft), the temperature is little above freezing and the pressure is enough to crush a human body instantly to pulp. And yet there is life, dominated by grotesque-looking fish with fierce fangs and huge jaws which hunt the smaller bottom-dwelling creatures in a world of perpetual darkness.

The best known of these monsters of the deep are the angler fish, so-called because they are equipped with a 'fishing rod' improvised from the modified front spine of its dorsal fin. At the tip of the spine, which dangles in front of the angler's gaping jaws, is the lure or 'esca' (from the Latin word for hook).

### Paying for light

As sunlight never penetrates below a depth of 1000 m (3300 ft), the lure would be invisible if it did not have its own lighting. This is provided by luminous bacteria that the fish houses and feeds in return for their light. The actual chemical enzyme that produces the light has been given the name 'luciferin' after Lucifer, the bringer of light. In the sunless depths, smaller fish are attracted by the shining lure, only to be snapped up in the angler's jaws.

Mysterious organs that glow in the dark have been discovered in many other parts of a fish's body. For instance, the shiny loose-jaw, found in the deep waters of the eastern Pacific, is equipped with two luminous organs. One is situated just below its eyes and produces red light – this may allow it to sneak up on fish and crustaceans that cannot see red light very well. The other is a luminous tip to the long barbel that protrudes from beneath its chin. This serves, like the luminous esca that the angler fish dangles in front of its mouth, to lure unsuspecting prey to its doom.

As its name suggests, the fish has massive, free-moving jaws that open to give it an incredible gape – many deep-sea predators are capable of expanding to swallow prey larger than themselves. Passing meals are such rare events in the depths of the ocean that they must not miss any opportunity to feed.

125

# A KEEN NOSE FOR BLOOD
*How short-sighted sharks home in on food*

A SPEAR fisherman swims over a coral reef beneath the clear waters of the Caribbean. Seeing a large butterfly fish, he aims, fires and spears it. As it struggles, and blood begins to cloud the water, he starts to pull the fish in towards him. Suddenly it is pulled from the spear by a reef shark that appears from nowhere, ripping and tearing at it, feeding in a frenzy of twisting and turning movements. Quickly the shark finishes the meal and is gone. Several other sharks have arrived, and they glide around threateningly as the blood disperses. Meanwhile, the frightened fisherman has retreated to the boat above, glad it was the fish and not him.

### Sensing movement

Not all sharks have such terrifying table manners as the reef shark, but all sharks have an extraordinary array of senses for detecting the whereabouts of food. Sharks that hunt in the open ocean have good vision, but species that feed on or near the sea floor, where the water is often turbid, have poor sight. In all sharks, however, the sense of hearing is acute; they can detect tiny low-frequency sounds, even the heartbeat of another fish. Closely connected with the shark's hearing is the so-called 'lateral line' organ, a series of receptors along either side of a fish's body, which responds to vibrations in the water made by the movements of other swimming creatures.

### Blood tests

Sharks' ability to hear underwater is certainly impressive, but, judging by the structure of their brains, their most highly-developed sense appears to be that of smell: the part of their brains that deals with that sense is twice the size of the rest. Tests have shown that they are able to detect one part of blood in a million parts of water. With the help of a favourable current or the motion of the waves, sharks can home in on prey that is injured or dying by following the smell of blood.

In nearly all kinds of fish that move in shoals, an injured individual gives off a chemical substance that warns others of its species to flee. Many kinds of shark can actually recognise these chemical alarm signals and use them to find prey. The defence mechanism is still effective, however, because, although the injured fish may perish, the other members of the shoal will have been alerted to danger.

One more remarkable ability sharks have is to detect tiny electrical currents and magnetic fields. This extra sense is provided by receptor cells found just under the skin of the shark's head. Awareness of magnetic fields not only helps sharks navigate, but is also used to locate prey, being accurate enough to detect the very weak fields created by the movements of a fish's muscles.

*Predatory senses A shark's ability to detect the tiny amounts of electricity around a moving fish, as well as its acute hearing and sense of smell, help it to close in for the kill.*

## DID YOU KNOW..?

*SPIDERS have fine hairs on their legs with which to sense air currents and vibrations. Other organs that respond to vibrations are located in tiny slits which, in some species, are distributed all over the body. Web-spinning spiders have most of theirs near the joints of the legs to alert them to the arrival of food.*

\* \* \*

*THE KIWI of New Zealand has an unusually acute sense of smell. Its nostrils are situated at the tip of its bill, which it uses to probe into holes in the ground and sniff out earthworms.*

# BORN AT A VERY EARLY AGE

*Not all marsupials have pouches, so what do they have in common?*

AMONG THE MAMMALS discovered by the first explorers of Australia and America were curious creatures the females of which possessed a pouch of loose skin on the abdomen where they sheltered and suckled their young. Zoologists in the 17th-century classified these animals as *Marsupialia*, from the Latin word for purse.

Of the 270 marsupial species in the world today, around two-thirds are found in Australasia; the rest live in Central and South America, apart from two species in North America. We now know that not all female marsupials have deep, bag-like, forward-opening pouches, like the kangaroo. Such pouches are found only in climbing and leaping species. In burrowing marsupials such as bandicoots and wombats, the abdominal pouch opens backwards, to avoid filling with soil. In mouse opossums, there are merely two narrow flaps of skin, and a few marsupials, such as the numbat (banded anteater), are completely pouchless.

## Not yet ready for the world

Rather than the possession of a pouch, what defines an animal as a marsupial is the immature, unformed state in which its young are born. In mammals like ourselves, babies develop for a relatively long period inside the womb. This extended development is made possible by the placenta, the womb's lining, through which the mother's blood passes nutrients to the foetus.

Marsupials have no placenta and babies spend a very short time in the womb – in the case of some opossums, only 12 days. At birth, marsupial babies are virtually embryos, with only rudimentary limbs, no fur, and closed eyes and ears. A kangaroo weighing 32 kg (70 lb) bears a baby only about 10 mm ($^1/_2$ in) long, while over a dozen newborn opossums would fit into a teaspoon.

## Forced feeding

But the newborn marsupial is not quite helpless. Its front legs are sufficiently developed for it to pull itself through its mother's fur from birth canal to teat. Once there, it fastens onto the teat tip, which expands to fill its mouth, preventing the young animal from falling off. At first, the baby is not even sufficiently developed to suck for itself – milk is expressed from the teat,

forcing it to feed. There the baby remains for many weeks or – in the case of larger species – months, until it has grown enough to begin a semi-independent existence. For young kangaroos, this means that they return to the pouch to sleep and suckle. On the other hand, when opossums have grown too large for the pouch, they ride in safety on their mother's back.

**Secure spot** *The 'joey' of a great grey kangaroo first leaves the pouch at the age of about ten months. For another six months, it occasionally returns to the pouch if frightened, or to sleep and suckle.*

127

# HANGING ON FOR A MEAL

## The honey mouse needs flowers every day of the year

IN THE HEATH and shrubland of southwestern Australia lives one of the smallest and oddest of all marsupials. Despite its name, the tiny shrew-like honey mouse does not raid bees' nests – it does not even eat honey. Like the bee, the honey mouse takes nectar and pollen direct from the flower. Its snout is an elongated tube for poking into blooms and sucking up the pollen grains and sticky nectar. On the end of its long tongue there is a 'brush' tip for scooping nectar and pollen from crevices at the petal bases.

The honey mouse is 150 mm (6 in) long, but more than half of this is tail, and it weighs less than 15 g (½ oz). This nimble forager moves securely between small twigs with the grasping thumb-like toes on its hind feet, holding onto larger branches by encircling them with its relatively long limbs. It often feeds hanging upside down, in order to poke its snout up into the head of a flower from below, supported only by its tail wound round a branch.

With no close relatives, the honey mouse is classified in a family of its own, *Tarsipedidae*. The origins of this maverick marsupial have long puzzled naturalists. Today honey mice live in specialised shrubland habitats where there is always some plant in bloom, providing a year-round food supply.

### Trail runs cold

Such habitats, now rare, were more common in the climatic conditions that prevailed 20 million years ago in Australia, which is possibly when the ancestors of the honey mice branched from some other marsupial line. Yet fossils of honey mice can be traced back only 35 000 years; before this there is no record of them or of any related species of marsupial.

Unless its unique habitat, limited to one small corner of Australia, can be protected from being taken over for agriculture, some scientists predict that the honey mouse will soon join the lengthening list of endangered animals.

---

## RETURNING TO THEIR ROOTS IN THE TREES

STUDY OF FOSSILS indicates that the kangaroo evolved from tree-dwellers resembling modern opossums. Over millions of years, the kangaroo's ancestors came down to the ground and evolved into the familiar fast-moving grazers of the open bush. The slender, grasping tail of their ancestors became the huge muscular balancing limb essential to the kangaroo's hopping form of locomotion. In a more recent and curious evolutionary reversal, one small group of kangaroos has climbed back up the trees, to resume life there.

### Walking on branches

There are seven species of tree-kangaroo, all of which live in the forests of New Guinea and northern Queensland. Lumholtz's tree-kangaroo, known affectionately to Australians as the boongary, is typical of the family. Its reddish-brown body is the size of a large dog, such as a labrador, but its most conspicuous feature is its long, bushy-tipped tail. It can hop on the ground, keeping its counterbalancing tail arched upwards, but in trees it 'walks', moving each foot independently – something no

ordinary hopping kangaroo can do. Its rear legs are shorter, and front legs longer, than those of its earthbound cousins. Also, its rear feet have rough, cushion-like soles to keep them from slipping, while the front ones have long nails to grip bark and branches.

### Night eater

The boongary sleeps during the day, nestled in a fork in the branches high among the tree-tops. At night it forages for leaves and fruit, descending to the ground to drink or to move to another tree. When startled, it scurries up the nearest tree-trunk like an enormous squirrel. If disturbed in the branches by a snake, it can jump from as high as 15 m (50 ft) to the ground, where it makes off swiftly through the undergrowth.

No species of tree-kangaroo has re-evolved the small, grasping tail of its distant opossum-like ancestors. Their tails are more slender than those of other kangaroos, but still extremely powerful. When sitting in branches, tree-kangaroos use these 'extra limbs' as props to help them balance; when they leap between trees, their tails act as 'rudders' for steering.

---

# AN ADAPTABLE FAMILY

## American marsupials are great survivors

THE SUCCESS story of the marsupial world is the Virginia opossum. During the past 50 years, this cat-sized opportunist has spread north as far as the Great Lakes region and New England. A second population introduced into California in the 1930s has advanced up the west coast to Canada. It is largely thanks to modern civilisation that the Virginia opossum has been able to extend its range; it is now often seen on the outskirts of cities, coming down from the trees at night to scavenge from refuse bins and tips.

### Not fussy

More than 70 species of opossum live in the New World. Most are sharp-eyed, furry climbers. They tend to lead a secretive nocturnal existence among the trees, especially in the Amazonian rain forest, where many different species exploit a variety of food sources. Some are carnivorous, some exclusively vegetarian, but most live on a mixed diet of fruit, seeds, insects and carrion.

Not all opossums live in trees. The yapok, or water opossum, found from Mexico to Argentina, has webbed rear feet and a powerful swimming kick. It dives for fish, frogs, shellfish and water insects. Under water, the female's backwards-opening pouch can be closed by a muscle that clamps together the waxy, hairy skin.

The monito del monte ('little monkey of the mountains') is a smallish opossum of southeast Chile, where it lives in cool mountain forests and bamboo thickets. It feeds mainly on bamboo leaves, but also catches worms and insects. The way it cares for its young places it in the group known as the 'parking opossums'. When the young become more developed, the mother monito, instead of carrying them on her back like the Virginia opossum, leaves them in a nursery nest of moss-lined bamboo leaves.

### Large families

Compared to larger marsupials, opossums are wasteful breeders. The average female Virginia opossum, for example, has 13 teats, but she may give birth to over 50 young. Many soon die, since they cannot latch onto a teat. On average, about seven offspring survive.

# FORM FOLLOWING FUNCTION

*Unrelated animal species leading similar lives can follow uncannily similar evolutionary paths*

**B**EFORE NORTH and South America were joined by a land bridge some 2 to 3 million years ago, the fauna of both continents included large sabre-toothed cats, very similar in appearance, but in no way related. In fact, the North American version, the smilodon, being a placental mammal, was more closely related to you and me than it was to its South American counterpart, the thylacosmilus, for the latter was a marsupial.

This prehistoric coincidence was a striking example of 'convergence', the way in which evolution by natural selection has worked on widely differing animal lineages in similar habitats to produce similar-looking creatures that lead similar lifestyles.

### Forest fliers

There are many examples of convergent evolution between the marsupials and the major mammal group, the placentals. Just as the forests of Asia or America have their flying squirrels, so the woods of eastern Australia have small marsupials that glide from tree to tree by means of outstretched flaps of skin – the sugar gliders. And whereas South and Central America have their anteaters, the termites of Australia are gobbled up on the long sticky tongue of the marsupial numbat.

Across Asia, Europe, Africa and the Americas, small carnivores, such as weasels and wildcats, feed on rats, mice and similar prey. The marsupial world has its small 'cats', too. The quoll, also known rather inaccurately as

**Design for digging** *Because the marsupial mole of Australia (above) and the unrelated European mole (right) both tunnel in search of food, the two creatures have evolved strikingly similar anatomies.*

the 'eastern native-cat', prowls the woodlands of southern and eastern Australia. With its dark brown-olive fur, spotted with white, this furtive nocturnal predator blends easily into the dappled moonlight and speckled leaves on the forest floor.

One of the most astounding convergences is between the moles of Africa and Eurasia, such as the familiar European mole, and the marsupial mole of deserts, shrub and saltbush country in southwestern Australia. Both creatures have almost functionless eyes, no ear lobes, slit nostrils, stocky bodies, and shovel-like nails on their front feet. The European mole is dark brown or black, to blend with the rich soils of its meadowland environment; the marsupial version has creamy-yellow or golden fur, displaying a silky sheen from the sand's continuous rubbing.

### Swimming underground

Because of the loose desert soils, the marsupial mole does not rely as much as its European counterpart on patrolling permanent burrows. Its technique is to 'swim' beneath the surface of the sand, chewing up worms, insects

and other small creatures as it travels, occasionally breaking to the surface to rest and breathe.

Convergence between animals that occupy the same ecological niche is not always possible. The constraints of an animal's original design limit the number of evolutionary pathways it can follow, and Australia has many creatures that look nothing like their placental counterparts elsewhere in the world. No marsupial, for example, ever evolved the hoofs characteristic of large, fast-running grazing animals, such as horses, antelope or deer. But large grazing marsupials have evolved an equally fast and efficient form of locomotion, using two feet rather than four – the kangaroo's hop.

---

### DID YOU KNOW..?

*WHEN RED KANGAROOS (and a few other marsupials) lose a baby, they do not need to mate again to start another pregnancy. Although the mother kangaroo carries only one baby at a time in her pouch, she can have a second fertilised egg, which does not develop beyond the stage of a few cells. A suckling 'joey' stimulates hormones that suppress any further growth of the second baby. But if the first dies, the hormonal messages stop, development proceeds normally and the 'spare' embryo takes the place of its brother or sister in the pouch. This can also happen when the first joey has grown up and left the pouch.*

# AGAINST ALL ODDS

*Man lends a hand – towards survival or extinction*

ONCE THE inhabitants of the eastern United States enjoyed the annual spectacle of migrating flocks of passenger pigeons so large that they took days to pass overhead. But in the late 19th century, the bird was the object of a campaign of ruthless slaughter – the nests were even shot out of trees so that the young birds could be fed to pigs. By 1914 the species was extinct.

Since 1600, man has been responsible for the extinction of at least 50 species of mammal and over 100 species of bird. Today the World Conservation Union considers about 4500 animals threatened species. The 507 mammals and 1029 birds on its list represent about one-ninth of all known bird and mammal species.

### Loss of homelands

In the past, the chief cause of extinction was hunting – for food, for skins and plumage, or for sport – but a greater threat now comes from the disappearance of the animals' habitat. Many species that survive will do so only in zoos or game reserves.

Some threatened species are, however, now being nursed back from the brink of extinction. In the 1960s, for example, the Seychelles brush warbler was one of the world's rarest birds. Only about 30 of these small brown birds were left, all of them on Cousin Island in the Indian Ocean. Then conservationists removed many of the coconut palms that, having been planted by settlers, had taken over the bird's natural scrubland habitat. By the late 1980s, there were over 400 birds. For good measure, conservationists successfully introduced the species to nearby Aride Island.

But only very rarely is it possible to devote such attention to the survival of a species. Other animals

*Price of a species* The black rhino is threatened by extinction because its horn is used in Oriental medicines. In South Korea, the horn sells for the equivalent of US $4400/kg ($2000/lb).

are threatened by far greater economic interests than the growing of coconuts, and conservationists have very limited means of fighting back. In Africa, the fate of the black rhino is dictated by the high price commanded by rhino horn, which is either made into dagger handles or used in Oriental medicines. The last 20 years have seen its numbers drop from around 65 000 to some 2000, and many local populations have been wiped out completely. In Namibia, game wardens have been forced to adopt a most desperate remedy, cutting the horns off local rhinos in the hope that this will save them from the poachers' guns – and extinction.

> ### DID YOU KNOW..?
>
> THE DEVIL'S HOLE pupfish – which is only about as long as the last joint of your little finger – has the most restricted habitat of any fish alive: just one narrow pool, about 20 m (65 ft) long, in the Nevada Desert. When pumping operations threatened to lower the water table and expose the rocky shelf where the fish feeds, the US Supreme Court stepped in to stop the pumping, saving the Devil's Hole and its unique inhabitants for posterity.

## CUDDLY AND TENACIOUS

THE KOALA has a slow breeding rate, producing a baby only once every two years. It is susceptible to disease and has a relatively small brain for an animal of its size. It is a fussy eater – usually eating only the leaves of certain species of eucalyptus – and consumes about 1.5 kg (3 lb) of leaves every day. And all the time its habitat is being reduced by the encroachments of man. Yet, despite all these apparent barriers to success, it manages to thrive.

When white settlers first arrived in Australia in 1788, they did not see many koalas, the animal having been widely hunted for food by the Aborigines. But the new Australians were not interested in eating it, and, left to itself around the settlements along the eastern coast, it became quite common.

What eventually aroused interest in the koala was its soft, silky fur. Early this century, hundreds of thousands of them were slaughtered each year for their skins. Two million pelts were shipped to Europe and America in 1924 alone, shortly before a policy of protection and reintroductions saved the day.

The koala's future seemed reasonably secure until the 1980s, when many populations became riddled with a dangerous sexually-transmitted disease, chlamydiosis. This infection causes kidney damage in the koala and can lead to infertility. So many koalas were infected that scientists started to predict the extinction of the species.

But these fears proved groundless; the majority of koalas succeeded in breeding despite their infection. Koalas, old and young, are able to tolerate their chlamydiosis. Australia's popular marsupial mascot had again escaped a threat that seemed to spell its doom.

# PADDLING IN CAUSTIC MUD
*Life in one of the most unwelcoming environments on Earth*

LAKE NATRON in northern Tanzania is no ordinary lake. As the African Sun beats down on it, water is evaporated far more quickly than any rain can replace it. The lake is replenished by springs as well as rain, but these add a strong solution of sodium carbonate (the basis of household washing soda). Natron is a soda lake, a hell-hole of hot, stinking, corrosive water and mud.

Despite the hostility of this landscape, half a million pairs of flamingos have been counted breeding on the mud flats of Lake Natron, which are transformed into an improbable lunar landscape by their nests – mounds of mud that bake hard in the Sun to look just like miniature volcanoes. From time to time a vast pink cloud of birds rises from the edge of the lake – an astonishing blaze of colour in such a barren terrain.

### Sole occupiers
In all, about three million flamingos – half the world's population – inhabit Natron and similar lakes along the length of East Africa's Rift Valley. Flamingos are highly specialised feeders, straining their food out of bitter, salty shallow waters. In other parts of the world, in the Caribbean or in the Camargue region of southern France for example, they share their environment with other water birds, but no other bird or mammal has evolved to cope with life on a soda lake as concentrated as Lake Natron.

Two flamingo species breed at Lake Natron, the greater and the lesser flamingo. The lessers feed on algae that flourish in the bitter water, and the greater flamingos eat tiny brine shrimps that harvest the algae. So efficient are the flamingos' bills, designed uniquely for use upside down, that they can trawl the shallows for food without drinking the water. The lesser flamingos' bills are equipped with fine hairs that act as a sieve, and the birds' tongues pump water in and out. The highly alkaline water is poisonous, even to flamingos, and in order to drink, they have to fly off to neighbouring freshwater springs.

The greatest flocks of all are to be seen at Lake Nakuru, 240 km (150 miles) north of Natron. Nakuru is a much more pleasant environment, with a far lower concentration of soda, and it is home to many other species of large bird, including pelicans and marabou storks. It is there that vast numbers of flamingos go through their elaborate courtship rituals. But in order to mate and nest, they head for the isolation of Natron, where the danger of a visit from their enemies – such as a scavenging jackal that might feed on the eggs, or a marabou stork that might kill a fledgling with its stabbing bill – is almost nil.

# PLAYING DUCKS AND DRAKES
*How the mallard is threatening to eclipse its drab relative*

SOMEWHERE in the Great Lakes region of North America, a colourful drake displays to a duck, nodding his head, grunting and whistling. Together they paddle away to feed. It is early winter, and the next spring the pair will raise a family.

There would be nothing unusual about this except for the startling fact that the drake is a mallard and the duck is another species altogether – an American black duck.

Mallard and black ducks are similar in size and shape. But the black duck drake lacks the shining green head, rusty back and white belly of the mallard drake. The difference in appearance between the females of the two species is far less marked, however. The female black duck looks like an unusually dark example of the drab mallard duck.

In recent years, mallard numbers have increased greatly in the eastern USA, the traditional haunt of the black duck. The species are closely related and are hybridising, so the numbers of true black ducks are decreasing. It may be that the female black duck responds more enthusiastically to the bright plumage of the drake mallard than to her own drake's drabber dress. Their hybrid offspring, unlike many hybrids, are not sterile, and merge well into the mallard population, having similar coloration.

### Back from whence it came
The black duck originally evolved into a separate species from the mallard in the isolation of its wet, woody breeding habitat. But now the expanding mallard hordes threaten to reabsorb the black duck, leaving only specimens and trophies as evidence that the species existed.

## DID YOU KNOW..?

*ONE OF the Earth's most extreme habitats is found in the ocean depths off the Galapagos Islands, where bacteria multiply in hot water vents from underwater volcanoes. So plentiful are these bacteria that they support an entire community of strange life forms. Among the creatures that feed on them are worms 3 m (10 ft) long.*

131

## ICEFISH WITH ANTI-FREEZE

THE ANTARCTIC blizzard rages and howls, blanketing the landscape in lifeless snow. Offshore, below the ice, in the dark of the bitterly cold water, a fish moves slowly across the seabed. The icefish is long and scaleless, with a snout like a duck's bill and strange white gills that give it its name.

Life in the freezing waters around Antarctica demands very unusual adaptations. Only about 120 species of fish manage to survive there, out of a world total of around 20 000 fish species. Of the 17 species of icefish known to man, most are between 450 and 600 mm (1½ and 2 ft) long, and are bottom-dwellers that prey on smaller fish and crustaceans.

The icefish is unique. It is the only vertebrate in the world that has no haemoglobin, the red oxygen-carrying pigment that gives our blood its colour. Although the amount of oxygen it can dissolve in its blood plasma is very small, the absorption of oxygen by its tissues is unusually efficient. And since the icefish has no red blood cells, its translucent, yellowish blood is thin, and is easily pumped round the body. Its heart is large, as are its blood vessels, so the icefish maintains good circulation, despite expending less energy than a red-blooded fish.

Scientists think that Antarctic fish, including the icefish, have another important weapon against the freezing waters – natural antifreeze. Chemicals called glycopeptides that circulate in their blood seem to prevent the formation of ice crystals in their body fluids.

# OVERCROWDING IN THE TUNDRA
### Do lemmings really commit mass suicide?

MORALISTS, keen to discover lessons for humanity in the behaviour of animals, have often perpetuated myths that give a very distorted picture of the natural world. For example, medieval bestiaries (books that treated animals and their behaviour as allegorical fables with a Christian message) described a mother pelican tearing the flesh and blood from her own breast to feed her young. This sacrifice was meant to illustrate Christ's own sacrifice for mankind. No pelican, of course, has ever made a heroic gesture of this kind.

### A lesson for man
Today, moralists sometimes seize upon the legend of lemmings rushing headlong over cliffs into the sea to draw a parallel with the problems of human overpopulation. According to this legend, lemmings deliberately give their lives to prevent their species becoming extinct through overpopulation.

It is true that roughly every four years, lemmings, like other small rodents that inhabit the Arctic tundra, suffer a dramatic population explosion. The consequences of these explosions are far-reaching, especially in the case of the Norway lemming, the species that gave rise to the legend.

### Search for food
The lemmings wear away the sparse tundra vegetation by overgrazing and by digging tunnels and burrows. So, each spring and autumn, they migrate singly or in small groups in search of better feeding.

Every three or four years they embark on much longer mass migrations. Just what triggers these spectacular population movements is not yet clear; it may simply be starvation, although some scientists think it is stress from the overcrowding of their environment.

The search for a new home often takes lemmings as far as the sea, but they do not hurl themselves in droves off cliffs. In fact, they can swim quite well and often cross fjords and lakes in the course of their journey.

However, although lemmings do not commit mass suicide, it is true that many do perish during the course of their migrations. Since they cannot swim for more than 15 to 25 minutes, many inevitably become exhausted and drown while attempting to cross large stretches of water.

## DID YOU KNOW..?

*NOBODY knows whether the thylacine – the striped, dog-like 'Tasmanian tiger' – is extinct or not. The last known specimen died in Hobart in 1936. Yet from time to time there are unconfirmed sightings of the animal, which may survive in more remote parts of the island.*

# SAVED IN THE NICK OF TIME
### The Arabian oryx, once extinct in the wild, has been given a second chance

AMONG the horned heads of deer and antelope with which hunters used so proudly to decorate their walls, pride of place in many collections went to a noble-looking animal with a black and white face and two long, slightly curving horns: the Arabian oryx. In antiquity, this creature was revered by the Arabs, who bound its horns together, creating the original unicorn.

For centuries the oryx had been a prized trophy for hunters living in the Arabian peninsula. A tough and elusive antelope, it was hard to track down on horseback in the desert, and to kill one with primitive firearms was considered a high test of manhood.

The oryx has remarkable stamina, migrating over vast tracts of desert in search of new feeding grounds, but it is not a fast runner. Against a new breed of hunter, armed with an automatic rifle and riding in a four-wheel-drive vehicle or even a light plane, it stood no chance. The animal was hunted to extinction in the wild, the last one being shot in October 1972.

Luckily, some far-sighted conservationists had prepared for this eventuality. They had started 'Operation Oryx' in the early 1960s, breeding a captive herd in the United States from animals brought in from the Arabian peninsula. By 1975, this herd was over 100 strong, while zoos and private collections in the Middle East had preserved a similar number of captive animals.

In 1980, five oryx were flown to Oman from the San Diego Zoo. To allow them to become acclimatised and establish their identity as a herd, they were kept in an enclosure for nearly two years, during which time five more animals were added to their number.

### Success story
This caution was rewarded, for, since their release, they have survived and bred. Jordan has a captive breeding herd, from which it is hoped animals can be released into the wild, and a programme of reintroduction also got under way in Saudi Arabia in 1989. Now, with the support of local people, the Arabian oryx is a wild animal again, its future safe in the hands of those who once hunted it.

# IN THE HEAT OF THE DAY
### Adaptations for keeping cool and finding water in the desert

IN THE SAHARA, nothing seems to move under the afternoon Sun – except the air itself, which shimmers endlessly in the distance. For a moment there is a flurry of activity, as a lizard darts from under a spiny bush to grab an unwary insect. Then all is still again, except for a string of slow-moving shapes drifting along the horizon – a caravan of camels driven by nomads.

In the daytime, deserts often appear almost totally lifeless, but this is because most desert animals actively avoid the heat, spending the day hidden in burrows and emerging only with the cool of dusk. A few animals are even capable of remaining underground without food or water for many months at a time, waiting for the rains to come. For example, the North American spadefoot toad digs itself an underground chamber, which it lines with a special mucus to prevent evaporation. Inside this chamber, the toad remains dormant throughout the summer. Long-term dormancy is practised only by amphibians, but small desert mammals like the kangaroo rats of the arid regions of North America and the jerboas of the Sahara are able to slow down their metabolism for a few days at a time.

Getting and keeping water is the greatest challenge, and desert animals have various ways of meeting it. Some seed-eaters, like the kangaroo rat and the gerbil, save the water they gain from their food by passing very little urine, while camels metabolise water from their reserves of fat. The 'ship of the desert' has another enviable advantage over its driver: it does not need to sweat to stay cool. The thick hair on its back keeps heat out and protects its skin from the Sun. Even so, the camel's body temperature rises by a few degrees in the blistering heat of the day. The excess heat is lost again at night.

Birds, of course, are able to fly in search of water, but when they nest in the desert they must somehow supply water to their young. Sandgrouse nest in extremely arid regions of North Africa, where they have evolved a unique method of providing their nestlings with drink. The male sandgrouse flies to an oasis, which may lie 80 km (50 miles) or more from the nest. After having a drink, he wades into the pool, where he rocks his body up and down to collect water on his belly feathers. The inner surface of these feathers is adapted to absorb water and minimise evaporation. When he returns to the nest, the chicks drink the cargo of water from his plumage.

*Keeping cool* Unlike the camel's back, its belly is covered with only very thin hair. This allows some body heat to escape into the shaded air beneath it.

## DID YOU KNOW..?

BEETLES in the dry Namib Desert of southern Africa obtain water from the moisture-laden winds that blow in from the Atlantic. On misty nights they stand, row upon row, on the tops of the sand dunes, facing the wind with their hind legs in the air and their heads to the ground. Any water that condenses on their backs trickles down to their heads, enabling them to drink.

✳ ✳ ✳

THE AUSTRALIAN native mouse gathers water by making a pile of small pebbles outside its burrow. The morning dew condenses on the pebbles, and the provident mouse finds its daily supply of water delivered to its doorstep like the morning milk.

133

# ANIMALS AND MAN

*Caring for pets can give people whose lives seem hopeless a will to live*

**A**NIMALS ABOUT the house help us relax and give us welcome company. In fact they do much more than that – keeping a pet has been shown to be beneficial to our health. For example, one American study in 1978 determined which social and psychological factors most influenced the survival of people who had been in hospital with coronary heart disease. Of all the variables studied – including sex, race, age, economic status and social isolation – pet ownership was the most significant factor in prolonging a patient's life. Of the patients who did not own a pet, some 28 per cent died within a year, compared to only 6 per cent of the pet-owners.

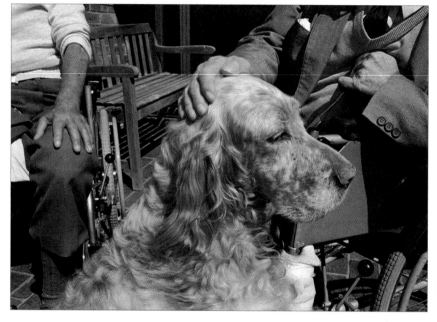

***Furry therapist** A spaniel enjoys a kind word and a pat from geriatric patients at a British hospital. Studies have shown that the companionship provided by pets can help prolong people's lives.*

Health care workers have long appreciated the role pets can play in providing company for the lonely, self-esteem for the insecure, and rewarding activity for those with time on their hands. In 18th-century England, an unusually forward-looking hospice for the mentally ill, the York Retreat, used to give its inmates small animals such as rabbits and chickens to look after. Having other creatures dependent on them gave the patients a sense of importance and responsibility.

### Welcome visitors

In more recent times, medical practitioners have started to make systematic use of pets as therapy – for the physically and mentally handicapped, especially children, for psychiatric patients and for the elderly. In 1983, a British charity, PRO Dogs, began to arrange for dogs to 'visit' hospital patients. Today, under the auspices of the Pets as Therapy Trust, more than 4500 dog-owners regularly bring their pets to hospitals, where some patients are encouraged to play with them and build up a

relationship as part of their therapy. The visits are especially beneficial to phobic and withdrawn patients, and to those undergoing cures for drug-addiction.

In several countries, including the United States and Britain, a well-established therapy for handicapped children is riding. When children with cerebral palsy, for example, are placed astride a pony, the world suddenly becomes a far more exciting place. For the first time they are on a level with other people, instead of looking up helplessly from a wheelchair. In time, learning to control a horse or pony frequently improves their ability to control their own bodies.

### Special friends

Mentally handicapped children benefit too. Communication and physical contact with an animal can make them more sociable and responsible in their own lives. Having another creature to love and care for gives even the loneliest people a powerful reason for living.

---

**DID YOU KNOW..?**

*WHEN CITY streets were narrow and badly drained, rainstorms had a dramatic effect. Water surged down the alleys carrying anything in its path – including stray dogs and the cats that haunted the gutters and rooftops. It is thought that the sight of their bedraggled corpses in the streets may have been the origin of the peculiar saying: 'it's been raining cats and dogs.'*

✳ ✳ ✳

*IN 1970, the editor of the British humour magazine* Punch *wrote a cheque to writer A. P. Herbert on the side of a cow. The bank was legally obliged to honour the cheque – in Britain, a cheque written on any object must be accepted by a bank, as long as it is made out correctly.*

## NOT QUITE AS FREE AS A BIRD

ALTHOUGH TURKEYS were imported from America in the 16th century, the festive roasting bird for most English people remained the goose. But at the tables of royalty and the nobility, geese were considered humble fare, and the dish that would be served at a grand banquet was roast swan.

Only the king and substantial landowners were allowed to keep swans, which were marked with nicks on their beaks to show who owned them. There were hardly any wild mute swans in the kingdom, since their wings were regularly pinioned. Even so, swans were not domesticated like farmyard poultry; they were free to swim wherever they liked, and matings between birds belonging to different flocks on the same river took place every year. The Royal Swan Master and his deputies travelled the country settling disputes over the ownership of each new crop of cygnets.

### Open space

In the 18th century, swan-keeping gradually declined, largely because swans are so much more trouble to manage than geese or turkeys – they require a lot of space, including a stretch of open water, and are difficult to handle and aggressive.

Today only the swans on the Thames are considered to be owned – either by the Queen or by the City of London livery companies of the Dyers or the Vintners. Every July, 'swan-upping' takes place: the cygnets are rounded up, their wings are pinioned and their beaks marked – two nicks for the Vintners and one for the Dyers. Royal birds are left unmarked. Everywhere else in Britain, away from the Thames, the mute swan is now wild.

# NATURAL EARLY WARNING SYSTEMS
## Animals might serve man as forecasters of earthquakes

'THE HORSES which were fastened in their stalls were greatly agitated, leapt up, and tried to break the halters with which they were attached to the mangers; those which were proceeding on the roads suddenly stopped, and snorted in a very strange way. The cats were frightened, and tried to conceal themselves, or their hair bristled up wildly.' Thus did a survivor of the great Naples earthquake of 1805 describe what had occurred minutes before the shocks were felt.

Animals are often credited with supernatural powers when they are really just using their senses. Horses may well be able to hear the low rumbles that foretell an earthquake, sounds we cannot hear. Cats may also be responding to these vibrations in the Earth, but it is equally possible that they sense changes in the Earth's magnetic field or the electrostatic charges produced by strains in the Earth in the build-up to a 'quake.

### Howls and brays

Accounts of animals' ability to sense an impending earthquake have been collected from every part of the world where earthquakes are common, from Italy to China to Peru. There are reports of dogs howling in chorus, donkeys braying, farm animals trying to break out of their pens, rats climbing onto telegraph lines and even of worms emerging en masse from the soil.

In China and Japan, pheasants have long been recognised as reliable indicators of seismic activity. This is consistent with other evidence that the birds are very sensitive to vibrations: in Britain, during the Second World War, it was noticed that pheasants frequently reacted to the sound of distant bombing – inaudible to human ears – with agitated alarm calls.

Many experts remain sceptical about these tales of abnormal behaviour minutes or even hours before a disaster. They point out that if we were to rely on animal behaviour to predict earthquakes, many of the supposed warning signals would turn out to be false alarms – animals have been known to become agitated for apparently no reason at all. Other scientists, especially in China, where earthquakes can cost so many lives, hope that a close study of animal behaviour will provide us with an infallible warning system.

### Crucial hours

On the whole, experiments have not been very successful, since many earthquakes do not have minor tremors before the major shock. The Chinese authorities were, however, able to give 5 1/2 hours' warning before the earthquake that struck Manchuria in 1975, minimising casualties by persuading people to evacuate their homes.

The best results in laboratory tests were obtained not with any of the animals normally cited in the stories that circulate after an earthquake, but with catfish, which appear to sense increases in static electricity. Japanese scientists, observing catfish in tanks over a period of seven months in 1978, reported that they behaved abnormally before 85 per cent of the earthquake tremors that were felt by human beings. This ties in curiously with the Japanese folk tradition that earthquakes are caused by the movements of a gigantic underground catfish.

## DID YOU KNOW..?

*WANTING to keep saboteurs out of Cam Ranh Bay during the Vietnam War, the US Navy posted unusual underwater guards – dolphins. The US Navy has also trained killer whales to recover lost torpedoes from the ocean bed. Intelligent and highly mobile, dolphins make good underwater auxiliaries; however, much detailed information on their training and intended roles remains top secret.*

\* \* \*

*KUBLAI KHAN, the 13th-century Mongol Emperor of China, kept 5000 mastiffs for dogfighting in arenas.*

\* \* \*

*IN 1519, Spanish explorer Hernán Cortés discovered a zoo in Mexico so large that it required 300 keepers.*

\* \* \*

*THE ANCIENT Egyptians worshipped cats as gods and kept them in great numbers. In 1888, 300 000 mummified cats were found in a necropolis in Egypt. One consignment of 19 tonnes was pulverised and sent to England for farmers to use as fertiliser.*

\* \* \*

*WHEN THE prickly pear was introduced to Australia, it spread so rapidly that huge areas of bush became impenetrable both for people and for grazing sheep. Luckily, nature had an answer to the problem in the shape of the cactus moth, Cactoblastis cactorum. When the moth was introduced from Argentina in 1925, its caterpillars ate their way through the prickly pear thickets and brought the alien under control.*

# WARTY INTERLOPERS

*Cane toads are guests who made themselves too much at home*

WHEN 100 marine toads were imported into Queensland, Australia in 1935, farmers were optimistic. They hoped that this large amphibian – twice the length of a common toad – would control the beetles whose larvae were ruining their sugar cane crops. When the toad had been introduced from Central and South America to the sugar plantations of Puerto Rico, its inexhaustible appetite for insects had kept pests down very successfully.

### Disappointment

From the imported toads, 62 000 baby toads were bred and released into the cane fields. Unfortunately, they did not perform quite as expected. With Queensland's abundant supply of insects of all kinds, they paid no special attention to the pests – and with no natural predators in their new home, they soon spread far from the cane fields.

The 'cane toads', as they became known, multiplied rapidly and are still going strong today, with populations building up to plague proportions over increasingly large areas. As yet they do not seem to have disrupted Australia's native ecology too drastically, co-existing happily with the local frogs.

On the other hand, predators that try to eat them are in for a nasty surprise. When tightly gripped, they squirt a blinding, poisonous spray from glands in their shoulders. Some reports say they have killed crocodiles, koalas, lizards and snakes. In spite of this, and

*Unlikely pets Marine toads did little to control the beetles once ravaging Australia's cane fields. But the 'cane toads' have made many friends, both young and old.*

the fact that people have died after eating its poisonous flesh, many Queenslanders treat the toads as lovable pets. Others consider them loathsome vermin and kill them on sight.

## LETHAL IMMIGRANTS

LIGHTHOUSE-KEEPER Lyall watched the small bird he had disturbed scurry off through the twilight to hide among the rocks. The bird never took to the air, but moved quickly and mouse-like among the stones.

This was not the first Stephens Island wren Lyall had seen since he had taken up his post there, in the Cook Strait between the North and South Islands of New Zealand. But it would be the last time he, or anyone else, would ever see one alive.

### Overzealous pet

Also watching the bird was Lyall's cat, Tibbles, which had already caught several of the little wrens and brought the bodies back to the lighthouse as trophies. Over the next few months, the cat would kill off the entire population of the tiny island, bringing home a total of 15 birds. The year was 1894, and within a few months the Stephens Island wren had been discovered – and then hunted to extinction by just one cat.

### Like sitting ducks

The arrival of domesticated animals on islands all too often heralds disaster for the native fauna. Local animals are not adapted to cope with alien predators like cats. This is especially true of birds isolated on tiny islands, such as the Stephens Island wren, which have – over the millennia – lost the power of flight. When cats arrive, the birds are easy picking.

The birds of New Zealand and its off-shore islands, where there were no native land mammals before the arrival of man, have been particularly prone to disasters of this kind. Ornithologists there recently received a chilling reminder of just how catastrophic the marauding of a domestic animal can be. It was especially galling as the bird that suffered was New Zealand's national emblem, the flightless kiwi.

In the Waitangi Forest of the North Island, 24 brown kiwis – out of a population of 800 to 1000 – had been fitted with radio transmitters so that they could be studied by conservationists. In the space of six weeks in the autumn of 1987, a single German shepherd dog killed 13 of the tagged birds. The researchers estimate that, before it was eventually shot, the dog had been responsible for the death of perhaps 500 birds.

# chapter five

# MIND
*and*
# BODY

IN 1628, William Harvey, an English physician, discovered the true nature of the body's circulatory system and identified the heart as a muscular pump (*page 156*). This ran counter to a belief that had held sway for some 2000 years: that the heart was home to the intellect. Only in the late 18th century did scientists begin to realise the importance of the brain. Today we know a great deal about the human body and how it works. But some of the amazing abilities of this most perfect of machines remain little understood, just as some of its bewildering frailties sadly remain impervious to modern medicine.

# THE MEDICAL FRONT LINE

## *When US troops gave their lives in the battle against yellow fever*

YELLOW FEVER used to be one of the most feared diseases of the Western hemisphere, vying with smallpox and the plague as the most deadly epidemic. Its most gruesome symptoms included black vomit and intense jaundice. When Major Walter Reed of the US Army Medical Corps arrived in Havana, Cuba, on June 25, 1900, to investigate the worst yellow fever epidemic there in 20 years, he had one vital lead to follow.

A local doctor, Carlos Finlay, had suggested at the time of the previous outbreak that the female of a particular mosquito, *Stegomyia fasciata,* was responsible for transmitting the disease. The cumbersome Latin name was often abbreviated to the familiar 'steg'. (The species in question has since been renamed *Aedes aegypti.*)

### *Send in the troops*

Following America's victory in the Spanish-American War of 1898, Cuba was under US military control. Yellow fever was a potential deterrent to American dreams of empire-building in the Caribbean. A blunt military offensive was needed to eradicate the disease, and Walter Reed supplied it.

Determined to prove that yellow fever could not be transmitted from an infected individual to a healthy person, Reed began one of the grimmest investigations in medical history. Medical colleagues and other army personnel volunteered to sleep in beds covered with the black vomit, urine and discharges of yellow fever victims. Some volunteers ran from their beds retching, but none caught yellow fever. The foulest leavings of fever victims clearly posed no risk to the healthy.

In a separate experiment, designed to test Finlay's theory, a house was divided in two. Stegs were allowed to enter one part of the building, but were excluded from the other by fine mesh screens. Only soldiers in the mosquito-filled half of the building went down with yellow fever, proving that stegs were indeed responsible for spreading the disease.

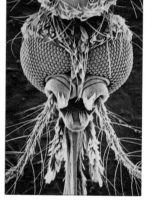

**Know the enemy** *Yellow fever is caused by a virus introduced into the blood by the bite of the female* Aedes aegypti *mosquito.*

The cost in human lives and suffering was high: two of Reed's co-workers developed yellow fever, and one died in agony. Several of the volunteers also died during the course of the experiments.

Havana's chief sanitary officer, William Gorgas, a fellow army doctor, used Reed's findings in an all-out campaign against the mosquito. Since mosquito larvae hatch in still water, he gave orders for all open barrels and tanks to be dumped, screened or covered in oil to prevent mosquito eggs being laid. All cases of yellow fever had to be reported. Houses were fumigated and sick rooms protected by wire screens to exclude mosquitoes that might pass on the fever. The results were dramatic. Within a year, Havana was free of the disease.

**Misguided panic** *Railway passengers, believing yellow fever to be contagious, flee from a victim during the Florida epidemic of 1888.*

### DID YOU KNOW..?

*THE NAME malaria comes from the Italian* mal aria, *meaning bad air. Until the turn of the 20th century, most people thought malaria was caused by bad air in the mist arising in marshes. We now know that, like yellow fever, the disease is spread by mosquitoes.*

# JUST A TINY SCRATCH

*How an aristocratic lady, an Eastern folk remedy and some humble
milkmaids helped to stop the spread of smallpox*

**A**S FAR BACK as 1000 BC, the Chinese knew about smallpox and had a way to combat the deadly disease: sticking smallpox-infected crusts up the noses of healthy individuals. What they were doing is now known as inoculation – transplanting infected matter from a sick patient to a healthy person to produce only a minor 'reaction' and then immunity. Other forms of inoculation had also been practised for centuries as folk remedies in Arabia, North Africa, Persia, India and Turkey. But the idea had failed to cross over into Europe. That it did at all is largely due to the publicising talents of a resilient aristocratic lady in the early 1700s.

Lady Mary Wortley Montagu witnessed the practice of inoculation in Turkey when her husband was Britain's ambassador there from 1716 to 1718. In 1717, she documented in detail how local Turkish women every year injected thousands of children with a needle. The children would then develop mild symptoms of smallpox, but would soon recover and would never come down with the disease itself. Her observations of 'grafting' (as she termed this method) were confirmed by several European doctors, including Charles Maitland, the embassy surgeon at Constantinople (Istanbul). He assisted in the inoculation of Lady Montagu's son later the same year – one of the first reported cases involving a European.

## Social acceptance

On her return to England, Lady Montagu herself suffered a severe attack of smallpox which marred her beauty just as she was setting up as a society hostess. This spurred her on to publicise the need for inoculation in England. In 1721, her daughter was inoculated by Maitland in London – the first known inoculation in Europe.

Thanks to Lady Montagu's court connections, it was not long before members of the British royal family heard of the successful demonstration of this means of preventing smallpox, and they had their own children inoculated. The medical profession were on the defensive – despite the stamp of royal approval – because this effective technique had not been discovered by one of their members, but had emerged from Eastern folk medicine by way of an English woman with no medical training whatsoever.

However, inoculation alone could not effectively eliminate all smallpox, chiefly because the transplanted infection often turned severe and even fatal, and an inoculated person could transmit the disease to others. It took the sharp observations of an English country doctor, Edward Jenner, to help secure total immunity against the disease.

Jenner had heard from his local farmer how dairymaids never contracted smallpox. They did, however, often catch cowpox – a relatively harmless infection – from the cows they handled. In 1796, Jenner extracted cowpox from the finger lesions of one dairymaid and inoculated James Phipps, an eight-year-old boy. The boy quickly developed a slight fever. Jenner then inoculated the boy with smallpox – but no disease developed.

## Gone for good

Through this experiment Jenner showed that an individual could be infected with a relatively nonvirulent virus, cowpox, and so become immune to smallpox. Jenner went on to advocate inoculation with cowpox – or vaccination as his method came to be called. In less than 200 years, widespread vaccination programmes enabled the World Health Organisation to declare officially the global eradication of smallpox.

---

## ROSS'S RUSTY MICROSCOPE

**T**HINK OF a medical pioneer and you will probably conjure up images of someone hunched over a microscope searching with single-minded determination for the great breakthrough, the cure for some deadly disease. Ronald Ross, who discovered the cause of malaria in 1898, might be considered the archetypal pioneer.

Ross was born in India in 1857 and learned his trade in the Indian Medical Service, with extra studies taken in English medical schools. He developed a close working relationship with Sir Patrick Manson, 'the father of tropical medicine', who encouraged Ross to explore the possible link between the mosquito and malaria.

Ross laboured for four years in a series of laboratories in various parts of India. Day after day, in what he described as a 'hand to hand fight with nature', Ross dissected every type of mosquito he could

*Patience rewarded For demonstrating the life cycle of the organism that causes malaria, Ronald Ross was knighted and, in 1902, awarded the Nobel prize.*

find. At one of the hospitals where he was stationed, he was forced to use a microscope that had a cracked lens and screws that had rusted from the sweat that continually dropped from his forehead. Ross could not turn on the overhead fan because the welcome air would blow away his dissected specimens.

Finally, dogged perseverance paid off: Ross hit on the right kind of mosquito. He found that the malarial parasite was present both in the intestines of the *Anopheles* mosquito, and, at a different stage of its development, in the insect's saliva gland. It was hoped that his discovery would lead to the eradication of malaria throughout the tropics, either by

eliminating the mosquito or by protecting people against it. In practice this proved harder to achieve. Nevertheless, Ross received many honours for his pioneering research, and an institute and hospital for tropical medicine was founded in England bearing his name.

## EXTRACTING A JOKE

**I**N THE EARLY 19th century, before general or local anaesthetics came into use, surgeons were said to need 'the heart of a lion and the hand of a lady' – the first to steel themselves against the cries of struggling patients, the second to work with speed and dexterity so as not to prolong the ordeal. A skilful surgeon could perform an amputation in less than three

***You won't feel a thing*** *This anaesthetic apparatus, based on the 1846 prototype of a Boston dentist, William Morton, used pieces of sponge saturated in ether.*

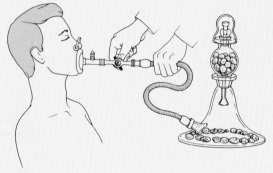

minutes. We now know that such virtuosity was, in fact, unnecessary. A perfectly good anaesthetic, nitrous oxide, was widely available and being used – but only to make people laugh.

Nitrous oxide was first prepared in 1772 by the English scientist Joseph Priestley, better known for his discovery of oxygen. As early as 1800, Humphrey Davy, inventor of the miners' safety lamp, suggested the gas might be used to relieve the pain of surgery. But its potential as an anaesthetic was ignored because of its more obvious property – that of inducing hilarious laughter when inhaled. 'Laughing gas' became a popular after-dinner entertainment and a feature of exhibitions given by travelling showmen.

There was hardly any serious research into Davy's suggestion until a young Boston dentist, Horace Wells, recognised the anaesthetic properties of nitrous oxide in 1844. At a public exhibition of the

effects of the gas, he noticed that one of its recipients had fallen and severely gashed a leg without showing any evidence of pain. After trying out nitrous oxide in his dental practice, Wells sought to gain wider attention by giving a demonstration of a tooth extraction under the influence of the gas at Harvard Medical School. But things did not go according to plan. The subject of the operation cried out in pain, the students hissed and booed, and Wells was denounced as a fraud.

In 1846, another Boston dentist, William Morton, performed a painless extraction at Harvard, using a liquid-based anaesthetic, ether, and the following year a British obstetrician, James Young Simpson, started to put patients under with chloroform vapour. It seemed that nitrous oxide would be consigned to oblivion, except as a chemical party trick. In 1853, Queen Victoria was given chloroform during the delivery of her eighth child. But, in time, ether and chloroform were both found to be too risky, and it is nitrous oxide that is the safest and most widely used anaesthetic inhalant today.

# A CHANCE REVELATION

*Roentgen's discovery of X-rays made him the first man to see through his wife*

**I**T WAS NOT so much as a physicist but rather as a keen amateur photographer that Wilhelm Conrad Roentgen uncovered the secret of the X-ray and its potential use as a tool in medical diagnosis in 1895.

As Professor of Physics at Würzburg University in Germany, Roentgen was working in his laboratory when he made his discovery – by accident. He was experimenting with an electric current flow through a gas-filled tube when he noticed a strange glow coming from a small screen, covered in a chemical called barium platino-cyanide, which he had left lying around. Putting his hand between the tube and screen he saw, to his surprise, the shadowy images of the bones of his hand in eerie outline. With his keen interest in photography, Roentgen hit upon the idea of substituting a photographic plate for the screen. Using his wife's left hand he took the first known X-ray picture: a clear, permanent image of the bone structure of her hand, obscured only at the place where she was wearing her gold ring.

At first he did not understand what the rays were – he simply called them

'X-rays'. We now know that X-rays are invisible rays of the same general kind as the rays of heat, light and radiowaves. Roentgen did not know this, but he appreciated their value for photography inside the living body and published a paper entitled 'On a new kind of ray' in the *Transactions of the Würzburg Physical-Medical Society*. X-rays were soon put to use in Vienna for medical diagnosis, gaining Roentgen worldwide fame for his chance discovery. The rays became known as 'Roentgen rays' and, in 1901, he received the very first Nobel prize for physics.

***Bare bones*** *Wilhelm Roentgen witnesses the power of X-rays in his darkened laboratory.*

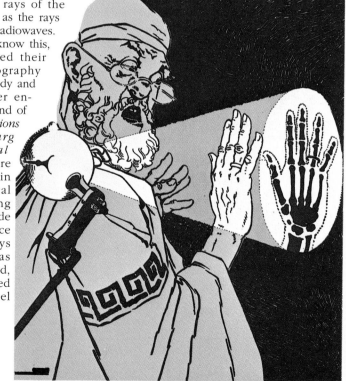

# HITTING DISEASE WITH MAGIC BULLETS

*The search for chemical agents that would kill bacteria, but spare human cells*

WE TAKE for granted the idea of a 'pill for every ill', but in 1875, when German chemist Paul Ehrlich began his medical experiments, the idea of a specific cure for an infectious disease was still considered preposterous. Many 19th-century doctors continued to be guided by the doctrines of ancient Greek and Roman physicians, who saw disease as a disharmony of natural forces in the body.

Over the centuries, a few independent thinkers had questioned this orthodoxy. One of the most remarkable was the 16th-century doctor and alchemist, Paracelsus, who was probably the first to think of diseases as real entities with their own distinct characteristics regardless of the person they attacked.

When Ehrlich began his experiments, nearly all the medicines prescribed by doctors were either useless or positively harmful. Ehrlich's dream was to find a 'magic bullet', the colourful phrase he coined himself to describe a drug that attacked a specific disease without harming the body's basic functioning.

As a boy, Ehrlich showed a keen interest in chemistry, and at the age of eight he devised a formula for cough drops, which was made up and sold by local pharmacists. At medical school he developed an interest in the new synthetic dyes being produced in a German chemical works. He started to explore ways in which these dyes could be used to stain living cells and so make it easier to study them under a microscope. In the course of his research for his doctoral thesis, Ehrlich discovered that a particular dye will attach itself only to certain types of

cell. He reasoned that there may also be chemicals which would kill off bacterial infection in the body while leaving surrounding healthy cells unaffected.

Ehrlich's early career coincided with the era in which many of the microorganisms responsible for disease were first discovered. His staining techniques were of enormous value in the identification of bacteria and protozoa under the microscope. He also made major contributions to the development of immunology, in particular the use of the blood of live horses to prepare anti-diphtheria serum.

### Arsenic arsenal

In the early years of this century, Ehrlich became convinced that certain arsenic derivatives would act as 'magic bullets' for specific diseases. With a team of chemists he began to produce hundreds of compounds containing arsenic. Each one was systematically tested on rabbits and mice infected with incurable diseases, such as sleeping sickness and syphilis. A lesser man

**Antibacterial warfare** *Visitors to Paul Ehrlich's laboratory were often surprised at the simple equipment used by the man who ushered in the age of modern drug therapy.*

would never have undertaken such a daunting task, but Ehrlich's formula for success was *Geduld, Geschick, Geld und Glück* (patience, ability, money and luck) – and he had considerable reserves of all four.

By 1907, Ehrlich's team had tested over 600 compounds. Only number 418 had proved of any value in combatting sleeping sickness. 'Magic bullet' 606 had, like all the others, been dismissed as useless, but it had not been tested against syphilis. Only when Japanese assistant Sahachiro Hata rechecked all the substances in 1909 was 606's effectiveness noticed. Ehrlich went on to test the compound, which he called Salvarsan, on humans with syphilitic lesions on their vocal cords. Within days, patients who had lost their voices could speak again. Ehrlich had found his 'magic bullet' and opened up the modern age of chemotherapy.

## DID YOU KNOW..?

*IN HIS WORK on toxins and antitoxins, Paul Ehrlich gave a precise definition of the 'minimum lethal dose', a concept still in use today. He defined it as the smallest quantity required to kill a guinea pig weighing 250 g (9 oz) within four days.*

141

# ETCHED IN THE MIND

## *People sometimes forget recent events, but remember the distant past*

**A**T DINNER one day in AD 48, the Roman Emperor Claudius became concerned about the absence of his wife, Messalina, and asked why she was not eating with him as usual. But Messalina was dead, executed for adultery on orders Claudius had issued only an hour before. He had already forgotten all about it. The emperor was a notorious drunk, and alcohol had destroyed his capacity to remember very recent events.

Although the extreme memory loss of this macabre story is very rare, many people suffer partial amnesia because of alcoholism, brain damage or disease, or merely as an embarrassing aspect of old age. But healthy people of all ages sometimes forget things from the recent past. Why, for example, do we often forget a telephone number we have looked up only minutes before?

### Creating continuity

It seems that we remember the past on two quite different levels. Claudius, after all, had not forgotten that he had a wife, that she was called Messalina, or that she usually dined with him. Only his short-term memory was affected by his fondness for wine, that part of the memory which, neurophysiologists say, gives minute-by-minute continuity to our lives.

Our short-term memory allows us to recall the last few minutes of a conversation, that the kettle is switched on – and the telephone number we have just looked up. In healthy individuals, events and experiences that affect us emotionally, as well as important facts and carefully acquired knowledge, are transferred to the long-term memory. Unfortunately we have only limited conscious control over which information the brain selects to be transferred.

The mechanism that shifts the contents of our short-term memory into a permanent store of facts, events and abilities is still somewhat of a mystery, as is our ability to unearth memories from the distant past. Most scientists

***Traffic stopper*** *In Budapest in 1938, a young woman suddenly stripped off her clothes and began to direct traffic, yet only a few hours later she had no memory of her shocking behaviour.*

agree that long-term memory is not a single entity. Mental abilities are retained in a very different way from facts. There are cases of people losing their memories who can still speak, even though they may have forgotten their own names.

Few cases of memory loss are as severe as this, but they can still be traumatic. After suffering a serious head injury, one woman could remember her childhood in Ireland vividly, but had no recall of her journey as a teenager to America, the man she had married there or the children she had borne. Our long-term memories are surprisingly tenacious, and the older they are the less likely they are to be lost through injury, illness or prolonged abuse of alcohol.

---

### DID YOU KNOW..?

*MOST OF THE things we are least likely to forget are predictable enough. They include our most pleasant experiences, matters that interest us and things we have a special motive for remembering. But we also remember particularly well the things we go over in our minds before going to sleep – a trick worth remembering.*

# THE ART OF FORGETTING

*Where were you when President Kennedy was shot?*

TEN YEARS AFTER the assassination of US President John F. Kennedy, the November 1973 edition of *Esquire* magazine reported that every one of the famous people they had asked could remember the exact details of how they first heard the news of the president's death on November 22, 1963. More rigorous academic studies later confirmed the finding: most people old enough to be aware of the assassination could recall precisely what they were doing and where they were when they heard the news.

We remember such startling and dramatic events better than any others. But why do we ever forget anything?

The things we most often forget are names (of things as well as people), numbers, dates, information learned by cramming, and things we do not understand. We also find it hard to remember anything when we are embarrassed, frustrated, ill or very tired. But forgetting happens to us all the time, and it is perfectly normal.

There is, it seems, a limit to what we can remember. If we could remember everything, all the time, life would become intolerable. As we get older, we shed more and more memories, leaving only the most significant in the mental space available.

# SECOND SIGHT

*Times you feel you have 'been here before'*

I WAS HAUNTED and perplexed ... by an idea that I had seen just this ... spectacle before. [The place] seemed as familiar as the decorous neatness of my grandmother's kitchen ... .'

So reported the novelist Nathaniel Hawthorne of a visit he made during the 1850s to the kitchens in the old castle at Stanton Harcourt, near Oxford, while he was serving as a US Consul in England.

Had Hawthorne been there before, perhaps in a former life? Had he experienced some psychic precognition of the old castle? Whatever the explanation, Hawthorne is by no means alone in having this uncanny experience. According to a 1967 survey, approximately one in three people has suffered from what is called déjà vu (French for 'already seen') – the eerie sensation of living through what seems to be a precise replay of a scene from the past.

### Past meets present

In *David Copperfield*, Charles Dickens described the experience as: 'a feeling which comes over us occasionally . . . of our having been surrounded, dim ages ago, by the same faces, objects, circumstances – of our knowing perfectly well what will be said next, as if we suddenly remembered it.'

What is the cause of déjà vu? The Greek philosopher Plato believed it was a sign of having lived previous lives – evidence for reincarnation. Modern science has not solved the mystery, but it does suggest various, rather more prosaic, explanations.

One theory holds that apparently forgotten memories are involved – and one such, in fact, caused Hawthorne's experience. As a young man he had read – and forgotten – a vivid description of the kitchen at Stanton Harcourt. But this does not explain the sensation Dickens describes, of knowing what will be said next during quite ordinary, even trivial, conversations.

Perhaps the best explanation for this phenomenon lies in the electrical activity of the brain. The feeling of déjà vu may be caused by a minute time lapse between our physical awareness of what is happening and our mental consciousness of the event.

It seems that the signals between our sensors – eyes, nose, ears, and so on – and the brain occasionally go out of phase. Our brains continually compare our experiences of the moment with similar experiences in our past, and, if the brain and the senses are out of phase, the present may appear to us like a memory of something that happened in the past.

*Déjà vu On his first visit to an English castle, the American author Nathaniel Hawthorne recognised it – possibly from a description he had read and forgotten.*

## FLASHING BEFORE YOUR EYES

THE AGE-OLD belief that a drowning man's whole life passes before him in a flash before he dies is perfectly true. Or so Canadian neurosurgeon Wilder Penfield, who pioneered research into the phenomenon in the 1950s, concluded. And it happens not only when a person drowns, but when he or she believes death is imminent, say those who have been saved at the last moment.

### Life in reverse

A curious feature of the experience is that in those final moments of consciousness one's life is replayed *backwards*; forgotten people, places and events crowd into the mind's eye with absolute clarity.

Penfield believed that this occurs because the brain normally stores all memories, but only a special trigger can recall them – death, or the belief that death is imminent, can be such a trigger.

Another theory is that the temporal lobes – where memories are stored – are especially vulnerable to interruptions in the supply of oxygen to the brain, and these in turn wreak havoc with the brain's electrical signalling system. People suffocating, drowning or being hung, for instance, remain conscious long enough to witness the bizarre effect of this oxygen starvation. This projects every available memory into the consciousness.

# REMEMBER, REMEMBER...

## Where do memories live in the brain?

SURGEONS usually perform brain operations with only local anaesthetic. (Local anaesthetic is enough to stop the initial incision hurting, and as the brain has no nerve endings, further cuts cause no pain.) It was because of this fact that Montreal surgeon Wilder Penfield discovered where memories are stored in the brain.

One day in the 1930s, Penfield was chatting to a patient undergoing brain surgery. He was probing her brain with an electrode, noting the areas where its mild current stimulated her to move or to speak, so that he could avoid these places when cutting away the diseased portion of her brain. Suddenly she began to describe looking into her yard, where she could see one of her children and hear all the usual neighbourhood noises. She recognised the scene as an event from her past. And as long as Penfield held the electrode in place, the patient continued to relive the scene.

### Chance find

Penfield realised that he had stumbled on a major discovery. Until that moment it had not occurred to anyone that memories might be physically locked into the brain. Since the 18th century, doctors and scientists had regarded memory as a purely mental function, and mind and brain as entirely separate entities. Now it

seemed that memory was in fact stored permanently in the brain cells. Penfield's electrode had released them from an area called the 'hippocampus', part of the temporal lobes that protrude on either side of the brain just below the temples.

Penfield tested his new discovery on further patients. One man was amazed to find himself back in South Africa, laughing and talking with his cousins there, just as he had in real life a month before. When Penfield switched off the current in the electrode, the memory stopped abruptly. When he restored the current, the memory began to unfold anew.

All the patients Penfield tested insisted that the experience felt like more than mere remembrance, or a waking dream. They felt they were actually reliving some event in their lives.

At first, Penfield's theory – that memories occupy a particular section of the brain – provoked scorn. But in the 1950s, surgeons removed both temporal

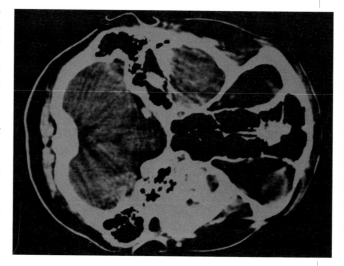

*Memory retrieval The temporal lobes, the bright wedge-shaped sections top and bottom in this brain scan, are vital in summoning up long-forgotten memories.*

lobes from a number of patients in the hope of relieving severe epilepsy. They succeeded, but only at the cost of also removing their patients' capacity to remember anything for more than a few minutes. This, together with evidence of the effects of strokes and head injuries on memory, convinced the medical world that Penfield was correct.

# SEARCHING THE MIND

## No amount of training or practice will give you a photographic memory

THE RUSSIAN neurologist A.R. Luria one day asked Solomon Veniaminoff – a newspaper reporter who first came to him as a patient in the 1920s – to repeat a long series of words that he had read to him previously. There was no sense in the words; they did not form a sentence, they were randomly ordered and their meanings had nothing in common. There was no logical reason why anyone should remember them at all.

The reporter paused, and remarked: 'Yes, yes . . . this was a series you gave me . . . when we were in your apartment . . .. You were sitting at the table and I in the rocking chair . . .. You were wearing a grey suit . . ..'

And, with that, Veniaminoff reeled off the long list of jumbled, nonsensical

words in precisely the same order as he had heard them on the previous occasion. It was an astonishing feat of memory – especially as the 'previous occasion' had occurred 16 years earlier.

A photographic memory like this is called 'eidetic' (from the Greek word meaning 'the same'). Only a few people are born with eidetic memories and one cannot be trained to have one. However, there are systems for increasing one's powers of recall that are modestly effective, but they all rely on devices – mnemonics – such as rhymes or simple sentences for lodging rather boring facts firmly in the mind.

The first letters of the words 'Richard of York Gained Battles In Vain', for instance, are a simple way to remember the first letters of the basic colours of

the spectrum – red, orange, yellow, green, blue, indigo and violet. Reciting the epitaph

*May his rest be long and placid*
*He added water to the acid*
*The other boy did what he oughter*
*He added acid to the water*

has helped chemistry students to remember how not to cause a horrible explosion when diluting acids.

We also remember things we turn over in our minds immediately before going to sleep. But perhaps the most disillusioning fact about learning is that, contrary to folklore, we do not absorb information while we sleep. If we did, every student who ever fell asleep during a lecture should have scored top marks afterwards.

# EYE EXPLORATIONS

*Gaining new insights into how we see*

SCIENTISTS may have glimpsed the nature of subatomic particles and witnessed the world of quasars and pulsars across the galaxies, but how we make visual sense of the world we see around us is still much of a mystery.

However, scientists are beginning to understand how the eye and brain work together to produce a seamless view of the world. Even when our eyes seem still, they are never at rest for more than a fraction of a second. But they move so fast – up to 100 times every second – that we are not aware of the movement. So how do we know about these movements, and what purpose do they serve?

### Unconscious movements

Scientists have recorded eye movements by fitting a mirrored contact lens to the eye. Parallel rays of light were reflected from the lens onto a moving film, registering the slightest movement. From this they discovered there are three separate types of

---

### DID YOU KNOW..?

*THE WORLD is literally turned upside down when the lens of the eye sends a picture onto the retina. At a very young age, we realise that we are seeing things upside down, and from then on the brain automatically turns the image the right way up.*

---

involuntary eye movement: irregular, high-frequency tremors; saccades, or flicks, that occur about once a second to correct the alignment of the eye when it has drifted too far from the object it is fixing on; and slow, irregular drifts that occur between these saccades. All these movements are entirely automatic and independent of the voluntary eye movements we make consciously when we read, drive or play a sport.

One experiment has shown that without these microsecond eye movements we could not see. Using special optical devices, scientists prevented the eye from moving at all, thus artificially stabilising the contours of an image on relatively few nerve cells in the retina. This caused the image to fade and disappear after a few seconds. They concluded that the involuntary movements of the eye are needed to allow light to fall on many different sets of cells in the retina. Otherwise, the eye cannot continue to generate a nerve signal for the brain to decipher as vision.

---

## LASERS VERSUS LENSES

EYE SURGEONS are looking at laser eye surgery as an alternative both to traditional eye surgery and to spectacles or contact lenses. Lasers have already been used to fuse detached retinas onto eyes, but surgeons are now experimenting with a technique that uses excimer lasers to change the shape of the cornea.

These lasers get their name from 'excited dimers' – volatile atoms in the gas mixture that is used to produce a laser beam of ultraviolet light. Excimers can be set to remove tissues in minute layers, and are so precise that they can carve a pattern into a strand of hair. The wavelength of the light beam determines where its energy will be absorbed and therefore which tissues it will affect.

Once the laser is set to penetrate the outer layer of the cornea it is incapable of entering the tissue behind it. The wound is very small and clean, so healing problems and scarring are unlikely.

But what is it like to be operated on by a laser? One procedure, still at the experimental stage, is surprisingly swift and painless, and the patient remains awake throughout. First, drugs are given to close the patient's pupil and anaesthetise the eye. Then the equipment is secured to the eye by vacuum suction, to prevent the eye from moving during the operation.

### Quick cure

In most cases, exposure to the laser lasts less than 12 seconds. The whole visit takes less than half an hour, and the patient does not need to stay in hospital. By the next day, all discomfort is gone and vision has returned to normal.

Although excimer laser surgery is still considered experimental in most countries, it is already available in Germany at a cost of about US $1700 for both eyes. Eventually the procedure could change life for millions of people. In fact, scientists predict that it could correct 90 per cent of all cases of myopia. Great news – except, perhaps, for opticians.

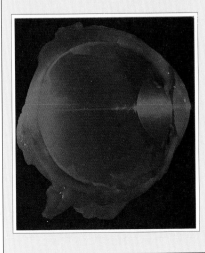

***Healing light*** *Lasers can help repair the retina. This image shows a beam crossing the centre of the eye from the lens (right) to the damaged area of the retina (far left).*

145

# THE VISUAL CLIFF

*Studying how babies perceive the world around them*

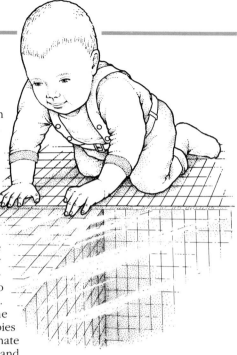

IT WAS a fine day, and Eleanor Gibson, a research scientist at Cornell University, USA, was picnicking with her baby beside the Grand Canyon. Watching the child crawling about, Mrs Gibson suddenly had a dreadful thought: what if the baby crawled too near the edge? Was a young child capable of gauging depths and recognising the danger of falling?

Eleanor Gibson's worries about her own child's safety gave her an idea. She would design an experiment to find out whether or not young babies can perceive depth. In order to do this, she would create a miniature, safe Grand Canyon in the university laboratory.

This famous experiment is known as the 'gingham cliff'. A narrow board was placed on a large sheet of strong glass which was about 300 mm (1 ft) above ground. To the right of the board, a sheet of gingham (a check-patterned fabric) was placed flush against the undersurface of the glass; this side thus appeared to be a solid surface like a table top.

But to the left of the board, the gingham was laid on the floor under the glass – thus creating the impression of

a cliff drop. A baby was placed on the board between the two sides. The question was: would the baby go over the 'visual cliff?

### Mother beckons

In the experiments, a mother encouraged her child to come to her over the gingham cliff. Out of 36 babies, ranging from 6 to 14 months old, all but three refused – most of the babies clearly perceived the left side as dangerous. However, all 36 were happy to crawl on the other side of the board.

Repeated experiments using the gingham cliff have shown that babies (and young animals) can discriminate depth as soon as they can crawl, and that they use this dependence on vision to perceive the danger of a steep drop and avoid it.

NOTE: *Eleanor Gibson was a scientist trying out her theory in the controlled conditions of a college laboratory – parents interested in the 'visual cliff' theory should not try to copy this experiment either at home or outdoors.*

**Depth perception** *Eleanor Gibson's 'visual cliff' experiments in the late 1950s showed that by the time babies can crawl they can discriminate depth.*

---

# A TREMENDOUS RECEPTION

*What our eyes have in common with a television set*

EVEN BEHIND a fixed gaze the eyes are in a frenzy of activity, as densely packed nerve cells respond to light in a neverending series of high-speed chemical reactions. The two main types of visual receptor cell are called rods and cones, and there are 125 million of them at the back of each eye, in the retina.

Rods are light-sensitive cells that help us to see in dusk and dark conditions. So sensitive are they that it has been estimated that, in total darkness, they would enable the eye to see a lighted candle 8 km (5 miles) away.

Cones are less sensitive than rods and help us to see in daylight or bright artificial light. They also filter colour.

Both types of cell contain light-sensitive substances called pigments. The pigments change rapidly when light hits them and this acts as a stimulus to send signals to the brain, where they are decoded and perceived as

pictures. Normally the rods and cones adapt automatically and instantaneously to changes in light and darkness. However, if the shift is dramatic, such as moving from, say, an indoor theatre to bright outdoor sunshine, there will be an adjustment that we may notice – the images we see may momentarily appear indistinct or bleached.

Exactly how cones contribute to colour vision is not fully understood. Rods have only one type of pigment and cannot discern colour, but cones have three pigments and each cone responds to a single primary colour – red, green or blue. The effect might be compared to what you see when examining a colour television image with a magnifying glass: the screen becomes a mass of tiny red, green and blue dots. Our cones too break down various hues into these three basic colours, and the brain interprets these sensations as the full palette of the world around us.

# A SECOND SIGHT

*What happens when the ability to see is regained after years of blindness?*

HE WAS in his fifties, active and independent, and every day in his work he used hand tools with skill and sensitivity, yet he had never seen them. For this man – known only by his case study initials of 'S.B.' – had been blind since he was nine months old. But all this changed dramatically at the end of the 1950s when the patient underwent two eye operations that successfully restored his sight after 51 years of blindness.

S.B.'s first blur of vision was the surgeon's face, but he did not recognise it as such. Even as his eyesight improved, facial expressions meant nothing to him and he failed to recognise people from their faces unless they spoke to him.

## DID YOU KNOW..?

*AN AFTER-IMAGE is a dark shape we see immediately after looking at something bright – a light bulb, say, or a camera flashlight. The intensity of the light 'bleaches' the photosensitive pigments in the retina momentarily and an after-image appears to hover in space. It will fade gradually, but can be restored by blinking or by looking at a different background.*

\* \* \*

*THE ABILITY to see details clearly develops during the first five years of a child's life. However, most of the significant development occurs during the first six to eight months. Studies suggest that girls develop more quickly than boys at first, but by the age of eight months the boys have caught up with them.*

## THE SHARP EDGE OF VISION

THE IDEA of correcting eye defects by surgery has been around since the turn of the century, and the first surgical correction for myopia (shortsightedness) was reported in a US medical journal in 1953.

In the 1970s, a Soviet eye surgeon, Svyatoslav Fyodorov, developed a 10-minute surgical procedure to correct the distortion of the cornea that causes shortsightedness. By making tiny radial incisions in the surface with a diamond blade, surgeons flatten the cornea, allowing the eye to focus properly.

Computers first collate precise measurements of the patient's cornea, such as its thickness, curvature and rigidity, which the surgeons use to judge the number and depth of incisions.

Over 25 000 patients in the Soviet Union alone had received the treatment by the late 1980s. The success rate is high – about 85 per cent do not need to wear glasses again – but some patients have reported difficulty with focusing on nearby objects or are bothered by glare.

Also, despite the computers' accuracy, there is some risk. It is still up to the surgeon's hand to make the incisions, and even for an experienced surgeon using a specially gauged diamond blade there is room for error.

S.B.'s story was reported by British neuropsychologist Richard Gregory in 1963. It illustrates the problems of people who have to learn how to use their eyes after years of blindness. One difficulty is that they cannot recognise anything that does not make a sound with which they are already familiar, or whose shape and texture they have not felt before. For example, S.B. recognised cars immediately, because he knew their engine noise, but did not recognise a crescent Moon when he first saw one.

Newly sighted people also have a distorted sense of scale when looking out from some distance above ground. S.B., looking down from his three-storey high window, was quite convinced that he could lower himself safely to the ground by his arms.

S.B. had coped enthusiastically with his blindness, relying on touch, taste, sound and smell for information about the outside world. Now he relied more and more on vision, and the world that he saw depressed him greatly. Everything appeared drab to him. As Gregory summed up the case: 'We felt that he had lost more than he had gained by recovery of sight.' Tragically, S.B. died a dispirited man less than two years after regaining his sight.

**Disappearing trick** *We all have a 'blind spot' in each eye. At the point on the retina where the optic nerve connects the eye and brain, there are no rods and cones, so light cannot be registered.*

To find your blind spot, hold this book at eye level as far in front of you as possible, and cover one eye.

Stare at the star at the bottom of this page, and slowly move the book towards you. At one point, the circle to the right of the star will disappear.

# SENSE AND SENSIBILITY

## *There are more sounds in the world than the human ear can ever hear*

OUR EARS are impressively sensitive pieces of apparatus. To make itself heard, a sound need only be strong enough to deflect our eardrum by 0.00000001 mm (40 thousand-millionths in). Our ears can pick up a rich variety of sounds from the breathing of a baby to the deafening boom of a supersonic jet. But compared with some of our fellow animals, even those of us with perfect hearing are effectively half deaf.

Sound is a vibration of the air and travels as a series of waves. The 'frequency' of the waves – the number of waves per second – determines whether the sound is high-pitched like a scream or low as a bass drum.

The human ear by no means picks up all the sound vibrations in the outside world. It can register waves of between 20 and 20 000 vibrations a second (v/s) – the highest C on a piano is 4096 v/s, so 20 000 is just a shrill hiss. But dogs can hear ultrasonic whistles of 35 000 v/s, which are totally inaudible to human beings. Bats are even sharper of hearing: they respond to frequencies of up to 75 000 v/s.

Yet no land animal can match the remarkable bottle-nosed dolphin. As dolphins communicate in their complex language of clicks and whistles, they can discriminate sounds from 20 up to a startling 150 000 v/s – nearly eight times the human limit. It is no use, however, wishing that dolphins could 'lend us their ears'. Extraordinarily, they hear through their jaws and throat, which pick up the high-frequency vibrations. Their ears are virtually atrophied.

# COMPLETELY OUT OF TOUCH

## *Deprived of our senses we begin to lose our minds*

FLOTATION THERAPY is one of the recent, New Age health crazes. People are shut in a dark sound-proof box where they float in a tank of salt water, relaxing from the stress of everyday life. With most input from their senses removed, floaters experience deep tranquillity and inner peace.

But in flotation therapy the senses are never entirely shut off – indeed, people often listen to music or watch videos inside their tanks. Total sensory deprivation has quite different effects, as psychologists at McGill University, Montreal, proved in the 1950s.

### *Dumb to the world*

Student volunteers were placed in padded clothing and lowered into completely soundproofed chambers of water maintained at body temperature. Their eyes were covered with goggles and their ears were plugged. They could not even hear their own breathing, and any feeling of body movement was masked by the bulky clothing and the buoyant mass of water. The students were told they could stay suspended for as long as they wished. Only a panic button linked them to the psychologists monitoring them in the outside world.

It turned out that being completely out of touch was anything but a recipe for relaxation. Most students pressed the panic button after a few hours and could not be induced to return to

**Block-out** *In one experiment, scientists monitored a subject wearing cardboard cuffs and a blindfold to reduce sensation.*

the isolation tanks for any amount of money. Lying in the tank they had been overwhelmed by vivid and bizarre hallucinations. One student held out for a whole day, but was temporarily a nervous wreck on his return to the normal world.

Why human beings should react with distress to sensory deprivation is not certain. Possibly the brain believes the body has gone to sleep and starts to dream. As the body is in fact wide awake, these dreams appear as hallucinations.

We may sometimes crave peace and quiet, but as social animals we only truly function in a stimulating environment. Total sensory deprivation makes sane people live the experience of a mad, mad world.

---

### DID YOU KNOW..?

*TOUCH RECEPTORS are not spread evenly over the body but are concentrated in those areas that need them most. There is a receptor on our fingertips every 2.5 mm (1/10 in), but the receptors on our backs are a massive 63 mm (2 1/2 in) apart. The tongue is especially sensitive: its receptors are 100 times denser than those in the back. This explains why even a tiny wound in the tongue can feel as though a massive chasm has just opened.*

# SMELLS WONDERFUL

## The nose is our most sensitive organ

OUR SENSE of smell is remarkably potent. Freshly mown grass, pine needles, Camembert cheese, burning rubber – even the memory of such smells can evoke powerful responses.

High inside our noses sit two patches of cells that act as smell receptors. The two patches comprise millions of cells, each with minute hair-like projections waving in a sea of mucus, like a mat of wafting reeds in a riverbed. These hairy cells, called cilia, are incredibly sensitive. A single molecule of some substances is enough to excite them into sending a message to the brain.

There are at least 14 different kinds of smell receptor cell, each of which is excited by a different type of smell molecule. This allows our brains to work out not only that something smelly has gone up our noses, but exactly what it is. Most familiar smells – freshly made coffee, cigarette smoke, and delicate perfumes – are complex mixtures of odours.

### Sum better than its parts

Some perfumes that we find highly desirable are made up of substances that on their own smell quite offensive. Civet, for example, which comes from the anal glands of a wild cat, has a vile smell in itself, yet it is a vital element in most expensive perfumes.

Humans are able to distinguish between more than 10 000 complex odours. Surprisingly, we do not seem to put this ability to any very significant use. Some scientists now believe that smells play an important hidden role in the relations between people, creating unconscious bonds. Experiments have shown that babies can already distinguish between their mothers and strangers at the age of six days using their sense of smell.

### DID YOU KNOW..?

*A HUMAN BEING can tell within three degrees the direction from which a sound is coming. Owls, which have one ear located slightly forward of the other, can locate sounds even more accurately – to within one degree.*

# WINDOWS OF THE SOUL

## We have more ways of sensing the world than we think

OUR SENSES were once known as the 'windows of the soul' and are universally prized as one of our most precious possessions. Few misfortunes excite our compassion more readily than the loss of sight or hearing.

But how many senses actually are there? The Greek philosopher Aristotle counted five – sight, hearing, smell, taste and touch – and this has remained the popular wisdom ever since. Scientists exploring the workings of the human nervous system, however, have uncovered a whole range of extra senses to add to this traditional list.

### Pain and pressure

All the senses depend on 'sense receptors', nerve endings that send back electrochemical messages to the brain. Every sense receptor is specialised to respond to a particular stimulus from the outside world – receptors in the eye respond to light, those in the nose respond to smells.

Spread throughout the body, in the skin, the joints and even the digestive system, receptors have been identified that react to a whole range of specific stimuli. There are some receptors that respond to heat and others that react to cold, receptors that register pain, and receptors that respond to pressure. Each of these can properly be called a different 'sense'. Some scientists also believe there are separate senses of hunger and thirst.

We talk of having a sense of balance – and this is quite correct. This sense is located in the ears; indeed, balance may be the ears' most important function. Deep inside the ear is a system of tiny chambers and canals containing fluid and lined with fine sensory hairs. When the head moves, these hairs are stimulated, firing messages to the brain telling it which position you are in and which way up you are. It is this mechanism that establishes your sense of balance.

There may be even more senses beyond the current range of science. Parapsychologists often talk of extrasensory perception (ESP) as a sense. There are people who claim to be clairvoyant, meaning that they can, for example, identify objects in a sealed envelope by 'seeing them'. Others say that they have the gift of precognition, the ability to 'see' events in the future. Despite much speculation and scientific research, no one has yet discovered any receptors in the human body that might correspond to these extrasensory senses.

One thing is certain. Even if the parapsychologists are right, we can no longer call any of these uncanny forms of perception a 'sixth sense' as we have in the past – by modern reckoning it will be more like the 14th or 15th.

*Famous five A French caricaturist, Louis-Léopold Boilly, depicted the five senses in 1823.*

# THE CHAIN OF COMMAND

*Our bodies' quick-thinking communication cord*

THE LINK BETWEEN the brain and the body is the spinal cord – a band of nervous tissue as thick as a little finger that runs through our hollow backbone for some 45 cm (18 in). Nerve cells called motor neurones convey electric impulses that travel from the brain to the spinal cord, leaving at the appropriate level and passing to the various parts of the body. Similarly, sensory neurones transmit messages from organs and tissues via the spinal cord to the brain.

But the spinal cord also functions without the intervention of the brain. It alone controls those actions, called spinal reflexes, that need to be taken very quickly in response to danger.

### Quicker than thought

When we touch a hot plate, for instance, the danger signal from the sensory neurones conveys the danger to the spinal cord, which sends a message back, via a motor neurone, telling the muscles to drop the plate immediately. This all happens so quickly that we may drop the plate before the brain has had time to receive the original message reporting the plate's heat.

It is this type of protective function that a doctor tests for when he taps a patient on the knee and watches his lower leg shoot up. Such a reflex is the spinal cord's way of ensuring that none of the tendons in our bodies become overstretched. By striking a knee, the doctor overstretches the patellar tendon. The leg muscles contract so as to take the strain off the tendon again.

The spinal cord also helps to manage routine reactions that may be considered too insignificant for the

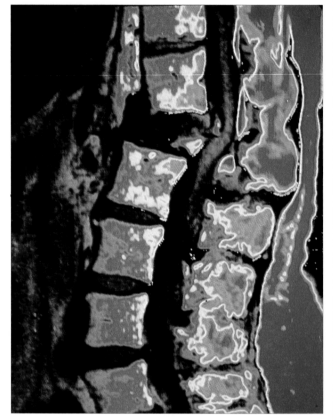

***Broken link*** *The backbone's 33 vertebrae (some of which appear on this X-ray as squares) protect a band of nervous tissue, the spinal cord, which controls the nervous system. A broken vertebra (seen below the second square from the top) will damage the spinal cord.*

conscious brain to deal with, making sure our bladder empties, our eyes blink, and our muscles hold our skeletons together. Thanks to the intervention of the spinal cord, the conscious brain is left free to occupy itself with more complicated tasks.

***Inner core*** *This section through the spinal cord – magnified 20 times – shows the outer white matter, consisting of a mass of nerve fibres, and an inner zone, consisting of nerve cells (shown in yellow).*

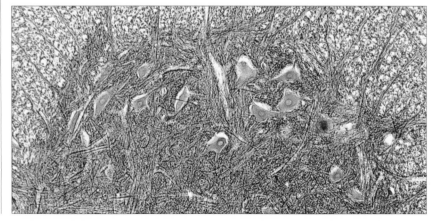

---

### DID YOU KNOW..?

*DOGS HAVE a finely honed 'scratch reflex' that helps them get rid of unwanted bugs. If you tickle a dog just behind its shoulders, it will immediately distribute its weight on three legs and start scratching until you stop tickling. Scientists have found that all breeds of dog, from the tiny Mexican hairless to the Great Dane, scratch at exactly the same rate – around five scratches a second.*

## WHEN A SURGEON'S MIND WENT INTO 'ERASE' INSTEAD OF 'RECORD'

IN 1986, a surgeon from Chicago with 20 years' experience was stitching up a patient after a routine gall bladder operation when he suddenly stopped and asked with curious detachment: 'Did I take out that gall bladder?' The assisting nurse calmly assured him that he had, and that he must put in another stitch. This he did, but after each new stitch he repeated the question. The quick-thinking nurse reassured him each time until the surgeon had completed the stitching.

Afterwards, the surgeon went to see a neurologist who diagnosed a rare type of immediate memory loss called transient global amnesia – transient because it will last only a few hours or days; global because the sufferer cannot remember what he sees, reads, hears, tastes or smells.

### Lost hours

In every other respect the functions of the surgeon's brain were perfectly normal. Although he was bemused by what was happening to him he showed no fear. He was kept under observation for a day and given various brain scans. During this time his memory recovered completely, except for a gap of 48 hours. Two days later the surgeon was back in the operating theatre.

Transient global amnesia is caused by a malfunction in the reticular activating system, a network of cells that are involved in registering and retrieving memory. Physical or emotional stress, immersion in cold water, sudden exposure to heat or cold or even sexual activity can cause the system to switch off, but how this happens remains a mystery. However, less than ten per cent of victims of a first attack will suffer further attacks, and the symptoms always disappear after a short time.

# REPLACING A NERVOUS LINK
## How doctors rigged up a scaffolding system for nerves to regrow along

HEART, KIDNEY and liver transplants are now established, and, at some hospitals, routine surgical procedures. But, in 1988, a Canadian medical team performed a transplant that formerly had only seemed possible in the realms of science fiction.

Surgeons successfully transplanted a sciatic nerve, which is the largest nerve in the body and runs from the lower back to the lower thigh, from a human donor into the leg of a nine-year-old American boy, Matthew Beech.

Matthew had suffered a rowing accident that had left a 230 mm (9 in) gap in his left sciatic nerve. In similiar cases, doctors would usually try to transplant other nerve tissue from the patient's own body. But they needed a very large amount of tissue to mend the gap, and decided that removing it from Matthew's body would leave him seriously debilitated. They either had to transplant a nerve from a donor or amputate Matthew's leg.

Nerves are perilously difficult to transplant because they end in hundreds of tiny fibres which are bound in bundles called fascicles. The grafted nerve must have the same number of fascicles as the severed nerve, and the surgeon must match and join each fascicle separately – an incredibly painstaking sewing job. Also, as with any transplant from one person to another, the new tissue may be rejected by the recipient's immune system.

The Canadian team was successful, and showed that nerve grafts actually stimulate a regrowth of the original nerve tissue. The graft was akin to erecting scaffolding along which Matthew's severed nerves could regrow. Helped by a drug that had been tested on monkeys who had had nerve transplants, Matthew's body did not reject the foreign tissue. A year after the operation this process was complete, and Matthew's severed nerves had grown back together.

**Bundle of nerves** *Our nerves contain hundreds of tiny nerve fibres in bundles known as fascicles. To repair a severed nerve, each fascicle must be joined. Each nerve fibre has a nutritive layer known as the myelin sheath.*

### DID YOU KNOW..?

*DR WALTER FREEMAN performed over 3500 lobotomies (controversial operations in which the frontal lobes of the brain are severed to calm those suffering from mental disorders) in the decade following the Second World War. Freeman once cut into 25 women's brains in a single day. He was convinced that the technique 'made good American citizens' out of 'schizophrenics, homosexuals, radicals …'.*

\* \* \*

*OUR BRAINS work harder than the rest of our bodies. For, although the brain comprises little more than two per cent of the body's weight, it uses up 20 per cent of the body's energy.*

\* \* \*

*FIGHTING BRAIN disease by brain transplants is not simply science fiction speculation. In Mexico, Sweden and the United States, brain grafts using a small quantity of cell tissue from the adrenal gland or foetal tissue are being used to alleviate the symptoms of Parkinson's disease.*

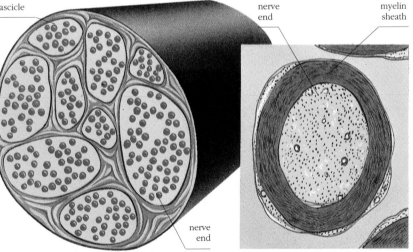

fascicle

nerve end

myelin sheath

nerve end

# ISLANDS OF GENIUS
## *The bewildering brilliance of the savant syndrome*

**H**OW CAN someone be able to calculate in an instant the day of the week for any given date over 40 000 years and yet be incapable of adding up two plus two? Or perform a complex classical piano piece after one listening and yet be severely mentally handicapped? Such individuals suffer from savant syndrome, a condition science has only recently begun to explain.

The syndrome has intrigued neurologists since Dr J. Langdon Down (who also gave his name to the mental handicap known as Down's Syndrome) first described such gifted but retarded geniuses in 1887, calling them idiot savants (savant means wise person).

One hundred years later, we know a great deal more about these 'foolish wise ones': idiot savants have a highly refined and efficient form of memory with which they can visualise paintings or a range of dates, or memorise a tune. These skills can be present from birth or acquired after an injury to or disease of the central nervous system. The condition can be caused by genetic abnormalities, sensory isolation, or defects in certain brain areas and structures that carry out intellectual tasks, such as the hippocampus (a seahorse-shaped structure directly linked to sensory inputs and memory).

Idiot savants are six times more likely to be male than female, and their skills can appear or disappear equally suddenly. Autism, a brain disorder that

*Sum savvy In the 1988 film* Rain Man, *Dustin Hoffman played an autistic savant (left) who astounds his brother, portrayed by Tom Cruise, by his ability to perform complex calculations.*

makes the individual withdrawn and virtually incapable of communicating with others, has also been linked to savant syndrome. About one in ten autistic children display savant skills.

One of the first descriptions of a 'human lightning calculator' was written in 1789 by Dr Benjamin Rush, a distinguished physician who was a signer of the American Declaration of Independence. His mentally handicapped patient, Thomas Fuller, was brought to Virginia as a slave in 1724. It took him a mere 90 seconds to work out that a man who has lived 70 years, 17 days, and 12 hours has lived 2 210 500 800

seconds – he even included the leap years in his calculation. Despite this incredible ability, Fuller died in 1790 without having learned to read or write.

### *Astonishing repertoire*
Another idiot savant slave became famous as a gifted pianist in the 1860s. Blind Tom could barely speak 100 words, yet he could play 5000 musical pieces flawlessly. His virtuoso performances took him to the White House and across America.

In 1964, American twins 'Charles and George' astounded neurologists with their calendar calculations. They could answer in an instant if asked, for example, when April 21 fell on a Sunday (1963, 1957, 1946 and so on as far back as 1700). The British neurologist and writer Oliver Sacks observed their skills when he accidentally spilt a box of matches in front of the twins. In unison they cried 'one hundred and eleven'. On picking up the matches, Sacks confirmed that exactly 111 matches had fallen from the box. Asked how they had counted the matches so quickly, the twins replied: 'We didn't count . . . we saw 111.' They also mentioned the figure 37 and, despite their inability to solve the simplest mathematical equations put to them, seemed somehow to sense that 111 could be seen as three groups of 37.

---

## TOO MUCH ON THE MIND

**J**OHN WAS 24, of more than average intelligence, witty and of strong character, but every few seconds or so he was taken over by violent spasmodic muscular contractions, or tics. Sometimes he could turn this to his advantage, such as when he played his drums, but most other times it caused him problems at work and at home. Apart from when he was asleep or in deep relaxation, he was free from these tics only when he was moving rhythmically – for instance, while performing certain tasks at work or when swimming.

While most neurological disorders involve a loss of some function – speech, short-term or long-term memory, language, identity and so on – there

is at least one brain disorder that comes from a surplus of brain function. John suffered from Tourette's syndrome, in which an otherwise normal person displays tics, jerks, grunts, grimaces and often frenzied behaviour.

### *Chemical control*
The syndrome is named after the French neurologist and playwright Gilles de la Tourette, who discovered it in 1885. Neurologists subsequently discovered that Tourette syndrome sufferers have an excess of the chemical transmitter dopamine in the brain. John was put on a course of drugs designed to lower dopamine levels and he was able to live a normal life.

## THERE, BUT NOT THERE

**A**LMOST EVERYONE who loses an arm or leg reports that they can sense their limb's presence immediately afterwards. But many such sufferers feel pain in the missing limb on and off for many years after the accident or amputation. For these people, the phantom limb, as this condition is known, is certainly not just something 'in the mind'.

Many neurologists believe that the trauma of a lost limb may affect the sensory cortex, the region of the brain that gives us our 'body image' – the awareness of our physical presence and its position in space and in relation to other objects. The sensation of a phantom limb may also result from disturbances in the spinal nerve-roots.

Numerous instances of phantom limbs have been documented over the past century. A case of unusually long duration was described by the neurologist George Riddock. A man had had his right leg amputated below the knee at the age of 14. When examined by Riddock 34 years later, the sensation of a limb was still present. The man said he felt he could bend and stretch the foot and toes. When wearing his artificial limb, he was able to differentiate between objects such as buttons or matches when he trod on them.

### Phantom predictions

So natural did the phantom limb seem that when getting up from his chair the man often stepped off with the 'right foot'. Sometimes it would itch and he would attempt to scratch it. The limb was remarkably susceptible to changes in the weather; before rain, for instance, he felt that the toes were being immersed in water that was being gently swirled round. In windy weather his toes felt separate from each other. So accurate were these sensations that he acquired a local reputation as a weather predictor.

Phantom limbs live up to their name in that they can give the sensation of passing through solids. One patient, who had suffered an amputation of the left arm, used to amuse himself by rotating his stump at the shoulder so that he felt his phantom hand pass through his own chest. In other cases, especially after accidental amputation, the phantom is immovable. A soldier whose right arm was blown off by the premature explosion of a bomb that he had been holding in his hand reported that the phantom hand still seemed to be grasping the bomb and he could not alter its position. Many people with phantom hands say that they can still feel the sensation of tight rings that they wore before the hand was removed.

# DRAWING CONCLUSIONS
## *The withdrawn children who flourish artistically*

**S**IX-YEAR-OLD Nadia's ballpoint drawings of horses and other animals were viewed with a mixture of marvel and disbelief by a team of child development researchers at Nottingham University in 1974. In spite of the fact that she could barely combine two words, and was extremely withdrawn and prone to screaming fits, she had an extraordinary ability to draw.

Psychiatrists noted that she was lethargic and exhibited obsessive behaviour. All this changed when she started to draw. Suddenly she would become animated. Holding her pen like an adult, and with her head close to the paper, she drew swiftly and displayed an advanced sense of perspective, depth and shadow. She would get inspiration from existing pictures but often arranged the subject in a new position. This showed that she could form a three-dimensional picture in her head even when shown only a two-dimensional drawing.

Nadia entered a school for autistic children at the age of seven. Slowly she learned how to speak and write and began to interact with other children – but as this happened her drawing skill disappeared. Cases such as hers have convinced some neurologists that autistic savants must trade off their genius when they are integrated into society. Their extraordinary talents are transformed into the more everyday skill of language.

### Budding architect

But the case of another autistic child, Stephen Wiltshire, suggests otherwise. Stephen is able to produce detailed architectural drawings with remarkable speed. His acute memory enables him to execute an accurate drawing after just one viewing. In 1987, at the age of 12, he was, in the words of an eminent architect and artist, Sir Hugh Casson, 'possibly the best child artist in Britain'.

Like Nadia, Stephen has also developed some language skills and is doing well at a special school. But Stephen's progress has not stifled his extraordinary drawing ability; in fact, his genius and social skills appear to progress in tandem. He now hopes to become an architect. A trust has been set up to help him train, funded in part by the sale of Stephen's own drawings.

*Autistic artist* Stephen Wiltshire, an autistic child, has amazed doctors and artists alike with his skilled architectural drawings. He made this drawing at the age of 11.

# ACTING ON IMPULSE
## *Understanding our cable and wireless cell system*

**F**OR FAST, effective communication, our bodies rely on what scientists have estimated as being between ten and 100 thousand million nerve cells, or neurones. Most of these are in the brain. Neurones relay electric messages called nerve impulses at speeds up to 100 m (300 ft) a second, making sure we can react quickly to ever-changing internal and external conditions.

### *Information network*

Under a microscope, neurones resemble frayed electricity cables. They consist of a cell body, which contains the nucleus of the cell, a long fibre called an axon that carries electric impulses to other cells, and thread-like protrusions named dendrites that receive incoming messages. A single neurone can receive messages from a great many others. The axon may branch many times, and scientists think there is at least one type of neurone that may have up to 200 000 axon branches, each leading to another neurone. Each axon is surrounded by a fatty layer, called the myelin sheath, which ensures that the electric impulses carried by the neurones do not escape.

For some neurones, it has been calculated that if the cell body were the

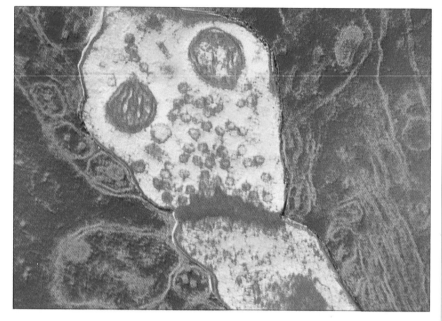

size of a tennis ball, the dendrites would fill an average-sized living room, and the axon, at that scale only 13 mm ($1/2$ in) wide, would be over 1.5 km (1 mile) long.

Sensory neurones receive stimuli in the form of electric signals from our sensory organs (such as the nose, eyes or skin) and convey them, as tiny currents of electricity, towards the spinal column and brain. Motor neurones despatch the brain's or spinal column's instructions back to our muscles or glands, also in the form of electric signals, so that we respond in an appropriate way to any stimulus – for instance, by quickly withdrawing our hand after touching something hot, or by producing more saliva when smelling food.

These electric messages travel through the body without the neurones actually meeting. When the message has travelled to the end of one axon it comes to a gap, called a synapse, which it somehow has to pass to reach the dendrites of the next neurone. So the electric

*Muscle bound* Nervous impulses travel along each of the hundreds of branches of a motor neurone. Each branch terminates on an individual muscle cell (seen here as bands).

*Nerve centre* Information is passed between two nerve cells by electrical impulses triggered by chemicals in the synapse (shown as a dense red band).

message converts to a chemical that can cross the gap; once on the other side of the synapse, the chemical is converted back into an electric signal. Scientists reckon that the simplest thought or action requires millions of such transactions to take place.

### *Breaks in the chain*

The system is intricate and vital, and should something interrupt the chain, the result can be devastating. For instance, multiple sclerosis – a disease of the central nervous system – can cause general paralysis. The disease attacks the myelin sheaths – which feed important nutrients to the neurones – causing them to become inflamed, and interrupting the nervous impulses. In particular, vision, sensation and limb movement are affected. It is thought that the disease is caused by a virus or by a deficiency in the fatty substances that make up the myelin.

In motor neurone disease the neurones that run from the brain stem to the muscles die. The muscles receive no messages from the brain, and gradually waste away from lack of use. Some sufferers are unable to perform any physical function. As yet, there is no cure for either disease.

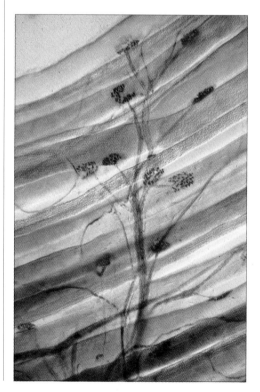

# READING THE MIND

## *When the pseudoscience of phrenology was all the rage*

I N THE EARLY and middle decades of the 19th century, it was widely believed that studying the bony protuberances of a person's skull would reveal his or her talents and character. Such analysis of the human psyche was called phrenology, and it was invented by Austrian doctor Franz Joseph Gall, who was born in 1758. Charles Darwin and many other prominent scientists were interested in Gall's theories, and Queen Victoria even had her children examined by a phrenologist to ascertain their chances of success in later life.

After examining the skulls of criminals and lunatics as well as average citizens, Gall mapped out the skull into 37 different areas, locating key character traits such as firmness, self-esteem and parental love on the top of

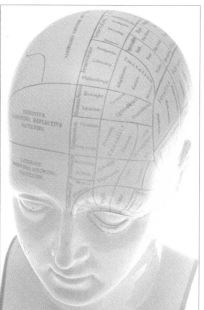

the skull, while secretiveness and cautiousness were placed on one side of the skull. His theory was that the protuberances of the skull reflected the bulges, and therefore the greater development, of different parts of the brain. However, the belief that you could 'read someone like a book' according to the contours of the skull rested on a fundamental error in anatomy that only later came to light .

### *Flawed system*

Gall's mistake was to believe that the skull was moulded by a growing brain, and that the contours of the skull therefore revealed underlying mental faculties. We now know that there is a barrier between the skull and brain called the subarachnoid space, which contains the cerebrospinal fluid that cushions the brain and protects it from contact with the skull. The brain does in fact possess different regions that govern different functions – however, they are not the ones identified by Gall's system of phrenology.

The discovery of cerebrospinal fluid, by a French physician named François Magendie, came in 1828, the year Gall died. But even this did not halt support for Gall's basic theory. As late as 1907, an electric 'phrenometer' was designed to measure the skull's bumps.

---

### DID YOU KNOW..?

*THE VICTORIANS believed that the heavier and larger the brain, the greater the intelligence. They were fascinated by the brain measurements of famous intellects. Those of the novelist William Makepeace Thackeray and the German statesman Otto von Bismarck, for instance, weighed 1658 and 1907 g (3 lb 10 oz and 4 lb 3 oz) respectively. However, post mortem measurements of the brain mean nothing, because after death the brain actually increases in weight as oedema (watery swelling of the tissues) sets in.*

---

**Character guide** *Gall's pseudoscience of phrenology divided the brain into 37 different areas based on the contours of the skull. Each area was responsible for a character trait.*

**Skull map** *In an English illustration from 1886, a child is about to have the protuberances of his skull measured by a phrenologist.*

# RHYTHMS OF THE MIND

*How to record the mind in motion*

THE SPECTACULAR developments in brain scanning in recent years have tended to eclipse the contributions made by the EEG (electroencephalograph) – yet in tracing some brain diseases the EEG can provide information no scanner can equal.

Electroencephalography was the brainchild of Hans Berger, a professor of psychiatry at Jena University in Germany, who made his discovery in 1929. It had long been known from animal experiments that the brain generated electric signals; Berger had found that by using a galvanometer, a very delicate device for detecting small electric currents, it was possible to pick

**Brain power** *The distinct wave patterns in these electroencephalograms show the changing electrical activity of the brain caused by different states of consciousness.*

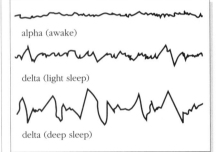

alpha (awake)

delta (light sleep)

delta (deep sleep)

up signals from electrodes placed on the scalp. When he amplified these weak signals and fed them into a machine that instantaneously made tracings onto a graph, he became the first person to view the awesome sight of the machinery of the brain in action.

### Changing patterns

Berger discovered that the electric messages of the brain are sometimes synchronised in distinct wave patterns. These vary in speed, depending on the patient's age, whether his brain is healthy, and the activity in which he is engaged. For healthy adults, the most prominent wave pattern on an EEG is the alpha rhythm. Its speed is 10 cycles per second and it is best detected when the subject is resting with his eyes closed. Tackling any mental challenge reduces the alpha waves, sometimes blocking them altogether. The resulting wave pattern of irregular frequency is known as the alpha block. With the onset of sleep and as sleep deepens, EEG waves become longer and slower in frequency – delta waves, whose frequency ranges from only 1 to 2 cycles per second, are dominant.

The EEG recording of the scientist Albert Einstein illustrates the phenomenon of alpha waves, although his example is hardly typical. While he was carrying out intricate calculations

which, however, posed him no challenge, his mind was relaxed and therefore a continuous alpha rhythm was present. Suddenly the alpha waves dropped out and he appeared restless. When asked if there was anything wrong, Einstein replied that he had found an error in the calculations he had made the day before and needed to telephone Princeton University immediately to report the mistake to his colleagues. Einstein's alpha rhythms had been replaced by irregular waves (alpha block) because of the mental challenge his error posed.

### Brainstorm

The EEG is still pre-eminent when it comes to detecting and monitoring epilepsy, which is, in effect, an electric storm in the brain. Perhaps its most spectacular success in this field has been in the widening of the definition of epilepsy. In the late 1940s, EEG investigations revealed an entirely new condition – temporal-lobe epilepsy – a variety in which the patient does not fall down, does not convulse, and may even be capable of walking and talking during the fit, but displays confused and often bizarre behaviour for which he afterwards has no recollection. States of depersonalisation, hallucinations and other strange phenomena often fall into this category of epilepsy.

## SEARCHING FOR THE SEAT OF THE SOUL

ANCIENT PHYSICIANS and philosophers might be forgiven for placing the location of intellect and consciousness or, as they termed it, 'the seat of the soul', anywhere in the body but the brain. After all, the human brain is comparatively small, averaging only about 1500 g (3¹/4 lb). On superficial inspection its gelatinous texture yields little evidence of the vast complexity of its operations and its supreme importance in making every bodily function happen.

Ignorance of anatomy in ancient times led to the belief, for example, that nasal secretions came directly from the brain, and the grey matter of the brain was thought to be composed almost entirely of phlegm. So the seat of the soul was assigned to apparently more interesting organs, such as the heart, liver or kidney.

The phrases heart-broken and lily-livered are relics of these beliefs. Although Hippocrates had – based on his observations of epilepsy in the late 4th century BC – placed the intellect in the head, a few generations later Aristotle placed it in the heart, dismissing the brain as an organ for 'cooling the blood'. In the 2nd century AD, Greek anatomist Galen discovered some of the functions of the brain, but Aristotle's views held sway for another 1500 years.

Only when English physician William Harvey discovered the circulation of the blood, in 1628, and showed that the heart is a muscular pump, did Aristotle's doctrines decline. Even then, almost every location apart from the grey matter of the brain itself was favoured as the seat of the soul – the ventricles, the hollow spaces in the centre of the brain, and the meninges,

its outer membranous coverings, being the preferred sites. The French 17th-century philosopher Descartes chose the pea-sized pineal gland as the contact point between the body and soul, because it is the only part of the brain that is a single organ rather than one of a pair. Anatomists performing autopsies were later dismayed to find that the gland thought to be the 'seat of the soul' was calcified.

It was Franz Joseph Gall, an accomplished Austrian anatomist specialising in the brain before he became diverted to the pseudoscience of phrenology, who, in the late 18th century, was the first to trace the origin of the nerves back to the brain. He pinpointed the cerebral cortex, the mantle of grey matter that covers the entire expanse of the brain, as the seat of the higher functions.

# Seeing into the Brain
### CAT scans reveal a slice of life

THE DISCOVERY of X-rays in 1895 made little impact on discovering how the brain functions. Although the first X-rays provided clear images of hard tissue in the body, such as bones, the soft tissue of the brain, being transparent to X-rays, did not show up.

The first breakthrough in X-raying the brain came in 1919 with the development by the American neurosurgeon Walter Dandy of the method known as air-encephalography. Dandy had been intrigued by the remark of a colleague that intestinal gas frequently obscured the X-ray appearance of bowel diseases. Dandy then conjectured that if air could be passed through the hollow spaces in the brain – the ventricles – the air would be opaque to the rays and the tissues surrounding the ventricles would be revealed.

### X-ray breakthrough

Dandy invented a machine to do just this, and found he could observe the ventricles' distortion or reduction in size, or shift to one side, when displaced by diseased brain tissue. This technique led to the development of angiography, the injection of an opaque substance into the blood vessels. This made possible X-ray detection of blood-clots (which cause strokes), tumours or other abnormalities in the blood circulation of the brain.

Although Dandy's technique provided the first detailed images of the brain, the procedure

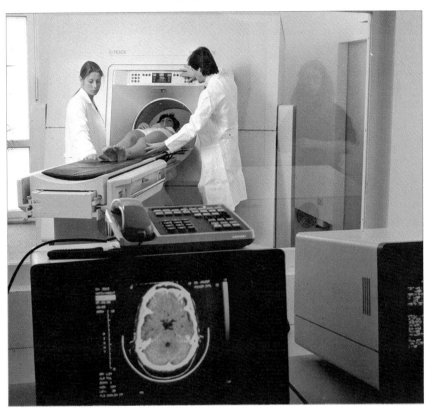

was distressing and dangerous for the patient. It was rendered virtually obsolete overnight by the development of the computer axial tomography (CAT) scan in 1973 by British scientist Godfrey Hounsfield and American scientist Allan Cormack. They were awarded a Nobel prize for medicine for this achievement.

### Absorbing matter

The CAT scan works on the principle that different tissues absorb different amounts of X-rays. For instance, as cerebrospinal fluid is less dense than brain tissue, it absorbs fewer X-rays and so appears as a dark area on the scan. But as tumours are denser than normal brain tissue, they appear on the scan as light areas.

For the scan, the patient is placed in a metal tube surrounded by a rotating X-ray machine that produces fan-shaped beams of

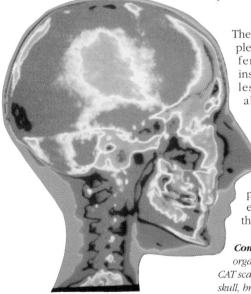

**Computer profile** *A computer has organised and coloured the data from a CAT scan's X-rays to produce this image of the skull, brain, neck, vertebrae and jawbone.*

**By degrees** *A CAT scan emits X-rays which pass through a cross-section of a patient's brain. The scan is linked to a computer that records the rays' degree of absorption and then analyses the information.*

radiation. Measurements of the beams' absorption as the machine circles the brain are made every few degrees – a CAT scan can store 1.5 million absorption point measurements – and an image of a wafer-thin 'slice' of the brain is thus produced. A computer then analyses further 'slices' from the base of the brain upwards, building up a complete image of the whole brain.

### Diagnostic tool

CAT scanning is painless and relatively risk free. It is now widely used for diagnosing tumours, haemorrhages and strokes and for investigating head injuries. It is also instrumental in helping neurologists understand the brain.

One incidental CAT scan discovery was that the two halves of the brain are not, as previously had been supposed, mirror images of each other, but have slight variations in the formation of the back area.

157

# TELEVISION ON THE BRAIN
*Visualising the living brain in action*

**N**OT ONLY can television images be bounced off satellites in space, but we can now get TV-type images from inner space – inside the brain. The PET (positron emission tomography) scan works on the simple principle that when one part of the brain bursts into activity, an increased supply of blood goes to that part to supply the extra oxygen and glucose needed for its exertions.

### Radioactive injection

In a PET scan, specially prepared radioactive oxygen or glucose is injected into the patient's blood vessels. Once this mildly radioactive 'tracer' has reached the brain, it emits positrons – positively charged atomic particles – that collide with the electrons of the brain cells and produce tiny bursts of energy that are detected by the PET apparatus surrounding the patient's head.

Pictures then appear on a monitoring screen showing the activated sections of the brain in glowing and expanding or shifting reds, blues and yellows as they perform a specific task – reading, writing or speaking, for example.

PET scans are particularly useful in identifying brain disorders characterised by unusual levels of energy use. For instance, they have shown that sufferers of schizophrenia have higher metabolic activity in certain parts of the brain than a normal person.

A team at the Washington University School of Medicine, USA, have used the PET scan to discover the seat of at least one of the emotions – fear. It is usually controlled by the temporal lobe that lies in the right hemisphere of the brain.

*Active mind The computer-synthesised colours in this PET scan show levels of activity in the different parts of a brain that has been injected with radioactive glucose. The glucose highlights the amount of energy each area is using.*

# MAPPING OUT THE MIND'S MALFUNCTIONS
*How the science of neurology began*

**T**HE WORK of a neurologist is like that of the ancient cartographer charting the unknown land masses and oceans of the world. Neurologists map out the brain when treating patients who suffer from abnormalities of the mind, and try to pinpoint exactly the part of the brain that has gone wrong. With this knowledge they can prescribe specific treatment and therapies.

### Separate functions

Until 1861, it was thought that the brain acted as a whole in its governing of the body's functions. But in that year Paul Broca, a French anatomist and anthropologist, discovered that different parts of the brain perform different functions. He reached this conclusion after carrying out an autopsy on a patient who, during his lifetime, had suffered from a severe speech impediment – he could only utter one syllable, though he fully understood spoken language.

As Broca had anticipated, the autopsy revealed damage to a section – now known as Broca's area – of the left frontal lobe of the brain. Three years later, Broca confirmed the correlation

*Brain sections In 1861, Paul Broca, laid the foundations of neurology when he discovered that different areas of the brain are responsible for different functions.*

of speech loss (aphasia) with defects exclusively situated in the left hemisphere of the brain.

Some 80 years later, Russian neurologist A. R. Luria mapped out in great detail all the functions of the left hemisphere of the brain, identifying the areas relating to hearing, sight and voluntary motion.

### Baffling brain disorders

Luria's case studies of patients with brain disorders provide a rich storehouse for analysing the workings of the mind. For example, some of his patients were completely unable to walk on a level floor but could walk upstairs or could step over lines drawn on the floor. Luria identified the various damaged parts of the brain that controlled each of these abilities.

Neurologists charting smaller and more localised areas of damage have uncovered much about the subtle complexities of the brain's functioning. For example, incomplete tissue wounds in the brain's speech and language centre, which is located in the left frontal region, present strange results. There are patients who, though able to write, cannot read even the words written by their own hand a moment before; or who cannot speak spontaneously yet can produce 'serial speech', such as reciting a prayer.

# INSIDE STORY

*Optical fibres that travel along the body's pathways*

UNTIL RECENTLY, if doctors needed to investigate the inner workings of the body, they could either carry out exploratory surgery (a potentially dangerous undertaking) or take an X-ray that gives only a static picture. But now, thanks to fibre optic technology, doctors can thread ultra-thin flexible fibres along the body's pathways – air passages, intestinal ducts, arteries, heart chambers – and see in fine detail the functioning or malfunctioning of the body's major systems and organs as if they were in a sealed capsule travelling along the pathways themselves.

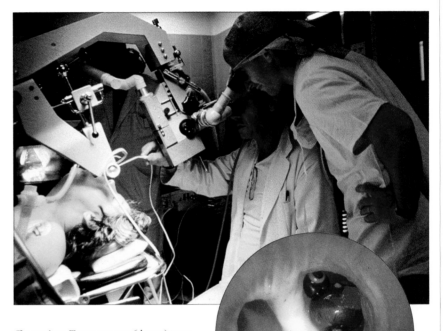

***Clear view*** *Two surgeons* (above) *peer through a fibrescope as they use a laser to eliminate growths on a patient's vocal cords. An endoscope allows surgeons not only to see inside the body, but to work with miniature scissors or forceps as well. The view through an endoscope* (right) *shows forceps retrieving an inhaled object from a windpipe.*

## Internal pictures

This major advance is due to the fibrescope, a flexible instrument resembling a thin cable. It contains two parallel bundles of optical fibres made of high-purity glass, along which light can pass, and is fitted inside a plastic or rubber tubing that is inserted into the body through a natural opening or small incision. Once the fibrescope is in place, light is shone down one bundle onto the subject, and a picture is reflected back up the other bundle to be viewed through an eyepiece, displayed on a television screen or recorded by a camera.

Fibrescopes can carry 10 000 fibres in a bundle less than 1 mm (0.04 in) wide, and send back images of minute areas of tissue such as a polyp in the colon. They can travel through our digestive, reproductive, circulatory and respiratory systems; for example, they can be inserted into an artery in the arm and directed towards the heart, so that a surgeon can detect any abnormalities in the heart valves or coronary arteries.

Fibrescopes are often incorporated into larger instruments called endoscopes. These have attachments that allow miniature surgical instruments (such as scissors, forceps or loops) to be inserted down the tube, and blood samples and small samples of tissue to be extracted.

## Diagnosis without surgery

The first fibrescope was constructed by an American, Dr Basil Hirschowitz. In the 1950s, he and his colleagues bought a few dollars' worth of optical glass and melted it down into fibres, which were wound round a cylinder converted from an empty breakfast cereal packet. The fibres were then given permanent glass coatings. Each of the resulting composite fibres could transmit light independently. The instrument Hirschowitz constructed was first passed down into a patient's stomach in 1957.

Doctors can not only view inside the body and diagnose a disorder, but they can also fire laser light through the optical fibres and treat ailments, such as stomach ulcers, without performing major surgery.

---

**DID YOU KNOW..?**

*LASERS have been used to improve the appearance of 'port wine' birthmarks – unlike other birthmarks these stains do not naturally disappear with age. Some doctors have even tried removing tattoos by laser, so far with mixed results.*

159

# THE ROBOT BRAIN SURGEON

*A medical advance that was inspired by a car factory*

DR YIK SAN KWOH, director of a CAT scan research unit in Long Beach, California, sits in front of a computer linked to a robotic arm in the operating theatre. A neurosurgeon pinpoints the area of a patient's brain tumour with the two-dimensional X-ray scanner and Kwoh then types in computer commands. Motors whirr and the mechanical arm swivels into a position above the brain. Ole the robot is about to remove the tumour.

The idea of using robots to perform delicate brain surgery came to Kwoh – an electrical engineer – after watching a robot assembly line in action on a TV documentary about car production. Thanks to a donation of US $65 000 from a Danish immigrant named Sven Olsen in 1981, Kwoh was able to adapt an industrial robot arm. He named his prototype robot neurosurgeon Ole, in honour of Olsen.

### Melon test

In 1985, Kwoh made the first tests of the robot's surgical skills. When commanded to extract pellets from inside a melon, Ole performed impeccably, confirming that the robot was ready to be used on a patient. A neurosurgeon located a tumour in a 52-year-old man, using a CAT scan that also superimposed an image of the path the surgical instrument should take. Kwoh keyed in commands for the computer to calculate the exact location of the tumour, and to transmit this data to the motors of Ole's six joints. Ole swivelled into the right position. Then, when the computer showed that the needle at the tip of Ole's arm was in precisely the right place, the neurosurgeon gently pushed the needle through Ole's arm guide and straight into the tumour.

### Perfect aim

Normally, a neurosurgeon would direct the surgical drill or biopsy needle himself to the right point and angle, but Ole's computer-guided accuracy – within 0.0125 mm (0.0005 in) – could not be bettered by a 'freehand' operation.

Ole has performed many tumour removals and biopsies since that first operation. He is so precise that only a very small incision is needed. The operation can be done under local anaesthetic, and some patients have been able to go home the next day.

*Skilled hand Yik San Kwoh demonstrates the robotic arm fitted with a needle to perform biopsies of brain tumours.*

---

## THE WRAP-AROUND HEART

SOVIET CITIZEN Vasily Fokin was 58 and suffering from serious heart failure. He could barely walk – his damaged heart could not handle the volume of fluid entering it, and this caused a backlog of fluid to build up in his legs.

Neither a suitable transplant donor nor an artificial heart were available. So doctors at the Kaunas Medical Institute in Lithuania 'trained' Fokin's back muscle – the *Latissimus dorsi* – to contract regularly by means of an electronic neurostimulator developed by the Moscow Design Bureau for Precise Machine Building. After a month of increasing stimulation, the muscle actually changed its structure to resemble cardiac muscle, which can be exerted continuously without tiring.

For the operation, previously only tried on dogs, the back muscle was cut away from the ribs, leaving the nerves and blood vessels attached. It was then wrapped around Fokin's heart, where it continued to work like a backup pump, providing the contractions for the heart. Surgeons reported a few months later that Fokin was leading a normal life and his legs no longer swelled.

### Electronic strengthening

This 'piggyback' heart is not solely a Soviet idea – scientists in Paris are experimenting with electronically-trained skeletal muscle to strengthen the heart, while researchers at a hospital in London have tested abdominal wall muscle. But surgeons admit that it will be a long time before they can use muscles to make an entirely new heart, with valves and chambers.

## DID YOU KNOW..?

*FIBRESCOPES can be combined with 'power fibres' carrying laser energy to perform laser surgery inside the body, such as shattering kidney stones and treating tumours.*

✳ ✳ ✳

*HISTORY RECORDS some interesting facts about ancient Babylonian medicine. For example, the 18th-century BC code of Hammurabi prescribed a stiff penalty for killing a patient while opening an abcess: cutting off the surgeon's hands. However, if the patient was a slave, the surgeon was required only to provide a substitute slave. And, some 1300 years later, the Greek historian Herodotus reported that it was customary in Babylon to place sick people in the street to allow passersby to offer medical advice.*

# THE POWER OF FAITH

## Can we will ourselves into good health?

TWO GROUPS of patients are suffering from gastric ulcers. One group is seen by a doctor who gives them what he describes as a potent drug. The second group is given pills by a nurse who warns them that the medicine may or may not be effective. Seventy per cent of the first group recover, but only 25 per cent of the second group – yet both groups have actually been given the same pills, which in fact contain only a completely inert substance and no medicine at all.

This story illustrates what is known as the placebo effect. A placebo (from the Latin word meaning 'I will please') is a dummy drug, such as a sugar pill, that works through nothing other than the patient's faith in the efficacy of the medicine. When patients believe that a pill will cure them, then that cure is more likely to happen. Exactly why has never been completely explained.

There have even been examples of placebo operations: in Kansas in the late 1950s, angina patients were invited to undergo a new surgical treatment for their heart pain. All the volunteering patients were put under anaesthetic, but only half actually underwent surgery. The rest were merely slit with a knife so that they had a scar leading them to believe that they had had major surgery. However, all of the patients experienced a measurable and significant improvement in their angina.

### Testing drugs

What placebos demonstrate is that healing is not simply a question of the body responding to prescribed chemicals, but can involve the mind and the will as well. The placebo effect makes it difficult to test the efficacy of new drugs – the health of some patients will improve simply from the act of participating in a drug trial, regardless of the merits of the drug itself.

So, in most trials, some patients are given placebos and others the real drug, and then doctors observe which patients recover more quickly or more fully. Since doctors also sometimes see a hoped-for improvement where there is none, this is best done under 'double-blind' conditions – neither the patients nor their doctors should know who has been given what until the end of the trial.

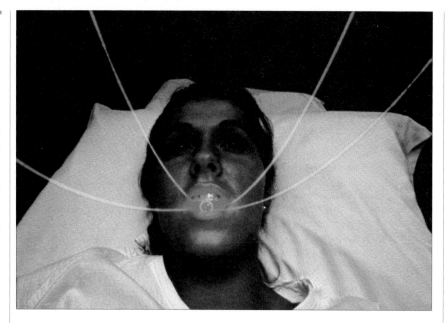

**Quadruple dose** *A low-power laser is directed through four fibre-optic strands to treat a cancerous throat tumour. The laser energy activates a cancer-killing drug that has previously been injected into the patient.*

# LASER LIGHT

## The invisible force that helps wounds to heal

LASER SURGERY is already well established for delicate eye operations, such as fusing a detached retina, but some doctors are now looking at lasers as a more general healing tool. Recent studies in Europe, the United States and the former USSR have suggested that there is a 'laser magic' that can help to heal burns and wounds normally unresponsive to conventional surgery.

### Stimulating growth

The wounds are exposed to low power lasers for only short periods, as long exposure at high power could seriously damage the tissues. Initial results show that the treatment stimulates damaged cells to grow and repair themselves. In one Hungarian study, 1300 patients with otherwise untreatable ulcers were given laser treatment. As a result, 80 per cent of the patients were completely healed, and a further 15 per cent showed a significant improvement.

Scientists are still puzzled at how laser healing works. But they have noticed that when white blood cells called macrophages are briefly exposed to laser light at low frequency, they release chemicals that somehow help to repair damaged tissue. It seems that low power lasers coagulate blood and cause protein to congeal. In this way, soft tissues are bonded together to seal wounds or join blood vessels.

Soviet experiments have concluded that laser light is particularly effective in stimulating ageing or malnourished cells, and cells of old wounds that are difficult to heal using other methods.

Doctors continue to search for new applications for lasers, including pain reduction, quick healing of sports injuries and the treatment of arthritis. Lasers have already been used in operations to reattach severed limbs: the clean cut a laser makes through delicate nerve fibres makes it easier for the fibres to regrow. Lasers may one day also remove or kill malignant tumours of the spinal cord and brain, for which conventional surgery would be impossible.

### DID YOU KNOW..?

*ALTHOUGH only low-powered lasers are used in healing techniques, surgical lasers can be extremely powerful. Surgical applications of lasers require from 10 to 100 watts of continuous laser power, or pulsed laser power reaching peaks of 10 000 to 1 000 000 watts. The power densities are roughly equal to those a 'Star Wars' laser would need to penetrate the casing of a guided missile, but the energy is concentrated into a narrow beam that can be directed with surgical precision.*

# THE WORLD OF THE WOMB

### *How we all grow from a single cell*

**T**HE BOND between a mother and the baby in her womb is so close that they could be described as a single biological unit. The most vital physical link is the placenta. This organ, joined to the baby by the umbilical cord, allows nutrients, oxygen and antibodies to pass from mother to baby, and allows waste products to flow back to the mother for disposal.

The bond is not just physical: a strong emotional link is also present. This was even recognised by ancient Chinese physicians, who encouraged pregnant women to engage in *tai-kyo*, the practice of speaking to the unborn baby. Today's scientists have confirmed that this communication is possible, as sound does penetrate the womb. Thus, even before birth the baby becomes familiar with its mother's voice.

But the unborn baby also has a life of its own: a heart that pumps blood, limbs that move, and a brain and nervous system that respond to stimuli.

*Weeks 5 to 12 (below right) At the beginning of this period, the developing baby is a tiny embryo just 2 mm (¹/8 in) long. It floats freely in the warm, protective amniotic fluid, which is encased in a thin membrane known as the amnion. By week eight, the embryo's soft cartilage has been replaced by bone, and its body structure is complete. It is now known as a foetus. It is still under 25 mm (1 in) long, yet its heart is beating, its spine can move, it has a brain and nervous system, and its major joints – hips, shoulders and knees – are visible.*

## THE FIRST WEEKS

**T**HE FIRST sign of life in the womb after conception is a single cell, which soon divides in two. Within a week, after repeated cell divisions, there are 150 cells. These cells attach themselves to the uterine wall, and by week 4 a tiny embryo has developed. The embryo will grow so quickly that by the end of the seventh week, it will be 10 000 times as big as the fertilised cell.

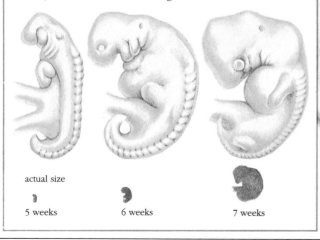

actual size

5 weeks          6 weeks          7 weeks

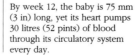

week 12

By week 12, the baby is 75 mm (3 in) long, yet its heart pumps 30 litres (52 pints) of blood through its circulatory system every day.

The baby is already using some of its muscles: it can kick, curl its toes, and clench and unclench its fists. It is able to make facial expressions.

**Weeks 13 to 28** (below) By week 13, the baby is 87 mm (3¹/2 in) long and almost completely formed, although it is too small and thin to survive outside the womb. In the next few weeks it will grow more quickly than at any time during the rest of its life. As the limbs strengthen, its movements are felt by the mother. By the 28th week, the baby's lungs would allow it, if born, to breathe.

**Weeks 29 to 40** (below) After week 28, the baby is able to survive outside the womb. In this final period, it will gain weight by laying down fat deposits. As it grows, it fills the uterus and its movements become restricted by lack of space. Around week 38, the baby settles into position for birth, which usually occurs in week 40. The average length of a newborn baby is 500 mm (20 in).

Doctors believe that the baby dreams by the 28th week, as tests show that brain waves associated with adult dreaming are present.

The baby acquires features – hair, eyebrows and eyelashes – that give it a distinctly human appearance. Its teeth begin to form.

Scientists believe that the rhythm of the maternal heartbeat forms the rhythmic beat from which our musical sense develops.

The baby's nails have grown to the end of its toes and fingers. The nails need to be cut soon after birth to prevent the baby scratching itself.

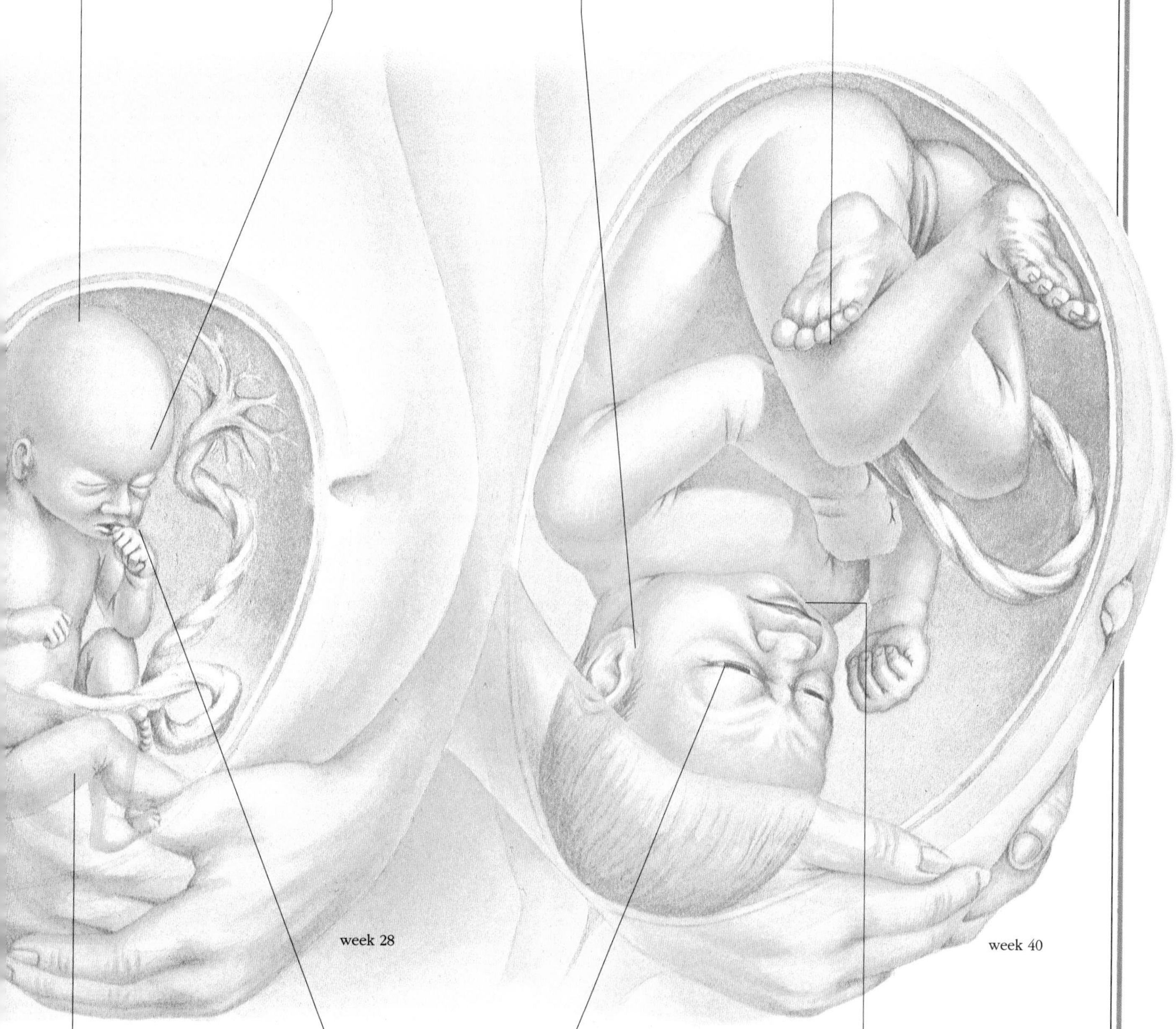

week 28

week 40

A thick grease called vernix covers the baby to prevent it from becoming soggy from the amniotic fluid. Most of the vernix will disappear before birth.

The baby sucks its thumb in preparation for feeding after birth. It can also cough and hiccup as it takes amniotic fluid in and out of its lungs.

The baby's eyes now open when it is awake. It can see light that has filtered through the mother's abdomen. This light will appear as a soft pink glow.

The baby has many more taste buds than its mother. It will be able to distinguish its mother's milk from that of a stranger soon after birth.

# THE BODY MIRACULOUS

## Blood tests help to unravel the mysteries of a 3300-year-old mummy

ON THE SURFACE of every red blood cell is a pattern of different molecules called antigens. The presence or absence of particular antigens can be used to classify blood according to 'blood groups'. The identification of an individual's blood group is a routine yet extremely important medical procedure – should a person require a blood transfusion after an accident or during surgery, he or she may only be given blood from a compatible blood group.

### Starting with 'A's and 'B's

The first antigens to be studied were called A and B, and their presence or absence determines which of the four main ABO blood groups a person belongs to: 'A', 'B', 'AB' or 'O'. Some people have A but no B antigens (group 'A'); some have B but no A antigens (group 'B'); some have both A and B antigens (group 'AB'); and the rest of us carry neither of these antigens and belong to group 'O'. (Other blood group classifications are independently based on the presence of still other antigens, such as M, N, S and s.)

We inherit our blood group from our mother and father, and our blood cells cannot possibly have an antigen that was in neither of our parents. Analysis of antigens cannot prove paternity or maternity, but it can sometimes show beyond doubt that a man or woman is not the parent of a particular child. For example, if a mother and father are both blood type 'O' (which means that neither carries A or B antigens), then their child cannot be 'A', 'B' or 'AB'.

### Identity crisis

Blood group analysis has been used to solve a case of mistaken identity involving an individual over 3300 years old. In 1969, a team led by R.C. Connolly of Liverpool University was asked to help identify a mummy in the Museum of Antiquities in Cairo.

In previous studies of the blood groups of Egyptian and South American mummies, Connolly's researchers had found that, long after red blood cells have disintegrated, minute quantities of antigens remain intact in other body tissues and can be identified. His team was asked to help confirm two hypotheses. Studies of ancient Egyptian letters and hieroglyphics had suggested, but not proved conclusively, that a mummy in the Cairo museum that had been thought to be the pharaoh Akhenaton could instead be his son-in-law and co-regent, Smenkhkare. And historians and anthropologists now wondered whether the child-pharaoh Tutankhamen and Smenkhkare, having similar body measurements, might have been brothers. If the blood groups of Tutankhamen and the mystery mummy were identical, it would be likely that both these hypotheses were true.

Connolly's team revealed that the two mummies belonged to the same blood groups in two different blood group systems: 'A' (in the ABO system) and 'MN' (in the MN system). As they also had similar body measurements, the odds were overwhelming that the two were siblings. Together with the other evidence historians had gathered, it was all but certain that the disputed mummy was Smenkhkare, and that Smenkhkare and Tutankhamen were indeed brothers.

**Transport system**
*Blood carries oxygen in arteries (shown in red) to all parts of the body, and carries away wastes in veins (in dull pink).*

164

# HARD TO SWALLOW

### How do showmen swallow swords and eat fire?

**M**OST PEOPLE could not swallow a sword without injuring themselves, for the secret of sword swallowing is not one of illusion but of long practice. Whenever an object enters the throat and threatens to obstruct breathing, a gagging reflex is triggered. Professional sword swallowers learn to desensitise this reflex, so that the throat muscles relax and allow the safe passage of the sword.

The path between the mouth and the stomach is not naturally straight. But by tipping back the head, the artiste can manoeuvre the sword past the Adam's Apple, down the oesophagus and into the stomach. The length of the sword that can be taken in is dictated by the

*Flames of glory Fire-eating has been practised since ancient times. When performed by experts, it is a relatively harmless stunt.*

distance between mouth and stomach. Some experts have managed to swallow swords up to 66 cm (26 in) long.

### A light inside

One particularly dangerous variation is the swallowing of lighted neon tubes, which, like sword swallowing, should only be attempted by a skilled professional performer. Audiences are amazed as the swallower's body glows from within, but this bizarre body contortion can be lethal if the tube should rupture.

Another test of the human body's amazing resilience is fire-eating, an ancient entertainment known to both Greeks and Romans. Spectacular variations have included eating hot coals and chewing molten metal.

### Avoiding a burn

The secret is that saliva helps the mouth withstand high temperatures without burning, while closing the lips tightly and holding the breath extinguishes any flames by cutting off the oxygen supply.

Fire-eaters are careful not to inhale through the mouth before performing their stunt: when they blow fire they

are igniting special fluids saturated on cotton wadding hidden in the mouth. They can blow fire as far as 9 m (30 ft), as was demonstrated by Reg Morris in 1986 in Staffordshire, England. The next year he succeeded in extinguishing over 20 000 flaming torches in his mouth in under two hours.

Harry Houdini, the great American escape artist who died in 1926, also learned the secrets of swallowing and regurgitating. In one trick, he would apparently swallow several needles and an unattached piece of thread, and then regurgitate the needles all hanging on the thread. What he was actually doing was bringing up a different set of needles, already strung to a thread, which he had swallowed prior to the performance.

---

## DID YOU KNOW..?

*SWEDE Birger Pellas has grown the longest moustache ever recorded. On February 3, 1989 it measured 2.86 m (9 ft 4 in).*

✳ ✳ ✳

*AN AMERICAN sailor called Cummings made a name for himself in the early years of the 19th century for his bravado in swallowing well over 30 knives. Some re-emerged through normal bodily functions, but when he died in 1809, after one knife had punctured his stomach lining, an autopsy revealed no fewer than 14 blades still in his stomach.*

---

## BARBERS VERSUS BARBARIANS

**T**HE ANCIENT Romans, with their clean-shaven faces and short hair, considered themselves the best groomed race. They frowned on the effeminate curled beards of the Greeks, but saved their true loathing for the 'barbarians' – by their definition, any foreigner who had a beard and long hair.

An unkempt hairstyle, the Romans reasoned, meant an uncivilised people. Wealthy Roman citizens got their slaves to trim their hair, while less well-off citizens visited barber shops – the first ones were started by Sicilians in 454 BC. Not all Romans were clean-shaven, however: philosophers and the recently bereaved customarily grew full beards.

Contrary to the Romans' prejudices, the so-called barbaric tribes – among them the Goths, Saxons and Gauls of western Europe – in fact took great care of their hair, their long flowing moustaches, and their beards. They used goats' grease and beech timber ashes to give their hair a glowing red colour. The Germanic kings of the early Christian era powdered their hair and beards with gold dust and adorned them with precious stones.

### Not just a whim of fashion

Various superstitions may have been at the bottom of the barbarians' reluctance to cut their hair. For instance, they believed that the head was the home of the 'protective

spirit', which they feared to disturb or injure by shaving or cutting their hair.

During the Middle Ages, beards and moustaches went in and out of fashion in quick succession. Consistent opposition came from the Roman Catholic Church, which issued edicts banning beards, but the Church never succeeded in enforcing its views on the laity for any length of time.

By the end of the 14th century, however, beards were no longer fashionable. One reason for this change may have been the increasing availability of soap, making shaving easier; another was the introduction of a new type of battle helmet, which came with a chinpiece that would not fasten securely over a beard.

# TO SLEEP: PERCHANCE TO DREAM

*EEGs help scientists to study what our brains are doing while we sleep*

HALF A CENTURY ago, scientists knew very little about dreams. They could not even say what proportion of the night was devoted to dreaming. But since the 1950s, they have started to unlock the closed door that hides roughly a third of our lives. This has been made possible by the invention of the electroencephalograph in 1929, by the German psychiatrist Hans Berger. The name means 'electric head writing', and describes quite aptly how the secrets of sleep are revealed.

The EEG, as it is known for short, is wired to the heads of volunteer sleepers in a laboratory. Groups of brain cells produce small electrical charges in patterns, and these can be detected by electrodes placed on the scalp. The electrical charges are converted into vibrations that are powerful enough to activate a number of pens, on electronic arms, to trace the movements on paper.

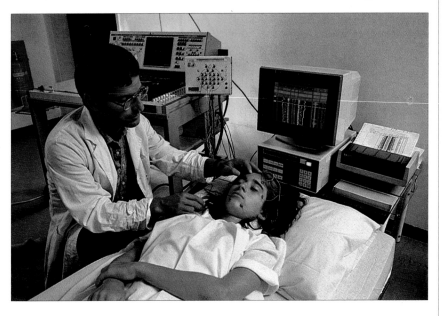

***The science of sleep*** *Computer analysis helps this doctor to decipher EEG patterns while his patient sleeps.*

### Signs of sleep

EEGs have detected that we go through several well defined stages of sleep in 90-minute cycles. When we are active with our eyes open, the EEG does not pick up any discernible pattern. But as soon as we close our eyes and begin to 'drift off' into sleep, alpha waves start to vibrate at 8 to 12 times per second, showing up on the EEG as a series of spikes. The onset of sleep itself is shown by the tracings of theta waves at a slower 3 to 7 times per second. Alpha and theta waves are associated with deep relaxation, creativity and tranquillity. Yogis and other experienced practitioners of meditation can, with practice, produce this level of relaxation when awake.

The deepest stage of sleep begins as the brain slows down to delta waves, vibrating at only 1 to 2 pulses per second. But then a curious thing happens: the EEG pens start tracing irregular spikes – similar to those recorded during wakefulness – as facial muscles and other parts of the body start to twitch.

This sudden burst of activity after a period of deep calm led scientists to name this stage 'paradoxical sleep'. But the darting about of the eyeball behind the eyelid, which is characteristic for this phase of sleep, gave it its better known name of rapid eye movement (REM) sleep. Scientists can monitor this stage on the EEG, and have discovered that if a person is awakened during REM sleep, he or she will be able to remember a dream eight times out of ten. By comparison, if interrupted during non-REM sleep, only about one in ten people recalled having had a dream. So it is thought that rapid eye movements are the response of the dreamer to the visual events of his or her dream-world.

We experience REM sleep about five times a night. The cycle of non-REM followed by REM sleep normally lasts about 90 minutes, but as the night goes on, the proportion devoted to REM sleep increases. So while our first dream may take only 10 or 15 minutes, just before waking we may have been engaged in a 45-minute epic.

> ## DID YOU KNOW..?
>
> *SCIENTISTS think that babies dream in the womb. Ultrascan tests to monitor foetal development during pregnancy have picked up rapid eye movements of the type associated with dreaming sleep.*
>
> ✳ ✳ ✳
>
> *BILL CARSKADON of Chicago has had the longest dream ever recorded in a laboratory. On February 15, 1967, sleep scientists recorded that he had a continuous rapid eye movement (REM) sleep lasting more than two hours.*

# VISIONS OF THE FUTURE?

*Danger signs in our dreams*

SOME PEOPLE say that if you dream about your own death, you will never wake up. Abraham Lincoln dreamt of his own death and lived to tell the tale to his biographer, Ward Hill Laman. 'Who is dead in the White House?' Lincoln recalled asking mourners around a draped corpse. 'The President . . . He was killed by an assassin,' came the reply in his dream. Lincoln had the dream in March 1865 – a few weeks before he was felled by the bullet of John Wilkes Booth.

The writer Mark Twain had a similar premonition, though his strange dream foretold the death of his brother, Henry. One night, while sleeping at his sister's house, Twain dreamt he saw Henry as a corpse, laid out in a metallic burial case supported by two chairs in a sitting room. A bouquet of white flowers, containing a single crimson bloom, was lying on Henry's chest.

### Special treatment

A few weeks later, Henry was killed in an explosion on a Mississippi steamer. As Mark Twain stood over the corpse in the makeshift burial room, he noted that while other victims of the disaster were placed in simple wooden coffins, his brother was lying in the same sort of metallic case he had seen in his dream. Then an elderly lady came up and placed a bouquet on Henry's chest.

Although the bouquet was a white one, it had a single red rose in its centre.

Many people are naturally sceptical about precognitive dreams, as these unconscious visons of the future are called. They argue that Mark Twain was a man of unlimited imagination who could tell a good story about almost anything. Lincoln's biographer, too, could have embroidered the details of the famous dream to make his own biography sell better. But as Lincoln's and Twain's accounts are just two of the many hundreds of well documented cases, it seems such dreams indeed warrant serious investigation.

Dr J.C. Barker, a British consultant psychiatrist, started his investigations

*Event foretold* *Novelist Mark Twain wrote of his many dream experiences, including the premonitory dream of his brother's death in the early 1860s.*

into precognitive dreams of disaster after the massive coal tip slippage at Aberfan, Wales, in 1966, in which 144 died. Impressed by numerous individuals' claims to have experienced dream warnings of the tragedy, he set up a special Premonitions Bureau, first in Britain and later in the United States, to act as an early warning system for future disasters. In the first six years, 1200 reports of apparent precognition were received in the UK alone, some of which did tally with later events.

## NOT GUILTY, ON ACCOUNT OF BEING ASLEEP

IN HIS DREAM, C.K. was chased by two Japanese soldiers, one with a knife, the other with a rifle. They eventually cornered him, but C.K. lurched at the knife-wielding soldier and tried to strangle him. As he did this the other soldier shot at C.K. The event described was all a ghastly dream – except that, on waking up, C.K. found his wife lying strangled beside him in bed.

C.K., an Englishman, had strangled her in his sleep, but when his case came to court in 1985, he was cleared of a charge of murder. The jury accepted the defence that the husband had committed the killing while still asleep, and therefore could not be held responsible.

This is not a unique story. As long ago as 1686, also in England, a sleepwalking Colonel Culpeper shot and killed a guardsman on his night patrol. At that time it was

still widely believed that during sleep the soul left the body and mingled with supernatural beings. It was therefore not unreasonable for the jury to think that the colonel's soul had become attached to some devil, making him innocent of the crime.

### Night terrors

Nowadays psychiatrists have a less fanciful explanation for such crimes. They call them 'night terrors'. These are sudden arousals from sleep with accompanying symptoms of deep anxiety. The night terror victim sits straight up in bed, heart thumping, and emits loud moans or piercing screams. Still asleep, the person may then get out of bed and carry out any number of complex acts, such as slashing furniture or even bodily assault. He or she may take up to ten minutes to come

round, and may recall very little of what happened. A nightmare, on the other hand, occurs during sleep and the sufferer usually remembers the disturbing vision vividly on waking.

The term used to describe these unconscious actions is 'automatisms', meaning actions performed without intent, and without the realisation that they are taking place. This was the defence used by C.K.

Morton Schatzman, an American psychiatrist who has researched this phenomenon, is concerned that night terrors could be used as an excuse by people who commit premeditated murder. He suggests that people who allege they were asleep when committing violent acts should be placed in a sleep laboratory where their sleep can be monitored to see if they do suffer from night terrors.

# THE WARNING ON SNORING

### An unexpected hazard to your health

**M**OST SNORERS are blissfully unaware of the noise they produce, and snoring could hardly be thought of as life-threatening. But for the few who suffer from a condition called obstructive sleep apnoea (OSA), snoring is potentially fatal.

OSA is caused by a weakness in the oropharynx. This is the upper airway at the back of the throat that includes the tongue and palate muscles. When we sleep on our backs and breathe through the mouth, the oropharynx sags inwards. It is then that snoring occurs, and the vibrations can reach a noise level of 70 decibels – close to the sound of a vacuum cleaner.

However, when a sleeper who suffers from OSA starts to snore, the oropharynx collapses, blocking the throat, and the sleeper is unable to breathe. Enormous pressure builds up in the chest cavity, and the flow of blood to the heart and lungs is impaired, sometimes causing heart failure. After about 15 seconds of such gagging, the sufferer will start to wake up, and partial wakefulness restores the muscle tone and opens up the airway automatically. The massive in-rush of air that follows produces a loud gasping snore, known as a 'heroic' snore, and about

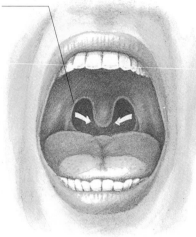

oropharynx

***Bad habit*** *In sleep our mouth muscles relax and, as we breathe, the oropharynx sags inwards. If we sleep on our backs and with our mouths open, we often snore.*

10 seconds later normal breathing and full sleep are both resumed.

OSA sufferers usually do not suspect that anything is wrong, as the waking periods are too short to be remembered the next day. They are unlikely to link the subsequent tiredness and lack of concentration with these interruptions to their sleep. Many doctors misdiagnose the condition and mistakenly send the sufferers to a psychiatrist.

In the United States, where most major cities have a special clinic to diagnose sleep disorders, and the problem is much better understood, people who suffer more than 35 such attacks a night are considered to be seriously at risk. In cases of over 100 attacks a night, doctors recommend that preventive action be taken swiftly.

### Cure for a snore?

Traditional remedies for snoring, such as strapping a hard object to the back to prevent a snorer from lying in a position that encourages snoring, might be a way to combat OSA, but this may be impractical for some people. As a last resort, a tracheotomy, a hole made surgically in the windpipe, allows the sleeper to bypass the obstruction when breathing. The most effective non-surgical treatment for OSA was invented by Colin Sullivan, at the University of Sydney. The sufferer sleeps wearing a mask fitted to an air supply at slightly above atmospheric pressure. As long as no leaks occur in the mask's air supply, the air pressure keeps the oropharynx from collapsing.

## DREAMING UP THE ANSWER

**W**HEN a problem preys on your mind and you just cannot find the answer, the solution might be to 'sleep on it'. This is not a mere figure of speech, because research has revealed that you are quite likely to find the answer popping up in your dreams.

Psychiatrists have devised various tests to help them study how people apparently solve problems in their dreams. One American doctor invited readers of the British magazine *New Scientist* to send in their dream solutions to two puzzles.

The first problem was mathematical: readers had to construct an object comprising four triangles by using six lines of equal length. Solving the puzzle required visualising a pyramid-like form known as a

*a tetrahedron*

tetrahedron. Eleven readers came up with solutions that they said had come to them while dreaming. One, a chemistry student, said she first dreamt of a wigwam, which gave her a clue to the shape. Another reader reported that she heard a voice saying 'try three-dimensional'. One reader wrote that she had no scientific skills, but in her dream she saw one of her colleagues flying up to the top of a bookcase from the floor. This, she reports, made her realise that her solution also had to fly up out of the page – in other words, become three-dimensional.

The second problem was a brain-teaser. Readers were asked what was remarkable about the following sentence: 'I am not very happy acting pleased whenever prominent scientists overmagnify intellectual enlightenment.' The answer is that each word contains one more letter than the previous one. One reader dreamt of scientists grouped around tables – one sat at the first table, two at the second, three at the third and so on. Another reader reported she had dreamt of a Count. On waking she realised that this was a pun: her dream had hinted that she should count the letters in the words.

### The science in dreams

Perhaps dreams reshuffle data in such a way as to provide a fresh perspective to a seemingly intractable problem. A dream solution certainly aided German physiologist Otto Loewi in 1920, when he literally dreamt up an experiment to show how nerves carry electrical impulses. Loewi awoke in the middle of the night to jot down his dream, but his notes were illegible. Fortunately, the dream recurred the next night, and Loewi awoke and immediately carried out an experiment with a frog's nerve. That experiment helped him to make discoveries for which he won a Nobel prize 16 years later.

## THE TIREDNESS OF THE LONG DISTANCE FLYER

SCIENTISTS used to think that jet lag occurred because cutting through time zones upset our circadian rhythm, the 24-hour cycle that acts as our body's natural timekeeper.

However, this conventional theory is now being questioned as it seems to contain a major flaw. Researchers have found that many people who fly from north to south (and hence not across any time zones) still suffer from all the symptoms of jet lag that east-west flyers do – fatigue, insomnia, lack of concentration and stomach upsets.

### Blaming the flight itself

In view of these findings, scientists have now come to blame the symptoms of jet lag on the process of flying itself: the high altitude, cabin pressurisation, the low humidity of the cabin, the vibration of the aircraft and the noise.

Carl Dransfield, a senior long-haul pilot with Qantas, has studied the problems of jet lag both on the ground and in the air. He believes that flying in the stratosphere, where the atmospheric pressure is only about 1 per cent of that at sea level, exposes us to increased radiation from the Sun – the equivalent of two chest X-rays on a transatlantic trip, he says.

It is this, along with cabin pressurisation, that causes upsets in our bodies' biochemistry, Dransfield believes. In particular, our bodies respond by producing an excess of toxic chemicals called free radicals. These chemicals are quickly broken down in a healthy, well-nourished body, but they can build up in the elderly, or in people under stress.

For years, many regular long-distance flyers have sworn that drinking large amounts of water, abstaining from alcohol, and exercising vigorously after landing eliminate jet-lag symptoms.

### Anti jet-lag diet

Dransfield points out that all these steps help to eliminate free radicals in the body. To decrease the effects of jet lag even further, he has developed a dietary supplement, based on a strain of wheat sprout, which supplies the body with enzymes that break down free radicals. Vitamin C and E diet supplements may also help, he says, as these are both powerful natural eliminators of free radicals.

# TRIBES GUIDED BY DREAMS
## *Where dreams are taken seriously*

AS WE FALL asleep, we lose contact with the outside world and enter the realm of dreams. Even people who consider their dreams important usually attach only a symbolic significance to them. But members of the Azande tribe of the Sudan, Zaire and the Central African Republic believe that the events they experience in their dreams are real.

The Azande consider that their pleasant dreams are prophecies of good events. But their unpleasant dreams are ill omened, and involve an encounter with witchcraft. The Azande believe that all misfortunes, and especially sickness and death, are caused by the spirits of witches seeking out innocent souls. As a tribe member sleeps, his soul is released from the body and is free to wander about. However, witches also allow their souls to roam during sleep, and when the two spirits meet, they struggle. It is this encounter that the Azande interpret as a real event.

The recipient of a bad dream must then consult a diviner who will help him to identify the witch who was responsible for the evil thoughts, so that he or she can be induced to call off the witchcraft.

Members of the Elgoni tribe on the Kenya-Uganda boundary also pay close attention to dreams. Carl Jung, the 20th-century Swiss psychologist who spent much of his life looking into the interpretation of dreams, spent some months with the Elgoni. He was overjoyed to find that their treatment of dreams confirmed his theory that there are two kinds of dream – those of a purely personal nature and those of a collective nature.

Jung observed that the Elgoni distinguished between 'big' and 'little' dreams. If an Elgoni had a dream that affected only himself – a 'little' dream – it was not regarded as significant. But if it was a 'big' dream, that is, if it appeared to have a wider implication for the whole community – such as a premonition of drought – then the other members of the tribe were called together to hear it and discuss what measures might be taken.

*Evil spirits Consulting a diviner is common practice among the Azande, who believe that everything is the result of some sort of magic or witchcraft. Here a diviner (right) advises one of his patients.*

### DID YOU KNOW..?

*THE PEOPLE of Germany and Transylvania once shared the belief that sleeping with your mouth open was dangerous. They feared that the sleeper's soul might escape – in the form of a mouse – through the open mouth and be harmed on its travels. Therefore, if the soul was permanently detained from returning, the sleeper would never wake up.*

# SOME ILL A-BREWING

### The mystery of a modern office malady

ROTHERHAM Council believed their new office block – Norfolk House – was such a well-designed building that they entered it for a British architectural award in the early 1980s. But when the staff moved in they soon started to complain of headaches, lethargy, skin rashes, wheezing, nausea and irritations to the eyes, throat and nose. A staggering 94 per cent of the workers complained of one or more of these symptoms that only occurred when they were at work. Norfolk House had got the Sick Building Syndrome.

### National epidemic

Ten years ago no one would have guessed that such symptoms could be caused by a seemingly harmless office interior, but now doctors and environmental health officers have verified that buildings can make people ill. A conference on the office environment in Washington, DC, in 1982 referred to Sick Building Syndrome as a national epidemic, and it is recognised as an illness by the World Health Organisation. Some researchers have suggested that sick buildings can even cause high blood pressure and miscarriages.

How can a building make its inhabitants sick? Investigators know that the syndrome is most common

> ## DID YOU KNOW..?
>
> *IF WE EAT raw or undercooked freshwater fish – but not sea fish – we may also unwittingly ingest fish tapeworms. These parasites can then grow up to 10 m (33 ft) long, lying curled up in our small intestines, where they can survive for up to 13 years. Anaemia may result in some cases.*

in modern office blocks with poor air conditioning systems. Environmental health experts blame fungi, microbes and dust mites in the air conditioning, as well as chemicals called biocides that are used in the humidifier system to kill off bugs. Modern building and furnishing materials such as chipboard partitions, as well as cleaning agents and commercial solvents such as chloroform and carpet adhesives, can give off vapours, including formaldehyde, that investigators have linked to skin and eye irritations.

Simply putting in a new synthetic carpet in a building can cause people to suffer extreme fatigue and loss of voice. This happened to 60 employees in – of all places – the Environmental Protection Agency building in Washington, DC, where they were badly affected by chemicals released from the new carpet. Pulses from fluorescent strip lighting and computer screens can also cause severe glare problems with attendant headaches and other complaints.

### Sick Building specialists

Sick Building Syndrome is so prevalent today that there are now special companies that employ indoor pollution squads to investigate and 'cure' sick buildings. They use fibre-optic technology to probe the normally inaccessible ductwork and then remove bacteria, fungi, dust and even dead mice. They also close down humidifiers, allow more fresh air to circulate, and take out fluorescent lights. Investigators at Norfolk House recommended changes along these lines: the result was a marked decrease in staff suffering the Sick Building Syndrome symptoms.

**Design flaw** *Rotherham Council's new building, Norfolk House, was well designed and modern, yet 94 per cent of the workers inside fell prey to Sick Building Syndrome.*

# WINE AND DECLINE
### *Was Rome brought to its knees by lead poisoning?*

**W**EALTHY ROMANS loved wine, and with around 370 varieties to choose from, according to Pliny the Younger writing in the 1st century AD, they drank prodigious amounts of it. In doing so they were unwittingly poisoning themselves with lead leached from the wine cask seals or linings by the acidity of the drink. One American researcher of occupational medicine, Dr S.C. Gilfillan, blames the lead thus consumed for the decline of the Roman Empire.

Gilfillan argues that lead poisoning specifically struck at the ruling classes who were the main consumers of expensive commodities such as wine, olive oil, honey-derived drinks and preserved fruits, all of which were stored in lead-lined jars. Such foods were too dear for the Roman poor and slaves, as were the lead-based cosmetics popular among upper-class women. Although all classes were to some extent vulnerable to the lead plumbing in the water supply systems, Gilfillan argues that Rome itself, where the aristocracy congregated, had soft water that absorbed lead from the pipes, while the poorer rural people had hard water that did not absorb lead.

The crucial date in the decline and fall, according to Gilfillan, was 150 BC, the year when Roman women were first allowed to drink wine. The gradual build-up of lead in their bodies, chiefly from wine, reduced their fertility and the few children they bore became weak and listless; the

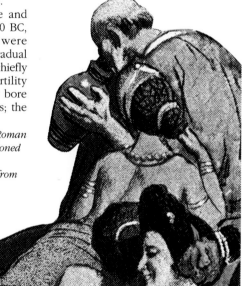

***Poisoned wine*** *The Roman aristocracy slowly poisoned itself by its abundant consumption of wine from lead-lined jars.*

ruling classes lost their vigour and grip on the empire. It is well known today that lead damages the brain, muscles and nerves, and causes anaemia.

The theory that the Roman Empire succumbed to a slow but fatal exposure to lead poisoning has been backed up by recent tests. A modern analysis technique called atomic absorption spectroscopy has detected lead in ancient bones.

---

## WHEN THE MIND GETS ALL TANGLED UP

**A**MANDA FAIRHURST was an outgoing, active old lady of 74. She attended church regularly and had many friends. Then she started to change: she gave up church and was even rude to the minister. She forgot to pay her utility bills, so the gas and electricity were repeatedly cut off. She could no longer recognise her nearest and dearest, and she became confused when performing the simplest chores around the house. Her distraught relatives called the doctor and Amanda was diagnosed as having Alzheimer's disease. She was put in hospital and within a few years she died.

### *Crossed wires*

Alois Alzheimer, a German nerve expert, first identified the disease in 1907, after a 55-year-old female patient of his had died exhibiting an unsettling combination of depression, hallucinations and memory loss. An autopsy revealed that the cells in the woman's thinking brain, the cerebral cortex, were hopelessly tangled up, like telephone wires blown down in a storm. Alzheimer's discovery lead to the realisation that there are basically two main types of dementia, the loss of mental faculties and of emotional balance. One is caused by strokes or other circulatory problems, the other is characterised by the tangled, degenerating brain cells of the Alzheimer's type. But whereas most dementias afflict those over 65, Alzheimer's even hits 40 and 50-year-olds.

Today, Alzheimer's is the major cause of admissions to US nursing homes, and the fourth leading cause of death in the US, killing some 100 000 people annually through complications such as pneumonia, accidents, and respiratory failure.

More than three million Americans over 65 are believed to suffer from it, and over 60 000 people in their forties and fifties. In the UK there are half a million people with Alzheimer's disease, and perhaps 15 per cent of people over 80 succumb to it.

### *Search for a cure*

Yet no one knows what causes Alzheimer's and there is still no cure. Some scientists believe that aluminium in water and in cooking utensils may accumulate in the brain and interfere with the chemicals that carry the brain's messages. Others believe the disease runs in families.

Other researchers have found, however, that Alzheimer's patients appear to be deficient in one or more of the chemicals that take messages across the brain, and are experimenting with drugs that can correct these abnormalities.

# RADIATING DEATH

## *When glowing was anything but healthy*

IN 1915, Sabin von Sochocky, a keen amateur painter, developed a paint that glowed in the dark, thanks to its special ingredient, radium, a brilliant white, highly radioactive substance discovered in 1898. Appropriately enough, Sochocky called his paint Undark. He went on to set up the US Radium Corporation to paint glowing numerals on wristwatch dials, crucifixes and light pulls. The craze for glow-in-the-dark objects took off, and soon Sochocky was employing hundreds of women and young girls to paint radium onto watch dials as well as luminous instrument dials for the US Army.

### *Poisonous cure-all*

At a factory in New Jersey, women and girls as young as 12 sat at rows of work-benches, tapering their radium-drenched brushes with their lips to ensure a fine luminous line on the dials. Their managers encouraged them, telling them that radium would make them sexually attractive, curl their hair, and improve their complexions. This was no cruel deception: radium at this time was considered by many doctors to be a cure-all for anything from waning sex drive to high blood pressure to 'debutante's fatigue'. No one believed that radium paint could cause cancer, although exposure to radiation from radium was known to destroy cells.

In 1924, however, New York dentist Theodore Blum noticed that one of his patients, who worked for US Radium, had a severe jaw infection. He wrote an article about her in the *Journal of the*

*Deadly mistake Technicians purify radium, unaware that it is carcinogenic. Discovered in 1898, radium was thought to be completely safe. But by the 1930s, deaths from cancer among radium workers had proved otherwise.*

*American Dental Association*, remarking in a footnote that he thought the infection was caused by a radioactive substance. This sparked a series of investigations, one of which found that the 'hair, faces, hands, arms, necks . . . even the corsets of the dial painters were luminous.' Dial painters began to suffer appalling cancers of the jaw, but the US Radium Corporation maintained that this was due to poor dental hygiene.

### *The bitter end*

In 1927, five former US Radium dial painters, now suffering from crippling bone diseases, filed a law suit against the company. Two of them were so ill they had to be carried to the courtroom, one was unable even to raise her right hand to take the oath. US Radium insisted that there was no scientific proof that the women's injuries were caused by radium. The case promised to drag on for years, until a sudden out-of-court settlement of $10 000 was awarded in 1928 to each of the women, plus medical expenses for as long as they suffered from radium poisoning.

---

# MAN'S OLDEST NUISANCE

## *The curse of the common cold*

COLDS HAVE always been a nuisance. And people have tried many curious remedies in the hope of curing them – all without success. The Greeks believed in bleeding them out, and Roman historian Pliny the Younger recommended 'kissing the hairy muzzle of a mouse'. But even though the cold is the illness we most love to hate, we are little closer to finding a cure for this mild and unglamorous infection than the ancient practitioners were.

But not through want of trying – especially through the efforts of the Common Cold Unit in Wiltshire, England. Set up in 1946, it was the first laboratory and research centre to concentrate exclusively on the cold. Since then, groups of up to 30 volunteers, usually isolated in pairs for up to ten days, have been given various strains of cold via infected swabs, as well as vaccines and anti-virals in the hope of solving this intractable medical problem.

### *The cold facts*

Thanks to the unit's annual 500 human guinea-pigs, we now know that a cold is not caused by a single cold virus but can be caused by many viruses – especially the 100 different rhinoviruses (rhino refers to anything nasal). The unit succeeded in growing and identifying these viruses and was able to begin the search for immunity and vaccines.

The unit has proved in trials that people under stress are more likely to catch colds – but why this happens is still unknown. Experiments also confirmed that women suffer more colds than men – but whether this is because they come into closer contact with children (who spread colds much faster than adults) or because their immune systems differ is not known.

Other experiments proved that introverts get more severe colds and excrete more virus than extroverts, and that getting cold does not cause colds. For this latter experiment, one group of volunteers was hosed down and had to stand in draughty corridors while another group remained dry and in a heated room. We now know that viruses are spread by water vapour from breath, which would explain why colds are more prevalent in the winter: people spend time closeted indoors away from the cold but also from fresh air.

Just as the unit was making progress with a synthetic antiviral compound that could suppress the virus from multiplying for six days, it was shut down in 1990 because of lack of funds.

---

**DID YOU KNOW..?**

*DESPITE the known risks, manufacturers of radium-based health foods and drinks did a brisk business in the US well into the 1930s. There was radium water (one New York company claimed to supply it to 150 000 customers), toothpaste, face cream, hair tonic and even a popular radium soft drink endorsed by an amateur golf champion, Eben Byers, who drank two miniature bottles of it every day. His jaw decayed rapidly and he died of anaemia within a few years.*

# TOP SPEED IN REVERSE

*The serious side of speaking backwards*

ANYBODY can painstakingly read words backwards, but how many can do it by ear? Professor Andrew Levine discovered his talent for speaking backwards in 1959 when, as a teenager watching the news on television, he admired the skill of the interpreters accompanying Soviet leader Nikita Khrushchev on his visit to the United States. Levine was keen to try his own hand at interpreting, so, as he could not speak Russian, he simply turned every English word he heard back to front.

### Word game

Amusements of this kind are not uncommon in children, especially between the ages of eight and ten, when they like to construct secret play languages. To do this, they do not have to be literate: in Panama, young Cuna Indians have a traditional game called *sorik sunmakke*, in which they reverse the order of the syllables in each word.

In Levine's case, the speed at which he spoke backwards was quite exceptional. He thought of his talent as nothing more than a party trick, until colleagues at the University of Wisconsin, where he taught political philosophy, decided to subject him to rigorous tests.

When asked to provide a simultaneous 'translation' of simple sentences, Levine started and finished less than two seconds behind the spoken model he was translating. Individual words he could reverse almost instantaneously, as if speaking normally. Turning words backwards often produces combinations of sounds that do not occur in English, yet his failure rate over long passages was only 7 per cent.

The reason for Levine's proficiency is that he does not allow the spelling to interfere with his backwards versions of words. Like many children who take up talking backwards, he reverses the phonemes, the units of sound considered to be the building blocks of speech: 'dollars' becomes 'srallod', and 'peace' becomes 'seep'. As Levine reverses only the sounds he hears, silent letters are ignored. This means he is almost as fluent in repeating foreign languages backwards, even ones he does not understand.

### Subconscious ability

Linguists were particularly interested in the fact that Levine, albeit subconsciously, was aware of the existence of phonemes. If the brain does cut spoken language up into segments of sound, further research may have practical applications in helping both the deaf and children who, through some mental disorder, have difficulty in acquiring normal forwards speech.

# LANGUAGE OF THE BIRDS

*Places where people 'talk' in whistles*

FANS OF the Marx Brothers will know the comic routines in which Harpo – the one who never speaks – communicates with his brothers through a frantic series of whistles and the honking of a horn. But they might be surprised to learn that there are places in the world where people really do speak to one another by whistling as part of everyday life.

The Mazateco Indians of Oaxaca, Mexico, are frequently seen whistling back and forth to one another, exchanging greetings, or buying and selling goods, with no risk of a misunderstanding. Mazateco children learn

*Dumb, but not silent* Harpo never spoke in the Marx Brothers' outrageous film comedies. He communicated with gestures, whistles, a horn or his harp.

the art of whistling almost as soon as they can talk.

Their whistling is not really a language or even a code; it simply uses the rhythms and pitch of ordinary speech without the words.

### Bilingual tunesters

A Mazateco can 'hear' the word that is intended because the whistler mimics ordinary speech so cleverly. Some of the Mazateco can actually whistle in two languages – their own Indian dialect and Spanish.

The Mazateco never use their fingers when whistling, relying entirely on their lips. When they were shown a photograph of people putting their fingers in their mouths to whistle, as Harpo always used to do, they could make no sense of it.

Although the Mazateco are unique in whistling to communicate over short distances, there are other regions of the world where people also 'talk' by

whistling: an area of northeastern Turkey south of the town of Görele, and La Gomera, one of the Canary Islands. These are both rugged, sparsely populated mountainous regions where people who might otherwise have to walk for two hours to speak with their neighbours simply whistle instead.

### DID YOU KNOW..?

*DOLPHINS can carry on two conversations at once. They whistle and make clicking noises, and are able to convey independent messages in both mediums at once. Each dolphin has a distinctive 'signature whistle' that identifies it to other members of the herd. Dolphins can also stun prey with intense bursts of sound, and can use sonar to locate objects in their environment.*

# SILENT CONVERSATIONS

*We often mean more as we do than as we say*

**W**E ALL NOTICE and respond to the expressions on peoples' faces, and these mean the same things round the world. But they are only one part of the non-verbal messages we are constantly sending out to the people around us. Our body language – the way we stand or sit, and the gestures that we make – very subtly reflects our feelings towards the people we are with and

the situation we are in. Body language messages are sent and received unconsciously and involuntarily. Their use varies somewhat from country to country – and even within a country – but their basic principles are universal.

**Showing affinity** *This woman reveals that she prefers the man on her right by standing close to him. Her crossed arms and legs are defensive reactions to the other man's assertiveness.*

**Insecure moment** *To show that he is listening, this young man faces the speaker opposite him. By scratching his wrist, he may subconsciously be revealing that he is unsure of himself.*

**Meeting of personalities**
*We all establish an 'intimate zone' around us, and expect strangers to stay clear of it. A man who lives in the countryside (above left) is likely to establish a relatively large 'intimate zone' around him. When greeting a stranger, he extends his hand beyond the zone. In contrast, a city dweller (above right) keeps his arm much closer to his body when shaking hands – he is accustomed to being in crowds, and therefore maintains a much smaller 'intimate zone'.*

**Persuader** *As this man speaks, he also communicates through gestures: one foot forward (an interest in winning over his audience), a hand on his hip (confidence), and an open hand (a desire to appear honest).*

## TELL-TALE SIGNS OF A DELIBERATE LIE

ONLY THE MOST accomplished liars can lie with their bodies as well as with their words. When we lie, we instinctively begin to fidget; it is therefore much easier to lie over the telephone than in full view. The most reliable indicators of a lie are hand-to-face gestures. The neck rub, for example, is a sign of uncertainty. Eye and nose rubs can be unconscious bids to cover up words the brain knows are untrue. The eye rub also prevents eye contact. Of course, any of these gestures may also be used quite innocently.

The neck rub

The eye rub

The nose rub

**Outsider looking in** *Although this woman looks towards her companions, her legs point away, suggesting that she feels isolated. Her crossed arms confirm that she is withdrawn from the conversation.*

**Know-it-all** *By placing both hands behind his head and reclining, this man communicates his feelings of strong self-confidence and superiority.*

**Two of a kind** *This man and woman reveal the close bond between them by sitting within each other's intimate zones, pointing their legs towards each other, and adopting similar postures. Both react to what has just been said. By placing his hand on his chin he shows that he is thinking, while she places the tip of her glasses in her mouth to stall before making comment.*

# JUST PUT IT IN WRITING

### Sorting fact from legend in the origins of written language

WHO INVENTED WRITING? Each ancient culture had its own legends. Chinese characters go back at least as far as 2000 BC, and there are several accounts of their origins. One tradition claims that writing was a gift to the Emperor Yu from a magical tortoise that he had saved from drowning. Another has it that Huang Di, the Yellow Emperor, received the first script from a dragon. Or did Cang Jie, taking inspiration for his strokes from bird tracks, invent Chinese characters?

In lands where writing was practised only by priests, the written word was believed to have magical properties. Indeed, the invention of writing was often attributed to gods such as the Egyptian Thoth, the Babylonian Nebo and the Mayan Itzamna. In northern Europe, Odin was credited with the invention of runes. Muslims believe that Allah Himself taught Adam to write.

The facts are rather less mysterious. Archaeologists believe that writing was first devised by the Sumerians around 3500 BC. They used it for accounting and

**Pictogram** *This Chinese character means 'a money offering', and shows a man carrying strings of shells on a pole.*

record-keeping, and it was then adopted by priests and story-tellers. Early writing took the form of stylised pictures of everyday objects (pictograms), or symbols to help the reader recall information he had memorised (mnemonics). Examples of these can be found in the rock paintings of Palaeolithic man. This unsophisticated writing was open to misinterpretation, and gradually more complex systems developed using symbols for abstract ideas (ideograms).

Because these symbols represented the meanings of words, rather than their sounds, early writing had very little to do with spoken language. But eventually phonetic symbols, notating words' sounds, came into use. Alphabets are phonetic systems: each letter represents a single sound, but has no meaning in itself. The Greeks were the first to use an alphabet that included symbols for all the sounds in their language, including vowels.

The invention of writing is not just something of the ancient past. Over the last 200 years, entirely new scripts have been devised for African and American Indian spoken languages that have no tradition of writing. Some scripts, such as that created in the 1840s by John Evans for the North American Cree Indians, were created by missionaries who wished to spread their message through the written word. Others, such as Sierra Leone's Mende script invented by tailor Kisimi Kamala in the 1930s, were produced by native speakers keen to prove that they were every bit as clever as the colonists who had settled in their lands.

***Scribe of the gods*** *The Egyptian god Thoth shapes human destiny with the 'stylus of fate'. Thoth, often depicted with the head of an ibis, was believed to have invented writing.*

# THE KEY TO CUNEIFORM

*Daring and dedication unlocked the door to a centuries-old script*

HENRY CRESWICKE Rawlinson held his breath and eased his way onto the topmost rung. With his ladder balanced precariously on the narrowest of ledges and a 300 m (1000 ft) drop below him, there was no room for error. Stretching up against the smooth rock, he used his left hand to support himself and his notebook, while his right hand slowly and meticulously began to copy the strange inscriptions.

Day after day, the Englishman clambered up the sheer rock face at Behistun in Iran, copying all the characters within reach. When he could no longer reach the inscriptions and despaired of success, a 'wild Kurdish boy' offered to help – scaling the rock like a monkey and copying the text for him.

### Soldier scholar

Rawlinson, who went to Iran in 1835 as military adviser to the Shah's brother, knew Persian, Arabic and Hindustani as well as Greek and Latin. He was also a fine athlete and soldier. Few men were ever better prepared to risk their lives in the pursuit of knowledge. But what was so fascinating about Behistun?

The inscriptions on the rock face at Behistun are written in an ancient wedge-shaped script – called cuneiform from the Latin *cuneus*, or 'wedge' – that has not been used since the first century AD. Like our own alphabet,

cuneiform was used to write more than one language. Rawlinson, along with other European scholars, was determined to find the key to its decipherment.

A few words in Old Persian cuneiform were already known. Ancient Roman and Persian texts provided the names of kings, and scholars had identified these in cuneiform characters, which were then used to work out other words. But most of the characters remained undeciphered, and reading cuneiform was like doing a giant jigsaw puzzle with most of the pieces missing.

The Behistun inscription, however, contained the names of more people and places than any other cuneiform text then known. It recounted the assumption of the Persian throne by Darius I in 522 BC, and this narrative text helped Rawlinson to understand the grammar of Old Persian. And there was a bonus: the rock face at Behistun provided the same text in three languages. Once the Old Persian text was understood, it was

***Lasting triumph*** *The basrelief and text at Behistun celebrate the 6th-century BC victory of Persian King Darius I over a usurper.*

used to decipher the accompanying Elamite and Babylonian texts. Rawlinson's exploits had borne fruit: by 1850, three languages that had seemed lost for all time could be read, yielding the history and literature of their peoples.

---

## SPELLING OUT OUR ABC

WE OFTEN say that things are 'as easy as ABC', but if it hadn't been for the Phoenicians, we might not have an alphabet at all. And without the ancient Greeks – who adapted the Phoenician alphabet before passing it on to us – all our letters would be back to front.

It is thought that the Greeks first encountered the alphabet around 1000 BC

Phoenician    Classical Greek    Latin

through trade with the Phoenicians, who inhabited what is now Lebanon. The Phoenicians wrote from right to left. When the Greeks borrowed their script, they experimented with boustrophedon (meaning 'plough-wise') writing: changing direction line by line, like an ox pulling a plough. Eventually, the Greeks settled on writing from left to right, and so their letters were mirror images of the Phoenician originals.

To adapt the alphabet to their own needs, the Greeks had to use some of the Phoenician letters in a different way. The Phoenicians only wrote down their

***To the letter*** *The Greeks reversed the shape of Phoenician letters when adapting them for their Classical alphabet, the forebear of our own Latin alphabet.*

consonants, leaving the reader to fill in the vowel sounds. But vowels had a far greater significance in Greek – for example, certain words could only be distinguished from others by placing the correct vowel at the beginning.

### Spare letters

Fortunately, Phoenician had several letters for consonant sounds that were not used in the Greek language, so the Greeks used these letters for vowels. The order of the Phoenician alphabet was, by and large, kept on, as were most of the names of the letters: *aleph*, *beth* and *gimel*, for example, became *alpha*, *beta* and *gamma*. The Romans, in turn, adapted the Greek alphabet for the Latin language, and are responsible for the shape of the alphabet as we know it today.

## FIRST IMPRESSIONS

JOHANN GUTENBERG, a 15th-century German goldsmith, was the European inventor of moveable type, the reusable letters that were assembled in rows to print books until recently. But a Chinese inventor, Bi Sheng, actually invented moveable type, using ceramic characters, in the 1040s. This system was abandoned, however, because Chinese books require many thousands of characters – it was simpler to print each page from a wood-block carved with the desired text than to locate and arrange all the ceramic pieces of type needed.

Gutenberg probably knew nothing of Bi Sheng's experiments, and can therefore be credited with independently inventing moveable type. Until the 1450s, all European books were either copied by hand, or printed from wood-blocks carved with the text of an entire page. Both methods were extremely time-consuming, and books were therefore very expensive.

Gutenberg realised that, as Western languages use only the relatively few letters of our alphabet, he could quickly assemble entire pages of words with separate letters of type that could be used again and again. Wooden type

would have to be laboriously carved by hand, and would wear out, but if the characters were made of metal, each letter could be cast many times in moulds and would last indefinitely.

Here Gutenberg's skills as a goldsmith came in. He succeeded in finding a hard-wearing alloy for the type, and in casting each letter with the precision required for a clear impression.

He also converted the traditional German winepress into a printing press, so that pressure could be applied evenly over the entire page. The effect of Gutenberg's technology was revolutionary: books could now be printed cheaply and in great numbers. By the end of the 15th century, 40 000 different editions of books had been printed in Europe.

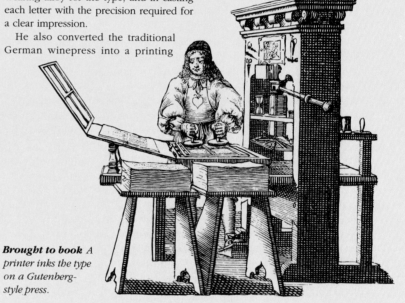

***Brought to book*** *A printer inks the type on a Gutenberg-style press.*

# GLORIOUS REMNANTS OF A DEFEATED PEOPLE
## *How a crusading missionary unwittingly preserved the secret of Maya glyphs*

DIEGO DE LANDA, a Spanish missionary among Mexico's Maya people, was contemptuous of native culture and beliefs. After arriving in the New World in 1549, he ordered Maya books burned, and flogged or imprisoned any natives who would not abandon paganism and embrace

***Maya ritual*** *The glyphs on the border of this Maya stone monument describe the ceremonial adornment of a lord, 'Jaguar Claw', possibly in preparation for sacrifice.*

Christianity. Yet, ironically, Landa preserved the only key to the decipherment of Maya writing.

Landa was a severe man – in fact, his suppression of the Maya faith was so violent that he was recalled to Spain and put on trial. Determined to convince the court that, despite his repressive measures, he actually had some respect for the Maya way of life, in 1566 he published his detailed observations of Maya customs and culture, including their form of writing, glyphs. That book is today the only source scholars have for translating the glyphs: although Maya is still spoken by some four million people, the written tradition has died.

Landa supposed that the glyphs were an alphabet, and asked a Maya informant to provide a glyph for each Spanish letter. Subsequent scholars soon realised that Maya does not have

an alphabet, but, in the 1950s, a young Russian scholar called Yuri Knorozov took a fresh look at Landa's discredited work. He had a hunch that, as Landa would have pronounced each letter in Spanish ('ah', 'bay', 'say' etc), the glyphs in Landa's text actually represented entire syllables. Applying this theory, Knorozov was able to decipher many words still recognisable in the Maya language as it is spoken today.

Unfortunately, Maya writing is very complex. Some glyphs are not syllables but 'logographs' – stylised word-pictures – and there is often more than one way to write a given word, so the meaning of many glyphs remains a mystery. Nonetheless, by reading the glyphs already deciphered, historians have uncovered much information about ancient Maya rulers and their conquests, and about Maya culture.

In 1573, Landa returned to Mexico a bishop. His book had not only won him his acquittal, but it also preserved for posterity the culture of which he so strongly disapproved.

# CATCHING UP WITH THE NEWS

*How our thirst for information was slowly quenched*

**M**OST PEOPLE would not associate Julius Caesar with the birth of newspapers, but it was he who introduced the earliest known official written news as far back as 59 BC. The *Acta Diurna* (Daily News) was a handwritten newssheet, posted daily in the Forum of Rome and in other prominent places within the city.

The *Acta Diurna*'s contents would not have been out of place in a modern newspaper. News ranged from accounts of battles, naval and military appointments, and political events, to a social diary announcing the latest births, deaths and marriages. Readers could check up on the result of a gladiatorial contest or even read about the fall of a meteorite. Citizens in distant parts of the Roman Empire sent scribes to copy the news and send it back by letter. Some scribes earned extra money by circulating news to more than one client. Many of these scribes were slaves, and a few used the money they earned from copying news dispatches to buy their freedom.

*Oyez!* Town criers, such as this one from a 19th-century English magazine (above), used this call – meaning 'hear ye' – to draw people's attention to the latest news.

**Broadsheet news** *A macabre border adorns this partially handwritten bulletin (below) of the death toll from seven plagues in London between 1592 and 1665.*

## Yesterday's papers

After the *Diurna*'s demise, it was left to travellers – and, later, troubadours and town criers – to spread the news by word of mouth. Newspaper journalism as we know it had to wait until German goldsmith Johann Gutenberg invented the moveable type printing press in the 1450s. This made publishing far cheaper and quicker. Even so, there were no newspapers for another 150 years, when several appeared almost simultaneously. One of these was the *Aviso Relation oder Zeitung* (Relation or Message), published

weekly by the Duke of Wolfenbüttel, a German town, in 1609. Around the same time, other newspapers with the same title appeared in Strasbourg and Augsburg.

These true newspapers featured topical news stories and were printed weekly or daily. The majority of readers were merchants, anxious to learn of events elsewhere in Europe and overseas that might affect business. By the end of the 17th century, Germany boasted 30 daily newspapers, thus founding a tradition for numerous local dailies which continues today.

The very earliest newspapers are now long defunct, but in 1645 the Royal Swedish Academy of Letters started publishing a regular official government newspaper, *Post och Inrikes Tidninger*, which today is still rolling off the presses.

---

### DID YOU KNOW..?

*A MURDERER was caught by electric telegraph as early as New Year's Day, 1845. A woman was found dead in her home in Slough, and the suspect – John Tawell – was seen leaving and boarding a train for London. Fortunately, the world's first public telegraph service had been installed between Slough and London in 1843, so police were able to alert their colleagues in London. Police arrested him and he was subsequently tried, convicted and executed.*

183

# BANNED IN BOSTON

## The rise and fall of America's first newspaper

ON THURSDAY, September 25, 1690, Bostonians awoke to find their city the home of America's first newspaper. A somewhat reckless journalist, Benjamin Harris, aimed to publish his *Publick Occurrences Both Forreign and Domestick* monthly, 'or, if any Glut of Occurrences happen, oftener'. Unfortunately, his first issue turned out to be his last.

Harris had enjoyed a colourful life as a London bookseller of seditious pamphlets and editor of a political newspaper. In 1678, he helped to whip up anti-Catholic hysteria by giving exposure in his paper to a fabricated plot to slaughter Protestants and burn down London. This early example of gutter journalism led to his arrest. After his release, his offices were again raided by the authorities and Harris fled with his family to Boston (then America's largest city), where he set up a coffee-house, bookshop and publishing business.

### Wide-ranging news

*Publick Occurrences* was well-written and lively, containing news of a smallpox epidemic that had hit Boston, a suicide, two fires, atrocities committed by Indians in the French and Indian Wars, and unrest in Ireland. It was printed on three pages, with one page left blank so that readers could jot down updates and pass them on to distant friends and relatives. Unfortunately, the governor of Massachusetts was not impressed by Harris's journalistic skills, while the Puritan clergy were aghast at his racy account of French King Louis XIV's amorous indiscretions with the wife of a prince. After only four days, Harris was banned from publishing any further issues. For that reason, some historians challenge its claim to be the first American newspaper.

No successor appeared until April 24, 1704, when dour Scottish postmaster John Campbell produced his weekly *Boston News-Letter* – the first continuously published American newspaper and the only one in the Colonies for 15 years. It finally petered out during the War of Independence in 1776. As for Harris, he returned to England and faded into obscurity as a seller of dubious medicinal cures.

*Press and suppress* Comprising only three printed pages and measuring just 150 by 260 mm (6 by 10 in), America's first newspaper brought Bostonians no-nonsense stories in the modern news style. It carried both local and foreign news. But publisher Benjamin Harris's revelations upset the local authorities, who swiftly banned the paper by proclamation (inset) after the first issue.

### DID YOU KNOW..?

THE JAPANESE newspaper Yomiuri Shimbun, launched in 1874, has the world's highest circulation, with close to 14.5 million buyers daily. It reaches 38 per cent of Japan's 34 million households. Yomiuri means 'selling by reading out loud', which is how the earliest broadsheets were hawked in 17th-century Japan.

✳ ✳ ✳

THE ORIGIN of the word 'gazette' for a newspaper or journal comes from the Italian gazetta: this was a small copper coin that residents of Venice paid in 1563 to hear public readings of one of the earliest regularly issued newssheets.

# CHAPPE'S SIGNAL SUCCESS

*A French revolution in communications*

**W**AR IS a mother of invention, and this was certainly true in the French Revolutionary Wars when, in 1792, the new republic faced enemies on all sides in the form of the forces of Britain, Austria, Holland, Prussia and Spain. What the Revolutionary Government urgently needed were good lines of communication.

Claude Chappe, a priest and engineer, had invented an optical telegraph system in 1791, but had not been able to test it fully. However, his older brother, Ignace, was a member of the Revolutionary Legislature, and arranged for Claude's system to be given a trial. It turned out to be a breakthrough in high-speed communications.

The two brothers had a series of watchtowers built, 5–10 km (3–6 miles) apart. Each had a vertical mast topped with a horizontal beam, known as the regulator, which could also be held vertically or tilted at 45 degrees clockwise or anticlockwise. At each end of the regulator was a vertical arm known as the indicator. Using ropes, the regulator and indicators could be moved to form 49 easily-recognisable shapes. Chappe named his system 'semaphore', which comes from the Greek words meaning 'bearing a sign'.

### All along the watchtowers

Operators in each tower watched neighbouring towers through telescopes and passed on messages to the next one in the chain. The first line

*Code book Chappe's original drawings show some of the 49 positions employed in his signalling system. Each position represented a letter or a symbol in code.*

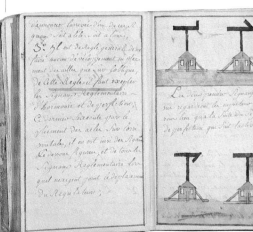

***Signs of the times***
*Claude Chappe demonstrates his two-armed telegraph system on a hilltop tower outside Paris in 1793.*

stretched 230 km (143 miles), from Paris to Lille, near the Austrian front. In August 1794, it conveyed the triumphant news of Napoleon's recapture of Le Quesnoy from the Austrians. Averaging three signals per minute, the good news was relayed in some 20 minutes – more than 90 times as fast as couriers on horseback.

The value of Chappe's semaphore was established, and it was adopted by countries as diverse as Russia, India and Egypt. Soon after Chappe's success, the British admiralty installed the first rival optical telegraph between London and the south coast, using six rotating shutters like venetian blinds. These were located at prominent points that are still named 'Telegraph' hills on modern maps.

By the time the electric telegraph had superseded Chappe's wooden signals some 60 years later, France alone had more than 550 semaphore stations, stretching 4800 km (3000 miles). Unfortunately, Chappe's system had drawbacks, such as the fact that it could not be used on a foggy day or during the night. Staff costs were high and it was also expensive to maintain and cumbersome to use. Criticism and claims by other engineers that they had invented the semaphore depressed Claude Chappe, and he committed suicide in 1805.

## DID YOU KNOW..?

*OCTOGENARIAN Dr Martha Voegli of Thun in Switzerland was amazed when the postman delivered a letter to her in 1978 – more than 27 years late. The letter was one of 60 contained in a small blue mailbag discovered by French gendarmerie recruits who were on a training exercise at 1200 m (4000 ft) on Mont Blanc's Bossons glacier. The bag had been part of a consignment of mail carried by the Malabar Princess, an Air India plane that crashed on the mountain in November 1950.*

\* \* \*

*THE HEAVIEST MAGAZINE on record ever to be published was the September 1989 edition of the American fashion magazine, Vogue. Its 808 pages weighed 1.51 kg (3 lb 5.4 oz).*

185

# FROM OUR OWN CORRESPONDENT

*How William Howard Russell's pen was mightier than the sword*

THE PROSE was anything but leaden: 'The silence is oppressive; between the cannon bursts one can hear the champing of bits and the clinks of sabres in the valley below.' This was how William Howard Russell described, for readers of *The Times* of London, the lull before the mayhem of the Charge of the Light Brigade in 1854. 'With a halo of flashing steel above their heads, and with a cheer that was many a noble fellow's death cry, they flew into the smoke of the batteries.'

### On the scene

Russell was the first accredited newspaper war correspondent. In the days before he was dispatched to cover the Crimean War of 1854–6, newspapers tended to compile war reports from letters sent by junior army officers, or from stories in foreign papers. In 1808, for example, *The Times* had sent a journalist to Spain to cover the Peninsular War, but he had not stayed long. Russell was not the only journalist on the Crimean scene, but he pieced together reliably accurate accounts of the fighting from confused eyewitness accounts.

'What has been the cost to the country,' he asked readers, '. . . of the men who died in their tents or in hospital of exhaustion, overwork, and deficient or improper nutriment?' Such dispatches, reporting the military command's gross mismanagement of medical supplies,

hospitals, food and clothing, were consistently supported in the editorial columns of *The Times* – the paper read by the government and the ruling and middle classes. The generals were accused of being preoccupied with petty rules and regulations instead of looking after their soldiers' welfare.

In January 1855, the government fell. Were Russell's reports to blame? Russell thought not, but the new Secretary for War made it clear to Russell that he was the culprit, and Prince Albert launched a furious counterattack on the 'miserable scribbler' to restore confidence in the establishment.

### A hero returns

But the truth in Russell's dispatches was indisputable, and he returned to England a popular hero. His vivid reports were backed by reliable facts and detailed descriptions. No one previously had provided such complete accounts of a war. Even a rival journalist in the Crimea, Edwin Lawrence Godkin, praised his influence: 'In his hands correspondence from the field really became a power before which generals began to quail.' As a result of Russell's reports, the army was comprehensively reorganised.

The war correspondent was now an unavoidable accessory to any military

*Eyewitness accounts William Howard Russell observes the scene of a battle during the Crimean War. He gathered information for his unprecedentedly vivid dispatches by talking to many soldiers and their officers.*

conflict. When the American Civil War broke out in 1861, just five years after the end of the Crimean War, no fewer than 500 war correspondents, Russell among them, turned out to report on it from the Northern side alone.

---

## FESSENDEN'S FESTIVE FEAT

IT WAS Christmas Eve, 1906. Sitting at his radio in mid-Atlantic, the ship's wireless operator could hardly believe his ears. Instead of Morse Code, he heard the strains of a violin, followed by a crackly voice that seemed to come from nowhere: 'If anybody hears me, please write to Mr Fessenden at Brant Rock.' The wireless operator had unwittingly tuned into the world's first broadcast of a programme of words and music.

Canadian-born Reginald Fessenden was a professor of electrical engineering and a prolific inventor with 500 patents to his credit. He invented 'radio telephony', which could broadcast words and music by using continuous waves of sound. This was quite different from Marconi's wireless telegraphy, which had been

demonstrated successfully in 1897, but which at the time could only transmit the dots and dashes of Morse code. By 1902, Fessenden had succeeded in using radio waves to broadcast the human voice across a distance of 1.6 km (1 mile).

### Professionals only

When Fessenden came to broadcast his 'show', the idea of voice transmission and broadcasting entertainment was unknown to the general public. His radio audience consisted of professional radio operators on board ships or at shore stations, monitoring navigation or military intelligence.

Fessenden's Christmas Eve concert was broadcast from a 128 m (420 ft) mast at Brant Rock, Massachusetts, and had a range of 320 km (200 miles). In it he

played the famous Largo from Handel's opera *Serse* on a phonograph – making him radio's first disc jockey – and a woman sang some festive carols.

Fessenden, and his broadcast, were well ahead of their time. The mass manufacture of radios did not begin until after the First World War, and the first radio broadcasting station – KDKA of Pittsburgh, Pennsylvania – did not come on the air until November 2, 1920. It was funded by Westinghouse, a manufacturer of radio sets. To promote the sale of radios, it broadcast both news and entertainment. KDKA still broadcasts to this day.

Fessenden himself went on to invent the radio compass, the sonic depth finder and signalling devices for submarines before his death in 1932 at the age of 65.

# SOUNDING RED ALERT

## *The telephone imagined to be an instrument of world destruction*

THE SCENARIO is not unfamiliar in screen dramas: deep inside the Pentagon (the United States's national military command centre), a red telephone sits on a table in a heavily guarded room. The telephone rings. The President of the United States of America picks it up and speaks directly to his Soviet opposite number. Their conversation is brief and to the point. The president puts the receiver down and presses the nuclear button. Civilisation as we know it disappears in a cloud of nuclear fallout.

This cinema image of the famous 'hot line' between the United States government and the Kremlin in Moscow is so well established that even Ronald Reagan once referred to a 'red telephone' while president. The reality, however, was quite different. The hot line was not a telephone connection at all, but a double satellite link that transmitted teleprinter messages, and, after 1984, fax messages as well.

### *Crisis contact*

Set up in the aftermath of the 1962 Cuban missile crisis, the hot line was designed to avert armed confrontation between the two superpowers. Precisely how many times the link was used since its inception is a closely guarded secret, but it is known to have been employed when Soviet troops marched into Afghanistan in 1979.

To rule out any possibility of distorted messages, the equipment was tested 24 times a day, with Americans and Russians taking it in turns to make neutral,

*Accuracy tests* Pentagon officials make regular checks on the American–Russian hot line for possible distortions.

unprovocative transmissions of, for example, the Professional Golfer's Association rule book, from America, and an encyclopedic account of women's hairstyles in Russia during the 17th century.

The message that most mystified the Russians, however, was one sent by the Americans on the day the hot line opened in 1963. In those tense Cold War days, the transmission that had Moscow's cipher experts working overtime was: 'The quick brown fox jumps over the lazy dog. 1234567890.'

*Hot line to Moscow* In the film Doctor Strangelove, *Peter Sellers, as the President of the United States, talks to the Russian premier, while the Russian ambassador (played by Peter Bull) listens in.*

187

## BIG BROTHER'S WHISPERS

IS A MESSAGE more powerful when we are not consciously aware that we have received it? Instead of displaying the customary notices warning that shoplifters will be prosecuted, a number of American department stores have taken to playing background music tapes interspersed with whispered exhortations to be honest. These are broadcast at such a low volume that the customers do not consciously hear them: they are subliminal, just at the threshold of normal human hearing. In some cases, the resulting reduction in theft has been dramatic.

Advertisers have been tempted to exploit the fact that people can absorb subliminal messages ever since the early 1950s.

The theory is that if you can penetrate the subconscious of your target audience, it cannot put up any rational resistance to your sales pressure.

The most publicised examples of subliminal advertising have so far been visual ones, where an image is displayed on a cinema or television screen for a fraction of a second. This kind of advertising attracted public attention for the first time in 1956, when it was learned that a New Jersey cinema had been showing subliminal advertisements for Coca-Cola.

Since that time the subject has raised its head periodically, caused a new outburst of moral indignation and then been forgotten again. In 1971, a gin manufacturer

was accused of artfully concealing the word 'sex' in the ice cubes illustrating an advert in an American magazine. This technique, known as 'embedding', is said to be commonplace, but no one knows how many people respond to such hidden messages.

Fears of brainwashing and pernicious political indoctrination have led several countries to ban subliminal advertising on the screen, but research into its effectiveness has been inconclusive. In the case of the notorious Coca-Cola advertisements, it was reported that sales of all soft drinks went up slightly after they were shown; apparently they triggered the audience's thirst without achieving the desired brand loyalty.

# LONG-DISTANCE INFORMATION

*How African musicians have transposed their languages into drumbeats*

THE DRUMS in many parts of Africa really do talk. Two drummers, separated by up to 32 km (20 miles), can hold a genuine conversation, reproducing in drumbeats the actual words of the language of their tribe. In Ghana, the range of this traditional form of communication has been extended by modern technology: radio news bulletins are introduced by the drummed message 'Ghana listen . . . Ghana listen'.

It is along the 'Bend' of West Africa, in countries such as Ghana, Benin and Nigeria, that the use of talking drums is most highly developed. Many of the languages spoken there are

'tonal': each syllable of a word is given a musical pitch, and the drummers can replicate both the pitches and the rhythms of each word on their instruments. It is therefore important that a drummer has a highly developed sense of pitch. It would be impossible to drum a message in a non-tonal language like English, because all the listener would hear would be the number of syllables in the message and their rhythm.

The most celebrated talking drummers of West Africa are the Yorubas, whose principal instrument is the hourglass-shaped drum known as a *dondon*. It is held under the arm and struck

with a hammer-shaped stick. In order to raise the pitch of the drum, the player exerts pressure on the leather strings running lengthways down the side; this tightens the skin of the drumhead. Slit-drums, shaped from hollowed-out logs, are widely used for telegraphic purposes among the Bantu peoples of Zaire and southern Africa.

Drums play a central role in African cultural and social life, and talking drums have many uses besides the sending of long-distance messages. During solemn rituals, they may play a hymn to a tribal deity or a song honouring a great chief; and, on more

**Musical message** *Talking drums, including dondons (on the right and far left), are used to comment on dancing during wedding celebrations in Tamale, Ghana.*

festive occasions, they can be used to make playful comments on the quality of the dancing or even to encourage the participants in a wrestling match. In some societies, notably the Mossi people of Burkina Faso, talking drums are the means of preserving the history of the tribe, which has been handed down in the form of epic drum narratives by successive generations of skilled musicians.

# A MYTH GOES UP IN SMOKE
### *The disappointing truth about Indian smoke signals*

M ANY PEOPLE, after watching Westerns as children, grow up believing that American Indians could communicate with smoke signals almost as easily as people nowadays talk over the telephone. Sadly, the idea that the individual puffs of smoke spelled out complex messages is a typical piece of Hollywood exaggeration.

Smoke signals were indeed used, especially among the seminomadic tribes of the Great Plains. But their content was limited to a few simple messages whose meaning had been agreed in advance. Returning Piman warriors in Arizona, for example, might signal the end of a successful raid by sending up a

---

### DID YOU KNOW..?

*PEOPLE WHO are accustomed to hearing the talking drums of West Africa can instantly recognise a particular drummer's nuances, in the same way that speakers can be identified by the sound of their voices.*

---

***Distant puffs*** *Despite his reputation for accuracy, this painting by 19th-century American Frederic Remington exaggerates the sophistication of smoke signal messages.*

column of smoke, and the village would reply with two columns of smoke.

Fires were fed with damp grass or boughs of evergreen and, although there are accounts of Indians using blankets to punctuate their signals, one or two simple, unbroken columns of smoke were normally all that was needed to send a message. It was the place the signal came from – whether, for example, the fire was on a hilltop or in a valley – that conveyed most of its meaning. When Apaches out hunting spotted another group of Indians in the distance, they lit a fire conspicuously to the right of their own party, which meant 'Who are you?'. The others, if they were friends, would then use a prearranged reply. Smoke signals were most commonly used to broadcast news of victory in battle, or to warn of sickness in a camp or dangers such as approaching enemies.

---

# MANY SHADES OF MEANING
### *What is the colour of happiness?*

I N WESTERN countries, red is for danger. Red is the colour of blood, the colour of fire and the colour of passion. It is the colour used for stop signs and traffic lights. It is also the colour of Mars, the Roman god of war. Red is the colour of anger – 'I saw red!' – and redheads are believed to have fiery tempers. But in China, red is the colour of happiness.

Colours mean different things to different cultures. In the West, black is the colour of mourning, and white is traditionally worn by brides; in China, the colour of mourning is white. In Europe, royalty is said to be 'blue-blooded'; in Malaysia, royal blood is white.

### *Compass colours*
Among the Pueblo Indians in the United States, colours are associated with the points of the compass. East is linked with white, north with yellow, west with blue, and south with red. The Cherokees associate abstract properties as well as direction with colours: success comes from the east and is red, the north is blue and means trouble, the black west is death, and the happy south is white.

For Westerners, blue is generally a happy colour (unless you have 'the blues'); it is associated with heaven, fidelity and peace. But the strongest curse of the Yezidis of the Caucasus and Armenia, who detest blue, is: 'May you die in blue garments!'

***Sad march*** *Mourners in a procession on Hong Kong's Cheung Chau Island are dressed in white, the colour traditionally worn at funerals in China.*

# FIERY WONDERS OF THE WORLD

*The towering beacons that warn seamen of danger*

DESIGNED to provide ships with a reference point, or to warn of dangerous rocks or currents, in ancient times lighthouses were simply beacons lit on high ground. But by the time of the great Greek and Roman civilisations, lighthouses were towering landmarks often associated with great cities or even empires. One such was the massive Pharos of Alexandria on the shores of the Mediterranean in Egypt. One of the Seven Wonders of the ancient world, it was built in about 280 BC of white marble and was 120 m (400 ft) high, and the fire kept beaming on its summit was said to be visible for 55 km (35 miles).

Light for the Pharos came from a fire in a metal basket, fuelled by wood carried up spiral ramps in horse-drawn carts and then hoisted to the very top with pulleys. The lighthouse's image can be found on many ancient coins and medals struck at the mint of Alexandria, and it survived for at least a millennium, although it was badly damaged by an earthquake in 796. Its foundations can still be seen today.

About the first century AD, candles and oil lamps began to be used to provide lighthouses' illumination. Today they are lit electrically or by gas flame. The colour and pattern of each lighthouse's flashing makes it distinctive to shipping.

Since 1948, the Dominican Republic has been building what it hopes will be considered a wonder of the modern world, a lighthouse memorial to the explorer Christopher Columbus. To survive the hurricanes and earthquakes common in the Caribbean, it will not be a spindly tower, but rather an enormous recumbent cross,

*Helping hand Lighthouses, such as this one on Anacapa Island, California, are an important aid to seamen, highlighting dangerous rocks and providing landmarks.*

some 1200 m (4000 ft) long and 35 m (120 ft) high. The leaders of this impoverished country opened the building in 1992, the 500th anniversary of Columbus's discovery of the island.

But many Dominicans believe that Christopher Columbus carries a *fucú*, or curse, and it seems that the *fucú* played its part in the building of the Columbus Memorial Lighthouse, which was designed by a British architect in 1929. At the ground-breaking ceremony, in 1948, the explosion used to move the first sod detonated prematurely, destroying an official's car. The US bank in which the architect's fee was deposited went bust, and years later his family received only a few dollars of the original $10 000 fee.

*Memorial to Columbus This hurricane-proof lighthouse in the Dominican Republic, opened in 1992 with the hope that it becomes a major tourist attraction.*

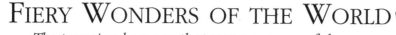

# INTRIGUE AND DECEPTION

*The real life of Sidney Reilly, master spy*

I N THE MURKY WORLD of espionage, Sidney Reilly stands out as a figure of extraordinary ambition. He aimed at no less a goal than the overthrow of communist power in Russia – and, by his own account, nearly succeeded.

The name Reilly was in fact only one of his many aliases – others included 'Comrade Relinsky', 'Georg Bergmann' or 'Monsieur Massimo'. He was born Sigmund Rosenblum in the Black Sea port of Odessa in 1874. He took the name Reilly from his first wife, Margaret Reilly Callaghan. He later claimed to be the illegitimate son of an Irish sea captain, but this was pure myth.

Unscrupulous in business and love, by the time of the First World War Reilly was operating as an arms dealer in New York, married bigamously to a second 'wife', Nadine. After the Bolshevik Revolution of November 1917, he was recruited by the British intelligence service to go to Russia to destabilise the government of Lenin and Trotsky.

### A tangled web of deceit

Arriving in Petrograd in the spring of 1918, he wove a fantastically complex web of conspiracy. Having established his cover as a Bolshevik sympathiser, he ingeniously managed to obtain papers that gave him the identity of a plain-clothes member of the *Cheka* – the Bolshevik secret police. At the same time, he plotted with disaffected elements in Lenin's Latvian guards to arrest the Bolshevik leaders – they were to be marched trouserless through the streets of the city – and establish an alternative government. Reilly believed that this plot might easily have worked; he later wrote: 'I had been within an ace of becoming master of Russia.'

But an attempt on Lenin's life by an anti-Bolshevik assassin, Dora Kaplan, on August 31, 1918, provoked investigations and arrests by Lenin's secret police. Reilly escaped by fleeing across the Baltic to Sweden on board a Dutch merchant ship. He was sentenced to death in absentia by a Soviet court.

The British intelligence service dropped Reilly from their ranks, but he remained obsessed with the overthrow of the Soviet government. In the 1920s, he became involved with an anti-government organisation inside the Soviet Union called 'the Trust'. On September 25, 1925, he clandestinely crossed the border from Finland into the Soviet Union to contact the leaders of the Trust in Moscow, not realising that it had been penetrated by the secret police. His every movement was watched. Unwittingly he talked freely to Soviet double agents. It was the end for Reilly – soon after entering the country he was arrested and shot.

# THE REAL MATA HARI

*The truth behind the legend of the female master spy*

I N JULY 1917, at the height of the First World War, Margaretha Geertruida Zelle, alias Mata Hari, went on trial for her life before a military tribunal in Paris. She was accused of having passed French military secrets to the German enemy – secrets so vital they had cost no less than 50 000 French lives, the prosecutor claimed. As a sensational tale of sex and espionage unfolded before the court, Margaretha's anguished declarations of innocence fell on deaf ears. The tribunal had no hesitation in pronouncing her guilty and sentencing her to death by firing squad.

### Dancing into danger

Yet the facts of Margaretha's life suggest she was more a harmless, bewildered victim of circumstance than a dangerous secret agent. Born in the Netherlands in 1876, she married a Dutch Army officer when she was 19 and lived for a time in Java and Sumatra. In 1905, back in Europe and separated from her husband, she embarked on a career as an oriental dancer, first under the name of Lady MacLeod and then as Mata Hari – a Malay expression meaning 'the eye of the day'.

Mata Hari was soon famous throughout the continent, not so much for the quality of her dancing as for her readiness to perform virtually naked on the stage. She acquired a string of lovers of various nationalities in the highest military and political circles, including Crown Prince Wilhelm, heir to the German throne.

After the First World War broke out in 1914, her international contacts made her a tempting target for spymasters looking to recruit agents. By this time down on her luck, she accepted money from both the German and French intelligence services. But she proved a hopeless secret agent. There is no evidence that either side ever got any worthwhile information out of her. Eventually, tired of paying money for nothing, the Germans deliberately allowed the French to discover her duplicity.

Although some of France's most influential men – many of whom were Margaretha's ex-lovers – appealed on her behalf, she was executed at Vincennes on October 15, 1917. Her unconcerned behaviour in the face of death fed the Mata Hari myth. Salacious journalists dwelt upon the black silk stockings and fur-trimmed cloak she insisted on wearing for the execution. As she courageously refused to be blindfolded, the story was put about that she believed one of her high-placed lovers had ordered the rifles to be loaded with blanks.

191

# INFIDEL INFILTRATOR

### The Swiss adventurer who rediscovered the lost city of Petra

IN 1809, Johann Ludwig Burckhardt, the son of a Swiss officer serving in Napoleon's Imperial Army, embarked for the Middle East to explore the hidden heart of the Islamic world. The Arab-ruled deserts and holy cities had been closed to Christian infidels for over a thousand years. The only way to penetrate them was to assume a Muslim identity. Burckhardt had learned Arabic and, arriving in Aleppo, adopted Arab dress and passed himself off as a Muslim trader, Ibrahim ibn Abdallah.

Ibrahim explained his strange accent in Arabic by claiming to be of Indian origin. When asked to speak Hindustani, Burckhardt rattled away in his native Swiss German, which fully satisfied his Arab listeners.

### Desert ruins

Burckhardt sustained his assumed identity for eight years, having many adventures, the most famous of which was the discovery of the lost city of Petra. This once flourishing capital of the Arab kingdom of the Nabataeans had gradually declined after its capture by the Romans in 106 AD. It was in Amman (now the capital of Jordan) that Burckhardt first heard tell of the magnificent ruined city in the desert, rumoured to hold a hidden treasure. No stranger was allowed to approach it by the desert tribesmen. But Burckhardt – or rather, Ibrahim ibn Abdallah – claimed a desire to sacrifice at a nearby Muslim holy place, the tomb of Aaron. Permission for such a sacred pilgrimage could not be refused.

Burckhardt progressed towards the lost city across the desert and the red

**Going native** In 1809, Swiss traveller Johann Ludwig Burkhardt donned Arab dress and embarked on a remarkable journey to sacred Arab sites, hitherto unseen by non-Muslims.

sandstone mountains, accompanied by suspicious guides. He kept notes furtively, writing under his loose Arab clothes. Had his true identity been discovered, his guides would certainly have killed him. On August 22, 1812, Burckhardt reached the awesome ruins through a cleft in the mountains. Cut into the red and ochre sandstone cliffs were nearly a thousand temples, tombs and monuments, with carvings of eagles and strange beasts, and black stones sacred to the sun god Dushara. Burckhardt's were the first Western eyes to enjoy this overwhelming sight since the time of the Roman Empire.

Burckhardt returned unscathed from his journey to Petra and went on to make the pilgrimage to Mecca in 1814.

**Sandstone city** In the ancient Arab city of Petra, in present-day Jordan, the Treasury, built after the Romans conquered the city in 106 AD, is one of the city's finest monuments.

He was the first infidel to enter the holiest city of Islam, his disguise by now impenetrable. By the time he died of dysentery in Cairo in 1817, Burckhardt's new identity had almost taken over his life. At his own request, he was buried in a Muslim cemetery. The name marked on his tombstone was Pilgrim Ibrahim ibn Abdallah.

### DID YOU KNOW..?

*POPULAR MYTH has it that an urn on top of the Treasury building in Petra contains great riches. Over the years treasure-seekers have tried and failed to shoot the urn down, leaving it pitted with bullet holes.*

# chapter seven

# The
# ADVENTURE
## *of*
# INVENTION

NO ONE CAN predict what fruits may eventually come of an inventor's unfettered imagination. Some 250 years ago, Parisians marvelled at a mechanical duck that rose upon its legs and even took food from people's hands (*page 201*). Today, the robot 'Manny', a distant relative of that whimsical duck, performs a deadly serious task: testing clothing against chemical weapons for the US Army (*page 202*). So even a seemingly useless or impractical invention may be a trailblazer for important and beneficial technology.

# OPPOSING CURRENTS OF THOUGHT

*How Nikola Tesla rather than Thomas Edison saw the way to develop electricity*

ONE OF Thomas Edison's most celebrated inventions was the electric light bulb, and his part in making electricity the principal form of industrial and domestic power is justly famous. But if Edison had had his way over how the new form of power should be distributed, the electricity supply industry would have been put back by many years. Edison was the champion of direct current, which, like the electricity from a battery, is a current of electrons flowing in one direction only. Alternating current, the form in which electricity comes from the mains supply today, flows for a fraction of a second first in one direction and then in the other. Chief among the advocates of alternating current was a Serbian-American inventor, Nikola Tesla.

When he arrived in America in 1884, Tesla was an admirer of Edison and even redesigned the dynamos that generated direct-current electricity for Edison's company. But Tesla was convinced of the superiority of alternating current. The lower the voltage at which electricity is

***Friend and foe*** *Tesla, shown sitting near his machine for generating artificial lightning, worked for Edison before becoming his rival.*

***Battle of the currents*** *Edison invited the press to witness dogs and cats being electrocuted by alternating current to prove that it was inherently dangerous.*

transmitted, the more power is lost along the cable that conducts it. Direct current was generated at low voltage; therefore, much power would be lost transmitting it over great distances.

Tesla recognised that alternating current, unlike direct current, could be generated at a low voltage and 'stepped up' by transformer to a high voltage for efficient transmission over very long distances. It could then be 'stepped down' by transformers in local sub-stations to a low voltage suitable for use in the home. He fell out with Edison after a year, and, in 1888, teamed up with an industrialist, George Westinghouse, to put his system of alternating-current dynamos to practical use. So began the 'battle of the currents'.

Edison exploited the public's ignorance and fears about electricity in his campaign against his rivals' system. Intent to show that alternating current was dangerous and unsuitable for the home, he even had one of his agents purchase Westinghouse dynamos and sell them on to prison authorities to provide the current for the first electric chairs. This underhand manoeuvre backfired badly – in 1890, the first man to go to the electric chair took eight minutes to die because the executioners had not delivered enough electricity. What kills people is the strength of a current; it makes no difference whether it is alternating current or direct.

It was soon realised that the transmission of high-voltage alternating current could be made safe by building power lines well out of human reach. Recognition of the superiority of Tesla's system came in 1893, when Westinghouse won the contract to build the first large-scale hydroelectric generating plant, at Niagara Falls, New York.

# PATENT GENIUS

*Successes and failures of a great inventor*

THOMAS EDISON was almost certainly the most prolific inventor of all time. He is best remembered for three inventions: the incandescent lamp, the kinetoscope (peep-show ancestor of the cinema) and the phonograph. But in a long life, lasting from 1847 to 1931, he patented more than 1300 inventions in the United States and abroad. At the height of his powers, in the 1880s, he was filing a patent every five days on average.

Needless to say, not all his ideas were successful. His first patented invention, devised in 1868, was an electric system to speed up the cumbersome process of recording votes in the United States Congress. Each Congressman was to be provided with 'yes' and 'no' buttons linked to an automatic central display. This eminently sensible system worked – but Congress was hostile to the innovation and declined to buy it.

### Word power

One of Edison's most bizarre ideas was the phonomotor, a spin-off from his famous phonograph. This 'vocal engine' attempted to harness the energy of sound vibrations from the human voice to drive machinery. Thus a sewing machine would be powered, not by a pedal or electricity, but by the seamstress talking in a loud voice. However, the device proved impractical.

Also related to the phonograph were the talking dolls made in the 1880s. Each tin doll contained a small phonographic cylinder with a recording of a nursery rhyme or other text, operated by turning a key.

When Edison focused his attention on the building industry in 1908, he was, as usual, startlingly innovative. He proposed replacing slum tenements with cheap new housing using concrete. Each house would be made in one piece, by simply pouring concrete into an iron mould – the whole process taking only three hours. Edison's proposal was much ridiculed, but he proved it actually could be done by casting a concrete house himself. While the use of concrete in buildings continued to increase throughout the early 20th century, Edison's single mould houses did not catch on.

*Edison's electric pen This device, imitated by many competitors, could make up to 3000 copies of handwritten documents. It was powered by a Bunsen battery (the two glass jars). The pen's vibrating needle perforated a sheet of tough paper with thousands of tiny holes. The sheet was then used as a stencil.*

His curiosity stretched beyond the bounds of the material world. In his later years, spurred on by the millions who had lost relations in the First World War, he applied his skills to attempts to contact the dead. Sceptical of ouija boards and other standard spiritualist equipment, he sought to invent a machine to amplify whatever weak vibrations might emanate from beyond the grave. Unfortunately, this last quest of the great inventor's lifetime proved a failure.

---

## PROFIT ON THE LINE

EDISON was not only a great inventor, but an inspired businessman. His entrepreneurial talent first showed itself about the age of 12, when he obtained the concession to sell newspapers and confectionery on the train running between Port Huron and Detroit, Michigan.

His profit on newspapers depended on exactly matching supply to demand. So, with characteristic enterprise, he persuaded a friend who worked on the *Detroit Free Press* to show him proofs of the lead stories in advance, so he could estimate the probable level of public interest and thus sales for the day.

His greatest triumph as a newsboy came in April 1862, when the first accounts of the bloody Civil War battle of Shiloh hit the headlines. Seeing the chance to make money, Edison bought 1000 copies of the *Detroit Free Press* on credit and arranged for news of the battle to be telegraphed up the line ahead of the train and posted in the stations.

Word spread fast through each small town and crowds packed the stations, frantic to read more details of the fighting when the newspapers arrived. Edison was able not only to sell all 1000 copies, but to hike up the price considerably as he went along.

Not content with selling newspapers, Edison moved into journalism, setting up a printing press in the train's baggage compartment to produce his own local newssheet, the *Grand Trunk Herald*. Retailing at three cents, it rose to a circulation of about 700 – the first newspaper ever printed on a train.

Edison finally overreached himself, however, by setting up a chemical laboratory in the baggage car where he would experiment in his spare time. When one of his experiments caused a fire, both he and his equipment were unceremoniously thrown off the train.

## GERM-PHOBIA AND DEATH RAYS

IN THE scientific world, Nikola Tesla is remembered principally for his work on the rotating magnetic field, which made possible the alternating-current generators that supply most of the world with electricity today. In honour of this achievement a scientific unit was named after him. The 'tesla' does not often crop up in layman's conversation, however, as it is used to calculate the force of a magnetic field. His name is also immortalised in the Tesla coil, a device that allows a transformer to generate high frequency current at a very high voltage. It is still used in televisions, radios and other modern electronic devices. He invented the coil in the course of his work on alternating current in 1891.

In later years Tesla was something of a solitary eccentric, often to be seen walking to the New York Public Library from his hotel, where his room had to serve as his laboratory. Although he developed a phobia for germs, it appears he did not suspect the city's pigeons of being carriers of disease; watching and feeding them were his greatest pleasures in life.

### Peacemaking weapon

Occasionally Tesla would emerge from his hotel-room with announcements of discoveries and inventions that people found increasingly hard to take seriously. In 1934, for example, he told the press that he had devised a deathray. This was to be the ultimate deterrent that would put an end to war. It consisted of a beam of high-velocity particles that would destroy squadrons of enemy aircraft at a range of 400 km (250 miles). The details of this weapon were never disclosed.

# SHAKING THE BIG APPLE TO THE CORE

*Tesla's demonstrations of the power of resonance*

THE EARTH and everything on it vibrate naturally, and when an external wavelike force is applied at the same frequency as this natural vibration, powerful, and potentially dangerous, sympathetic resonances can build up. Nikola Tesla was fascinated by the extraordinary power of all forms of invisible energy, and, in 1898, he conducted experiments, largely for his own amusement, which exploited the Earth's natural resonance.

When Tesla attached a small oscillator – a device for generating vibrations – to one of the iron pillars supporting the building that housed his New York laboratory, he expected the resonance to be transferred to nearby objects in the room. At first the oscillator seemed to be having hardly any effect. Little did he realise that in several surrounding blocks of Manhattan, the inhabitants were experiencing what appeared to be a major earthquake – complete with trembling buildings, falling plaster and shattered windows.

### Knock-on effect

The vibrations had travelled down through the iron frame of the building into the layer of sand on which Manhattan is built. Sand is a particularly effective transmitter of vibrations, and a powerful resonance had been set up in other buildings before it was felt in Tesla's own.

### Disturbing the peace

When Tesla finally felt his own workshop beginning to tremble, he knew it was time to stop. The oscillator was powered by compressed air, and rather than waste time disconnecting the pressurised tanks, Tesla decided it would be better to destroy the machine with a sledgehammer. Just as he was doing so, the police, who were familiar with Tesla's eccentric ways, arrived to see if he was, as they suspected, the cause of the panic on the streets outside.

On another occasion, the irresponsible inventor attached a similar device to the skeleton of a building under construction in New York's financial district, omitting to inform the men working up above on the steel girders. The workmen descended in a state of panic, and once more the police were required to intervene.

Tesla claimed that, given the opportunity, he could flatten Brooklyn Bridge with his tiny oscillator. He also said that, given the time and a reasonable supply of dynamite, he could exploit the natural vibrations of the whole Earth to split the planet in two.

# WIRELESS FOR THE WORLD
*A radio station half a century ahead of its time*

ON DECEMBER 12, 1901, the historic day on which the Italian inventor Guglielmo Marconi transmitted the letter 's' in Morse code from Cornwall to Newfoundland, Nikola Tesla was working on a far more ambitious application of wireless telegraphy. His 'World Broadcasting System' was not going to be limited to sending messages in Morse code: he intended it to link all the world's telephone and telegraph systems and broadcast stock exchange prices and weather reports round the globe. With his remarkable understanding of the potential of radio waves, he foresaw the use of radio for entertainment and predicted such futuristic wonders as television, letters delivered from terminal to terminal in the manner of today's electronic mail, and the faxing of photographic images through the air.

When Tesla heard the news of Marconi's triumph, he was unconcerned, remarking dismissively to a friend, 'Marconi is a good fellow. Let him continue. He is using 17 of my patents.' Tesla's own broadcasting service was to be coordinated from a futuristic tower that he was having built on the coast of Long Island. Between 1901 and 1903, thanks to the generous support of the financier J. Pierpont Morgan, the tower – a wooden structure 57 m (187 ft) high crowned with a wide copper dome, giving it the appearance of a gigantic mushroom – was actually built. But at that point the money ran out, and the tower stood as a forlorn monument to Tesla's genius until the First World War, when it was pulled down.

### Impractical approach

Had Tesla concentrated on a series of small-scale applications of his inventions, instead of conceiving grandiose projects that never came to fruition, his name would be as familiar today as those of Edison and Marconi. In 1943, at the end of a patent dispute, the US Supreme Court found that the principles that enabled Marconi to make his transmission in December 1901 had all been described in detail by Tesla as early as 1893. But this official recognition came too late for the Serbian-American genius: he had died earlier that year, aged 86.

# FIRST IN THE FIELD

## *Who really invented the world's first electronic computer?*

DR JOHN VINCENT Atanasoff is hardly a name known to millions round the globe. Yet, according to a decision by an American court in 1973, he can claim the credit for inventing the electronic digital computer, the most important technological development of the modern age.

The invention of the first true computer has normally been attributed either to British code-breakers working at Bletchley Park, Buckinghamshire, during the Second World War, who in 1943 created the Colossus machine, or to the University of Pennsylvania team of John W. Mauchly and J. Presper Eckert, inventors of the Electronic Numerical Integrator and Calculator (ENIAC) between 1942 and 1945.

### *Research aid*

Atanasoff had, in fact, got there before them. He was a professor of physics at Iowa State University, working on complex mathematics relating to quantum mechanics. In an attempt to avoid performing years of tedious calculations, he set out to construct an electronic device that would do the sums for him. By 1942, when America's entry into the war interrupted his work, he had produced a primitive but functioning machine that had most of the essential elements of a modern computer, including binary logic (in which all numbers are reduced to a code consisting of a series of zeros and ones) and an electronic memory.

***First memory*** *Atanasoff holds the memory drum of the electronic computer he invented in 1942. Despite the size of the drum, it could hold only one-tenth as much information as a modern pocket-calculator.*

Atanasoff's work on computers was completely forgotten until 1971, when it came to public attention in a dispute over patents. After six years of litigation, a judge decided that the ENIAC computer had in fact been based on Atanasoff's pioneering efforts and that it was he, therefore, who deserved to be known as the father of modern computing. Thirty-five years late, Atanasoff was given the credit he deserved.

---

## SPINNING THROUGH THE AGES

IN 1927, a Philippine porter in a Los Angeles hotel, Pedro Flores, began making wooden Yo-yos and selling them to hotel guests. Two years later, Donald F. Duncan, a visitor to Los Angeles from Chicago, became so fascinated by the toy that he bought Flores's factory.

Soon Duncan had persuaded the newspaper magnate William Randolph Hearst to offer the Yo-yo as a promotion to boost his papers' sales. The result was a craze for the Yo-yo that quickly swept through the United States and Europe and has never quite died out.

Bing Crosby recorded a song about the Yo-yo, and celebrities such as actors Douglas Fairbanks and Mary Pickford were photographed playing with it. Passion for the toy even reached Iran, where a newspaper denounced it as a 'time-consuming and immoral novelty', citing examples of mothers neglecting their children in favour of the Yo-yo.

### *Chinese-French connection*

But the toy that Duncan promoted so successfully was no 20th-century invention. While the exact origins of the Yo-yo remain unknown, some historians claim that, like gunpowder and paper money, it was invented in ancient China. Missionaries returning from Peking (Beijing) during the late 18th century are said to have brought it to France. Whether or not this is true, it was a favourite toy of the French nobility and their children, and was nicknamed *l'émigrette* (after emigré, or emigrant) when it became associated with aristocratic families fleeing the guillotines of revolutionary Paris. Even King Louis XVI and his wife Marie Antoinette were Yo-yo enthusiasts.

It is just as likely, however, that the Yo-yo was invented independently in ancient Greece. An image on a vase dating from 500 BC in a Berlin museum depicts a small boy playing with a Yo-yo.

### *Foul play*

But the Yo-yo has not always been a harmless toy. In the 16th-century, it was used as a weapon in the Philippines. The attacker hid in a tree and spun a Yo-yo down onto his victim's head as he passed beneath. These Yo-yos were sometimes as heavy as this book; if handled skilfully, they returned to the attacker.

# THE PROFITS OF INVENTIONS
## *Practical genius has often gone unrewarded*

THERE IS a compelling fascination in the magic moment at which an original idea crystallises in someone's head and a new invention is born. Sometimes the moment comes after months or years spent searching for a solution to a clearly-defined problem; in other cases a need is perceived and an answer provided for it almost simultaneously. But a flash of inspiration does not necessarily bring a happy or a prosperous future. For many gifted inventors, legal wrangles over patents have soured the original joy of their discoveries; others, as employees of large corporations, never saw any of the profits made from the commercial exploitation of their ideas. Still others have made large fortunes from their inventions, yet have continued to live their lives much as before.

### WIRED UP
The creator of the first wire coat-hanger received not a cent for his ingenious invention. In 1903, Albert J. Parkhouse was working for a company in Jackson, Michigan, manufacturing wire lamp-shade frames. The firm was too mean to provide enough hooks for its employees to hang up their coats, so one day, rather than throw his coat on the floor, Parkhouse twisted a piece of wire into the now familiar shape of a hanger. His employer noticed what he had done, immediately grasped its potential and patented the idea. Parkhouse just went on working on the shop floor of the factory.

### KEEPING TIME
In the early 19th century, many inventors were competing to produce a practical and reliable metronome – a device that helps musicians learn to play in a steady rhythm. Dietrich Winkel, a German organ-builder living in Amsterdam, finally solved the problem in 1814. He placed two weights on a clockwork-driven pendulum, one fixed and one sliding, on opposite sides of a pivot. Each time the pendulum swings, it produces a clicking noise. The position of the sliding weight affects the speed of the pendulum, so musicians can adjust the metronome to produce a series of clicks at the speed they wish to play. Unfortunately for Winkel, he demonstrated his invention to Johann Nepomuk Maelzel, a German rival in the same field. Maelzel unscrupulously

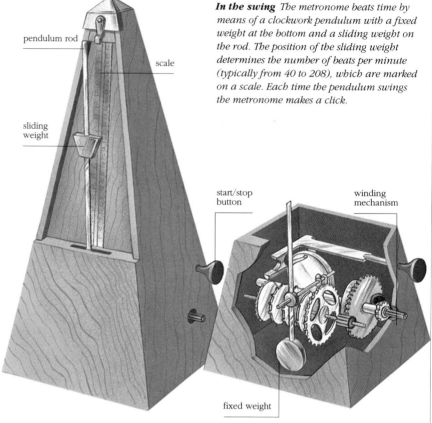

**In the swing** *The metronome beats time by means of a clockwork pendulum with a fixed weight at the bottom and a sliding weight on the rod. The position of the sliding weight determines the number of beats per minute (typically from 40 to 208), which are marked on a scale. Each time the pendulum swings the metronome makes a click.*

pendulum rod

scale

sliding weight

start/stop button

winding mechanism

fixed weight

patented the metronome in his own name and began mass production. The gadget, which still uses the principle devised by Winkel, has been known as the Maelzel Metronome ever since.

### SEEING IN THE DARK
One dark and foggy night in 1933, Percy Shaw, a road-repairer from Yorkshire, England, was struck by the sight of a cat's eyes gleaming brightly in the light of his headlamps. This everyday experience inspired him to develop a revolutionary form of road-marking for night driving – a convex lens backed by an aluminium mirror. These are embedded in a rubber pad, which is mounted in a cast-iron housing set into the road. The lens and mirror are positioned so as to direct reflected light from car headlamps back to the driver. A year after he first had the idea, Shaw was ready to patent his invention. He opened a factory to manufacture his 'catseyes' in 1935. Although the invention made him rich and famous, his style of life was completely unaltered. He continued to lead a simple existence in a small house in his native

Halifax, and spent only a fraction of his vast accumulated wealth.

### RIDING ON AIR
The pneumatic rubber tyre was first invented by a London engineer, Robert W. Thomson, in 1845, for use on the wheels of carriages. The invention failed to catch on at first – rubber was expensive at the time, so Thomson's idea was not marketable. In 1887, the pneumatic tyre was re-invented by John Boyd Dunlop, a Scottish-born veterinarian, who had a flourishing practice in Ireland. Dunlop noticed how his son's tricycle jarred its rider as the solid rubber tyres bumped over the unevenly paved streets of Belfast. He substituted rubber tyres filled with air and patented his invention the following year. Dunlop's pneumatic tyres were an immediate success with bone-shaken cyclists and should have made him a millionaire. But he sold his interest in the business in 1896, and gained nothing from any of the subsequent developments of his invention, such as the automobile tyre – a multi-million-dollar business that made his name famous throughout the world.

# INVENTING HISTORY

*How a new type of wire helped cause millions of deaths*

IN THE late 1860s, settlers flooded into the Great Plains of the American West and began to cultivate crops on what had been virgin grassland. The government favoured the development of settled agriculture, but cattle ranchers had been grazing their herds across the unfenced prairies, and the ranchers and new farmers soon came into conflict.

Existing forms of fencing were totally inadequate to keep cattle away from fields under cultivation; wood was too scarce and expensive for fencing, and the kinds of wire available tended to snap in the cold winters of the prairies. The most effective barriers were hedges made of

*Wired for war Placed atop trenches, barbed-wire fences were an effective obstacle to attacks during the First World War. The wire was used by both sides and led to stalemate.*

*Barbed barrier In 1873, Joseph Glidden patented a new type of wire set with spikes. A farmer from Illinois, Glidden developed the wire to keep cattle away from crops.*

prickly shrubs. As these took time to grow, the race was on to manufacture a durable wire to do the same job.

Several patents for forms of barbed wire had already been filed when Joseph Glidden, a farmer in De Kalb, Illinois, came up with his version in 1873, in which spikes or 'spurs' were held in place along a double-stranded wire. Glidden made no claim to have thought up the idea of using 'spurs' himself, but his wire had enough original features to be granted a patent the following year. Since the 'Glidden fence' was the first that could be mass produced, he is often credited as the inventor of barbed wire.

The invention was to have consequences far beyond the concerns of neighbouring farmers and cattlemen. Without it, the government's policy of encouraging permanent settlers would have been difficult to enforce – one of its immediate effects was to help bring the open, lawless prairies into the domain of private property.

Even more dramatic was barbed wire's influence on the character of modern warfare. Military strategists soon realised that a form of fencing that kept out cattle could also stop advancing horses and men. In Flanders and northern France during the First World War, troops dug into trenches behind barbed wire entanglements were able to resist almost any offensive. This absolute superiority of defence over attack created a military stalemate that neither side would accept, prolonging the war at the cost of the lives of millions of young soldiers. Barbed wire had changed the course of history.

## DID YOU KNOW..?

*IN 1830, Edwin Budding of Stroud, England, filed a patent for 'a new combination and application of machinery for the purpose of cropping or shearing the vegetable surface of lawns, grass-plats and pleasure grounds' – in other words, a lawn mower. Budding worked in the textile industry and had intended to produce a machine for finishing off or 'napping' heavy cloth. Handworkers in the industry, however, resisted the new machinery that, they felt, might threaten their employment. So Budding transformed his invention into an efficient grass cutter instead. Chain-driven cylinders of cutting blades like Budding's are still found on many modern lawn mowers.*

# MECHANICAL MADNESS

*The weird and wonderful world of Heath Robinson*

WHO INVENTED a device to remove gravy stains from gravel paths? Or a machine for pulling Christmas crackers? Or a system for eating peas without the use of either knife or fork? These were all the brain-children of William Heath Robinson – and none was intended to work.

Born in London in 1872, Heath Robinson was an inspired cartoonist who satirised machines instead of people. He specialised in drawing plans for elaborate but useless machinery, involving a wealth of pulleys and levers connected with knotted string. These bizarre contraptions were mostly 'labour-saving' devices that involved far more labour than a straightforward way of achieving the same result. Their ingenuity was matched only by their total impracticality.

### Automated life-style

His masterpiece was probably the miniature house he built in 1934 for the Ideal Home exhibition in London. Its occupiers, a staid middle-class couple, descended to breakfast on ropes through trapdoors in the ceiling. As they landed on their chairs, their weight depressed springs that put a record on a radiogram and squeezed milk from a concertina to feed the cat. In the nursery, a machine powdered the baby's bottom.

*Just for fun Heath Robinson satirised useless machines in this 1934 book. His name is now in the dictionaries as a word describing 'an over-ingenious mechanical contrivance'.*

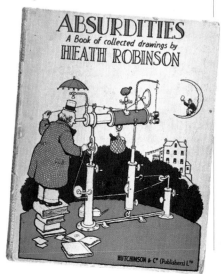

# SHOWMEN AND SLAVES

*Robots don't just entertain: they can put in a good day's – or night's – work*

**M**EMBERS of the staff of the Franklin Institute in Philadelphia, Pennsylvania were puzzled. The museum had acquired what seemed to be a mechanical doll, but no one knew how old it was, who had made it, or exactly what it was meant to do. Once its mechanism was restored, however, the figure wrote out a short poem in French – and eerily signed it with the words, 'written by Maillardet's automaton'.

This robot, and others made by Henri Maillardet in the early 19th century, were by no means the first mechanical devices designed to mimic the actions of living creatures. As long ago as the second century BC, Hero of Alexandria wrote of a theatre manned by mechanical performers, and Leonardo da Vinci is said to have built a mechanical lion to greet the King of France on his visit to Milan in 1507. By the 18th century, the art of automaton-building had reached new levels of sophistication, as French and Swiss inventors constructed ingenious figures that played musical instruments or performed complicated feats of draughtsmanship.

Not until the 20th century did such inventions come to be known as 'robots'. The word first appeared in 1921, in a Czech play about rebellious humanoid machines, and is derived from the Czech word for 'forced labour'. It is mainly as helpmates, though, that robots have found their way from fiction into the real world. In particular, they are used to perform many tasks too dangerous, difficult or boring for humans.

## Tireless workers

For example, robots have explored the wreck of the Titanic, and a robot even helps doctors to perform brain surgery. But the main use of robots has been in industry, where – after teething problems such as painting one another rather than the cars on the production line at General Motors – they are now widely used for tasks such as welding, machining and assembling electronic parts. In Japan, which employs twice as many robots as the rest of the world put together, one company has built a factory in which robots work night-shifts all on their own.

But the dream of the future is of robots which can build other robots – a prospect that would open up such exciting possibilities as the exploration of deep space by machines which could renew themselves unendingly.

**'The Scribe'** *This automaton can be programmed to write a text up to 40 letters long. It was built by a Swiss clockmaker, Pierre Jaquet-Droz, in 1774. It dips its pen in ink, and its eyes follow the movements of its hand across the page. The mechanism, seen from the back (above), is driven by springs.*

---

### DID YOU KNOW..?

*THE UNIVERSITY of Western Australia has developed a sheep-shearing robot. The device, which consists of a mechanical arm incorporating sensors and cutting equipment, has to perform a million calculations a second in order to follow the shape of the sheep without nicking it. Even then the robot has been known to make the occasional mistake. Researchers are delighted with it, saying that although it takes longer to do its work than a human shearer, it can work much longer hours. The reactions of the sheep are not recorded.*

## THE DUCK THAT ASTOUNDED PARIS

IN 1738, Jacques de Vaucanson presented a duck to the Royal Academy of Sciences in Paris. Like any duck, this one rose upon its legs, threw its neck to the right and left, plumed its wings, made gurgling noises, played in the water with its bill, took food from people's hands and occasionally excreted. But this duck was completely mechanical.

Unfortunately, Vaucanson's duck no longer exists, only the description and drawings of it he published. The gilded-copper duck 'digested' food, but only after a fashion – it dissolved food in its stomach, but absorbed no energy in the process, and needed to be wound up.

Vaucanson must have been an inventor of considerable genius; the same year, at the age of 29, he demonstrated an automaton that could faultlessly play 12 'airs' on the flute. He also built a shepherd that could play 20 tunes on his pipe with one hand and beat a drum with the other.

However, he did not restrict his talent to such whimsical projects. Applying himself to the challenge of building a machine to weave silk, he eventually designed an important forerunner of the modern automated loom. It was guided by perforated cards and powered by animals or falling water.

# FLYER FROM A DISTANT PAST
## *A pterosaur makes one last flight*

IT IS DIFFICULT to imagine what life was like in the Mesozoic era, when pterosaurs, the largest living things ever to fly, took to the skies. But, on May 17, 1982, some 65 million years after their extinction, a pterosaur was to fly again. Or was it?

Thousands of spectators at Andrews Air Force Base outside Washington, D.C. watched as a robot model of one of the reptiles was towed to a height of 120 m (400 ft) – only to plummet almost immediately, the disappointing result of two years' work and an investment of $700 000. Paul MacCready, the aeronautical engineer who designed the model, wryly commented: 'Now we know why pterosaurs are extinct.'

The radio-controlled robot was named *QN*, after *Quetzalcoatlus northropi*, a pterosaur with a wingspan of 11 m (36 ft) whose fossil remains were found in Texas in 1972. The living prototype had a huge head, slender beak, long neck and no tail – in short, experts say, an anatomy unsuited to flight.

### Starting small
MacCready had nonetheless been determined to build a mechanical pterosaur that could fly. He began with a gliding model with a 2.4 m (8 ft) wingspan,

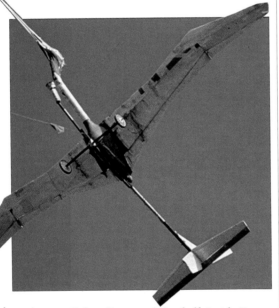

**Robot dinosaur** QN, *a half-size plastic model of a giant pterosaur, flew without mishap 21 times in a row. But it crashed during its public unveiling.*

and then built larger versions carrying wind sensors, a computer, gyroscopes and batteries for a five-minute flight. These needed a tail boom for stability on take-off, but this would be jettisoned once an auto-guide came into play.

*QN*, which had a 5.5 m (18 ft) wingspan, proved that MacCready's efforts had not been completely in vain. The 16 kg (35 lb) wing-flapping robot made 21 successful test flights in a row before its humiliation in front of the air-show's expectant crowd.

# A DANCER INFILTRATES THE HIVE
## *The robot built to talk to honeybees*

THE TIME may be coming when beekeepers will be able to go down to their hives not just to collect honey but to give orders to their industrious charges. After years of research, scientists have found a way of talking to honeybees.

Bees communicate with one another by a sort of elaborate song-and-dance routine. A bee that has discovered a food source – such as a field of flowers – will perform a 'wagging dance' to indicate the location of that source to its co-workers. Now a team of German and Danish researchers has succeeded in building a robot bee that can mimic the sounds and actions bees make during this dance.

### Waxy disguise
The mechanical impostor is made of brass covered in beeswax, with a piece of razorblade for wings. The robot does not fly (it is simply placed near the entrance to a hive), but it moves its wings to make the sound of a bee. The intricate details of its actions and song are computer-controlled, and, in experiments performed in West Germany in 1988, real bees successfully followed the robot's directions towards food sources up to 1 km (0.62 mile) away.

## DID YOU KNOW..?

*JAPANESE scientists have designed a robot to make sushi, a traditional Japanese dish of rice and raw fish. Working at full tilt, it can pat into shape 1200 lumps of rice per hour. Another robot to demonstrate culinary skills is a robotic hand developed in the United States. The hand can crack an egg into a bowl, then beat it with one of its fingers, which is capable of 65 strokes a second.*

\* \* \*

*AT A BAR in San Francisco, the waitress communicates with a voice-activated robot barman via a radio headset. The robot can mix 150 different drinks, and also tallies the bill.*

# WORKING IN THE DANGER ZONE

*Robots come into their own where humans fear to tread*

IN 1942, the biochemist and science fiction writer Isaac Asimov laid down the three rules of robot morality:
1. A robot may not injure a human being or, through inaction, allow a human being to come to harm.
2. A robot must obey the orders given to it by human beings except where those orders would violate the first law.
3. A robot must protect its own existence as long as such protection does not conflict with the first and second laws.

### Hazardous work

Today's robots are still too primitive to have any moral sense, but in performing jobs far too dangerous for human beings they nonetheless meet Asimov's demanding standards.

For example, remote-controlled robots have been built in the United States and Britain to perform bomb disposal. These are powered by batteries or by electricity from a mains supply. Some run on caterpillar treads rather than wheels, and are capable of going virtually anywhere – even up flights of steps. Because bombs can differ

tremendously in their design, human operators must tell the robots what to do step-by-step.

The robots therefore carry television cameras, and a cable or radio link allows operators a safe distance away to see the bomb and to instruct the robot on how to defuse it. This can be

***Suspect package** The camera on this bomb-disposal robot allows its operators to see it handle a suitcase. The robot receives its directions by remote-control.*

accomplished by removing anything that may be covering the bomb's detonator, which is then destroyed with a shotgun or by other means.

Remote-controlled robots are also working inside many nuclear power plants in highly radioactive areas which people cannot enter. The robots transmit television images of the inside of the reactor, maintain fuel rods, clean up nuclear waste, clear drains, and weld or cut metal to make repairs.

## THE MANNEQUIN WITH A WARM PERSONALITY

SCIENTISTS working for the US Army have developed a man-size robot, named 'Manny', that is so much like a human being that it even sweats when it exerts itself. Under computer control, Manny can walk, run, crawl and even kick a ball. It simulates breathing, its chest expanding and contracting as moist air is exhaled through its nose and mouth. Its body is warm to the touch, thanks to 12 small heaters implanted under its rubber skin.

The more Manny moves, the faster it breathes and the warmer it becomes, and capillary tubes inject water through its skin to simulate perspiration.

The purpose of all these sophisticated functions? Manny's job is to measure the effectiveness of protective clothing under conditions soldiers might experience in combat.

The movements of its joints (which are driven by hydraulic pumps), and the accompanying perspiration and warmth, subject its clothes to stresses identical to those imposed by a person in motion.

Manny performs its exercises in a carefully sealed enclosure the size of a small room. When the enclosure is contaminated with chemical or biological weapons, sensors on Manny's body detect any harmful substances that leak through the clothing it is wearing.

***Catching its breath** 'Manny' was built by the US Army to test protective clothing.*

### DID YOU KNOW..?

*JAPANESE robots have found their way into the world of the arts. 'Wasubot' can sight-read a musical score and play it on the electric organ, using both the keyboard and the pedals. Another robot can sketch a portrait of a human face after examining its sitter by video camera for only 20 seconds.*

✳ ✳ ✳

*RESEARCHERS in the United States have built a robot that can unscramble Rubik's cube. The robot, known as 'Cubot', holds the cube in its hands, reads and interprets the colour patterns and manipulates the faces to solve the puzzle. It can unscramble even the most complicated combinations in less than three minutes.*

# UNCOMPLAINING HELPERS

*Robots can help meet the needs of disabled people*

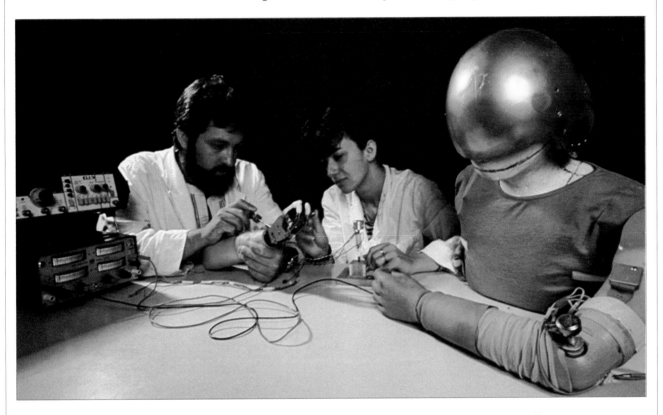

ROBOTS CAN help disabled people to lead more independent and comfortable lives. For example, Japanese inventors are developing a robot that can replace a guide dog for the blind. Named Meldog, it 'sees' obstacles using sonar, the same technique bats use to navigate and hunt: emitting very high-pitched sounds and discerning shapes from the echoes. Meldog is programmed with a detailed map of its owner's surroundings, and it identifies landmarks by recognising the walls and signposts it 'sees'.

Meldog moves on wheels, and, as it can sense how fast its owner walks, is always able to remain a short distance ahead. It communicates with its owner by means of a radio link to a special belt that the owner wears. The belt emits a code in the form of mild electric pulses felt through electrodes placed on the skin. The blind person must learn which series of pulses is an instruction to stop, for example, or to turn right or left.

In the United States, a robotic workstation helps quadriplegics to work as computer operators. It responds to voice commands and can perform such tasks as page-turning, disk-handling, and

**Mechanical aid** *A robot that can pick up and replace a telephone receiver can allow a limbless person greater independence at work or at home.*

**Sense of touch** *Conventional artificial limbs are somewhat clumsy, but a robotic limb, like the one shown here, could have tactile sensors that could 'feel' an object.*

making a cup of coffee. One such robot even brings its owner a paper tissue when he says 'ah choo!'.

Robots have been used in American hospitals to perform such tasks as shaving patients and brushing their teeth. Robotic replacement limbs are also being developed for amputees.

At a hospital in Connecticut, a robot delivers meals from the kitchen to patients' rooms, finding its way along corridors and even negotiating the elevators on its own. Nicknamed 'Roscoe', it has a complete map of the hospital stored in its computer memory. Should Roscoe happen upon an object that does not fit the map, such as a wheelchair along a corridor, it either amends its course to avoid collision, or waits until the object has passed.

Robots will never replace human help, but they can free nurses and therapists to carry out tasks requiring greater judgment and compassion, thus enhancing the quality of life for both carer and patient.

# PATENTLY CRAZY

## *Some of the wonderful inventions humanity never learned to appreciate*

THE WORLD'S patent offices are full of highly detailed descriptions and drawings of inventions that never went into commercial production. Some were built in prototype, but many never progressed beyond the drawing-board stage. Most 19th-century inventions that now seem quite ludicrous to us were deadly serious in intent.

Their proud inventors applied for and were granted patents on devices they hoped would prove invaluable boons to mankind. In the 20th century, however, designing ridiculous pieces of machinery has become something of a hobby. English eccentrics are especially fond of dreaming up fantastic machines merely for their own satisfaction, with no thought of gain.

**Musical rest** *This combined 'piano, couch and bureau' was patented on July 17, 1866 by Charles Hess of Ohio. The bed rolled out from under the instrument and there was a dressing table directly beneath the horizontal piano strings with storage space on either side of it. The inventor assured sceptics that: 'This addition to a pianoforte does not in any way impair its qualities, but on the contrary, adds considerably to its reverberatory powers.' The piano stool was equally versatile: the seat lifted up to reveal a mirror and a sewing box, while the frame below contained drawers and a flap that could be secured at any angle to serve as a writing desk or table.*

**Side by side** *An unusual tandem bicycle was patented on December 19, 1979 by Robert C. Barrett of California. The machine would no doubt give the riders a strong sense of togetherness, but, as the inventor realised, 'the steering is preferably arranged to be done by one rider only with the other rider being given handlebars of a nonrotatable nature.' The same would apply to the brakes.*

**Warm and snug** *In 1896, Quimby Backus of Massachusetts patented his combined bedstead and fireplace. The ornate wooden surround of the fire folded down to form the bed. The contraption was lined with asbestos, and Backus claimed that the fire could be left alight even when the bed was folded down on top of it.*

**Shot in mid-flight** *This photographic rifle was made by Professor E. J. Marey of Paris in 1882 to help in his study of bird flight. When the trigger was pulled, rotating discs in the drum exposed up to 12 photographic plates in rapid succession as the professor tracked a bird with the gun.*

**Space chronometer** *This giant solar-powered space clock, with three aluminium hands but no face, was designed in 1987 by Chris Coles and Alan Jefferson. Everyone in the world would see it seven times a day as it orbited the Earth, but, being British, it would show only Greenwich Mean Time.*

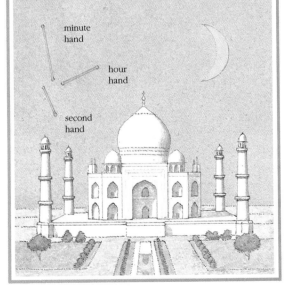

minute hand

hour hand

second hand

**Off the tee** *Arthur Paul Pedrick of Surrey, England, received a patent in 1974 for a golf tee linked to a Van de Graaf generator, which was operated by the golfer's foot. The electrostatic charge from the generator would make the ball hover above the tee, reducing the risk of hitting with slice. Unfortunately, this invention, like many of Pedrick's other proposed improvements to golfing equipment, was not permitted by the rules of the game.*

# SECOND-GUESSING THE FUTURE

*Scientists and storytellers alike have a penchant for flights of the imagination*

IN MOST people's minds, science is fact, science fiction is make-believe, and an unbridgeable gap separates the one from the other. But scientists and writers of science fiction often borrow ideas from one another, and a few individuals have even managed to combine the two professions. For example, Konstantin Tsiolkovsky, whose pioneering theories of astronautics and rocketry provided the foundation stone for the Russian space programmes of the 1950s and 1960s, was also a science fiction writer. His novel *Beyond the Planet Earth*, written in 1920, looked beyond even the achievements of our own time to the prospect of vast space stations in which generations of people could live.

### Keeping pace with the times

Other science fiction writers may not themselves have made important contributions to science, but many have drawn their inspiration from a keen awareness of the most recent scientific developments. For example, when Jules Verne wrote his novel *Twenty Thousand Leagues Under the Sea* in 1870, he knew, as most of his readers did not, that the latest developments in submarine technology had placed his characters' journey within the realm of the possible.

It is perhaps not surprising, then, that science fiction should often have predicted inventions many years – and sometimes even centuries – before they actually happened. Take Aldous Huxley's most famous novel, *Brave New World*. Written in 1932, Huxley's prediction of test-tube babies seemed a chilling fantasy at the time. Some half a century later, however, scientists turned it into a reality. Huxley also introduced the idea of cloning people from a single cell. Although human cloning is not yet possible, the genetic engineering of plants and animals from single cells is now an established branch of practical science.

Other inventions have first seen the light of day in the pages of science fiction. H.G. Wells was particularly far-sighted. His novel *The World Set Free*, written in 1914, gives an uncomfortably accurate picture of the

***Fiction meets fact*** *Jules Verne's science fantasy stories brought many scientific ideas into the public domain, such as the submarine and aqualung shown on this stamp from the Republic of Guinea.*

effects of radioactive contamination after a nuclear war. And, in 1895, the year before Henri Becquerel discovered radioactivity, Robert Cromie predicted the atom bomb in his novel *The Crack of Doom*.

There are many other examples of unnerving foresight. In 1893, E. Douglas Fawcett's story 'Hartmann the Anarchist' predicted the aerial bombardment of London, and the first flight to the Moon was foreseen by Edgar Allan Poe in 'The Unparalleled Adventure of One Hans Phaall' in 1835. Given these successes, what other science fiction predictions may yet come true? We would need Wells's time machine to know the answer.

# GIFTS FROM THE SEA

*Scientists find unlikely sources for restoring human bone*

SEA URCHINS, coral and even algae are now being used to help people with damaged or diseased bones. The skeletons of these sea creatures and plants have proved better replacements for human bone than any purely man-made material.

The human body has only a limited ability to regenerate damaged or lost bones, and always needs to have some healthy bone tissue on which new bone can grow. So when the jawbone has wasted away, for example, surgeons must implant a material, such as man-made hydroxylapatite ceramic, on which natural bone can grow.

Both natural bone and this ceramic are calcium phosphates. There is, however, a significant difference between the two: bone is very porous, and the ceramic is not. Bone tissue grows best and strongest when blood cells can permeate the bone, but, in the case of ceramic implants, the new bone grows round the implant rather than inside it.

### Skeleton structure

Now scientists have come up with better artificial bone tissue. Researchers have discovered that certain sea urchin, coral and algal skeletons have a pore structure closely matching that

*Helping to build new bone Because of its porosity, material derived from algal skeletons is ideal for artificial bone implants. Here, new bone tissue permeates the minute holes in a jawbone implant (coloured pink), forming a strong and durable bond.*

of human bone. Although these skeletons are made of calcium carbonate, which would break down in the human body, they can either be used to create a mould for casting a better material, or they can be chemically converted into calcium phosphate. In either case, the result is a stable, porous material that provides an ideal implant for bone replacement.

## A 'LIVE WIRE' MADE OF RUBBER

RUBBER is an excellent electrical insulator, yet an American scientist, Minal Thakur of AT&T Bell Laboratories, has developed a way of converting it into a conductor of electricity. He achieved this through a process known as 'doping', the changing of a substance's atomic structure by the addition of an impurity – in this case, iodine. The resulting compound conducts electricity ten thousand million times better than the original rubber.

### Replacing copper

Rubber is only the latest, though perhaps one of the most unlikely, polymers to show potential as a conductor. Polymers are substances, such as concrete, glass and plastic, which have very large molecules made up of multiples of simpler chemical units. Since the early 1970s, scientists have been working to develop new plastics with the capacity to act as electrical conductors. In 1987, researchers

in West Germany used doping to create a polymer that conducts electricity twice as well as the same weight of copper, one of the best conductors found in nature.

Since copper is both heavy and very expensive, many industries would welcome cheap, lightweight substitutes to use in electrical circuits. Conducting polymers have also been used for a new type of rechargeable battery: it is lighter and lasts longer than conventional batteries, making it particularly suitable for use in electric cars.

An important characteristic of some polymers is that they only conduct electricity at certain temperatures. These can be fitted to an ohmmeter, which measures the flow of electricity, to monitor changes of temperature during the shipment of drugs or frozen foods. Polymers may one day even be implanted inside the human body, where they could function as artificial nerves.

## DID YOU KNOW..?

*A FRENCH company has developed a new type of concrete that is made with dried blood. The powdered blood, mixed with certain chemicals, introduces evenly spaced air bubbles into the concrete. A silicate shell forms round every bubble, and the shell's hardness and uniformity make the concrete stronger than traditional concrete.*

\* \* \*

*COCA-COLA can replace oil in cars. This unlikely theory was proved by British scientist Dr Jack Schofield in 1989 when he completed a 115 km (70 mile) round trip between Liverpool and Manchester in a car whose engine was lubricated with Coke – and a special additive. Dr Schofield has developed a chemical that reacts to Coke – or even tea – to produce a lubricant that he claims can make engines last longer than they would with oil.*

\* \* \*

*IN A FEW years' time, people may well be willing to pay good money for 'flat batteries' – at least, for batteries that look flat. Japanese researchers have invented flexible paper that works as a battery. Instead of containing liquid or jelly, as in today's batteries, paper batteries are a completely dry sandwich of copper-impregnated plastic between sheets of metal foil, all sealed in plastic.*

# THE CAR THAT BOUNCES BACK TO SHAPE
*Plastic is no longer just the stuff of toy cars*

CARS BUILT in the year 2000 should have one crucial advantage over vehicles of today: thanks to their plastic body panels, they will simply bounce back into their original shape after a minor collision.

The resilience of plastic is only one of its advantages over steel. Today more than 80 per cent of European cars are built with plastic bumpers, making them lighter and therefore more fuel efficient than earlier models, and manufacturers around the world are increasing the number of plastic parts in their cars. A French firm is already making low-cost, plastic-body commuter cars. One has a maximum speed of 65 km/h (40 mph), and prototypes exist for larger and faster plastic cars.

In contrast to steel, which must be laboriously pressed and then spot welded – sometimes in thousands of places – to form a desired shape, plastic can be manufactured in moulds.

### Design freedom
This process is not only less expensive, but it also eliminates restrictions on the subtlety of a car's design. Lightweight cars need to be designed with careful attention to aerodynamic principles so that they will hold the road in a strong wind. The freedom to use moulded plastic will enable designers to make

cars of the future both aerodynamically sound and pleasing to the eye.

The greatest difficulty facing manufacturers of plastic cars is completely superficial: although plastics can be made in any colour, they do not have much lustre, nor can they withstand the high-temperature painting necessary to achieve the glossy finish of today's cars. However, scientists are coming up with ways to give plastics more lustre.

Plastic cars will never have to be scrapped because of corrosion. They will, in any case, never totally outlive

*City special The plastic body of this French commuter car is held together by glue, rivets and screws. One model can go no faster than 50 km/h (30 mph), and can be driven without a driving licence in France.*

their usefulness: some of the plastics being developed for use in cars can be shredded and used for new vehicles.

In spite of these benefits, we will probably never see advertisements for a 'plastic car' – it would sound cheap and low quality. But do be on the look-out for cars made from 'space-age materials'.

# THE PINK FLAMINGO'S BLUE-GREEN FRIEND
*Humble algae are helping mankind in ways both great and small*

ONE SIMPLE microorganism is playing an important role in combatting both world hunger and air pollution, is an ingredient in food colouring, and may one day produce oxygen in space for astronauts to breathe. This miracle worker is a blue-green alga, called *Spirulina*, that lives in some African and American lakes.

A Swiss environmental group has championed *Spirulina*, which is a traditional food in Chad and may have been eaten by the ancient Aztecs in Mexico. The group calls itself 'Green Flamingo', a name inspired by the fact that wild flamingos derive the beta-carotene pigment that makes them pink from the *Spirulina* that they eat. Green Flamingo has developed a system of growing

*Spirulina* in troughs of slightly salty water, feeding it on the by-products of biogas generators that produce methane gas for fuel from organic waste, such as decaying weeds or manure.

Biogas generators are an important source of energy in China and parts of the Third World, but they normally have a serious environmental drawback: the large quantity of carbon dioxide they produce contributes to the greenhouse effect, the potentially dangerous gradual warming of our environment. *Spirulina*, however, consumes large quantities of carbon dioxide, and is therefore an ideal crop to raise alongside a biogas generator.

*Spirulina* is also used in Israel to purify waste water, and scientists hope that

it could be grown on spaceships and submarines as an efficient producer of oxygen. It is already grown commercially in France and the United States for use in cosmetics and food colouring.

The alga is also an excellent food for fish and for humans. It contains much high quality protein, essential fatty acids, vitamins A and B, and little saturated fat. As it is a primitive organism, it is easy to digest, and has saved babies close to starvation who have not been able to digest other foods. Although it is grown in water, it is a suitable food source for desert areas: with a small investment of water, it yields more nutrients than any other crop. The diet that turns flamingos pink could yet feed the world's hungry.

# THE HARDER THEY COME

*Diamond coating is forever, say scientists, and could be put into everyday use*

ONE DAY we may all use razor blades that never dull, spectacles that cannot get scratched, and machine tools that will last and last. The reason for the durability of these products will in all cases be the same: all will be coated with man-made diamond.

Scientists have attempted to manufacture diamond, nature's hardest substance, ever since 1798, when it was discovered to be a form of carbon. They believed that diamond was made deep in the Earth at very high temperatures and pressures. Although some scientists late in the 19th century claimed to have made diamond, the first undisputed success was in 1955, when American researchers at the General Electric Company submitted graphite to pressures 55 000 times as great as our atmosphere and temperatures of 2000°C (3600°F).

### Breaking up a gas

Only a year later, scientists at the Soviet Academy of Sciences managed to grow diamonds at low pressures and a temperature of only 1000°C (1800°F). Their process, known as chemical vapour deposition, involves breaking up molecules of methane gas in such a way that the carbon atoms form a film of diamond on a piece of existing diamond, steel or other material. Some geochemists have revised their theories about diamond's origins: they now think that natural diamond could be the result of chemical vapour deposition inside the Earth.

## DID YOU KNOW..?

*CAR ENGINES of the future could be made partially from plastic. A Canadian firm claims its part-plastic engine is more efficient and durable than conventional engines, and, in the United States, a racing car has been powered by an engine with plastic connecting rods, timing gears and piston rings. Scientists are also experimenting with ceramic diesel engines that do not need a cooling system.*

## PRINTED ELECTRICITY

ELECTRIC cars, noiseless aeroplanes and fridges that can be lifted with one hand – these are only some of the products that could become reality if the claims of an American scientist prove true.

Dr Kenneth Wilson, a physicist from Florida, is the inventor of a process whereby electricity could effectively be generated in paper panels. The theory behind the technique goes back to the early 19th century, when it was discovered that electricity is generated across the junction of two different metals when one of the metals is heated.

In the past, this has been an inefficient way of generating electricity, a 'thermopile' of thousands of wires being needed to create sufficient current to power a large vehicle such as an aircraft.

The Wilson process, however, aims to simulate such a thermopile by printing the wires onto treated paper in a special metallic ink. If exposed to heat, these thin panels of 'paper wires' could generate electric current.

Such 'thermopanels' could be used in any number of ways. In the engines of cars or aircraft, for example, the heat of the engine itself could be used as a source of energy.

Crude oil releases heat when it is brought to the surface, and this could be applied to thermopanels to provide the power for offshore oil platforms. Also, thermopanels could be wrapped around the waste pipes of existing power stations, providing an inexpensive new way of generating electricity.

Japanese researchers at the Nippon Industrial University have taken the process a step further. They have used other gases that contain carbon, such as alcohol vapour, and have established the world's record for growing diamond film: 30 micrometres (one thousandth inch) an hour. And in the former Soviet Union, scientists created a new form of carbon that is even harder than diamond.

A Japanese company is already applying a coating of diamond, which is sensitive to extremely high frequencies, to loudspeakers to improve their performance in the high range.

Other commercial uses may not be far off. Windows with a diamond coating would not scratch. Diamonds can be made to conduct electricity, and, since diamond is unaffected by radiation, diamond circuits could be used in nuclear reactors or in space. Diamond also conducts heat very well, and would be an excellent material for keeping electronic equipment cool.

*Chemical vapour deposition To build a thin diamond coating on a silicon wafer, methane and hydrogen gases are first pumped into a silica-glass bell jar at very low pressure. Microwave radiation bombards and excites the gases, generating a blue plasma ball, and heats the silicon wafer to about 900°C (1700°F). Carbon atoms separate from the methane molecules and form a layer of diamond one atom thick on the silicon wafer. The process is repeated over and over to increase the thickness of diamond.*

Microwave radiation

Silica-glass bell jar

Plasma ball

Silicon wafer

Inlet for gases

## PICTURES IN THE BLINK OF AN EYE

WOULDN'T it be fun to be able to snap a photograph, view the result on your television and, if you are satisfied with it, print out copies in your own home? Several camera manufacturers have been working for years to develop such technology. They are designing cameras that, instead of using light-sensitive film, store still images electronically in a form similar to that used by video cameras to record moving images.

The difficulty is in achieving an image of the same quality as a conventional photograph. Whereas video films create a convincing image by capturing 25 imperfect pictures a second, which the eye and brain combine into a clear moving image, a still video camera must take a perfect picture on each frame. So far, researchers have designed cameras that can sense and store 800 000 pixels (the units of digital information that make up an electronic image), but one frame of conventional colour film represents the equivalent of up to 20 million pixels.

The difference may not matter all that much to some photographers. Still video cameras, even with their inferior images, have distinct advantages. An amateur photographer could very quickly put together a 'photo album' on his television screen. Some still videos can record ten seconds of sound with each picture, so he could add a spoken commentary. And the 'film' can be used again and again.

Journalists could use the camera to great effect: immediately after a news event, the camera's electronically stored images could be transmitted over the telephone to a newspaper office and be cropped or retouched by computer to prepare them for publication.

*Disk camera Pictures taken by this Sony still video camera are stored on a floppy disk in digital form, allowing them to be viewed instantly on a TV screen with no need for any chemical processing.*

# DROPPING IN TO WORK
### *Small aircraft could be the commuter transport of tomorrow*

FOR YEARS, flying saucers have been symbols of the unknown, conjuring up pictures of mysterious aliens and worlds beyond our imagination. But they are about to enter the real world – and might one day be as common a sight in our cities as cars.

A company in California, Moller International, which develops 'vertical takeoff and landing' (VTOL) aircraft, has come up with one prototype that bears an uncanny resemblance to the popular image of the flying saucer. The vehicle, which holds two people and fits into a single car garage, is driven by eight rotary fan engines arranged round its rim. The airflow from the fans is directed downwards to provide the lift necessary for takeoff or to hover in midair. With the help of a computer, each fan is operated independently to control the craft's speed, altitude, balance and direction. When the craft is travelling forwards, its shape helps to provide lift in the same way that the wings of an aeroplane keep it airborne.

While this two-person VTOL demonstrates the feasibility of this futuristic form of air travel, the company is developing a four-person vehicle with horizontally-mounted engines, which will have a top speed of 645 km/h (403 mph) and will be able to fly at 9500 m (31 000 ft). This model looks like a hybrid between a light aircraft and a racing car; its aerodynamic design means that it cannot easily be blown off course by gusts of wind. At optimum cruising speed, it should be reasonably fuel-efficient, consuming about 15 litres of petrol per 100 km (15 mpg).

### *The sky's the limit*
At the moment, the cost of one of these high-speed 'volantors', as the company calls them, would be as high as that of a helicopter. But Paul Moller, their inventor, hopes that, with sufficient demand, manufacturing costs could come down to within the range of those of a luxury car. If this is possible, personal VTOL aircraft may one day provide an attractive way of commuting to work. However, their future depends very much on whether civil aviation authorities will allow such aircraft to use public air space.

Several British manufacturers are developing rivals to Moller's VTOLs. If the craft prove as popular as their manufacturers hope, they would pose novel problems in traffic control. Imagine the skies over London or Los Angeles filled each morning with flying saucers.

*Just testing If vertical takeoff and landing craft become the transport of the future, they may not take the shape of the Moller 200X, but will owe much to its pioneering flights.*

# THINKING MACHINES

## *The ever-accelerating computer revolution*

**T**HE FIRST MACHINE invented by human beings to do brain work for them was the abacus, probably developed in ancient Babylon as early as 5000 BC. It took nearly seven millennia for mankind to progress from this ingenious but primitive counting device to what is generally accepted as the prototype of the modern computer – Babbage's steam-driven 'analytical engine'. A British mathematician and inventor, Charles Babbage produced the first designs for his calculating machine in 1834. Although the analytical engine was never built, its basic mechanical principles – with information fed in through cards punched with holes – were still being followed by computer pioneers a century later.

### *Size and power*

By 1946, technology had advanced to the Electronic Numerical Integrator and Calculator (ENIAC), built at the University of Pennsylvania. In such an electronic computer, figures and information can be stored and manipulated in the form of electrical impulses, a great leap forward from earlier mechanical devices with thousands of moving parts. Although not the first electronic computer, ENIAC was immensely powerful compared with previous designs and could perform several thousand calculations a second. But, to achieve such speeds, it had to be huge; it contained 18 000 valves and occupied 150 sq m (1600 sq feet) of floor space – bigger than an average house.

Since ENIAC, however, the rate of progress in computing has accelerated astonishingly. By 1976, only 30 years after ENIAC, the world's most powerful computer, the Cray 1, was performing 100 million

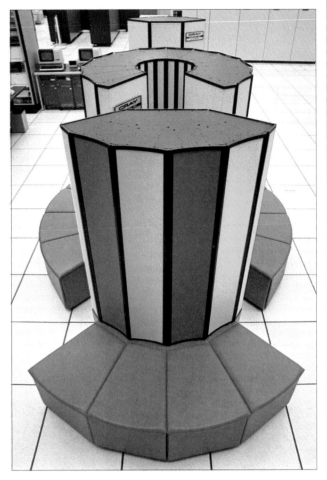

***Computer sculpture*** *The manageable dimensions of modern computers, like this Cray X-MP/48 at a physics research centre near Geneva, allow them to be housed in distinctive style.*

calculations a second. And this was quickly surpassed. The Cray 4, expected to be functioning by 1993, will be a thousand times more powerful than the Cray 1.

As they have become more powerful, computers have got smaller and cheaper. The microchip, introduced in the 1970s, allowed entire electronic circuits to be put onto a 6.35 mm (¼ in) square piece of silicon – small enough to balance on a fingertip. As a result, it was possible to build a computer as powerful as ENIAC but 16 000 times smaller. The shrinkage in price has been as dramatic as the shrinkage in size. Computing power that would have cost US $100 000 in 1960 was down to around $1000 by 1985.

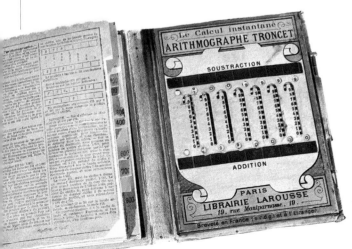

***Pocket calculator*** *Owners of this* Arithmographe, *patented in France in 1889, could add and subtract by inserting the stylus into the holes opposite the numbers and pulling up or down.*

# BREAKING AND ENTERING

*How computer hackers are able to penetrate secret records*

IN 1988, a US Department of Defense spokesman revealed that a German student had been regularly reading top secret defence files from American and other military bases round the world. The culprit had been able to carry out his break-ins without ever leaving home. Sitting at a computer terminal connected to the telephone system, he had been able to link in to at least 30 such restricted computer networks worldwide and gain access to all kinds of highly sensitive information.

What appeared a disturbing case of espionage was a prime example of 'hacking'. A 'hacker' is an amateur computer buff who spends his leisure time exploring confidential files. It turned out that Hamburg in West Germany was a hotbed of talented hackers capable not only of reading secret files, but also, should they wish, of altering or erasing them altogether.

Any computer network connected to the telephone system is vulnerable. The hacker needs only to discover the coded password that gives entry to the network. With intelligent guesswork and a little perseverance, this can often be cracked by simple trial and error.

Most hackers are only in it for fun – like Britons Robert Schifreen and Steve

*Chaos Computer Club These two members of a Hamburg computer club broke into NASA's computers, but changed no data, as that would be against 'hacker ethics'.*

Gold, who penetrated British Telecom's Prestel computer system in 1984 and were able to read all the material in Prince Philip's electronic mailbox.

But the potential for crime is enormous. Some experts believe that American financial institutions are losing up to $5 thousand million a year to computer fraud. At its simplest, once a hacker has gained access to a bank's

computerised filing system, he can order it to transfer large sums of money to an account in a foreign country – just what a traditional bank robber might do, but far less risky than a stick-up.

---

## BUILDING A BRAIN

ALTHOUGH COMPUTERS can perform mathematical calculations of unbelievable complexity in seconds, in other ways they are frustratingly stupid. When it comes to recognising an individual human face, taking part in a conversation, reading untidy handwriting or getting the point of a joke – tasks that human beings can perform without consciously needing to think about them – traditional computers are very slow indeed.

### Flexible response

It is very easy to confuse a computer by feeding it misleading or incomplete information, because the machine can only respond inflexibly according to the rules of its program. The human brain, on the other hand, is capable of learning from experience. Instead of responding rigidly according to a set of rules, it interprets everything its owner sees or hears in the light of the wide range of background

knowledge it has built up over the years. It can make an informed guess as to the best course of action, even when confronted with a totally unfamiliar or unexpected situation.

Many scientists believe that future technological progress lies with computers and programs that work in a similar way to the brain. Rather than carrying out a sequence of operations governed by a strict program, these 'neurocomputers' can be trained. Each time they perform a task, the experience is stored in a 'neural network'. Ideally they will be able to bring this experience to bear on each new problem they have to solve.

### Making connections

The practical difficulties of building such computers are daunting. The human brain is the most complex system known to science, with more than 10 thousand million neurons (nerve cells), each one connected

to 10 000 others. The wiring for an electronic replica of such a neural network would be impossibly complex, but it is hoped that laser beams can make the connections instead of wires.

Neurocomputers no longer belong to the world of science fiction – prototypes were already in operation by the end of the 1980s. At Californian airports they have been tested as a means of spotting explosives hidden in luggage. Plastic explosives contain large quantities of nitrogen, so the computers were linked to sensors that detect the amount and location of nitrogen inside a bag. They were then 'taught' by a process of trial and error to distinguish between a likely bomb and a harmless object that gave off a similar pattern of signals. Their strike rate improved with each successive test, but computer scientists have a long way to go before their creations can begin to match the all-round ability of the human brain.

## A COMPUTER IN THE EAR

FOR PEOPLE who suffer from total deafness, there was until recently no hope of relief. Hearing aids were powerless to help, because no level of amplification of sound had any effect.

In recent years, however, microchip computer technology has at last offered a chance for some of the profoundly deaf to hear. The crucial element in this new system is a silicon chip, with a titanium shield to protect it from corrosion by body fluids. The chip is surgically implanted in the mastoid bone behind the ear.

The vibrations we call sounds are picked up by a speech processor, worn like a personal stereo and wired up to a coin-sized 'transmission coil' worn behind the ear. The processor turns the sounds into a digital code, which is transmitted by the coil to the implanted silicon chip. The chip then decodes the digital message and relays it to one or more electrodes attached to the cochlea – the part of the inner ear that both analyses the various frequencies that make up complex sounds, and transforms the vibrations into

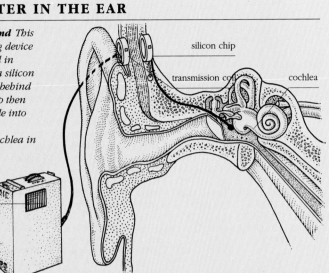

*Electronic sound This modern hearing device transmits sound in digital form to a silicon chip implanted behind the ear. The chip then converts the code into vibrations that stimulate the cochlea in the inner ear.*

silicon chip

transmission co[il]

cochlea

microphone

speech processor

nerve impulses to send to the brain. Some sophisticated models of this new system have as many as 16 electrodes.

The electrodes stimulate the nerve ends in the cochlea, just as sound would in a person with normal hearing. The simpler

systems cannot restore normal hearing, but can help a deaf person to monitor and improve his or her own speech. With more complex versions, what the person hears is similar to the computer-generated voice heard in some science fiction films.

# WORMS AND VIRUSES
## *The sinister world of computer infection*

IN 1972, American science fiction writer David Gerrold wrote a story about a malign program that would spread from computer to computer like an infectious disease. He christened this fictional program 'Virus'. As so often in the history of computing, reality has caught up with fantasy. By the 1980s, computer viruses had become a fact of life, causing companies to lose hours of working time and spreading panic among computer-users worldwide.

Properly speaking, a computer virus is a program devised by a mischievous

computer buff to attach itself secretly to another existing program. It spreads whenever the host program is copied onto a plastic diskette from one computer, then loaded into another. Many viruses lie dormant until triggered in some way – often by the computer's built-in clock. One strain, the 'Italian' or 'Ping-pong' virus, will set a little ball bouncing across the computer screen whenever the clock reaches a certain time. Another strain was dubbed the 'Friday the 13th' virus, because it became active whenever a Friday fell on that day of the month.

There are, in fact, several distinct varieties of computer infection, although all are usually referred to loosely as viruses. Each kind works in a slightly different way. A particularly insidious pest is the 'worm'. This is a program designed to infiltrate an entire computer network and reproduce itself over and over again. Some proliferate so fast that they quickly occupy almost all the operating space in the network, rendering it unusable. On November 2, 1988, a large American network, Internet, which links computers at universities, the Pentagon and other government agencies, was infected with a

worm that closed down much of the system for 36 hours.

Even worse is a 'Trojan' – named after the wooden horse that, according to legend, was used to smuggle Greek warriors into the city of Troy. A Trojan is a program that claims to do one thing, but in reality does another. When the unsuspecting operator introduces it into the computer, the machine can be taken over by the alien program.

### *Innocent prank?*

What motivates a person to foist a virus on innocent victims is often simply the desire to prove that it can be done. Many do no more than print a message of peace and goodwill on the computer screen. But Trojans have been known to cause all the other information stored in a computer to disappear.

Appalled at the thought of the havoc a destructive virus might wreak in their accounts or records, companies now invest heavily in 'inoculation' programs to protect their computers against infection. But, just as natural viruses mutate to keep one step ahead of medical advances, determined computer virus-manufacturers will doubtless devise ways of circumventing such precautions.

# COMPUTERS WITH HUMAN SENSES

*The race to make machines that can see, hear and understand*

EVERYONE HAS SEEN films in which space travellers chat to their computers and the computers answer back. For the time being, such technology is no more than a distant dream. Computers have enormous difficulty just in distinguishing the syllables and words that make up speech, let alone understanding their meaning.

It is relatively easy for computers to speak, by synthesising sounds that are recognisable as words – a computer that says 'please' and 'thank you' in the right places is no miracle of science. But recognising the words that make up normal, continuous human speech is another matter. No existing machine could be relied on to distinguish between the sentences, 'This new display can recognise speech,' and 'This nudist play can wreck a nice beach.' However, computers are already reasonably efficient at making out words that are spoken separately.

Some of the coming generation of voice-responsive computers will be programmed to react to a range of spoken commands. Many companies are also hoping to bring out machines that will produce printed copy from dictation. Until recently it was thought that these 'cybernetic secretaries' would have to be tailored to the idiosyncratic accent and speech habits of each user

*Sight and sound This computer laboratory is working both on systems that recognise human speech and the even more difficult task of mimicking human vision.*

and would only respond accurately to their master's or their mistress's voice. Now, it seems, this may not be necessary; rapid progress is being made with systems programmed to adapt easily to each new speaker.

The IBM Tangora system, under development at the end of the 1980s, was claimed to recognise a spoken vocabulary of 20 000 words with 95 per cent accuracy. The speaker still has to pause slightly between words, but the system includes a processor that enables it to make informed guesses as

*At your command A researcher at IBM works on a prototype 'talk-writer' computer. The machine interprets and acts on verbal instructions given through the microphone.*

to what is a likely sentence. The system has been programmed with grammatical rules, and vast quantities of office correspondence have been subjected to statistical analysis. Acting on the basis of this information, the machine can calculate the probability of one particular word following another.

Similar use of statistical probability is necessary for computers to interpret visual data. Security systems can distinguish between faces they have been taught to recognise, but no computer can yet match a human's ability to make sense of a cluttered three-dimensional scene by identifying all the objects in it.

## DID YOU KNOW..?

*UNTIL RECENTLY, the most information that could be stored on one silicon chip was one million bits (one megabit), equivalent to around 20 000 words. This seems extraordinary enough, but in 1988 the Japanese company Toshiba began production of a chip with a massive four megabit capacity – able to encode the contents of a 160-page paperback on its fingertip-sized surface.*

# chapter eight

# CITIES

## *and*

# CIVILISATIONS

EVERY YEAR millions of brides are carried by their new husbands over the threshold of their first home. Whether this custom was once a measure taken to outwit evil spirits (*page 243*), or merely a way to ensure that the bride did not stumble at such an important moment in her life, matters little today – carrying the bride is simply a practice that helps to mark an event in our lives. Rites, customs, beliefs, how people live, how they govern themselves, the homes they build – a look round the world, from the ancient past to the present, reveals a variety of human experience that is truly mind-boggling.

# THE WORLD'S FIRST CITIES

### *What made the first farmers move into town?*

IN ABOUT 10 000 BC, the world's weather changed drastically – and for the better. The sheets of ice that for millennia had covered much of the Northern Hemisphere began to melt. In a section of the Middle East now known as the Fertile Crescent, one eventual result of this warming was something never seen before: the rise of true cities.

For thousands of years, people had fed themselves by hunting, fishing and gathering edible plants. But in the Fertile Crescent, new weather patterns – cool, rainy winters followed by blisteringly hot summers – helped to change this ancient way of life. Plants such as wild wheat and barley were highly successful, for they flourished in spring and were able to reseed themselves before the earth grew parched again.

The cave-dwelling people of the region soon realised that it was easier to move their homes to the fields of wild grain than to drag the harvest to their caves. To complete the harvest quickly, groups of families settled and worked together. In time, these villagers increased their food supply by sowing the grain themselves.

One more step was necessary before these farming villages could grow into cities. About 9000 BC, when farmers discovered how to irrigate the soil, the food supply was finally assured. Indeed, there was a surplus of food. So unprecedented was this circumstance that those who gained control of the surplus were treated like gods. At the same time, people gravitated to the villages where food was kept.

The villages became towns, and specialised trades developed to serve the well-fed population. By 3500 BC the fertile areas of the Middle East were dotted with settlements that, in their organisation and economy, were recognisable as cities.

# THE GIFT OF IMMORTALITY

### *Why writing was invented in a land of plenty*

AHEAD of the car, the computer, nuclear energy or the steam engine, writing is the greatest of all human inventions. Writing has allowed people to preserve their ideas, culture and techniques, and to defy time – even death – by transmitting knowledge in all its precise details from one generation to another.

But how and where did writing originate? Who invented this incomparable method of communication?

About 5500 years ago, the Sumerian peoples settled between the Euphrates and Tigris rivers in southern Mesopotamia. No one knows where they came from, but they irrigated their fertile land and farmed it expertly – indeed, they produced more food than they could eat. The Sumerians stored their surplus grain in warehouses, where they also stored their most sacred objects. The warehouses became

*Urban pioneers The alluvial plain between the Rivers Tigris and Euphrates was home to the ancient Sumerians. Their irrigation canals assured a bountiful supply of food.*

centres of trade as well as places of religious pilgrimage and large settlements grew up around them. The population of the city of Ur, for example, grew to more than 20 000 by 1750 BC.

The Sumerian king was the ultimate owner of the land the people tilled. To them, the king was also a god – and so were his servants. A huge priesthood served this divine household, and administered the land. Contributing one's surplus harvest to the royal granaries became a form of tax, or tithe. As the cities grew, so did the complexity of ensuring that everyone had paid their taxes, and of keeping track of what was in the granaries.

And so the priests devised a system of marks for counting and keeping a record of their god-king's riches. Had the Sumerians not created a complex urban society, with its strong distinctions between city and country life, they probably would not have needed to invent writing. But having done so, they progressed from numbers and signs for contents of the royal warehouses to written forms for names, dates, and words for doing and being. They wrote on clay tablets, pressing the wedge-shaped ends of sticks into the soft material and then baking it.

From such simple beginnings the writings grew until all the myths and laws of the Sumerians' cities, as well as their endless inventories, were preserved for us to read today. Such was the power of their written language that it was still understood in the first century BC, more than 1600 years after the civilisation had been destroyed.

### DID YOU KNOW..?

*THE SUMERIANS invented writing, built the world's first real cities – and invented the wheel, in about 3500 BC.*

# THE OLDEST CITY ON EARTH

*Like a phoenix, Jericho has come back to life time and again*

'JOSHUA fit the battle of Jericho,' says the old spiritual, 'and the walls come tumblin' down.' The Biblical account is more explicit, describing how the people shouted when the priests blew with the trumpets, and how 'the wall fell down flat, so that the people went up into the city . . .. And they utterly destroyed all that was in the city, both man and woman, both young and old, and ox, and sheep, and ass, with the edge of the sword.'

This celebrated massacre really did take place, say archaeologists, in about 1400 BC. But the city Joshua captured was already phenomenally ancient – the walls that 'fell down flat' stood on foundations nearly 7000 years old.

And this was neither the first nor the last occasion on which Jericho was besieged and sacked. But time and again the excellence of its site lured people to rebuild the city.

### A time to sow

The reason for Jericho's attraction was that it lies on the edge of the Fertile Crescent, a great sweep of land incorporating the Nile Valley, the eastern Mediterranean coast and the Tigris and Euphrates river basins. Plants grow easily here; and here, 11 000 or so years ago, the art of agriculture was born.

People had gathered and ground wild grains – ancestors of our modern wheats and barleys – for generations before it occurred to anyone to sow the ears themselves and nurture them to ripeness. This brilliant idea, together with taming animals such as the sheep, pig and goat, gradually transformed the people's way of life from that of the 'old' Stone Age hunters and gatherers to that of the 'new' Stone Age farmers.

These people had no knowledge of how to use metals, but they did recognise a good place to live. The town that became known as Jericho was one, and it attracted more and more people. Eventually, by about 8000 BC, they were sufficiently wealthy to build a massive stone wall around their thriving town, along with a huge stone tower to help to defend it.

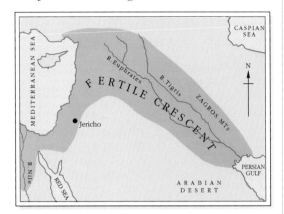

**Border town** *Jericho's position on the edge of the Fertile Crescent meant it was often the scene of conflict between advanced city civilisations and desert nomads.*

Indeed Jericho, if small – in ancient times the population rarely exceeded 3000 – can fairly be called the oldest known city in the world, antedating the larger and more advanced metropolises of Sumer by about 5500 years.

That first township was sacked and destroyed in about 7000 BC. New peoples settled there, to be ousted in turn; on occasion the city was left empty for centuries at a time: from roughly 6000 to 5000 BC nothing but grass made its home in Jericho's ruins.

### Fresh blood

It was in about 2000 BC that an entirely new culture discovered Jericho. The new immigrants came from Mesopotamia, bringing with them advanced techniques of building houses, and the ability to fashion tools and weapons out of bronze. These were the Canaanites, ancestors of the people Joshua attacked so successfully with sonic warfare.

But even Joshua's occupation did not last. This oldest of cities has fallen, and risen again, upon or near its ancient stones, many times since, and the exact site of the city has moved more than once. Who knows how many may follow the present Jericho, a bustling place of more than 10 000 people, 1.6 km (1 mile) south of the Old Testament town, in times to come?

**Sonic boom** *Joshua and his Israelites had good reason to rejoice at the razing of Jericho's walls: by capturing the oasis city, they wrested control of the year-round spring that nourished its people.*

217

# SECRET CITIES OF THE INDUS

*A civilisation that has disappeared even from legend*

EVEN IN RUINS, the ancient cities of Pakistan's Indus Valley look better planned than most modern cities in the Indian sub-continent. Indeed, they recall the symmetry of modern American towns, with regular grids of streets, brick buildings and sewers for sanitation.

The archaeologists who uncovered the Indus Valley ruins early in this century realised they had stumbled on an original culture, contemporary with ancient Sumer and Egypt (around 2400 BC). But in some ways (such as in its plumbing and town planning) it was more advanced than either. It had its own system of writing – so far undeciphered – and trade links with ancient Mesopotamia, as well as outposts near modern Bombay, more than 1000 km (600 miles) distant.

Where did the creators of this civilisation come from? What language did they speak? Did the same rulers govern all its remarkably similar cities – more than 100 built on the same pattern have been discovered, stretching over an area larger than Egypt or Sumer? And why did the civilisation collapse around 1700 BC? These mysteries all remain unsolved.

### Town planners

The major cities, which include Harappa and Mohenjo-Daro, had citadels with huge walls, with towers at regular intervals, set on mounds about 12 m (40 ft) high. Archaeologists have

***Made to measure*** *Great distances separated the cities of the Indus civilisation in what is now Pakistan and India (right). Yet the cities were remarkably similar – even their bricks were a standard size. And many cities were dominated by a citadel – a religious and administrative centre – like the one overlooking the ruins of Mohenjo-Daro (above) in Pakistan.*

also found remains of gigantic granaries and of huge public baths.

It has been suggested that the idea of building cities came from Mesopotamia, along the trade routes. Trade links with Sumer became so close that there were official Sumerian translators of the Indus language. But the few surviving examples of Indus writing are too fragmented to give us any real clues as to what that language was like.

Why did this culture collapse so completely? Possibly the River Indus altered its course, condemning the cities to either flooding or desert; possibly the desert was man-made, caused by excessive tree-felling to provide fuel for baking bricks; perhaps epidemics and famines played a part.

### Grisly clue

The end, however, may have come more violently. At Mohenjo-Daro, archaeologists found 13 skeletons, some with axe or sword blows to the head. These may have been inflicted by the invading Aryans – ancestors of the modern Hindus – who dominated India after the Indus civilisation.

Except in Hindu myths like the Rig-Veda, which speaks of a dark-skinned, wealthy people overcome by the Aryan invaders, and in the worship of Siva, a Hindu deity who in his aspect as Lord of the Beasts is strikingly like the god of the Indus religion, this short-lived, mysterious culture has vanished almost without trace.

---

## WHAT IS A CITY?

WE ALL THINK we know what the word 'city' means – but do we really? In Britain a city traditionally signifies a town, of any size, with a cathedral. So London today includes two cities – those of London and Westminster. But St Asaph in North Wales, with a population of fewer than 4000, is a city with a cathedral. And because of its sheer size, Birmingham was specially made a city in 1889, despite having no cathedral then.

In Australia, a city is simply an administrative district. Here lies Mount Isa, the world's largest city by area, spreading over 40 978 sq km (15 822 sq miles).

In the USA, 'city' is purely a legal term no matter how large or insignificant the township concerned. The US Census, however, terms any place with a population over 2500 as a city, no matter how rural. (By contrast, Kidlington in England, with a population of 17 500, is officially a village, because it is run by a parish council.) The world's most populous city is the Keihin Metropolitan Area (containing Tokyo and Yokohama) with an estimated 27 000 000 inhabitants in 1991. Tokyo is first in another way – it is the most expensive city on Earth, costing a visiting businessman about $362 in daily living expenses in 1989. By comparison, London cost $318 and Johannesburg in South Africa only $88.

So what is a city? It all depends, it seems, on where you live.

# THE GOLDEN AGE OF ATHENS

### Fifty years of unrivalled political and cultural achievement

The all-marble Parthenon temple

**N**EARLY 2500 years have passed since the goddess Athena's temple, the Parthenon, first rose in all its glory above the ancient city of Athens. Today tourists flock to the city in their thousands every year, to marvel at the sheer scale of the Athenians' architectural achievement. Surely a society that produced such perfection must have endured for hundreds or even thousands of years? Amazingly, the period that we now call the Golden Age of Athens lasted less than half a century.

The building of the Parthenon was essentially an expression of Athenian civic pride. In the middle of the 5th century BC, Athenians had every reason to feel proud, since their democracy fostered political and cultural achievement on a scale never before matched in the ancient world.

The statesman Pericles voiced the Athenians' feelings about their city. In a famous speech in 431 BC, he praised Athens for being 'an education to Greece' – the pinnacle of civilisation and democratic government. Because of this tremendous pride, the Athenians believed it was their duty to band together and beautify their city.

The Parthenon, built from 447 to 432, was paid for with public funds, and thousands of contracts were awarded to individual citizens. Each person took responsibility for a small part of the building work – perhaps transporting a few blocks of marble, or fluting one of the columns. With such community spirit it was completed, except for some details, in only nine years.

But the Golden Age proved too good to last. Plague struck the city in 430 BC, killing thousands of people. The Spartans' invasion in 404 BC brought all the Athenians' other building projects to an end. Never again would Athens recapture the brief but dazzling glories of her Golden Age.

***Pillars of wisdom*** *Great philosophers, such as Plato (centre left), and Aristotle (centre right) – depicted here in Raphael's* School of Athens *– later helped to sustain the city as a focal point of intellectual activity.*

# THE CRADLE OF DEMOCRACY
## *Citizens band together to run their state successfully*

WE ARE used to hearing Athens described as the 'cradle of democracy'. Yet what we call democracy would have been unrecognisable to the ancient Athenians. There were no political parties as such, and only a very restricted franchise.

All citizens had a part to play in the running of the state. Every citizen had a place in the Assembly – the main decision-making body – and each had the right to ask questions and raise important issues. But if you happened to be female, a slave, or not of Athenian parentage, you did not qualify for citizenship. Of the 350 000 or so people who lived in ancient Athens, there were some 40 000 adult men (over the age of 18) who qualified as citizens.

### Administering Athens

The citizens appointed a council, or Boule, made up of 500 members, to deal with administration. Membership was limited to one year. The senior members of the Boule formed an inner council (the Prytany) and took it in turns to be chairman of the Assembly.

Besides his political activities, each able-bodied citizen had to serve in the army or navy for part of the year. But, unlike modern-day soldiers, Athenians had to provide their own equipment. For most citizens this meant paying for

**Wheels of democracy** *Athenian citizens took pride in their civic duties, which included voting on judicial and administrative matters. These tiny bronze wheels were their public ballot papers.*

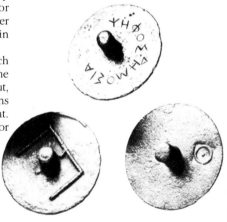

a suit of armour and a sword – but wealthy men might have to keep a warship in commission for a year.

Athenians extended their democratic ideals into their armed forces. In fact, the top military and naval commanders were elected annually. And it was not unusual for an unpopular or unsuccessful commander to find himself reduced to the ranks the following year.

Living in the Athenian democracy was like being a part of a very large family in which everyone took responsibility both for himself and for other people. Athenians had a real passion for public life: if they had not, their system of government would never have worked. The ancient Athenians would not have known what to make of our so-called modern democracies; the idea of electing someone else to make important decisions would have seemed like tyranny to them.

---

## WHAT'S IN A NAME?

IT IS HARD to imagine the Greek capital being called anything but Athens. Yet, according to legend, the city might well have been named not after Athena but after the sea god Poseidon.

Once, many thousands of years ago, Poseidon and the goddess Athena were deadly rivals, each one constantly trying to get the better of the other. Both claimed ownership of the province of Attica, which contained the city that we now call Athens. To end the feud the gods decided that whoever gave the province the more valuable gift could claim the land. Poseidon struck the earth

with his trident, creating a salt-water spring; Athena made the very first olive tree sprout up beside the spring.

The gods decided that the olive tree was the better gift, but only by one vote. Athena was given the province, and the city of Athens was named after her. Poseidon was so enraged that he took his revenge by making all the rivers but one dry up in the summer time. To this day, you can see the saline spring. And the rivers still dry up in the summer – Athens has to obtain her mains water from the hills outside the city – so Poseidon got his revenge after all.

---

# GET OUT OF TOWN!
## *How to handle a difficult politician*

THE CITIZENS – that is the free men of ancient Athens – were proud of their equality; so what happened when some citizens threatened to become more equal than others?

Democracy was frequently jeopardised by the development of factions and vendettas in the Assembly. Professional politicians (called 'orators' or 'demagogues') were charismatic men who often inspired great personal loyalty. It followed that there were sometimes bitter arguments between rival supporters. If feuds were allowed to become too bitter or an unpopular politician became too strong, the business of government would be disrupted – and that would endanger Athenian democracy. So a system called 'ostracism' was invented.

### Banishing acts

Any prominent citizen who had become unpopular could be 'ostracised' by his fellow citizens – banished from the city for a period of ten years. The system worked like this: without specifying anyone's name, any citizen could propose that an ostracism be held. If the Assembly agreed to the proposal, the Agora – the market place that also acted as a civic centre – was fenced off. Each of the ten tribes of Athens had its own gate through which the members would pass to vote. Each citizen voted by writing the name of the person he wished to see exiled on a fragment of pottery called an ostracon.

At least 6000 'votes' had to be cast before a citizen – the one with the highest score – could be banished. But when his ten-year exile was over, he could return and resume his life as if nothing had happened – without any dishonour or loss of rights or property.

**Casting out opponents** *A vote scratched on a piece of potsherd (ostracon) singles out the flamboyant writer Aristides for ostracism – banishment from Athens for ten years.*

## WHEN CROWS WERE WHITE

CROWS ARE instantly recognisable by their glossy black plumage; but in Greek mythology there was a time when all crows were white.

The god Hephaistos was overcome with passion for the goddess Athena and, having tricked her into coming alone to his workshop, he fell upon her in a frenzy of lust. But his attempted violation went disastrously wrong. His seed fell on the ground, and it was Mother Earth who conceived and gave birth to Hephaistos's child.

Although the baby – Erichthonios – was hideously ugly and had a serpent's tail instead of legs, Athena felt obliged to see that he was taken care of. She asked King Kekrops's daughters to bring him up; but first she put the child in a covered basket and gave strict instructions to the daughters never to look inside.

Of course, they were unable to resist lifting the lid to have a look. The sight of Erichthonios – half-boy, half-snake – drove them mad and they flung themselves off the summit of the Acropolis.

This is where the crow – once the goddess Athena's favourite bird – comes in. Thinking he was doing Athena a service, a crow flew straight to her with the sad tidings. Athena was building the Acropolis, and the news came as such a shock that she dropped the enormous boulder she was holding: it can still be seen today in the form of Mount Lykabettos. She took out her anger on the bearer of this awful news, the unfortunate crow. She banished all crows from the Acropolis forever, and turned their beautiful white feathers black. For proof of this story, one has only to look at the hooded crows in Greece today. Although their heads, wings and tails are black, the rest of their plumage is off-white: a reminder of how they looked before the day they upset the goddess Athena.

# AT HOME IN ANCIENT ATHENS
## A day in the life of an average Athenian

TODAY'S TOURISTS, gazing up at the splendours of the Acropolis, may think that the ancient Athenians led a life of luxury. But they would be quite wrong. The average Athenian in the 5th century BC lived in a simple house built of mud bricks, with no bathroom or kitchen and hardly any furniture.

Take the *andron*, or dining-room, for example. There were no carpets on the mosaic floors, the couches were hard and the rest of the room was bare save for a few low tables. A typical meal might consist simply of home-baked bread, served with eggs, poultry or fish cooked in olive oil.

### Skilled slaves

Slaves were regarded as valued members of the household, and were given wages that they could save to buy their freedom and become citizens. Some slaves were Greeks, captured in wars with other city states; most came from the slave markets of the East. They were often well educated, and many of them worked as skilled secretaries, entertainers and teachers.

To an Athenian, the ultimate luxury was leisure – and having slaves enabled a citizen to find the time to pursue his interests.

The citizen's day began at dawn, when he got off his hard bed and dressed in his cloak (which he also used as a blanket). Then to work – as a stonemason or potter, perhaps, or an administrator of the state-owned silver mines; or as a landowner, overseeing vineyards and olive groves. With the exception of the silver mines, all 'industry' in ancient Athens was on a tiny scale: even the largest factory, which made shields for the army, employed no more than 120 workers.

By the afternoon, the citizens would have time for those things they enjoyed best: engaging in sport, philosophy and – especially – politics. Most would try to set aside a few hours each day to attend the gymnasium – a cross between a sports centre and a debating society – where they would argue about the issues of the day. Lively debate on public affairs as well as poetry, song and revelry then continued long into the night at the symposium, or drinking party. Time to take part in the running of the city – not work – was what mattered most to the Athenians; and without their simple, uncluttered way of life, they would never have had time to govern their city so successfully.

*Light relief* This 5th-century BC cup depicts a boy playing music for his master – the less serious side of an Athenian symposium. More pressing matters such as political debate were also conducted at such 'social clubs'.

### DID YOU KNOW..?

*ATHENIAN COURTS had no judges and no lawyers. Plaintiffs and defendants conducted their own cases, in front of a jury made up of their fellow citizens. Juries varied in size from 101 to 1001, according to the importance of the case. If the accused was found guilty, the prosecutor proposed a punishment, but the defendant could suggest an alternative: it was up to the jury to choose. There was no appeal.*

✳ ✳ ✳

*PLATO, in his philosophical work* The Republic, *said that the ideal democratic city-state should contain only 5000 citizens. Aristotle, on the other hand, believed that every citizen should know all the others by sight.*

✳ ✳ ✳

*THE ATHENIANS used a form of taxation to maintain their city, pay public servants and keep up their army and navy. Any man whose wealth exceeded a certain sum had to perform a number of duties or 'liturgies'. He had to choose between keeping a warship in commission for a year, financing the production of plays, or equipping a religious procession.*

# THE BIG APPLE

*How New York City grew from a bag full of beads*

THE MOST famous bargain in American history was the native Indians' sale of Manhattan Island in 1626 to Peter Minuit, of the Dutch West India Company, for a song – or, more exactly, for a sack of beads, cloth and ironware then worth 60 guilders, or about $24. The entire island, now part of the most populous city in the United States, cost him just 41 cents per sq km, about $1.06 per sq mile. Today, Manhattan's 58 sq km (22 sq miles) of real estate are worth over $945 thousand million.

The Dutch were the first colonists to govern Manhattan, but were not the first Europeans to see, or even claim, the island. An Italian explorer, Giovanni da Verrazano, first discovered Manhattan in 1524. He was in the pay of King Francis I of France, in whose name he claimed the land. One hundred years later, the Dutch took Manhattan and the surrounding area by enlisting the Mohican Indians to help them defeat rival French interests. The Dutch held the colony until the English wrested it from them in 1664.

According to one story, it was as a result of the Dutch presence that the city has become known as the Big Apple. The governor of the Dutch colony, Peter Stuyvesant, began planting apple orchards in 1647. In due course, the state of New York became famous for the quality of its apples. In the 1920s, jazz musicians identified New York City, with its rich variety of life, as the biggest and juiciest of all of the state's produce, and they coined the phrase.

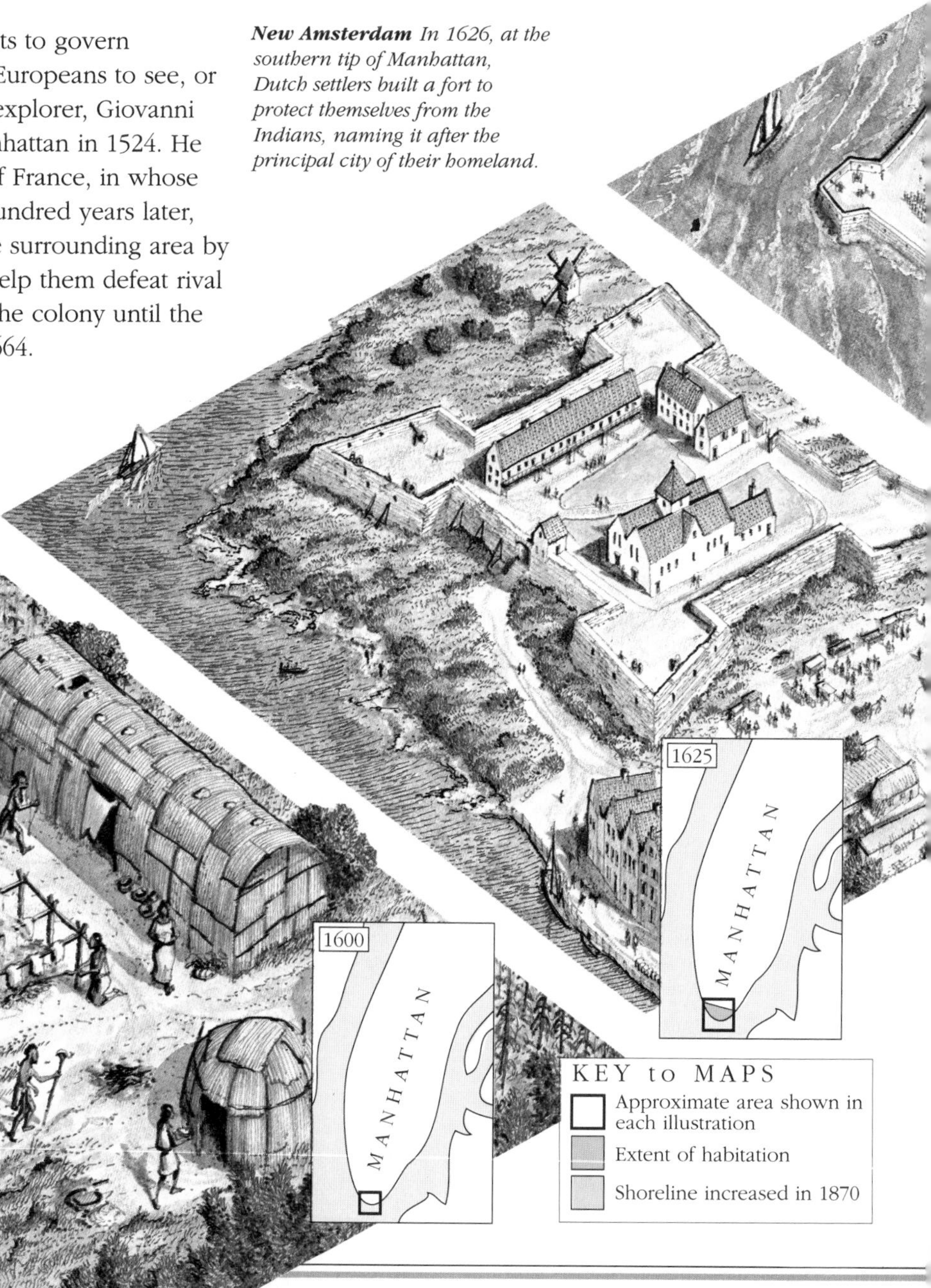

*New Amsterdam In 1626, at the southern tip of Manhattan, Dutch settlers built a fort to protect themselves from the Indians, naming it after the principal city of their homeland.*

*Ancient origins When Europeans first reached the island of Manhattan, they found only an ancient Indian settlement on its marshy plains.*

1600

1625

MANHATTAN

KEY to MAPS

Approximate area shown in each illustration

Extent of habitation

Shoreline increased in 1870

**Modern Manhattan**
*Today Manhattan is only a part of New York City, yet 20 238 people live in each sq km (52 378 in each sq mile), a density of population almost three times that of the city as a whole.*

1990

CENTRAL PARK

MANHATTAN

1773

MANHATTAN

***Changing fortunes*** *The British took over the settlement in 1664 and renamed it New York. Although it passed back into Dutch hands in 1673, the British reclaimed it the following year. A little over a century later, New York had seen such expansion that, albeit briefly, it became the capital of the United States.*

# COSMOPOLIS
## *The great melting pot*

FOR CENTURIES, the port of New York has been the gateway to the New World for countless immigrants from many nations. Even in the 17th century, when there were only a few hundred settlers, 18 languages were spoken in the city. The first large group of immigrants after the Dutch and English settlers were the Italians who began to arrive in the early 1800s. People from all over Europe, fleeing poverty and religious and political persecution followed. The Irish came in their hundreds of thousands to escape starvation when the Irish potato crop failed in the 1840s. By 1910, the city of New York had twice as many Irish as Dublin, and more Italians than Naples.

Today, about one-fifth of New York's 7.3 million residents were born outside the USA. Among the city's inhabitants are Italians, Russians, Irish, Asians, Canadians, and Hispanics. More Greeks live in Astoria in the borough of Queens than in any other city outside Greece, and Astoria's high schools teach children from more than 20 countries.

### THE WAY IN

In 1892, the federal government opened an immigration station on Ellis Island in Upper New York Bay. In the 64 years of its existence, it was the first stop in America for 12 million people. Its peak year was 1907, when 1 004 756 people passed through its gates. Of these, only two per cent were not permitted to settle. Grounds for refusing entry included professing a belief in anarchy or polygamy.

### CHANGE OF RESIDENT

Not all of New York's immigrants came from abroad. Harlem, a section of Manhattan which was first settled by the Dutch in 1658, and by other immigrants from Europe in the 1880s, was the destination of black people from the southern states in the 1890s. Liberated from slavery after the American Civil War, they too came in search of a better life. In the 1920s, the black population rose from about 83 000 to 204 000, and Harlem became the centre of an artistic movement known as the Harlem Renaissance. Today, nearly a quarter of a million black people make their home there.

## THE VANISHED RACE

MORE than 27 000 Indians from all over the USA live in New York City. But where now are the people whose ancestors were the city's first inhabitants?

Two surviving groups of Indians do have a connection with Manhattan. They are the Delaware, who now live, after enforced migration, over 2000 km (1250 miles) away in Oklahoma, Wisconsin and Ontario; and the Ramapough, a community living on the border of New York and New Jersey, direct descendants of Manhattan's original inhabitants. When the Dutch first settled the island, two

groups of Indians, the Canarsee and Wickquaasgeek, came seasonally to settlements in the south and north respectively, to hunt, fish and grow crops.

By the 1740s, disease, the spread of European settlers and warfare had emptied the island of its first Indians. Yet Indians and New York's most famous modern feature are indelibly associated. As the skyscrapers began to rise over Manhattan, descendants of New York State's Iroquois Indians became renowned as supremely skilled steelworkers in the construction industry.

# THE CAPITAL OF THE EAST

## *Japan signalled its opening up to the West by naming a new capital city*

ONE DAY in 1873, the playwright Hasegawa Shigure received a terrible shock when her mother appeared 'with a different face'. She had stopped shaving her eyebrows, was wearing her hair loose, and her teeth – which, like every Japanese woman's, had always been artificially blackened – were now gleaming white.

What Hasegawa was witnessing was just one example of the myriad changes taking place as the modern age dawned in Japan. The epitome of Eastern traditionalism, Japan had decided to open its doors to

*Dress sense* In the 1860s, just as Japan begins its rapid modernisation, a group of young men from Satsuma prepare for study abroad by donning formal Western attire.

the West – ending a centuries-old policy of isolationism – and to modernise the nation as fast as possible.

The seat of government was moved from Kyoto to Edo in 1868 and renamed Tokyo, 'eastern capital'. Situated at the heart of a bay, Edo was the gateway to the Pacific and to the West. Even in 1800 the town was no backwater – with a population of over a million it was then probably the world's largest city.

A modernisation programme followed, which often meant a slavish imitation of Western ways. Everything from chairs – first used in government offices in 1871 – to morning coats and high collars was enthusiastically taken up. In the 1880s, the diplomatic corps and the political elite were even encouraged to learn ballroom dancing as a patriotic duty. A fancy-dress ball in 1887 put an end to such extremes: Japanese conservatives were outraged at their fellow citizens prancing about dressed as insects. There was a strong public reaction, and the westernisation programme was hastily relaxed.

### *Linguistic legacy*

The word for fashionable in Japanese remains *haikaru* (high collar) to this day, and many similar Western phrases from this period have also entered the language. Female office workers are still known as *O-eru* (from the initials O.L. for 'office lady'); their male counterparts are known as *sararimen* (salary men). These workers may not refer to their city as Edo, but modern Tokyo has one thing in common with its predecessor – with a metropolitan area population of 27 million, it can claim to be the world's largest city.

---

## ENTERTAINMENT WITH A TOUCH OF CLASS

MOST WESTERNERS think of the word 'geisha' as being a euphemism for a prostitute. In fact geisha means 'art person', the term the Japanese use to describe a female entertainer skilled in the arts of singing, dancing and playing the samisen (a three-string Japanese guitar). Geishas enjoy a high social status in Japan.

Originally their function was to provide men with early evening entertainment before a night with a licensed prostitute. After prostitution was outlawed in 1958, geishas continued to flourish, providing an exotic and very

expensive form of entertainment. Men tend to club together to pay to keep a geisha, because her exclusive services are beyond the means of all except the very rich.

A geisha nowadays begins her career as a teenage *maiko* or dancing girl, whose job is to look after groups of wealthy men. As well as singing and dancing for them, she will sit at their table, pour their drinks, serve them food and sit quietly while the men talk.

If a client takes a fancy to a *maiko*, and she to him, then her days as a *maiko* end. The man has to provide her with expen-

sive gifts of food and clothing as well as provide somewhere for her to live. By taking up with a man, a *maiko* gives up the chance of becoming a geisha.

Geishas are becoming increasingly rare: faced with the prospect of spending years learning the arts of flower arranging, calligraphy, music and ancient dances; sleeping motionless on wooden pillows to preserve their elaborate hairstyles; wearing tight, restrictive kimonos; and spending their time in the company of elderly men, most young girls are opting for discos, boyfriends and Western-style clothes instead.

## AN $80 MILLION FUNERAL FIT FOR AN EMPEROR

ON FEBRUARY 24, 1989, Hirohito, the Emperor of Japan, was buried in front of dignitaries from 163 countries. He was laid to rest close to his father's grave in the Shinjuku Gyoen Imperial Gardens in west Tokyo. His state funeral was the most expensive funeral ever, at an estimated cost of $80 million. It was also the final act in a long and traumatic period of Japanese and world history.

When he succeeded to the Chrysanthemum Throne in 1926, Hirohito's divinity was fully acknowledged by the Japanese people. He was said to be descended from the mythological first emperor, Jimmu Tenno, who ruled from 660 BC and who, according to legend, was himself descended from the sun goddess Amaterasu Omikami. All Japanese emperors were therefore of divine origin,

**Mortal remains** *An honour guard escorts the palanquin bearing the body of Hirohito through the funeral gate.*

and when the Japanese drew up their first constitution in 1889, its foremost principle stated that 'The emperor is sacred and inviolate.'

Exactly 100 years later, however, it was a mere mortal who was laid to rest in the Imperial Gardens. The constitution of 1947 – imposed by the United States after the Second World War – ended the emperor's divinity and made him instead 'the symbol of the State and of the unity of the people'. The Americans were keen to establish a clear division between religion and state in order to undermine the once militaristic influence of the Shinto cult of emperor-worship.

They were not entirely successful. Many Japanese adhered to the old ways, and in fact two very different ceremonies were held at Hirohito's funeral. One was a secular, state event, the other a traditional Shinto ceremony. And in response to Hirohito's death, at least two old soldiers committed suicide to show their devotion to the former emperor-god.

# ALL THE TEA IN...JAPAN?
## *The philosophy behind Japan's national beverage*

TO THE JAPANESE, tea is much more than just a pleasant drink. It is a religion, a way of life, and its serving and drinking is an elaborate cultural exercise. Tea ceremonies are so complex that many Japanese themselves do not always understand what is going on in them.

Tea was introduced to Japan in the 12th century, along with Zen Buddhism. Monks used the drink to help them to stay awake during long periods of meditation. Then the practice of drinking tea spread to the upper classes, where it quickly became fashionable. Tea was served in a specially built house, about 3 m (9 ft) square, amid complicated rituals designed to induce a sense of peace and tranquillity among the carefully chosen guests.

Tea is no longer drunk only by the upper classes – everyone drinks it. But it remains at the heart of Japanese society, and professional tea masters, who conduct the ceremony, are highly respected. Great attention is paid to all aspects of the four-hour ceremony – the surroundings, the decorations, the utensils, the textures of the foods, the choice of tea, and even the choice of conversation to go with it, must not be left to chance.

The importance of tea is so great that many Japanese girls do not think themselves fit for marriage until they have learned all of the ceremony's labyrinthine complexities.

**Kettle culture** *Geishas demonstrate their skills in the subtle and elaborate art of the tea ceremony.*

# SHAKEN TO THE ROOTS

*The Japanese have learned to cope with the ever-present fear of earthquakes*

ONLY A FEW of the survivors of the great Kanto Plain earthquake of September 1, 1923, are alive today. Those who are will never forget the day when 5000 buildings in Tokyo were destroyed, and many more were set on fire. By the next morning, two-thirds of the city had been devastated and 99 331 people lay dead.

Earthquakes are common in Japan. The islands straddle three shifting geological plates, whose movement gives Tokyo one of the highest rates of earth tremors in the world. Tokyo averages about three noticeable earthquakes a month; the fires that often follow have come to be known as 'flowers of Edo'.

### Building confidence

Since 1923, however, only the earthquake of August 8, 1983 – which killed one person – has caused any serious damage. Although approximately 844 000 homes were without electricity as a result, it was only a matter of hours before all services were restored.

The Japanese lead the world in the field of earthquake protection. If a serious 'quake occurred, seismologists are confident they would be able to predict it in good time to be able to alert the emergency services.

Great attention is paid to the design of 'quake-proof buildings. Since the 1923 disaster, many tower blocks have been built on rock foundations, with deep piles for extra sturdiness. The after-effects of an earthquake often include a series of devastating tidal waves, or tsunamis, so breakwaters and wharves have been raised and strengthened.

Nobody can say how well Tokyo would cope with another 'quake as serious as the one in 1923. Until there is another major tremor, planners will not know how successful their precautions have been.

*Matchbox city* Tokyo's wooden frame houses, with their paper walls and straw mats, were easy prey to the fires that followed the 1923 earthquake.

## GRIM FOUNDATIONS

WHEN THE MEN repairing Edo Castle after the earthquake of 1923 lifted one of the foundation stones, they found a group of human skeletons crushed beneath it. The skeletons were lying with their hands in an attitude of prayer, and gold coins were scattered over their heads and shoulders.

The skeletons were those of servants of the Tokugawa shoguns, the most powerful family in Japan. When the castle was built (it was finished in 1640) the servants had volunteered to be buried alive in the belief that a building constructed on living flesh would be impregnable.

A Frenchman, François Caron, reported in the 17th century that: 'They go with joy to the designated place and, lying down there, allow the foundation stones to be laid upon them.' Many similar stones may still be seen today by the castle's Hirakawa Gate. But nobody knows how many bodies lie beneath them or beneath Japan's other castles and temples.

# THE TROUBLE WITH TOKYO
## A dream city faces increasing problems of overcrowding

TOKYO is the richest city on Earth and land is so expensive that, according to the British news magazine *The Economist*, during a property boom in 1987 it would have cost more to buy Tokyo's metropolitan area than to buy all the land in the United States. Japan's capital is therefore also one of the world's most overcrowded cities. Tokyo has one-tenth of the open space of London per resident and suffers grave pollution.

The city's commuter problem is so severe that 'pushers', distinguishable from the guards by their white gloves, are employed to cram people into the trains. Overcrowding is becoming so great a problem that there is serious talk of moving the capital city elsewhere in an attempt to relieve the strain.

### Economic hub

The trouble is that Tokyo is the headquarters for all Japan's major industrial companies, as well as being home to the country's most prestigious university. Every ambitious Japanese person wants to live there.

Most people still work a six-day week and, as they have 12 to 14 days' national holiday a year, regard more than five days' additional holiday as a sign of disloyalty to their employer. A typical businessman's day might begin with a lengthy journey from the suburbs, followed by long hours at his desk. In the evening he might visit one of the city's 500 000 restaurants with a few colleagues – to continue their business discussions. Very little time is spent at home. But people are happy to live like this, if it means they will get ahead.

Enjoying leisure time in Tokyo is difficult. For example, the Japanese are fanatical golf lovers, but there are few courses in the country and membership of a club is prohibitively expensive. A cheaper alternative is the multistorey practice ranges that are becoming increasingly popular in the capital. This is the nearest that most Tokyo residents will ever get to a round of golf.

**Driving a bargain** *The high cost of some Western luxuries has inspired the Japanese to search for alternatives. They can now boast a high quality domestic whiskey and, with their multistorey driving ranges, have also found a solution to the lack of space for golf courses.*

### DID YOU KNOW..?

*THE JAPANESE have the longest life span of any people on Earth. Men can expect to live for 75 years, while women reach an average age of 81 years.*

# LIVING WITH LIMITS
## Looking behind the doors of Japanese homes

JAPAN HAS one of the richest and most powerful economies in the world, but the density of the population means the average Japanese lives in extremely cramped conditions. In Tokyo particularly, home to one in every four of the population of Japan, the demand for housing far exceeds supply. As a result, accommodation tends to be small – 90 per cent of the houses have less than 100 sq m (1075 sq ft) floor space.

Traditionally, the internal walls of Japanese houses are made of paper mounted on wooden frames. While the houses are cool in summer, they can be very cold in winter. They are not designed to last for more than about 40 years, but have one major advantage: they are quick and easy to rebuild if damaged in an earthquake.

Today many Japanese houses have Western-style interiors, but in virtually all homes one or two rooms have traditional tatami mats on the floors. The mats measure 1.8 m (6 ft) by 1 m (3 ft 3 in) and are 750 mm (3 in) thick. They are made of straw and reed, edged with cotton or silk. Rooms are measured by the number of mats they can hold: a room measuring six or eight mats, for instance, would serve as the living room by day, and the bedroom for a family of six (often including grandparents) by night.

When someone builds a new house it is quite usual to call in a Shinto priest to purify the ground before work begins. Owners often pray to the god of the land to allow the building to go ahead without mishap. It is also customary to place little cones of salt around the site, each containing a lighted stick of incense.

More than one in three of the homes in the Tokyo area never receive any direct sunlight. And many have sanitation that is primitive by Western standards.

227

# LIVING OUT AN IDEAL

## *Great thinkers apply their minds to creating a perfect city*

IMAGINE A PLACE where everybody is looked after. Imagine a place where food, clothing, housing and medical treatment are provided for all, where no one has to work for more than six hours a day.

The 16th-century English statesman Thomas More, who defied King Henry VIII and was beheaded, dreamed up just such a society. He called it Utopia (Greek for 'nowhere'). As ideal societies go, it also had its drawbacks.

If you did not have green fingers, you would not enjoy Utopia. Everybody had to garden. Two years of 'country living' were mandatory for all citizens. Spare time was to be devoted to learning, through private studies and public lectures. No consumer goods were available in the shops, and everyone was to dress in black. Once a month, all wives had to kneel down in front of their husbands and beg forgiveness. The punishment for pre-marital intercourse was celibacy for life. Adultery was rewarded with slavery. And, as in George Orwell's *1984*, somebody was always watching you to make sure you behaved yourself.

An earlier proposal for an ideal society, Plato's Republic, was hardly more enticing. In the Republic, what Plato called 'philosopher kings' were the elite. Then came the army. Last of all were the ordinary citizens. There was not much scope for social mobility. If you used your mind, you were not supposed to use your hands. If you were a stonecutter (as, in real life, the philosopher Socrates was apprenticed to be) you stayed a stonecutter. There was rigid censorship of all literature – and music and poetry were actually forbidden. The family was abolished, to be replaced with state nurseries. People

**Island paradise** *On Thomas Moore's Utopia, no town was isolated by more than a day's journey on foot.*

did not marry: they just 'bred' children when it seemed necessary.

Did More or Plato really expect people ever to live in the way they prescribed? More's Utopia was, as much as anything else, a critique of Tudor morals, assailing greedy kings and religious hypocrisy. Plato's ideal society, however, was a cold abstraction, denying human feeling.

Plans for ideal societies have usually involved suitable physical surroundings, too. More took care to describe how the cities of his Utopia looked. There were 54 of them, all exactly alike, with solid protective walls, terraced houses with large gardens, warehouses, communal dining halls and churches. Plato was more circumspect: the nearest he came to a town plan for his ideal republic was probably in his descriptions of the circular, moated city of Atlantis, but he included these in quite separate books. Neither Plato nor More, however, were to be the last to envision either the perfect life, or the perfect place to live it.

---

## CITIES OF RHYME AND REASON

POETS ARE DREAMERS, they say, but two at least – first Samuel Taylor Coleridge and, more than a century later, D.H. Lawrence – made practical plans to set up communities that would answer to their own ideals.

Indeed, Samuel Taylor Coleridge was practical enough to propose charging an entrance fee of £125 to anyone who wanted to join his 'pantisocracy', a community in which everyone would have equal powers. Coleridge envisaged 12 liberal, educated men emigrating to America with their wives to establish the settlement he called Susquehanna.

Coleridge was serious about his plan until his collaborator, the poet laureate Robert Southey, suggested that going to America was too drastic a first step. The

idealists should start more modestly with a co-operative in Wales. Vexed by this, and by Southey's intention to add servants to the community, Coleridge abandoned the scheme.

Lawrence had slightly grander plans: to sail away with 20 kindred souls, also to found a colony in America. He christened it Rananim. His hopes were perhaps too grand: at one stage he fixed on Fort Myers, Florida, as the site for Rananim. But as a millionaires' fishing resort it was hardly the ideal location.

Finally, Lawrence settled near Taos in New Mexico, where for a brief period he lived happily, building, tilling the land, painting and writing. But his ideal 'community' there consisted solely of himself, his wife Frieda, and occasional visitors.

# FORGING A NEW ORDER

*An architect takes on the ultimate design challenge: the reshaping of daily life*

IN THE LATE 1920s, a penniless fugitive from justice, an architect who had no home of his own, began drawing plans for a perfect city.

The new community, named Broadacre City, was to consist of innumerable homesteads. The houses themselves were to be simple and functional, in harmony with their environment. But Broadacre was to be more than a model of fine architecture; it was also to embody a new way of life.

### The good life

For the people who lived there, there would be no drudgery, no chasm between work and leisure. Farms – and every homestead was a farm – would be extensions of gardens. Factories would be centres of craftsmanship. Government would exist only to deal with essential administration. Such was the life in Broadacre as envisioned by the American architect Frank Lloyd Wright, who had achieved international renown for building houses that, despite their ultra-modern design, blended perfectly with their natural setting. But when he began work on his dream city, he had had more than a fair share of misfortune.

Wright had suffered broken marriages and messy divorces, and his mistress had died in a fire that had razed his own dream house, Taliesin, near Spring Green, Wisconsin, to the ground. After the First World War his reputation had plummeted; work was hard to find. The supreme indignity came when he was arrested for adultery at the age of 60. Broadacre was his response to the mauling that fate and the modern world had handed out.

Wright summed up his sense of all that was wrong with modern cities in one word: rent. Ideas, land, even money (if it was borrowed) had to be paid for. For Wright, such a system was inherently exploitative. He believed that modern city dwellers had no sense of themselves as productive individuals, and so were slaves to rent.

### Barter economy

But in Broadacre, such slavery would be impossible. Everyone would own enough land to grow food for himself and his family. There would be no opportunity for outsiders to come between the citizen and what he produced and exploit both for money. Goods and services would all be exchanged, not bought and sold for monetary profit.

Did anyone ever build anything like Broadacre in reality? The answer is no. But the stunningly original houses that Wright built remain, along with the elaborate drawings he made of Broadacre, to hint at the possibilities he dreamed of and that might have been.

***Dream builder*** *Drawn in the 1930s, Frank Lloyd Wright's sketch for Broadacre City incorporates buildings from earlier stages of his career – and helicopters resembling spinning tops as transport for the town.*

# THE LONDON THAT NEVER WAS

*Why was Christopher Wren's plan for rebuilding London rejected?*

'IF YOU SEEK his monument, look around you,' reads the translation of Christopher Wren's epitaph in St Paul's Cathedral in London. In the wake of the Great Fire of 1666, Wren had built a new cathedral, along with 51 of the 84 churches that the fire had destroyed. However, this was but minor repair work compared to what Wren had wanted to do – to recreate London from scratch. On September 11, 1666, just nine days after the fire started, Wren had presented King Charles II with his plan for a new metropolis.

### Lost opportunity

The plan was rejected but, over 200 years later, when there was an outbreak of cholera in London, health experts claimed that had the king adopted Wren's scheme, thereby doing away with the maze of cramped and overcrowded alleyways, the mortality rate might have been as much as a third lower. After Wren's death in 1723, his

son lamented that the opportunity had been lost for making the city 'the most magnificent, as well as commodious for health and trade of any upon Earth'.

Wren's plan was nothing if not expansive. All new streets would conform to one of three widths: 27, 18 or 9 m (90, 60 or 30 ft). Narrow alleys, one of the great characteristics of the old London, would vanish. A big, open, public quay would grace the riverside, between the Tower and Temple.

Its sheer scope, as much as anything, made the plan an impossibility. Such a scheme would have been colossally expensive. At a time when families were homeless and when many were struggling simply to survive, rapid reconstruction of the city was vital.

### Forgotten dreams

King Charles had alternative plans to choose from. John Evelyn presented the monarch with a scheme not unlike Wren's, but on a smaller scale, and with more concern to preserve London's traditional character. Dr Robert Hooke came up with a stern scheme for making London's streets into gridiron patterns. Valentine Knight had an idea for an arc-shaped canal that would run from Billingsgate to Fleet River. The king accepted none of these plans.

But in 1675, the rebuilding of St Paul's, to Wren's design, began. More than 86 000 tonnes of building stone, 500 tonnes of rubble, a lot of marble, bricks, and £750 000 and 35 years later it was complete. If not an entire city, this magnificent building is a monument indeed to Wren's genius.

---

## A LEGENDARY CITY OF GOLD

GOLD is the sweat of the Sun. Or so the South American Chibcha Indians believed, and the 16th-century Spanish conquistadores took this to mean that the Indians' supplies of the precious metal were boundless. After discovering the huge wealth of the Aztecs and the Incas, they became convinced that even more treasure was to be found further into the interior of South America, where entire cities, entire countries of gold were just waiting to be plundered. They called the mythical place El Dorado. But in fact, El Dorado was not a city or country at all. The name originally belonged to the ruler of Colombia, an Indian town near Bogotá.

### Coronation ritual

Tradition had it that when a new king of the Chibchas came to the throne, his tribesmen would smear him from head to toe in a mixture of sticky resin and gold dust, until he glistened magnificently, reflecting the rays of the Sun god that the tribe worshipped. Then the king would be rowed out into the middle of nearby Lake Guatavita. He would slowly remove the gold from his body and throw it into the water. At last he would dive in, washing off all the gold that remained stuck to his skin. The tribesmen would then hurl yet more gold into the water. Subsequent attempts to drain the lake and recover the gold have all failed. As far as we know, the treasure is still lurking down there, an enduring testament to El Dorado, the man of gold.

Not only the Spanish, but Germans, Portuguese, and even Queen Elizabeth's courtier Sir Walter Raleigh, made many fruitless journeys into the jungles of South America in search of the gold. Despite their failure to uncover further wealth, these explorers did help to put the continent on the map by bringing back priceless information about the geography of the land through which they travelled.

The English poet John Milton used the myth of El Dorado in *Paradise Lost* in 1667; a century later, the French philosopher

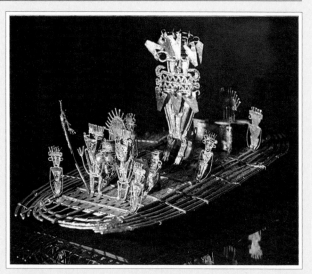

*Royal trappings Discovered in a cave near Bogotá in 1969, this golden model of a raft bears El Dorado; his oarsmen face away out of deference to his glory.*

Voltaire used it in *Candide*. By then, the legend of the city that never existed was as deeply embedded in European tradition as the gold in the mud of the Colombian lake.

# AN ODD PLACE TO LIVE

## *With the 'space race' the answer may be down not out*

EVERYONE needs somewhere to live and work, and humans are adept at making the best of their circumstances – they will live in houses of ice, mud huts, in tents or on cramped houseboats, if that is the best they can find.

In the industrialised world, the problem is not materials for building but limited space, and the prohibitive price of land. The answer in most industrial cities has been the skyscraper – building *up* rather than *out*. But what can be done in an overcrowded city like Tokyo, where earthquakes prevent real skyscrapers from making economic use of the world's most costly real estate?

The Japanese are thinking of turning the world upside down. The government is financing two business corporations, Taisei and Shimizu, to plan huge underground cities to accommodate 100 000 people, along with offices, theatres, libraries, hotels, sports centres and a complete transport network. Taisei have christened their project Alice City, after Lewis Carroll's heroine who found a 'Wonderland' in a rabbit hole. They expect their city to be built some time in the 21st century.

The underground city is technically feasible, but there is a massive psychological barrier to overcome. Will people be able to cope with living away from the Sun and sky? At present, the planners intend residential buildings to be on the surface, with residents commuting down to workplaces or entertainments. But even being buried just for working hours may not seem an attractive idea.

### *It's all done with mirrors*

However, in Minneapolis in the United States, the University of Minnesota has already built its Civil and Mineral Engineering Building 95 per cent underground, to a depth of 35 m (110 ft). Even the subterranean floors get some sunlight and a view out of the window,

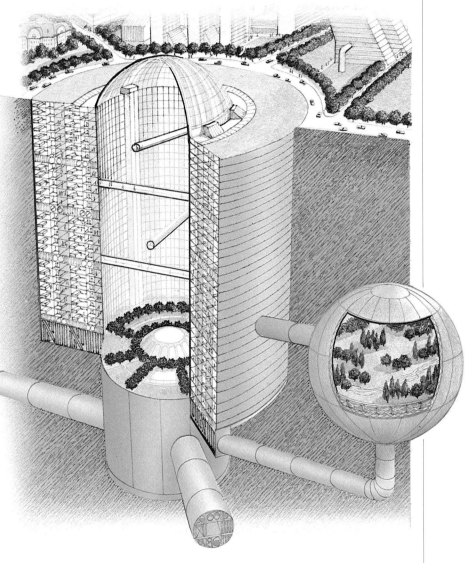

***Earthquake-proof housing*** *One of the great advantages of a subterranean city, particularly for the Japanese, is that the shaking from earthquakes is far less below 30 m (100 ft) than at surface level.*

thanks to an elaborate system of mirrors. In the United States and Canada, not only commercial buildings are going underground. More than 6000 houses have now been dug into the earth there, providing comfortable, secure and energy-saving homes.

Perhaps the problems of subterranean living are best revealed by the immense efforts made to mimic life above ground. Tokyo's Asahi television centre, 20 m (65 ft) below the surface, is even designed to provide an imitation of the weather. On a rainy night, a special shower – carefully insulated from the electrical systems – creates the impression of rain in the studio as well.

231

# CITY IN THE SKY

*Where you could spend most of your life without ever coming down to Earth*

IF YOU have a taste for high living, an apartment on the 92nd floor of the John Hancock Center skyscraper in Chicago might be just the place for you. A resident with a preference for an air-conditioned lifestyle need hardly ever step outside the building. A ride down in the lifts takes you to your office or your neighbourhood shopping centre on the 44th floor – with a bank, a post office, a laundry and a grocery store that delivers to your door. After that, why not take a dip in the pool on the same floor? And for dinner you can zoom up to the restaurant on the 95th floor and look out over an unobstructed 100 km (60 mile) view beyond the Chicago skyline and over Lake Michigan.

### Tower of power

Chicagoans have christened the Hancock Center 'Big John', and the building's vital statistics certainly show why. A black tower 344 m (1127 ft) tall, it was the first 100-storey building in the city. By the time it was completed in 1968, it had consumed 5 million man-hours of work and enough steel to build 33 000 cars. The building has 2000 km (1250 miles) of electric wiring and 11 459 panes of glass, which cover nearly 3.2 hectares (8 acres) of the tower's surface.

The safety of the 2000 people who live in the Hancock Center and the 5000 more who work there is a major priority ('Big John' was the inspiration for the disaster movie *Towering Inferno*). While the Hancock may sway and creak in storm-force winds, its innovatory design – a series of x-shaped trusses stacked on top of each other – provides sound support.

Still, no one could spend their whole existence in the Hancock. Three things it does not have are a church, a maternity ward and a funeral parlour.

---

## DID YOU KNOW..?

*THE THREE lifts servicing the Hancock Center's 94th-floor observatory are the fastest in the world. They make the trip from the ground in about 39 seconds, travelling at about 30 km/h (20 mph). Half a million visitors a year make the high-speed ascent.*

---

## RADICAL CHIC

FASHIONABLE Parisians are going underground. Not into the Métro or the Resistance, but into the caves their ancestors lived in. In search of holiday retreats, the modern city dwellers are moving into attractive little villages just north of the Loire valley, where the inhabitants have for many centuries lived like troglodytes in their *caforts* (short for *caves fortes*, 'cave strongholds') carved out of the soft white tuff rock.

The centre of this region is the pretty but strange little town of Trôo. Here the cave houses rise in tiers, with flowered terraces, and are connected by narrow passageways, steps and secret tunnels. Each house has a principal chamber with a fireplace. Other smaller rooms open off the main room or a side corridor. In recent years ceilings have been added, but the walls are generally bare stone.

A cave has much to recommend it as a holiday home. Today's troglodytes have added bathrooms and central heating, and television aerials are everywhere on the outside. The rock keeps the home an even temperature all year round – and once locked up, it is almost burglar-proof.

---

# STONE AGE SURVIVORS

*Were the cave dwellers of the Philippines a hoax that fooled the world?*

WE ALL KNOW that our prehistoric ancestors lived in caves. But are there really any people alive today in some remote area of the world who still follow the same habits and customs as the cavemen of 35 000 BC, untouched by the progress of civilisation? Scientists would certainly like to think so. A chance to study prehistoric man in the flesh would help to answer so many questions about the nature of humanity – for instance, were human beings naturally peaceful, until corrupted by civilisation?

### Noble savages

So there was great excitement in scientific circles when, in 1971, a Philippine hunter called Dafal announced the discovery of the tiny Tasaday tribe in the forest on the island of Mindanao. Here were 27 people living in isolation, untouched by knowledge of agriculture or animal husbandry. They lived in caves. They could make fire, but had no weapons, only primitive stone tools. They had no leaders or social hierarchy, living a simple life of total equality, sharing their few worldly goods in a spirit of peace and happiness.

Manda Elizalde, the Minister for Tribal Affairs in President Ferdinand Marcos's Philippine Government, intervened to save the Tasaday from the loggers who were threatening to destroy their area of rain forest. Anthropologists, journalists and television crews poured in from across the world to witness and record the Stone Age spectacle. Then, in 1972, the Tasaday's forest was declared a reserve and most outsiders were excluded. There the matter rested for 14 years.

In 1986, after the collapse of the Marcos Government, a Swiss journalist called Oswald Iten published a sensational report denouncing the Tasaday as a hoax. He claimed the cavemen had told him they were ordinary local tribesmen who had been persuaded by Elizalde to pose as Stone Age people. Elizalde then, allegedly, creamed off the government grants that he arranged for the newly discovered tribe. According to Iten, the supposed cave-dwellers really lived in houses and wore modern underwear beneath their 'primitive' leaf aprons.

### A convincing performance?

Scientists, many of whom had certified the genuineness of the Tasaday, quarrelled in public. They argued about the Tasaday's stone tools. Some said they were too badly made to be useful, that they must be fakes. They argued about the Tasaday's language. Was it ancient or invented? And if it was invented, how did the children manage to give such convincing performances? And they argued about research techniques – can you get people to give you the answers you want by loading the questions you ask?

Meanwhile, the Tasaday moved from their forest caves to Elizalde's mansion in the Philippine capital, Manila, and became involved in complex litigation over the claims and counterclaims about their identity. Even if their Stone Age life ever was real, they can surely never go back to it again.

# FROM THE MUD, AN EMPIRE

*Venice rose from marshland to become one of Europe's grandest and most powerful states*

NO CITY conjures up more romantic images than Venice – gondolas gliding down the Grand Canal, crumbling Renaissance palaces reflected in the still waters, peaceful squares lapped on one side by the waters of a quiet lagoon. But there was nothing romantic about the founding of the city. Venice was born of fear. About 1500 years ago, Italy was going through deeply troubled times. The Roman Empire was collapsing as ferocious barbarian invaders swept down from the north, laying waste all that lay in their path. The area that is now Venice was then simply a collection of islets and mud flats in a crescent-shaped lagoon, an inhospitable wasteland, marshy and malarial.

But it had one vital attraction – it could offer safety. When Attila and the Huns sacked the city of Aquileia on the mainland in AD 452, the inhabitants fled to the marshes. And the Lombard invasion a century later brought still more frightened people from the burning cities to seek refuge on the islets of the lagoon.

The newcomers quickly learned to deal with their waterbound environment, protecting the mud flats with stakes, constructing buildings on piles, connecting islets by filling in channels. Situated near the centre of the lagoon, Venice forged ahead of the other small settlements and by the 8th century had become an independent aristocratic republic under an elected ruler, the doge. Centuries of empire, trade and culture were to follow.

Venice is now one of the tourist magnets of the world – a strange fate to have befallen an area that must once have seemed among the loneliest and most desolate on Earth.

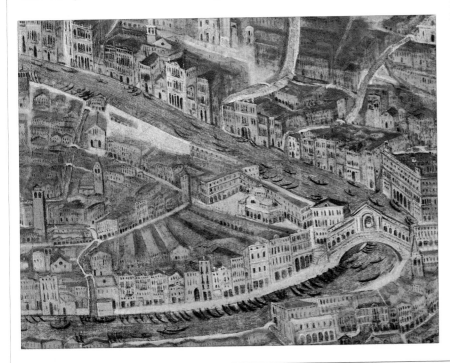

***Swamp city*** *By the late 1700s, some 200 palaces had been erected on the archipelago of mud banks and islets that make up the historic city of Venice.*

## A HOLE AWAY FROM HOME

IF YOU ARE male and looking for somewhere cheap and clean to spend the night in Japan's capital city, you might consider checking in at one of the capsule hotels that have been springing up both in Tokyo and in other Japanese cities over the last ten years. Accommodating up to four times as many customers in the space of a conventional hotel, they are Japan's answer to urban overcrowding.

But what is it like to spend the night in one of these hotels? A guest being led to his room is confronted by long corridors with two tiers of plastic capsules on each side. The boxes are air-conditioned but tiny, measuring 1.5 m (5 ft) in height and width, and 2 m (6 ft 6 in) in length.

Once the hotel guest has crawled inside, he will not be able to stand up, but at least he should be able to sleep fully stretched out on the mattress on the floor. For their size, the mini-rooms are remarkably well equipped, with radio and television, a folding desk, an alarm clock and a telephone. Nearly all luggage, however, has to be left at the hotel reception.

The capsule hotels have been a great success with customers because of their low rates. (Astronomical land values have pushed up the price of hotel developments – and so the cost of a standard hotel room.)

***Confined luxury*** *A young Japanese enjoys the cleanliness and amenities of Osaka's Capsule Inn.*

Will the sleeping capsule spread to other countries with a more spacious lifestyle? American businessmen have certainly started to take an interest in the idea and think it might have a future.

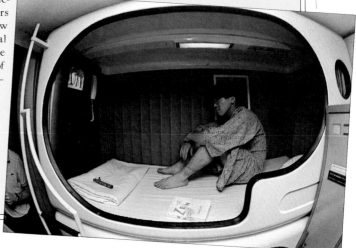

# AT HOME IN CEMETERY CITY

*Of all the world's cemeteries, Cairo's is the most 'lively'*

DRIVING into central Cairo from the airport, visitors pass through what looks like a huge poverty-stricken suburb on the eastern fringes of the city. The mud-brick houses are brown and dusty, and the narrow streets swarm with the typical life of a poor district of Cairo – the hustle and bustle of children playing, women balancing their shopping on their heads, men smoking hookahs in cafes.

But the district is not quite what it seems. Above the chaos and the squalor rise domes and minarets, marking the magnificent tombs of Egypt's medieval rulers, the Fatimids and Mamelukes. For this lively, crowded part of town is Cairo's famous 'City of the Dead' – a vast sprawling cemetery.

The more important of the historic mausoleums are carefully protected as religious monuments, but the more commonplace family tombs, mostly solid structures the size of a small house, have long provided excellent accommodation for the living as well as the dead. Sometimes families inhabit their own tomb, adding a patio and a roof terrace to make it more like a villa. Others have taken over tombs deserted by their owners, or pay rent for a two- or three-room burial chamber – usually on the understanding that they leave for the day whenever the landlord comes to honour his dead ancestors. And, after a funeral, they must move out for some weeks while the body decomposes in Cairo's extreme heat.

The habit of living among the tombs is almost as ancient as the 800-year-old cemetery itself, but the population explosion in Egypt has driven ever more people to search for living space in the necropolis. The City of the Dead is now reckoned to have about 300 000 living inhabitants and their number is still growing (although most live in mud-brick houses built between the tombs).

For those supplied with electricity and running water, the cemetery can be a perfectly comfortable place to live.

## DID YOU KNOW..?

*SOME districts of Cairo and its suburbs have a population density of as much as 104 000 people per sq km (260 000 per sq mile). This means the Egyptian capital is almost four times more crowded than Manhattan Island, New York.*

## POLAND'S MIRACULOUS SAINTS IN SALT

MORE THAN 100 m (325 ft) below the ground, in the depths of a mine in Poland, stands the magnificent chapel of the Blessed Kinga with its 17th-century altar. In the maze of tunnels around it are other underground shrines, statues of saints and movingly represented religious scenes. The siting of these sacred objects is astonishing enough, but even stranger is how they were made. The chapels and statues have been carved out of rock salt. This is the famous Wieliczka mine near Kraków, 150 km (100 miles) of tunnels hewn out by generations of miners since the 11th century. The salt carvings were an expression of their religious devotion and their desire for supernatural protection in their perilous daily toil.

Nowadays the mine is not only a popular tourist attraction but also serves as an underground leisure centre. The man-made warren of Wieliczka features a snackbar, a ballroom, a tennis court and even a sanitorium where asthma sufferers can be effectively healed from their ailments thanks to the salt mine's beneficial microclimate.

***Cellar chapel*** *The underground nave of the Blessed Kinga chapel in Poland is 54 m (177 ft) long and carved from salt. Kinga was a nun who came to Poland from Hungary in the 13th century.*

# A HUMAN WARREN

*Why would anyone choose to live under the ground?*

VISITORS to some of Coober Pedy's hotels in South Australia find they are staying in tasteful accommodation, with wall-to-wall carpeting, comfortable furniture, paintings on the walls, and modern electronic gadgetry. But it is no use asking for a room with a view, because there are no windows – everything is *underground.*

Coober Pedy is a remote mining town that produces almost 90 per cent of the world's total supply of opals. Ever since the gemstone was discovered there in 1915, many of the miners have lived in 'dugouts' beneath the desert. Amused aborigines named the place *kupa piti* – 'white man in a hole'.

### Merits of cave life

Carved out of soft, pink sandstone, the miners' dwellings are much more than just holes in the ground. As well as standard modern conveniences, they have a few special advantages. Billiards players can chalk their cues by twisting them against the ceiling, and home improvers can extend a room simply by taking a pickaxe to the wall.

Lack of wood for building may be one reason for going underground (Coober Pedy's last tree died in 1971). But the main reason is to escape the

heat. Summer temperatures can soar to 50°C (122°F) in the desert above, but the underground homes maintain a comfortable temperature of about 25°C (77°F). About a third of Coober Pedy's 4000 inhabitants live underground.

In other hot places around the world, people have taken to the underground life, although in less luxurious style. On the borders of the furnace-like Sahara desert, for instance, in the Matmata area of southern Tunisia, the local Berber people have dug deep to escape the fierce climate. Their two- and three-storey houses, cut into the soft

**Tunisian tunnels**
*Berbers escape the summer heat and winter winds in their underground abodes at Matmata.*

rock, form a circle around a central courtyard where communal village life is carried on. There are about 700 of these pits which, one theory suggests, were constructed because building material was scarce and the rock soft. It was therefore simply easier for the Berbers to build down than up.

# THE TUNNELS OF CU CHI

*The Vietcong's underground resistance*

FOR AMERICAN soldiers, one of the most frustrating aspects of the war in Vietnam was the elusiveness of their communist foe. In January 1966, for instance, 8000 US troops were airlifted into the Cu Chi district, 30 km (20 miles) from Saigon, an area known to be thick with Vietcong guerrillas. Yet despite the speed and scale of the operation, virtually no enemy troops were sighted. The Vietcong seemed able literally to vanish into thin air. In fact, they had vanished into thick earth.

### Guerrilla fortress

Underneath Cu Chi the Vietcong guerrillas had dug a complex network of tunnels about 320 km (200 miles) long, an extraordinary feat of military engineering. The horror of living in this underground fortress can be readily

imagined. Yet some Vietcong stood the conditions for years at a time.

Many of the tunnels were hardly big enough for a man to pass through – they were rarely wider than 1 m (3 ft), and often no higher than they were wide. They opened out into chambers, usually about 3 m (10 ft) square, where weapons were made or repaired, papers and pamphlets printed, or meetings held. The atmosphere underground was hot, stifling and smelly, especially where the tunnel complex reached four 'storeys' into the earth. Food was often in short supply, and the guerrillas had to eat what they could. One Vietcong commented: 'I found grilled rat had a better flavour than chicken or duck.'

While the war raged overhead, everything possible was done to make

the Vietcong soldiers feel at home. There was even a troupe of actors and entertainers that toured the tunnels putting on performances to improve morale. For Cu Chi was only the largest of a huge series of tunnel complexes that surrounded Saigon, from the coast as far as the Cambodian border.

### Effective defence

For ten years the tunnels of Cu Chi defied large American forces. Although many Vietcong died underground, the network survived bomb and gas attacks and penetration by specially trained US fighting men, the 'tunnel rats'. After the communist victory in 1975, the whole district was formally honoured as the 'Iron Land of Cu Chi'. Ironically, the tunnels have since been restored as a showpiece for overseas visitors.

# WELCOME TO THE WORLD

## The strange customs and superstitions associated with childbirth

ADVOCATES of 'natural' childbirth in Western countries urge midwives to put a newborn child straight into its mother's arms as soon as it is born. Such a notion would appal the Akha tribe of Thailand. A newborn Akha baby must cry three times before anyone will touch it. The three cries are thought to be noisy requests to the god Apoe Miyeh, asking for a soul, a blessing and a long life.

Once the baby has performed that duty, the midwife will pick it up and give it a temporary name. This is to keep evil spirits at bay: they would assume an unnamed child is unwanted, and try to claim it. The baby is given its permanent name at a later ceremony, when it is clear that it is healthy enough to survive.

All over the world, people have traditionally taken elaborate precautions to keep a newborn child and its mother safe from supernatural harm. In European countries, midwives would untie all knots in the house to help the expectant mother to relax and to ensure a smooth delivery, while bolting the doors and windows to lock out evil.

### Easing childbirth

A curious 19th-century British custom involved hanging a document called *Our Saviour's Letter* over the bed during childbirth. Purportedly written by Jesus to one Agbarus of Edessa, the text was probably a medieval invention. It was supposedly effective against witchcraft as well as an aid to trouble-free childbirth.

All these precautions might ease the birth, but the time that a child was born was still thought by many to have an influence on the kind of life it would eventually have.

In India, a child born during an eclipse was distinctly ill-omened, and only after performing certain rites was the father allowed to see his child. A German tradition says that if the clouds resemble sheep when the child is born, it will enjoy good fortune. Many cultures believed that a child born on a Sunday would have a happy life, while an old British tradition has it that a child born when the clock strikes three, six, nine or twelve will be able to see ghosts – a doubtful privilege which is, however, offset by imperviousness to spells and charms.

Many cultures had purification ceremonies for both mother and child immediately after birth, but perhaps the most unexpected is the Philippine tradition of 'mother roasting'. The mother lies near a specially built fire for a week. Then, water is poured over the hot rocks of the fire, and the steam purifies her.

**Out demons out** *A 19th-century Welsh collection of legends recounted the trials of Jennet Francis, who, after a desperate fight, rescued her newborn son from the clutches of goblins and ghouls.*

### DID YOU KNOW..?

*IN 19TH-CENTURY WALES, the bone from a shoulder of mutton was thought to help predict the sex of an unborn child. After being charred in a fire, the bone was hung over the door of the house. The child would have the same sex as the next person (other than a member of the family) to come through the door.*

\* \* \*

*IN GERMANY, it was once believed that a wife who carried one of her husband's socks would never give birth prematurely.*

# OF MAIDENS AND MIRACLES

*What do Jesus, Buddha and Zoroaster have in common?*

FOR CHRISTIANS, the conception of Jesus is just as significant an event as His birth. That Jesus's mother, Mary, was a virgin when she conceived Him is a certain sign that Jesus had a divine origin, that He truly is the Son of God. But belief in a miraculous birth is by no means unique to Christianity, and can in fact be found in religions the world over.

Buddha, it is said, went through thousands of incarnations before he took the form of a small white elephant and entered his future mother's womb through her right side. The event was accompanied by other miracles – musical instruments that played by themselves, rivers that stopped flowing, and a sudden, unseasonal blossoming of trees and flowers.

### Shining light

Zoroaster, the prophet of the Parsee religion, also existed in spirit before his birth in the 7th century BC. His father was believed to be Ahura Mazda, the supreme god, and his mother a 15-year-old maiden named Dughda. During her pregnancy Dughda dazzled onlookers with divine light radiating

*Divine birth The birth of the Indian god Krishna is attended by astrologers who consult their almanacs to foresee the fortunes of his life. Krishna means 'dark as a cloud', as this painting shows.*

from her body, and her parents swiftly married her off to a man from a nearby village to avoid a scandal.

A divine light burned too from the Indian maiden Devaki, after the Hindu god Vishnu entered her womb. He was born in earthly form as Krishna, to live both as a warrior and philosopher before returning to the spiritual realm as a Hindu god in his own right.

In South America, the mother of the Aztec god and hero Quetzalcoatl was a virgin when a deity took the form of morning, breathed on her, and made her pregnant so that Quetzalcoatl could take human form.

The ancient Greek supreme god, Zeus, turned himself into a shower of golden rain in order to impregnate Danae (who gave birth to the gorgon-slayer Perseus), and into a swan before he raped Leda. One of the twins born as a consequence was Helen, over whom Greece and Troy went to war. Perhaps Zeus's most brazen effort was to impersonate the warrior Amphitryon on the very night that he was at last going to consummate his marriage to

*Precious love The Greek god Zeus transforms himself into a shower of gold to press his amorous advances on the virgin and symbol of chastity, Danae. Her attendant catches the coins.*

Alcmene – who had barred Amphitryon from her bed until he had avenged the deaths of her brothers.

Zeus watched the battle, and in Amphitryon's shape entertained Alcmene with tales of 'his' exploits. At the same time he ordered the sun god Helios to take a day off, so stretching the night, and his time with Alcmene, from 12 to 36 hours.

When Amphitryon himself arrived home victorious, he was extremely disconcerted at Alcmene's coolness, while she found him tiresomely repetitive in the accounts of his feats. But the prophet Tiresias soon managed to reconcile the couple by explaining what had actually happened.

It was, in fact, an ancient Greek habit to ascribe divine fatherhood to any highly distinguished person. The philosopher Plato and the mathematician Pythagoras, for instance, were both said to be sons of the god Apollo.

### Magical flower

Some of the world's ancient civilisations created myths of miraculous conception that involved no divine powers and had political rather than religious significance. In such cases, some magical object was generally held to be the father. For example, Fo-hi, a legendary emperor of China, was conceived when his mother swallowed a flower that had clung to her clothes as she was bathing.

237

# THE SAVIOUR OF MOTHERS

*The surprisingly simple solution to the problem of puerperal fever*

IN EUROPE in the mid 19th century, any woman who went into hospital to have her baby stood a one-in-four chance of dying there from puerperal fever. But the man who virtually eradicated it from his own hospital was ridiculed and died mad.

Ignaz Semmelweis made his discovery at the obstetric clinic in Vienna, where he began work in 1844. Puerperal fever was, as elsewhere, rife there. The disease sets in when bacterial infection attacks the mother's inevitably vulnerable birth-passage after the child is born.

Semmelweis noticed, however, that the fatal fever was two or three times more common in the one section of the clinic where medical students were taught. They would come here to assist during labour – straight from the dissecting room. Semmelweis concluded that somehow the students were carrying something – he did not know what – from the bodies of the mothers who had just died from puerperal fever to those giving birth. That 'something' caused the fever.

### A clean break

His solution was stunningly simple. He ordered the students to wash their hands in a disinfectant of dilute chlorinated lime before examining any of the patients in the maternity ward. As a result, deaths on the ward dropped from nearly one in five patients to just over one in every hundred.

Amazingly, his superiors at the clinic were unimpressed, failing to understand Semmelweis' ideas – bacteria were unheard of then – and clinging to the belief that the disease was unavoidable. Semmelweis' liberal political opinions were also deemed suspect and increased opposition to his work. In 1850, frustrated and disillusioned, he returned to his native Hungary.

There, his work was endorsed to the full, but medical opinion in the rest of Europe remained set against him. Semmelweis spent a further 15 years battling the medical establishment, and then his spirit finally broke. In July 1865 he went into a mental hospital, and within a month was dead.

Yet Semmelweis was actually in the vanguard of contemporary medical thinking. Around the time of Semmelweis' death, Joseph Lister in England established the principles of antiseptic surgery, while Louis Pasteur in France discovered the existence of bacteria. Had Semmelweis lived just a few years longer, he would have heard himself acclaimed as a pioneering genius.

There was one last irony in his life. Before going into the asylum Semmelweis had cut his hand while dissecting the body of a woman who had died of puerperal fever. The wound became infected, and Semmelweis died, of all things, from the very disease he had done so much to eradicate.

## DID YOU KNOW..?

*TO BE BORN with a caul (part of the foetal membrane, which sometimes surrounds the head of a newborn baby like a hood) was once believed to be a sign of good luck. And, in the 19th century, cauls were prized by sailors as protection against drowning, and were bought and sold for large sums of money.*

## WHEN MEN GIVE BIRTH

LONG BEFORE the advent of modern anaesthetics, the expectant mothers of Dumfries, Scotland, had the good fortune to experience totally painless childbirth. According to a 1772 report, the local midwives had the power to transfer the pains of labour from wife to husband. How they managed this remains a mystery, but the babies 'kindly came into the world without giving the mother the least uneasiness, while the poor husband was roaring with agony and in uncouth and unnatural pains.'

**Ritual pregnancy** *This Zairean headboard depicts a man lying beside his wife giving birth – a representation of the curious couvade syndrome.*

The extraordinary spectacle of husbands suffering more from pregnancy and childbirth than their wives has not, by any means, been limited to one town in Scotland. Known as couvade (from the French for 'brooding' or 'hatching'), the phenomenon occurs in various forms all over the world.

In some African tribes, the men will take to their beds for the entire duration of their wives' pregnancy. The women continue to work as usual until a few hours before giving birth. They believe that men are cleverer as well as physically stronger than women, and are therefore better able to defend unborn children against malign and evil spirits – which is their task during the pregnancy.

The symbolic activity undertaken by fathers is not always so extreme. Some Pacific islanders do no more than separate husband and wife during the birth and for several days afterwards; and during this time the man will avoid certain foods and certain tasks that the islanders regard as 'man's work'.

In medieval Europe a woman would put on her husband's clothes when labour started, hoping to transfer the birth pangs to him. The belief that all fathers feel sympathetic labour pains had a practical use, too. Villagers in the north of England would find the father of an illegitimate child simply by waiting for the mother to go into labour, and then scouring the village for any man lying ill in bed.

# TRYING TIMES

### Earning your place in a tough society

**F**EW PEOPLE announce their place in society as unmistakably as a Masai warrior from East Africa. His face and body are covered in red ochre, his hair, similarly reddened, is elaborately braided. He wears a simple red cloth, and a mass of bright bead jewellery. He is one of the Masai elite. His job is to defend the village against its human enemies and its cattle against marauding lions.

All Masai belong to an 'age clan' within their village. The village medicine man announces the formation of a clan every few years, which means that boys may be as young as 13 or as old as 17 when they join. To

**Future fighter** *A Masai boy sits patiently while his hair is shaved off. This is only one of the ceremonies he undergoes before becoming a warrior.*

become a *moran* – a warrior – each boy has his head shaved, takes a ritual bath and is then publicly circumcised with a sharp stone. His main goal during this ordeal is to remain entirely silent, although his parents may howl and wail on his behalf.

Once this test is over, the boys grow their hair again and dye it and their bodies with ochre. During this period the group is also allowed to indulge in unruly behaviour, showing little respect for their elders or the traditions of the tribe. Then the group sets about building its own compound. Here, as the village's current defenders, the new 'junior warriors' will live with girls of their own age group. The older warriors – those aged about 25 – go through a further ceremony to become fully fledged members of the tribe, making decisions on its business affairs and grazing lands, while belonging to the reserve defence force.

### Changes in status

The age clan before them give up their distinctive, red-daubed appearance, leave their *moran* compound – and are now allowed to marry. These ex-warriors are junior elders; their main task is to prepare the boys of the tribe for initiation. In due course, they will become senior elders, who act as lawyers, judges and counsellors to the village group. Eventually they will retire from public duties, to be 'venerable elders'.

Few societies are as rigidly structured as the Masai, who suffer very little internal friction. Part of the reason for their success in this respect may lie in such rites as the public initiation into adulthood that all Masai men have to endure. The rite signals the end of childhood, and binds them irreversibly to the life of their fellows. And that is what all initiation rites do: they sever the initiate from the past, and mark the beginning of a new and promising life as a member of a group.

---

### DID YOU KNOW..?

*BOYS OF THE Kukata people of Australia traditionally undergo a ritual of walking through fire to make them fearless. In other Aboriginal tribes, women press the boys down onto a fire, or hurl flaming sticks over the boys' heads.*

# STUNG INTO ACTION
*Taulipáng Indians consider pain a tonic*

ADOLESCENCE is difficult enough without its onset being greeted by a whipping, having your chin, arms and chest scored with cuts, and having an open basketwork frame of stinging ants pressed against your body.

That is how the Taulipáng Indians of the Guianas in South America initiate boys into manhood. And if any boy shows signs of fear or of feeling the pain, his ordeal is repeated. Each part of the ceremony has its significance. The whipping purifies the boy and gives him strength. The cuts on the chin are believed to help to make him expert with his blowpipe, and those on the arms improve his archery. The agony of the ants is said to 'refresh' him, keeping him active and wide awake.

The Taulipáng Indians do not reserve these painful encounters with insects solely for puberty rites. Most people voluntarily undergo it whenever they feel in need of an invigorating tonic. Once, an entire village went through the ceremony before an important visitor arrived. The Taulipáng also claim that it helps fend off disease and improves their humour and hunting skills.

*Painful rite* A Taulipáng boy undergoes the ceremony in which stinging ants are placed on his chest. This is the last of a series of torments suffered to attain adult status.

# AN EDUCATION IN ITSELF
*German students learned a sharp lesson before class*

A NEW STUDENT arriving at a German university at any time between the 14th and late 17th centuries might reasonably expect to have his intellectual powers put to the test. But first he had to be admitted to the student body – and that involved an ordeal that did not tax his knowledge or intelligence at all.

The new student had to undergo a humiliating ceremony known as the *depositio beani* or 'laying aside the yellow beak' – the *beanus* or 'yellow beak' being a nickname for the uninitiated. He would be obliged to dress up as an animal, in a hat with horns, and wear large wooden teeth. Then the older students would hunt the 'animal' down, beat him, saw off his horns, and pull out his teeth with pincers. The student's body was then smeared with a noxious ointment and he was force-fed pills made of cow dung.

### The final break

The new student was then accused of being a thief and sexual pervert; a student garbed as a priest heard the initiate's confession and absolved him.

The proceedings ended solemnly. A grain of salt, symbolising wisdom, was placed on the student's tongue and wine, symbolising the joy that wisdom brings, was dripped on his head. The former *beanus* was now a full member of the student body. But there was a final twist. To confirm his new status, the student had to pay for a supper for all his tormentors.

## DID YOU KNOW..?

*BOYS OF the South American Maue tribe have to perform seven dances with one arm thrust into a sleeve swarming with ants – and undergo the ritual several times before they marry.*

✳ ✳ ✳

*ON REACHING puberty, Omagua Indian girls in Peru were traditionally sewn into hammocks suspended from the ceiling of their huts. There they had to remain motionless for eight days, receiving only a little food and water once a day.*

# MYSTERIES AND PRIVILEGES

*The odd things a man must do to become a Freemason*

A T THE TEMPLE door a grown man removes his money, his watch and any other metal objects from his person. He is blindfolded, and a hangman's noose is tied round his neck. He stands in his trousers and shirt, his left breast bared, the right sleeve of his shirt rolled up past his elbow and his left trouser leg pulled up above the knee. On his left foot he wears a shoe, on the the right a slipper, so that when he walks he limps.

He is led just inside the door of the temple by its outer guard, the 'Tyler'. The Tyler announces him as 'a poor candidate in a state of darkness' who is seeking admittance to the 'mysteries and privileges of Freemasonry'.

### Character building

The Freemasons are a secret society, descended from the guilds of European stonemasons who built the great cathedrals and castles of the Middle Ages. They insist that their intentions are to encourage their members' moral growth and to promote good works in society. But their complicated initiation ceremonies almost defy belief.

Once inside the temple, the candidate is led by the hangman's rope into a windowless, candle-lit room, and paraded – with a dagger at his bared breast – past the lodge members.

He then swears 'in the presence of the Great Architect of the Universe' not to 'write those secrets, carve, mark, or otherwise them delineate . . . under no less a penalty . . . than that of having my throat cut across, my tongue torn out by the root and buried in the sand of the sea at low water mark . . .'.

Having so sworn, the candidate is accepted as an Entered Apprentice, the 'first degree' of Freemasonry. Most move up within a matter of months to become next a Fellow Craft mason and then a Master mason. It is said that the ceremony for entering this last is so gruesome – it apparently involves being symbolically hanged on a gallows and raised out of a coffin from the dead – that it gave rise to the popular term 'third degree', meaning torture.

*Solemn ceremony As depicted in this early 19th-century French painting, novices are blindfolded to symbolise the spiritual 'state of darkness' that Freemasonry will enlighten.*

## DID YOU KNOW..?

*AMONG THE HOPI Indians of North America, a girl enters womanhood only after she has spent four days in isolation, grinding corn in the house of an aunt. During her seclusion the girl is not allowed to scratch her body or head with her hand, but must use a stick. When she finally emerges, she wears her hair differently to show that she is ready to marry.*

✳  ✳  ✳

*IT USED to be widely believed in England that if a child did not cry during baptism, the rite had failed to drive the Devil out of him. In Germany, on the other hand, it was held that a child who cried during the ceremony would die young.*

241

# FOR BETTER OR FOR WORSE

*Why the moon is important when choosing a wedding date*

FOR MOST PEOPLE their wedding day is the most important planned date in their lives. Small wonder then that, down the ages, its correct timing has always been of great significance. Both the ancient Greeks and Romans favoured marriages at full Moon because they believed that the Moon influenced fertility. And today country folk in Germany and parts of the USA still look to the Moon for a blessing. Similarly, in coastal areas of Holland and eastern Scotland, weddings were once arranged to coincide with the high tide – a symbol of the good fortune that it was hoped would flood towards the couple in their married life.

Sometimes mystical and practical concerns coincided. The Romans favoured June weddings. Not only was the month dedicated to Juno, the goddess of marriage, it also meant that the bride would be able to help with the harvest before she was too many months pregnant. And as she would usually give birth to her first child in the early spring of the following year, she would have enough time to recover to assist with the next harvest too.

Man has long looked to the seasons for wedding-day inspiration. In the Swiss Alps and rural Ireland it is still the rule that weddings are conducted before harvest, and the people of southern Finland also avoid harvest time, marrying later in the year when the weather makes work impossible. The life-renewing spring encouraged, among others, the ancient Chinese, the Irish and the Scots, who have the rhyme: 'Marry when the year is new, always loving, always true.'

Not only the time of year but also the day of the week is said to influence wedding fortune. Although in the West Saturday is now the most convenient day, according to an old English rhyme it was ill-starred and bode the early death of one partner. Monday, Tuesday and Wednesday were then the recommended days. By contrast, in Italy superstition had it that the children of a Monday marriage might turn out to be idiots, while those of a Tuesday union could be clubfooted. And it was unthinkable to marry on December 28, Childermass, the anniversary of the slaughter of the children by Herod. In fact, the day of the week on which December 28 fell remained unlucky throughout the following year.

***Fun for all*** *In rural 19th-century Germany, the whole village would often join in the wedding celebration.*

## 'SOMETHING OLD, SOMETHING NEW...'

EVERY YEAR thousands of American and British brides go to the altar wearing, as the old verse dictates, 'Something old, something new, something borrowed, something blue'. But how many are aware of the special significance that each 'something' has?

'Something old' recalls the past happiness of the bride's courting period and symbolises the transfer of these feelings to her marriage. Lace is the conventional 'old' item, either in the form of a decorative frill or as a handkerchief or veil. The 'something new' is probably the most important symbol, representing the hoped-for success of her marriage. And the adoption of a completely new wardrobe on the wedding day is a universal custom, which the groom also frequently follows. By tradition, a few threads of the wedding dress are left hanging until the last moment so that the dress will be as new as possible.

A veil lent by a happily married woman is a popular choice for 'something borrowed'. This is a symbol of the loyalty of friends continuing in the bride's new life. Lastly, blue is the colour of constancy and fidelity and nowadays is often represented by a blue garter. This was also commonly borrowed, as the marriage prospects of single women were believed to be improved if they were to lend a bride one of their garters. As a result, popular brides would go to church with their legs completely ringed by their friends' lucky lace bands.

Scandinavian people did not adopt the wedding ring until the late 17th century. Instead they preferred to break a gold or silver coin, one half being kept by each partner.

# HERE COMES THE BRIDE
### Embarking on marriage in the right spirit

WHEN THE BRIDE leaves home on her wedding day she must literally start off on the right foot: to step out on the left foot brings bad luck. The journey to the wedding can be strewn with omens, both good and bad. Sunshine is a good sign, but the bad luck forecast by rain is cancelled out if the bride sees a rainbow. The horses (or horseless carriage) must then start without any problem, or the marriage will be a failure. En route, a black cat crossing in front of the bride is a good omen, as is a chimney sweep or an elephant – although either is an unlikely event these days. Fortunately, the bride is just as unlikely to have a pig cross her path: this would be a definite sign of bad luck. But if she sees a funeral, she may as well call the wedding off, as it is the worst omen of all.

### THE BLUSHING BRIDE

An old custom, prevalent in England and parts of the United States, held that a husband could not be liable for any of his wife's debts from a previous marriage, as long as she married him wearing nothing but a smock. The reasoning went that if she brought (virtually) nothing to the new marriage, her creditors could take nothing. Some brides took this to its logical extreme by marrying completely naked. In one case in 1789, in Vermont, USA, the bride stood naked hidden inside a closet, and had to put her hand through a hole in the door to accept the ring. When the ceremony was over, the bride was able to dress in all her wedding finery and leave the church a solvent woman.

### MIND THE STEP

The threshold of a house has long been considered an unlucky place where evil spirits are likely to lurk, and this may account for the old tradition of the new husband carrying his bride over it. A more practical explanation for the custom is that it prevents the bride tripping over the step and stumbling into her new home – an action that may seem ominous even to those not normally inclined to superstition.

### GHOST MARRIAGES

If a Zulu tribesman is engaged to be married but dies before the wedding, his fiancée will marry one of his kinsmen who will father a child on the dead man's behalf. Similarly, in ancient China, if the prospective groom met an untimely death, the bride would go ahead with the wedding ceremony, marrying his ghost instead. She would then live with her dead husband's parents. The Hopi Indians of the American South West believe that marriage and death are fundamentally linked. The bride saves her wedding clothes for use as her funeral shroud; without them her spirit cannot enter the afterworld.

# WITH THIS RING
### The wedding ring – a symbol of love, or possession?

THE IDEA of the wedding ring as a symbol of love is relatively modern. The ring was originally regarded as both a down payment on the bride and a sign to other men that she was no longer available. It was, in effect, a 'property sold' sign. Even the word 'wed' comes from the Anglo-Saxon term for a security given in order to bind a promise.

The ancient Hindus were among the first to use wedding rings, and the tradition was exported to the West by the Greeks and Romans. The ring remained a 'property sold' sign until the 9th century, when the Christian Church adopted it as a symbol of fidelity.

It is hardly surprising that to lose, break or remove such a powerful symbol was thought to have dire consequences. In parts of Scotland there is a belief that if a woman loses her ring she will also lose her man. If the ring is dropped at the wedding ceremony and it rolls away from the altar, this is a terrible omen. And if the ring ends up on a gravestone, one of the newlyweds faces an early death – the victim is determined by the sex of the person buried in the grave.

The choice of the ring finger is also connected with various myths. The fourth finger of the left hand was chosen by the ancient Greeks and Romans as they mistakenly believed that a vein ran directly from it to the heart. That a woman's ring is generally, but by no means universally, worn on the left hand, stems from the belief that this was the weak hand, symbolising woman's submission to man.

### DID YOU KNOW..?

*THE TIWI PEOPLE of Melville, an island off Australia, marry off girls before they have even been conceived. The contract for the first daughter's future marriage is made at the mother's wedding ceremony. If the first children are boys, the fulfillment of the contract is delayed.*

\* \* \*

*AT SOME GERMAN country weddings the bride and groom are still made to saw through a wooden log to prove that they can work well as a team.*

243

## THE HEIGHT OF WEDDED BLISS

ONE OF the most unusual marriage ceremonies ever held must surely be the mass wedding that took place in mid air between Tokyo and Bangkok in 1972. This was a publicity stunt organised by the German airline Lufthansa to launch the first commercial jumbo jet flight of a European airline.

Inviting Japanese couples to take part in a 'jumbo wedding', the airline found itself besieged by eager applicants. Twenty couples were selected and on the appointed day headed across the tarmac of Tokyo airport, led by a Shinto priest.

The event was a curious mixture of ancient custom and commercial enterprise. After take-off, the couples were married one by one in full traditional dress before a Shinto shrine erected inside the cabin. Following the lead of marine captains who are permitted to conduct marriages at sea, the pilot of the aircraft also assisted in the ceremony, via the intercom. At the wedding feast, the ritual drink of rice wine was served in cups decorated with a crane – the Japanese symbol of happiness and the motif emblazoned on all Lufthansa aircraft.

After a stop in Bangkok, where the wedding party was blessed by a Buddhist monk, the newlyweds took off for Germany and a free honeymoon in the Black Forest. One couple, it seems, were especially grateful to their German hosts, naming the baby boy who arrived nine months later 'Lufthansa'.

# A SHOWER OF GOOD WISHES

*If you have run out of rice, throw shoes*

DURING an Anglo-Saxon wedding ceremony the bride's father would pass the groom one of his daughter's shoes to signify the transfer of 'goods'. The groom would then rap her over the head with it to show that he was her new master. The bride's parents might then throw an old shoe after their newlywed daughter to indicate that they had relinquished their responsibilities to her.

The Inuit (Eskimo) people of North America also throw shoes after the bride. But here the custom has a different meaning. The Inuits regard the shoe as a fertility symbol, and a piece of an old shoe is carried by a woman who wants to bear many children.

More common is the custom of throwing confetti – a colourful mix of small pieces of paper, sometimes in the form of horseshoes, slippers and hearts. The word confetti is derived from the Italian for sweetmeats, and the practice comes from the Roman tradition of throwing almonds and nuts as fertility symbols. In many countries the wedding guests throw grain – often rice – although increasingly they use a paper substitute. The wedding pair represent a new field from which future generations will grow, and the scattering of seeds encourages a fruitful marriage.

An extension of the tradition is the breaking of wedding cake over the bride's head: people in the west of Ireland use oat cake, while the Scots favour shortbread. However, in some parts of the world there are other reasons for throwing sweet things. In Morocco, for example, raisins, figs and dates are scattered to 'sweeten' the general proceedings and, at the same time, to make the bride sweeter to the groom and his family.

***Hundreds and thousands*** *Large sheets of paper are put through a shredder at this late 19th-century confetti factory.*

# AGAINST THE EVIL EYE

## *Why some men marry trees, and some brides hide inside boxes*

**M**ANY OF the rites and customs practised at wedding ceremonies even today were originally designed to protect the bridal couple from evil influences.

Probably the most universal talisman still in use is the veil. It was used both as a disguise, to hide the bride from evil spirits, and also as a protective shield, to ward off the 'evil eye'. The Chinese are particularly wary of evil presences during what they see as the 'limbo period', the time from when the bride leaves her house until her arrival at the ceremony, so she travels inside a closed sedan chair. If she is especially fearful, the bride will travel 'Russian-doll' fashion, inside a box inside the chair! Evil spirits are also literally shut out in some Russian ceremonies in which all the doors, windows and chimneys are sealed to prevent witches entering the wedding.

### *Role playing*

A subtler way of warding off evil spirits is to divert their attention by the use of 'false brides'. This sometimes involves substituting the bride with one of her playful brothers – a favourite ploy in the Baltic republic of Estonia, which has also deceived many a bridegroom, to the great hilarity of the bride's family. In southern India the bride herself is

dressed as a boy, and in Fès, Morocco, the groom is dressed as a girl. However, the most bizarre type of deception is practised in northern India: here, people conduct mock marriages with trees or objects. These usually occur only when the omens are especially bad: for example, if a widower wishes to marry for a third time, his new bride may be cursed by the jealous spirits of his departed wives – to prevent this the groom will first 'marry' a tree so that the spirits attack the tree. Similarly, if the bride's horoscope predicts an early widowhood she will perform a mock ceremony with a large water pitcher that she has dressed in her future husband's clothes. Then the real wedding can take place.

Some people prefer to take a more offensive stance against evil. A favourite spirit antidote is the noise of gunfire. Once heard at country weddings throughout Europe, it is sometimes still delivered with great gusto in Morocco where the poor bride must be almost shell-shocked by the end of her wedding day. Volleys from muskets are fired first across her procession, then right beside her, and finally in the bridal chamber. The smoke is believed to purify the bride herself, while the noise frightens off the evil spirits. The battery of assault does not stop even when the bride is alone with her husband. He now slaps her on the forehead and shoulders with the flat of his

***Portable hide-out***
*A Chinese bride dressed in red shelters from the 'evil eye'.*

sword and tucks a pistol beneath the pillow just in case any determined spirits are still lurking.

At least she does not have to endure the Slavonic tradition in which the wedding guests gather outside the bedroom door and make as much noise as they possibly can while the marriage is being consummated.

---

## DID YOU KNOW..?

*AS A DEFENCE against the 'evil eye', Moroccan brides have to keep their eyes tightly closed throughout the wedding ceremony.*

---

## THE BRIDE IN BLOSSOM

**O**RANGE BLOSSOM has been the 'traditional' wedding flower in Mediterranean countries for many centuries. It symbolises all the old-fashioned virtues and qualities a man would hope to find in a wife – purity, beauty and motherhood. While the pretty white blossoms signify innocence and virginity, the tree produces a prolific amount of fruit, which symbolises fertility. Furthermore, the orange tree is one of the few plants to produce flowers and fruit simultaneously –

the perfect combination of beauty and usefulness at the same time.

Legend has it that the first bride to wear orange blossom was a poor Spanish girl, the daughter of the king of Spain's gardener. She was in love but her father was too poor to give her a dowry, so her marriage could not go ahead. Meanwhile the king had just received the country's first orange tree, a prize rarity of which he was very proud and quite protective. The orange tree was much admired by the

French ambassador, but when he asked for a cutting, the king refused.

The gardener's daughter heard about the refusal, and one night she crept into the garden and secretly took a cutting from the tree. The next day she sold it to the ambassador, and so acquired her dowry. On her wedding day, she did not forget that her happiness was due to the orange tree. To express her gratitude she arranged its blossoms in her hair, little expecting that she would create a new fashion.

# THE LIVING AND THE DEAD

## How people around the world deal with death

TO WEAR anything but black at a funeral seems to us disrespectful of the dead. Black reflects our dark sense of grief, and the seriousness of such a sombre occasion. But the custom began for quite a different reason – not from respect, but from sheer fear of the departed.

Our ancestors believed that the ghost of the newly dead lingered near the corpse. And the ghost was so lonely that it was ready to snatch one of the living for the sake of companionship when the chance presented itself. Few people were willing to risk that fate, and so everyone dressed in the same drab colours to remain as inconspicuous as possible.

### Taking evasive action

Fear of haunting dictated several curious customs. At funerals of the North American Menomini Indians, the nearest relative of the deceased would slip away early, while the ghost was still watching the ceremony, to avoid being ensnared. At Sacs or Fox Indian funerals, relatives would be sure to drop an item of food or clothing into the grave, lest the spirit come at night to claim such gifts itself.

In some parts of the world, people took the corpse out of the house through one of the windows rather than the door. In this way they hoped to confuse the ghost and prevent it from finding its way back home. And

**Beware the dead** *The black clothes of a funeral cortege offer a mark of respect, but they also protect the mourners from the unwelcome attention of the spirit of the deceased.*

in China, mourners traditionally set off firecrackers on their way home from a funeral service to fend off the spirit of the departed.

The notion was taken to extremes by the Yakut people of Siberia. There, a dying person would have the finest food and best seat at his own funeral feast, before being taken out and buried alive. Food and possessions – even a horse to ease the journey to the next world – were buried with him, so that he had no excuse for returning to his home.

The black funeral clothes of modern Europe and America are by no means the only relics there of this ancient and profound fear of the dead. The pennies that undertakers placed on corpses' eyes served another purpose besides keeping them closed. The pennies were the spirits' fare to the next world. And if modern funeral orations sometimes seem unusually complimentary to the departed, it may be because something more than a desire to honour the dead is at work. Perhaps we still share a lingering, half-conscious fear that somewhere, nearby, invisible but attentive ears are listening to every word.

---

### DID YOU KNOW..?

*AFTER Horatio Nelson's death at the Battle of Trafalgar in 1805, the British naval hero's body was shipped home to England for burial – carefully preserved in a large cask of brandy.*

# CATACOMB COUNTRY
## *The many ghosts that encircle Rome*

AROUND the original perimeter of Rome lies a secret, foreign country of the dead. This is the 250 km (150 mile) long labyrinth of catacombs, where 750 000 people lie buried. And it is a foreign land, for since 1929 the catacombs have been an outpost of a sovereign state – the Vatican.

The majority of the Roman catacombs date back to between the 2nd and 4th centuries after Christ. Why were they built, and why outside the walls of ancient Rome?

### Force of circumstance

All but the wealthiest Romans cremated their dead, a practice that the early Christians, who believed in an eventual resurrection of the body, regarded with horror. At the same time, it was illegal to bury anyone inside the city walls, and land around Rome was expensive. So the Christians tunnelled underground. They started digging from wells, quarries and sometimes private underground tombs, into the soft volcanic rock that lies under Rome.

Chambers large enough to take the remains of the deceased were cut out of the rock on each side of a gallery. As need arose, further galleries and chambers were added, branching off the originals or burrowing farther into the ground. Some catacombs are as many as six storeys deep.

Catacombs are not, by any means, exclusive to Rome – or even to Christians. They can be found all around the Mediterranean, some dating from long before the Christian era, in Tunisia, Lebanon, Egypt and Malta, as well as in both ancient Etruria and in the city of Naples in Italy itself. The most populous catacombs of all lie beneath the streets of Paris.

There the curious tourist can take a guided tour, through a macabre series of chambers and galleries lined with skulls and bones, to a huge ossuary

*Frightened to death The millions of bones in the catacombs in Paris were arranged into an exhibition for the curious in the early 19th century, as illustrated by the English caricaturist George Cruikshank.*

where lie the skeletons of some three million people. The Paris catacombs were originally not a graveyard but underground quarries, and were converted only in 1787. In the Second World War they found yet another use – as a refuge for members of the French Resistance.

---

## TOWERS OF SILENCE

THE PARSEES in India – followers of Zoroastrianism, the religion of ancient Persia – believe that corpses should not desecrate either earth, which is sacred, or flame, which is a symbol of God. But these beliefs leave them with a problem: how to dispose of their dead without burying or burning them. The answer is the 'tower of silence'.

Shortly after someone dies, corpse-bearers (the only people permitted to touch the body) wash and dress the cadaver. Next, they bring in a dog – a holy animal to the Parsees – to look the corpse in the face and so drive away evil spirits. Then the bearers carry the corpse to the tower of silence, on a bier that they break up and bury afterwards.

The towers are huge circular structures, some 90 m (300 ft) in circumference, built

of stone or brick. They are roofless and have a thick outer wall surrounding a central pit, which is lined with masonry.

The towers are closed to everyone except for the corpse-bearers, who bring the body into the tower and lay it on one of three concentric circular platforms: the outer for men, the inner for women and the central one for children. There the body is exposed to the baking, purifying Sun – and to the vultures. In a matter of hours the birds

*Old versus new The Parsee funeral tower in Yazd, Iran (top left) overlooks a modern tomb built during the last shah's reign.*

will strip the body of all its flesh. Months later, the corpse-bearers will throw any remains into the central pit, lined with sand and smouldering charcoal. The task is accomplished: the body has gone, without once touching earth or flame.

# ALL DRESSED UP...

### How the ancient Egyptians prepared for the afterlife

TO ENJOY the new life that he believed followed death, an ancient Egyptian needed one thing more than any other: his physical body. The body was an inseparable part of the personality; the Egyptians dreaded the idea that it might decompose. And so, with meticulous care, they embalmed – mummified – their dead, rich and poor alike.

The embalmers had a grisly job. They removed all the internal organs, including the brain, heart, lungs and stomach, embalmed them and stored them separately in jars. They packed the body itself with spices and bitumen – the word 'mummy' comes from an Arabic word for bitumen. This made the body black, heavy, and all but indestructible. Then they washed the body and wrapped it in linen bandages, which were gummed into place.

### Hung out to dry

The practice lasted from about 2400 BC until the 4th century AD. But the Egyptians were by no means alone in preserving their dead. Peruvian Indians embalmed and worshipped their dead, as did the aboriginal Guanche of the Canary Islands, using methods similar to the Egyptians'. The Aleuts of North America preserved their dead by drying them out – hanging the corpses on poles or putting them in dry caverns.

In Egypt, the dead took everything necessary for the afterlife with them to the tomb, from clothing to worldly wealth. Much of this fell prey to grave robbers in the course of time. Even the mummies themselves became a money-making commodity: in the Middle Ages the remains were powdered and sold as a healing agent for wounds.

---

### DID YOU KNOW..?

*WE OWE much of our knowledge of ancient Egyptian furniture to a burial custom practised by the wealthy. To ensure comfort in the afterlife, they were buried with a selection of their own furniture.*

✳ ✳ ✳

*IN THE CONGO, professional corpse-painters decorate the dead with elaborate and startling masterpieces of their art – and charge people to see the results.*

---

## CAUSE FOR CELEBRATION

CHILDREN receive gifts of chocolate coffins bearing their own names, sugar skulls grin merrily, and families enjoy picnics in the cemetery to sing and chat to the corpses there. These are all part of the extraordinary festivities that take place on Mexico's *El Dia de los Muertas*, the Day of the Dead.

Mexicans believe that on this day the dead return briefly to the land of the living – and since their visit is but a short one, they deserve a joyful reception.

The Day of the Dead – held on what other countries call All Souls' Day – is no more than an enjoyable reminder of the brevity and insignificance of life. The Mexican author Octavio Paz even goes as far as to say that: 'The Mexican frequents death, mocks it, caresses it, sleeps with it, celebrates it.'

Such an attitude has its roots deep in Mexico's history. Between the 3rd and 8th centuries AD, long before the rise of the Aztec civilisation there, the Totonaca Indians believed that the 'underworld' of the dead was a parallel world to this. A dead person would repeat his previous existence, even marry the same partner as before. Dying was nothing to be feared; and, as if to prove it, the Totonaca god of death was always portrayed as a skeleton wearing a broad grin.

---

# DIFFICULT DUTY

### Widows once followed their husbands into the grave

MONUMENTS all over India testify to the devotion of Hindu widows to their husbands. Each of the suttee (virtuous women) had made a supreme gesture to expunge her own and her husband's sins and ensure eternal bliss for them both: each had hurled herself onto the flames of her husband's funeral pyre.

Whether these women sacrificed themselves voluntarily or not is a moot point. Any Hindu widow who might have questioned her expected duty may also have decided that death was preferable to life as the reviled outcast she would have become had she refused. And if, in the end, her courage failed her, there were men at hand with poles to pin her down among the flames.

This grim practice dates back at least to the 4th century BC. It was a progressive Hindu sect, the Brahmo Samaj, who first agitated against suttee and, in the face of orthodox Hindu opposition, persuaded the British to prohibit it. In 1829, suttee was outlawed in British India, but remained legal in some princely states for 30 years. And there are unconfirmed reports that it still secretly occurs today.

*The ritual fire The Hindu practice of burning a woman who outlives her husband began at least 2300 years ago – and may still continue even today.*

# LIVING DEATH

*Locked up, bricked up or buried alive as punishment or stunt*

THE EVENING of June 20, 1756, saw the start of perhaps the hottest, sultriest night of the year in Calcutta. The monsoon was overdue; the heat was stifling. For the few dozen British soldiers in the city, that had been perhaps the least of their worries when the day began. For they, together with perhaps 500 local troops, were huddled in Calcutta's Fort William, facing a besieging force of 30 000 infantry, 20 000 cavalry, 400 elephants and 80 cannons, under the leadership of the Bengali nawab, Siraj-ud-Dawlah.

When the nawab's soldiers stormed the fort, they refrained from murdering the Europeans; instead, they thrust them into the fort's punishment cell, a grim coop that measured just 5.5 by 4.6 m (18 by 15 ft) and had only two small barred windows. The garrison had nicknamed it the 'Black Hole'. No less than 64 people were crushed into this suffocating place and left, without water, to survive the hottest night of the year. By 6am next day, only 21 were left alive.

Long cited as an example of British heroism and 'native' brutality, the incident in fact probably stemmed from oversight and stupidity rather than deliberate barbarism by the nawab.

### An age-old punishment

If the Black Hole of Calcutta became a legend because of negligence, it was a rare instance in the history of such punishments. In Europe in the Middle Ages, to be buried alive was a common, and legal, punishment. Monks, nuns and girls of noble blood suffered being bricked up to starve to death in private rather than face the shame of public execution. But the practice was not new. In ancient Rome, any of the six vestal virgins (who tended the goddess Vesta's sacred fire) who broke her vow of chastity faced the same fate.

In Mexico, Germany and China at various times, the wives of noblemen simply had to be unfortunate enough to outlive their husbands – and then were buried, alive, in the same grave.

Incredibly enough, it seems that it is possible to survive a full-scale burial. Reports describe how Indian fakirs, in a supreme demonstration of the power of mind over body, have reduced their heartbeat and breathing to barely detectable levels. In this state of suspended animation, they have remained underground for days on end.

### Barley and diamonds

In 1835, at the maharajah's palace in Lahore, the fakir Haridas spent 40 days buried in a locked and sealed chest. According to the *Calcutta Medical Times*, before his incarceration, Haridas fasted for days, swallowing and regurgitating a 27 m (90 ft) strip of linen to clean out his stomach. After sealing his nose and ears with wax to protect himself from invading insects, he rolled back his tongue – whose muscles he had cut away specially – to seal his throat, and relaxed. Within seconds, said one witness, 'he was physically dead.'

Barley seeds sprinkled on the ground above the buried chest had sprouted undisturbed before Haridas saw daylight again. He was shrivelled and rigid but, after an hour's massage and manipulation, he had returned entirely to normal – to receive a gift of diamonds from the maharajah.

*A test of survival Irishman Mike Meaney is examined by doctors after being buried alive in a coffin for a record 61 days in London in 1968. He had been supplied with air, food and water throughout the ordeal.*

# THE VOICE OF THE PEOPLE

## Revolutionary spirit ushers in democratic bodies

KING JAMES I of England declared wryly in 1614: 'I am surprised that my ancestors should have ever permitted such an institution to come into existence.' That 'institution' was the English Parliament, which frequently thwarted the king's designs. James believed that kings were appointed by God and had a 'divine right' to rule.

How did modern Western democracy emerge in the face of such a belief? The answer lies largely in 17th-century England, which saw King Charles I beheaded for attempting to usurp the powers of Parliament. This turbulent period ended in 1689 with the principle firmly established that the monarch ruled in partnership with Parliament. Crucially, the king could not impose taxes without parliamentary consent.

'No taxation without representation' became the war-cry of revolutionary America, and the fledgling United States declared the equality of man along with its independence in 1776, and wrote popular elections into its constitution in 1787. Two years later, King Louis XVI summoned the States-General – the legislative assembly of pre-revolutionary France – for the first time since 1614 in the hope of raising taxes and averting bankruptcy, and ended by losing his head to shouts of 'liberty, equality, fraternity'.

Between them, the principles and slogans of these revolutions in England, America and France fuelled demands for democracy across Europe that, by the end of the 19th century, few rulers had the will or the power to resist. The monarchies that did ignore their peoples' desire to choose their own governments did not long survive the First World War, especially those on the losing side. Some sovereigns did keep their thrones, but only by ceding power to the people and their representatives. And so strong is the ideal of democracy that even the most oppressive regimes have usually held elections of some kind, however corrupt, to give themselves a semblance of popular support.

# WHO COUNTS, WINS

## Absolute power corrupts absolutely

GENERAL Alfredo Stroessner, Paraguay's dictator for 34 years (until ousted by a coup in 1989) was acknowledged to be a harbourer of Nazi war criminals, torturer of dissidents and probable drug baron. Yet he insisted on holding presidential elections every five years to give his authoritarian regime some legitimacy.

### Magic majorities

The elections themselves were sheer theatre. The register of voters was a carefully guarded state secret and, once Stroessner was deposed, was found to include the names of large numbers of people who had magically continued to vote (for Stroessner) long after they had in fact died. Even children voted for him. The 'opposition' parties regularly won one-third of the seats in both chambers of the Paraguayan Parliament, irrespective of the number of votes they received, and Stroessner paid their campaign expenses and large salaries to the chosen deputies.

Paraguayans used to say cynically in Stroessner's time: 'Our elections are more advanced than in the United States. In the US, computers know the results of an election just two hours after the polls close. In Paraguay, we know the election results two hours before the polls open.'

Grotesque as Stroessner's claim was to have been elected democratically, he is by no means alone in the annals of political corruption. Britain, the 'mother of parliaments' herself, had a far from democratic system of representation until reforms swept away its most bizarre aspects in 1832.

The least of the evils was a series of 'pocket boroughs' where rich landlords – often peers of the realm, who already had seats of their own in the House of Lords – were able to nominate their own candidates without opposition.

### DID YOU KNOW..?

*THE MOST unambiguous election of all time was held in North Korea on October 8, 1962. One hundred per cent of the voters turned out, and all voted for the Workers' Party of Korea.*

Some of these boroughs were deemed so valuable in terms of political influence that they were bought and sold in the manner of playing cards.

### Rotten to the core

Most extraordinary were the 'rotten' boroughs, where the electors numbered no more than a handful. A notorious example was Old Sarum in Wiltshire, where for hundreds of years a population of precisely zero had faithfully returned a Member of Parliament chosen by the landowner, who lived elsewhere.

Successive reforming acts after 1832 further improved the situation, but it was not until 1918 that all men over the age of 21 and all women over 30 secured the right to vote.

As bizarre as some electoral systems have been, none can beat the astounding efficiency of that organised by Charles D.B. King of Liberia in the presidential elections of 1927. Mr King beat his opponent by 234 000 votes. This was a remarkable margin given that the total number of voters added up to only about 15 000. Mr King was duly elected.

# THE LONG MARCH FOR WOMEN'S RIGHTS

## Millions of women are still without a political voice

EYEBROWS were raised all over the world when the tiny principality of Liechtenstein granted all its women citizens over the age of 20 the right to vote. For Liechtenstein made this grand concession only in 1984, and many people must have wondered how such an elementary right had been denied them so long. Yet the struggle to give women everywhere this most basic voice in politics is far from over.

A long tradition of popular representation in a country has never been a guarantee that women would be included among those represented. Greece, the 'cradle of democracy', granted women the vote in national elections only in 1952. In the United Kingdom, whose Parliament dates back to 1265, women were not able to vote until 1918. Even then (until 1928) they had to be aged over 30, whereas men could vote from the age of 21. The fledgling United States declared that 'all Men are created equal' in 1776, but it was 144 years before women won the right to vote in federal elections.

In Iceland, whose legislative body, the Althing – the world's oldest – was first established in AD 930, women finally gained the right to vote in 1915. In the 1980s, Iceland boasted the only specifically women's political party in the world, and the world's first democratically-elected female president.

### Leaders of men

None of this disregard for women's political acumen seems to have had any basis in logic or in historical evidence. Cleopatra in ancient Egypt, Elizabeth I of England and Catherine the Great of Russia were all shrewd, even ruthless monarchs, who had little difficulty in outwitting their male rivals.

Forceful leadership has come in modern times from Indira Gandhi of India, Golda Meir of Israel and Margaret Thatcher of Britain. Corazon Aquino of the Philippines and Pakistan's Benazir Bhutto are two women whose popular appeal helped to topple authoritarian regimes. The latter became the first woman prime minister of a Muslim country, yet in many parts of the Islamic world women are still legally barred from voting, let alone holding political office. In Bhutan, the constitution allows one vote 'per family'

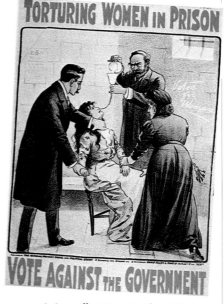

**Force fed** *A suffragette campaign poster from 1909 depicts the harsh response of the British authorities to women who were prepared to die for their right to vote.*

– an arrangement that keeps the expression of political opinion largely in the hands of men.

Other nations, notably South Africa, deny the vote on the basis of colour and race, but there are still countries in the world where no one has any kind of vote. Some, like Guinea in West Africa, are ex-colonial powers that have been victims of anti-democratic coups. But a few, such as most of the Gulf States, are ruled directly by royal families without any electoral systems at all.

---

## DID YOU KNOW..?

*ALEXANDRA KOLLANTAY of the Soviet Union was a pioneer in women's politics: in 1917 she became the world's first female minister of state as commissar of social welfare in Lenin's newly-established Bolshevik Government. Seven years later she became the world's first woman ambassador when she represented the Soviet Union in Norway in 1924.*

**Hard road** *American women had to fight long for the right to vote. Only in 1920 was women's suffrage written into the US Constitution.*

PRESIDENT WILSON SAYS: "This is the time to support Woman Suffrage."

PRES...NT WILSO...

## FIRST WITH THE NEWS

**A**T THE END of the first Tuesday after the first Monday in November every four years, Americans tune in to television and radio newscasts to discover who will be their next president. But the election returns they hear, county by county and state by state, are not in fact the official election figures.

Official vote tallies are rarely complete until two or three weeks after the election. This is largely because absentee votes – although they rarely affect the final outcome of the election – have to be included in the official count and need to be carefully checked.

How, then, does the American public hear an accurate election result only a few hours after voting has finished?

Counting does take place immediately after the polls close at all 181 000 polling places. And in 1964 the three major broadcasting networks, ABC, CBS and NBC, created the News Election Service (NES) to gather these individual results as soon as they were known at each polling place and total them as quickly as possible, county by county and state by state, ready to broadcast.

It is a prodigious task, involving massive telephone and computer resources. In the 1988 election, NES counted more than 90 million votes for president, nearly as many again for the House of Representatives, 50 million for the Senate and millions more for the 12 states holding elections for governor.

## THE AMERICAN WAY

### The complicated process of electing a president

**T**HE PRESIDENT of the United States is not elected by the people, but by the electoral college. This is because the Founding Fathers, who framed the American Constitution, wanted the president and vice-president elected by the more 'judicious' sections of society. The voters select in the first place a number of electors to form an electoral college. It is the 538 votes of the members of the electoral college that decide who will be president. The 435 seats in the House of Representatives are apportioned to each state according to its population; while each of the 50 states has two senators, regardless of size or population. (Washington, the District of Columbia, has three electors and is a special case.)

So where does the popular vote come in? What happens is that the ordinary voter in the United States does not vote directly for the presidential or vice-presidential candidate, but for a candidate for the electoral college who has already pledged his vote to a particular presidential candidate. He in turn votes on behalf of his own state. To become president, the candidate must first secure a majority of the electoral college votes.

Because all the electoral college votes in a state go to the candidate with the largest share of the popular vote within that state, and because only a handful of perhaps a dozen of the most heavily populated states controls a majority of votes in the electoral college, it is possible to get some rather strange results. If the winner has only a very slim majority in the key dozen states, it can turn out that, across the country he has fewer popular votes than his opponent. Nevertheless, this opponent loses the election, as he has failed to gain a majority of votes in the electoral college. On three occasions the winning candidate has polled fewer popular votes than his opponent; this last happened in 1888, when the Republican candidate, Benjamin Harrison, defeated his Democratic opponent, Grover Cleveland.

*George Bush* The 41st US President acknowledges his 1988 victory, which gave him 426 of the 538 electoral college votes. He won 38 states and took 54 per cent of the popular vote.

## VOTE – OR ELSE!

### Cast your ballot now or pay later

**I**N MOST Western democracies, a political party has two problems to solve at election time: it has to win more votes than its rivals to achieve power, but it also has to persuade people that it is worth going out to vote at all. In some countries, however, not to vote in an election is actually against the law – and punishable as such.

Failure to vote in certain countries, such as Austria and Australia, results in an automatic fine. In both these countries voter turnout is rarely less than 92 per cent, and in Australia has been as high as 98 per cent.

Penalties in some countries take a practical form. In Greece, passports may be withdrawn or not granted. In Bolivia, non-voters may be prohibited from using banks or schools for up to three months. As Bolivia suffered 191 coups between independence in 1825 and 1984 (an average of one every 10 months), the citizens may regard this law, and possibly the elections themselves, with some cynicism.

Until the recent revolution, one single-party communist state had compulsory voting: Romania. Turnout rarely fell much below 99 per cent, and the majorities by which candidates won their seats were much the same. President Nicolae Ceausescu won a 100 per cent majority in the 1985 elections – there was no other candidate.

### DID YOU KNOW..?

*THE FIRST country to give women the vote was New Zealand, in 1893.*

✳ ✳ ✳

*AMERICAN Indians were not considered citizens and, despite their service in the US Army during the First World War, could not vote until 1924.*

✳ ✳ ✳

*IN BOLIVIA, you must be 21 to vote – unless you are married, in which case you can vote from the age of 18. In the Dominican Republic, even those under the statutory voting age of 18 may vote if they are married.*

✳ ✳ ✳

*ANDORRA has the world's highest age qualification for voting – 25.*

# STEEPED IN STRANGE TRADITIONS

*Peculiar practices of the British parliament*

THE PROCEEDINGS of the British Parliament are full of elaborate ritual and bizarre customs. Perhaps the most striking of these occurs at the State Opening of Parliament, when both Houses, the Lords and the Commons, assemble before the sovereign. The Lords send a messenger – Black Rod, so called because of his symbol of office – to summon the members of the Commons to attend the sovereign in the Lords. But before Black Rod can enter the Commons, the Serjeant at Arms slams the door in his face. Black Rod must then knock three times, and be peered at through a grille by the Serjeant at Arms, before being admitted. Thus the House of Commons symbolically asserts its independence from the House of Lords.

### SHARE A BOAT?

When the House of Commons 'rises' at the end of the day, an official calls 'Who goes home?' This is repeated by the police round the building. The practice began so members could band

together to cross what were then the dangerous unlit fields between Westminster and the City of London or to share the cost of a boat on the Thames.

### KEEP YOUR DISTANCE

Two red lines run down the central aisle in the Commons between the Government and Opposition benches. Members may not address the House from between the red lines. This is ostensibly for their own safety, for the lines are a relic of more violent times and are two swords' lengths apart.

### HAT TRICK

If a male member of the House of Commons wishes to raise a point of order while voting is taking place after a debate, he must do so wearing a hat. This shows that he is not attempting to restart the debate, since members are not allowed to speak during debates with a hat on. As few members wear hats these days, top hats are kept on hand in the House for members wishing to raise a point of order.

### WHO SPEAKS TO THE SOVEREIGN?

The official representative of the House of Commons to the sovereign is not the prime minister (who represents only the Government of the day), but the Speaker of the House. Hence his title and, since he speaks to the sovereign on the Commons' behalf, his role as 'chairman' of debates in the House. He is elected by the Commons.

***King vs Commons*** *The House of Commons asserted its rights against the monarchy when Charles I personally attempted to arrest five of its members in 1642. The Black Rod ceremony dates from this acclamation of parliamentary power.*

# FORWARD INTO BATTLE

*People go to war for the oddest of reasons*

MOST PEOPLE would agree that war is hell, yet occasionally nations have found the strangest reasons for pitting themselves against one another. The ear of an English sailor, for instance, sparked a war between Great Britain and Spain in the 18th century. Hostilities between the two countries began in 1731, after Robert Jenkins allegedly had his ear cut off in Havana by a Spanish captain named Fandino. The British officially declared war only in October 1739, when Jenkins told his story before Parliament. The conflict continued for another nine years, as part of the war of the Austrian succession in which Britain and Spain were enemies, until 1748.

Pigs have played a part in starting two wars. The 'Pig War' of 1906–1909 was a trade dispute between Austria-Hungary and Serbia over the import of Serbian pork, but it fuelled existing antagonisms between the opponents' supporters (Germany and Russia) and so contributed, however little, to the tensions that erupted in the First World War. On a smaller scale, in 1974 in Papua New Guinea, a tribal dispute over the ownership of a single pig – a symbol of wealth and prestige – led to a fierce four-day battle that resulted in four deaths, 60 wounded, 70 arrests and the destruction of 200 houses.

In 1969, the famous Latin passion for football boiled over as El Salvador and Honduras competed in an important World Cup qualifying match. Riots after the game led to a five-day war between the two countries' armies, with a final score of 2000 dead and the destruction of much of the Honduran air force.

**The war of Jenkins's ear** *Britain declared war on Spain in 1739 after sailor Robert Jenkins told Parliament how his ship had been boarded by Spaniards, who cut off his ear and spoke ill of the king.*

### DID YOU KNOW..?

*THE ANCIENT female warriors known as Amazons were said to live completely apart from men, only visiting them for a few days when wishing to become pregnant. Their male offspring were either strangled at birth or given to their fathers; the girls were kept by their mothers and continued the race.*

# WARRIOR WOMEN

*The soldiers who struck fear in the hearts of their enemies*

NO ONE had seen an Amazon within living memory, but the original Amazons were a source of fear among the ancient Greeks. Their very name spelled terror: for it means 'breastless' – a reference to the legend that this alarming race of warrior women had one breast removed so that they could throw a spear or use a bow and arrow more efficiently.

### Always beyond reach

More myth than reality, these daunting fighters were mentioned by Homer – their queen had sided with Troy and had helped to destroy the great Greek hero Achilles – but they remained elusive. As the Greeks became more and more familiar with the territories around them, so the purported land of the Amazons receded beyond the known world.

Archaeologists and historians have now come to believe that the Sarmatians, who lived roughly in what is now Poland, may have inspired the Greek stories of fearless women soldiers, for women did fight in the Sarmatian armies and were buried with their weapons.

One band of real-life 'Amazons' was the female army of Dahomey (now Benin) in West Africa. In the middle of the 19th century, the Dahomian king, Gezo, ordered that at a certain age (believed to have been 18) every girl in his kingdom should be presented for possible recruitment into the army.

Those with the necessary physique underwent a rigorous course of training, the climax of which included crossing a 5 m (15 ft) barrier of thorns and a pit of smouldering wood – naked! Gezo formed his elite force of women for a simple enough reason, if one that might irritate modern opinion: the women had never known independence, and so would always obey orders. They were also – if only to protect them from

*African Amazons The female army of Dahomey had a reputation as fearless fighters who would defend their king to the last.*

others' attentions – officially numbered among the king's wives. But there was another side to this. Dahomey had always had female soldiers, and Gezo saw that they fought longer and harder than most men in his army.

Their greatest battle was also their last. In 1851, Gezo attacked his rivals, the Egba tribe, at Abeokuta. At one point, a division of a few hundred women routed 3000 Egba warriors, and then, outnumbered by 15 to one, took on another force of defenders – who had to clamber over the piles of their own dead before they could finally vanquish these formidable females.

### The final conflict

All in all, nearly 5000 'Amazons' died in the bloody assault. Although enemy losses were five times that number, the women's corps was drastically weakened, and began to fade from prominence – a disappearance hastened by the growing resentment of Dahomey's men at being forbidden to marry the finest of the country's women until they left the army at the age of 35.

Amazons made their last appearance on the battlefield during the Boer War in South Africa at the turn of the century. A women's unit called the Boer Amazons fought side by side with their menfolk against the British from 1899 to 1902, most effectively in guerrilla actions. Since then, the traditional name, if not the prowess, of fighting women has faded from military history.

## THE MAID OF ZARAGOZA

IN THE STRUGGLE between Spain and Napoleon's armies the city of Zaragoza lay under siege, continuously bombarded by enemy fire. As demoralised soldiers started to leave their posts, a young Spanish girl, 22-year-old Augustina Domonech, took over a cannon and began to return fire at the French, vowing never to leave the gun as long as she remained alive.

Augustina's heroic action brought the Spanish soldiers back to their posts, and the battle raged on. Eight months later, in February 1809, Zaragoza finally fell, overwhelmed by the might and persistence of the French. Augustina, however, escaped the ruined city to continue fighting for Spain.

Lord Byron celebrated the maid of Zaragoza in his poem *Childe Harold*, and her bravery earned the love and respect of all who met her.

Augustina's exploits continued during the guerrilla war against the French. Attacked in 1813 by three bandits, she left two dead, escaping with a wound to the cheek. In her words, it was only 'a severe scuffle'.

*Spanish heroine Augustina Domonech received three medals and a soldier's salary for her courageous acts.*

## THE BIG PEOPLE OF MIN TOP

THE SOLDIERS of South Vietnam's Women's Army were a remarkable, and unsung, part of the Vietnam War. Founded in the early years of the war, this 3000-strong army fought with a ferocity typical of the entire conflict. The women were tough, well-trained and, knowing the treatment they could expect if they were taken prisoner, would fight to the death. Typical of their actions was the one at Hoc Nom in 1962, when 15 soldiers wiped out 25 Vietcong men.

Perhaps the most formidable element of the Women's Army were the so-called 'big people of Min Top'. Larger and fairer than other Vietnamese, they were descendants of mixed-race children born when a Swedish mining company had come to Min Top three generations before. Min Top women were superb soldiers, once killing 22 Vietcong at Kong Loc for the loss of a single female warrior. One woman, Dho Minde, is said to have run 70 km (45 miles, or nearly two marathons) through thick jungle in order to avoid being captured. Their toughness matched their ruthlessness: they were never known to take prisoners.

# ANYTHING YOU CAN DO...

## What is the hardest secret for a soldier to keep?

THE BRITISH general Lord Marlborough was winning the Battle of Ramillies against the French in his inimitable style, but for one badly wounded cavalryman the fight was already over. Surgeons worked feverishly to staunch the flow of blood from his head, ripping away his uniform to make their task easier. When they did that, it was certain that Dragoon Cavanagh of the Scots Greys would not be returning to his regiment. For the surgeons had uncovered his great secret: 'he' was a woman.

### In search of a husband

Kit Cavanagh's secret was discovered in 1706. She had disguised herself as a man and become a soldier in 1693, to find the husband who had deserted her to join the British Army. In the course of her army career she was twice wounded and once a prisoner of war. Two years before fighting at Ramillies, she had in fact met her husband, but had not revealed her true identity.

Once she had recovered from her wound at Ramillies, Kit Cavanagh remarried her husband and was given a job as an officer's cook. This proved too dull, however, and she returned to battle. This time she dressed as a woman – which saved her life at the Battle of Malplaquet in 1709, when her stays stopped a bullet in its tracks. After this she lived another 30 years, died a peaceful death, and was buried in England with military honours.

Kit Cavanagh is neither the only woman who went to war disguised as a man, nor the only one who did so to seek out her husband. Hannah Snell, the English wife of a Dutch sailor, did the same in 1744, using the name James Gray. She fought against Scottish rebels in 1745, and later as a British marine against the French at Pondicherry, India.

In this battle she was wounded, but removed the bullet herself rather than risk discovery. After five years of warfare, and having learned that her husband was dead, she left the sea in 1750, sold her memoirs and married twice more before her death in 1792.

Sarah Edmonds, on the other hand, joined the Grand Army of the Republic to escape her tyrannical father and, as Franklin Thompson, fought in the American Civil War for the Union against the Confederate states. The inspiration for this scheme apparently came from a romantic novel, and within two years Sarah Edmonds had found army life disenchanting enough to desert. Her story does have a fairy-tale ending, however, for in 1867, once the war was over, she married her childhood sweetheart.

### A double agent

The Confederate Southern Army had its secret heroine, too. When Loreta Velasquez's husband joined the Southern cause at the outbreak of war, she adopted the identity of Harry T. Buford, raised her own regiment, fought in several battles, was wounded and, finally, worked as a spy. At one point she amazed her husband by turning up at his camp as 'Harry Buford'.

Latter-day stories of such intrepid women are rare, possibly because most countries' armed forces now include units for women. Or is it that these soldiers with a special secret to keep are more adept at disguise?

# SILLY WAR

## The world's longest war was extraordinarily peaceful

IN APRIL 1986, the Dutch ended their longest war ever, and possibly the longest war in history. Their ambassador in London flew to St Mary's in the Scilly Isles, off the southwestern coast of Britain, with a declaration of peace that formally ended a war between Holland and the placid islands that had, in theory, lasted 335 years.

Not a single shot was fired and not a drop of blood was shed in the whole duration of the conflict. It began as a bizarre side show to the English Civil War. In a bid to fill their depleted coffers, the Royalists granted the Scilly islanders (who supported the king against Parliament) the right to engage in 'legitimate privateering' – or, in plain language, piracy.

### A threatening presence

From this piracy, the Dutch suffered most, as their ships passed close to the islands on their way to the East Indies. Thus, in 1651, a Dutch admiral, Maarten Tromp, ordered the Scillonians to desist. They refused, and he declared war on the islands. Shortly afterwards, Tromp was himself seen off by the British Navy with a curt message that the British could look after their own problems.

It was only in 1985 that anyone realised that the 'war' had never officially ended. Cynics claimed that it did end only because the islanders hoped to attract some extra Dutch tourists – having themselves long since forgotten to worry about the possibility of Dutch warships appearing on the horizon.

## DID YOU KNOW..?

*DURING THE Hundred Years' War between England and France – a series of wars actually lasting for 116 years, from 1337 to 1453 – Flanders, which was under French rule, rebelled against the French king and supported England. The Flemish depended on English wool for their textile industry.*

✳ ✳ ✳

*THE SHORTEST ever war was fought on August 27, 1896, between Britain and Zanzibar (now part of Tanzania). Faced by a rebellious sultan, the British fleet bombarded his palace until he surrendered, after just 38 minutes.*

# AN ARMY OF MEN WITH NOTHING TO LOSE

*The Foreign Legion was established to give a home to homeless refugees*

ROMANTIC and swashbuckling, totally loyal, terrifying to its enemies, and fearless in the face of death – this is the popular image of the French Foreign Legion. But how far does the reality match the legend?

The birth of the Legion in 1831 was far from romantic, and as a fighting force it was a disaster. King Louis Philippe founded the Legion for two cynical reasons. First, he hoped that a force consisting primarily of foreigners might absorb the mass of refugees who had flooded into France in previous years. Secondly, and more importantly, the Foreign Legion could be sent to fight the colonial war in Algeria, thus freeing the regular Army to protect the king's precarious hold on the French throne.

### Bad start

When the first battalion of this peerless force landed in Algeria, it reminded one eyewitness of a circus; the men were aged anywhere between 16 and 60, and were decked out in an assortment of antiquated uniforms.

When a second battalion arrived a few months later, 35 men deserted immediately, and one company drank itself into a mutiny; the ringleaders were promptly executed. In the

*'The Legion is our country'* Founded in 1831, for service outside France, the French Foreign Legion now numbers about 8500 men, each of whom has sworn to serve, not France, but the Legion itself.

Legion's first attempt at combat, 28 legionnaires tried to defend a position just outside Algiers – only one survived.

And yet it was from this unpromising beginning that the French Foreign Legion built its mystique. The authorities lauded the ineffectual dead legionnaires as heroes – and at the same time sent officers and sergeants from the French Army to instil discipline and real fighting strength into the Legion.

### No place to go

Throughout its history, men have joined the Legion, as often as not, because they have had nowhere else to go. Criminals, disgraced noblemen, professional soldiers who would rather fight than 'keep the peace' were taken in and, at one time, were even offered an official list of alternative identities to choose from. Most, in fact, kept their own names, but it remains a matter of honour never to enquire about a fellow legionnaire's past.

Once in the Legion, they learned – from the discipline and the battles they had to fight – that they had only themselves to depend on during the five years of their initial contract. Legionnaires were always given the French Army's most impossible missions; they were expendable, and they knew it. And so, with nowhere to go and nothing to lose, legionnaires *did* fight their battles to the last man.

The legionnaires' most heroic stand was when they were sent by Napoleon III to fight on the side of the newly appointed emperor of Mexico, Maximilian of Habsburg, at Camerone in 1863. A mere 65 of them held off a force of 2000 Mexicans until only three legionnaires were left alive; but 300 Mexicans lay dead, and another 500 had been wounded.

More than 90 years later, in 1954, Legion troops were sent to help defend the village of Dien Bien Phu in northeast Vietnam, then a French colony, against Communists fighting for independence. Of the 16 500 troops in the garrison, nearly 10 000 were legionnaires. Encircled by the Vietnamese, they endured eight weeks of artillery bombardment before the final onslaught. In one encounter in those last terrible hours, 400 legionnaires were reduced to hand-to-hand fighting with bayonets; only 70 survived.

### Victorious defeat

For the French Army, Dien Bien Phu was a disaster that cost them the war. For the Legion, it was a victory. The reality matched the legend: these were men who preferred death to surrender. But the reality is also that the Legion was made up of men who retained only one cause for pride in life: they knew how to die bravely.

This fierce self-reliance almost destroyed the Legion. In 1961, after bitter fighting against Algerian nationalists, the Legion's 1st Parachute Regiment rebelled against the French government's decision to pull out of the North African colony, where the Legion had had its headquarters for over a century. Hauled back to France in disgrace, the Legion took years to rebuild its morale.

Today, it is once again a proud, elite fighting unit, and over 100 nationalities are represented among its ranks (all are entitled to French citizenship on their retirement). The legend lives on, but the Legion is a more sober, more professional and less reckless home for the homeless than once it was.

## DID YOU KNOW..?

*NEW RECRUITS to the Foreign Legion are vetted to ensure that they are not joining to escape punishment for a serious crime. Petty criminals, however, may sometimes be allowed to join. Under French law, the Foreign Legion may deny the existence of any individual serving with it. And anyone betraying the true identity of a legionnaire may be prosecuted under the French penal code.*

✳ ✳ ✳

*TO HELP alleviate language problems inside the Foreign Legion, each non-French-speaking legionnaire is allocated a French-speaking 'buddy'.*

# CRIME AND PUNISHMENT

## A 4000-year-old system of justice

'AN EYE for an eye, a tooth for a tooth, a hand for a hand ...'. The Old Testament concept of a punishment to fit the crime was central to the Jewish law handed down by Moses, and central also to the code of Hammurabi, the ruler of Babylon from 1792 to 1750 BC. The Babylonians had a whole range of punishments that, while they seem draconian now, were really a way of limiting personal vengeance: they chopped the fingers off sons who had struck their fathers, and plucked out the eyes of men found guilty of blinding someone. The Babylonians did not believe in humane punishment – and neither did most ancient peoples.

But there was one exception. In about 2050 BC – 300 years before Hammurabi, and perhaps 750 years

*Ancient code Dating from the 18th century BC, this stone tablet is believed to be the oldest set of laws in existence. The section shown here depicts the Babylonian ruler Hammurabi (standing) receiving legal advice from the god Marduk.*

before Moses – the Sumerian King Ur-Nammu formulated a set of laws that were strikingly modern in their approach to crime and punishment.

The laws laid down a scale of damages to be paid by the perpetrators of violent crime to their victims. Thus a man who had chopped off someone's foot would have to pay his victim ten silver shekels; the fine was one shekel for breaking a bone, two-thirds of a silver mina for cutting off a nose, and so on. Ur-Nammu's code is the first known example of a monetary fine being imposed instead of a physical punishment.

---

### TURNING SINNERS INTO SEAMEN

SLAVE LABOUR in the galleys was a common punishment for European criminals from Roman times right up until the 18th century. And all over the world, it was common practice for prisoners of war to be sent to the galleys.

In 1602, Queen Elizabeth of England set up a commission to ensure that criminals, 'except when convicted of wilful Murther, Rape, & Burglarye', should be spared execution and despatched to the galleys 'wherein, as in all things, our desire is that justice may be tempered with clemency & mercy . . . and the offenders to be in such sort corrected & punished that even in their punishments they may yeld some profitable service to the Comon welth.'

But conditions aboard a galley were far from merciful. The slaves remained at their oars in all weather and were chained together for up to six months at a time. Their life expectancy was usually not more than three years. And when they died, they were simply tossed overboard.

*Forced labour For centuries, European criminals and prisoners of war were sentenced to slavery. Many saw service as oarsmen.*

---

### DID YOU KNOW..?

*TWO-THIRDS of all the lawyers in the world live in the United States. Los Angeles alone has more judges than the whole of France, and in Washington, DC, there is one lawyer for every 25 men, women and children of the population.*

✳ ✳ ✳

*THE PILLORY and the stocks used to be a common sight in market places throughout Europe. Petty offenders would be pelted with fruit and vegetables. More serious criminals – such as the publishers of treasonable pamphlets – might be nailed up by their ears, which would later be cut off and left dangling on the pillory. When William Prynne, an English lawyer, wrote a controversial book in 1633, he was fined £5000, prohibited from practising law and suffered 'the loss of both ears on the pillory'. One famous writer sent to the pillory was Daniel Defoe, author of Robinson Crusoe. He was ordered to be pilloried three times for writing a pamphlet promoting the rights of dissenters against the Church. The crowd was on his side, though: they threw flowers instead of fruit.*

# STAIRWAY TO HELL

*The Victorian treadmill was intended to break both body and spirit*

ONE, TWO, THREE steps … four hundred, five hundred, six hundred. The treadmills of Victorian England seemed endless to the prisoners who had to walk on them for up to eight hours a day – with five minutes' rest after every quarter of an hour, and 60 minutes for lunch – and they still ended up exactly where they started.

The mill was a gigantic cylinder, 2 m (6 ft) high, with steps on the outside that turned under the prisoners' weight. Depending on its width, as many as 36 people might be on the wheel at any one time. They were kept apart by wooden partitions, each person having a compartment no more than 600 mm (2 ft) wide.

### Futile exertion

The first 'eternal staircase' was designed by William Cubitt in 1818. It was intended to be a form of hard labour, so tiring and monotonous that prisoners would be broken in both body and spirit and would think twice before breaking the law again. No one who had broken the law could escape the rigours of the treadmill: even pregnant women and young children were forced to climb the eternal staircase.

All prisoners were at the mercy of the warders, who could make the work more difficult by adjusting the vanes of a huge fan that was turned by the wheel.

By changing the angle of the fan's vanes the warders could increase or reduce wind resistance. If the warders thought that the mill was turning too quickly, they simply increased the resistance.

Even worse than the mill was the crank, invented at Pentonville prison in 1846, and designed for use in solitary confinement. Unlike the treadmill, which was sometimes used to grind corn or pump water, it served no purpose other

*Wheel of misfortune When 19th-century English judges sentenced prisoners to 'hard labour', the term was all too accurate. A French engraving illustrates the barbarism of the British penal system of the day.*

than punishment. The handle had to be turned, by adults and children alike, 1800 times for a prisoner to earn his breakfast, 4500 for lunch, 5400 for supper (adults were forced to make another 2700 turns afterwards). One man who repeatedly failed to meet his quota ate only nine meals in three weeks. The crank's revolution counter was often faulty, sometimes making the task of completing the required number of turns almost impossible. Men were driven insane, and some even committed suicide.

Prison reformers managed to have both the treadmill and the crank outlawed by the end of the 19th century.

# DANGEROUS VICES

*Why was smoking bad for your feet?*

IT IS COMMON knowledge that smoking and drinking are bad habits, and that people should avoid bankruptcy if they can. But few people in the West today think of smokers or drinkers as criminals, any more than they would expect a bankrupt to be humiliated in public.

It was not always so. In Britain in the 17th century, for instance, undischarged bankrupts were required to wear a distinctive uniform of brown and yellow until they had paid their debts. The aim was to prevent them obtaining credit from unsuspecting tradesmen, although the law was usually enforced only when the bankrupt was also guilty of criminal fraud.

Drunkards fared little better. In the 17th century in England and other parts of Northern Europe, they were sometimes made to walk around dressed in a wooden barrel that had a hole in the top for the head, and two holes in the sides for the hands. The idea behind the so-called drunkard's cloak was to shame the victim into sobriety.

Smokers in the 17th century sometimes suffered the worst fate of all. Tsar Michael of Russia hated the habit so much that he decreed the bastinado (beating the soles of the feet with a stick) for a first offence, a slit nose for a second, and death for the third. Around the same time, the Sultan of Turkey found the tobacco habit so offensive that he ordered snuff takers to have their lips slit, and smokers to be hanged – with a pipe shoved through their nose.

---

### DID YOU KNOW..?

*ABOUT 1685, the bell of the Huguenot church at La Rochelle, long a Protestant stronghold on the west coast of France, was soundly whipped for the crime of having given assistance to heretics. It was found guilty under a French law that considered inanimate objects, as well as animals, capable of criminal behaviour. The bell was buried and then disinterred to symbolise its rebirth into the services of the Roman Catholic church.*

## CATCHING A TRAIN

WHEN TWO railway engines collided in 1838, killing one of the drivers, the English legal system of the day made it quite clear who was to blame. The guilty engine was seized and ordered to be forfeit, under the ancient law of deodand.

*Deo dandum* (a gift to God) was a Saxon precept requiring any chattel that had caused the death of a human being to be surrendered to the king, who would put it to some good use. So the widow of a man who had been run over by a cart might receive the cart as financial compensation. Or, if a farmer fell on his scythe and died, the scythe was sometimes given to charity, as happened in England in 1218.

In Victorian times, however, the law was used by opponents of the new railways. After the 1838 collision, and a similar incident involving an explosion on a ship, Parliament eventually abolished the law in 1846.

# A COCK AND BULL STORY
### Bringing animals before a court

THERE was never any doubt as to the guilt of the accused. In the French county of Valois, in the year 1314, he had wilfully killed a man. Several people had witnessed the extremely bloody and savage attack. The accused was duly sentenced to death and hanged soon afterwards by order of the provincial parliament. The accused was a bull.

Modern law does not recognise the idea that animals can commit a crime, but in medieval Europe it was quite common for animals to be arraigned on all sorts of charges – everything from witchcraft and sorcery to murder.

Cattle and pigs were the most frequent victims, but other creatures went on trial too. The Swiss, for example, often prosecuted worms for destroying crops, while in 1487 the authorities in the French duchy of Savoy brought a case against some beetles that had been ravaging the local vineyards. Almost a century later, the rats of Autun in central France were summoned before the court on a charge of infesting local houses and barns. When they failed to appear, their lawyer explained that their lives would have been endangered by the number of cats in the neighbourhood. He said that the court would have to guarantee the safety of each and every one of his clients on their way to and from the trial. The case was adjourned indefinitely.

In the 15th century, a cock in the Swiss town of Basel was not so lucky. He was accused of laying an egg, which the superstitious townsfolk saw as a sure sign that he was a sorcerer. After due process, the cock was tied to a stake and burned, along with the egg. And in Lavegny, France, in 1457, a sow that had killed and partly eaten a child was hanged for murder. Her six piglet accomplices were spared, however, on the grounds that they had been too young to know any better.

*This little piggy was guilty* In medieval Europe, even animals could be convicted of crime. The legal profession took such cases seriously, but they were naturally open to ridicule, as this 19th-century etching of the trial of a sow and her piglets shows.

# TO CROWN IT ALL
### Why a king spared the man who crushed his crown

AT SEVEN o'clock on the morning of May 9, 1671, four men paid a formal call on Talbot Edwards, Keeper of the Crown Jewels at the Tower of London. Edwards, who was acquainted with the men and believed that they had come to arrange a marriage with his daughter, did not hesitate to let them in. But he soon found out that they had come for a less jolly reason. Their plan was to steal the jewels.

As soon as the doors closed behind them, the robbers threw a cloak over Edwards's head and thrust a gag in his mouth. When he still tried to call for help he was beaten over the head with a mallet and stabbed.

### Caught in the act

The gang's leader was an Irish desperado named Colonel Thomas Blood. Leaving Edwards for dead, he grabbed the king's crown and squashed it flat so that it would fit under his cloak. One of his companions thrust the royal orb into his breeches, while another seized the sceptre. They were trying to saw it in half when Edwards's son came home unexpectedly, found his injured father, and raised the alarm.

Blood fled with the crown and would have got away if his horse had not slipped. He was captured, after a struggle, by young Edwards and his men. Upon his arrest Blood boasted: 'It was a bold attempt, but it was for a crown.'

### Audacious burglar

Blood was imprisoned in the Tower, but when questioned refused to answer to anyone but the king himself. Intrigued, Charles II sent for him. Blood explained that he had fought against the king in the Civil War and had been rewarded with Irish estates, which he had had to forfeit on Charles's restoration to the throne. To get revenge, he had determined to steal the crown jewels. He had disguised himself as a parson and had struck up a friendship with the Keeper of the Jewels. The idea of marriage between Edwards's daughter and Blood's 'nephew' was simply a ruse to enable Blood to carry out the robbery.

Charles was so amused by the audacity of Blood's explanation that he set him free and saw to it that his estates were fully restored.

# BLOODY JUDGE JEFFREYS

*The merciless judge whose loyalty to the king clouded his sense of justice*

DAME Alice Lisle was a kind and gentle widow of 70, liked and respected by everyone who knew her. In 1685, however, after the failure of the Duke of Monmouth's rebellion against the English King James II, she was beheaded for the crime of harbouring a wounded rebel.

In fact, the evidence against her was not strong, but Dame Alice was a victim of the infamous Judge George Jeffreys. The judge had been appointed by the Roman Catholic king to try the Duke of Monmouth's Protestant rebels – a travesty of justice known as the Bloody Assizes. Jeffreys browbeat defence witnesses and twisted the law to suit the king's purpose. By the end of the assizes, he had sentenced 200 rebels to be hanged, 800 to be sold into slavery, and countless others to be whipped and imprisoned.

### Pay up – or hang

Not all the sentences were carried out, for Jeffreys made a fortune out of the sale of pardons. Not surprisingly, he is remembered as the most hated judge in English history.

Although Jeffreys was doubtlessly cruel and corrupt in his persecution of Protestants, he was widely regarded by his colleagues as a very able man. He had a first class brain, an unrivalled grasp of the law, and was capable of conducting himself with great dignity and good humour.

Jeffreys's fatal flaw, however, was his single-minded devotion to the monarch. He gave himself heart and soul to James II and was ruthless in his

master's cause. But Jeffreys's loyalty was not entirely disinterested. He was almost certainly spurred on by the prospect of being made Lord Chancellor as a reward for his support. While this expectation came true, his fortune did not last. When James was deposed in 1688, Jeffreys went too. He shaved his bushy eyebrows and disguised himself as a sailor in an attempt to escape to France. But he was recognised on a

*A harsh sentence Judge Jeffreys dispensed the death penalty to some 200 rebels following a failed insurrection against King James II in 1685. He sentenced hundreds more to slavery in the colonies.*

London street, arrested and taken to the Tower of London, followed all the way by a jeering, outraged mob. He died in prison four months later, remembered more for his cruelty than his ability.

---

## PRIDE AND PREJUDICE

JUDGE ROY BEAN, of Langtry, Texas, was in no doubt as to where justice lay in the case of a man brought before him for the murder of a Chinese labourer. 'There ain't a damn line here nowheres that makes it illegal to kill a Chinaman,' he thundered, flourishing his law book. 'The defendant is discharged.'

Nor did Mexicans fare any better: 'It served the deceased right for getting in front of a gun.' And as for the happy couples who came to him to be married: 'May God have mercy on your soul.'

Bean, it may be gathered, was not an orthodox judge. Born around 1825, he killed several men in his youth and dabbled in the slave trade before fighting on the Confederate side in the Civil War. He organised a guerrilla band called the Free Rovers – known to everyone else as the Forty Thieves – and worked as cotton smuggler, Indian fighter, butcher, dairyman and petty swindler before ending up in the small town of Langtry.

The town was named after a railwayman, but Bean, who was very fond of

women and named the courtroom-cum-saloon that he built The Jersey Lily, after the famous actress Lillie Langtry. (The name was misspelled due to the ignorance of the drunken sign painter who had been sentenced to do the job.)

For many years, Bean dispensed whiskey and justice in equal measure from his seat on the porch. He had managed to get himself elected as a justice of the peace by claiming that, having been in and out of prison so often, he knew the legal system back to front.

# TAKING THE BLAME

*Employing a scapegoat was once a princely privilege*

WHEN the Yoruba people of West Africa wanted to free themselves of their problems, they would make a human sacrifice to please the gods. According to Sir James Frazer in *The Golden Bough*, once the inhabitants of a village had chosen their victim, or *oluwo*, they made sure that he had everything he wanted before his execution.

On the appointed day, the *oluwo* would have his identity concealed from the villagers by being showered with chalk and ashes. Then he would be paraded through the streets and all the villagers would rush to touch him, believing that they would thus transfer their problems and sins to him. Finally, they would chop off his head, and all the troubles of the community would die with him.

The idea of a scapegoat to take the blame for everyone else is probably as old as civilisation. The word itself has its origins in an ancient Jewish practice: every year on Yom Kippur, the Day of Atonement, a high priest would lay his hands on the head of a live goat and confess the sins of the Children of Israel over it. Then the animal was driven into the wilderness, where it was left to fend for itself.

In Europe, schoolboy princes who had been misbehaving had a different idea: they employed 'whipping boys' to take their punishment for them. For example, when Edward VI of England was a student, his whipping boy was Barnaby Fitzpatrick. But when the young James I made a mistake with his Latin, his teacher, George Buchanan, spared the whipping boy and punished the prince instead – and vowed that he would do it again if the prince did not work harder.

King Henry IV of France used whipping boys even as an adult. When he converted from Protestant to Roman Catholic in 1593, he sent two ambassadors to Rome to be symbolically whipped by the pope for Henry's previous heresy. The ambassadors were made cardinals soon afterwards, to show that there was no ill feeling towards them.

*Rough justice* Edward VI's whipping boy unbuttons his tunic as he prepares to take the young prince's punishment for making a mistake during his school lessons.

---

## DID YOU KNOW..?

*EVERY YEAR, the ancient Greek islanders of Leucas used to throw a criminal who had been sentenced to death off an enormous cliff as a sacrifice to the gods. To temper justice with mercy, they tied feathers and live birds to him to 'lighten' the fall. If he survived, they hauled him out of the sea and gave him his freedom, on the condition that he left the island.*

---

## GUILT BY RESEMBLANCE

OTTILIE MEISSONIER was walking along a London street one night in the mid 1890s when she spotted a middle-aged man under the light of the street lamps. She recognised him at once as a confidence trickster who had defrauded her several weeks earlier of two watches and some valuable jewellery.

The man denied the charge. He insisted that he was a Norwegian named Adolph Beck, and that he had never seen the lady before. But the case against him was overwhelming. Ten different women picked him out at identity parades, and the police soon decided that he was John Smith, a notorious criminal. He was tried at the Old Bailey and sentenced to seven years in prison.

In prison he continually protested his innocence, but none of his petitions to the Home Secretary for exoneration were successful. And three years after serving his sentence, another woman accused him of stealing money and jewellery, and Beck found himself in court once again, charged with the same offences as before.

It was while he was awaiting sentence that an extraordinary coincidence occurred. Another man was arrested while trying to pawn some stolen rings. He was Wilhelm Meyer, an Austrian who looked remarkably like Beck and who sometimes used the alias 'John Smith'. He had stolen the rings from various women, using exactly the same technique as in the previous robberies.

And that was not all. Meyer was a Jew and, like all Jewish men, he was circumcised. So, according to police records, was John Smith. But Beck – as he had pointed out at his trial – was not. Moreover, Beck's handwriting did not match specimens said to be written by Smith. Experts had dismissed this as an attempt by the accused to cover his tracks. But by now it was obvious that a miscarriage of justice had taken place. Meyer eventually pleaded guilty to all charges and Beck was officially exonerated in 1904. He stepped from the dock a free man, and with £5000 (more than $24 000) compensation for his long years in prison.

Unfortunately, the experience had broken him. He spent the money recklessly and died soon afterwards in near penury. Some good did come out of the affair, however: soon after Beck's death, the Court of Criminal Appeal was established in an attempt to ensure that such mistakes never happened again.

# GETTING BY ON CHARM ALONE

## *The magical objects people hope will ease their way in life*

FOOTBALLERS display team mascots. Travellers, soldiers and lovers carry good luck charms. Houseowners nail up horseshoes over front doors. All these objects are mascots, a word derived from the Provençal word *masco*, meaning sorcerer, for it is sorcery that is required to combat evil and bring good luck.

Originally there were two kinds of mascot. Talismans, from the Greek *telesma*, meaning mystery, were supposed to attract good fortune. Amulets were meant to shield their wearers from the 'evil eye', a devil said to exert a malign influence on all who were subject to its glance. (The word amulet probably derives from the Latin *amuletum*, a colloquial word for cyclamen – a plant thought to protect against poison.) In medieval Europe, the 'evil eye' was blamed for many a misfortune.

### Power of belief

Talismans and amulets are common to all societies. What varies are the objects and symbols that are chosen. Some amulets are quite revolting to look at, their hideousness intended to avert the gaze of even the most ardent devils. Other amulets, especially beads and jewellery, may be exquisite – these wield their power through the symbols emblazoned on them.

A common symbol on talismans is the cat. In ancient Egypt, cats were considered sacred and were revered. In medieval Europe, however, it was thought that witches could appear in the form of a cat. That such a symbol can be interpreted in contradictory ways suggests that it is not the talisman itself that wields the power, but rather the belief invested in it by its owner.

Talismans can also be used as a coded signal for a particular belief. For example, the fish is an ancient symbol of Christ, and it was used by Christians as a secret sign when the Church was persecuted by the Romans.

Talismans and amulets do not have to take the form of engraved ornaments. They can also be the limbs or organs of animals. For example, the Eskimos of Greenland used to sew a hawk's head onto a boy's clothing. This was supposed to make him a better hunter.

Over the years, symbols can change in meaning and even gain an opposite connotation. A notorious example is the swastika. Its name derives from a Sanskrit word meaning 'bringer of good luck', and in many cultures it has symbolised happiness. But since it was adopted as the Nazi symbol, it has come to mean not a protection against the 'evil eye', but the 'evil eye' itself.

***Waving danger away*** *This 3500-year-old Egyptian ivory wand was thought to protect against dangerous animals.*

---

## LUCK OF THE IRISH

VISITORS to Blarney Castle in Ireland used to engage in a particularly irrational and dangerous practice: they would climb the 37 m (120 ft) high keep, and then lower themselves head first over the parapet. As friends held them by their ankles, they would kiss a stone set in the wall which they believed would grant them 'the gift of the gab'.

Several legends explain just how this particular stone came to be endowed with magical powers. One has it that Cormac MacCarthy, who built the castle in the 15th century, was worried about a forthcoming legal case. He dreamt that if he kissed the first stone he saw in the morning, words would pour from him, and he would easily be able to talk his way out of the law suit. When he awoke, Cormac found a stone and kissed it. His words did indeed pour out, and he won his case. Now fearful that all Ireland would start kissing the stone, he set it in the parapet of his castle, well out of reach of any intruders.

A century or so later, Queen Elizabeth I of England was trying to get Cormac's descendant, Dermot MacCarthy, to surrender the castle as a proof of loyalty. Dermot, who obviously had 'the gift of the gab', always managed to put the queen off, coming up with ever more elaborate excuses. Elizabeth eventually grew tired of all this talk, retorting that: 'This is all Blarney. What he says he never means,' and blarney entered the English language as a word for wheedling talk.

Nowadays, aspirant wheedlers can reach the Blarney Stone without risking life and limb. Although no longer dangerous, kissing the stone is still an awkward procedure, requiring the visitor to lie down on his back, take hold of an iron handle and bend his head back until his lips touch the orator's rock.

# FORBIDDEN FOOD

### One man's meat is another man's poison

A SPECIALITY at one of London's oldest and most famous restaurants is steak and oyster pie. Traditionally, this would be accompanied with a glass of stout. But members of no fewer than four major world religions would find this seemingly innocuous meal repulsive.

Hindus object violently to eating beef. Orthodox Jews will not eat shellfish. Muslims refuse to drink alcohol. And Buddhists will not eat animals at all. On the other hand, that same restaurant would never dream of serving horsemeat. In Britain that is fit only for dogs, but in France horsemeat is part of the human diet.

Offer a plate of best roast dog to a French or English person, however, and they will be outraged

**Acquired taste** *Water beetles are pounded into paste for a Southeast Asian dish.*

and disgusted. But in China, dogs – called 'hornless goats' – are a delicacy, as they once were among the ancient Phoenicians, Greeks, Romans and Aztecs and, until recently, in the South Pacific. The Tahitian islanders kept one breed of dog especially for the table, and the 18th-century explorer Captain Cook found it as tasty as English lamb.

All societies regard certain foods as untouchable. Few North Americans or Europeans would relish a menu of ants, caterpillars, locusts, raw ducks' feet and dragonfly larvae, but all are eaten every day somewhere in the world: ants in Latin America, Asia and Africa; caterpillars among the Australian aborigines, who call them 'witchety grubs'; locusts among the Navaho Indians in North America and in north Africa; raw ducks' feet in China, and dragonfly larvae in Laos.

**Insect proof** *A giant centipede is added for piquancy to this home-made Thai rice liquor.*

# SAFE FROM THE BUTCHER

### The versatile cow is too valuable for Hindus to eat

ONE-THIRD of the world's cows live in India – one of the poorest countries in the world, where famine is a regular occurrence – yet no one dares to inflict the slightest harm on these animals, let alone kill and eat them. Cows are sacred to the Hindu population in India, and are protected as such by law.

To Hindus, cows are a symbol of fertility and motherhood. Cows are revered, loved and protected. They wander about freely and have even been known to hold up trains for hours, while passengers wait for them to move off the track. Hindus hang garlands round cows' necks at festivals and pray for them when they are sick.

If this seems strange to non-Hindus, it seems even odder in the light of the fact that the Brahmans, the Hindu priestly caste, originally oversaw the slaughter of cattle. But that was before a huge increase in the population, and

a consequent shortage of grazing land, made growing vegetables a much more economic source of food.

This radical change in the economy occurred during the 6th century BC. During the 5th century BC, however, the Buddhist religion – among whose tenets was a profound aversion to killing for food – began to spread throughout India. Its appeal was undoubtedly increased by the scarcity of beef and the lordly insistence of the Brahmans on reserving what beef there was for themselves. After a struggle for religious domination in India that lasted nine centuries, the Hindus finally reversed their position.

**Protected species** *Indian tribesmen take their colourful cow to a festival.*

By the 4th century AD they had declared cows to be sacred animals.

It did not escape the Hindu sages that cows are more productive alive than dead. They provide milk for food, calves to sell, oxen to pull ploughs (they are more efficient on the small Indian farms than tractors), dung for fertiliser, fuel and building materials, and – once they have died of old age – leather too. Who would not be grateful for such a useful animal, and revere it?

# PAPUAN PIGS ARE POLITICS
*Where pork is perceived to tell friend from foe*

IN MANY PARTS of Papua New Guinea, the pig rules. Not directly, but as a symbol of wealth and power. Some tribes, such as the Ebei, keep pigs as big as Shetland ponies and look after them like pets to show how rich they are. In the Western and Southern Highlands, pigs bind together political alliances – although, to do so, they first have to be cooked and eaten.

The highland pig festivals are gatherings of friendly tribes, held to demonstrate their loyalty to one another and to warn potential enemies of the sheer numbers they may have to face if they start a conflict. The festivals take enormous planning, which is why any one tribe will hold one only every ten years or so.

### Long build-up

A pig festival starts with the host clan building several long houses to accommodate the guests. Construction may take some years; once it is complete, the hosts send out invitations to neighbouring communities. Meanwhile, the members of the host clan have been gathering pearl shells and money to give as presents to their guests, and preparing body decorations of feathers, paint and shells.

Once the hard currency of the festival is prepared, the pigs are fattened. If the hosts do not have enough of their own, more are bought on credit from neighbours. And when all the pigs are ready, the guests arrive.

The festival itself has three stages. First, the hosts display their gifts of money and shells, and their pigs, for all to see. Next, the pigs – as many as 2000 of them – are slaughtered, cut up,

*Peace symbol Pork is cut up to be cooked communally and shared by local tribes seeking to maintain friendships in the Southern Highlands of Papua New Guinea.*

***Preparing the oven*** *At pig festivals in the Southern Highlands of Papua New Guinea, pork is traditionally cooked in earth ovens – deep pits filled with hot stones. The meat is placed on the preheated stones and covered with layers of leaves and earth.*

and hung on poles to be counted. Finally, there is the cooking and eating.

The pigs are communally cooked in long earth ovens for several hours. Then each male host divides up his pork among his relatives and guests, with especially large portions going to guests from whom he himself has received pork at past festivals.

The guests take the meat home, recook it, and distribute it in smaller portions among family and friends. Following this, neighbouring villages often stage their own smaller pig festivals to show their political sympathy for the host clan.

Thus fortified, everyone can look forward to the next highland pig festival, solid in the knowledge that such excellent hosts will make the best of allies. And the hosts, too, can take comfort from the thought that their generosity will not be forgotten in times of peril. As for the potential enemies, their mouths must be watering from one year's end to the next.

---

## DID YOU KNOW..?

*PIGS, given the right diet, convert their food into flesh more efficiently than any other animal.*

✳ ✳ ✳

*DESPITE the abundance of pigs in ancient China, at one time only the emperor was allowed to eat pork.*

# THE UNPOPULARITY OF PORK

*Why are pigs forbidden food for some?*

IF YOU EAT in a French or Cantonese restaurant, you will be sampling some of the finest cuisine in the world. On the menu will be at least one, and often many, pork dishes. In France, even small villages have their own charcuterie, a butcher's shop that specialises in cooked and cured cuts of pork. In China, pigs are everywhere, and everyone eats them. Yet Judaism and Islam consider pigs 'unclean' and their followers may not eat pork. How has this come about?

The book of Leviticus in the Old Testament lays down that among 'clean' animals are those that both chew the cud and have cloven hooves. Pigs, while cloven-hooved, do not chew the cud and so are 'unclean' and not to be eaten. Among other 'unclean' animals are birds that do not fly and fish that do not swim – in other words, creatures such as ostriches and shellfish.

Besides abjuring pork, Muslims will not eat carnivorous animals, birds that seize their prey with talons, or the flesh of the domestic ass. Islam and Judaism have a number of laws and rituals in common, and it is reasonably certain that Islam borrowed some directly from its older neighbour. But this does not explain the original underlying reason for the ban on eating pork.

### Unhygienic habits

One theory suggests that the taboo arose because pigs are, literally, dirty animals, and dangerous to eat too. They wallow in mud, and eat all sorts of rubbish from which they contract parasitic worms that can cause disease in humans if the meat is not cooked properly. But people had domesticated the pig – and eaten its flesh – in the Middle East for about 4500 years before the book of Leviticus was written in roughly 450 BC. As a health warning this seems a little belated.

The real explanation, some anthropologists suggest, does have something to do with pigs' eating habits and their love of wallowing in mud. Animals that chew the cud – cattle, goats and sheep – do so as part of an elaborate digestive process that is designed for a high-cellulose diet – that is to say, grass. Pigs cannot survive on grass; they tend to eat the same vegetables as people do. The nomadic Hebrews simply could not afford to maintain animals that would, in effect, compete with them for food.

Besides, pigs need a lot of water if they cannot establish a decent mud-bath. The reason is that they do not sweat (despite the expression 'to sweat like a pig'). Mud helps to dissipate their body heat – in fact, wallowing in mud is a more efficient way of losing heat than a regular bath in water. The Hebrews, who lived on arid grasslands, had few resources for indulging a water-hungry animal like a pig.

Islam was founded in a strikingly similar environment. Both religions had good economic reasons for discouraging pig-keeping. Both had excellent religious reasons for wanting to set their adherents apart from their neighbours. For both, strict dietary laws were a simple and effective method of reminding their believers of their difference from others, but in a way that did not greatly inconvenience them.

## KEEPING TWO WORLDS APART

THE INUIT PEOPLE of Alaska (the Eskimos) hunt caribou in spring, and whales during the winter. They also believe that land and sea animals find each other repellent. Whether out of respect for the animals' supposed prejudices, or to avoid detection in the hunt, the Inuits remove all traces of their pursuit of the one kind of animal when hunting for the other.

So, in spring, before going out in search of caribou, an Inuit hunter will clean his body of all traces of the whale grease that has accumulated over the winter. In April, before going whaling, he removes all scent of the caribou.

He will also avoid taking the weapons he uses for hunting caribou to sea with him. He may, however, use his sea-going weapons on land, but he must ritually cleanse them between seasons. The Inuits believe that infringement of these rules may jeopardise the hunt.

Just as the seasons dictate what the Inuits hunt, so other significant points in time dictate their diet. After childbirth, for instance, a woman is forbidden to eat raw meat. Instead, she should eat food that is deemed good for the growing child – such as ducks' wings which, the Inuits believe, will help make the child a good runner or paddler.

*Lethal disguise* *In the vast expanse of northwest Greenland, an Inuit slides his hunting rifle along the ice, hoping to catch his prey unawares. The rifle is set up on a sleigh-screen called a* utoq.

### DID YOU KNOW..?

*CARIBS and Zulus once shared Jews' and Muslims' aversion to pork – but for other reasons. The Caribs shunned pork for fear of growing small, pig-like eyes, while Zulu girls believed that if they ate pork their future children would resemble pigs.*

# MARKING TIME

## *Different ways to count the changing of the seasons*

THE WORLD has much reason to be grateful to the French Revolution. Besides the victory of egalitarian principles for which the Revolution is renowned, among its benefits was the adoption of the metric system of measurements. This system is used today by scientists worldwide and, in many countries, by people in their everyday lives. The metric system is decimal – everything is based on the number ten – and is therefore consistent within itself and easily understood. French revolutionaries, intent on destroying all ties with the old regime, found the decimal principle so attractive that they even applied it as far as they could to measuring time.

September 22, 1792, the day France was declared a republic, was the first day of Year One in the new Republican Calendar. The year still had 12 months, but all were 30 days long, and there were ten days to the week or *décade*.

The last day of a *décade* was devoted to rest, and five more days (six in a leap year), scattered throughout the year but not part of any month, were festival days. There was also a scheme to divide the day into ten hours, but that never really caught on.

The Republican Calendar worked well enough inside France, but was abandoned after 13 years. Because its leap year fell in a different year from that of the conventional calendar, it was difficult to convert from one system to another, causing confusion in diplomatic and business dealings with other countries.

Our present calendar was adapted by Pope Gregory XIII in the 16th century from an earlier system introduced by Julius Caesar. A completely decimal calendar is an impossibility, since we measure time with a combination of two quite different units – the year and the day. A year is counted as the number of days it takes for the Earth to make one complete circuit of the Sun. A day, however, is the time the Earth takes to rotate once on its axis, and each year it does this 365.24219878 times – a number that plainly will not divide by ten. The extra day in leap years helps to correct the error in the standard 365-day calendar year, but, because we have a seven-day week, January 1, for example, falls on a different weekday each year.

There have been several proposals to make this system more logical. The International Fixed Calendar would divide the year into 13 months of 28 days each, with one additional 'year day' at the end. Months would always begin on a Sunday and end on a Saturday. Leap years would have an extra 'leap day' in the middle.

The World Calendar would divide the year into quarters of 91 days each, with an extra day at the end of the year and an unnumbered 'leap day' in the middle every fourth year. Each three-month quarter would start on a Sunday, and the first month in each quarter would have 31 days.

Neither proposal has made much headway. The Gregorian Calendar works reasonably well and will probably continue to be a world standard. In any case, we do not experience the year merely in terms of numbers, but in seasons, solstices, and equinoxes – times marked by customs and festivals the world over.

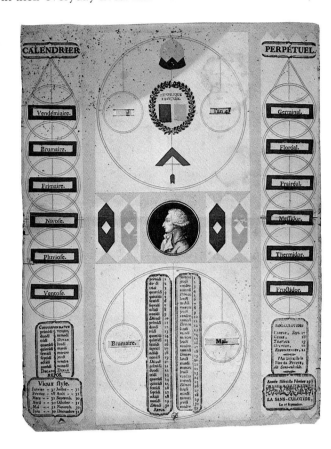

***Changing times*** *This French chart, printed shortly after the Republican Calendar was introduced, aided conversion between the new calendar and the Gregorian one used elsewhere in Europe.*

# A SYMBOLIC HARVEST

*The Jewish festival of Succoth harkens back to a time of wandering*

USING THE SIMPLEST of materials, some observant Jews build a booth, or *succah*, outside their house or near the synagogue in autumn. The *succah* is a plain hut constructed from branches, twigs and leaves, and decorated with fruit and flowers. Those who do not have space to build one outside sometimes decorate a symbolic trellis in their homes. This is part of the celebration of Succoth, the feast of Tabernacles.

### Fruitful celebration

Tabernacles is the last of the three great festivals of the Jewish year, following Passover and Shavuot. Beginning five days after Yom Kippur, the most solemn day of the year, the festival lasts for seven days and is both a joyous occasion and a time for contemplation. It takes place at harvest time and commemorates a successful farming year.

But a deeper meaning of Succoth lies in Israel's long and dramatic history. It is a time when Jews remember their forefathers wandering in the desert, living in simple tents, drawing hope only from their devout belief in their God and His mercy.

Succoth is therefore an expression of thanksgiving for the Israelites' preservation, as well as a time for remembering those who are still homeless and without shelter. In former days, and especially in warm climates, many Jewish families lived for seven days within their *succah*, worshipping, eating and celebrating there. Even today, some families take some of their meals out of doors during the festival.

There is much symbolism in the events that make up the feast of Tabernacles. The humble booths are constructed so that the stars in the night sky can be seen through their flimsy roofs, as a reminder of the frailty of man and the vastness of creation.

Four plants also have special significance at this time: citron, palm, myrtle and willow, whose different characteristics serve as reminders of the variety and brotherhood of mankind. For example, citron, as it has both taste and fragrance, symbolises people who have learning and perform good deeds. Those with good deeds but no learning are represented by myrtle, which has fragrance but no taste.

### Continuity of the faith

Immediately after Succoth comes another holy day, *Simchat Torah* – 'the Rejoicing of the Law'. On each Sabbath throughout the year, Jews read a selected portion of the books of Moses. Over a year, they will have read them through from beginning to end.

The readings are arranged so that the very last verses (from Deuteronomy) and the very first verses (from Genesis) are read together on *Simchat Torah*. This is itself a symbol of the Jewish faith – in God, and the law of God, there is no beginning and no end.

# THE ELUSIVENESS OF EASTER

*The difficulty of finding a date for Easter*

EASTER, although one of the most important dates in the Christian calendar, can occur on any weekend between March 22 and April 25. Calculating the exact date of Easter has caused controversy and bewilderment, even in Church circles.

The date of Easter, the commemoration of Christ's Resurrection three days after the Crucifixion, is based on the lunar calendar, and originally could fall on any day of the week. The earliest Christians celebrated it during Passover, the eight-day Jewish festival that begins on the day of the first full Moon after the vernal equinox (March 21).

### Always on a Sunday

It was during Passover, which commemorates the Jews' Exodus from slavery in Egypt, that Christ was crucified. But gradually some Christian leaders wanted to distinguish their holy days from those of Judaism, and it was therefore decided that Easter would always fall on a Sunday, the day of the Resurrection, and that it would be celebrated after Passover. This rule was agreed by the Council of Nicaea in 325.

**Holy fire** *Easter pilgrims in Israel carry ritual Paschal candles made of beeswax.*

Thus, in countries where the Church has accepted the Gregorian calendar, Easter Day is the first Sunday after the first full Moon on or after March 21. If the full Moon occurs on a Sunday, Easter Day falls on the following Sunday. But Eastern Orthodox Churches in Greece and Romania still calculate Easter with the old Julian Calendar, while recognising the modern Gregorian Calendar for fixed feast days. There is a difference of about 13 days between the two systems.

This century, several attempts have been made to find a single date for Easter – either by making it a fixed feast, like Christmas, which is always celebrated on a certain date, or by introducing a completely new calendar. The Roman Catholic Church recommended making Easter a fixed feast back in 1963, but only on the condition that the world's other Christian Churches would agree, which they have not.

Neither has the more radical proposal of a fixed World Calendar made much progress. In this system, each date would fall on the same day of the week every year, and Easter would always be on Sunday, April 8.

And so the possibility of settling on a fixed date for Easter is remote. Apart from keeping close track of the Moon's phases, a good diary remains the only way to know when to buy Easter eggs.

# NEWTON OF THE ORIENT
## The stone observatories of the Maharajah Sawai Jai Singh

I N THE GROUNDS of the royal palace at Jaipur, capital of the Indian state of Rajasthan, tourists today wander through what looks like the abandoned stage set of some science fiction spectacular – a scattering of impressive stone structures in strange and varied geometrical shapes. The uninformed visitor could hardly guess that these monuments are precision astronomical instruments for the study of the Sun, Moon and stars.

For Hinduism, as for many other religions, the calendar of religious ceremonies and festivals depends upon a knowledge of astronomy. Many worshippers visit the holy sites of the Ganges whenever there is an eclipse of the Sun, for example, and therefore want to know when an eclipse is imminent. In the early 18th century, an Indian prince, the Maharajah Sawai Jai Singh, was worried that accurate astronomical observations had not been made by Hindus for many centuries.

### Importance of astronomy

Jai Singh set out to revive Hindu astronomy and to perfect the calendar and the official tables showing the movements of the heavenly bodies. He was an exceptionally able man – his second title 'Sawai' literally means 'one and a quarter more', because he was 'more' in every way than his contemporaries. But he had his eccentricities, notably a deep distrust of the small brass instruments usually employed by astronomers of his day. He believed that the most accurate measurements would be achieved on the largest scale, and ordered the construction of massive astronomical instruments in stone.

A total of five observatories were built to Jai Singh's instructions. The most important were at Delhi, Jaipur and Ujjain. At Jaipur, the monumental structures include the largest sundial in the world, with a gnomon (the projecting arm that casts the shadow) that is 27 m (90 ft) high. This tells local time to within a few minutes – it cannot be more precise because the huge shadow

### DID YOU KNOW..?

*A SMALL MODEL of an umbrella, symbolising divinity or royalty, can be offered as a gift to the goddess of smallpox during the Hindu month of Sravana. Coconuts, flowers, salt and grain are also offered by mothers as thanks for protecting their children from disease during the previous year.*

***Back to the future*** *This modern-looking sundial at Delhi, the first of Maharajah Sawai Jai Singh's observatories, was built in 1724. The time of day is calculated by noting the shadows cast by the straight walls in the centre onto graduated markings on the curved inner walls.*

is blurred at the edges. Jai Singh's weather observatory, a precursor of the modern meteorological office, is still used today, producing long-range weather forecasts that are included in Hindu calendars and almanacs.

### Far-reaching expertise

Although not accurate by modern standards, Jai Singh's observatories plotted the movements of the heavenly bodies with enough precision to be very respectable for their time. Their results appeared in his astronomical table, the *Zij Muhammad Shahi*, compiled both in Persian and in Sanskrit.

On at least one occasion, Jai Singh was able to improve on observations of the Moon and planets made by his contemporaries in Western Europe, with whose work he was well acquainted. Ujjain is still known to orthodox Hindus as the 'Greenwich of India', and Jai Singh himself is remembered as the 'Newton of the Orient'.

# FUNNY MONEY

## *Where a tiger's tongue will settle the bill*

I N 1642 the General Assembly of Virginia solemnly passed a law declaring tobacco the only valid currency in the colony. To save people having to carry large bundles of leaves around with them, paper money called 'tobacco notes' was soon in circulation. But tobacco remained the solid basis of the Virginian currency for over a century. This was not the strange aberration it might seem. History shows that virtually anything scarce, durable and desirable can become money.

Back in prehistoric times, polished axeheads served Stone Age man as currency – understandably, since an axe was probably the most useful object around. The ancient Chinese went one better: instead of exchanging actual goods, they substituted imitations of them. Small pieces of bronze were cast in the shape of a shirt, a knife, a spade or a hoe, and these 'coins' were worth the same as the objects they represented. So a miniature bronze shirt would buy a shirt – or a shirt's worth of anything else!

### *Rare as whales' teeth*

In more recent times, the most varied objects have functioned as money – dogs' teeth in New Guinea, whales' teeth in the Pacific islands, spearheads in Africa, drums in Burma and on the island of Alor in Indonesia. In Thailand, most parts of a tiger could be

***All that glitters*** *In parts of Africa, all manner of beads and bangles are sometimes exchanged as money in local transactions.*

***Heavy debts*** *The largest coins ever made were the limestone discs used on the Pacific island of Yap. These varied in size from 'small change', a mere 230 mm (9 in) across, to colossal coins whose diameter was twice the height of a man.*

used as cash, including the claws, the tail, the teeth and the tongue. In the course of time, as in China, the real thing was replaced by a replica. Pieces of silver in the shape of a tiger's tongue were still changing hands in Thailand only a few years ago.

In China and Tibet, tea was used as a currency for about 900 years. The 'tea brick' consisted of tea and wood shavings pressed together into a block weighing just over 1 kg (2½ lb). In 1800 it was worth approximately one Indian rupee. Pieces could be broken off to provide change. Asian banks continued to issue tea bricks until little over a century ago.

***Token value*** *This miniature Chinese bronze spade, made in 450–400 BC, was a substitute for barter goods.*

But the greatest success story among strange currencies was undoubtedly the cowrie shell. For many centuries it was accepted in payment through much of Africa and Asia. Fifty cowries were worth about one British penny. In the French Sudan, cowries remained an acceptable currency for paying taxes until 1907, when they at last succumbed to the relentless advance of paper money and coins.

## DEAR SKINS

ONE HUNDRED YEARS before the birth of Christ, China was ruled by the Han Emperor Wu Ti. To his embarrassment, Wu Ti found himself desperately short of cash and sought some ingenious device to milk his noblemen of their excess wealth.

It was his wily Prime Minister who devised the cunning plan that saved the imperial finances. As a first step, the emperor appropriated all the white deer in his domain, enclosing them in the royal park. Then he decreed that all princes and courtiers wishing to enter

the imperial presence must, as an essential point of protocol, wear a white deerskin mask. The deerskin could, of course, be bought – at an extortionate price – only from the emperor himself.

In an attempt to avoid impoverishment by the emperor's new decree, a nobleman who had bought one of the expensive skins would offer to pass it on to a colleague, in return for goods or services. And in this way, the deerskins became established as a form of currency, one of the world's best-attested examples of leather money.

# THE VANISHING MARK

### Time is money when inflation gets out of control

IN THE EARLY 1920s, an inhabitant of Berlin went into a local cafe and ordered a coffee priced at 5000 marks. By the time he came to pay, the bill had risen to 8000 marks. Prices were rising by 60 per cent an hour!

The collapse of the German currency after the First World War is the world's most famous example of hyperinflation. At the height of the crisis, money was literally not worth the paper it was printed on. Germans thought inflation was bad at the end of 1922, when the US dollar was valued at 18 000 marks. But by August 1923 a dollar would buy a million marks, and by November it was worth a staggering 130 thousand million.

In practice, all metal currency disappeared from circulation. People simply hoarded any traditional coinage they had, because the metal's value was bound to be far higher than the face value of the coin. The government made coins of cheap porcelain instead. Eventually notes were printed on almost any material that was available – shoe leather, cloth, cardboard, even old newsprint.

The problems of living with hyperinflation were enormous. Workers were paid daily with large bundles of notes, which

they had to spend immediately, before their wages became virtually worthless, and shoppers were seen pushing heaps of money through the streets in wheelbarrows.

Although Germany presents the most famous inflation horror story, it is not the worst. That record belongs to Hungary after the Second World War. In 1946 there were Hungarian bank notes in circulation with a denomination of 100 000 000 000 000 000 000 pengo. When a new unit of currency was introduced, the forint, it was valued at an astronomical 200 000 000 000 000 000 000 000 000 000 pengo.

***Petty cash problem*** *In Germany during the early 1920s, a time of runaway inflation, paper currency was so devalued that even a newsstand needed an oversize basket for the daily takings.*

# BANKING ON BEEF

### *Taking a healthy interest is nothing new*

OUR MODERN banks are named after the bench (*banco*) where an Italian moneylender would once have sat in the marketplace of a Renaissance city. But some historians claim the world's first banks date back much, much further, to the Egypt of some 6000 years ago. Here, a customer's account was kept not in coins or notes, but in cattle – cows and oxen being accepted as local currency.

Borrowers have probably always accused banks of charging excess interest. A clay tablet from ancient Babylon, from about 700 BC, records a loan made by bankers Egibi and Son, of 'two-thirds of a manna of silver … at an interest of one shekel monthly upon the manna'. Since a manna was worth 60 shekels, this implies an interest rate of about 20 per cent per year – much like the rates charged by banks today.

## DID YOU KNOW..?

*THE 'GIZZI PENNY', a thin rod of iron about the length of an arm, was used as money in parts of West Africa until the 1930s. It was often called the 'penny with a soul'. If the penny was damaged, it was considered to have lost its 'soul'. A witch doctor had to be engaged to 'reincarnate' the money and thus restore its value. Two Gizzi pennies would buy 20 oranges or a large bunch of bananas, but the currency also had practical worth: once you had enough pennies, you could take them to the local blacksmith and he would forge them into an iron spear or tool.*

✳  ✳  ✳

*IN 1810, the Welsh 'Bank of the Black Sheep' – the Aberystwyth and Tregaron Bank – issued bank notes that carried pictures of sheep, so that illiterate local shepherds could readily grasp their value. The 10-shilling note showed a lamb, the £1 a sheep, and the £2 two ewes. The notes were not popular, however, and circulated only for a few years.*

✳  ✳  ✳

*RUSSIA was the first modern state to introduce the decimal system, in 1700. One rouble was worth 100 kopeks. Britain adopted decimal currency in 1971.*

# PAPER VALUES

*When was money printed on playing cards – and where was there a currency you could eat?*

THE INVENTION of paper is traditionally attributed to a Chinese government minister, T'sai Lun, in AD 105. So it is not surprising that China also introduced the first paper currency, in about AD 650.

The Chinese nicknamed their paper notes 'flying money' – because it was so easy to move around. By the 12th century, there were enough notes in circulation to cause serious inflation. When the famous Italian traveller Marco Polo visited China from 1275 to 1292, during the rule of the great Kublai Khan, he marvelled at the sophisticated use of paper money throughout the emperor's domain.

Europe was slow to catch up with China's advanced financial methods. From about 1400, bankers in Barcelona, Genoa and Florence began to honour 'bills of exchange' – in effect, a form of private paper money. But it is the Swedes who are normally credited with issuing the first proper European bank notes. A private banker in Stockholm, Johan Palmstruch, began printing notes in 1661. Lamentably, his novel venture went bankrupt within six years.

It was not until 1695 that the newly established Bank of England showed how to do it properly. With government backing, bank notes were issued with denominations between £10 and £100. They have continued to appear, in unbroken sequence, ever since.

### Legal and tender

Paper is not the only material that has been used for printing money, however. Long before the Chinese paper currency, the ancient Egyptians, the Romans and the Chinese themselves had all produced monetary notes on papyrus and animal skins.

One of the strangest note issues occurred in French Canada in 1685. Short of cash to pay his troops, the administrator of the Quebec garrison, Jacques de Meulles, decided to write out promises-to-pay on the back of playing cards. This expedient proved so successful that playing-card notes were still circulating as valid money in Canada more than a century later. Nor is this the only place where playing cards were turned into currency – the revolutionary government of France repeated the ploy in 1790.

### Short change

The world had to wait until the 20th century for the first edible bank note. This was the Tibetan srang, hand-printed on rice paper. The srang might not suit every gourmet's palate, however, since the printing dyes were made by mixing vegetable matter with yak dung!

Lastly, the unchallenged record for the shortest-lived issue of bank notes belongs to Panama. The country's usual currency has been the US dollar, but in October 1941 President Arnulfo Arias decided to print his own notes in various denominations of balboa. Unfortunately, immediately after initiating this bold experiment, the luckless President Arias was overthrown and the dollar reinstated. The balboa notes had lasted just one week.

*Fair deal Playing-card currency was introduced in Canada in 1685; later, blank cards were turned into currency (left). In France, playing-card money (below, left and right) was used after the 1789 revolution.*

*chapter nine*

# TRAVELLING WAYS

DURING THE SECOND World War, a young
Chinese sailor named Poon Lim, the sole survivor of a torpedoed British ship, drifted on a
raft in the Atlantic for 133 days (*page 278*). He
survived on rainwater and the raw flesh of
seagulls and fish. Yet, despite his self-reliant
character and obvious ingenuity, he was later
turned down by the US Navy – because he
had flat feet. Poon Lim's story bears the hallmarks of many of man's great journeys: coping
with whatever circumstances arise; arriving at
an unexpected destination; and developing
abilities and character traits well beyond the
call of everyday life.

# A RATE OF KNOTS

## *Why did tea make ships sail faster?*

ARLY IN OCTOBER 1869, the sleek lines of the clipper *Sir Lancelot* were sighted off Falmouth. It had arrived in British waters roughly two weeks earlier than expected – having made the 26 000 km (16 000 mile) journey from Fuzhou (Foochow), China, in a record-breaking 85 days. The *Sir Lancelot* had won the great race to bring the first tea crop of the year to the West.

Speed was essential in the tea trade: dealers were prepared to pay high prices to have the first tea of the season. Some ship owners paid off the entire costs of a ship's construction with the proceeds of just one voyage.

Clippers were built to carry high-value cargoes that needed to be moved quickly: legal cargoes, such as tea, and illegal loads of opium. To gain speed, clippers were built on radically different lines from traditional ships.

### Built for speed

For hundreds of years, merchantmen had been heavy and squat. They rode over the waves, whereas the clippers were light, long and slim, with sharp bows and concave hull lines that let them cut through the water. And they carried as much as 5500 sq m (60 000 sq ft) of sail on their tall masts, enabling them to keep moving in breezes that would have left other vessels dead in the water.

The new clippers first made their name after the California Gold Rush of 1849, when the sea journey from New York to San Francisco was generally faster and safer

***Joining the rush*** *During the 1849 Gold Rush, clippers, such as the* Flying Cloud, *carried prospectors, machinery, food and even dance-hall girls from America's east coast via Cape Horn to California. They carried Chinese tea and spices on their return journey.*

than the overland trail. The ships were called 'clippers' because of the hours they 'clipped off' a voyage. They could average 20 knots or 37 km/h (23 mph), twice the speed of an ordinary windjammer.

Clippers broke records wherever they went. The *Flying Cloud*, in 1851, completed the New York–San Francisco run in 89 days. In 1868, the *Thermopylae*'s maiden voyage from London to Melbourne took 59 days, a record still unsurpassed by any sailing ship.

Ironically, four years before the *Sir Lancelot*'s triumph on the China run, a supremely efficient marine steam engine had been introduced, which signalled the end for sailing ships. In 1865, the first ships equipped with the new engines were cutting the journey from China to England to just 64 days, and were carrying three times as much cargo.

Then, in 1869, the Suez Canal was opened, lopping 8000 km (5000 miles) off the route. By 1875, construction of square-rigged ships had all but ceased, but they sailed for 50 years more.

***Hands together*** *Sailors aboard the* Garthsnaid *furl the fore course, the lowest of the clipper's sails, during a storm.*

# PILGRIMS' PROGRESS
## *Life below deck on the* Mayflower

TRY TO IMAGINE some 100 men, women and children crammed into a single room, with barely enough space to sit down. The ceiling is so low that anyone taller than 1.5 m (5 ft) has to stoop. Imagine spending day after day there with no sanitation, no natural light and bad ventilation. This was the scene below the decks of the *Mayflower* – the ship that took the Pilgrim Fathers from Plymouth, England, to the New World in 1620.

The Pilgrims were a band of Puritans who had originally left England in 1609 to escape persecution for their religious beliefs. They had settled in Leiden, Holland, but returned to England 11 years later – only to leave Europe for good, in search of a world free from what they considered the corrupting influences of other faiths and ways of life.

### *Haphazard navigation*

The *Mayflower* was tiny by modern standards. It was 27 m (90 ft) long and weighed little more than 180 tonnes, yet it crossed the North Atlantic during the worst season to sail.

In 1620, navigating the oceans was not easy. Compasses (the *Mayflower* carried two) were reasonably advanced, but charts were extremely unreliable, so once a ship drifted off course, the crew had no way of knowing exactly where they were.

On September 16, 1620, the Pilgrims set out from Plymouth for America in fine conditions. But the weather turned and they were soon in the grip of violent storms and mighty seas. The hatches were battened down and the emigrants huddled together, cold, wet and seasick. Down in the stinking hold, they ate, worshipped and tried to sleep. In this squalor, Elizabeth Hopkins gave birth to her fourth child.

The *Mayflower* sailed along for 55 days before a call of 'Land ho' came from the lookout. The Pilgrims had reached the northern tip of Cape Cod, Massachusetts. The following day they rounded the Cape and dropped anchor in a wide harbour just off what is now known as Provincetown.

But the Pilgrims' troubles did not end here, for it took them more than a month to find somewhere suitable to settle. Eventually, their choice fell on a place they called Plymouth. Here the Pilgrims established a settlement under the guidance of John Carver and William Bradford.

### *A bleak welcome*

Tragically, although only one Pilgrim died during the hazardous voyage, 44 perished during the first four months on land. The Pilgrims were exhausted and weak when they landed and, as the first winter approached, America seemed a cold and hostile place.

William Bradford's summing up of their arrival speaks volumes: 'They had now no friends to welcome them nor inns to entertain or refresh their weatherbeaten bodies; no houses or much less towns to repair to, to seek for succour . . .. Besides, what could they see but a hideous and desolate wilderness, full of wild beasts . . . the whole country, full of woods and thickets, represented a wild and savage hue.' And the Pilgrims were city dwellers unaccustomed to working the land. Only with the help of friendly Indians, who taught them how to fish and plant corn, did the Pilgrims survive. After their first harvest, the Indians and Pilgrims held a joint celebration of Thanksgiving – a November holiday that Americans have celebrated ever since.

---

## SICK OF THE SEA

ADMIRAL LORD Horatio Nelson paid a heavy price for his courage and determination. He lost an eye, an arm and ultimately his life while serving his country. But, perhaps surprisingly for Britain's greatest sailor, he suffered throughout life from seasickness.

He endured five months of seasickness on his very first voyage. And as late as 1801 – 30 years after his first voyage – he wrote of 'a heavy sea, sick to death . . .. I shall never get over [it].' Yet he was not deterred from a naval career.

Seamen were constantly exposed to deprivation, malnutrition and disease. And Nelson was as prone to them as the next sailor. During a voyage to the Caribbean in 1780, Nelson and 87 of his crew came down with yellow fever; fewer than ten survived.

Among other ailments, Nelson suffered from recurrent malaria, scurvy, temporary paralysis and possibly tuberculosis. He also frequently suffered from depression – hardly surprisingly, considering his medical history.

**Fallen hero** *Horatio Nelson was mortally wounded during his finest hour: the naval battle that defeated the combined French and Spanish fleets off Cape Trafalgar in 1805.*

# A HARBOUR AT HIGH ALTITUDE

### The search for the mountain-side home of Noah's ark

'THE WINDS BLEW for six days and nights, flood and tempest overwhelmed the world.' These words are not from the Bible, though they resemble the account of the Flood in Genesis. They come instead from the world's oldest written legend, the Sumerian epic of Gilgamesh from the 3rd millennium BC. The myths of many ancient cultures tell a similar story: when a deluge threatens to wipe out life on Earth as punishment for mankind's wickedness, catastrophe is thwarted only by the heroic construction of an immense ark by one man, called Noah in the Biblical version.

### Bald mountain

For centuries, people have searched for Noah's ark where the Bible says it came to rest: on Mount Ararat, in present-day Turkey. In 1876, for example, James Bryce, an Englishman, claimed to have found a large piece of wood from the ark there. But Ararat had been treeless for hundreds of years, and any timber found by shepherds would have been burned for fuel.

Today, the search goes on, largely on behalf of Christian fundamentalists who believe that discovering the ark would help prove the literal truth of the Bible.

### A breakthrough?

In August 1984, an American explorer, Marvin Steffins, announced that he had found the ark, 1500 m (5000 ft) up Mount Ararat. The remains of the enormous ship's hull are clearly visible from the air, he said, and correspond exactly to the Biblical measurements of the vessel. He has visited the site and collected fragments that he claims are made of a cement-like substance with which Noah would have encased the ship's wooden frame. Although scientific analysis has identified Steffins's samples as limestone, he still hopes that excavation of the site will one day confirm that the ark is there.

Some historians, however, believe that Noah would never have been able to find enough timber locally to build the large vessel described in the Bible. They suggest that the ark was a raft of papyrus reeds on which wooden shelters were built, and that such a raft would never have survived through the ages.

# SAILING ON THE WINDS OF CHANGE
### A blast of fresh air for the shipping industry

**Into the wind** *The three 14 m (46 ft) wings atop the cargo ship* Ashington *function as sails. They are covered with the same man-made fabric used to construct lightweight aircraft wings.*

HIGHER OIL PRICES, and growing concern for the environment, may be just what it takes to put wind into the sails of freight shipping. In 1984, a two-masted sailing cargo ship, the 33 m (109 ft) *Atlantic Clipper*, was launched in Britain. Its 420 sq m (4500 sq ft) of sail give it enough power to average eight knots on transatlantic crossings.

Eight knots is a slower speed than the 12 to 23 knots diesel-powered vessels can average. But if oil once again makes the leap in cost that that it did in the early 1980s, sailing ships like the *Atlantic Clipper*, whose diesel engines need only be used during 15 to 18 per cent of a voyage, may become far cheaper to run than conventional vessels. The savings on fuel would be tremendous, and would considerably outweigh the increased spending on the crew's wages for the slower, and therefore much longer, voyage.

Meanwhile, a British firm, Walker Wingsail, has designed vertical wings that serve the function of sails, only with greater efficiency. The wings are computer assisted and can be operated by a single crew member. The computer processes information about the speed and direction of both the wind and the boat itself, and adjusts the angle of flaps on the wings to achieve the most power.

Walker's wings were installed on a cargo ship, the *Ashington*. Its three 14 m (46 ft) high wings have been designed with sophisticated aerodynamic principles in mind, and are made of lightweight but extremely durable man-made materials (such as glass-reinforced plastic) also used in the aircraft industry.

# LUCKY BREAKS

*Even an ill wind can blow some good*

OUTSIDE A VILLAGE church on the coast of Cornwall in England, a cry went up: 'Wreck!' Inside, the vicar's sermon came to an abrupt halt. The congregation – no strangers to shipwrecks – rose to the alarm. Perhaps some hapless sailors were in need of rescue. Yet the vicar entreated them to wait. The sailors' salvation, he said, must be delayed – not by a prayer, but by the time it would take the vicar to change clothes. He knew as well as any Cornishman that a wreck's cargo could include precious metals and all sorts of luxuries, and he wanted his fair chance at the plunder.

### Treacherous coastline

Such is the stuff of legend, and, in fact, this mercenary vicar probably never existed. But before modern navigational aids were invented, the treacherous coast of Cornwall saw countless shipwrecks, and the Cornish, from the impoverished tin-miners to the gentry, were renowned for their resourcefulness in plundering wrecks. An 18th-century prayer from the nearby Isles of Scilly summed up their attitude: 'We pray Thee, O Lord, not that wrecks should happen, but that if any wreck should happen, Thou wilt guide them into the Scilly Isles for the benefit of the inhabitants.'

Once a ship in distress was spotted, crowds of men and women would gather with axes, crowbars, sacks and carts, and follow it – sometimes for days – along the coast. This earnestness led some sailors to believe that the Cornish actually helped to steer ships onto the rocks by displaying false lights or extinguishing familiar beacons. But

little evidence backs these claims, which, as is often the case, may well have grown in the telling.

The most convincing evidence of a deliberate wrecking was in December 1680. A Virginian trader hit rocks because a lighthouse keeper failed to light the fire in the lighthouse; the keeper later looted the wreck's cargo and was subsequently sacked from his job.

As soon as the plunderers reached a ship, no time was wasted removing its cargo. Gold, silver, jewellery, casks of wine – anything of value would be carried off. Plunderers were even known to strip timbers from a ship's hull. They would hide the loot in mines, caves, millponds or under water wheels.

If a few plunderers did, on occasion, rob the surviving sailors and even take the shirts off their backs, many times the Cornish risked life and limb to save lives. Through frequent practice, they were adept at manoeuvring small boats along the rocky coast, and they were renowned both for the heroism of their rescues and the subsequent generosity they showed to shipwreck survivors.

**Tidal harvest** *Plunderers show no qualms in stripping the clothes off the corpse of Sir Clowdisley Shovell after his ship was wrecked in 1707.*

The plunderers' enemy was the customs officer. Soon after the Dutch *Lady Lucy* was wrecked off Porthleven in 1739, four large casks of fine Cognac from its cargo were found by customs in a cellar a short distance away. Oddly enough, it was a vicar's cellar.

---

## RELIC OF A PREHISTORIC LOG JAM

THE OLDEST KNOWN boat of any description is in fact a hollowed-out log that dates back to between 6590 and 6040 BC. Logs make ideal boats – they float easily and can be carved to the required shape or moulded by heating. In some ancient cultures, sides, bows and a stern were added and the inside fitted out with rowlocks and a thwart, or seat. Some had figureheads, usually shaped like an animal's head with holes for eyes.

Other holes in the sides of log boats were probably for mooring poles or a

**Dug-out discovery** *This hollowed-out pine log, found in a peat bog in Holland in 1955, is about 3 m (10 ft) long. It may be the world's oldest boat.*

fishing line. A somewhat more sophisticated refinement was the fish well, a small compartment with a series of holes bored below the waterline, in which the catch could be kept alive.

As the oldest boat – which was found at Pesse in Holland in 1955 and is now in the Assen Museum – has none of these extras and indeed was extremely narrow, experts have cast aspersions on its being a boat at all. It may simply be a coffin, a cooking trough or a sledge.

## WATER, WATER, EVERYWHERE ...

POON LIM, a young Chinese sailor serving in the British Merchant Navy, survived alone on a raft for a record 133 days. His ship, the *Benlomond*, had been torpedoed by a German submarine in the Atlantic on November 23, 1942. Poon Lim grabbed a lifebelt and searched for other survivors: there were none.

By some miracle, Poon Lim happened upon a life raft stocked with provisions – enough food and water for 50 days. The next 83 days he survived thanks only to his inventiveness and his unfailing instinct for self-preservation. He found a piece of floating debris, and pulled a nail out of it. Using his teeth, he fashioned the nail into the shape of a fishing hook. For a while he used biscuit paste for bait to catch small fish, which he then used as bait for larger fish. When the paste ran out, he used the spring from a lamp to tempt the fish. For nearly three months all he ate was raw fish

and the occasional seagull; he drank only whatever rainwater collected in cans.

Somehow, Poon Lim managed to stay alive and sane for nearly 4½ months. Several times he came frustratingly close to being rescued when he spotted ships or aeroplanes. But none of them saw him until, on April 5, 1943, he was picked up by a fishing boat off the Brazilian coast near Salinópolis. Although very weak, he was able to walk, and was suffering only from an upset stomach, a doctor said. He was awarded the British Empire Medal that same year.

Poon Lim later tried to enlist in the US Navy, but was turned down because he had flat feet.

*Canny castaway* Poon Lim spent 133 days drifting in the Atlantic on a raft, surviving on fish and birds whose meat he dried to make it more palatable.

# AN ATOMIC FAILURE
### *How a nuclear success failed to impress*

THE US FREIGHTER *Savannah*, launched in 1959, was the first merchant vessel to use nuclear energy to generate steam for turbine propulsion. Before being decommissioned in 1970, it had logged more than 800 000 km (500 000 miles). The vessel's power plant was fully operational for 99.9 per cent of the time at sea. Refuelling was necessary only every two years. The future for nuclear ships looked rosy. Why, then, are there so few nuclear-powered civilian vessels in the world today?

Following the success of the *Savannah*, numerous ship owners expressed interest in nuclear power. West Germany built the *Otto Hahn* in 1968 and the Japanese followed in 1973 with the *Mutsu*. The Greek shipping tycoon Aristotle Onassis had planned to install a nuclear reactor in his supertanker, the *Manhattan*, but he changed his mind and the ship received a conventional boiler plant. By 1982, all countries had converted their nuclear ships to diesel, with the exception of the Soviet Union and Japan.

The reasons were largely economic. Development costs were enormous: in the case of the *Manhattan*, then the largest ship in the world, research showed that conventional power would be cheaper. In the 1980s, new technology brought the costs down, but by this time there was growing awareness of the hazards of nuclear power and more stringent safety demands made nuclear-powered ships impractical.

But economics play only a small part in military circles. Many of the world's submarines are powered by nuclear energy and can travel over 600 000 km (380 000 miles) without refuelling.

***Powerful precedents*** *The first nuclear-powered cargo ship, shown here under construction in a New Jersey shipyard in 1959, is the second* Savannah. *Its earlier namesake became, in 1819, the first ship to cross the Atlantic under steam.*

# RECONSTRUCTING THE TRIPLE THREAT

*The trireme made the ancient Athenian Navy   invincible – now two Britons
have solved the riddles of   its design*

NEAR THE port of Piraeus in Athens, an elegant wooden boat, 37 m (120 ft) long, pushed out to sea, powered by 170 sweating oarsmen. They could be confident of the seaworthiness of their ship, the *Olympias* – vessels exactly like it had, they knew, soundly defeated the powerful Persian Navy at Salamis and saved Athens from invasion. The oarsmen, who were seated in three decks, one above the other, with great physical effort and skilful coordination of strokes reached a speed of seven knots.

Had any casual observers of this event in 1987 not already known of the existence of the *Olympias*, they could be forgiven for thinking they had entered a time warp. The ship was a precise reconstruction, based on contemporary images found on ancient vases, coins and monuments, of a 5th-century BC Athenian trireme.

### Design debate

It was designed by two British experts, Professor John Morrison, a Cambridge classicist, and John Coates, a naval architect. They were spurred on by a debate on the design and capabilities of the trireme through the letters' page in *The Times* of London in 1975.

History records that a Greek fleet of 380 triremes defeated a Persian fleet perhaps three times that size at Salamis in 480 BC. Morrison and Coates took up the challenge of designing a trireme for

the Greek Navy, and, with the help of a British and Greek crew, making it go.

In the 5th century BC, naval battles were won by ramming – and thereby crippling or sinking – enemy ships. Trireme crews required both immense muscle power and precision timing: attacking too quickly risked jamming their bronze ram in the enemy's hull, while a slow attack gave the enemy enough time to escape.

Scholars have long debated the arrangement of the trireme's banks and oars – some theorised that there was just one bank, with three men rowing each oar. Morrison showed that there were indeed three banks on a trireme, that each oar was manned by only one rower, and that, contrary to what one might expect, the oars for the middle

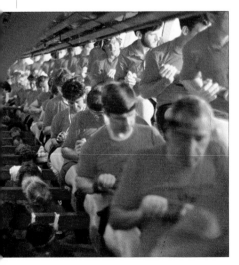

***Economy of space*** *Coordinating the three banks of rowers so that their oars would not collide took much practice, especially since only the rowers on a trireme's top bank could actually see their oars reach the water.*

***Easy riders*** *Travelling at full sail through the Aegean, the* Olympias's *170-strong crew rest their oars. In ancient times, the sails and masts were often left ashore before battle – sheer muscle power provided greater speed and manoeuvrability than wind, and spars and ropes on deck would have hindered the efforts of the fighting men.*

and upper banks were the same length as those for the lower bank.

The *Olympias*'s crew soon discovered, however, that rowing the heavy oars was exhausting and that getting three banks of oars to move without colliding was in itself no mean feat. The 62 rowers of the upper bank had the most taxing stroke – and in ancient times were the best paid. All would, though, occasionally get some rest: when the wind was right, the trireme could hoist its two sails for power.

After a few discouraging tries, teamwork finally prevailed and the *Olympias* glided through the water with as much ease as the ancient trireme

279

# THE LAST SOS
### *Radio distress signals have outgrown Morse's dots and dashes*

IN MARCH 1899, the steamer *Elbe* ran aground off the southeast coast of England. Out of sight of other ships, things could have gone badly for the *Elbe*'s crew but for the fact that a nearby lightship was equipped with Guglielmo Marconi's new radio equipment and was able to send a distress message. A lifeboat was sent out in response, and the *Elbe*'s crew was rescued.

Marconi's development of radio technology, just a few years before the *Elbe* incident, revolutionised safety at sea. Until then, communication between vessels had been strictly limited: signalling by flags, lanterns or fog horns (which are still used today to complement more modern methods) worked within sight or hearing. But ships sometimes go for long periods at sea without seeing or hearing another vessel and, before the advent of radio, could go for days or weeks without communication.

### *Morse alphabet*
The coming of radio, coupled with a signalling system invented by Samuel Morse in 1838, changed all that. Consisting of a system of dots and dashes signifying the different letters of the alphabet, by the end of the century Morse code had proved itself easily adaptable to the new medium of radio.

Radio remains a lifesaver, but the era of Morse code is coming to an end. The International Maritime Organisation has introduced the Global Maritime Distress and Safety System (GMDSS). Instead of dots and dashes, properly equipped ships can communicate with radio telex, which is relayed via satellite to other ships and coast stations. Digitally-encoded distress messages, which give the position of the ship and the nature and time of the distress, can now be sent at the touch of a button or with an abbreviated dialling code. The last official Morse code message will be sent in 1999, the year GMDSS becomes compulsory on all ships.

Many ships are already equipped with 'emergency position-indicating radio beacons' which, in the event of the ship sinking, float free and automatically send a distress signal. Polar-orbiting satellites can pick up these signals anywhere in the world, and since 1982 have helped save more than 1000 lives.

***Ship to shore*** *INMARSAT satellites enable ships to communicate with other ships or land-based radio stations. The two polar-orbiting COSPAS-SARSAT satellites pick up messages from emergency radio beacons, which automatically float free should a ship sink.*

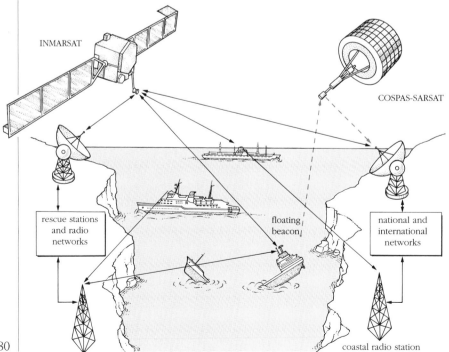

INMARSAT

COSPAS-SARSAT

rescue stations and radio networks

floating beacon

national and international networks

coastal radio station

# SPEED OF LIGHT
### *How a news flash swept across England in 1588*

THE LONG rivalry between Queen Elizabeth I of England and King Philip II of Spain came to a head in 1588 when Philip sent 130 ships towards England with orders to invade. The feared Armada was on its way.

The English had known since 1586 of the likelihood of a Spanish invasion and were well prepared. Yet the Spaniards could attack anywhere along the south coast, and it was clearly impossible to deploy defence forces everywhere. In the event of an attack, everything would depend on the speed with which information could be transmitted and defences mobilised.

### *Tried and tested*
The usual method of communication – messengers on horseback – was far too slow. So an older, quicker way, which had often served England well in times of threat, was pressed into service: a network of beacons, on headlands and hills, stretching all over the country.

On July 29, when the Armada was spotted making its way up the English Channel, the first beacon, on the Cornish coast, leapt into flame. Immediately the flames were seen, the next beacon was lit. Beacon answered beacon as the signal flashed northwards and eastwards; these in turn were a signal for the ringing of church bells. By the next morning, the message that the Spaniards had arrived was known as far away as Durham, some 450 km (280 miles) from the south coast, and local militias were out in force. As it happened, the Armada was defeated at sea, and Spanish soldiers did not set foot on English soil.

In July 1981, beacons were lit on many of the same sites for a happier reason, to celebrate the marriage of Charles, Prince of Wales, to Lady Diana Spencer.

### DID YOU KNOW..?

*THE FAMOUS distress message, SOS, doesn't actually stand for anything. It does not, for instance, mean Save Our Souls – it is simply an easy Morse code message to remember and recognise, even if badly distorted by adverse radio conditions : '. . . - - - . . .'. 'Mayday', the distress call used in radiotelephone messages, is a corruption of the French m'aidez, or 'help me'.*

# PLANS OF ACTION

## *Maps have helped to change the course of history*

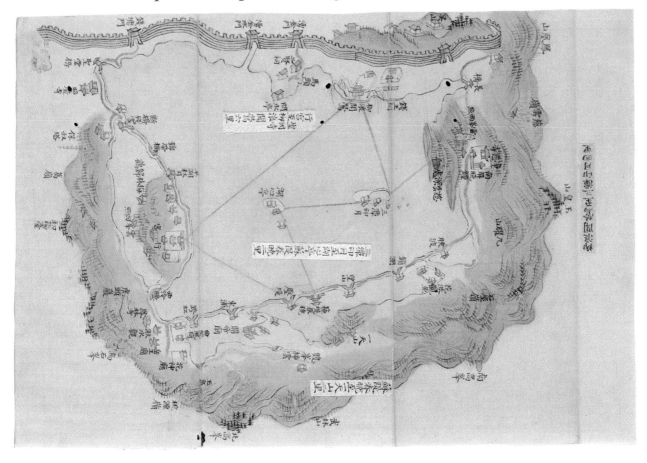

N 227 BC, a man entered the living quarters of Cheng, king of the Ch'in state in northwest China, bearing a gift of considerable value: a silk map. The visitor, however, had a secret mission. Concealed in the map was a poisoned dagger, and the man was an assassin.

The assassination attempt did not succeed, and King Cheng went on, in 221 BC, to unite a half dozen rival states under his sole leadership. He took the name Shih Huang Ti, which means 'first emperor', for Cheng was the first imperial ruler of a country he renamed China, after his Ch'in people.

Chinese maps from Shih's time do not exist, but in 1973 three silk maps dating from about 168 BC were found in a tomb in the province of Hunan. Only two of the maps have been properly restored: one of them shows topographical features such as rivers and mountains, while the other indicates the locations and strengths of military posts.

Silk, or sometimes bamboo, continued to be used for Chinese maps even after the invention of paper

*Delicate detail* This 18th-century Chinese silk map, shown at close to actual size, depicts towns in the Hangzhou district. The Great Wall and some of its watchtowers can also be seen.

around AD 100. As late as the Ch'ing dynasty (1644–1911), silk was preferred because of its strength and its suitability for detailed work. In addition, it could be seamlessly woven to almost any length.

Europeans, however, did not know of silk, or indeed paper, until many centuries after the Chinese, and instead used parchment (made from animal skins) for their maps. The earliest surviving fragment of a parchment map dates from around AD 260 and measures 180 by 450 mm (7 by 18 in). It clearly shows the north shore of the Black Sea and the River Danube, with towns indicated by stylised brick walls.

The distances shown on early maps are often completely out of proportion to the ground they are meant to depict. But although they seem primitive in comparison to modern maps, it was maps like these that helped the Romans and the Chinese to administer two of the greatest empires the world has ever seen.

281

## GAINING A BETTER PERSPECTIVE

HOW IS IT possible to make accurate maps of the most inaccessible parts of the globe, where no man has ever set foot? The answer is photogrammetry, the science of drawing up maps from aerial photographs. Today photogrammetry is the most versatile and accurate method of making maps.

Photogrammetry works in much the same way as human sight. Because our eyes are set slightly apart in the face, each eye sees the same object from a slightly different angle and thus relays a different image of its shape to the brain. The closer the object is to our eyes, the more the images will differ from each other. By comparing the two images, the brain forms an impression of depth and is thus able to form a single, three-dimensional picture.

In photogrammetry the eyes are replaced by a camera that takes a series of aerial photographs of a particular geographical feature or stretch of land. Because the camera is mounted on a moving aircraft or satellite, each picture it takes of the same feature will be from a slightly different place, and therefore from a different angle. These differently angled pictures can then be combined into a three–dimensional image that allows the cartographer to assess the height of features on the ground. In this way, a topographical map can be drawn using contour lines to describe the height of every feature.

Initially, this complex process involved detailed and time-consuming mathematical calculations and complex pieces of optical machinery, but most of this work is now done by computer.

Photogrammetry can be used not only to chart unknown territory, but also to plot changes to the Earth's surface over time. For example, it can map changes to the landscape after an earthquake.

# MERMAIDS AND MONSTERS
*Early maps explored the byways of man's imagination*

UNTIL THE 19th century, when steamships and transcontinental railways made foreign travel a possibility for many people, only a few intrepid adventurers, mainly sailors and traders, ever travelled great distances. 'Abroad' was a truly foreign place about which the vast majority of people knew very little. Early cartographers therefore had little fear of being accused of inaccuracy, and could allow their imaginations to wander somewhat when they compiled their maps.

Nowhere is this more apparent than in old maps illustrated with mythical animals and bizarre human forms. In 1493, for example, a German cartographer named Hartmann Schedel peopled Asia with such legendary creatures as men with horns, birdmen, and bald yet bearded women.

### Ancient sources

An important source of information for Renaissance cartographers was the 2nd-century AD *Guide to Geography* of Ptolemy, which provided the locations of about 8000 places as well as instructions on how to prepare maps. Several Latin editions of this eight-volume work were published in the late 15th century.

But other, more fanciful sources would also be consulted. For example,

Sebastian Münster, a German cartographer born in 1489, fleshed out Ptolemy's work with grotesques described by the 1st-century AD Roman author Pliny the Elder. Near India, Münster drew curiously afflicted people who had only one foot, but one large enough, if hoisted above the head, to form a sunshade. Elsewhere, a race of men sported dogs' heads and barked instead of spoke.

Some of the illustrations on old maps were so fantastic that it is doubtful that anyone actually believed them. Did the Chinese of 350 BC really believe, as a contemporary map shows, that they shared the world with people who had holes through their stomachs so that they could be carried from place to place by poles poked through their bodies and held at shoulder height by two bearers?

*Artistic licence*
*Sebastian Münster drew in fantastic creatures on his 16th-century map of Asia.*

And did European cartographers of the 17th century truly believe that the Pacific Ocean was full of mermaids disporting themselves in the ocean waves? Münster simply brushed aside his readers' doubts with the comment that 'God is marvellous in His work.'

Other grotesques and fantastics were not entirely of the imagination, however. Many 16th- and 17th-century maps depict a strangely horned breed of animal that we know today as the rhinoceros, although some maps give it two horns, and others only one. Arguments arose among early naturalists as to whether the one-horned variety was in fact a unicorn, and the debate was only settled in the late 18th century, when it was discovered that some rhinoceros species have two horns, some just one.

This sort of misunderstanding occurred frequently in the days when very few Europeans had ever seen a rhinoceros, let alone visited its homelands. Such was the ignorance of many people about the world they lived in that when a cartographer wrote 'here be dragons' on a part of his map, most of his readers believed him.

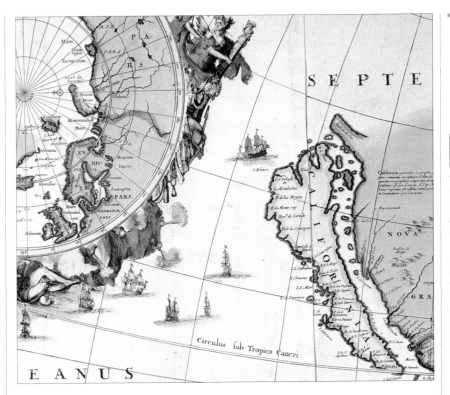

# CALIFORNIA DREAMING

## Early explorers mistook a peninsula for an island

**W**HEN A FLEET of Spanish ships sailed north from their recently acquired empire in Mexico along the California coast in 1533, its sailors became the first Europeans to explore the west coast of what is now Mexico and southern California. They assumed that the land they were charting was an island, for they had earlier discovered a stretch of water that ran northwards to the east of this new land and which, they guessed, rejoined the sea at some point farther up the coast.

Seven years later, another Spanish fleet sailed up the uncharted water intending to circumnavigate the island. But after a journey of some 1100 km (700 miles), the fleet came to a dead end. There was no outlet to the sea. What they had sailed up was therefore an inlet, and the land they had thought an island was in fact a huge peninsula, which is now known as Lower California and is part of Mexico.

### Common mistake

This fact was recorded on contemporary maps. It was neither the first nor the last time mariners had confused peninsulas with islands – indeed, Florida had been charted first as an island before sailors discovered its connection to the mainland of America.

***Misleading source*** *A Dutch map, published by Gerard Valck in 1686, shows California as an island, repeating an error made by an English map maker 61 years earlier.*

But in the case of California, cartography took a definite step backwards. In 1625, an Englishman named Henry Briggs published a map showing California separated from the mainland, explaining that it was 'sometymes supposed to be a part of ye western continent, but scince by a Spanish Charte . . . it is found to be a goodly Islande.'

### Errors compounded

This error was repeated by cartographers such as Pieter Goos of Amsterdam, who showed California as a huge wedge-shaped island in his *Zee Atlas*, first published in the 1660s. So convinced was he of the insularity of California that he mapped out several dozen miniscule islands between California and the coast of what was then known as New Granada.

It was not until the early 18th century that the mistake was corrected. Goos's small islands were finally discarded as fictitious, and the 'goodly Islande' known as California was returned to its rightful place as part of the mainland of North America.

# A MAP OF THE MEDIEVAL MIND

## The Mappa Mundi and its old world view

**I**N 1988, the Dean and Chapter of Hereford Cathedral in England announced plans to sell a map of the world at auction. The map in question is far from accurate – for example, it does not even include America or Australia. Yet it was expected to sell for some £7 million (US $12 million).

The Mappa Mundi is no ordinary map. It was made about 1290, when Europeans still believed that the world was flat and did not know of the existence of America or Australia. The map was drawn in black ink, with red and blue colouring and highlights in gold leaf, on a sheet of vellum measuring 1630 by 1370 mm (64 by 54 in).

### Pilgrims' priorities

In accordance with the views of the medieval Christian church, Jerusalem was placed at the centre of the habitable world, while other towns and cities in Europe and the Middle East were included because they sat astride the routes taken by pilgrims to the Holy Land. But the scribe of the Mappa Mundi carelessly labelled Europe and Africa the wrong way round.

Geography aside, the map is a fascinating glimpse into the medieval mind. Drawings and short captions recount the history of the human race and the marvels of the natural world, and, at the top of the map, the Blessed are shown ascending into Heaven while the Damned descend into Hell. At the extremes of our planet, strange people with big ears and cloven feet inhabit isolated islands, while the people of Norway appear to be sharing their country with a race of monkeys.

It is not known how the Mappa Mundi came into the possession of Hereford Cathedral, where it has been well preserved. The cathedral, however, has not survived in such a good state of repair, and in November 1988 its authorities decided to sell the map to raise funds for the building's restoration and maintenance. But many people in Britain were alarmed by the possibility that a part of their heritage might leave the country. The cathedral authorities were eventually persuaded not to sell the map and to use other means to raise the estimated £7 million that they needed.

## THE LANDS THAT NEVER WERE

ONE SUMMER night in 1726, a package was left on the doorstep of Benjamin Motte, a London publisher. Inside was the manuscript of a book written by one Lemuel Gulliver and entitled *Travels Into Several Remote Nations of the World*. Gulliver described himself as 'first a surgeon, and then a captain of several ships', but other than a few brief biographical details given in a foreword to the book, nothing else was known about this mysterious sea captain, nor the travels he claimed to have made.

The account of Gulliver's voyages was extraordinary. He described the people of hitherto unknown lands, such as Brobdingnag, said to be connected to North

America by a land bridge, and Lilliput, an island apparently near Sumatra.

Motte enjoyed the book so much that, without ever meeting the author, he decided to publish it, even if the author did demand, through an intermediary, the then exorbitant fee of £200. *Gulliver's Travels*, as the book soon became known, sold out within a week of publication.

Speculation soon arose as to the identity and whereabouts of Lemuel Gulliver. The author, however, was unavailable for comment, for he had returned to his home in Ireland, fearful of the reception the book might enjoy. The reason for this trepidation was that *Gulliver's Travels* was no innocent travelogue, but an often

biting, if somewhat disguised, comment on the political and social climate of early 18th-century Britain. Its author was Jonathan Swift, the foremost political satirist of his day.

Swift was not the only English writer to possess a vivid geographical imagination. In 1687, Captain William Hack invented Pepys's Island, supposedly in the South Atlantic, in honour of the then Secretary to the Navy, Samuel Pepys. In his *Description of the Coast & Islands in the South Sea of America*, Hack even named parts of the island Admiralty Bay and Secretary's Point, and ships of the British Navy searched in vain for the 'very pleasant' island as late as 1764.

# DISCOVERING HIDDEN DEPTHS
### Seasat-A *went into space in order to explore the ocean floor*

OVER THE centuries, man has attempted to map the whole of his world, painstakingly surveying each hill and mountain and measuring each river and road. But one part of the world proved impossible to map in its entirety: the oceans. On June 26, 1978, all that changed.

On that date, the US National Aeronautics and Space Administration (NASA) launched the *Seasat-A* satellite, designed to study the world's oceans. *Seasat-A* orbited the Earth at a height of 800 km (500 miles) and, as it crisscrossed the world in a trajectory that returned it to the same flight path every three days, it built up a picture of the height of the sea's surface and the contours of the seabed itself.

The surface of the sea is not uniform, but varies considerably in height according to the strength of the Earth's gravitational field. Even allowing for waves, tides, strong winds and currents, the sea's surface bulges in some places and dips in others.

*Seasat-A* set out to measure these differences. It took readings of the sea's height every 3 km (2 miles), producing millions of readings in total, each one accurate to 100 mm (4 in). These were used to compile a global map of the surface of the sea.

In addition, scientists have used *Seasat-A*'s data to investigate the seabed itself. They soon discovered that features on the seabed, such as trenches and ridges caused by movements in the Earth's crust, produce different gravitational effects on the height of the sea's surface. Where there is a depression on the ocean floor, the surface of the sea dips. Conversely, where there is a ridge on the ocean floor, the surface of the sea rises as well. Thus information about the sea's surface helps scientists to understand in detail the movements of the Earth's crust.

Unfortunately, the electrical supply system on *Seasat-A* failed after 100 days in orbit, ending its observations. Nonetheless, the pioneering work of *Seasat-A* has enabled scientists to investigate fully, for the first time, just what is happening at the bottom of the sea.

***Getting its bearings*** *A tracking station (left diagram) helped to establish* Seasat-A*'s precise altitude – only then could the satellite (below) make accurate readings of minute variations in the height of the sea's surface. These variations were signs of trenches and ridges on the ocean floor.*

orbit of *Seasat-A*

tracking station

# WAYS AND MEANS
## *Stumbling across prehistoric pathways*

PEAT-DIGGING has gone on for centuries in the Somerset Levels, near Glastonbury in the southwest of England. But in 1970 the diggers turned up more than they had bargained for: the well-preserved remains of the oldest man-made network of roads in the world, dating back to 3800 BC.

These timber trackways were made of brushwood and logs, laid across marshes to form 'bridges' between isolated settlements on islands of dry ground. There are many other examples of such constructions, including prehistoric wooden pavements in Switzerland and a medieval log road across the Hungarian Pamgola swamps.

Log roads may seem primitive compared with modern motorways but, remarkably, the same technique was used as recently as 1942 to build parts of the Alaska Highway, which links Alaska with the northwestern United States. Log bridges provided a quick and effective way to 'float' parts of the highway over treacherous swampy ground.

However, the timber trackways were exceptional examples of early road-building. Most early roads were not deliberately built at all. They were simple earth

***Fortified path*** *All along the Silk Route fortresses once protected ancient travellers and their goods. Here the road leads past the ruins of the Jiaohe citadel east of Turpan, China.*

tracks that developed naturally over the years through continual wear by animals and men. As long-distance trade grew, the tracks sometimes developed into extensive international trading routes.

The greatest of these was the Silk Route from Shanghai to Istanbul, which linked the distant empire of China to the Western world across the wastes of central Asia. From the 1st century BC, when Chinese silk first reached Europe, through to the late Middle Ages – a period of about 1500 years – caravans attempting to follow this hazardous road were frequently obstructed by blizzards, burning desert sands and bandits.

Yet the Silk Route, one of the world's greatest roads, which measured about 10 000 km (6250 miles), was created without the work of a single engineer.

***Forest clearance*** *Thousands of trees were felled by prehistoric man to build trackways in the Somerset Levels some 4500 years ago.*

### DID YOU KNOW..?

*WHEN SILK was first brought to the West from China, in the 1st century BC, it became so popular that the Roman Emperor Augustus issued edicts restraining its use by men – it was considered effeminate.*

285

# THE INCAS' WEB OF POWER

*A network of roads but no wheels*

TO THE 180 Spanish conquistadores who invaded the South American Inca Empire in 1531, the native rulers seemed in many ways primitive. They had no written language, no horses, no wheels and no gunpowder. Yet these technologically backward people had built a sophisticated road system to rival the greatest achievements of the Romans.

The Incas' network of roads ran the length of their empire from modern-day Peru in the north down to Chile. The two main routes were a coast road 4000 km (2500 miles) long and the truly awesome Royal Road, stretching 5200 km (3250 miles), the longest trunk road built anywhere until the late 1800s.

### Engineering miracles

The Royal Road was not only long – it was also built through some of the most difficult terrain in the world, traversing the heart of the Andes mountains. The problems posed would daunt a modern engineer. The Incas hacked tunnels through rock. Rather than loop around the steepest gradients, they cut stairways into the sheer mountain side,

> ## DID YOU KNOW..?
>
> *KING SANHERIB of Assyria was extremely proud of his processional road. Built around 700 BC, it was about six times as wide as a three-lane road today, well paved and lined with lofty pillars. So anxious was he to preserve its grandeur that he decreed that anyone who built even a balcony overhanging the royal highway would be impaled on the pinnacles of his own roof.*

which their beasts of burden, the llamas, could climb comfortably. And they constructed extraordinary rope suspension bridges over deep gorges and mountain torrents. The most spectacular was the San Luis Rey Bridge, which would not have looked out of place in a fairy tale. It was made from fibre ropes and wooden slats 45 m (150 ft) long, swaying perilously 90 m (300 ft) above the Apurimac River.

Most of the road users were soldiers and *chasquis* – government messengers. Highly trained runners, the *chasquis*

were stationed at intervals of about 3 km (2 miles) along the main highways and carried messages in relays to and from the court at Cuzco. Since the Incas had no system of writing, the messages were carried as *quipus* – colour-coded arrangements of knotted threads. Relay teams could cover up to 320 km (nearly 200 miles) a day. At this speed, they were able to bring fish from the coast to the Inca court – 400 km (250 miles) inland and high in the mountains – within two days, to be served fresh at the royal table.

But it was not only for transporting food that the Incas created good roads. The road network carried soldiers who kept the peoples of the empire under control. It was like a vast web of power thrown over South America – and it eventually helped the Spanish conquistadores when they took over the Inca Empire for themselves.

**Without wheels** *A modern Inca religious procession, in which a man playing the role of a Christian saint rides in a litter, is a reminder that the wheel was unknown to the ancient Incas.*

## ON THE TRAIL OF THE DEMON DOGS

**F**OLKLORE TELLS of many ancient pathways in Britain that are haunted by demon black dogs – sometimes headless. The dogs seem to patrol 'green lanes' – ancient grassed-over roads that were boundaries to churches or country estates. These canine spectres often disappear into a hedgerow, bridge or gateway – traditional points of transition between the mortal world and the supernatural one – and they are also said to haunt churchyards, because of the ancient practice of burying a sacrificed dog to guard a newly consecrated graveyard.

The black dog has many regional names – Trash, Skriker, Barghest, Black Shuck, Moddey Dhoo, Padfoot – but it is always calf-sized, dark and shaggy, with blazing eyes. The counties of Suffolk and Norfolk in eastern England are especially prone to haunting by black dogs. Legend has it that, in the 1800s, a man called Finch from Neatishead in Norfolk was once walking along a green lane when he mistook Black Shuck for a friend's dog that had snapped at him. He aimed a kick at it – and his foot went straight through the phantom.

*Phantom marks Some people say that the large scratches at the side door of this church in Suffolk were made by the claws of the black dog.*

Another black dog is described in a contemporary pamphlet as having visited St Mary's Church in Bungay, Suffolk, on Sunday, August 4, 1577, during a terrible storm. This evil apparition 'wrung the necks' of two parishioners and left a third 'as shrunk up as it was a peece of lether scorched in a hot fire'. Another demon dog (or perhaps the same one?) disrupted a church service at nearby Blythburgh during the same storm; it killed three people and left behind claw marks on the church door, where they can still be seen to this day.

Some say the black dog is the ghost of a prehistoric hound set to guard holy sites and wayside shrines common on roads all over the world. Others say it is the Devil himself, perhaps on the lookout for solitary and vulnerable travellers. Norfolk tradition has it that no one can set eyes on Black Shuck and live. It used to be said when someone was dying: 'The black dog is at his heels.' But, in Essex, Black Shuck was thought to protect lost travellers.

# MALTESE MYSTERY
### *Strange grooved tracks scar the landscape of Malta*

**T**HE SMALL Mediterranean island of Malta is patterned with grooves, etched into the bare rock to a depth of up to 600 mm (24 in). They run in pairs across the landscape and disappear into fields, roads or houses, over cliffs and even into the sea. They

are frequently found beside modern roads. At one site – nicknamed 'Clapham Junction' after a busy London railway station – there are scores of them, forking and intersecting like complex railway sidings. Is it possible, then, that these strange grooves are the remains of an ancient civilisation's transport system?

One clue to the intriguing puzzle is that many of the grooves run up to the entrances of Bronze Age villages. From this archaeologists have concluded that the tracks were made by the

***Furrowed land***
*According to one theory, the deep V-shaped ruts covering the Maltese landscape were made by the trailing poles of primitive sledges.*

Bronze Age inhabitants of the island in about 2000 BC. But they cannot tell how or why the tracks were made.

One theory was that the grooves were used as a method of water drainage. But experts have had to rule this out, as the grooves show no sign of water erosion. Transport seems to be the most likely answer, although wheeled vehicles could not have used them because the pairs of grooves are not exactly parallel – the gauge varies so wheels would lock or be wrenched off. And sledges with fixed runners could not cope with the hairpin bends.

The answer to the problem could be a 'slide-car', a kind of primitive sledge consisting of two poles with a load slung in the middle. The poles would be supported at one end and drag along the ground at the other – wearing deep ruts in the rock. But what could have pulled these slide-cars? Animals' hooves would have worn down the rock, and even bare feet would have polished the surface – but apart from the grooves there is not a mark to be seen. The mystery remains to fascinate archaeologists and tourists alike.

# PAVING THE WAY FOR ROMAN RULE

*The roads that built an empire are still in use today*

THE ROMAN mania for roads began in 312 BC, with the building of the Via Appia from Rome to Capua, about 210 km (130 miles) to the south. As the empire spread throughout Europe, North Africa and the Middle East, so did the road system. By about AD 200, the Romans had built an estimated 85 000 km (53 000 miles) of road.

The builders were a mixture of skilled professionals – the *architectus* (civil engineer), *agrimensor* (surveyor) and *librator* (leveller) – and soldiers who did the manual labour. The emperors felt road-building would keep the legions usefully occupied between campaigns, but the soldiers did not always do this work willingly and there were several mutinies.

### Bedrock of empire

Foundations for the road varied according to the soil and the terrain, as well as the amount of traffic that was expected. For a main road, the standard technique was to dig down to solid rock, and then fill the ditch with rubble, packed down with sand or gravel. Next came small stones, followed by more gravel and a final layer of massive polygonal stone blocks. Away from major cities, a road might be paved only when it approached a town or at a crossroads; otherwise its surface might be of gravel or logs, or sometimes simply of dirt. The width varied too, from just over 1.5 m (5 ft) to about 7.5 m (24 ft). Roman roads are legendary for being straight, but although there were several straight stretches of 40 km (20 miles) or so, the roads would just as likely follow the contours of hills or deflect to cross a river at a more suitable location.

### Keeping a record

Using the simplest tools – picks, hammers and spades – the Romans performed spectacular engineering feats.

They hewed massive rocks, drained marshes and hacked out tunnels for their roads. At Terracina, south of Rome, a slice of rock 38 m (126 ft or 120 Roman ft) high was removed from a headland to allow the Via Appia to run straight along the coast. The labourers carved numerals in the cliff face every ten Roman feet to record their progress down from the top. The road ran along at the level CXX (120) mark.

### The end of the road

Roman roads were built to last and they outlasted the Roman Empire itself. But they could not survive one simple innovation – the horse collar. This

*Polygonal paving Many of the large black stones with which the Via Appia is paved have not worn away in the more than 2000 years since they were laid.*

medieval invention meant that horses could pull much heavier loads than ever before, and put a burden on the roads that they had never been intended to bear. The heavy wheeled traffic gradually broke up the surface of the roads.

But many of today's highways in Europe still follow the old Roman routes. For instance, the modern-day road between Rome and Rimini in central Italy uses a tunnel carved out in AD 77 – more than 1900 years ago.

# THRILLS AND SPILLS

## The perils of stagecoach travel never deterred travellers in a hurry

A STAGECOACH bound from Pittsfield to Albany in the eastern United States tore down a mountain pass out of control. The coach overbalanced on a corner, and only a tree stump prevented it plunging down a sheer precipice. The trembling passengers scrambled to safety as luggage tumbled into the abyss below.

That horror story from the 1830s was not untypical of the experience of stagecoach travel. Overturnings and runaway horses were most common, but bad weather and floods caused problems too. In Britain, three passengers and four horses were lost when the Liverpool mail coach was washed downstream from a flooded bridge in 1829.

There were human perils for the traveller as well. Passengers faced not only the threat of bandits and highwaymen, but also the risk of sharing a lengthy journey with some strange companions. There are stories of passengers packed into a stagecoach with convicts in irons, corpses and, apparently, even a performing bear.

Yet for all its dangers and discomforts, stagecoach travel had the great advantage of offering unprecedented speed, sometimes as much as an average of 16 km/h (10 mph). As companies competed for passengers, speed became an obsession. Stops for changing the horses were cut to a

**All aboard** *During a refreshment stop at an English inn, passengers pass on the latest news before re-boarding their stagecoach.*

minimum and coaches ran through the night. Journey times were reduced by ten times or more between the early 1700s and 1800s, with scant regard for safety. In one case, five passengers were injured when the Albany mail coach raced a rival coach.

### Expert horsemen

Although they were sometimes irresponsible, stagecoach drivers were well respected. Their salaries and skills made them the elite of horsemen. Western folklore is full of colourful characters with names like Sage Brush Bill and Cherokee Bill, hard-living drivers who took passengers and the mail across the Far West.

The age of the stagecoach lasted a little over two centuries. The first regular service in Britain probably appeared in the 1630s; in America it started about 100 years later. In both countries, numbers swelled until the coaches' heyday in the early decades of the 19th century. The arrival of the railways in the 1830s brought a swift decline for the stagecoach, though it remained the premium mode of transport in the Far West until the Pacific railway was completed in 1869.

**Daily run** *In the middle of the 19th century, the concord coaches of the American West provided an efficient postal service as well as a 'bus service' to individual homesteads.*

289

# ANIMAL MAGIC

*The art of stopping an unruly horse in its tracks*

THE STABLE door was locked. Everyone had been driven from the stall by a frantic horse, rearing and kicking. Then the old farmer arrived. Ignoring warnings about his safety, he opened the stable door and threw in his cap, whispering 'sic iubeo' – Latin for 'thus I command'. The horse came quietly to the door and allowed the farmer to put on its bridle.

Such scenes have been recorded many times in different parts of Britain since at least the 6th century AD. Men with command over horses are known as horse-whisperers, members of a secret brotherhood whose skills were well attested but nonetheless exceedingly difficult to explain.

It is now thought that the whisperers' power lay in 'charms' that exploited the horse's sharp sense of smell. The farmer's cap would have been impregnated with one of these charms and thus have dominated the horse's spirit.

### A special something

While one smelly substance would attract or 'draw' a horse, another would repel or 'jade' it. The best drawing substance was milt – a spongy wedge of tissue found in a foal's mouth immediately after birth. Impregnated with the aromatic oils of plants such as tansy,

rosemary and cinnamon, milt would prove irresistible to any horse.

Jading required equally mysterious charms, such as the bones of a frog or toad thrown into a stream at midnight under a full Moon. The bone that floated became the charm or talisman. It would be carried either in the horse-whisperer's armpit or in a leather pouch with a piece of raw flesh. If a suitable bone could not be had, a few stoat or rabbit livers and some stale urine might suffice. By means of these jading charms, a horse-whisperer could apparently stop a horse dead in its tracks and keep it stock still, as if bewitched.

*Fair whispers* Annual horse fairs, such as this one held at Skirling, Scotland, provided a natural setting for the activities of the horse-whisperers. Here they would gather to show off their mysterious skills.

Fear of being accused of witchcraft was one reason why the whisperers cloaked their methods in secrecy, developing a special handshake and password. The main reason, however, was to guard the tricks of their trade. This they have successfully done – so much so that there may be no one left alive who really understands the old horse-whisperer's art.

---

## THE LURE OF GOLD

WHEN THE Far West of the United States was opened up in the second half of the 19th century, law and order lagged far behind the growth of wealth and population. Robberies were especially a problem for the Wells Fargo stagecoach company, with its enticing freight of gold dust and nuggets on its long journey from the mines of California to banks in the east. Between 1870 and 1884, over $400 000-worth of goods were stolen from Wells Fargo, and 16 drivers or guards were shot in raids.

The company went to great lengths to catch the thieves, employing detectives such as J.B. Hume. Hume's most famous case was the tracking of 'Black Bart', the scourge of Wells Fargo, which offered $800 reward for his capture. Hume used a handkerchief left at the scene of a hold-up to find his man. He visited 90 laundries to track down the tell-tale laundry mark on the handkerchief and finally identified Black Bart as a prosperous miner, C.E. Bolton, who ended up in prison.

But such successes were few and far between, so merchants resorted to their own ingenious methods of protecting their gold. One trader put live rattlesnakes in the trunk containing his gold dust – and the consignment got through safely.

*Self defence* In the hope of deterring attackers, stagecoach drivers and guards would prominently display their arms.

# RACE AGAINST TIME

*The short-lived success of the Pony Express*

'HAVE DETERMINED to establish a Pony Express to Sacramento, California, commencing 3rd April – time, ten days.' So ran the laconic telegram by which, on January 27, 1860, William Russell announced his 240-hour pony mail service between St Joseph, Missouri, and Sacramento, California, a distance of 3165 km (1966 miles) across some of America's wildest country. In little over two months, stations were in place along the route where horses and riders could be changed at regular intervals.

### The mail must go through

Daring young men flocked to ride the famous ponies, attracted by the chance of adventure and the good pay – $50 a month plus a room and board. They had to be skilled horsemen, capable of riding stages of up to 160 km (100 miles), stopping only momentarily every 25 km (15 miles) or so for a swift change of horses. This elite body of riders included such legendary figures as 'Buffalo Bill' Cody and 'Wild Bill' Hickok. Their motto was 'The mail must go through,' and, in spite of all hazards, the teams of horsemen rarely failed to meet the exacting 240-hour deadline for delivery.

Only a month after the Pony Express started up, it faced its most severe test when the Pah Ute Indians in Nevada attacked and burned isolated Pony Express stations and harassed riders. In all, seven stations were destroyed, 150

horses lost and 16 men killed. But the mail nonetheless got through.

It was neither the Indians nor the harsh weather of the winter of 1860–61 that closed the Pony Express only 18 months after its launch. Needing more than 80 riders and 500 horses, it was too expensive to run.

Yet the Pony Express was worthy of its legend. In its brief period of operation, its

riders raced a total of 985 000 km (616 000 miles) – a distance equal to 24 times around the Earth. And only one bag of mail was ever lost.

**Determined faces** *Iron resolve and bravery sometimes verging on recklessness characterised the drivers of the Pony Express, which made a twice-weekly run between St Joseph, Missouri, and Sacramento, California, delivering the mail.*

---

### DID YOU KNOW..?

*THE WILD WEST produced some unusual characters but few as surprising as one-eyed Charlie Pankhurst, a hard-bitten stagecoach driver noted for tobacco chewing, drinking whiskey and uttering profanities. When he died in 1879, his friends arranged an elaborate funeral, only to discover that Charlie had been a woman!*

# JOURNEY'S END

### *Arduous travels bring pilgrims closer to their god*

BACK IN THE Middle Ages, travel was slow and hazardous. Yet many Christians, rich and poor alike, were ready to embark on arduous journeys to distant lands, travelling for six months or a year, to visit the holy places of their faith. In spring the roads were thronged with pilgrims, mostly on foot, heading for the three most sacred sites – the Holy Sepulchre in Jerusalem, St Peter's in Rome, and Santiago de Compostela in northwest Spain.

Like modern tourism, medieval pilgrimage gave rise to an organised business. There were guides, souvenirs and hotel and travel facilities. Conditions were often harsh, but most pilgrims did not expect comfort. The hardships of the pilgrimage earned merit in the afterlife.

Besides the three major pilgrimage sites, there were a myriad other holy places to be visited. Perhaps the strangest was St Patrick's Purgatory in northwest Ireland, at the edge of the known world. The Purgatory was a cave on a desolate island in Lough Derg, Donegal, where, in the 5th century, St Patrick was reputed to have fasted for 40 days to drive the Devil out of Ireland. Pilgrims usually spent some time fasting and praying before entering the narrow cave. They were promised that if they stayed there

***Common quest*** *By the turn of the century, the number of Muslim pilgrims worshipping each year at the cube-shaped Kaaba sanctuary in Mecca is expected to reach four million.*

for 24 hours, they would be granted visions of purgatory and Hell. While many pilgrims saw nothing, a considerable number did report visions, and visitors came from far and wide. Pilgrims still go to Lough Derg today – but they no longer seek visions in a cave.

The healing centre of Lourdes, at the foot of the French Pyrenees, became a place of pilgrimage in the 19th century when a local miller's daughter, Bernadette Soubirous, had visions of the Virgin Mary. The number of people who make the pilgrimage to Lourdes increases every year, but in general over the last 500 years, Christian pilgrimage has declined drastically.

### *Mass movements*

Outside the Christian world, however, the custom flourishes. Every year nearly two million Muslims from all over the globe gather in the holy Saudi Arabian city of Mecca to worship at the Kaaba sanctuary – the most sacred place of Islam. Hindus in India travel great distances by bus, railway, bullock cart or on foot to visit their sacred shrines, believing that this will guarantee them a vision of paradise before their next incarnation on Earth. And all devout Hindus desire to wash in the sacred waters of the River Ganges.

Perhaps the strangest place of pilgrimage was in an atheistic state. Every day and in all weathers, the communist faithful from all over the Soviet Union queued in Red Square, Moscow, to visit the tomb of Vladimir Ilich Lenin, the founder of the Marxist state.

***Himalayan climb*** *Every year, thousands of lightly clad Hindu pilgrims offer prayers to Siva at the 3800 m (12 500 ft) high Amarnath Cave.*

# THE GREAT WALKABOUT

*Stone Age voyagers discover Australia*

WHEN the British explorer Captain James Cook led his men to Botany Bay in 1770, they were the first Europeans to set foot on Australian soil. But some 60 000 years before Cook's voyage, the vast island continent had already been discovered by an even more extraordinary group of explorers, the ancestors of the present-day Aborigines.

Australia has not always been an island. About 200 million years ago it was joined to India, Antarctica, Africa and South America in the huge continent of Gondwanaland.

### Break away

But the gradual movement of the tectonic plates that make up the Earth's crust broke up this great land mass. By the time man had evolved in Africa and was spreading across the planet, Australia had drifted clear and was isolated by the ocean. Nonetheless, in around 60 000 BC, some intrepid Stone Age adventurers, migrating southward from Asia, began to populate this often harsh and empty country.

The first immigrants are the world's earliest known seafarers, and must have come either from China via the

Philippines or from Southeast Asia through Indonesia, island-hopping as far as the north coast of New Guinea or Australia. They would have needed to cross stretches of ocean up to 400 km (250 miles) wide.

It is still a mystery how people who had only the simplest stone tools could have built an adequate ocean-going canoe or raft – or what could have

*Canoe craft* A group of Aborigines sew the ends of a bark canoe together with strong twine. Some 60 000 years ago, their ancestors made a spectacular ocean journey, island-hopping from Asia to New Guinea.

inspired them to embark on a risky venture beyond the narrow limits of the world they knew.

Once in New Guinea, the Aborigines had no more need of boats. The sea level was then far lower than it is today, so New Guinea was linked to Australia in a single land mass, known to geologists as Sahul. Through tens of thousands of years, the Aborigines spread over the whole of Australia, migrating vast distances on foot, until there were about half a million of them inhabiting the wide empty spaces down to the southern coast.

## JOURNEY TO MECCA

EVERY YEAR, at the start of the last month of the Muslim calendar, almost two million people journey to the east coast of Saudi Arabia for the *hadj*, the holy pilgrimage to Mecca which all devout Muslims should, if they can, perform once in their lifetime. This host of visitors comes from every corner of the globe where Islam is practised, an astonishing mixture of nationalities.

The city of Mecca was the birthplace of the prophet Muhammad, founder of Islam, in AD 570, and it was he who decreed it should be a site of Muslim pilgrimage. The focus of the pilgrimage is the sanctuary of the Kaaba, a cube-shaped building in Mecca which, according to Muslim tradition, was built by Abraham. (It is towards the Kaaba that all Muslims, no matter where in the world they are, turn to pray five times every day.) Especially holy is the sacred black stone set into one wall of the building by Muhammad. As the first and

last acts of their pilgrimage, all Muslims visit the Kaaba and walk around it seven times; those who can get close enough to the black stone kiss or touch it as they pass by, but because of the crowds most have to be content with waving in its direction. The principal days of ceremony, prayer and meditation are those between the 7th and 10th of the month – and for much of this period, all the pilgrims must be in the same place at the same time.

The annual *hadj* is an extraordinary feat of organisation. The sheer numbers of people involved pose enormous problems of health, transport and policing. A vast tent city is erected to house the visitors, who outnumber the ordinary inhabitants of Mecca by three to one.

Yet despite the problems, the pilgrimage is becoming ever more popular. The pilgrim returns to his own country with new honour, having fulfilled one of the most sacred obligations of his faith.

## DID YOU KNOW..?

*THE MUSLIM calendar begins from AD 622, the date of the Hegira, Muhammad's flight from Mecca to Medina. In Muslim terms, we are now living in the 14th century. Each Muslim year is divided into 12 months of 29 or 30 days, so the year is only 354 or, occasionally, 355 days long. As a result, although the pilgrims always enter Mecca in the last month of the Muslim year, this does not always happen in the same season – if the pilgrimage is in mid-winter one year, it will be in mid-summer 16 years later.*

# GOING FOR GOLD

*The rush that led more often to ruin than to riches*

ON JANUARY 24, 1848, James Marshall discovered gold at Sutter's Mill in California's Sacramento Valley and sparked off the greatest gold rush in history. When news of Marshall's find leaked out, would-be prospectors in their tens of thousands set out from around the globe for the golden land.

Americans from cities on the coasts of the Atlantic and the Gulf of Mexico crowded into often unseaworthy sailing vessels offering passage around Cape Horn; others joined ramshackle wagon trains that struggled through the Rocky Mountains or across the deserts of Arizona. Many died on the journey, lost in storms at sea, struck down by disease or perishing from thirst during the overland journey. But by 1849, some 80 000 had made it through to California and spread out through the mountain valleys, mining and panning the rivers for gold.

*Glimmer of hope* 'Forty-niners' sift pans of soil and water until, if they are lucky, specks of gold are visible.

Although some of the first 'forty-niners' did strike it rich, most of the later arrivals barely made even a living, let alone a fortune. What they did earn was quickly spent on essential supplies sold at grossly inflated prices – eggs, for example, retailed at the extraordinary sum of $1 a piece. The real fortunes were made by the businessmen who charged these extortionate prices.

Yet the lure of gold was undiminished. The prospectors moved on to a whole series of gold rushes in North America that followed through the rest of the century; the most spectacular were to Pike's Peak, Colorado, in 1859; Deadwood, South Dakota, in 1876; and the Klondike, in Canada's Yukon Territory, in 1897.

Wherever a gold rush occurred, boom towns sprang up overnight, wild places where tough adventurers from every race and many different countries drank, gambled and fought hard, with little interference from the civilising influences of women or the law. Such a place was San Francisco, turned from a tiny village called Yerba Buena into a town of 55 000 inhabitants almost overnight, where there were reported to have been 1400 murders committed between 1850 and 1856. Deadwood was another boom town noted for its frontier violence. It was there that the legendary scout and federal marshal Wild Bill Hickok was shot in the back by Jack McCall while playing poker in a saloon on August 2, 1876.

Once the gold rush faded, Deadwood was abandoned – from boom town to ghost town in a matter of weeks. But in other cases, the brave (if deluded) efforts of the early gold prospectors opened up many inhospitable areas to human settlement, not only in North America but also in Australia, where gold was discovered in 1851, and South Africa, where rich deposits were found in 1884. And the lust for gold founded great cities like Denver, now the capital of Colorado, and Johannesburg, South Africa's largest city. Yet only a tiny minority of those intrepid fortune hunters ever struck the golden vein of their dreams.

## DID YOU KNOW..?

*THE LARGEST gold nugget ever discovered was the Welcome Stranger, weighing 78.4 kg (172 lb 13 oz). It was found in the state of Victoria, Australia, in 1869 – lying in a cartwheel rut.*

*Frontier justice* Wild Bill Hickok, said to be the fastest gunslinger in the West, was shot from behind by Jack McCall during a poker game in 1876. McCall hanged for the murder.

# SPREADING THE WORD
## *The prehistoric mystery of the Indo-Europeans*

AN ITALIAN calls his mother *madre*; a German says *Mutter*; a Pole calls her *matka*; an Iranian says *madar*; and the Hindi word is also *madar*. Why is the word almost the same in widely differing languages spread across half the globe?

In the late 18th century, this question started to fascinate European scholars, who were struck by the similarities between Sanskrit, the ancient language of India, and classical Greek and Latin. They suggested that, back in prehistoric times, there must have been a single people, the Indo-Europeans, from whose speech such diverse languages as Russian, Persian, Hindi and English eventually evolved. Ever since the existence of such a people was first proposed, linguists and archaeologists have devoted lifetimes of detective work to trying to track them down.

By comparing the vocabularies of different languages, linguists identified the common roots of many words. These root words, they deduced, came from the original Indo-European language, and they provided several clues to the identity of the people who used them. The Indo-Europeans had words for snow and tree, for wolf and bear, but they apparently had no word for sea. So it was assumed they must have lived in the dark forests of central Europe or Asia. Similar linguistic evidence suggested they were a warrior race, riding horsedrawn chariots into battle.

Many candidates have been put forward as the original Indo-Europeans. Most scholars now favour a semi-nomadic people who lived in the Kurgan region north of the Black Sea. Around 3000 BC, they started to migrate into Europe. It is possible that they also moved eastwards to Iran, and, eventually, India, spreading their language as they conquered other tribes.

Strong as the case for Kurgan as the home of the parent language appears, there is not sufficient archaeological evidence to prove beyond doubt that these people were the original Indo-Europeans. In 1987, a British scholar, Colin Renfrew, stated his belief that the idea of the Indo-European warrior race was a myth. He said the starting point of the Indo-European language was Turkey, from where it spread gradually through peaceful contact between one agricultural community and another.

Fortunately, science may soon be able to provide valuable new evidence in the dispute. Modern genetic techniques make it possible to establish and trace historical relationships between peoples now widely scattered round the globe. Scientists also believe they will soon be able to analyse the genetic make-up of human remains found in ancient burial sites. If no genetic markers are found to indicate a common Indo-European ancestry, then it was probably the language, carried by peaceful contact between peoples, that travelled to Europe from Asia, and not the people themselves.

---

## BLUE GOLD

IN 1850, a 21-year-old immigrant from Bavaria named Levi Strauss arrived in San Francisco, intending to cash in on the Gold Rush by selling canvas tents and wagon covers to prospectors. But when he realised that sturdy trousers were in short supply among the miners, he decided his stock of canvas might prove more profitable if it was made up into trousers and other garments. Soon 'those pants of Levi's' were a byword for hardwearing durability.

A few years later, Strauss shifted from using canvas to denim. His first trousers had been brown; adding an indigo dye produced the original blue jeans. However, it was not until a tailor from Carson City, Nevada, called Jacob Davis, hit upon the ingenious idea of strengthening jeans with copper rivets that they assumed the form we are familiar with today. Legend has it that Davis was fed up with repairing miners' trousers over and over again because they filled their pockets with heavy rock samples. Davis and Strauss patented a method of 'fastening the corners of pockets in wearing apparel in order to prevent them from tearing' in 1874.

By the time of Strauss's death in 1902, Levi's jeans had made their inventor a millionaire. But he could hardly have guessed that, by the 1970s, his heavy-duty work clothes would have become fashionable garb for everyone from students to princesses.

**Levi's originals** At first, Levi's were sold, not as 'jeans', but as 'waist overalls'.

---

## DID YOU KNOW..?

*BETWEEN 500 and 250 BC, the most numerous and widely dispersed of the Indo-European peoples in Europe were not the Greeks, the Romans, or the Germanic tribes, but the Celts. Although not allied by anything more than language and culture, Celtic communities extended from Northern Ireland to Turkey. Their influence on the development of European culture was immense, especially in the spread of ironworking and the use of four-wheeled carts with iron-rimmed wheels.*

# AT THE ENDS OF THE EARTH

## *A papal decree neatly sliced the world in two*

**H**AVE YOU EVER wondered why Brazilians speak Portuguese and the rest of Latin America speaks Spanish? Was it that Spain was a much more enterprising colonial power during the Age of Exploration?

Not at all. During the 15th century, Portugal led the world in voyages of discovery. The Portuguese charted the west coast of Africa, reaching the Cape of Good Hope in 1488, and opened up the Indian Ocean. Under the flag of Spain in 1492, Christopher Columbus sailed west in the belief that he would reach India – and inadvertently found the New World. On the homeward journey, bad weather forced him into Lisbon, where King John II of Portugal heard of Columbus's discovery before his Spanish patrons. John immediately asserted Portuguese rights over all land west of Africa.

Spain applied to Pope Alexander VI to intervene. Alexander was ambitious, greedy and, conveniently, Spanish. He issued two papal decrees, or bulls, called *Inter caetera*, that granted Spain dominion over all unclaimed lands 100 leagues west of the Azores (a league is about 5 km or 3 miles).

**Spheres of influence** *The Alexandrine Line, shown by a vertical dotted line on this Portuguese chart from around 1535, separated the interests of Spain and Portugal in the New World. Portugal secured only the northeastern corner of South America in this agreement – but won the right to colonise Africa.*

The so-called Alexandrine Line caused uproar in Portugal and King John made hasty preparations for war. The threat led Spain to reconsider her position and, in 1494, the two countries signed the Treaty of Tordesillas, which moved the demarcation line 370 leagues further west, thereby increasing Portugal's share east of the line.

Yet even the revised Alexandrine Line barely cut into South America. In hindsight, the division seems to be unfair to Portugal, for the Portuguese were only allowed to colonise what is now the northeastern coast of Brazil. However, at the time no one knew how far the Americas extended in any direction. And much further east of the line, as the Portuguese knew, lay the continent of Africa, which was now theirs, in theory, to exploit. This explains why there were Portuguese colonies in Africa and India from the 16th century onwards.

The pope's authority to partition the world came from an 8th-century document called the *Donation of Constantine*. Ironically, this document was later proved to be a forgery. In any case, Alexander's 'division of the world' did not deter the English, Dutch or French from sailing forth over the next hundred years or so to claim their own portions of the Americas, Africa or Asia.

# A LAND OF MARVELS

*Venetian Marco Polo's sensational account of 13th-century China*

I N THE MURKY light of the Chinese emperor's dining hall, Marco Polo watched in awe as wizards murmured incantations over a row of fabulous golden drinking cups ranged upon the floor. Ten paces away and raised on a high platform sat the emperor himself, Kublai Khan, supreme ruler of all China and most of the rest of Asia. The cups rose magically, drifted across to the Khan's table, and gently set themselves down in front of him. Not a drop of the liquid within was spilt. And the wizards had ensured that no inferior being had touched the cup from which the emperor would drink.

### Family journey

This is just one of the marvels recounted by the 13th-century Venetian traveller Marco Polo in his book *Il milione*, known in English as *The Travels of Marco Polo*. Polo was not the first European on record to reach China: his father Niccolo and uncle Maffeo hold that honour. Marco Polo's fame lies in being the man who revealed the wonders of Cathay, as China was then known, to the West. He accompanied his father and his uncle on their second journey to the legendary court of Kublai Khan and travelled throughout the empire as an emissary of the Khan.

*Gifts for the mighty On their second visit to Kublai Khan (shown in an ermine-lined dark blue robe), the Polo brothers took with them sacred oil and a papal letter requested ten years earlier, as well as 17-year-old Marco (kneeling, and wearing a green robe).*

The flying cup routine was, no doubt, an elaborately contrived illusion, perhaps made more plausible to the spectators by their consumption of kumiss, a fearsome ferment of mare or camel milk. But this was not the only magic the wizards could perform. According to Polo, they could also control the weather, driving clouds away from the Khan's palace, even though torrential rain fell all around it.

### Model of efficiency

Kublai Khan may have enjoyed the magic of his court wizards, but he also presided over a startlingly modern state. Paper money, for instance, had existed in China from the 7th century AD. It was made from the bark of the mulberry tree, which was pounded flat and glued into sheets. These were then stamped with an elaborate series of seals to guarantee their authenticity. Attempts at counterfeiting were rewarded with the death penalty – not only for the forgers themselves, but for their children and grandchildren too.

The Khan kept in touch with events in his vast empire by means of a postal system that few, if any, modern states could match. Polo claims that, on all the main roads of the empire, the Khan maintained sumptuous accommodation

and stables of up to 400 horses for his messengers at stages no more than 50 km (30 miles) apart. Some 10 000 stages and more than 200 000 horses served this massive communications system, which was supplemented by yet more runners on foot.

Polo reckoned that with these resources Kublai Khan received news in less than a sixth of the time normal travellers might take over such distances, and that in times of national emergency a horseman could gallop as many as 400 km (250 miles) a day – a speed of communication scarcely matched until the arrival of the railway.

Was Marco Polo exaggerating? There is no reason to think he did so deliberately. He dictated his story while a prisoner of war (he had been captured by the Genoese – great rivals of the Venetians – during a battle in the Mediterranean), with little hope of living to see home or freedom again. He had nothing to gain from telling anything other than the truth.

# 'DR LIVINGSTONE, I PRESUME?'

*What happened after Stanley found Livingstone?*

HENRY MORTON Stanley stared at the sick old man standing in the throng of tribesmen in the village of Ujiji, in what is now called Tanzania. Unwell himself, Stanley was momentarily lost for words. Then he raised his hat and said calmly: 'Doctor Livingstone, I presume?'

The man hesitated and finally spoke the one word that meant success for Stanley. 'Yes,' he replied with a smile.

This famous exchange on November 10, 1871, was the end of an arduous search for David Livingstone. The Scots missionary and explorer had set out to find the source of the Nile five years previously and had disappeared in the region of Lake Tanganyika. In October 1869, Stanley, a reporter for the *New York Herald*, was dispatched to locate him and bring back his story as an exclusive. Stanley reached Zanzibar, off the east coast of Africa, in January 1871 and began to organise his expedition. Two months later, he and a small army of porters, soldiers and pack animals left the port of Bagamoyo, opposite Zanzibar, and headed west. The march was difficult, through countryside disturbed by tribal wars. Many of Stanley's men deserted him; others were killed or perished from disease. Faced with illness himself, Stanley was ready to turn back when news of a white man at Ujiji spurred him on.

Only days later, the trail ended. Stanley, wanting to give the villagers ample warning of his approach lest they suspect his party were stealing up on them with ill intent, entered the village with a clamour of horns and volleys of musket shot. Livingstone was pleased to meet him and anxious for news from home.

## Parting of ways

The two men spent four months together, exploring the northern shores of Lake Tanganyika. When Stanley left in March 1872, he implored Livingstone, already a very sick man, to return with him. But Livingstone refused. Stanley was the last white man to see Livingstone alive.

Before his return to the USA, Stanley had a mixed reception in England. He was lionised by some, but lampooned in the press and ridiculed by the Royal

*Jubilant welcome Stanley and his bearers bring desperately needed food and medical supplies to Livingstone's encampment on the banks of Lake Tanganyika in 1871. The American flag symbolises that nation's financial support for Stanley's expedition.*

Geographical Society. Many doubted the truth of Stanley's extraordinary story. It was said that Stanley had not found Livingstone, but that Livingstone had himself rescued Stanley. Some even suggested that Stanley had not been to Africa at all.

He was vindicated, however, when Livingstone's family verified letters and papers brought back from the bush. Queen Victoria thanked him personally for his services and gave him a gold snuff box. And eventually, even the Royal Geographical Society acknowledged his achievement.

When Stanley heard of Livingstone's death in 1873, he returned to Africa to continue the search for the source of the Nile. In that, he did not succeed – but between 1874 and 1884 he did discover the Congo and follow it for 2400 km (1500 miles) to its mouth.

# THE UNCONVENTIONAL EXPLORER

*The Victorian adventurer who left her visiting card on top of Mount Cameroon*

WEST AFRICA, 1893: the White Man's Grave – a vast, largely uncharted region of mangrove swamps and tropical rain forest. Fatal diseases such as malaria, black-water and yellow fever were endemic. Europeans rarely penetrated the interior. Those who did so faced cannibals and ferocious wild animals. Droves of native porters and huge quantities of equipment accompanied the few explorers brave enough to venture into this daunting territory.

Yet Mary Henrietta Kingsley, a 30-year-old English traveller, hacked her way through this most hostile, unhealthy jungle, on foot or by canoe, with only a small band of African bearers.

She made two expeditions to Africa, in 1893 and 1894. The first took her to what are now Angola, Nigeria and the island of Fernando Po. She waded through stinking black crocodile-infested ooze in her long Victorian skirts, often sinking up to her neck. She was almost continually plagued by blood-sucking leeches and mosquitoes.

Every day brought alarming encounters with dangerous man-eating beasts. When crocodiles threatened to overturn her canoe, she beat them off with her paddle. On another occasion, she scared off a leopard that came into her tent by hurling a water jug at it.

On her second expedition, in 1894, she explored the French Congo and

became the first European to enter parts of Gabon. She taught herself to manage a canoe single-handed and was the first person to navigate the Ogooué River. This was a hazardous trip through long stretches of rapids and whirlpools.

Mary Kingsley had been obsessed by Africa since childhood, but her travels had a scientific purpose. Many of the specimens of plants and animals she collected were previously unknown. Three species of fish she discovered were named after her.

### Narrow escape

Kingsley's primary aim was to study the religion and customs of the Fang, a tribe of cannibals, few of whom had ever seen a white person. While cautiously skirting a Fang village one day, she slipped over a cliff and plunged through the roof of a hut. Fearful of ending up in the cooking pot, she placated the startled occupants with gifts of tobacco, handkerchiefs and her knife. She escaped with nothing more than a skinned elbow.

But Mary Kingsley soon made more conventional contact with the Fang. She traded Western goods for information, food and shelter. She gamely ate the magotty Fang dishes served to her and was once dished up smashed snail on a plantain leaf – a repast she described as 'a slimy grey abomination'.

Her lodgings were even more disturbing. One night, she found the stench of a Fang hut overpowering. The pungent odour emanated from some small sacks

*Dress sense* While on the whole ignoring the conventions of her time, Mary Kingsley never swapped her Victorian skirts for men's clothes. And with good reason, too. Her thick skirts once prevented her from being spiked after falling into a game pit.

hanging near the ceiling. She emptied the contents into her hat and found, to her horror, 'a human hand, three big toes, four eyes, two ears and other portions of the human frame'.

Despite their forbidding habits, Mary Kingsley spent much time among the Fang and made the first detailed study of their way of life. At the end of this tour, she became the first white woman – perhaps even the first woman – to climb to the top of Mount Cameroon. Typically, she made much of the ascent alone – and left her visiting card on the peak.

On her return to England, she wrote two accounts of her experiences, *Travels in West Africa* (1897) and *West African Studies* (1899), which became immediate best sellers. And the lectures she gave to audiences around the country were warmly received.

In an age when women were expected to remain firmly in the home, Mary Kingsley ventured where few men dared. She died of typhoid fever on June 3, 1900, while nursing Boer prisoners of war at Simonstown, South Africa.

**Trade party** *Mary Kingsley (seated left of flag) travels down the Congo River.*

# DEAD MEN'S TALES

*What the bodies of three long-buried seamen may have revealed about antibiotics*

IN AUGUST 1984, in freezing temperatures and a 15-knot wind, a small band of Canadian scientists under Dr Owen Beattie of Alberta University carefully exhumed the remains of 20-year-old Petty Officer John Torrington from his grave on Beechey Island, Canada, far inside the Arctic Circle.

John Torrington had lain in his grave since 1846, but the chill of the Arctic permafrost had kept his body almost perfectly preserved. The scientists were thus able to perform a thorough postmortem examination – 138 years after Torrington had died. And then they buried him again, reconstructing his grave as they had found it.

Two years later, Beattie returned to Beechey Island and uncovered two more bodies, the remains of seamen John Hartnell and William Braine. They too had died in 1846. The three sailors were among the earliest victims of the ill-fated attempt by British explorer Sir John Franklin to find a Northwest Passage linking the Atlantic and Pacific Oceans. This passage, conventional wisdom insisted, would lie somewhere between the wasteland of the northern icecap and the barren and inhospitable northern coast of Canada.

Franklin had set sail in two ships, HMS *Erebus* and HMS *Terror*, on May 18, 1845, from Greenhithe on the Thames in England. The ships were provisioned for a three-year voyage. Neither Franklin, nor any of his men, ever returned. Exactly why the voyage was a disaster, and what happened to the crews of the two ships, will perhaps never be known.

### Resistant strains

The autopsies on the three crew members may have helped to solve an enigma of modern medicine: why people and animals seem to build up a resistance to antibiotics. The usual explanation is that some antibiotics kill only the weaker germs, leaving stronger bacteria to proliferate. For example, some scientists have blamed the widespread use of antibiotics in the livestock industry for the development of hardier strains of bacteria.

Dr Kinga Kowalewska-Grochowska, also from Alberta University, found that some of the bacteria taken from the sailors' cell tissue resisted antibiotics. The resistant organisms had been in suspended animation for 140 years – whereas antibiotics have been in use only since the Second World War.

Beattie and his team had also found extremely high levels of lead in the sailors' bodies. They concluded that the men may have died from lead poisoning coming from the solder used in their food tins. (Until the bodies were discovered, scurvy and starvation were thought to

be responsible for many if not all of the deaths.)

Kowalewska-Grochowska's investigations led her to believe that the high levels of lead may have caused the bacteria to evolve an ability to withstand antibiotic attack.

### Pollution and antibiotics

Kowalewska-Grochowska concluded that the ability of modern bacteria to resist antibiotics may result from the high levels of lead and other heavy metals in our environment, rather than from overexposure to the antibiotics themselves. This theory, however, remains unconfirmed at present.

Much of the lead in our atmosphere comes from the exhaust of cars burning leaded petrol. So from the white, frozen wastes of the Arctic there may be a message from the past in favour of a green planet: by reducing our consumption of leaded petrol, we may help reduce the resistance of bacteria to modern antibiotics.

*Doomed expedition The three sailors whose bodies were recently discovered on Beechey Island died during the first winter of Franklin's 1845 Arctic expedition. The remaining 106 men searched for the Northwest Passage until their two ships got trapped in the ice. They continued on foot but perished in the arctic conditions.*

---

## DID YOU KNOW..?

*JOHN ROSS, a British visitor to the Arctic in 1818, was doubted on his return home when he spoke of large areas of 'red snow'. In fact, a unicellular plant (Protococcus) covers large tracts of snow in Arctic and alpine regions, giving it a bright crimson hue.*

✳ ✳ ✳

*MOST PEOPLE who go to the North Pole get there by aircraft. Some have been less conventional: a Japanese, Fukashi Kazami, made it on a 250cc motorcycle in 1987. In 1989, the British explorer Robert Swan became the first man to walk to both Poles.*

✳ ✳ ✳

*THE NORTHWEST Passage – goal of countless expeditions since the late 15th century – was first successfully navigated in 1903–6, by the Norwegian explorer Roald Amundsen.*

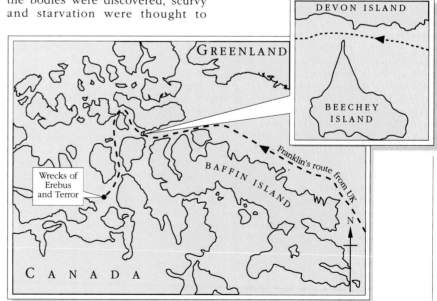

# THE COLD SHADOW OF DOUBT

*For Robert Peary, making it to the North Pole was only half the battle*

IT HAD BEEN a fascinating evening. The guests at the banquet at the Tivoli in Copenhagen had heard a gripping tale of adventure and exploration, as Dr Frederick Cook described the journey that had made him, on April 21, 1908, the first person to set foot on the North Pole. But then a telegram arrived: Commander Robert Peary of the US Navy, Cook's former colleague, claimed the Pole as his own – and was, by implication, calling his rival a liar.

Peary was a distinguished polar explorer with 20 years' experience. Cook was a charismatic man, a popular hero who in 1906 had led an expedition to climb Mount McKinley, the highest peak in North America. But he had had only two and a half years of arctic travel. Peary challenged Cook to provide proof of his claim to have reached the Pole.

### Battle of rivals

The bitter controversy that followed divided America. Cook's case began to collapse in October 1909, when his two Eskimo companions on the polar expedition testified that at no time during the trip had they been out of sight of land. (The ice cap around the North Pole covers an ocean, not dry land, and is constantly in motion.) Cook disputed their claims, but was unable to produce his logbooks for verification, having left them behind in the Arctic. His credibility suffered further when Ed Barrille, his guide on the McKinley expedition, swore an affidavit that Cook had got no nearer to the summit than 23 km (14 miles). Photographs that Cook presented as proof of both conquests were shown to have been designed to deceive.

Peary was triumphant. With Cook dishonoured, his own claim was upheld. He received 22 gold medals from geographical societies around the world and was promoted to rear-admiral in recognition of his achievement in reaching the North Pole.

So the record stood until 1985. Then Wally Herbert, a British explorer who had himself been to the Pole, scrutinised Peary's logbook. An explorer's log, with its daily navigational observations and on-the-spot record of progress, is the most vital proof of success in any polar expedition. When Herbert looked for the entries in Peary's log that described his time spent near and at the Pole, he found nine blank pages, with only a loose-leaf entry, possibly a later addition, recording Peary's triumph. Equally disturbing was Peary's apparently slack navigation. The only way of knowing which way the ice covering the Pole is drifting (and in which direction to travel to compensate for it) is to take careful and regular sightings of the Sun to determine latitude and longitude.

### Off course?

Peary's method of navigation ignored the movement of the ice. He took a compass reading and then marched in a straight line towards the Pole until he had covered the required distance. He took only three sightings for latitude on the way and none for longitude, and so he had no real way of knowing precisely where he was.

When Peary reckoned he and his team had come the right distance, they made camp and he went off to make the Sun sightings that would confirm

**Nagging doubts** *There was never any question that Peary got as far as the Arctic Circle, but did he ever reach the North Pole?*

**Title fight** *Cook and Peary contest the title of first man to reach the North Pole in this French cartoon of 1909. The public were divided in their support for the claims of the two explorers.*

that they really were at the North Pole. Wally Herbert believes that Peary's sightings told him that they had indeed come the right distance but had travelled in the wrong direction and were, in fact, about 80 km (50 miles) to the west of the Pole. Herbert further assumes that Peary did not have the heart to tell his bone-weary companions the painful truth and falsified his log to support his claim.

The controversy does not end here, however. A report by the National Geographic Society published in December 1989 produced new evidence in support of Peary. Scrupulous examination of Peary's photographs has convinced experts that he really reached the North Pole. Further proof is seen in the explorer's measurements of ocean depths near the Pole, which compare favourably with modern charts. More than 80 years after Peary's claim to the North Pole, the tables seem to have turned once more in his favour.

# STEAMING TO SUCCESS

## Stephenson's track record was built on the foundations of other inventors

BETWEEN October 6 and 14, 1829, five ungainly looking machines gathered at Rainhill in northwest England for a competition that was to make railway history. The Rainhill trials were organised to decide the best type of locomotive to run on the new Liverpool and Manchester Railway. Pitted against one another were some of the greatest engineering talents of the age.

Among the competitors was the father-and-son team of George and Robert Stephenson. On the third day of the trials, their new engine, the *Rocket*, whose revolutionary boiler design set the pattern for all subsequent locomotives, steamed to victory, reaching a top speed of 47 km/h (29 mph). The success of the *Rocket* has led to its designer George Stephenson being called the 'father of the locomotive'. However, for all its originality, the *Rocket* was really only a development of the work of earlier inventors.

### Let down by flimsy rails

The man who can most accurately be called the 'father of the locomotive' is Richard Trevithick, a Cornish engineer. A quarter of a century before the *Rocket*'s victory, Trevithick had worked out the basic principles for – and built – a high-pressure steam engine that was efficient and powerful enough to haul a train. In 1804, he demonstrated a locomotive that could move a load of 20 tonnes at 8 km/h (5 mph). The engine was mechanically sound, but the flimsy track of the time shattered under its weight. Trevithick, disillusioned, abandoned locomotive design.

Achieving the right relationship between the engine and the rails was crucial to the Stephensons' success in 1829. Trevithick's train had flat-rimmed wheels running on a flanged 'L'-shaped track. The weight of the engine had created the friction that the wheels needed to grip the rails; but, as the rails were too weak to sustain such a load, another way of providing traction had to be found. In 1812, Yorkshire engineer John Blenkinsop came up with a solution to the problem: a lightweight

engine, driving a cogged wheel that engaged with a toothed rail set alongside the running track.

Such an arrangement still could not move heavy loads at very high speed. William Hedley succeeded, in 1813, in building the *Puffing Billy* locomotive with smooth driving wheels that did not tax the rails unduly. But it was Stephenson who put the flange on the inside of the wheels, so that they took some of the stress previously taken by the rails, and patented a flat-topped cast iron 'edge' rail, whose shape helped it bear heavy loads. He also abandoned the clockwork-like gearing systems other pioneers had used to power the driving wheels. Instead, he used much more efficient driving rods.

The engine itself was his great masterpiece. Stephenson was the first engineer to run 'fire tubes' (the *Rocket* had 25 of them) through the water in the boiler, heating it so that steam pressure was maintained at a higher level and more consistently than ever before. This basic design principle remained unaltered in steam locomotives ever after.

*Steam speed* A replica of Stephenson's Rocket, *as it appeared at the 1829 Rainhill trials, where it achieved a top speed of 47 km/h (29 mph).*

# FLYING OFF THE RAILS
## Trains that travel as fast as planes

WILL RAILWAYS ever win back the passengers and freight lost to motor and air transport? Perhaps – if the trains could travel from one city centre to another at up to 500 km/h (300 mph). And perhaps they soon will, if research in western Europe, Japan and the USA comes to fruition. These ultramodern trains will achieve such phenomenal speeds because they will not touch the rails at all – they will literally fly through the air.

One, the French *Aérotrain*, has already reached 400 km/h (250 mph) in test runs. This high-speed monorail train is powered by jets and rides on a virtually frictionless cushion of air, like a hovercraft.

### Magnetic lift

A yet more radical way to raise a train and so dispose of the friction from conventional rails is magnetic levitation, or maglev. The system works on the simple principle that magnets will repel or attract one another. If the magnets are sufficiently powerful, they will lift even

*State-of-the-art transport* Japan's HSST (High Speed Surface Transport) maglev has reached 500 km/h (300 mph) during trials.

the hundreds of tonnes of a loaded passenger train into the air.

Japanese maglev trains work on the 'repellent' principle. One set of magnets sits in the track, while the train carries another set. Each generates an identical magnetic field, which forces the two sets of magnets apart and lifts the train into the air. The Japanese train runs on wheels at speeds up to 100 km/h (60 mph), at which point it generates sufficient power to lift off.

### Energy saving

The train then rises a full 100 mm (4 in) into the air and rockets along at up to 500 km/h (300 mph). It rises so high to maintain a smooth ride in the face of Japan's notorious earthquakes, which can shift the tracks up or down by as much as 20 mm (3/4 in). The train's designers say that it can take passengers from one town to another as fast

as an intercity jet – while consuming less than half the energy.

The German *Transrapid* floats on the 'attractive' system. A series of electromagnets is set in the 'wings' of the train, which hang below the track. When the magnets are switched on, they draw up towards the track – lifting the train off the rails in the process. The *Transrapid* has achieved speeds of up to 400 km/h (250 mph) in trials. Both the repellent and attractive types of maglev are propelled by electric motors. These have several advantages: they are quiet, smooth running, easy to maintain and emit no toxic fumes.

# VELOCITY FROM A VACUUM
## The silent and smokeless 'atmospheric' railways of the 1840s

THE GREAT Victorian engineer Isambard Kingdom Brunel proclaimed: 'I have no hesitation in taking upon myself the full and entire responsibility of recommending the adoption of the Atmospheric System on the South Devon Railway.' This was, perhaps, not his wisest decision.

The idea of 'atmospheric' railways, promising fast, smoke-free, quiet travel, became something of a vogue in the 1840s. The principle was a simple one. A continuous length of iron tubing, with a slot along the top, was laid between the rails. An arm from the bottom of the leading carriage of the train passed through the slot and connected to a piston in the tube, and a leather flap was fitted over the slot, making it airtight. Steam-pumping engines situated at various intervals along the track expelled the air from the tube in front of the train; the pressure of the air remaining behind the piston forced it – and the train – forward.

But right from the introduction of the system in the mid 1840s, several

practical problems arose. Engines proved unreliable, with passengers sometimes having to get out to push. The problem of maintaining the vacuum at junctions and crossings was never solved, and the pumping engines repeatedly suffered breakdowns.

Worst of all, however, the leather flaps deteriorated rapidly in very hot or very cold weather and also became a favourite meal for rats. Just one damaged flap weakened the vacuum needed to power the train. In 1848, it was found that every flap along the entire length of the railway needed to be replaced, and Brunel was forced to abandon the whole project.

The railway pioneer George Stephenson described the atmospheric railway as 'a great humbug'. But perhaps it was simply an idea ahead of its time. If it had been introduced a decade later, vulcanised rubber would have been readily available to replace the leather flaps, and the problem of the leaky seal, at the very least, would have been solved.

# A RAIL LEGEND IS REBORN

*Travelling back in time on the world's most luxurious train*

**E**VER SINCE the Orient Express first steamed out of Paris in 1883, its great opulence made it the stuff of legend and the inspiration for books like Graham Greene's *Stamboul Train* (1932) and Agatha Christie's *Murder on the Orient Express* (1934).

Even so, fiction could hardly match a reality that included the seductive dancer Mata Hari on a First World War spy mission for Germany, the British general Baden-Powell sketching Turkish naval defences disguised as the patterns on butterflies' wings prior to the same war, and, during the Second World War, the deposed King Carol and Queen Marie of Romania fleeing with two carriages of valuables.

Reports of the train's unrivalled comfort, its splendid interiors, haute cuisine dining car and attentive staff all helped to ensure its reputation as the premier luxury express. In the early years, passengers had to leave the train at Giurgiu in Romania. There, they would cross the Danube by boat, then take another train to the Black Sea port of Varna in Bulgaria. A short steamer ride to Istanbul finished the crossing into the Orient and ended the adventure.

The completion in 1921 of the enlarged Simplon Tunnel between Italy and Switzerland enabled passengers to make the entire journey overland via a more southerly route through Venice, Trieste, Zagreb, Belgrade and on to Istanbul. The era of the Simplon-Orient-Express, which was to last for nearly 20 years, had begun.

With the coming of the Second World War, the opulence of the train began to decline, as the luxury coaches were replaced by ordinary carriages. By the 1970s, the Orient Express barely existed, the service being made up largely of different interlinking local expresses.

But, in 1982, the legend was reborn with the Venice Simplon-Orient-Express. Over a period of five years, shipping magnate James Sherwood had bought more than 30 original coaches, many built in the 1920s, and restored them in every detail, from the colour of the paintwork to the wooden wall panelling.

Today, the journey is made in three stages: passengers take the train from London to Folkestone, then cross the Channel by ferry to Boulogne; there they board a train, which, in about 27 hours, takes them through to Venice.

## THE TRAINS THAT DRIVE THEMSELVES

**I**N 1910, the world's first fully operational driverless railway opened below the streets of Munich. Although the train carried no passengers, only mail for the Post Office, it was hailed as having revolutionary implications for the future of rail travel in general.

Decades later, despite the use of modern technology – closed-circuit televisions to monitor the movement of passengers on both the train and the platform, and microprocessors that can perform all the tasks of a human crew on a conventional train – just 20 passenger-carrying railways around the world use automatic trains and only a few of these are completely unmanned. An attendant is usually on board to control doors, start the train and cope in an emergency.

Why is it that such a labour-saving and therefore economical system has had such little success? Research shows that passengers are reluctant to travel on trains without drivers because they fear they are not safe. But, since the first fully automatic unmanned system was introduced, in Lille, France, in 1983, the indications are that these trains are as safe as – if not safer than – those with drivers. Once an automatic computerised system detects an object on the line, for example, it can operate the emergency brake far faster than the most alert driver.

*In the driver's seat Opened in 1987, London's Docklands Light Railway runs for 12 km (7 miles) without a driver, though there are guards on board to monitor station stops.*

# MODELLED ON PERFECTION

*The amazing accuracy of detail of miniature railways*

**T**HE MAKERS of model railways have always aimed for realism, so much so that, at the time of the Boer War, the German firm Märklin made not only model armoured trains, with quick-firing cannon and automatic mortars fitted with cap-firing mechanisms, but also sold a model ambulance car complete with a surgery compartment and miniature figures of wounded soldiers on stretchers.

In the 1890s, a French firm had brought out a luggage van that burst asunder if it came off the track, and, in 1901, Märklin took this a stage further with a model train in which compressed springs exploded the whole train to bits. The company's brochure proclaimed that reassembly would be 'a pleasant task' for children. Fortunately, the firm also made cranes and breakdown wagons that could be rushed to the scene of the 'accident'.

### Drink-driving ban

Creating a miniature railway world included crafting details such as a passenger waving a handkerchief from the rear of a coach, and, in one case, realism was insisted upon by American law when the word 'beer' was removed from model beer wagons to conform with Prohibition regulations. Locomotives made in the 1890s blew real smoke from a cigarette concealed in their smoke stacks or whistled convincingly, while an electric model made by American Flyer in 1936 had a continuous whistle powered by a fourth rail.

Size was no barrier to authenticity. The smallest working model railway, built by Jean Damery of Paris after the Second World War, had an engine 8 mm ($^5$/16 in) long – small enough to stand on the nail of a little finger.

### Record-breaking journeys

Some models can run distances comparable to full-size trains. The record for a model steam locomotive is 232 km (144 miles) in 27 hours 18 minutes: this is held by the 184 mm ($7^1$/4 in) gauge, coal-fired *Winifred* built in 1974 by Wilf Grove of Surrey, England. Electric models run even further, and, in 1978, a Yorkshire toyshop owner ran a loco and six coaches nonstop for 37 days, covering 1091 km (678 miles).

# THE EAST–WEST CONNECTION
### The railway that really opened Russia

THE Trans-Siberian Railway, which runs for 9297 km (5777 miles) from Moscow in the west to Nakhodka, close to the Pacific port of Vladivostok in the east, is the world's longest railway. The line is a vital commercial artery running across the former Soviet Union, linking it with Japan via the Nakhodka–Yokohama sea route and with Beijing, China, via a major branch line across Mongolia. It is also nowadays a popular tourist attraction, with many railway enthusiasts and foreign travellers making the eight-day journey across seven time zones.

The railway passes by much rugged terrain, skirting the bare hills and mountains of Chinese Manchuria and crossing the torrential waters of such great rivers as the Amur and the Ob. It borders part of Lake Baikal – the world's deepest lake – and traverses the barren fringes of the Gobi Desert and the taiga – the vast forests of Siberia. It calls at major industrial cities such as Irkutsk and Novosibirsk, and at timber-built Siberian stations with their intriguing glimpses of rural life.

In 1891, when the future tsar Nicholas II ceremonially dug the first turf of the proposed new railway in Vladivostok, Siberia was still a remote, undeveloped region. In those days, the trip to Vladivostok (and Japan) from Western Europe took at least six weeks by mail steamer.

Before the railway, Russians travelling across their vast country had to endure the indignities of sitting on their luggage in unsprung mail carts as they negotiated the rough trail, or else, in winter, face severe winds as they made slow progress in their open sledges. All year round, convicts and deportees could be seen trudging along the route to begin their period of exile.

### Tigers, bandits and disease

The railway was built in eight main stages, often against fearsome natural odds. Its construction was a bitter struggle against marshy virgin forest, permafrost, insects and disease. The workers – made up of Russians (chiefly convict labour), Chinese, Turks, Italians, Persians and Koreans – were struck down by bubonic plague and cholera and also fell victim at different times to the assaults of bandits, Manchurian tigers and catastrophic floods. Heavy artillery also wreaked havoc and destruction during China's Boxer Rebellion and the Russo-Japanese War.

*Tracks across the ice* In 1904, Russian troops laid 40 km (25 miles) of track to take trains loaded with soldiers and munitions across the frozen Lake Baikal during the Russo-Japanese War.

One particularly intractable obstacle was the vast expanse of Lake Baikal, in southeastern Siberia. To construct this part of the line, the highest point of the railway at 1025 m (3363 ft), labour gangs had to work on cliffs that fell sheer into the water. It took five years to finish this loopline. While this section was being built, a train ferry service across the lake was launched. The *Baikal* was built in Britain, then dismantled and transported across Russia by train, barge and sled. The 7000 parts were reassembled, and the ferry, carrying the entire train and passengers, began a regular service in 1900.

A final 1930 km (1200 mile) stretch following the Amur across Russia was completed in 1916. The railway had cost the equivalent of US $585 million, more than three times the original estimate. The cost in human lives over the 25 years of construction – so easily forgotten by foreign travellers in the comfort of their Trans-Siberian 'soft-class' carriage – can never be measured.

# A CITY IN MINIATURE

*Exploring the world's largest railway station*

NEW YORK's Grand Central Terminal was planned as a city within a city and it was said that you could spend days without leaving the 20 hectare (48 acre) site: there were hairdressers, shoe shiners, baths, private dressing rooms, dozens of shops, restaurants, a post office, a cinema, an emergency hospital, and even a police station in this multilayered labyrinth.

### Filling a need

In 1871, the railway magnate Cornelius Vanderbilt opened a railway station on 42nd Street. This terminus was constantly in need of enlargement. Beginning in 1903, the old station was therefore demolished and foundations were laid for the current Grand Central, which was opened in 1913.

An immense cavern, blasted out of solid rock, contained some 60 tracks on two levels leading to the main concourse. This vast elegant room is 114 m (375 ft) long, and its vaulted ceiling is 38 m (125 ft) high. It has been estimated that the concourse area could hold up to 30 000 people at one time. On several occasions, it has been used as an auditorium, exhibition or concert hall, and even as a giant ballroom.

Below the main and lower concourse area, complex multiple levels of tunnels, tracks and looplines keep trains, subways and passengers on the move. The station was a great engineering marvel of its age and was said to draw more professional interest at the time than even the contemporary Panama Canal. Loops of track enable trains to turn round without backing out of the station, and the exact position of each train is registered electronically in the terminal's control towers from the moment it enters the tunnel at 96th Street.

### Providing the juice

Also beneath the lower concourse is the giant power plant that moves trains and lights and heats the building, as well as the vast network of service tunnels.

Tenants of the six-storey main terminal building have included a radio station, a gymnasium, tennis courts, a

*Cavernous concourse In the 1950s, a staggering 54 million people would pass annually through New York's Grand Central Terminal, on an average 500 trains a day.*

photographic studio and an art gallery, while suites of private rooms enabled the suburbanites to change into evening dress before going out on the town or perhaps frequenting the terminal's famous Oyster Bar, which still serves some 12 000 oysters a day. When Grand Central was the terminus for two major railways, the upper level was reserved for glamorous long distance trains like the 20th Century Limited, while the lower level served the city's commuters and handled freight.

The station has since become a commuter terminal, and it now serves about 180 000 passengers a day. But, gazing at the huge blue vaulted ceiling with its figures of the constellation, or at the vast chandeliers, it is not hard to feel the sense of imperial grandeur of this architectural monument to the heady days of the American railway.

# PALACES ON WHEELS

*Travelling in style in the golden age of the railway*

*Sumptuous saloon In the splendour of their private carriage, Queen Victoria and her husband, Prince Albert (left), receive Louis Philippe of France (right).*

I N THE MID-19th century, monarchs were as fascinated by the railway as the common man. But when members of royalty travelled by train, they did so in carriages that were just as comfortable as their palaces.

The lavish interiors reflected the personal tastes of the royal traveller: King Ludwig of Bavaria created what was virtually a mobile version of his famous fairy-tale castles, and he continually added extra touches of luxury (even the lavatory seats were cushioned with pure swan's-down). So proud was he of it that he is said to have had the empty train driven around his kingdom so that his subjects could admire it. More magnificent still was the train built for Said Pasha, the Turkish Viceroy of Egypt. The saloon housed his own apartments at one end and those of his harem at the other; the engine was liveried in purple and silver with elaborate decorations in red and gold.

### Decorum and decoration

Queen Victoria made her first rail journey in 1842 amid tremendous pomp and ceremony. One carriage of the royal train, provided by the London and Great Western Railway, featured crimson and white silk hangings, and elaborately carved sofas in the style of Louis XIV. The journey itself was rather slow, since the queen insisted the train go no faster than 70 km/h (40 mph).

Many other heads of state enjoyed such opulence. The Austro-Hungarian Emperor Franz-Josef I had a train that incorporated a 16-seat state dining room, a serving room and a kitchen car with sleeping berths for the chefs. The last of the great royal trains, built for King Victor Emmanuel III of Italy in the 1930s, was a miniature Renaissance palace, with a red-and-gold banqueting hall, and other rooms furnished in gilded leather, silks, tapestries and exotic woods.

Lavishly appointed private coaches were not restricted to members of royalty, however. The carriage built for Pope Pius IX in 1859 had an interior throne room, furnished in white velvet, and a dome supported by sculptured pillars fronted by life-size statues of Faith, Hope and Charity. And by the turn of the century, ownership of at least one lavishly appointed carriage, with marble baths, gold plumbing, solid silver dinner services, organs, priceless paintings and specially commissioned murals, had become an important status symbol for very rich Americans.

# GETTING ALL STEAMED UP

*The extraordinary calculations of Dr Lardner*

T HE PIONEERING railway and steamship engineer Isambard Kingdom Brunel was bedevilled by a popular science writer of his day called the Reverend Dr Dionysius Lardner. Lardner was cautious to the extreme, not especially profound in his thinking, and slightly inflated by a sense of his own importance – all of which proved to be an irksome thorn in Brunel's side. The two men exchanged barbed comments when, in 1834, Lardner claimed to have proved, by elaborate calculations, that if the brakes were to fail on a train entering Brunel's proposed tunnel at Box, near Bath, on the downward gradient, the train would emerge at 215 km/h (120 mph); at this speed, Lardner asserted, passengers would not be able to breathe and would be asphyxiated.

### False alarms

Brunel pointed out that Lardner had omitted to take into account the factors of friction and air resistance that would reduce the speed to 100 km/h (56 mph). Brunel proceeded to build the tunnel, which is still in use today.

In 1836, when Brunel had already laid the keel of his transatlantic liner, the *Great Western*, Lardner presented 'irrefutable' mathematical proof to the British Association that an Atlantic crossing of approximately 5000 km (2770 miles) was impossible because the maximum range of a steamship without taking on coal was 3600 km (2000 miles). Again, Brunel had to demonstrate practically what Lardner could disclaim – at a whim – theoretically.

### Learned, but wrong

Lardner's influence was based on an academic background that included two doctorates, 15 educational prizes and a gold medal for a course of lectures on the steam engine. But when Lardner was wrong he was spectacularly wrong, and never more so than in 1838 when he told the British Association: 'Men might as well project a voyage to the Moon as attempt to employ steam across the stormy North Atlantic.' Even so, people flocked to hear him on tour in the United States in the early 1840s, and his scepticism was shared by many well-educated people.

# MEANS OF ESCAPE

## *The thrills and delights of unorthodox forms of transport*

THERE ARE people who complain continually about the inconvenience of travelling to work, but, come the weekend, many of them just cannot wait to go travelling again – not by car or train, but by racing bike, power boat, hang-glider or hot-air balloon. Some, more adventurous still, may set out on a land yacht or a powered parachute. Travelling by these unconventional means gives them the sense of fun and freedom lacking in their daily journeys to work. Inventors, too, enjoy turning their backs on convention in order to experiment with radically new designs for cars, flying machines and bicycles –building, for example, a wooden car or an aeroplane shaped like a pancake. The alternative forms of transport pictured here have not revolutionised the way we live, but they have given people enormous pleasure and presented them with some of the greatest challenges of their lives. Imagine the exhilaration of sailing a land yacht across the Sahara, or of pedalling furiously, entombed in a glass fibre shell, in pursuit of the world cycling speed record. To be borne aloft by a team of eagles might surpass all these other thrills, but as yet no eagles have been found willing to oblige.

**Economy drive** *The Africar was designed by British photo-journalist Anthony Howarth as a cheap, sturdy vehicle for use in countries where roads are rough, the climate harsh and spares difficult to come by. The coachwork and most of the chassis are built of wood strengthened with polyester. Despite a successful test drive of 16 000 km (10 000 miles) from the Arctic to the Equator in 1984, developing countries have not yet been persuaded to take it up.*

**Boat of the desert** *This French sail-powered tricycle is no modern invention. The idea of wind-driven chariots occurred to the ancient Egyptians, the Chinese and to a 16th-century Dutch mathematician called Simon Stevin. Sailing on land is far more efficient than sailing on water. On firm surfaces land yachts can reach 130 km/h (80 mph). The sport is popular in many countries, and regular 'regattas' are held on sandy beaches or in deserts.*

**Flight of fancy** *This heavier-than-air flying machine was the apparently serious idea of a Baltimore man, who sent it to the Scientific American in 1865. Basing his calculations on the fact that an eagle can carry a lamb in its talons, he thought ten eagles would be enough to lift the pilot and his craft.*

**Parachuting upwards** *Devised purely for fun, the powered parachute can fly safely up to heights of 3000 m (10 000 ft). Unlike a balloon, the craft is not at the mercy of the wind – the propeller at the rear fills the parachute for takeoff and gives a cruising speed of 55 km/h (35 mph).*

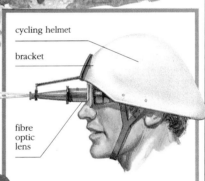

cycling helmet

bracket

fibre optic lens

**Flying Flapjack** *This curious plane was built by the American Chance Vought Company in the 1940s. Its experimental shape was designed to provide stability and enable it to fly at greatly varying speeds. The prototypes were dogged by unforeseen problems, and the 'Flapjack' never went into production.*

aperture for fibre optic cable

**One eye on the road** *An extreme solution to the racing cyclist's problem of air-resistance is the Cyclops, designed by Briton Mike Burrows in 1984. The three-wheeled machine (left) has an aerodynamic, wedge-shaped cover, which prevents its driver from seeing, except through one tiny hole at the front. This is connected by optical fibres to a lens on the driver's goggles (above), giving him a rather poorly-defined image of what lies ahead.*

309

# LIVING DANGEROUSLY

*People who challenge death for money or fun*

THE DANGEROUS Sports Club is a group of eccentrics based in Oxford, England, who endeavour to 'act boldly in a timorous, over-protected world'. 'Acting boldly' to the Dangerous Sports Club means acting like madmen to most other people. Why else would David Kirke, one of the club's founding members, have hurled himself from the Royal Gorge Bridge in 1982, 320 m (1030 ft) above the Arkansas River in Colorado? He was attached to the bridge by a length of elasticated cord tied to his ankles. At 260 m (860 ft) the cord was stretched to its limits, and so was Kirke: virtually unconscious, he dangled for over two hours before his companions could haul him back to the bridge.

### Grabbing the bull by the horns

History is full of such daredevils. The 'bull leapers' of ancient Crete, for example, used to grab the horns of a charging bull and somersault over its back. These were the forerunners of circus acts such as Hugo Zacchini, whose fame was due as much to his showmanship as to his acrobatic skills. In 1929, Zacchini was shot from the mouth of a cannon, propelled by compressed air. He travelled over 40 m (135 ft) through the air at a speed of 130 km/h (80 mph). In the 1870s, the American circus performer John Holtum would catch cannonballs fired at point-blank range – in his own hands.

But death-defying acts can go wrong. The escapologist Harry Houdini used to invite people to punch him hard in the stomach, resisting the blow by tensing his muscles. On October 22, 1926, however, Houdini was struck in the stomach before he had time to prepare himself, and died six days later of a ruptured appendix.

Circus folk perform their dangerous deeds to make money. But people like George Willig, who climbed up the outside of the World Trade Center in New York in 1977 without ropes, or Jaromir Wagner, the Czech who flew the Atlantic strapped to the pylon of a light aircraft in 1980, have no other motive than a love of danger.

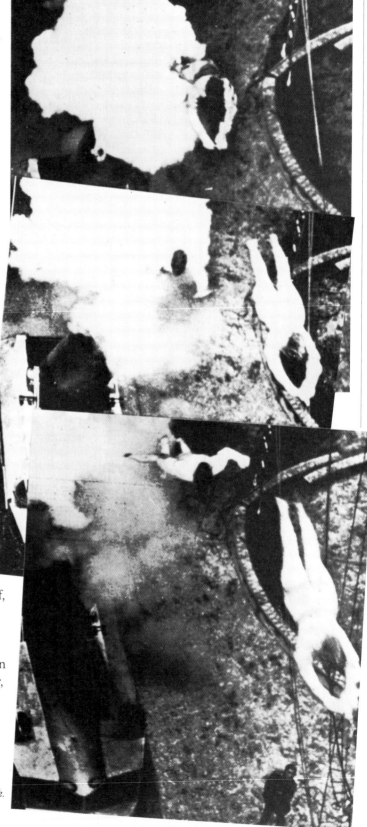

***Double trouble*** *In 1934, Hugo Zacchini and his brother amazed audiences by being simultaneously shot from a cannon in the Ringling Bros and Barnum and Bailey Circus in New York.*

# THE LONG AND WINDING ROAD

*Where pigs are more dangerous than jaguars*

ONE OF the most ambitious peacetime expeditions ever undertaken by the British Army ended in triumph on June 9, 1972, when two Range Rovers carrying an exhausted team arrived at the southernmost point of South America, Cape Horn. They had set off from the north coast of Alaska 188 days earlier in an attempt to become the first people to drive the full length of the Americas, using the 22 000 km (14 000 mile) Pan-American Highway. The real triumph of the expedition was the crossing of a mere 400 km (250 mile) stretch of country from Panama to Colombia, known as El Tapon (The Stopper) or the Darien Gap.

The Gap's mixture of jungle, swamp and river slices the Pan-American Highway in two, presenting a seemingly insurmountable barrier. Road builders had decided that the Gap was impossible to cross – and the British team would soon find out why.

### Team effort

Six members of the task force covered the first stage of the journey, from Anchorage in Alaska to Canitas in Panama, where the northern section of the Highway stops, in 40 days. There, in January 1972, they were met by a team of engineers, medical staff, jungle experts, as well as scientists to study the plant, animal and human life of the Gap. The support team travelled independently from the task force who used the Range Rovers. These were equipped

*Deep water Swamps and rivers failed to stop the intrepid team. Their two Range Rovers were floated on a makeshift raft.*

with motor-driven winches, water tanks, aluminium ladders for bridging ravines, exhaust 'snorkels' for fording streams and an inflatable raft for deeper water.

The struggle to cross the Gap began on January 17, with teams of people on foot hacking a path for the Range Rovers and guiding them through it. The Gap proved to be worse than anyone had imagined: flooded rivers, thick jungle, ravines and swamp made their progress painfully slow; they were plagued by vicious hornets, biting ants, scorpions, mosquitoes and deadly snakes – even some of the plants were poisonous. And, feared even more than jaguars, were the wild pigs that roamed in stampeding packs of up to 300. The team suffered terribly from the heat and were occasionally subject to diseases caught from the swamp and insects.

The expedition was supported by supplies dropped from aircraft,

*Constant perils Fording rivers was only part of the problem faced by the team who crossed the Darien Gap in 1972. Vicious insects and alligators were an ever-present danger.*

and the team was driven on by a determination that bordered on madness. In conquering obstacles such as the aptly named gradients of the Heartbreak Hills and the ravines of the Devil's Switchback, only a fierce team spirit kept mental breakdown at bay. Mechanical breakdown was also a constant problem. One of the Range Rovers had to be winched out of a fast-flowing river where it had sunk almost out of sight, and the final swamp could only be crossed after vegetation had been blown out of the way with dynamite.

The expedition finally and jubilantly reached the end of the Gap at Barranquilla on April 23, 96 days after entering its green prison.

# WALKING A THIN LINE

*The man who cooked an omelette above Niagara Falls*

ON JUNE 30, 1859, 35-year-old Jean-François Gravelet – better known as Blondin – walked the 335 m (1100 ft) separating the two banks of the Niagara River on a rope stretched 50 m (160 ft) above the raging waters of the Falls. The precarious walk took 20 minutes. When Blondin finally reached safety, he was applauded by thousands of excited spectators. For Blondin it must have been an exhilarating moment – he had been in training since his acrobat father began to teach him the art of tightrope-walking at the age of five.

After this first success, crossing the Niagara became almost a regular stroll for Blondin. Not content simply to walk across, he devised ever more audacious stunts, including crossing while blindfolded or pushing a wheelbarrow, or with his feet in a sack or on stilts. On one occasion, he carried his business manager Harry Colcord on his back. According to Colcord, the episode was a nightmare from beginning to end. Six times, Blondin nearly lost his balance. Fittingly for a Frenchman, Blondin's most bizarre crossing involved cooking: he carried a small stove halfway across, and calmly prepared and ate an omelette.

Blondin performed equally astonishing feats away from Niagara. In 1861, crowds in London's Crystal Palace watched in amazement as Blondin – on stilts and without a net – performed somersaults on a rope strung 52 m (170 ft) above the ground. Blondin's 50th year saw him walking a rope strung between the masts of two ships in a storm at sea. He gave his final performance in Belfast in 1896, at the age of 72. He died in London a year later – in no more dangerous a spot than bed.

*Piggyback ride On August 19, 1859, Blondin carried his manager across Niagara Falls.*

### DID YOU KNOW..?

*TIGHTROPE -WALKING is one of the most ancient of human entertainments, dating back at least to Roman times, and almost certainly originated in ancient Greece. A Roman tightrope-walker would have been known as a* funambulus *– from the Latin* funis, *for 'rope', and* ambulare, *for 'walk' – which gives us the English term 'funambulist'.*

# ALONE ON EVEREST

*One man's struggle with the world's highest mountain*

ON AUGUST 18, 1980, a 35-year-old Italian climber, Reinhold Messner, set off alone up the north face of Mount Everest, which lies on the border of Tibet and Nepal. He had come to his upper base camp at 6500 m (21 500 ft) with three companions, but now he would have no further assistance. Messner was determined to achieve the first solo ascent of the world's highest peak, 8848 m (29 028 ft) high at its summit.

In his rucksack were supplies for a week, but only the bare necessities. He would have no rope to hold him if he fell into a crevasse, no Sherpa guides to prepare a bivouac or carry heavy loads, and no radio with which to call for help. And Messner carried no oxygen, deeming it an unworthy artificial aid. His total kit consisted of two ski sticks, a lightweight ice axe, a sleeping bag, a tent, food and a camera. Even this weighed 18 kg (40 lb), a heavy load in the debilitating thin atmosphere of the high Himalayas.

All Messner's meticulous preparation was almost wasted from the start. Setting out in the darkness, he slipped into a 500 m (1650 ft) deep crevasse and would have been killed, had he not landed on a small snow ledge only 8 m (26 ft) down. From here he managed to clamber out and continue his ascent.

### Will to succeed

Over the next two days, Messner laboured upwards through worsening weather conditions. In the thin air, the slightest physical effort made him breathless. Even setting up his tent for the night was a herculean task. The functioning of his brain, too, suffered from shortness of oxygen, and he began to imagine voices in the frozen solitude. Yet sheer willpower kept him moving. Sometimes reduced to crawling on all fours, he finally reached the summit on the afternoon of August 20. Another day's agonising effort brought him back to base camp and relative safety.

By 1986, Messner had climbed all the world's peaks over 8000 m (26 250 ft), yet he could give no explanation of the force that drove him to continue risking death on the snowclad peaks. The most he could say was that 'the inexplicable gives meaning to life'.

# SURVIVAL IN THE SKY

*The stowaway who lived through an ordeal that should have killed him*

**A**RMANDO Socarras Ramírez and a fellow student flew from Cuba to Spain on June 4, 1969. Unlike the other 143 passengers on the nine-hour flight, however, the Cuban students travelled under rather than inside the Iberia Airlines DC-8: Socarras had stowed away with his companion Jorge Pérez Blanco inside the aeroplane's wheel compartment.

When airport mechanics opened the compartment during the aeroplane's routine post-flight service in Madrid, only one very cold stowaway dropped onto the tarmac; tragically, Pérez had fallen from the plane on the approach to Madrid. But, by some miracle, Socarras was still alive. He was rushed to hospital to be treated for exposure and shock.

Dressed only in a shirt and trousers, Socarras had endured a temperature of -40°C (-40°F), pressures a quarter of those at sea level, and a lack of oxygen that had rendered him unconscious for almost the entire journey. Any one of these should have killed him.

Airborne at 8800 m (29 000 ft), Socarras had experienced stresses familiar only to mountaineers on the highest Himalayan peaks. But when mountaineers climb to such heights, they do it gradually and have time to acclimatise to the decreasing pressure. Socarras's aircraft had climbed at a rate of 455–610 m (1500–2000 ft) per minute.

Baffled scientists could explain Socarras's survival only as a remarkable example of human hibernation. When the body's temperature decreases, so does its demand for oxygen. Socarras's temperature had, it seems, dropped by just the right amount. This did not freeze him, but it reduced his need for oxygen and enabled him to live.

**Miracle man** *Doctors were amazed to find that after his high altitude flight in a jet's wheel compartment, stowaway Socarras suffered from no more than exposure and shock.*

## GOING OVER THE TOP

**O**N THE AFTERNOON of October 24, 1901, several thousand people watched as a large wooden barrel careered through violent rapids towards Niagara's Horseshoe Falls. Swept along by the current, the cask disappeared over the edge. Seconds later the barrel rose up to the surface in the calmer waters 54 m (160 ft) below: it had survived its battering. And miraculously, for the first time in Niagara's long history of daredevils, so had its passenger.

Strapped and cushioned inside, schoolteacher Anna Edson Taylor had just celebrated her 43rd birthday with a death-defying plunge into the history books. Taylor was shocked and badly shaken and had a gash in her head; but she was alive, conscious, and within a few days had fully recovered.

Anna Taylor's bravery did not bring her the cascade of riches she had hoped, and she died penniless in 1921. She is buried in a 'stunters' section of Niagara Falls' Oakwood cemetery, remembered still as the first person – and only woman ever – to survive the Niagara fall. Her advice to potential imitators was: 'Don't try it!'

***Taking the plunge*** *Schoolteacher Anna Edson Taylor was badly shaken after her 54 m (160 ft) descent in a barrel over the Horseshoe Falls on October 24, 1901.*

# REACH FOR THE SKY

*Mankind has always dreamed of flying like a bird*

**A**T THREE MINUTES past six on the evening of April 25, 1937, Clem Sohn, the 'Birdman' from Michigan, USA, jumped from a light aeroplane 3000 m (10 000 ft) above an airfield near Paris. His wings, made of fabric, were stretched between his arms and body and between his legs, after the style of a flying fox. A crowd of 200 000 spectators watched breathlessly. Sohn descended to an altitude of 300 m (1000 ft), using his wings to glide in wide, perfectly controlled sweeps. But then he plumetted like a stone, his parachute uselessly entangled – another victim of the dream of flying like a bird that has haunted humanity for thousands of years.

Before balloons or aeroplanes were invented, manpowered wings seemed to be the obvious and only way to fly. Early scientists, such as Leonardo da Vinci, observed the flight of birds and bats and drew what seemed an obvious conclusion: human beings would one day soar into the sky by flapping wings. They therefore devised extraordinary mechanisms that used arm or pedal power to move the wings, but these always failed.

This obsession with flapping wings led inventors up a blind alley. Even in Leonardo's day, all the materials and technology required to build a successful fixed-wing glider already existed, but no one thought of constructing such an aircraft.

Yet something very close to the eternal dream of birdlike flight has at last proved possible through the invention of hang-gliding. Had Leonardo ignored how birds flapped their wings, and concentrated instead on how they picked up air currents to glide and soar, the challenge of human flight might have been solved much earlier.

*Leonardo's sketch for a man-made wing*

*Fatal illusion* 'Birdman' Clem Sohn confidently spreads out the wings that minutes later failed him in his descent from a height of 3000 m (10 000 ft) onto an airfield near Paris in April 1937.

## DID YOU KNOW..?

*AT THE CRYSTAL Palace, London, in 1875, inventor Thomas Moy demonstrated his Aerial Steamer, a monoplane with two large propellers driven by steam. There was no pilot and the craft never really flew – but it did rise about 15 cm (6 in) off the ground while following a circular track.*

# RUNNING ON AIR

*At several times the speed of sound, an engine may be a waste of space*

TO POWER flights at subsonic speeds, jet engines work by igniting fuel and forcing hot gases out of an exhaust to create thrust. But when an aircraft accelerates beyond the speed of sound, the propulsive thrust increasingly comes not from the engine, but from the airflow through the engine inlet and out of the jet nozzle at the rear. This is known as a ramjet, sometimes called a 'flying stove-pipe'.

Take Concorde as an example. At takeoff, each Concorde engine puts out about 17 500 kg (38 000 lb) of thrust. The engine inlets and the nozzle contribute next to nothing. But as the aeroplane picks up speed, the flow of air into the engines also accelerates. By the time the plane is cruising at Mach 2 (twice the speed of sound), only 30 per cent of the thrust comes from the engine. The rest is provided by air pressure built up by the high-speed air flow in the specially shaped engine inlet and through the nozzle.

### Record holder

Another supersonic aircraft is the US Air Force SR-71 Blackbird, which holds the world speed record at 3509 km/h (2193 mph). At full speed (Mach 3.2), the Blackbird's two engines are providing only 17.6 per cent of the total thrust. At a slightly higher speed, the engine's contribution would fall to zero, and it would then be much better to remove it altogether.

So would it be possible to construct an aircraft propelled by a ramjet alone, without any complex engine? The answer is a simple 'no' – because such an aircraft could never take off.

*Sight and sound* Travelling at more than thrice the speed of sound, the gloomy outlines of this SR-71 Blackbird may have disappeared over the horizon by the time its sound waves reach our ears.

## DID YOU KNOW..?

*ON DECEMBER 14, 1986, the monoplane* Voyager, *designed and piloted by Dick Rutan and Jeana Yeager, took off from Edwards Air Force Base, California, for the first nonstop flight around the world without in-flight refuelling. For the enormous distance involved,* Voyager *had to carry 3181 kg (7012 lb) of fuel. Even with an extra engine, which provided power for the takeoff and was then shut off, the aircraft covered 4300 m (14 200 ft) of runway before it lifted off the ground – even more than a jumbo jet requires.* Voyager *completed the 40 212 km (24 987 mile) flight on December 23.*

## FALLING INTO FLIGHT

THE 18TH-CENTURY Swedish philosopher, mystic, theologian and scientist Emanuel Swedenborg is often credited as the first man to attempt a truly logical design for a heavier-than-air flying machine, even though he believed it incapable of flight. Swedenborg was inspired by an incident at the Swedish town of Skara, when a student who fell off a church tower in a strong wind floated to Earth unharmed, carried by his cape which billowed out like a parachute.

This set Swedenborg to calculating the mathematics of flight. Reasoning that a large enough area of 'sail' would lift a man's weight, in 1714 he produced an aircraft design. He imagined a sail spread over the top of the pilot's 'car', and paddle-like wings providing minimal motion. The machine would be launched from a roof or lifted off by a following wind.

The strength of Swedenborg's design was his understanding of the importance of lightweight materials – cork or birch

bark – and his appreciation of the need to balance the machine. But it was really more of a glider than an aircraft. And it was totally impractical – he never even tried to build a prototype.

Swedenborg rejected the idea of balloon flight as against nature, and did not live into the 1780s to see himself disproved by the first manned balloons. But now that technology has caught up with the Swede's impractical imagination, any errors of judgment on his part can be forgiven.

# THE FLYING COACHMAN

*How the inventor of the glider kept his own feet on the ground*

LIVING at Brompton Hall, Yorkshire, in the first half of the 19th century, Sir George Cayley was in most respects a typical English gentleman. He was such a powerful, kind and respected person that nobody thought him crazy – despite his eccentric interest in flying.

Cayley's obsession with flight lasted throughout a long lifetime. In 1804, at the age of 31, he produced the very first sketch of a recognisable modern aeroplane, with a single wing and a proper tail fin and tailplane.

By his old age, his study of aerodynamics had led him to all the right conclusions for designing a powered heavier-than-air flying machine. Unfortunately, no engine yet existed that could make his plans a reality – the steam engine was the best available, and Cayley's own calculations had proved a steam-powered plane would be simply too heavy to fly.

So Cayley was restricted to constructing the first manned glider. After testing a small model that carried a boy across a Yorkshire valley, he moved on to a man-sized monoplane design. It might have been better if Cayley himself had flown this big glider, built in 1853, but by then the scholarly baronet was 80 years old. Instead he thrust his apprehensive coachman, armed with detailed instructions, into the machine.

The glider flew, but could not really be controlled. It did land in one piece, but was never again to fly. Distinctly shaken by the experience, the coachman resigned. 'Sir George,' he explained, not unreasonably, 'I was hired to drive, not to fly.'

# PARASITES OF THE AIR

*The piggyback aircraft that inspired high hopes*

TODAY a jumbo jet can fly hundreds of people nonstop from Britain to Australia, but, before the Second World War, not even the biggest airliners could cross the North Atlantic with anywhere near such a large load on board – the fuel needed for such a long flight took up too great a share of the carrying capacity.

Seeking a solution to this problem, British air expert Major Robert Mayo hit on the idea of putting a small, heavily loaded seaplane on top of a much bigger, lightly loaded flying boat. The flying boat had powerful engines and a large wingspan, which enabled it to lift off with enormous loads, but, as it consumed fuel very quickly, it could not make long-distance journeys. The shorter wingspan and weaker engines of the seaplane meant that, once airborne, it could make a long journey on relatively little fuel.

Mayo's brainchild was christened the Short-Mayo Composite Aircraft. It first flew on January 4, 1938, and the two components, the big flying boat *Maia* and the seaplane *Mercury*, first separated in the air on February 6 of that year. Later, the seaplane flew nonstop to Montreal, and then set a world distance record with a nonstop flight from Scotland to South Africa.

But although it was a technological triumph, the Composite never went into airline service. For one thing, it was too expensive.

Most other examples of a 'parasitic' relationship between small and large aircraft have, in the end, proved just as impractical. After the Second World War, for example, the US Air Force experimented with a tiny jet fighter, the XF-85 Goblin, which was designed to fold up and fit inside the bomb bay of a giant B-36 heavy bomber. Only 4.6 m (15 ft) long, the Goblin was supposed to swing down from the bomb bay, unfold its wings and zoom off. It was then meant to hook back onto the bomber for the ride home, but hooking back proved insuperably difficult.

---

### DID YOU KNOW..?

*IN 1935, Soviet air engineer Vladimir Vakhmistrov developed a scheme for a giant TB-3 bomber to carry no less than five other aircraft – two I-5 fighters above the wing tips, two I-16 fighters hung below the wing tips, and an I-Z fighter on a trapeze under the fuselage. All five were released into flight simultaneously.*

**Hitching a ride** *Prior to the 1940s, most runways were too short for long-distance planes to take off, so most long-distance aircraft were seaplanes. In Mayo's design, a flying boat takes off with a seaplane on its back. Once in the air, the seaplane is launched from the flying boat and goes off much more heavily laden than if it had had to get airborne under its own power.*

A passenger-carrying seaplane (*left*) balances on a 'mother' ship

The seaplane (*above*) is then detached from the airborne 'mother' ship

Once it is fully launched, the long-distance seaplane goes its own way

## COAST TO COAST BY HOOK OR BY CROOK

THE FIRST aircraft to fly across the United States from coast to coast was a biplane in 1911. However, it crashed so frequently en route from New York that, by the time it arrived in California, the only parts remaining from the original aircraft were the rudder and the oil drip pan under the engine.

The flight was inspired by the newspaper magnate William Randolph Hearst, who offered a prize of $50 000 to the first man to fly across the continent in 30 days. The challenge was taken up by Calbraith Rodgers, who had raced cars, horses and yachts. He bought an aircraft

and took off on September 17, 1911, followed by a special train, provided by his sponsor, loaded with spare parts.

The United States must have seemed impossibly big as he spluttered into the air in his frail biplane of wood, wire and cloth. And he had not foreseen some of the greatest difficulties of his journey. Time after time, his plane overturned while landing on potholed fields. Bits of his aircraft disappeared into the homes of souvenir hunters. He was repeatedly blown off course, or got lost through his inability to navigate. He was slowed to walking pace by fierce winds, damaged

by storms and even chased by an eagle. In the Rocky Mountains, he nearly collided with a jagged precipice and, a few days later, his engine exploded, shooting splinters of steel into his right arm.

At last, the much-rebuilt aircraft came in to land at the agreed destination, Pasadena, a suburb of Los Angeles. Rodgers was fêted, wrapped in a huge Stars and Stripes and given a bouquet – but he did not get the $50 000 cheque. His journey had taken 50 days, far beyond the agreed time limit. Even more sadly, Rodgers was killed five months later while stunt flying.

# WHERE THE WIND BLOWS
### *The world's greatest balloon race*

JAMES GORDON BENNETT was an American newspaper magnate, founder of *The New York Herald*. But his name is also remembered for the great annual balloon race he sponsored, the Gordon Bennett Cup. Beginning in 1906, the cup was awarded each year to the balloon landing farthest from the starting point, which was always in the country of the previous year's winner. The balloonists' lack of control over the direction of flight, entirely at the mercy of the wind, made the competition very unpredictable.

### Wet start

The first flight of 16 balloons took off from Paris on September 30 and was carried northwest towards England. The winner, US Army Lieutenant Frank Lahm, reached Fylingdales Moor, Yorkshire, a distance of 647 km (402 miles). But he was one of only three starters who managed to cross the English Channel. Fortunately for those who preferred not to risk a ducking, the next year's race took off from St Louis, Missouri, where there was almost no chance of running out of dry land.

After being interrupted by the First World War, the competition resumed in 1920. The vagaries of the weather ensured some eventful races. In 1923, the balloons took off in a violent thunderstorm; five competitors were killed and a further five injured. In 1925, one balloon was hit by a train, while another unsuccessful competitor managed to land on the bridge of a ship at sea. And in the 1935 race, which started from Warsaw, the wind carried all the leading balloons off to an area of the Soviet

Union so remote that they were not retrieved for a fortnight.

The last Gordon Bennett race was held in 1938, leaving the record for the longest flight still with the 1912 winner, A. Bienaimé of France, who had travelled 2191 km (1361 miles) from Stuttgart to a village outside Moscow. Today's record-breaking balloons have totally outstripped such a performance: on November 9–12, 1981, the huge gas

***Winds of fate*** *During the 1925 Gordon Bennett Cup, one balloon collided with a train near Boulogne, France. Fortunately, nobody was seriously injured.*

balloon *Double Eagle V* flew 8383 km (5209 miles), from Nagashima, Japan, to Covelo, California. But it is doubtful that contemporary balloonists will ever surpass the sheer excitement of those magnificent men of 1906.

# PEDALLING THROUGH THE SKY

*The spectacular progress of manpowered flight*

I N 1960, a British industrialist, Henry Kremer, offered a prize of £5000 (US $14 000) for any manpowered aircraft (MPA) that could fly a figure-of-eight course around two pylons at least 800 m (2500 ft) apart. For 17 years this prize, regularly updated to keep pace with inflation, remained unclaimed. But it spurred many people to build MPAs.

The original Kremer prize was finally won on August 23, 1977, by *Gossamer Condor*, designed by an American team led by Paul MacCready, an aeronautical engineer. Like most MPAs being developed at this time, it had a giant wing, yet weighed almost nothing, and was driven by a propeller. The pilot, Bryan Allen, rode it like a bicycle, pedalling to turn the propeller and thus create the forward thrust.

To maintain the momentum of progress in manpowered aircraft, Kremer then offered a much higher prize – £100 000 ($280 000) – for the first manpowered flight across the English Channel. *Gossamer Albatross*, from the same design team as *Gossamer Condor*, carried off this prize as well. Bryan Allen took off from Folkestone on the south coast of England and landed at Cap Gris-Nez in the north of France, a distance of some 36 km (22 miles).

MacCready then turned his attention to a possible means of improving the speed and range of his MPAs with a little assistance from the Sun. He designed *Solar Challenger*, a pedalled aircraft whose wings were covered with solar cells on their upper surface. The electricity generated by these cells provided additional power, which, on July 7, 1981, helped Steve Ptacek to pedal from Cormeilles en Vexin, near Paris, to Manston, Kent, in the south of England, a distance of 262 km (163 miles).

By the end of the 1980s, MPAs equipped with electric batteries for an extra boost were regularly registering speeds of around 50 km/h (30 mph), and better performances were being achieved all the time.

*Prize winner* *On June 12, 1979, Bryan Allen successfully pedalled* Gossamer Albatross *across the English Channel for nearly three hours in order to win the second Kremer prize.*

## THE ONE-HOUSEFLY-POWER ENGINE

O N JULY 24, 1977, the smallest aircraft ever built took off for a demonstration flight at Kirkland, Washington, in the United States. Weighing just 0.1 gram (0.04 oz), its engine and pilot were one and the same: a common housefly.

The designer of the flyplane, Don Emmick, made no claim to have originated the concept – the Croatian-American inventor Nikola Tesla, for example, had experimented with insect power back in the 19th century. But Emmick, an engineer for an aircraft manufacturer, did bring an expert knowledge of aerodynamics to a previously little-explored field of air engineering. The frame of the tiny machine was made of balsa wood, with the two wings, fore and aft of the pilot/engine, covered in transparent film.

Gaining the cooperation of the housefly required a certain ingenuity. Caught under a glass, the insect was stunned with ether and then glued to the airframe by its stomach. When it came round, the fly needed no further encouragement to flap its wings and take off.

One insectonaut, the most successful of several, flew for a full five minutes outdoors, circling and manoeuvring to avoid obstacles. Conscious that he might be condemned for cruelty to the housefly, Emmick very carefully freed the test pilot from its machine once the experiment was completed.

*Live engine* *With a wingspan of only 76 mm (3 in), this flypowered aeroplane holds the current record for the world's smallest powered model aircraft.*

# THE BIRDMAN OF CRETE

*How modern technology and pedal power recreated Daedalus's flight*

ACCORDING to ancient Greek legend, the first manpowered flight was made by Daedalus, an inventor of genius, some 3500 years ago. Imprisoned on the Mediterranean island of Crete, Daedalus devised a bold escape plan. With wings of bird feathers glued together with wax, he took to the air together with his son Icarus. Poor Icarus flew too close to the Sun and his wings melted, but Daedalus made good his escape.

### Where to land?

In 1984, scientists at the Massachusetts Institute of Technology (MIT) decided to see whether they could reproduce Daedalus's flight from Crete, using a specially designed pedal-driven aircraft. Where exactly Daedalus landed is unclear, so the MIT team settled for the volcanic island of Santorini, 117 km (73 miles) north of Crete, for touchdown.

The idea of a manpowered flight over such a distance required a daring leap of the imagination. The previous longest manpowered flight, by *Gossamer Albatross* across the English Channel in 1979, had covered only 36 km (22 miles). Pedalling from Crete to Santorini in the air would be equivalent to running two consecutive marathons.

The aircraft was computer modelled for maximum aerodynamic efficiency and built from the most advanced lightweight materials. *Daedalus 88* ended up weighing 31 kg (69 lb), less than half as heavy as its pilot. Yet its wingspan of 34 m (112 ft) was greater than that of a Boeing 727.

It took four years of work and an investment of a million dollars before the team finally arrived in Crete in the spring of 1988 ready to attempt the Daedalus flight. Just after 7am on April 23, with Greek cycling champion Kanellos Kanellopoulos at the controls, the strange spindly aircraft, like a pink and silver dragonfly, rose silently from a runway at Iráklion airport, and headed off northwards out to sea. Kanellopoulos pedalled at about 5 m (15 ft) above the Sea of Crete, tracked by a fleet of small support craft, and constantly drinking a glucose solution to replace the 1 litre (1¾ pt) of fluid lost each hour through sweat.

### Natural assistance

The flight was expected to take five hours at best, but with a following wind Kanellopoulos did it in less. Averaging 30 km/h (19 mph), he approached the beach at Santorini only 3 hours 55 minutes after leaving Crete.

The sole mishap during the trip occurred at the very last moment. As *Daedalus 88* came in to land, a sudden

*Stuff of legends* Squeezed into the cabin of the fragile-looking Daedalus 88 aircraft, 30-year-old Kanellos Kanellopoulos pedals his way across the Sea of Crete in April 1988 in imitation of Daedalus's famous flight.

gust of headwind broke up the aircraft just 7 m (23 ft) offshore. Kanellopoulos emerged exultant and unharmed. The myth of Daedalus had become a reality.

---

## DID YOU KNOW..?

*THE FIRST jet fighter designed for operation from aircraft carriers, the American McDonnell XFD-1 Phantom, was not ready for its first test flight on January 25, 1945 – one of its two engines had still not been delivered. The test pilot refused to regard this as a problem, however, and the first flight was made with one engine missing.*

✳ ✳ ✳

*THE MOST engines ever fitted to one aircraft are the 12 engines of the giant Dornier Do X flying boat of 1929. The Do X was the biggest aeroplane of its day. At a time when few airliners carried more than a dozen passengers, it once took off with 169 people on board: ten crew, 150 passengers and nine stowaways.*

# BUILT FOR SPEED

*The competition to be the fastest thing on land*

**K**ARL BENZ proudly displayed his new creation, the first successful petrol-engined motor car, to the public in Mannheim, Germany, in 1886. The car chugged and rattled along the 1 km (3000 ft) road test at a top speed of 15 km/h (9 mph). How could he have foreseen that less than a century later, a British car would break the world land speed record at over 1019 km/h (633 mph)? Richard Noble achieved this speed in the jet-engined car *Thrust 2* on October 4, 1983, at Black Rock Desert in Nevada, USA.

Perhaps the most famous high-speed driver was Sir Malcolm Campbell. Between 1924 and 1935, he broke the land speed record nine times, taking it from 235 km/h (146 mph) to 485 km/h (301 mph) in his Bluebird cars. Almost 30 years later, Sir Malcolm's son followed in his footsteps. On July 17, 1964, Donald Campbell reached 649 km/h (403 mph) in another

*The big push The* Thrust 2 *in which Richard Noble broke the world land speed record in 1983 was designed by John Ackroyd in 1980. The space-age car is powered by a Rolls-Royce Avon 302 engine capable of producing some 7700 kg (17 000 lb) of thrust.*

Bluebird. Campbell's record still stands as the fastest speed ever reached by a wheel-driven car; all faster speeds have been reached in jet-propelled vehicles.

The land speed record changed hands six times in the last six months of 1964, and a further four times in 1965, by which time the American driver Craig Breedlove had taken the top speed to 966 km/h (601 mph). This record stood for five years until Gary Gabelich became the first man to break the 1000 km/h barrier. In October 1970, he drove the *Blue Flame* at 1002 km/h (622 mph), a land speed record that lasted for 13 years – which is a record in itself.

---

# ON THE ROAD

*The man who revolutionised road building*

**W**HEN John Loudon McAdam was appointed as a road trustee in Ayrshire, Scotland, in 1783, he was so horrified at the poor condition of the highways that he determined to find a way of making better roads. After nearly 30 years of experiments, most of which he financed himself, he came up with a system for building the best roads since those of the ancient Romans.

His technique was first to lay a 250 mm (10 in) thick foundation of broken stones, each about 50 mm (2 in) in diameter. A second layer of smaller angular stones would interlock with the foundation stones when pressed down. The final layer consisted of pebbles. The weight of the vehicles would grind these into dust, which would fill the gaps in between the stones. The traffic would then compact the surface. McAdam's system was first used in

England in 1815; it enabled mail coaches – an essential communications link – to increase their average speed by about 50 per cent, from 8 km/h (5 mph) to 13 km/h (8 mph).

But McAdam was not responsible for the invention of tarmacadam (or Tarmac, as it is more popularly known). The world's most common road surface was not invented until 1854, 18 years after McAdam's death, and then, so the story goes, it was discovered only by chance.

A British surveyor named E.P. Hooley noticed that some tar that had been accidentally spilled onto a rough surface had solidified to a smooth, hard finish. He added a layer of tar to McAdam's roads; it proved to be an effective means of bonding and sealing against water. Hooley called his system tarmacadamising in honour of the Scottish road pioneer.

---

### DID YOU KNOW..?

*IN 1979, Stan Barnet touched 1190 km/h (740 mph) at the Edwards Airforce Base in California. He reached this astonishing speed in the* Budweiser Rocket, *with a little help from a Sidewinder missile that provided an extra 2700 kg (6000 lb) of thrust. However, the vehicle did not keep up the speed long enough for this performance to qualify as a record.*

# THE TIN LIZZIE

## *One man's crusade to make the common man a car owner*

'I DON'T NEED a speedometer for my Ford: at 5 mph the fender rattles; at 10 mph my teeth rattle; at 15 mph the transmission drops out!' Despite the abundance of jokes such as this that prevailed at the height of the Model T Ford's popularity, no one could deny that Henry Ford had fulfilled the promise he made when announcing the birth of the Model T in 1908: 'I will build a motor car for the great multitude.'

The success of Ford's car is surprising, as it was extremely hard to handle. Some American states even considered the Model T to be so difficult to drive that they insisted on special Ford driving licences. The car had only two forward gears, separate pedals with which to engage forward and reverse gears, a handbrake that also activated the clutch and a crank start that was capable of dislocating a man's wrist.

There were few concessions to styling, and between 1914 and 1925 there was not even a choice of colour – hence Ford's famous saying: 'You can have one in any color you want, so long as it is black.' And yet by 1927,

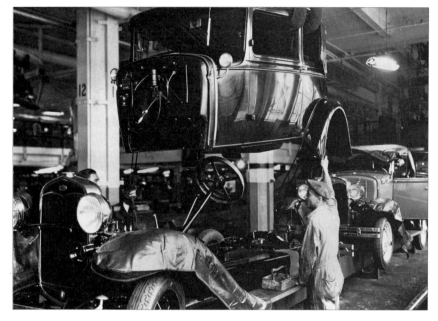

**All lined up** *Ford introduced the moving assembly line to his Model T factory in 1913. Here, workers supervise the lowering of the coachwork onto the chassis – once the chassis was bolted on, the car was finished.*

when the last Model T was made, Ford's dream had long since become reality. Over 15 million of the car had been sold in the United States and another 1.5 million in Canada and Britain. By bringing the means of private transport to the common man, Ford had permanently transformed the lifestyle of millions.

The Tin Lizzie, as the Model T was affectionately known, boasted many technological advances: the body was built of vanadium steel, which is stronger and more shock-resistant than ordinary steel; it had a relatively smooth 'crash-free' gearing system; and the car's special engine suspension gave it the ability to travel the rough American highways without suffering serious damage

to the chassis. It was also the first American car to have left-hand drive.

The secret of Ford's success lay in the introduction of the moving assembly line in his factories. This reduced the time taken to produce the chassis of a Model T from 728 to 93 minutes. At the peak of production a chassis was rolling off the line every 24 seconds. In 1922, one million Model Ts were built and in 1924 the number rose to over 2 million – a record figure for annual production that lasted for 32 years.

## DID YOU KNOW..?

*A ONE-OFF attempt at car safety, the US-built* Sir Vival *of 1960 featured separate engine and passenger compartments, rubber bumpers, a raised driver seat and a swivelling third headlight.*

## BUMPER TO BUMPER

HAVE YOU ever wondered what would happen if all the cars in a country were out on the road at the same time? Divide the total length of a nation's roads by the number of registered vehicles and you arrive at some terrifying statistics.

Italy boasts the world's most crowded roads. Drivers there would, in theory, have only 13 m (43 ft) of clear road before they bumped into the car in front. The second most congested

country is Germany, where motorists would have just slightly more room at 17 m (56 ft).

Even in the wide open spaces of the USA, the statistics are no more encouraging. There are just under 30 m (98 ft) of highway for every American vehicle. One of the few places in the Western world where the driver still has plenty of road space is Ireland. The fortunate Irish motorist has a whole 111 m (364 ft) of road to call his or her own.

# THE CAR OF THE CENTURY

## What makes a Rolls-Royce so special?

THE FIRST Rolls-Royce motor car, produced in 1904, had a two-cylinder, 1.8-litre engine. Just three years later, the firm produced the Silver Ghost, which had a *six*-cylinder, *seven*-litre engine. This model was considered to be the last word in reliability and smoothness. In a publicity stunt designed to demonstrate the car's reliability, it completed a world record 23 127 km (14 371 miles) of continuous driving without breaking down. In 1987, the Rolls-Royce Phantom VI became the world's most expensive production car. It now costs £350 000 (more than US $550 000) for the 'basic' model.

### THE FLYING LADY

The Rolls-Royce mascot, the silver flying lady or Spirit of Ecstasy, has never been made from solid silver. The Phantom of 1910 had a silver-plated mascot; since then it has been made of copper, zinc and nickel alloys, and more recently of stainless steel. The mascot was created after a craze started in 1910, when Rolls-Royce owners placed their own mascots such as a black cat, a golliwog and a policeman on their venerable vehicles. Since 1911, nearly every Rolls-Royce radiator has borne the Spirit of Ecstasy. A notable exception, however, is Queen Elizabeth II's ceremonial Rolls-Royce, which carries a steel figurine of St George slaying the dragon.

### IS THE ENGINE RUNNING?

In the 1950s, the most famous Rolls-Royce advertisement of all proclaimed: 'At 60 miles an hour the loudest noise in this new Rolls-Royce [the Silver Cloud] comes from the electric clock.' However, 40 years earlier, in 1910, two experiments had already proved that Rolls-Royce engines were remarkably smooth-running. In the first experiment, three glasses full to the brim with ink were placed on a sheet of paper on the bonnet of a Rolls-Royce. The engine ran for four minutes at 1150 rpm. A camera with its shutter open was pointed at the glasses, exposing the film for the whole four minutes. Not a single drop

**Safety-conscious lady** *To prevent serious injury in an accident, Rolls-Royce Silver Spirit and Silver Spur cars built since 1980 have a special mechanism that pulls the statuette of the flying lady into the car's body at the slightest impact.*

of ink was spilled, and a crystal-clear photograph testified to the total absence of vibration. In the second experiment, a penny was balanced on its edge on a Rolls-Royce radiator cap. The engine ran for two minutes, but the coin, to everyone's amazement, remained standing.

### BEAUTY OR BEAST

The most notorious 'Rolls-Royce' was the 'Beast', built by flamboyant English businessman John Dodd in the late 1970s. It was actually not a Rolls-Royce at all. Dodd justified the use of the world's most coveted brand name by fitting a 27-litre Rolls-Royce Merlin 61 aero engine under his customised car's 4.3 m (14 ft) long bonnet. Apart from that, he added two of the famous Rolls-Royce trademarks, the Spirit of Ecstasy and the radiator.

Although it was never proved, the 'Beast' was reputed to be the fastest car ever to travel on the public highway, at speeds of over 320 km/h (200 mph). Its engine was the same as those used to power the Spitfires that fought in the Second World War.

Rolls-Royce were outraged, and turned to their lawyers. The 'Beast', totally unreliable in traffic, constantly broke down on its way to court, and the publicity-seeking Dodd once arrived on a horse. However, Dodd eventually lost the case, and in 1983 fled to Spain. The 'Beast' went with him, but without the famous Rolls-Royce insignia.

***Rolls in a Royce*** *Car manufacturer Charles Rolls sits at the wheel of one of the three models designed by the enterprising electrical engineer Henry Royce in 1904. Rolls was so impressed with the quality of the car that he agreed to take Royce's entire output and to sell his cars under the name Rolls-Royce.*

# FOUR-WHEELED CINDERELLA

### The 'ugly' car that sold 21 million worldwide

***Dictator's dream*** *In May 1938, Hitler inspected one of the first Volkswagens. But his 'people's car' was not mass-produced until after the war – the Volkswagen factory made military vehicles instead.*

'THE VEHICLE does not meet the fundamental technical requirements … its performance and qualities have no attraction for the average buyer. It is too ugly and too noisy. Such a car can, if at all, only be popular for two to three years at the most.' This was the opinion of the British commission set up at the end of the Second World War to report on the future of the German car manufacturers' principal product, the Volkswagen.

The Americans agreed, with their own derisory conclusion: 'It isn't worth anything.' Twenty-seven years later the car, long since known as the Beetle, had passed the legendary Model T Ford's sales figure of over 15 million vehicles.

The idea for the Volkswagen, or 'people's car', originated in May 1934 at a meeting between Adolf Hitler and Ferdinand Porsche, a designer better known today for his luxury cars. Hitler, who had always been passionately interested in cars, envisaged the 'people's car' as a propaganda vehicle. He stipulated that the Volkswagen must carry two parents and three children,

achieve at least 8.3 litre/100 km (35 mpg) and cruise at 100 km/h (60 mph). It also had to sell at 1000 Reichsmarks (about $400 at the time), an unrealistically low price that was made possible by heavy sponsorship from the car industry – at Hitler's command.

But Hitler never saw the Volkswagen become the 'people's car' he dreamed of. German citizens were encouraged to pay instalments on cars, but never received them. Until the end of the war the factory built only military vehicles. The money went into the government's coffers. By the end of the war Hitler was dead, and the Volkswagen plant had been reduced almost to rubble.

### Postwar success

While the Allies initially revived production of the vehicle they spurned the chance to invest in it, and Volkswagen passed back into German hands. Its domestic success contributed to the revival of the German economy. But the links with Hitler, and the car's unconventional shape, made the market for exporting the vehicle very limited.

## DID YOU KNOW..?

*THE WORLD'S most durable car is a diesel-engined 1957 Mercedes-Benz 180D, which travelled 1 906 879 km (1 184 880 miles) in 21 years – the equivalent of five times the distance to the Moon.*

The breakthrough was achieved in 1959 when a US advertising agency chose the name 'Beetle' and began a hugely successful advertising campaign. They focused on the consumer benefits of the car's small size (previously seen as a disadvantage in the USA) and on its air-cooled engine, which made it extremely reliable. The Beetle became America's leading imported car and remained so for many years, providing the capital for Volkswagen's conquest of other world markets.

Today, more than 50 years and 21 million vehicles since the first Volkswagen, vintage Beetles are avidly collected.

323

## KEEP ON TRUCKING

I N THE SPACE of a year, American truckers may travel 800 000 km (500 000 miles) in their 18-wheel 'big rigs' – the equivalent of driving round the world more than 20 times.

The speed limit in the USA is between 88 and 104 km/h (55–65 mph) and a coast-to-coast journey can be 5000 km (3000 miles) each way. So truckers often work in pairs: one sleeps while the other drives. Husband-and-wife teams are not uncommon.

Many trucks have a specially designed living space attached to the back of the driver's cabin. These 'sleepers' can be up to 3 m (10 ft) high and 2.4 m (8 ft) square. Their fittings may include a television, cooking facilities, shower, toilet and bed. The trucks' fuel consumption is enormous too: a large rig uses 30 litres of diesel per 100 km (9 mpg).

Truckers are a breed apart. Spending so much time on the road away from their families creates enormous stress, so they have developed their own trucker community, conversing on CB radio and meeting at the many truck stops that dot American highways. They have even developed their own language. For instance, a policeman is known as a 'bear', the brakes are called 'anchors' and small cars are known as 'roller skates'. When a truck carrying dangerous cargo overtakes a small car, it is referred to as a 'suicide jockey blowing the doors off a roller skate'.

# STRETCHING LUXURY TO THE LIMIT
### Customised limousines that will never see the open road

I F YOU HAVE money to burn and want a truly luxurious customised car, you can approach one of the specialised limousine stretching businesses that flourish around Los Angeles and order a fully-fitted hotel suite on wheels, complete with a swimming pool in the boot.

The urge to transform a standard factory-built car into a personalised vehicle unlike anything else on the road became an integral part of American culture after the Second World War. Do-it-yourself customising techniques have usually aimed at creating cars that look fast, mean and dangerous, but some rich drivers have gone in for limousines that realise the wildest fantasies of Hollywood.

### Dream boat

Competition to create the world's longest and most absurdly luxurious car is keen, even though US law does not allow cars over 13 m (42 ft) in length to be driven on public roads. The title was formerly claimed by the aptly named *American Dream*, built by Jay Ohrberg

Show Cars of Newport Beach, California. This was a Cadillac stretched to 18 m (59 ft), which had 50 passenger seats and a swimming pool.

Even the fabulous *American Dream* is dwarfed by another 50-seater customised Cadillac, the *Hollywood Dream*, bought secondhand in 1988 by Kenji Kawamuda, the owner of a sports and health centre near Osaka, Japan. When he was shown the car while visiting Australia, Kawamuda realised that a 22-wheeled leisure complex might attract new customers to his sports centre. So he bought the car for about US $750 000, had it cut in two to ship it back to Japan, and now keeps the reassembled car on permanent display at his centre. He has since recovered much of his outlay by charging visitors to look round it.

Powered by an 8-litre engine, the car is 20 m (66 ft) long and houses a cinema, a TV lounge, a cocktail bar and a bedroom that sleeps four. The impressive outdoor facilities include a swimming pool, a hot tub and a one-hole golf course on the roof.

**A car to live in** *With its helipad, satellite dish, bedroom, bar, whirlpool bath and swimming pool, the 16-wheeled stretched Cadillac known as the* American Dream *can provide every possible convenience of modern life – except space.*

# A VISION OF THE FUTURE

*Why did the American dream car fail?*

IN JUNE 1947, Preston Tucker, a former racing car engineer from Ypsilanti, Michigan, boasted to the American nation that he was about to introduce the first completely new car in 50 years, the Tucker '48.

With this announcement he immediately caught the public's imagination. Even today the Tucker '48's sleek body lines are regarded as classic; it stands only 1.5 m (5 ft) high on a 3.3 m (10 ft 6 in) wheelbase, and it was 30 mm (2 in) longer than the largest Cadillac then made.

The Tucker '48 was a revolutionary design. Gone were standard parts such as clutch, transmission and differential. The wheels were to be driven direct from the rear-mounted engine by means of a revolutionary form of automatic transmission that would give an infinitely smoother ride than any other car on the market. The car's safety features were also innovatory, with disc brakes (not common until the 1950s), a rounded windscreen, a padded dashboard and an 'uncrushable' front passenger compartment.

Other unique features included three headlights, which automatically dimmed when another car approached, and an engine capable of propelling it at a cruising speed of 160 km/h (100 mph), yet using no more than 8.3 litres per 100 km (35 mpg). All this for $1800; no wonder Tucker had a reputed 300 000 advance orders.

Tucker was a natural salesman. He quickly raised over $25 million in funding and sponsorships, and the Tucker became a household name.

## Government probe

But things began to turn sour when it became obvious that despite all the promises, Tucker was not actually producing the cars. The US Government Securities and Exchange Commission

*Night vision Long before safety became a major selling point, the Tucker '48 had many innovatory safety features. For example, a third headlight, directed by the steering wheel, improved vision at night.*

became suspicious and consequently opened an investigation. By the end of 1948, a meagre $2 million of the investors' money was left. There were a few cars in various stages of completion on the production line, but far from being originals, they used the body and engine of the Oldsmobile and the Cord – motor cars made by rival manufacturers.

## The end of the dream

The commission came to the conclusion that, as the finished car would differ materially from that described in the fund-raising prospectus (principally because of the engine), Tucker was committing fraud, and he was forced into liquidation.

Four months after the commission's decision, Tucker appealed and was acquitted. Nevertheless, his dream was over. Only a few of the 50 Tucker '48s that were made are running today. They still make heads turn. And so they should: they cost $510 000 each to produce in 1948.

---

## THE FORMULA ONE PHOENIX

AT KYALAMI stadium in March 1977, Austrian racing driver Niki Lauda won the South African Formula One Grand Prix. Yet eight months before, Lauda, the reigning world champion, had been pulled from his blazing car at the Nürburgring track during the 1976 German Grand Prix. He had suffered multiple injuries, including severe burns. No one had expected him to survive, and he had been given the last rites.

That Lauda did survive was due mainly to his indomitable will. After just six weeks he put his physical and mental scarring behind him, and stepped back into a Formula One racing car. He completed a remarkable season by winning, of all races, the German Grand Prix (although this time at the Hockenheim circuit). Lauda went on to become the 1977 world champion. He retired the following year, only to return to the racing track in 1982. To crown it all, he completed a remarkable hat-trick in 1984 by winning the world championship for a third time.

# THE WAY AHEAD

### The search for an alternative to petrol

O N NOVEMBER 1, 1987, 25 of the strangest-looking vehicles ever seen in Australia rolled into Darwin. They were about to take part in the world's first transcontinental race for solar-powered cars. When the 'space-age' *Sunraycer* crossed the finishing line in Adelaide five days and 3060 km (1900 miles) later, it was hailed as a major turning point in the quest for an alternative to petrol as the fuel of the future.

General Motors' US $15 million investment in *Sunraycer* shows how serious the leading motor manufacturers are about finding an alternative fuel. As the Earth's natural fuel resources decline and concern grows about the detrimental effects that traditional fuels have on the environment, the race to find new, cleaner sources of energy has begun in earnest.

### Welcome sunshine

At first glance, solar power looks to be the cheapest, cleanest and most inexhaustible option. However, the technology is still too expensive for the average motorist: the *Sunraycer*'s 27 kg (60 lb) battery alone costs $10 000. Moreover, during the race the car's performance depended heavily on how much solar energy its battery could accumulate during its two-hour recharging period each morning; if the weather had been poor, the *Sunraycer* might not have performed so well.

Electric vehicles have had their advocates ever since an electrically powered car became the first car to break the 100 km/h (60 mph) barrier in 1899. Research shows that electric vehicles are quieter and emit less pollution, but few can travel farther

**Solar power** *Highly aerodynamic in design, the* Sunraycer *is powered by solar energy derived from 9500 solar cells covering an area of 27 m² (90 sq ft).*

than 80 km (50 miles) without recharging the battery, and it will be many years before more efficient types of battery are available. Scientists are trying to develop a car that can run partly on batteries, partly on electricity generated by solar energy. But the lead-acid battery that would be necessary to provide adequate range would itself weigh about half as much as a small car.

### Weighing the costs

Alternative combustion fuels are also being considered. But hydrogen, for example, though clean and plentiful, is expensive to extract (from natural gas, coal or water) and, as it is highly flammable, difficult to handle. Compared to fossil fuels, oxygenated fuels such as ethanol and methanol release fewer of the chemicals that cause acid rain. But they release other harmful gases that contribute to the 'greenhouse effect', the gradual increase in the Earth's temperature that could imperil the world's fragile ecosystems. Methanol also melts soldered joints in fuel tanks.

All in all, it looks as if we are stuck with petrol for the foreseeable future.

**Featherlight frame** *Weighing less than 7 kg (15 lb), the* Sunraycer's *aluminium chassis helps to increase efficiency while being strong enough to support the car's gross weight of almost 270 kg (600 lb).*

# GULPING AND SIPPING

## The world's hungriest and most frugal vehicles

THE US space shuttle, a revolutionary combination of aircraft, launch vehicle and spacecraft, is the most powerful vehicle on Earth. Its three main engines are capable of delivering enough thrust to drive seven and a half jumbo jets. The liquid hydrogen and oxygen fuel for these engines is housed in an external tank that holds 2 million litres (440 000 gallons). Each engine is more powerful than the entire *Atlas* rocket that put John Glenn into space in 1962, when he became the first American astronaut to orbit the Earth. Together with two giant rocket boosters, the engines can lift the shuttle to an altitude of 45 km (28 miles) within two minutes of takeoff. By this time the craft is travelling at 4800 km/h (3000 mph) and devouring more than 234 000 litres (51 500 gallons) of fuel every minute. After eight minutes, most of the primary fuel supply has been used, but by this time the shuttle is in orbit. The external tank is jettisoned, and is destroyed as it re-enters the Earth's atmosphere.

### Frugal flyer

Compared with the shuttle, the Boeing 747 – the undisputed king of the airways – is a modest consumer. The jumbo jet, which weighs 340 tonnes with a full load of nearly 500 passengers, is about the same size as the shuttle's orbiter, but with a fuel capacity of 203 900 litres (44 850 gallons), its tanks hold only just over a tenth of the fuel carried by the shuttle. The 747's fuel consumption is also moderate by comparison, amounting to a mere 207 litres (45 gallons) per minute at the maximum cruising speed of 920 km/h (570 mph).

### Least thirsty of all

Down on the ground, even the world's largest trucks, such as the Peterbilt giants of the United States, are moderation itself when compared with their airborne cousins. Despite carrying loads of up to a third the weight of a fully laden Boeing 747, they can achieve about 30 litres per 100 km (9 mpg). And at the very bottom of the scale, the prototype Volkswagen *Okopolo* positively sips at its petrol. To save fuel, this frugal little car turns off its engine when the driver takes his foot off the accelerator or when the engine management system decides no more power is required, and turns it back on when the driver puts his foot down again on the accelerator. The *Okopolo*'s rate of diesel consumption is a mere 1.7 litres per 100 km (162 mpg).

*Letting off steam Leaving behind huge clouds of exhaust fumes, a US space shuttle climbs towards orbit after takeoff from the Kennedy Space Center in Florida.*

---

## THE TOUGHEST CAR RALLY IN THE WORLD

ON NEW YEAR'S DAY 1988, more than 600 cars, motorcycles and trucks gathered at the Palace of Versailles outside Paris for the start of the annual Paris–Dakar Rally – the toughest race in the world. Ahead of the competitors lay about 14 000 km (8700 miles) of some of the world's most desolate terrain, taking them across France and Spain, and down through the blazing heat of the Sahara to Senegal in northwest Africa, by which time more than 60 000 litres (13 200 gallons) of diesel and 40 000 litres (8800 gallons) of petrol will have been consumed.

For this, the tenth annual rally, the organisers had determined to make the already notorious course more gruelling than ever. They were tragically successful.

By the time the victor, Juha Kankkunen of Finland, had crossed the finishing line on the beach in Dakar three weeks later, the event had claimed the lives of six competitors and spectators and had left a number of others seriously injured.

### Braving the dunes

The death toll led to a stepping-up of safety precautions. The rally, however, will always be treacherous. There may be rescue teams standing by, but drivers must still battle with such hazards as 18 m (60 ft) sand dunes, blinding sandstorms and daytime temperatures averaging 27°C (80°F). Some of the most dangerous driving is on *fech-fech*, a hard crust of sand with deeper soft sand below: driving on it is like skating on thin ice. In 1988, 150 competitors abandoned the race on the fourth day after getting stuck in *fech-fech*.

Among the innumerable dangers that each driver faces is the risk of sand blocking the car's radiator and causing the engine to overheat. Another problem is the difficulty of finding reference points on which the eye can focus while driving for hours across the desert sands. One entrant described driving for minutes on end at speeds of 190 km/h (120 mph) with his eyes completely shut.

Even though the rally's safety precautions are now better than ever, with flying doctors and in-car emergency radios, the Paris–Dakar rally still deserves its reputation as the world's most gruelling race.

# THE AUTOGUIDE

## How tomorrow's motorists will get from A to B

**I**MAGINE yourself driving along a road in the centre of a major city. As you approach an important junction, a display panel on the dashboard tells you which way to turn to reach your destination. It warns you visually that there is traffic congestion ahead. The display panel shows you a diagram of the road layout and indicates the best alternative route to avoid the traffic jam. This is the Autoguide, the driver's guidance system of the future.

The system is currently being tested in Berlin and London, and by the end of the century it could be in regular use throughout Europe. Cars participating in the tests are each equipped with a computer that receives up-to-the-minute information about routes and
•traffic conditions from a network of electronic beacons along the roadside.

***Route guidance*** *To use the Autoguide, the driver simply enters his destination on a handheld control unit. An in-car transceiver continually transmits the car's location – established with the help of a magnetic sensor – to roadside beacons which receive*

These beacons transmit a 'map' to the Autoguide's computer, which decodes it and on a digital screen displays the best route to the driver, together with detailed guidance at each junction. One Autoguide prototype even gives verbal instructions with a synthesised voice. Motorists have only to enter their destination into the Autoguide at the beginning of the journey and then follow its advice. The system might also assist public transport by, for instance, pinpointing the location of the vehicles in a bus fleet.

The Autoguide's advocates say it will help improve road safety and reduce fuel consumption by preventing unnecessary detours on unfamiliar journeys. But the biggest beneficiary would be the daily commuter, who would face less congestion, less aggravation and shorter journey times.

*traffic and route information from a control centre. The beacons transmit the information to an in-car microcomputer, called a processor, which decodes it. The driver then sees detailed route instructions on the car's display unit.*

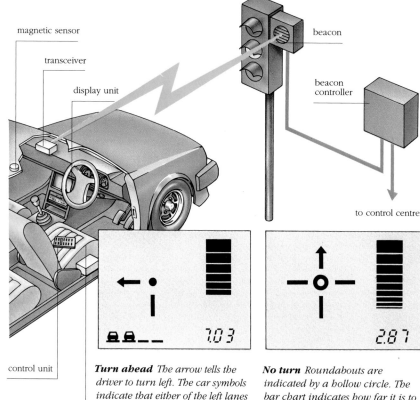

magnetic sensor

transceiver

display unit

control unit

processor

beacon

beacon controller

to control centre

***Turn ahead*** *The arrow tells the driver to turn left. The car symbols indicate that either of the left lanes may be used. The figure is the distance to the destination.*

***No turn*** *Roundabouts are indicated by a hollow circle. The bar chart indicates how far it is to the roundabout, where the driver must continue ahead.*

# BUILDING BRIDGES

## Record-breaking spans around the world

**T**HROUGHOUT history, man has been a builder of bridges. From the simple log across a stream came the basic girder design still used for many bridges. And the circular arch principle developed by the Romans is the basis of even such sophisticated structures as the Sydney Harbour Bridge in Australia, whose 49 m (160 ft) width is greater than that of any other long span bridge.

The world's longest bridge is the second of the two Lake Pontchartrain Causeways, completed in 1969. Linking Lewisburg and Metairie in Louisiana, USA, it is 38 km (24 miles) long.

The central span of the Humber Bridge in northeast England is the longest of any suspension bridge. The structure hangs from two 162 m (532 ft) towers, which are 1410 m (4626 ft) apart at the base, but are 36 mm ($1^3/8$ in) further apart at the top because of the curvature of the Earth.

By the end of this century, the projected Akashi–Kaikyo Bridge in Japan will be longer than the Humber Bridge; it will be a suspension bridge whose main span will be 1980 m (6496 ft) long. There are also plans for a bridge over the Strait of Messina connecting Sicily to the Italian mainland. Its single span will be 3320 m (10 892 ft).

### Connecting continents

Another astounding project at drawing board stage is a bridge that would link Europe and Africa across the narrowest part of the Strait of Gibraltar. Planned by a Swiss engineer, Urs Meier, the structure would be made entirely from reinforced plastic and have a central span of colossal length: 8400 m (27 600 ft).

---

### DID YOU KNOW..?

*THE WORLD'S longest rail tunnel is the Seikan tunnel in Japan, linking the islands of Honshu and Hokkaido. It is 54 km (34 miles) long and runs 100 m (328 ft) below the seabed of the Tsugaru Strait. The longest road tunnel is the St Gotthard tunnel in Switzerland, which was opened in 1980 and runs for 16 km (10 miles) under the Swiss Alps.*

*chapter ten*

# MASTERS *of* THEIR ART

THE 15TH-CENTURY Italian artist Andrea Mantegna would probably be astonished to know that coachloads of 20th-century tourists queue up every day to view his painted room of illusions, the *Camera degli Sposi* in Mantua (*page 367*). This masterwork was typical of the Renaissance: an unabashed celebration of the world in the form of a painstaking imitation of it. Today Mantegna's achievements – and those of all the artists, writers, musicians, dancers, craftsmen and sports heroes who preceded and followed him – continue to entertain and surprise us.

# ALL THE WORLD'S A STAGE

## *The magic of the theatre – in words and painted canvas*

**T**HE AUDIENCE is hushed; the curtain rises. It reveals a brilliant set: a crowded street scene in Renaissance Venice, perhaps; or the drawing room of an English country house. At once, as the action begins, the audience is transported to that place, the lifelike sets helping to create and sustain the illusion that what is happening on the stage is real.

Although Western drama has existed for more than 2500 years, scenery, as we know it today, is a relatively recent innovation. Greek and Roman actors performed against a background of pillars and porticoes, but the scene was stylised and unchanging. Sets designed to suit each play were first seen at the courts of the great Italian princes of the Renaissance. In 16th-century Italy, it became fashionable to put plays on indoors, on what we now think of as a conventional stage – a box with one side missing. Artists and architects provided painted backdrops and wings that created the illusion of a three-dimensional scene.

In other countries, however, theatre remained an outdoor entertainment. The stage at Shakespeare's

**Open-air entertainment** *The theatre of Dionysus, built in about 330 BC at the foot of the Acropolis in Athens, was an outdoor structure. A semicircular dancing ground called the orchestra separated the audience from the stage.*

**Exposed art** *A modern production at the Young Vic in London aims to recreate the intimate contact between the players and the audience of the theatre of Shakespeare's day.*

Globe, for example, thrust out into the audience. As scenery would have interfered with the audience's view of the action, scene-setting was achieved through costume, a few simple props, and careful mention of location in the actors' speeches. Only in the second half of the 17th century, decades after Shakespeare's death, did English theatre begin to follow the Italian fashion for lavish sets. Yet Shakespeare was very much a success in his own time, proof enough that great poetry and acting can draw an audience into the world of the dramatist just as effectively as a breathtaking set.

## DID YOU KNOW..?

*THE OLDEST known play is a religious drama written in ancient Egypt in 3200 BC – more than 5000 years ago. It tells the powerful story of the murder of the god Osiris by his evil brother Seth. Osiris's body is cut up and scattered over a wide area, but his wife Isis and his son Horus gather the pieces together and the dead god is resurrected. The play ends with the crowning of Horus as king of Egypt. The text of this drama was discovered by archaeologists on a papyrus at Luxor (ancient Thebes) in 1895.*

# QUICK TO THE PUNCH
*The origins of the theatre of Punch and Judy*

THE KNOCKABOUT farce of a Punch and Judy show delights the child in all of us, young or old. But an adult spectator can hardly help be struck by how strange a children's entertainment this is, in which the hero strangles his child, beats his wife to death, hangs the hangman, and often sees off the Devil himself.

No one is absolutely certain of Mr Punch's origins, but his true ancestor seems to be an Italian puppet, Pulcinella, created by comedian Silvio Fiorillo around 1600. It took another 60 years for Pulcinella to migrate to England as the hump-backed, hook-nosed puppet Punchinello, soon abbreviated to Punch.

The famous diarist Samuel Pepys first saw Mr Punch in London's Covent Garden in 1662 and recorded his enthusiasm for a puppet play that was 'the best that ever I saw'. Many other people must have thought the same, for Punch was summoned to appear at court before King Charles II that same year. Once established, his popularity was never seriously to wane.

### Entertaining violence

The search for the meaning of Punch's violent exploits has provoked some wild speculations. It was once seriously suggested, for instance, that Punch represented Pontius Pilate and Judy was Judas Iscariot, in a Christian allegory.

But probably it is all just violent, anarchic fun, irresistible as many things in the worst possible taste are. Certainly, however many million times Punch has killed his Judy over the last 300 years, there is no sign of her giving up the ghost for good.

***Fun figure*** *The hook-nosed Pulcinella, here dressed in his typical apparel, was a familiar character in the commedia dell'arte, the Italian comic theatre of the 17th century.*

## DID YOU KNOW..?

*THE WORD 'tragedy' comes from the Greek for a goat (*tragos*) and a song (*ode*), so it literally means 'goat-song'. This name for the drama either refers to an early custom of sacrificing a goat on stage at the climax of the performance, or to the goat skins worn by the satyrs who appeared in the Dionysian rites that were the forerunners of Greek theatrical drama.*

# A SINGULAR SUCCESS
*The effort behind a record-breaking one-man show*

IT IS JANUARY 16, 1967. In the space of a mere three hours, a smooth-faced 44-year-old turns into a shrivelled septuagenarian – and the 17th-century historian and gossip John Aubrey lives again. But this is not black magic; it is simply the magic of modern stage make-up.

This is the first night of Roy Dotrice's one-man show *Brief Lives* – adapted from Aubrey's biographical sketches of eminent people – at the Hampstead Theatre Club in London. Dotrice is undergoing a painful process involving large quantities of latex, a false nose, blacked-out teeth, a bald pate and false whiskers. He will spend just two hours on stage, followed by a further hour to remove his make-up.

A three-hour make-up session is not a record by the standards of the film industry: it took 20 hours to prepare Rod Steiger for his lead role in *The Illustrated Man* in 1969; his whole body had to be covered with mock tattoos.

However, Steiger did not have to endure the ordeal night after night. Dotrice did: between 1967 and 1974 he portrayed Aubrey no less than 1700 times, with performances in London's West End, on New York's Broadway and on a world tour. In doing so, he broke the record for the greatest number of one-man shows. Dotrice took so long to make up for his role that he spent twice as much time in the chair (equivalent to 850 eight-hour days in total) as he did on stage.

## HARDLY TIME TO BREATHE

IF YOU WENT to see the world's shortest play, you would hardly have time to sit down before it was time to go home again. For *Breath*, by Samuel Beckett, lasts just 35 seconds.

*Breath* does away with such theatrical conventions as dialogue, plot or actors. The play's stage directions run to only 120 words. The curtain rises on a stage strewn with rubbish, and the only 'action' consists of lighting effects and a soundtrack that starts with the cry of a newborn child, followed by a 10-second breath in, a 10-second breath out, and ends with the cry of a dying person.

Beckett wrote the play in 1969, as a contribution to Kenneth Tynan's controversial revue, *Oh! Calcutta*. But Tynan altered Beckett's script without telling him. Beckett was so annoyed that he called Tynan a 'liar' and a 'cheat'. What was it that made him so furious? Beckett discovered that Tynan had staged the play using actors. Whether he was also upset by the fact that all the actors were naked, we shall probably never know.

# THE BARD FACTS

*How many words does the Prince of Denmark speak?*

THE NEXT TIME you see a production of Shakespeare's *Hamlet*, you could spare a thought for the prince. In this, the longest of the bard's plays, the actor playing the hero has to speak 1530 lines – a total of 11 610 words. By comparison, *Comedy of Errors*, Shakespeare's shortest play, is only 1778 lines long, less than half the length of *Hamlet* (3931 lines).

Between about 1590 and 1610, Shakespeare wrote over 100 000 lines of drama and brought to life 1277 characters, major and minor. His vocabulary was one of the richest of any English writer. There are over 30 000 different words used in his works, double the average vocabulary for an educated individual in the late 20th century.

Nearly half Shakespeare's plays were individually published during his lifetime in 'quarto' format – about half the size of a modern magazine. The source of these texts was often pirated scripts or notes hastily scribbled during a performance, and they were hopelessly inaccurate. A quarto *Hamlet* contains the immortal line: 'To be or not to be, I there's the point.' Fortunately, seven years after Shakespeare's death in 1616, his friends produced an accurate collected edition of his plays, the First Folio, which has been the basis for most subsequent performing editions.

### Doubts about authorship

Some critics still refuse to believe that a mere actor, educated at a grammar school in the English midlands, with 'small Latin, and less Greek', could have written such powerful plays. All or part of his work has at various times been attributed to a whole range of possible alternative authors, including the Earl of Oxford, the philosopher Francis Bacon and an Elizabethan nun.

In soberly realistic terms, it has to be admitted that Shakespeare's plays are packed with anachronisms and

*Alas, poor Yorick!* Hamlet, here played by the British actor Laurence Olivier in a 1948 film, ruminates on the fact that death will reduce man to dust.

*Helping hand This cartoon from the early 20th century shows Shakespeare receiving assistance from Francis Bacon, allegedly one of the real authors of Shakespeare's plays.*

minor absurdities. For instance, a clock strikes in ancient Rome, ten centuries before clocks were invented, and Cleopatra plays billiards. In *A Winter's Tale,* a ship lands on the coast of Bohemia – a totally landlocked country. And in *King Lear*, the Duke of Gloucester, supposedly a pre-Christian nobleman, talks of 'spectacles', although eyeglasses were not used in Britain before AD 1400.

But all this counts for nothing. Shakespeare is apparently indestructible: his plays are performed more than those of any other playwright in the history of the world, and are as popular today as at any time in the last 400 years. He was truly, as his contemporary Ben Jonson wrote, 'not of an age, but for all time!'

## WILL'S LAST WILL

BY THE TIME Shakespeare died – on his 52nd birthday, April 23, 1616 – he was a prosperous man, as his will bears witness. His bequest to his eldest daughter Susanna, for instance, included 'all my barnes, stables, orchards, gardens, landes, tenementes and hereditamentes ...'.

But for his wife Anne Hathaway there was only one mention in the will: 'Item: I give unto my wife the second best bed with the furniture.' Did this reveal a lack of marital love? Probably not. As Shakespeare's widow, Anne would have received a substantial inheritance as of right, which did not need to be specified. And the 'second best bed' would have been the couple's lifelong marriage bed, the best bed being reserved for guests. So perhaps it was a touching love-token after all.

Completely absent from the will is any reference to Shakespeare's great legacy of plays or poems. With no law of copyright, the works belonged to no one and had no monetary value.

## DID YOU KNOW..?

MACBETH *is considered an unlucky play because it is traditionally believed that the text includes a real black magic spell. Actors always avoid referring to the play by name, calling it 'the Scottish play' instead, and they never quote from it in the dressing room.*

# THE ROSE AND THE GLOBE
## The buoyant theatre scene in Shakespeare's London

I N 1599, near the end of the reign of Queen Elizabeth I, a German visitor to London noted the flourishing theatrical scene: 'daily at two in the afternoon,' he reported, 'London has two, sometimes three plays running in different places, competing with each other, and those which play best obtain most spectators.' There were plenty of spectators to compete for: in 1605 about 21 000 stage-struck Londoners went to the theatre every week – roughly one in ten of the city's population.

Rather like today's television audience, the Elizabethans expected to see new plays all the time, creating an enormous demand for playwrights to meet. William Shakespeare was one of the most successful dramatists of his day (as well as being an accomplished actor and part-owner of the most prestigious London theatre, the Globe). But his output of 37 plays in little over 20 years, impressively prolific by modern standards, pales into insignificance beside some of his contemporaries, such as Thomas Heywood who claimed to have been involved in the writing of no less than 220 plays.

As theatre was frowned on by the City of London authorities, playhouses were built outside the City limits, eventually congregating near Southwark, on the south bank of the river Thames. On this Elizabethan version of Broadway, the Rose was founded in 1587, and its famous rival, the Globe, 12 years later.

### Stand or sit
By the standards of the time, these playhouses were massive structures – the Globe could hold an audience of about 2000 – but most of the stage was open to the sky, so rain was liable to stop the play. The spectators sat in a circle of galleries three storeys high or stood in front of the stage. As the German visitor related, where you stood or sat depended on how much you could afford: 'For whoever cares to stand below only pays one English penny, but if he wishes to sit he enters by another door, and pays another penny. . ..' Prices went up to sixpence for the most exclusive gallery seats in the 'lords' rooms'.

### The power of words
With the mob of 'groundlings' – those who had paid only one penny – swarming in front of the stage and the sophisticates in their finery chattering in the galleries, the atmosphere of a Shakespearean playhouse was very different from that of theatre today. To hold the attention of this socially diverse and excitable crowd, the players could call on only a very limited – although very effective – range of props or special effects. The stage was bare for much of the action, and the success or failure of a play depended almost entirely on the magic of words. Fortunately, although most of the groundlings were illiterate, they were intensely responsive to verbal wit and magnificence of language.

On occasion, however, the theatre could be exciting in more unpredictable ways. In 1613 the Globe was burned down after a cannon, fired as a special effect, ignited thatched roofing over the stage. Only one man was hurt – his breeches caught fire, but he poured beer over them to douse the flames.

---

### DID YOU KNOW..?

*IN 1787, at the Richmond Theatre near London,* Hamlet *was performed without Hamlet, when the actor supposed to play the prince proved too nervous to appear. Novelist Sir Walter Scott was in the audience – and found that most spectators thought the play improved by the absence of the melancholy hero.*

❋ ❋ ❋

*IN ACTOR-manager Herbert Beerbohm Tree's painstakingly realistic 1900 production of* A Midsummer Night's Dream *in London, there were flowering shrubs, a carpet of real grass and rabbits running around the stage.*

---

*Global reconstruction A look inside a model of the Globe Theatre, now being reconstructed on London's Bankside, reveals a stage partly covered by a large canopy, an open courtyard and covered galleries.*

# THE WHOLE WORLD IN A FAN

*Unlocking the secret of Japan's traditional theatre*

THE CULTURE of Japan has produced two startlingly original forms of theatre – Noh and Kabuki. Noh, the older of the two, has continued almost unchanged for the last 600 years. The founders of the tradition, Kannami Kiyotsugu and his son Zeami Motokiyo, refined their theatrical style to suit the taste of the fastidious Japanese aristocracy, which had turned even such everyday activities as tea drinking and flower arranging into an elegant artistic performance.

As a consequence, Noh is a minimal spectacle, more a ritual than a drama, with every movement and intonation formalised and fixed for all time. There is little spoken dialogue and no scenery or special effects. Simply by manipulating a fan in different ways, a performer is expected to suggest falling rain, rippling water or the rising Moon. The actors are all men, wearing masks to represent their characters – a woman, a god, a devil, an old man. For much of the play, a chorus sings the main performer's lines while he executes the solemn ritual movements of a dance.

There are five types of Noh drama: plays about the gods, about warriors, and about women; miscellaneous plays, usually about mad people; and plays

**Colourful story** *Traditional Kabuki theatre uses make-up instead of masks to define its characters as good or bad, male or female, serious or comical.*

about devils, strange beasts or other supernatural beings. Traditionally a programme would feature one play of each type, but today it is more likely to consist of only two or three plays.

Kabuki theatre is very different in tone. Based on the melodramatic style of puppet theatre, Kabuki always appealed to the people, rather than the aristocracy. Its origins go back to 1603, when a female dancer, Okuni, organised some very successful erotic plays and dances in a dry riverbed at Kyoto. The theatre became associated with

prostitution, however, and in 1629 women were forbidden to appear on stage. But the idea of popular theatre had been established and was later developed in plays with an all-male cast.

Being a Kabuki actor is an hereditary profession handed down from father to son, and the acting families are the custodians of the Kabuki tradition. With its long performances – originally 12 hours at a stretch, now normally around five hours – and its heavily made-up actors and stylised action, Kabuki is still very far from the traditional Western idea of theatre. As in Noh, dance, movement and song play a greater part than dialogue.

A Kabuki programme usually has four parts: an historical drama followed by one or two dance plays, a domestic play and a striking dance drama.

Both Noh and Kabuki have repeatedly toured the West, and their influence is evident in modern Western minimalist theatre. Kabuki at least has lost some of its purity through its contact with Western cultures. But the Japanese tradition remains as exotic and impenetrable as ever to the theatre-goer on Broadway or in London's West End.

**Lavish minimalism** *The elaborate costumes of Noh actors stand in sharp contrast to the typically bare stage designs.*

# A BETTER MOUSETRAP

## What is the secret that 8 million people will not tell?

THE THOUSANDTH performance of Agatha Christie's mystery play *The Mousetrap* at the Ambassadors Theatre in London, on April 22, 1955, attracted only one newspaper critic. 'The biggest mystery of the evening,' he wrote, 'is why this play has run so long.' In December 1970, *The Mousetrap* became the world's longest-running play when it notched up 7511 continuous performances. Twenty two years later the play was still running, having celebrated its 17,000th performance in 1992. So far, around 8 million people have seen it in London's West End.

This legendary whodunit opened at the Theatre Royal in Nottingham, England, in October 1952, moving to the Ambassadors in London in November that year, where it received good reviews. But there was no sign of what was to come, and Agatha Christie herself predicted a run of no more than six months.

### Counting up the years

While actors have come and gone, the set looks much as it did in 1952. There has been only one complete change of scenery, although furniture and furnishings are replaced as they wear out. Two items – a clock and a leather armchair – are survivors from the first production.

In the play's first 36 years, wardrobe mistresses ironed more than 106 km (66 miles) of shirts, theatregoers consumed over 269 tonnes of ice cream and 220 000 litres (48 000 gallons) of soft drinks. In January 1985, the original 'murder weapon' (a Colt New House .38 revolver, dropped from the production after real firearms were banned from the stage in 1962) fetched nearly US $700 at auction – six times its normal value.

### Secret of success

Why does *The Mousetrap* continue to attract audiences night after night? Perhaps because impresario Sir Peter Saunders was careful to court publicity in the early years. The 10th anniversary party at the Savoy Hotel boasted a cake weighing more than half a tonne. One actress in the cast was persuaded to marry under an archway of mousetraps. And a blaze of unexpected attention followed a performance of the play at Wormwood Scrubs prison when two of the inmates took the opportunity to escape. As each anniversary passes, the publicity given to the play draws more people to see it, which in turn leads to another anniversary, and so on.

The greatest mystery of all is 'whodunit?' Although the play has been translated into 22 languages and performed in 41 countries, the millions who have seen it are careful not to reveal the secret. There is one recorded exception: an enraged taxi driver whose passengers failed to tip him.

**Distinguished ancestry** *Since the days of the original cast of 1952 – led by Richard Attenborough and Sheila Sim – 251 actors and actresses have appeared in* The Mousetrap, *and 117 understudies.*

Leaving them at the theatre where *The Mousetrap* was showing, he shouted after them: 'The butler did it!' But he was not as vindictive as he seemed: there is no butler in the play.

---

# A CONFEDERATE'S CURTAIN CALL

## How one young actor changed the course of history

APRIL 14, 1865: at Ford's Theater in Washington, DC, the young actor John Wilkes Booth was preparing to give the greatest performance of his life. He was about to assassinate the President of the United States.

Unchallenged, Booth reached the box in which Abraham Lincoln and his wife were enjoying the final act of *Our American Cousin*. He waited to hear a line in the play that always brought the house down, then, silently, opened the door of the box, aimed the gun at the back of the president's head and fired. Then Booth leaped from the box to the stage beneath and escaped on a horse he had waiting behind the theatre.

President Abraham Lincoln died the next morning: Booth had made history.

But who was he, and why did he want to kill the president? Booth was a successful actor, earning more than $20 000 per year. But he was also a strong opponent of Lincoln's Emancipation Proclamation, which promised freedom to all slaves in the southern (Confederate) states.

### Revised plans

Booth's original plan, hatched a month earlier, was to kidnap Lincoln and hand him over to the Confederate government which could exchange him for prisoners of war. He recruited several accomplices to help with the abduction. They made their first attempt on March 17, intercepting the president's carriage on its way to a theatrical production in Washington. But Lincoln was not in the carriage. Booth now decided to abduct Lincoln from Ford's Theater. But by the time he was ready, the Confederate government had fallen and Booth decided that only desperate measures could now help the South. By killing Lincoln, he thought, he might instigate a revolution in the North that would benefit the South.

At first it looked as if the assassin, having crossed the Potomac River into nearby Virginia, would elude capture. But on April 26, 1865, Booth was surrounded by Union troops in a Virginia tobacco barn. As he refused to be taken alive, the barn was set on fire and Booth was shot as he tried to escape from the flames.

# THE CITY OF DREAMS

## How Hollywood grew from orange groves into Tinseltown

F THERE IS ONE word that symbolises films and film-making, it is Hollywood. The place in the world most adept at publicising itself, Hollywood has even erected a sign on the nearby hills that advertises its name in letters five storeys high. And yet this glorified centre of the film business started life as nothing more than a series of dusty orange groves on the outskirts of Los Angeles.

The place was bought up in the 1880s by property developer Horace H. Wilcox. His wife, Daeida, named the purchase Hollywood after the home of a friend in Chicago. Wilcox, a fervent supporter of Prohibition, had hoped to develop Hollywood as an alcohol-free religious community, but events were to prove otherwise.

In 1910, Hollywood was incorporated into the city of Los Angeles. By this time, the early film-makers had already begun to move in, having recognised that conditions in southern California were ideal for their purposes: almost uninterrupted sunshine, a diversity of stunning and natural landscapes – desert, ocean, mountains, forests – providing perfect backdrops.

### Stardom amongst the sprawl

In 1913, Cecil B. De Mille's *The Squaw Man* was released. It was Hollywood's first full-length film and box-office success. With De Mille at the helm, the newly formed Paramount Pictures Corporation prospered. It was soon followed by six other film companies: Universal, Fox, MGM, Warner Brothers, United Artists and Columbia. By the 1920s, Hollywood was established as the undisputed film capital of the world.

Over the next three decades, Hollywood attracted the world's best writers, producers, directors and actors – drawn by both the glamour and the money to be made. Yet despite the fame of its star inhabitants, Hollywood – the town – is just an extension of Los Angeles's vast, smoggy urban sprawl with, as crime writer Raymond Chandler once put it, 'the personality of a paper cup'.

**Studio barn** *Cecil B. De Mille (seated) produced* The Squaw Man *in 1913. Hollywood's first full-length film was a box-office success, and put the town on the map for film-makers.*

## DIGGING FOR FILM MEMORABILIA

A DOCUMENTARY film-maker, Peter Brosnan, and an anthropologist, Dr Brian Fagan, are trying to raise funds for an archaeological dig with a difference. It is not an ancient city they wish to uncover, but Hollywood's idea of an ancient city – made with wood, plaster, nails, cable and wire.

If the budget target is reached, a team of scientists will start combing the sand dunes of Guadeloupe, California, 320 km (200 miles) north of Los Angeles. Here they hope to examine the massive set for Cecil B. De Mille's epic silent film *The Ten Commandments*, which was made in 1923.

In that year, the director and 2500 artisans, extras and actors set up Camp De Mille as a base camp from which to build the ancient Egyptian city of Rameses. A 1000-strong construction gang set about building four statues of Rameses three storeys high, as well as numerous sphinxes, some of which towered 30 m (100 ft) over a broad avenue leading to the pharaoh's palace.

De Mille had a simple alternative to the difficult and expensive task of demolishing the enormous city after shooting the film: bury it in the sand. He also anticipated the efforts of men like Brosnan and Fagan: 'If in a thousand years from now archaeologists happen to dig beneath the sand of Guadeloupe,' he wrote in his autobiography, 'I hope they will not rush into print with the amazing news that Egyptian civilisation, far from being confined to the Valley of the Nile, extended all the way to the Pacific Coast of North America.'

# SET PIECES AND SCENE STEALERS

*When the stars are upstaged by the sets*

O F ALL Douglas Fairbanks's historical epics, perhaps the most impressive for its set pieces was his *Robin Hood* (1922). The centrepiece, erected in Pasadena, California, was a re-creation of Nottingham Castle, faithful in historical detail and absolutely massive in size – in fact, to this day it remains the biggest single structure ever built on a film set. Designed by Wilfred Buckland, the 140 m (450 ft) long and 30 m (90 ft) high castle was built of plaster in only two months by a team of 500 men working day and night.

### Competing for attention

When taken to view the newly built set, Fairbanks was impressed, but as he looked it over his awe began to change to unease. The castle was just too good. 'I can't compete with that,' Fairbanks declared, and he was all for scrapping the project until persuaded otherwise by his production staff. *Robin Hood* was a great success, memorable for its scenes of swashbuckling derring-do and stately pageants within the castle fortifications.

A more recent film involving a crusader almost dwarfed by the set design was *Batman* (1989). Production designer Anton Furst had to build Gotham City – the film's futuristic metropolis based on all the worst aspects of New York City – an enormous undertaking which required more than 90 km (60 miles) of tubular scaffolding just to strengthen the building shells. The sets took up most of the 38 hectare (95 acre) backlot at Pinewood Studios, England. Two models of Gotham City were required: one a miniaturised set 1.5 m (5 ft) high, the other comprising life-size streets and four-storey-high buildings. This enabled the director to shift from computerised miniature photography showing Batman's aircraft, the Batwing, flying over the city, to a live-action sequence where Batman emerges from the crashed aircraft in front of the City Hall building.

The biggest set of all time remains that built for Samuel Bronston's 1964 production, *The Fall of the Roman Empire*. For this, the Roman Forum was reconstructed on a 9 hectare (23 acre)

**Unequalled grandeur** *The largest set ever built was designer Veniero Colosanti's Roman Forum built for the 1964 Hollywood epic* The Fall of the Roman Empire.

set built outside Madrid. Over seven months, 1100 workmen erected over 350 statues, laid 6700 m (22 000 ft) of concrete stairway and built 27 buildings.

## DID YOU KNOW..?

*STARS' SALARIES have always been a major part of a film's budget, but it was in 1963, when Elizabeth Taylor demanded US $1 million for* Cleopatra, *that they began to escalate. Marlon Brando was paid $3.7 million for 12 days' work on* Superman *(1979). Sylvester Stallone earned nearly $16 million for starring in, directing and writing* Rocky IV *(1987) – yet by his own account he received only 25 T-shirts in payment for his first major role, in* The Lords of Flatbush.

## THE CHASE THAT SET THE PACE

GIVEN AMERICA'S great love of the automobile, it is hardly surprising that the car chase has become a standard feature of so many Hollywood films. Carey Loftin is considered one of the great car chase stuntmen, and it was his expertise, together with actor Steve McQueen's own stunt driving, that made the car chase in *Bullitt* (1968) the one that other directors have emulated ever since.

The then standard technique of filming car journeys was to sit the star in a car bolted to the floor of the studio, while a filmed driving sequence projected onto a screen behind the car filled the area of the rear window. *Bullitt* broke new ground by being filmed entirely on location with cameras bolted onto the chase cars.

In the 12-minute chase, McQueen pursued gangland killers across the steep inclines of San Francisco's roads at speeds approaching 200 km/h (125 mph). The cars, which actually became airborne at times, had to be strengthened to withstand the terrible strains and shocks imposed upon them. In the finale, in which the killers crash and are engulfed in a fireball, a driverless car was remote-controlled to explode on cue. Even by today's standards this stunt sequence is spectacular.

# DEFYING DEATH FOR A LIVING
### *From dare-devil pioneers to risk-assessment professionals*

ACTION-PACKED scenes, ranging from barroom brawls to the most hair-raising aerial exploits, have always been a key ingredient of films. Almost from the start there have been stuntmen – individuals able and willing to carry out feats of skill and danger, often doubling for the studio's prize asset, the leading actor.

In the pioneering days of the film industry immediately after the First World War, stuntmen were known in Hollywood as 'fall-down boys', a mixed band of former cowboys, army pilots, racing drivers and acrobats – each with his own speciality that could be employed to exciting effect in the films.

### Bumps and bruises

As the fame of the film stars increased during the 1920s, stuntmen were increasingly called upon to undertake the work that the studios considered too dangerous for their leading actors. Although the more action-orientated stars liked to say they did their own stunts, this was often not the case; even the athletic Douglas Fairbanks sometimes relied on his personal stunt team.

Bruises, bumps and broken bones were the worse injuries that usually befell a stuntman – fatalities were rare. Stuntmen soon developed ways of making their stunts look spectacular while ensuring that they were as safe as possible. Nonetheless, accidents still can happen, and for this alone today's stuntman is a highly respected and well paid member of the film business.

Within the film world certain stunts have become legends, amongst them Paul Mantz's extraordinary single-handed crash-landing of a B-17 'flying fortress' bomber for the 1950 production *Twelve O'Clock High*. Mantz, doubling for Gregory Peck, was paid the then considerable sum of US $6000. Mantz's luck did not hold, however, for he was killed when crash-landing an aircraft in *The Flight of the Phoenix* 15 years later.

Another breathtaking stunt was successfully carried out by Dar Robinson when he made a 360 m (1170 ft) free-fall jump from Toronto's CN Tower for *Highpoint* in 1979. Said to have been paid a fee of US $150 000, Robinson assessed the risks involved by practising free falling from a low-flying airplane. He correctly estimated six seconds free falling, three seconds to open his parachute, and just one second to make his safe landing.

*Precarious living Early stars like Monty Banks – seen here hanging from a car – often did their own stunts.*

# CRASHING TO SUCCESS

*The stuntman who became famous for safety*

A FAMED STUNTMAN who had often doubled for John Wayne, Yakima Canutt left stunting in 1945 to take responsibility for staging and directing action scenes that were later edited into the main picture. As what is known as a 'second-unit director', Canutt organised a succession of brilliant stunt sequences.

Canutt, who was himself an expert horseman, was determined that stunts should appear daring and spectacular yet always be safe. For the film *Ivanhoe* (1952), he showed his stunt team how to make horses fall without hurting either the horse or the rider. His trick was simple but effective: dig sand-pits where the falls were to happen, and then pack them with grass to disguise them and to cushion the impact.

Canutt was appointed second-unit director for the 1959 remake of *Ben Hur*, which featured a 12-minute chariot race watched by 8000 extras and won by Charlton Heston in the title role. Canutt bought 78 horses for the race and gave Heston and the other riders lessons in handling the horse teams. For the most spectacular moment in the race, when Heston's chariot had to leap over the wreckage of two crashed chariots, Canutt's son, Joe, doubled for the star. Although the stunt did not go as planned – Joe Canutt fell out of the chariot and suffered a gash on the chin – the footage was breathtaking and was incorporated into the film to universal acclaim. No other stuntman or horse was injured during the filming of this sequence.

In special recognition of his talents, Canutt received an Honorary Academy Award in 1967 – not only for his achievements on screen, but for his work in designing safety devices to protect stuntmen.

***Learning the ropes*** *In* Ben Hur, *actor Charlton Heston did all his own stuntwork, except for a jump over two crashed chariots, executed by Yakima Canutt's son, Joe.*

## DID YOU KNOW..?

*H. B. HALICKI'S* The Junkman *made in 1982, features the most destructive car chase sequence ever filmed – a total of 150 vehicles ended up on the scrapheap. However, over the whole TV series of the* Dukes Of Hazzard *more than 300 cars were wrecked.*

*✳ ✳ ✳*

*THE FIRST stuntman, an American called Frank Hanaway, was hired in 1903 for* The Great Train Robbery *simply for his ability to fall off a horse without hurting himself.*

# DOLLAR DISASTERS
## From blockbuster to budget-buster

THE STORIES behind the staggering sums spent on shooting a big budget film, especially if it ends up a box-office disaster, can be as fascinating as the film itself. *Cleopatra* (1963) had been planned as a US $2 million blockbuster, with big-name stars, a cast of thousands, and sets intended to do justice to the wonders of the ancient world. From the outset, however, costs soared way above budget, not least because leading actress Elizabeth Taylor demanded a $1 million fee, plus two penthouse suites, and a Rolls-Royce to ferry her between hotel and film studio. A wardrobe bill of $130 000 just for Cleopatra's 65 costume changes did not help matters either.

### Success at a price
Leading actors and directors were hired and fired or just left, locations switched from California to Rome and London, scenes were scrapped and sets had to be rebuilt, so that after eight months in production only ten minutes of the final film had been shot. By the time of its release, *Cleopatra*'s costs approached $44 million – an extraordinary sum in the early 1960s.

Fortunately, the film made money on the international box-office circuit, in contrast to what is generally considered to be the biggest flop in film history, Michael Cimino's 1980 western, *Heaven's Gate*. Since its release it has become the yardstick against which other film disasters are measured. The film's total costs added up to around $57 million, but it earned a mere $1.5 million from cinema ticket sales in North America.

### Painstaking authenticity
Director Cimino decided that no expense was to be spared in making *Heaven's Gate* as visually authentic as possible, and this meant building an entire frontier town, painstaking research to ensure all costumes were historically accurate, and teaching hundreds of extras how to skate, waltz and use period firearms. All in all, 200 hours of footage, equivalent to 400 000 m (1.3 million ft) of film, were shot and Cimino had to edit this down to a commercially viable two-hour film. At first he only managed to prune the film to 5 hours 25 minutes, but eventually it was released at 2 hours 30 minutes.

All the director's efforts did not make any difference, because *Heaven's Gate* was roundly slated by American film critics, and film-goers stayed away. For some years Cimino was known as the 'man who killed the Western', and the studios abandoned this genre through most of the 1980s.

Yet it appears that the lessons of *Heaven's Gate* have not been learned. *The Adventures of Baron Munchausen* (1989) was director Terry Gilliam's attempt to recreate the fabled exploits of an 18th-century German soldier. Offscreen disagreements bedevilled the making of the film, as did the vastly expensive changes of location and the departure of key actors just as shooting was to begin. The director's quip that it cost 'less than $40 million. Maybe by only a dollar, though,' gives some idea of the enormous sums still lavished on film-making. The haste with which the film was subsequently released on video reflected its abysmally low takings at the cinema.

*A drain on resources* Costumes and dance lessons for the extras in this lavish scene in Heaven's Gate *helped make the budget soar.*

# CINEMA-IN-THE-ROUND
## At an IMAX film, the screen comes to life

**A**S HOLLYWOOD is the centre of the film business, one might also expect it to be the source of technological innovation in film-making. Yet, surprisingly, the most exciting development in years, IMAX, has come not from southern California, but from a small company in Toronto, Canada.

The audience at an IMAX (from 'Maximum Image') film sits back in steeply pitched seats to see dazzling half-hour documentaries like *Nomads of the Deep* (1979), in which the viewers travel underwater with humpback whales, and *The Dream Is Alive* (1985), where they are taken on an extraordinary low-orbital flight with space-shuttle astronauts. These documentaries are shown either by wide-angle projection onto a flat screen, known as IMAX, or by fish-eye projection onto a dome-shaped screen, known as OMNIMAX.

### Vast screen

The screen can be up to seven storeys high – ten times the size of most cinema screens. The resulting image is so vast that it almost fills the audience's field of vision, thereby giving them the impression that they are actually part of the film. IMAX and OMNIMAX films have proved immensely popular with audiences; in 1987 they were viewed by 25 million people. But, as yet, neither system has been used to make a feature film – the cost would be millions of dollars more than a conventional film.

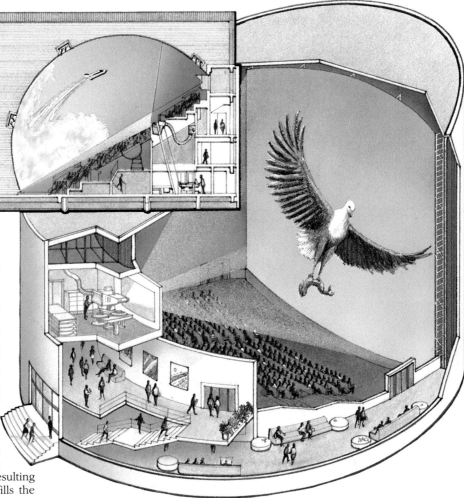

*Enveloping screen Inside a typical 500-seat IMAX theatre (above), the flat screen stretches wall-to-wall and floor-to-ceiling. During an OMNIMAX film (inset), a vast dome-shaped screen is filled with images projected with a fish-eye lens.*

IMAX uses the largest existing camera format, 70 mm, but its frame area is three times that of standard film and this is why IMAX can project a much larger image. While a normal frame has five perforations – holes punched along both sides that slot into a sprocket as it pulls the film through the projector – the IMAX frame has 15, which ensure a much steadier picture. As it is guided through the powerful IMAX projector, the frame is also held firmly against the rear element of the projector lens by a vacuum to enhance the clarity of the image. A digitally-recorded six-channel sound system makes the film's soundtrack especially vivid.

The origins of IMAX go back to the Montreal Expo of 1967 where multi-screen films had been a great success. Some of the film-makers involved determined to develop ideas in this field further, and were commissioned by the organisers of the 1970 Osaka Expo to come up with a radically different screen format.

IMAX films can only be shown in specially built cinemas. By 1990, over 90 IMAX cinemas had been opened in 14 countries, including Japan, Britain and the United States. Although unlikely to replace conventional cinemas, the IMAX system has brought a new experience to cinema-going, one that 'not even the best Hollywood special effects wizard could equal', according to one American newspaper.

# THE SPORTING SPIRIT

### *It took a French baron to revive an ancient Greek spectacle*

IT ALL BEGAN in 776 BC, with a simple foot race of about 200 m (660 ft) held on a single day at Olympia in the southwest of the Greek mainland. Every four years from that date, athletes as well as poets and artists met there for a festival in honour of the god Zeus. Apart from foot racing, the event, later extended to five days, came to include wrestling, boxing and the pentathlon (running, jumping, discus, javelin and wrestling). Winners became overnight heroes, and the festival merited a permanent place in the Greek calendar to mark a span of four years which they called the Olympiad.

The games lasted for nearly 1200 years, until AD 393, when the Christian Roman Emperor Theodosius I banned all such 'pagan' celebrations. A millennium and a half later, a French baron began a campaign to recreate that spirit of good-natured but serious competition. Through sheer persistence, he succeeded.

Baron Pierre de Coubertin's family wanted him to become an officer in the French Army. But de

> ### DID YOU KNOW..?
>
> *THE ANCIENT Greeks regarded the Olympic Games as so important that they would call a truce between warring cities for up to three months – time for athletes to travel to the stadium at Olympia in the Peloponnese, compete, and return home to continue fighting.*

Coubertin believed that the cause of peace would be better served by a regular meeting of amateur, world-class athletes, and dedicated his energy to realising this dream. During the 1890s he made speech after speech to international sports associations, and at last persuaded them to revive the name and the spirit of the ancient Olympic Games. In 1896, King George I of Greece opened the first of the reborn Olympics, appropriately enough in Athens.

Unlike the original games, the new Olympics did not overcome enmities between states, and were suspended during the two World Wars. Economic realities have also eroded the principle that only amateurs should take part. And more than once politics has dictated who would, or would not, participate. But, thanks to de Coubertin, winning a gold medal at the Olympics is once again one of the highest sporting achievements.

***First to the finish*** *At the first modern Olympics in 1896, the Greek runner Spiridon Louis won the marathon in just under three hours.*

# BREAKING THE RECORD

*How would ancient Greek athletes fare at today's Olympics?*

ABOUT 2600 YEARS ago, two Greek athletes set sporting records at the Olympic Games that were not to be surpassed until the 20th century.

The record-makers were a discus thrower named Protiselaus and a long jumper called Chionis. Both set their records in the same Olympiad, in 656 BC. Protiselaus would have won the gold medal at all the modern Olympic Games until 1928, when his staggering 46.32 m (152 ft) Olympic record was broken by the 47.32 m (155 ft) throw of the American Clarence Houser. Another American, Alvin C. Kraenzlein, broke Chionis' long-jump record in 1900. And even then Kraenzlein exceeded Chionis' 7.05 m (23 ft 1½ in) jump by only 115 mm (4½ in).

Protiselaus' and Chionis' feats must have been truly remarkable, for the ancient Greeks normally kept records only of the winners of the foot races at the Olympic Games. All that usually mattered to the athletes was winning, not whether they had outshone some previous competitor in the same event.

The early games comprised very few athletic events. There were three running races – one length thought to be about 200 m (660 ft) called an *agon*, two lengths (called a *diaulos*) and an endurance race just under 5 km (3 miles) called a *dolichos* – plus the long jump, discus and javelin.

### Ahead of their time

Would those two athletes of the ancient world, transported in a time machine to a modern Olympic stadium, still astonish today's spectators? The answer for both of them is probably 'yes'.

Protiselaus could easily break his own record by using a modern discus, with an aerodynamically more efficient design. Archaeological records indicate too that the one he used was probably also heavier than the standard 2 kg (4½ lb) discus used by Olympic athletes today.

And when Protiselaus amazed the ancient Greeks with his performance, he would have made his throw while standing virtually still. By using the modern circling style of throw, together with a present-day discus, he would certainly shatter the record he set all those centuries ago. Chionis' case is more problematic. It is very likely that when he jumped he was holding dumbbell-like weights in each hand. He would have swung these at precisely the right second to increase his body's momentum through the air. Whatever his method, it was still an impressive leap, and most 20th-century long jumpers would regard him as a real threat.

But two modern Olympic record-breakers in particular could probably

*Record setter At the 1936 Berlin Olympics, Jesse Owens jumped 8.05 m (26 ft 5¾ in), creating a new Olympic and official world record – his longer 1935 jump had still not been officially accepted by then.*

*A giant leap Bob Beamon made his record-shattering long-jump of 8.9 m (29 ft 2½ in) in the rarefied air of Mexico City – nearly 2500 m (8000 ft) above sea level. Perhaps his achievement can be bettered only by a jump at a similar altitude.*

shrug off any contender from the ancient world. That includes Chionis, for both these consummate athletes were long-jumpers. The legendary Jesse Owens set a record on May 25, 1935, that stood for 33 years, 4 months and 18 days – which is itself a record length of time for a modern athletic achievement to remain unsurpassed.

Owens' phenomenal leap of 8.13 m (26 ft 8¼ in) – Owens was the first man ever to jump more than 8 m – was eventually beaten by Bob Beamon on October 13, 1968. In the thin air of Mexico City, Beamon jumped a magical distance of 8.9 m (29 ft 2½ in). Experts regard this feat as a virtually unbeatable performance.

Just the same, a time machine that could transfer all these outstanding athletes to some future Olympics might produce very interesting results.

# WHOSE GAME IS IT, ANYWAY?
## *The dubious origins of national sports*

TO SAY that baseball is as American as apple pie sums up the problem of taking too seriously a country's claim to have invented a particular sport. Americans did not invent apple pie either, of course. And so it is with the English claim to have invented soccer, or the Scots' claim to have invented golf. Other sports, too, have unlikely origins.

### HIGHLAND FLING?
The first reference to golf in Scotland is a decree banning it. In 1457, the Scottish Parliament issued an edict against the sport because people were neglecting their archery practice – vital to the country's defence – in favour of the game.

But golf almost certainly did not start in Scotland. The Chinese trace their own similar sport of *Ch'ui Wan* as far back as the 3rd century BC. When the Roman legions came to Britain some 200 years later, they brought the game of *paganica* – played with a bent stick and a feather-stuffed leather ball similar to the ones used in early golf. The name itself may come from Holland, where *kolf* means 'club', although the Dutch played their 17th-century version of the game with a ball the size of a grapefruit. And finally, the English like to annoy the Scots by saying that they invented golf – a claim based on a stained-glass window from 1350 in Gloucester cathedral that depicts a figure resembling a golfer.

### HIGH STAKES
Basketball, they say, is a Canadian game, but the 10th-century BC Olmecs of what is now Mexico would probably have little difficulty in picking up the rules. Their version of the game – the earliest known to be related to basketball,

**Prisoners' pastime** *Union prisoners of war play baseball in a Confederate camp in North Carolina in 1862. In the decades before the American Civil War, baseball acquired rules and organised clubs, but during the war it languished except in army camps.*

and called *pok-ta-pok* – might provide entertainment of a different sort to a modern audience, however. It was a fertility rite performed at religious festivals.

The Aztecs and Maya, too, had a version of basketball. They played *tlachtli* or *ollamalitzli* with a solid rubber ball on a court flanked with high walls, in which two stone rings were set at right angles to the court. The first team to get the ball through one of the rings won the game outright. This probably happened only rarely. The rings were small and 6 m (20 ft) above ground, and touching the ball with the hands was forbidden – somehow, knees, elbows and hips were used to pass it between players. However, the rewards for scoring a goal were high: the successful

**Symbolic spiel** *A group of players in 17th-century Germany indulges in* Kegelspiel *(pin-game), adopted by the Church to signify the battle of good against evil.*

player was reputedly entitled to claim the spectators' clothes and jewellery.

Where does that leave the Canadian claim? In 1891, a Canadian, Dr James A. Naismith, introduced basketball as we know it today – but he was living in Springfield, Massachusetts, USA, which is where the first game was played.

### ILLEGAL PLAY?
Nine-pin bowling reached America from Germany in the 17th century. By

the time of its first mention in literature, in Washington Irving's story *Rip Van Winkle* from 1819, people were playing it all over the United States. By the 1830s, Americans were gambling large sums of money on the outcome of games.

Perhaps predictably, bowling alleys soon attracted the underworld, who rigged games and the betting to their own advantage. Several states banned the game in the 1840s and the gambling that went hand in hand with it. The promoters promptly added an extra pin to the game, so creating the 'new' sport of ten-pin bowling and side-stepping the law.

### CAUGHT OUT?

The search for the origins of baseball resulted in one of the greatest hoaxes of all time. Sports-goods manufacturer Albert Spalding set up a commission in 1907 to trace the game's roots. It came to the unequivocal conclusion that the great Civil War soldier Abner Doubleday had invented baseball in Cooperstown, New York, prior to the civil conflict, in 1839. Cooperstown became a tourist centre and built a baseball stadium and museum on the basis of the commission's report.

The bubble burst on the eve of baseball's centenary celebrations in 1939 when a researcher discovered that the Spalding commission's findings were largely the invention of its chairman, Abraham G. Mills. He had been a close friend of Abner Doubleday – but Doubleday had probably never heard of baseball or even visited Cooperstown in 1839.

The earliest reference to a game called 'base-ball' comes from a vicar in Kent, England, who in 1700 disapproved of it being played on Sundays. People in England, particularly children, had been enjoying the game since the Middle Ages under its more usual local name of rounders.

### VILLAGE CONTEST

One of England's national sports, cricket, was certainly invented in England. The country's other sporting obsession, football, comes from much further afield. It was the Roman legions who brought football to Britain. And it too has its origins in China, where it has been played since at least 200 BC.

The earliest games of English football were wild and disorganised matches between neighbouring villages and parishes, in which teams of up to 500 players tried to kick or otherwise transport the ball to their opponents' goal – which might be 5–6 km (3–4 miles) from their own goal. Some villages in England still play games like this.

# MOUNTAIN MEN
## *Ritual and reward for the Sumo wrestler*

THE SIGHT of two mountainous Japanese Sumo wrestlers colliding can leave the spectator wondering how they survive the match. Indeed, in Sumo's earliest days, fights were often to the death. Today, the ultimate goal of the 800 or so professional fighters in Japan – the *rikishi* – is to attain the rank of *yokozuna*, supreme Sumo champion, and a rare honour indeed.

So high are Sumo's standards that there have been only 62 *yokozunas* in the entire history of the sport – and that stretches back over 2000 years. In all that time, little has changed about Sumo, the first martial art. Its origins are bound up with the Japanese belief in Shinto, the 'way of the gods', where winning gains favour with the gods. Hence the very elaborate ritual that surrounds a Sumo match.

### *Fight of the pure*

The clay fighting ring is itself a sacred shrine. On entering it, the *rikishi* first claps, to attract the gods' attention and indicate his own purity of heart. Then he shakes his apron to drive away evil spirits, and raises his arms to show he carries no weapons. Next comes his most dramatic gesture, *shiko*. With his left hand on his heart and his right arm extended to the east, the huge fighter raises his right leg as high as possible – to send it crashing down with all his force. Then he performs the same earth-shaking stamp with the other leg. After that, the *rikishi* purifies himself and the ring by throwing salt, wiping himself, and rinsing his mouth with water. Finally, the opponents spend three or four minutes trying to intimidate each other with grimaces and threatening postures.

### *Seconds out*

The fight itself is brief and brutal. The wrestlers may not punch with a clenched fist, pull hair, poke eyes, kick to the stomach, grab the part of the loincloth that covers the genitals, or choke their opponents. Anything else is fair game. The result is a thunderous collision that rarely lasts more than 10 seconds. The *rikishi* hurl themselves at each other, and the contest ends when one giant is pushed to the ground or outside the circle, which is 4.6 m (15 ft) in diameter.

Despite their enormous size, Sumo wrestlers must be speedy and supple. Weight is obviously a crucial factor in winning, and *rikishi* eat huge portions of protein-rich stews to gain weight low on the body and depress their centre of gravity. The average *rikishi* weighs about 135 kg (300 lb). In 1988, the heaviest-ever fighter, Konishiki, tipped the scales at 252 kg (556 lb) – about the weight of four normal men.

---

### DID YOU KNOW..?

*ALL SUMO wrestlers are obliged to join a so-called stable or* heya. *And, with the exception of the most successful* rikishi, *they live a celibate life together in a kind of barracks.*

✳ ✳ ✳

*ONCE their professional careers are over, Sumo wrestlers slim rapidly, reaching the normal weight for their height and build in only a few months. The years of carrying enormous weight do take their toll, however: the average ex-wrestler is only 64 when he dies.*

**Sumo stamp** *A Sumo wrestler performs the high* shiko *stamp to drive evil spirits out of the ring.*

# THE MAGIC OF DANCE

## Entering into the rhythm of the gods can bring rain or heal sickness

**W**HEREVER there are people, there is dancing. For most 'civilised' people, dancing is rarely more than a pleasant pastime. But far from the modern ballroom and disco, ritual dances are still vital in many societies to mark the stages of life and to communicate with the gods.

People dance for help with crops and hunting forays, to bring rain to their parched land, to overcome sickness or enemies. These dances are a form of prayer, and they have magical powers.

Typical are dances that imitate animals. For example, to entertain the animal spirits before the hunt and appease them afterwards, boys of the Australian aboriginal Kemmirai tribe leap about, scratch themselves, and hold their hands in front of their chests like the kangaroos they are about to kill. And the Tewa Indians in New Mexico dance like the deer they hunt, galloping and then standing, trembling and shifting their heads about in fear.

### Arousing the elements

The North American Indians of the Great Plains also dance for rain: the Sioux fill a pot with water and dance around it four times before throwing themselves on the ground and drinking from it. There are dances to assist the survival of individuals or whole tribes. Both the Inuit of the Arctic and the Amazon Indians have shamans, or priests, who will dance themselves into a frenzy in order to enter the spirit world and bring back the soul of someone who is sick. The task of the 'devil dancers' of Sri Lanka, too, is to exorcise evil spirits, whereas the Iroquois

***Dagger dance*** *In pursuit of ecstasy, dancers on the island of Bali work themselves into a frenzied trance, pressing their sharp daggers, known as krisses, towards their chests.*

Indians of New York State are singularly good-humoured about their approach to healing: first the shaman decides what has caused an affliction – often the spirit of an animal – and then he prescribes a ritual dance to appease the animal's offended spirit. The dance imitates the animal, even down to the dancers eating its favourite food, and ends with everyone cheering the patient noisily.

In such societies, dancing marks all of life's critical stages. Birth, puberty, marriage and death are all assisted by dancing. What strikes a Westerner about these dances is that men and women rarely act as partners. And in all of them, traditional steps and gestures remain rigid and unchanging. So strict can this code be that, it is said, the old men of Gaua in the New Hebrides would watch the dancers with special vigilance, ready to shoot an arrow into anyone unlucky enough to make a mistake.

> ### DID YOU KNOW..?
>
> *IN ITALY between the 14th and 18th centuries, the belief grew that wild music could counter the effects of the tarantula spider's poisoned bite. Reduced to a state of lethargy, the victim's only hope of cure was to dance out of his torpor. We know the music today as a conventional dance – the tarantella.*

# NIGHT AND DAY

*Dancing mania swept the streets of medieval Europe*

PEOPLE HAD COME to Aachen, as they always did, from all over Germany to celebrate the midsummer feast of St John. But the festival in 1374 was different. Suddenly, people began to dance. For no apparent reason, they carried on dancing until they dropped, foaming at the mouth. Wherever they went through the streets, others joined in the mania, until the town was alive with leaping and gyrating people – and littered, too, with the supine forms of the exhausted.

### All join in

A hard core of these manic dancers moved on to other towns once the festival was over. A gang of people followed, ready to take any advantage they could of those afflicted. But, as in the streets of Aachen, wherever the dancers went, otherwise sane and ordinary spectators would suddenly be infected by the mysterious hysteria and join the throng in its contortions.

By the early 15th century, towns all over Europe had seen outbreaks of dancing mania. In 1418, when compulsive dancers in Strasbourg were taken to chapels of St Vitus, a 4th-century saint credited with curing convulsive diseases, the affliction became known as 'St Vitus dance'. (Today this term is used for a nervous disorder.) The mania lasted for centuries: there were outbreaks in Belgium, Holland, Italy, France and Scotland up until the 18th century.

Historians and psychologists have offered several reasons for these bizarre epidemics. The feast of St John was a thinly Christianised version of an ancient pagan midsummer festival; the year 1374 saw the last outbreak of the Black Death, which wiped out roughly a third of Europe's population. The festival may have been simply the spur for the people of Aachen to express, to the point of madness, the emotional and economic strain they had suffered during the years of the plague. That 'madness', and the release it brought, was catching, for hardly anywhere in Europe had escaped the scourge.

### Mouldy bread

There may be more prosaic explanations. Some of the dancers may have had convulsive nervous diseases to begin with. Others may have been victims of a particularly grim form of food poisoning. 'Ergot' is a deadly fungus that can grow on damp rye; among other things it causes spasms and cramps, typical symptoms among manic dancers. Bread made from damp rye was almost certainly on sale in Aachen in the wet summer of 1374. But none of this explains why the outbreaks of dancing mania continued for so long.

# THE GREATEST DANCER IN THE WORLD

*A dramatic talent that seemed to defy gravity*

VASLAV NIJINSKY literally leaped to fame and glory in St Petersburg in 1907, when, at the age of 16, he danced solo for the first time in public. The stunned audience went wild, and hailed him as the 'eighth wonder of the world'.

He had enormous success in his lifetime. The lightness and expressiveness of his style, his physical beauty, his virtuosity and dramatic talent amazed all who saw him dance. But it was his extraordinary ability to leap high and, apparently defying gravity, remain in the air before drifting to Earth, that took audiences by storm. As one admirer put it, Nijinsky went 'up like a rocket . . . down like thistle-fluff'.

### Tailored for the part

Nowhere was Nijinsky's prowess seen to greater advantage than in his Paris performance of *Le Spectre de la rose*, a ballet created specially for him in 1911. In this, clad in a costume covered in rose petals, Nijinsky made a spectacular leap from a window onto the stage. His dresser is said to have made a fortune by selling the petals to fans.

Nijinsky was no stranger to controversy. In 1912, for instance, his mildly erotic choreography for *L'Après-midi d'un faune* shocked many and delighted others. Critics spoke of 'a lecherous faun, filthy, crude movements' – but the show was a sell-out. And when the Paris police were requested to prevent further performances on grounds of obscenity, they declined.

A year later, *The Rite of Spring*, which Nijinsky choreographed in a revolutionary style to the no less avant-garde music of Igor Stravinsky, inspired insults, howls, whistles, and fights among the Paris audience that drowned out the music and left some of the dancers in tears. Yet today it is one of the classics of modern ballet.

Nijinsky's career as a dancer and choreographer was shortlived. In 1916, he suffered a nervous breakdown. Within a year, he was diagnosed as schizophrenic. After one last private recital in 1919, he gave up dancing for ever. He died in London in 1950, but the legend lives on.

***Rosy phantom*** *The great Nijinsky dances in* Le Spectre de la rose *with prima ballerina Tamara Karsavina.*

# ENDURANCE TEST

*Dance marathons were a painful and humiliating way to get rich quick*

IN 1932, a young American man dropped dead after 48 hours non-stop dancing in a dance marathon. During these competitive dancing sessions, some of the contestants had teeth extracted; others got married. And a few even went mad. The first dance marathon was held in England in 1923. It lasted 9½ hours. Later the same year, in New York, Alma Cummings kept going for 27 hours, wearing out six partners in the process. By the 1930s, dance marathons – dramatised by Hollywood in 1969 in

*They Shoot Horses, Don't They* – had become big business. In the Depression, competing meant a chance to win a cash prize and a way to get free meals for a while – up to eight of them a day. To win or to survive almost to the end promised instant celebrity – even if the price was the loss of human dignity and, often, physical injury.

Rules were strict: in every hour, contestants had to spend 45 minutes in constant motion. Just 15 minutes were allowed for rest (but not sleep), first aid

***Bop till you drop*** *A contestant in a dance marathon collapses of exhaustion. Marathons held a morbid fascination for spectators who paid to watch the dancers suffer.*

and toilet needs. And this gruelling schedule went on for 24 hours a day.

In the first days of a marathon, competitors would dance genuine tangos, foxtrots and waltzes. As the ordeal wore on, all pretence at real dancing was abandoned and contestants just had to keep their feet moving.

Audiences paid between 25 and 50 cents admission, and could number up to 5000 people at a time. They would bring presents for their favourite competitors and place bets on the outcome. Everything the dancers did was scrutinised by the audience – even the bandaging of blistered feet and collapsing ankles in the 'hospital' area.

If interest flagged, the 'floor judges' – whose job it was to goad the contestants and arouse the audience's emotions – would ensure capacity crowds for the next day by promising elimination dances, races, comedy sketches, mock weddings and even wrestling in mud between the already exhausted participants. The floor judges would mercilessly victimise the weaker contestants by speeding up the music or flicking wet towels at swollen legs.

### Going pro

Despite these humiliations, many contestants turned professional. One, a tap-dancing newspaper boy named Stan West, notched up 2000 hours of 'dancing' in a single contest in 1933.

According to *The Guinness Book of Records*, the longest marathon, held in Pittsburgh, Pennsylvania in 1930, lasted over 30 weeks, with rest periods progressively cut from 20 to 10 to 5 to nil minutes an hour. The prize was $2000.

Marathon dancing was a mixture of gladiatorial contest, sport and soap opera. In 1933, this entertainment was banned in the USA, although it flickered on illegally until the late 1940s.

PHOTOS SOLD HERE MADE BY
'Rdm' Studio
OPEN DAY & NIGHT.

## DID YOU KNOW..?

*WHEN New York police raided the Roseland Ballroom during a Marathon World Championship, the promoters simply transferred the contestants – still dancing – into a van and from there onto a sloop, which sailed out of territorial waters and so beyond the jurisdiction of the police. The ruse worked perfectly until the contestants got seasick.*

# THE DANCING COMPUTER
### *Choreography takes a leap into the future*

WHAT STEPS did the dancers perform during the first production of Tchaikovski's *Swan Lake* in 1877? The answer, surprisingly enough, is that no one knows. No written choreography exists for most of the world's repertoire of dance, whether classical or modern. Dancers have traditionally learned their routines from the choreographer's own demonstrations or from other dancers who are familiar with the work.

Systems of dance notation do exist but they are rarely used. Because dance involves the whole of the human body moving in three dimensions, the task of recording even a short ballet is extremely complex. A single minute of dancing may take as long as six hours to record on paper.

However, the advent of sophisticated computer graphics has opened a way of making the job both simpler and faster. Since the early 1980s, computer scientists have been creating animated figures that simulate sequences of steps, body movements and even the dancer's position on stage – all on a computer screen.

A dance composition is also faster to plan and learn using a computer rather than through months of rehearsal.

However, the programs developed so far require large computers that, at around US $100 000, are beyond the moderate budgets of most dance companies. So choreographers are only now beginning to experiment with computer dance compositions. But as dancers become more familiar with the new system, and its costs shrink, electronically inspired dances may well catch on.

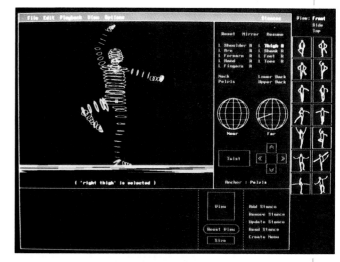

***Fast forward*** *The dance computer uses the principle of a motion picture camera: movements are composed one by one in still frames that are later 'played back' at speed. Unlike film-makers, computer choreographers can view the stage and figures from all angles.*

## RHYTHMS OF WAR

DRUMS BEAT OUT a hypnotic rhythm, voices chant a strange incantation, flames throw grotesque shadows across the carvings on a totem pole. Around it the frenzied braves, daubed in paint, swinging tomahawks, circle endlessly. That is Hollywood's picture of an American Indian war dance. It is undoubtedly a caricature, but it also contains a grain of truth.

War dances are indeed hypnotic, frantic affairs. Their aim is not only to strengthen communal feelings between the warriors, but to induce fearlessness in the face of the enemy by an orgy of wild music and dancing before the battle.

War dances are not exclusive to American Indians. Nor are warpaint, drums, or a bloodthirsty mime of the fighting to come. The headhunters of Prince of Wales Island, in the Torres Strait between Australia and New Guinea, would paint themselves, dance around a fire to the music of an orchestra of drums, and end their ritual by acting out the beheading of their enemies with their bamboo knives.

From New Zealand, the vigorous war dance of the Maori, the *haka*, has travelled all over the world. The national rugby football team, the All-Blacks (so called from their black kit) perform the *haka* before every match they play.

While it may not be a battle to the death that the players are about to face, the dance, and the bloodcurdling war cry that goes with it, probably have much the same effect on the team. It may entertain the crowd, but rugby is a deadly serious sport to New Zealanders.

***War dance*** *Maori rugby players in the New Zealand All-Black strip perform their pre-match* haka.

# THE SOUNDS OF EARTH

### *The universal language of music even reaches out into space*

**H**OW COULD you make an alien inhabitant of a planet belonging to a distant star system understand what it was like to be a human being on the planet Earth? This was the question posed to a committee of experts in 1977, when the American spacecraft *Voyager 1* and *Voyager 2* were about to be launched on a journey into the depths of space, carrying messages of greeting to any intelligent life form they might meet. To many people's surprise, the experts decided that one of the best ways to communicate with an alien would be not with words or pictures, but with music. They devoted 87½ minutes of the *Voyager* video message discs to a selection of the 'Earth's greatest hits'.

Why choose music? First because the structure of music – from the simplest eight-bar blues to a complex Bach fugue – is based on numbers, and musical harmony is easily analysed in mathematical terms. The scientists argued that, as

mathematics is the most universal of languages, aliens were more likely to understand the mathematical structure of our music than anything else about us.

But the experts also felt that music expressed human feeling better than any other medium and that it could represent the full variety of human cultures. There has never been a society without its own distinctive music to express its sadness and pain, its happiness and tranquillity.

When it came to selecting the music that would represent humanity to the Universe, variety provided the keynote. The committee chose Aborigine songs from Australia, the Navaho Indians' *Night Chant* and a wedding song from Peru. They added Javanese gamelan music, panpipes from the Solomon Islands and Peru, a raga from India and ch'in music from China, bagpipes from Azerbaijan, bamboo flutes from Japan and percussion from Senegal. There were songs from Georgia, Zaire, Mexico, New Guinea and Bulgaria. There was blues singer Blind Willie Johnson with *Dark Was the Night,* the jazz trumpeter Louis Armstrong performing *Melancholy Blues* and rock 'n' roller Chuck Berry singing *Johnny B. Goode.* From the Western classical tradition, they chose Renaissance recorder music, three examples of Bach, two of Beethoven, an aria from Mozart's *The Magic Flute* and Stravinksy's *The Rite of Spring.*

Were these really the Earth's greatest hits? At least they are now potentially the longest-lasting. The disc, which is made of gold-plated copper, is built to last a 1000 million years.

*Gold disc The 'Sounds of Earth' record (above), encased in a gold-plated aluminium shield, is installed (left) on the* Voyager 2 *spacecraft. From here it was dispatched into space, where, scientists hope, it will be received by nonhuman intelligences.*

# 'A NIGHTINGALE WITH TOOTHACHE'
## Composers with a sense of humour

**S**ERIOUS music is mostly no laughing matter. But one or two composers have proved that a touch of humour is not always out of place in music of lasting value.

One such was the Frenchman Erik Satie. Born in 1866, he spent years as a pianist in a Parisian cabaret, while composing in his spare time. In both his life and his music he displayed an unusual sense of humour. He gave his works strange titles, such as *Three Pieces in the Shape of a Pear*, and peppered the music with bizarre instructions to the performer. In one piece, the pianist is asked to 'play like a nightingale with toothache'.

Satie's private life was equally eccentric. He was never seen without an umbrella, of which he owned hundreds, and for the last 30 years of his existence he lived in a single room in a Paris suburb, where no visitors were ever allowed. When his friends at last went there after his death in 1925, they found only a bed, a chair, a table, a broken piano – and 12 identical grey velvet suits that had all been bought on

**Erik Satie** *A caricature of the eccentric French composer, with a manuscript page of one of his most popular works, the first* Gymnopédie, *a piano piece of strange, haunting beauty.*

the same day and never worn. Yet despite Satie's oddness, his music was appreciated by his more gifted contemporaries and influenced many later composers – and is still highly popular.

The 20th-century American composer Charles Ives was, by contrast, far more eccentric in his music than in his life. Ives trained as a musician but decided the insurance business offered a better living – in fact it made him a millionaire. He still devoted almost every spare moment of his busy working life to composition, writing music on commuter trains and in the evenings at home. He gave little thought to the publication or performance of his works, most of which came to light only after his death in 1954.

Ives found his inspiration in the sounds of everyday life. His music mixes the ringing of church bells and the blaring of brass bands, the whistling of errand boys and the chanting of hymn tunes, in a glorious experimental cacophony. In other words, like every true eccentric, he did exactly what he pleased when he pleased – and the result was music that is unique in its energy and originality.

### DID YOU KNOW..?

*ONCE MOZART, while rehearsing* Don Giovanni, *could not elicit a convincing scream from the singer playing the part of Zerlina as she resisted Giovanni's advances. So Mozart crept up behind her and seized her round the middle at the crucial moment. She shrieked. 'That,' he said, 'is the way an innocent maiden screams when her virtue is threatened.'*

\* \* \*

*WHEN BRAHMS was in his early teens and studying music, he used to play the piano in a sailors' tavern and dancing saloon. He would prop a book of poetry in front of him to distract himself from the noisy crowd – for he played everything by heart.*

\* \* \*

*SCHUBERT was incredibly industrious as a penniless young composer, writing as many as eight songs a day. He even slept with his spectacles on, in case he got an idea for a song in the night and wanted to write it down.*

# FROM BRANDY GLASSES TO DOOR HINGES
## *The serpent that sounds like a buffalo – and other odd instruments*

**A**T SOME TIME in the Stone Age, a man tied a bone to a piece of cord and whizzed it around his head to make an exciting sound, thus inventing the first 'bullroarer' or 'thunderstick'. Ever since, human beings have realised that anything that will produce a noise or a note can be used as a musical instrument.

From the sackbut to the saxophone, craftsmen have created a dazzling range of often outlandish instruments to bang, blow or scrape. One of the most bizarre is the 16th-century serpent, a curved, black object which, if stretched out, would measure 2 m (7 ft).

### No temptation
The serpent has been described by one enthusiast as looking like an elephant's intestines and sounding like a snorting buffalo. When the composer Handel heard it play, he is said to have remarked: 'Well, that is not the serpent that tempted Eve.' But he used the instrument in his *Music for the Royal Fireworks* all the same.

In 1761, the American inventor Benjamin Franklin took the simple idea of producing a sound by rubbing a moist finger around the rim of a glass, and adapted it to create a mechanical instrument which he called a glass harmonica. This soon attracted the attention

of famous composers, and Mozart wrote a quintet for the instrument with woodwind and strings. In the 1980s, an American, Jim Turner, made a bold effort to revive the art of glass playing, performing the Mozart quintet and other pieces, including jazz classics, on 60 brandy glasses.

Twentieth-century composers have often looked beyond traditional instruments for their inspiration and have

**Snorting snake** *The serpent takes its name from its long S-shaped tube. Once a common instrument, its muffled bass sound was heard in musical backwaters up to the end of the 19th century.*

searched for new sounds wherever they can – even in everyday objects. For his ballet *Parade*, Erik Satie employed typewriters, pistols and factory sirens. American composer George Antheil scored his *Ballet Mécanique* for eight pianos, a Pianola, eight xylophones, two electric doorbells and an aircraft propeller. In his *Acustica*, Mauricio Kagel featured the rattling of a board covered with door hinges.

The use of such novel 'instruments' has always exercised a fascination. At one of humorist Gerard Hoffnung's packed concerts in London's Festival Hall in the mid 1950s, a piece was performed entitled *Grand Grand Overture for Hoovers, Rifles, Cannon, Organ and Full Orchestra*.

## THE SOUND OF SILENCE

**O**N AUGUST 29, 1952, pianist David Tudor sat still and silent in front of the grand piano at the Maverick Concert Hall in Woodstock, New York. He made no attempt to touch the keyboard. After precisely four minutes 33 seconds, he got up and left – having completed the world premiere of *4' 33"* by the avant-garde American composer John Cage.

Writing a totally silent piece of music might seem extreme, but for John Cage this was only a beginning. In *Fontana Mix*, for instance, first performed in New York in 1959, the music is created out of the everyday sounds that people make – coughing, swallowing, putting spectacles on, even dropping ash in an ashtray. These tiny sounds are then amplified on tape. As the composer said: 'Now I go to a cocktail party, I don't hear noise, I hear music.'

Perhaps Cage's most famous works are his pieces for 'prepared piano'. Before the performance, the instrument is stuffed with all sorts of commonplace objects – nuts and bolts, spoons, clothes pegs, pieces of paper, wood. The pianist then plays on the keyboard in the usual way, but the sound that comes out is a long way from normality. The effect is strangely attractive, rather like some oriental percussion instrument.

Cage made music out of radio static, the sounds of pouring water or of a lion roaring, and from notes chosen at random by throwing dice. His *0' 0"* calls for anyone to ad lib anything. But of all his experiments, the silent *4' 33"* may well be the one the composer himself prized most. 'My favourite piece', he once wrote, 'is the one we hear all the time if we are quiet.'

## DID YOU KNOW..?

*THE LARGEST musical instrument in the world is the organ in the Municipal Auditorium, Atlantic City, on the eastern seaboard of the United States. Designed by Senator Emerson L. Richards and completed in 1930, the organ has 33 112 pipes ranging in length from 6 mm to 19.4 m (¼ in to 64 ft).*

# THE PIPES OF WAR

*How Scottish are the bagpipes?*

THE SHRILL skirl of the bagpipes has accompanied the kilted Scottish Highlanders into battle for at least the last 400 years, giving fresh courage to the fierce mountain warriors and striking fear into the hearts of their enemies. At the Battle of Pinkie in 1549, it is recorded, 'the wild Scots incited themselves to arms by the sound of their bagpipes.' And the pipers were playing too when Highland troops advanced across desert minefields against Rommel's Afrika Korps at Alamein in 1942.

### From Sweden to Tunisia

Bagpipes have become as much a symbol of Scotland as haggis or whisky. But the Scots have no claim to be the inventors of the instrument. Some version of the bagpipe was almost certainly flourishing in the Roman Empire as long ago as the 1st century AD. The Emperor Nero is believed to have played the instrument – he is more likely to have piped than fiddled while Rome burned. By 1300, bagpipes of one kind or another were droning and screeching from England to India and from Sweden to Tunisia – almost everywhere, in fact, except Scotland. It was not until another century had passed, and the rest of the world had started to tire of the pipes, that the Scots took them up and made them their own.

Bagpipes were popular partly because they could be made with materials that were to hand in a rural society. All that was needed was the skin of a sheep or the stomach of a cow to make the bag, and a few hollow reeds for the pipes. The principle of the instrument is clever but simple. The piper blows into the bag, which acts as a reservoir to maintain a steady flow of air to the pipes. The pipes are of two kinds, 'chanters' and 'drones'. In a basic two-pipe version, the piper plays the tune on the chanter while the drone produces the single constant bass note that is so characteristic of the bagpipe sound. In some variants, the flow of air for the bag is provided by a bellows.

Bagpipes are still used for folk music in many countries – they accompany, for instance, the traditional dances of the Breton people in northwest France. For most people the sound of the bagpipes rising over the din of battle is indelibly associated with Scottish regiments. But they have no exclusive claim to this: for centuries the Irish, too, have used bagpipes as a call to arms.

*Tunes of glory* Piper Laidlaw rallies the King's Own Scottish Borderers to continue advancing through a mustard gas cloud on the Western Front in 1915. His valour with the bagpipes won Laidlaw the Victoria Cross.

# A JEWEL OF AN INSTRUMENT
## *The secret behind the greatest violin in the world*

A VIOLIN MADE in the 18th century by Antonio Stradivari of Cremona, Italy, can be worth as much as US $1 million. 'Strads' are so extraordinarily valuable because they are still considered to be the finest violins ever produced.

Stradivari trained his two sons to make stringed instruments as well, but they failed to achieve the same magical quality, outstanding as their work was. Exactly what gives a Stradivarius its unique quality has long been a mystery – although suspicion has largely centred on the varnish used in the instruments. Stradivari wrote his formula for the varnish on the flyleaf of the family Bible – but unfortunately one of his descendants destroyed it.

### Venetian timber

However, Joseph Nagyvary, professor of biochemistry and biophysics at the Texas A&M University, believes he has discovered the secret of Stradivari's success. Nagyvary points out that the spruce wood Stradivari used came from Venice, where timber was stored in the sea. This created minute holes in the wood – which Nagyvary found only with an electron microscope magnifying 2000 times. These holes are absent from the dry-seasoned wood used in modern violins, but are present in a Stradivarius. This, reasons Nagyvary, must give an extra richness and resonance to the sound.

When he examined the varnish, Nagyvary made another remarkable discovery: it contained tiny mineral crystals. He concluded that these came from ground-up gemstones, added by

***Violin superstar** This late 19th-century artist's impression of Stradivari's workshop in Cremona shows the master craftsman, charming the ears of his admiring assistants, as he tests the sound of a new violin.*

the alchemists who made the varnish in the belief that the stones had magical properties. On a violin, the crystals would filter out high-pitched harmonics to give a purer, smoother sound.

Nagyvary tested his theory by building his own violin out of wet-seasoned wood, coated with varnish containing gemstone powder. One expert called the result 'the best new violin I've heard'. Internationally renowned violinist Zina

Schiff was impressed enough to play the Nagyvary instrument in public concerts.

Were Stradivari, or any of the other famous craftsmen in Cremona, such as the Amatis and Guarneris, aware of the unique qualities of the materials they used? Nagyvary says: 'I honestly think the old violin makers did not know anything more about violin making than the modern violin maker . . . . They were just the lucky beneficiaries of the greatest historical coincidence.'

If craftsmen take up Nagyvary's discoveries will the value of an original 'Strad' fall? Almost certainly not. For no one else seems to be able to recapture that magic ingredient – his genius.

---

## SCALING THE DEPTHS

'MOST of our members still don't know which end of a violin to blow.' This is the proud boast of the Portsmouth Sinfonia, an orchestra in the south of England that claims to be the worst in the world. Founded by art students in 1969, the Sinfonia has made a successful career out of being unbelievably bad. Some of its musicians are of professional standard, but they try not to let their skills show.

By 1981, the Sinfonia felt that some other British orchestras had slipped so disastrously that its reputation was under threat. In that year, when the Royal Philharmonic Orchestra recorded a medley of popular tunes backed by a disco beat, the Sinfonia responded with its own *Classic Muddly*, a truly awful, slipshod recording that guaranteed its status as the very worst for years to come. At the time, Sinfonia conductor John Farley freely admitted his own incompetence: 'I'm a very bad conductor,' he told a reporter, 'but the orchestra has got what it deserved.'

## DID YOU KNOW..?

*JEAN BAPTISTE LULLY mortally wounded himself while conducting his* Te Deum. *He was beating time by banging a staff on the floor. Unfortunately, he missed the floor, and crushed a toe. Gangrene set in and he died.*

\* \* \*

*THE YOUNG Schumann tied up his middle finger in order to strengthen the others. The result was a badly damaged finger, and the end of any hopes of becoming a first-rate player. Instead he became a brilliant composer.*

# BREAKING THE SOUND BARRIER

*When today's avant-garde may seem old hat*

ON MAY 15, 1913, a Parisian theatre staged the first performance of a new ballet, *The Rite of Spring*, with music by Igor Stravinsky. Almost as soon as the orchestra started playing, members of the audience began to whistle and shout their disapproval. Fights erupted, the police were called, and the evening ended in a near riot. The main reason for all the uproar was the revolutionary nature of Stravinsky's music. His jagged, aggressive score had broken the narrow boundary that marks off what is 'acceptable' as new music from what sounds discordant and even offensive. Yet nowadays, *The Rite of Spring* is a standard work in the concert repertoire – it would seem that familiarity has bred acceptance.

It may be difficult for the modern listener, confronted by the often puzzling experiments of the late 20th-century avant-garde, to believe that these too will one day become concert hall favourites. Composers have swung from the extremes of 'serial' music, in which every detail of pitch, rhythm and volume has been mathematically determined, to 'aleatory' music, where everything is supposed to happen by chance. Sometimes performers have been as puzzled as audiences – as, for instance, when they were asked to play a piece in which the lines of the musical staff were drawn on the side of a fish tank and the fish swimming behind the glass acted as the notes.

Yet some modern experimental techniques have already found their way into popular music. English composer David Bedford is in some ways a typical member of the avant-garde. His works have bizarre titles like *The Tentacles of the Dark Nebula* and *A Horse, His Name Was Henry Fenceweaver*. In one of his pieces, Bedford instructs singers to perform at any time and at any speed. In another, the audience joins in playing on kazoos. But Bedford has also worked with rock musicians, such as Mike Oldfield, who have a massive popular following. And many pop groups now use electronic sounds that were once the preserve of the avant-garde.

Perhaps it will happen, then, that to the next generation brought up on computers, the music of today's avant-garde will sound old hat. There are always new barriers to be broken.

---

## DID YOU KNOW..?

*MENDELSSOHN lost the score for his* A Midsummer Night's Dream *overture by leaving it in a cab. He rewrote every note from memory.*

\* \* \*

*TOSCANINI, the Italian conductor, was notorious for his rages. In a temper he once thrust his fist through a door in New York's Carnegie Hall. A sentimental fan kept the splintered wood as a souvenir.*

---

## THE MUSICAL SWAN

IN 1774, Cox's Mechanical Museum in London exhibited the 'Silver Swan'. A life-size, working model, the graceful bird would curve its long neck to plunge its head down to a 'lake' of glass rods, and appeared to seize a silver fish in its beak. The elegant routine was accompanied by music played on a set of bells. Such elaborate automata were the origin of a craze that was to sweep the world in the following century – the musical box.

**Silver swan** *Cox's mechanical bird sat on a lake of glass rods, where silver fish wriggled back and forth. The musical accompaniment to the swan's graceful movements was partly intended to mask the sound of the mechanism. The swan can now be found in the Bowes Museum in County Durham, in the north of England.*

Interchangeable Cylinder Musical Box, designed for an envoy of the Shah of Persia in 1901, had 20 cylinders, each capable of playing six tunes. As well as two steel combs, it incorporated an entire percussion section of drums, cymbals and bells, a reed organ worked by miniature bellows and, as if this were not enough, two singing birds perched in an imitation garden.

For all this lavish artifice, the musical box could not compete with the phonograph and by 1914 it had almost died out. The more elaborate models remain treasured collector's items, however. In 1985, the Grand Orchestral Interchangeable Cylinder Musical Box was auctioned at Sotheby's, London, for a remarkable £19 000 (about US $30 000).

The basic mechanism for the musical box was reputedly invented by the Swiss watchmaker Aristide Janvier in 1776. It consists of a rotating cylinder with projecting steel pins that pluck the tuned teeth of a steel comb. The tune played depends on the arrangement of the pins.

At first musical boxes were very simple, but by the late 19th century they had developed into sophisticated devices offering a range of tunes that could be selected by the turn of a knob. The most luxurious models were of a truly fantastic complexity. The Grand Orchestral

# DIVINELY GIFTED
*Paganini's performances were out of this world*

IN 1829, a music critic wrote that the 47-year-old Italian violin virtuoso Niccolò Paganini's playing opened a world through sound that had only been experienced before in dreams. He added: 'there is something so demonic in his appearance that at one moment we seek the hidden cloven hoof, at the next, the wings of an angel.'

Nothing like Paganini's playing had ever been heard before. Like most other great composers of his day, he wrote virtuoso pieces whose technical demands ideally suited his own prodigious abilities. Using every conceivable technical device, he played with incomparable expressiveness. So astounding was his playing that many people believed his talent to be drawn from divine or satanic forces. A popular rumour that Paganini had sold his soul to the Devil was given further credence by his pale, gaunt looks – which in later life were accentuated by illness – and by his extraordinary personal magnetism. Far from denying these rumours, Paganini encouraged them by openly pursuing a dissolute lifestyle, gambling and chasing women. Once he was so deeply in debt that he pawned his violin.

It was only when he was in his mid-forties that he tried to give due credit to his own industry and genius. He sent numerous letters to music journals disclaiming all stories of a pact with the Devil.

But by then it was too late. On his deathbed in 1840, the 58-year-old Paganini repeatedly refused to see a priest. When he died, the Church refused to allow his burial in consecrated ground. His body was stored ignominiously in a cellar for five years before being properly interred.

*Fabled fiddler Niccolò Paganini's technically brilliant and expressive violin playing coupled with his extraordinary looks led to rumours of a pact with the Devil.*

## THE MAGICAL MECHANICAL PIANO

AS RECENTLY as the 1920s, player-pianos were one of the world's most popular forms of entertainment. With their keys moving up and down as if played by phantom fingers, these 'Pianolas' (actually the trade name of one make) poured out their music in shady bars and respectable parlours alike. In the United States alone, half a million player-pianos were manufactured in the early 1920s. Yet by the 1930s, with the increasing popularity of the radio and gramophone, the once prevalent player-piano had disappeared almost as completely as the dinosaurs.

The first player-piano was patented in France in 1863. It consisted of a cabinet placed in front of a piano with a line of felt-covered 'fingers' projecting over the piano keys. Inside the cabinet, a tracker bar 'read' holes that had been punched into a rotating paper roll (like the holes in a computer punch card). The bar then activated a system of bellows that made the 'fingers' strike the appropriate piano keys. In later models, the whole mechanism was incorporated into the piano itself.

*Family fun In the 1920s, the Pianola was a focal point for home-entertainment.*

In some models the user would be required to pedal the bellows to control both the volume and speed – quite a skilful business, and one that was rarely totally successful. In more sophisticated models, known as reproducing pianos, the expressive effects of pedalling were incorporated into a punch card that was able to reproduce every nuance of a performance, such as a change of tempo.

Famous pianists from all styles of music – from Rachmaninov and Debussy to George Gershwin and 'Fats' Waller – queued up to record their performances on piano rolls, which were then reproduced for sale like modern-day discs or tapes. The enormous advantage of the roll was that it was played back on a real piano – even today's compact discs inevitably lose some of the quality of a live instrument, despite a highly sophisticated recording process.

Late 20th-century computer technology has caught up with the player-piano. In the 1970s, the Japanese company Marantz developed the Pianocorder – a computer and specially encoded magnetic tape that is installed in a piano to enable pianists to record themselves while they play. They can then sit back and listen as the performance is repeated by the instrument on its own – mistakes and all.

# A REASON TO WRITE

## *What inspires authors to put pen to paper?*

**T**HE POWER that drives novelists or poets can vary as much as the subjects they choose to write about. And by no means all writers are concerned above all to create works of art. Some write purely for the money. Anthony Trollope used to say that a writer was like a shoemaker: 'His primary object is a living.' He once declared that he wanted to excel 'in quantity if not in quality', and succeeded in so far as he habitually reeled off 3000 words before breakfast. During the 1860s and 1870s this industry earned him £4500 (about US $230 000 today) in an average year, but that did not stop him bombarding his family and his publishers with letters about all kinds of trifling financial matters.

Harold Robbins has always had a talent for making money. In 1936, at the age of 20, he became a millionaire from his dealings in the food industry, but he lost it all three years later. His first novel was published in 1948. Today he earns at least $500 000 a year from an output that critics have described as 'throwaway' and even 'disgusting', but that sells 30 000 copies a day worldwide. Commercial success is presumably what makes Robbins feel justified in calling

**Author's retreat** *To write his novels, Thomas Wolfe would often escape from the hectic atmosphere of New York to the seclusion of his log cabin in Oteen, North Carolina.*

himself 'the world's best novelist' who has not 'the faintest idea' why he has never won a literary prize.

Some authors are best inspired by themselves. Thomas Wolfe once described an unfinished 500 000-word autobiographical novel as 'a mere skeleton of a book' and, when his publisher asked him to cut it, he simply added more. Despite ever-increasing pressure from his publisher, Wolfe repeatedly refused to agree to the cuts. When he was told that his autobiography might not sell widely because of its length, he disdainfully replied that any fool could see that the book was not written for money.

### *Hiding a creative urge*

John Keats is an excellent example of the writer driven purely by creative inspiration. He would scribble verses, none too legibly, on scraps of paper – and then hide them. A friend with whom Keats was staying noticed this odd behaviour and managed to save several of his greatest poems, including his *Ode to a Nightingale*, from possible oblivion by searching the house from top to bottom. Yet even Keats hankered for recognition, and was deeply hurt by the critics' hostility to his poetry. In 1821, as he lay dying from tuberculosis at the age of 25, he ordered engraved on his tombstone the words: 'Here lies one whose name was writ in water.'

**Awaiting death** *Only a few days before his death at the age of 25, John Keats was painted by his friend Joseph Severn in his Rome hotel. Keats had come to Italy in hopes of finding relief from his tuberculosis.*

# THE DANGEROUS EDGE

*The man who found writing more exciting than
playing Russian roulette*

'**A** GAMBLE with a 16 per cent
chance of failure' was how
Graham Greene regarded his
early experiments with a revolver, loaded with one cartridge, that he had
found in his elder brother's cupboard.
Not that Greene had any apparent reason for playing with the possibility of
killing himself. He was a successful
undergraduate at Oxford, editing a student magazine and leading a full and
active life. But, as one friend put it,
Greene, by playing Russian roulette,
'wasn't trying to get out of life; he was
trying to get more kick out of life.'

### Seeking out hot spots

Graham Greene always suffered from
excruciating boredom. Fear of boredom
and a fascination with death were the
determining factors in his career. Once
he had given up gambling with pistols,
he was drawn irresistibly to the most
dangerous places on Earth. From Spain
in the Civil War to the conflict in the
Belgian Congo, from the wars in
Vietnam to the appalling corruption of
Haiti, from Batista's Cuba to pre-
Sandinista Nicaragua, and from the
Suez Canal in the Six-Day War to the
strife-torn streets of Belfast, Greene
roamed the world with boredom snapping at his heels.

Greene, however, was more than a
random traveller engaged in *Boy's
Own* adventures. To keep boredom at
bay, Greene had himself dispatched to
what he called the 'dangerous edge' of
things. He was fascinated by unstable
regimes, and saw many crumble. But
Greene was not merely a detached
observer; he also had a strong impulse
to become involved. This led him to
take winter clothes to Cuban revolutionaries hiding out in the mountains,
to provide Nicaraguan Sandinistas with
ammunition, and so mock the dictator
Papa Doc that the Haitian government
denounced him as a pervert and, still
more implausibly, as a torturer.

### Distilling his experience

Often, Greene's novels arose out of his
travels. Sometimes he travelled in search
of a novel. For *A Burnt-out Case* he
spent three months in a leper colony in
the Congo. But, just as Greene needed
to travel, he needed to write: to him,
both were forms of action. And for him
writing was a way to make sense of
what he referred to as the 'madness and
melancholie' of human existence. He
also claimed to be unable to understand
how other people can cope without trying to interpret their lives through writing, composing or painting.

Greene may have seen life that way,
and may have been terrified of boredom:
the irony is that he entertained, intrigued
and enlightened millions of readers
through his inspired writing.

*Great adventurer Graham Greene, who
acquired a following at the age of 28 with the
1932 thriller* Stamboul Train, *could look back
on a life full of adventures.*

# A SEASON IN HELL

*The gunrunner who was
a great poet*

**I**N MARCH 1891, a 37-year-old gunrunner with a cancerous leg was
being carried across the Arabian
desert towards Aden. Arthur Rimbaud
was making his painful way home to
France after a decade in Arabia and
Africa, where he had worked as a merchant, travelled on expeditions to
gather ivory, and provided arms for
obscure African wars. A moderately
successful entrepreneur, he had managed to amass some 30 000 francs
(equivalent to about US $90 000 today).

No one – least of all Rimbaud himself –
on that last journey would have suspected that this adventurer and businessman
was soon to be acclaimed one of
France's greatest lyric poets. He had not
written a line of poetry since 1874. In
France itself, he was assumed to be dead.

### Early creativity

Rimbaud wrote all his poems between
the ages of 15 and 20. Coming to Paris
from his native Charleville, he had
taken up with fellow poet Paul
Verlaine. Together, the two writers
scandalised the literary establishment,
drinking copious quantities of absinthe,
smoking hashish and ridiculing prominent academicians. Both gained notoriety, but Rimbaud's poetry was ignored.

In 1873, during an argument, Verlaine
shot and wounded Rimbaud, and was
sent to prison. Rimbaud was blamed by
his fellow writers for Verlaine's imprisonment and ostracised by them; he
reacted by pouring out his visionary
poem, *A Season in Hell*, and then
renounced poetry for good.

As he confesses in that poem,
Rimbaud had tried to reinvent language,
to 'give colours to the vowels and make
words operate on all the senses'. But he
felt his work had been a complete failure. One night, in despair, he burned all
his manuscripts, and then left France to
wander around Europe and Africa.

Thanks largely to his old friend
Verlaine, from the late 1880s Rimbaud's
work began to be published and appreciated. Gunrunning in Africa, he never
tasted his long-delayed success. When
he finally arrived in France in May
1891, his right leg was amputated, but
the cancer had now spread throughout
his body. Three months later, Arthur
Rimbaud was dead.

# CHARACTER IN SEARCH OF A PLOT
### *Who killed the unconventional Kit Marlowe?*

**'A** WOUND over his right eye of the depth of two inches and of the width of one inch.' That, an inquest determined, had caused the death of 29-year-old playwright Christopher Marlowe in an inn near London on May 30, 1593. Four centuries later, the question of exactly why Marlowe was killed remains unanswered.

Marlowe – besides having a reputation second only to Shakespeare's for plays such as *Dr Faustus* and *Edward II* – was a drinker, brawler, roustabout and intriguer. He was also notoriously irreligious in an age when religious loyalties could make or break a man. Any of these unconventional aspects of his character could have led to his murder.

### New evidence

For the best part of 350 years, the favourite suspect – on no concrete evidence – was a jealous homosexual lover. Then, in 1925, a long-lost report of the inquest on Marlowe's death came to light. It described his last hours in detail and identified his killer. But it raised yet more questions.

Marlowe had spent the last day of his life at Eleanor Bull's tavern in the company of three men: Robert Poley, Ingram Friser and Nicholas Skeres. They began drinking at 10am, and continued throughout the day. Then Marlowe and Friser fell out over the bill. Marlowe snatched Friser's dagger and struck him with the hilt. Friser responded by seizing the knife and driving it into Marlowe's skull.

### Anti-Catholic sentiment

On the face of it, the killing seems to have been no more than the tragic climax to a day of drunken idleness. But Poley was a government agent and had just returned from a mission abroad. Under the Protestant queen, Elizabeth I, all Catholics were regarded as potential enemies of the state. Friser was a Catholic spy and a swindler; Skeres a petty thief. What was Marlowe doing in such company in the first place?

Marlow had once been a spy himself. Espionage had interfered with his studies at Cambridge to the extent that only under pressure from the government did the university grant him his degree. Perhaps surprisingly, for a self-confessed atheist, he had lately been in the company of prominent, politically

*Fatal brawl A Victorian illustrator depicted the death of Christopher Marlowe in a tavern. But, contrary to this etching, he was stabbed with a knife, not a sword.*

active Catholics and, accidentally or otherwise, may have discovered something compromising about them.

At the time of his death, Marlowe was about to face charges of heresy. For, under torture, his fellow dramatist Thomas Kyd had implicated Marlowe in the production of anti-Protestant propaganda. Marlowe may have been about to trade information for his own freedom; or, at least, someone feared he would, and so had charged Friser with silencing him.

None of this really explains the role of Poley in the affair. Possibly he was there to hear what Marlowe had to reveal about current Catholic schemes, and Friser took the opportunity to protect his paymasters. But that would not account for the unseemly haste with which Friser was pardoned for the murder.

Was it a political killing, or simply the result of tempers flaring after too much to drink? Perhaps, somewhere, another official report lies gathering dust.

# EVERLASTING POETRY

*The book that was brought back from the grave*

WHEN Lizzie Siddal died of an accidental overdose of the drug laudanum in 1862, she had been married to the painter and poet Dante Gabriel Rossetti for just two years. Despite a long engagement, the marriage had been as turbulent as it was short. And in 1861, the couple's only child was still-born. Lizzie's already nervous disposition was further undermined. In the end, she had to take laudanum both to sleep and to give herself an appetite for food.

When she died, Rossetti was devastated. He burned every letter she had sent him and destroyed every photograph of her that he owned. None, he claimed, did her beauty justice. In a final poignant gesture, he threw the only manuscript of his poems into her coffin.

### A purer medium

Rossetti was first and foremost a painter, but he came to believe that poetry was a purer form of expression. Over the course of the next few years, he decided to publish a volume of his own work – but many of his best poems were deep under the ground with Lizzie.

The artist was also a great eccentric – he kept wombats and kangaroos in his

London house – with a predilection for the supernatural, for which he had shown a marked fondness since boyhood. Particularly after Lizzie's death, he often experimented with spiritualism and mesmerism. In 1869, when he was working hard on some new poems, he

*Drowned beauty In 1852, Millais asked Lizzie Siddal to model for Ophelia, the heroine who drowned herself in the belief that Hamlet did not love her.*

came across an unusually tame chaffinch while out walking and was instantly convinced that it was the spirit of his wife. This seems to have made him decide to seek the opening of her grave, in London's Highgate Cemetery, and the exhumation of his poems.

Rossetti was not present when Lizzie Siddal was dug up. But a friend told him that her famous golden-red hair was longer than it had ever been in life, and that she was as beautiful as she had been on the day she died.

The news of the exhumation leaked; a curious public flocked to buy Rossetti's 'underground' poems when they were published. And the legend of the woman whose beauty not even death could alter was born and has flourished ever since.

## MIRROR OF LIFE

WHILE at work on a novel, Charles Dickens would frequently rush to a mirror. In front of it, he would contort his face in a series of grimaces. Then he would rush back to his desk, to continue writing frantically.

At such moments it was as if the creatures of his imagination had temporarily possessed him. Dickens claimed actually to hear every word the characters in his novels spoke. He did not invent his stories, he said: he saw them.

Dickens would weep at the misfortunes and sufferings of the children of his brain and rejoice at their good fortune, as if he held them as dearly in his heart as his own children. Often, too, the men and women who crystallised out of his pen would irritate him, for they would not leave him alone.

*Strange guests Terrified of losing his imaginative gift, Dickens put up with everyday intrusions from his characters.*

## DID YOU KNOW..?

*THE WORLD'S top-selling author is the British writer Barbara Cartland, who has sold over 500 million copies of her 500 romantic novels. Since 1976, she has also held the record for writing the most books a year: an average of 23.*

# THE LONG VOYAGE OF ULYSSES
### *The world's most censored masterpiece*

**A**LTHOUGH his novel *Ulysses* was concerned with the events of a single day – June 16, 1904 – James Joyce calculated that he had spent 20 000 hours writing his epic set in the city of Dublin. That represents about 2500 normal working days, or eight years working a six-day week without holidays.

More than 16 years passed from the time Joyce published the first part of the book in March 1918 until it was freely available in its entirety in 1934. This was not because Joyce was a slow writer – he finished *Ulysses* in 1922 – but because the sexually explicit novel was censored, banned and burned before it reached the bookshops in one piece.

### *Postal service scruples*
The first instalments of *Ulysses* were published in an American magazine, the *Little Review*, in 1918. In 1921 the US postal service exercised its power to prosecute anyone who sent obscene material through the post and took the magazine to court. The editors were convicted and fined $50 each.

Other writers were sympathetic enough: Virginia Woolf, herself a pioneering novelist, and her husband Leonard would have been happy to publish *Ulysses*, but it would have taken two years just to set the type by hand on their antiquated press. But no established publisher would take the book unless Joyce made cuts, and that he refused to do.

### *Limited editions*
Finally, in 1922, the tiny Parisian firm of Shakespeare & Co. brought out a limited edition of 1000 copies. The same year, the Egoist Press in London published an edition of 2000 copies, only to have 500 of them confiscated by the US postal service in New York. Egoist Press soon brought out a further printing of 500 copies, and the British customs seized and burned 499 of them.

To add insult to injury, an unscrupulous American, Samuel Roth, began printing expurgated and unauthorised versions of Joyce's text in his magazine, *Two Worlds*. Joyce's standing was such

that he was able to raise a petition against Roth that was signed by 167 luminaries, ranging from physicist Albert Einstein to novelist E.M. Forster.

Only in December 1933, in a celebrated court case, was *Ulysses* cleared of obscenity charges. This paved the way for Random House in New York to publish an unexpurgated edition. However, it was not until the 1960s that *Ulysses* was available in Dublin.

***Uncompromising figure*** *After* Dubliners *and* A Portrait of the Artist as a Young Man, Ulysses *was James Joyce's third prose work to run foul of the censors. But he refused to accept any alterations in his works.*

# THE ULTIMATE REFERENCE BOOK
### *It was born in Edinburgh, inspired by a Parisian, lives in Chicago, and calls itself British*

**T**HE *ENCYCLOPAEDIA* Britannica is renowned all over the world. But it is not British. An American company has owned the title since 1902, and the huge work is published today by the University of Chicago. The latest edition runs to 30 volumes and 43 million words, and it cost $32 million to plan, write and edit – and that does not include the printer's bill.

### *Scottish origins*
*Britannica* started rather more modestly in Edinburgh, Scotland, in 1768, when two men – printer and bookseller Colin Macfarquhar, and an engraver of fine collars for gentlemen's dogs, Andrew Bell – joined forces. They believed they could emulate the success of the French *Encyclopédie* edited by Denis Diderot and published between 1751 and 1765.

They advertised their forthcoming work as 'A New and Complete Dictionary of Arts and Sciences', and hired a 28-year-old scholar and scientist, William Smellie, to be editor.

In December 1768 the first part of the new encyclopedia appeared. It was issued in 100 instalments, and the three-volume set was complete by 1771. Enlivening the 2659 pages were 160 engravings by Andrew Bell.

### *Mixed coverage*
The contents were comprehensive indeed. Toothache, said the text, might be cured with 'laxatives of manna and cassia dissolved in whey or asses milk'. A recipe was offered for making fake emeralds. 'Woman' was defined simply as 'the female of man', and sex as 'something in the body that distinguishes male from female'. But Smellie made up for these two dismissive entries with a 40-page illustrated article on midwifery; many readers demanded its removal.

Controversy and shortcomings apart, the new encyclopedia was a fair success, selling 3000 copies of the first edition – enough to justify the second edition of 1776 and to inspire several unauthorised American editions.

# BATTLE OF THE GIANTS

*Which is really the world's tallest statue?*

**A**SKED WHICH is the tallest statue in the world, most people will almost certainly answer the Statue of Liberty, or perhaps the Great Sphinx at Giza, Egypt. But while both of these have enormous reputations, neither is the world's tallest statue. For over 1250 years, that distinction belonged to the Dafo Buddha in Leshan, China. Since it was built in AD 713, the Buddha dwarfed all other contenders, until its title was taken, in 1967, by Motherland Calls in the Soviet Union – by far the tallest statue in the world. The sword held in the figure's outstretched hand reaches nearly 12 m (40 ft) higher than the Buddha. America's famous beacon stretches only halfway up the side of the colossal Russian sculpture, and the Great Sphinx does not even reach her knees.

**The Statue of Liberty**
Height: 47 m (155 ft)
*Visible for up to 95 km (60 miles), the Statue of Liberty welcomes visitors to New York Harbour. Liberty, which sits on a 45 m (150 ft) plinth, was presented to the USA by France in 1884 to commemorate 100 years of American independence. Its internal frame was built by Gustave Eiffel, architect of the Eiffel Tower.*

**The Mount Rushmore Memorial**
Height, chin to top: 18 m (60 ft)
*If any of the four heads carved on Mount Rushmore, South Dakota, USA, were given a body, the figure would stand nearly 152 m (500 ft) tall. The heads, which took 15 years to make, depict George Washington, Thomas Jefferson, Theodore Roosevelt and Abraham Lincoln. They were almost complete by 1941 when their sculptor, Gutzon Borglum, died. His son finished the fine details.*

**The Corcovado Christ**
Height: 30 m (100 ft)
*On the summit of Mount Corcovado (which means 'hunchback') overlooking Rio de Janeiro, Brazil, stands the world's largest statue of Christ. With arms outstretched, the imposing figure of Christ the Redeemer stands some 743 m (2452 ft) above sea level. French sculptor Paul Landowski built the figure in concrete in just four years, completing it in 1931.*

**The Bamian Buddha**
Height: 53 m (175 ft)
*In the cliffs of the Bamian River Valley, in Afghanistan on the border with India, there stands the second largest Buddhist sculpture in the world. Built around AD 600, when the town was a centre of Buddhism, this huge rock carving is set back in a cave hewn from the cliff face. In the same valley there is a second statue, identical in everything but size, being 15 m (50 ft) shorter.*

### The Crazy Horse Monument

*When complete, the statue of the Sioux Indian chief Crazy Horse will be a dizzying 171 m (563 ft) tall. At present the rough form is very gradually taking shape on Thunderhead Mountain in South Dakota. American sculptor Korczac Ziolkowski began the monument in 1942, thinking it would take seven years to build. But Korczac died in 1982 and his family have vowed to complete the work. To date, eight million tonnes of rock have been blasted away.*

### Motherland Calls

Height: 82 m (270 ft)

*Well over twice the size of the Corcovado Christ, Motherland Calls is the world's tallest statue. The concrete figure was built in 1967 to commemorate the 1942–43 Battle of Stalingrad, in which the Russian army suffered heavy losses while defending the city. It stands atop a hill overlooking the city of Volgograd (called Stalingrad until 1961).*

### The Dafo Buddha

Height: 70 m (231 ft)

*The big toe of the seated Dafo ('grand') Buddha in Leshan, China, is over 8 m (26 ft) long. In fact you could comfortably stretch out on one of the Buddha's toenails, which are 1.8 m (6 ft) wide. The statue, which took 90 years to build, sits majestically on the banks of the river Min. It was designed by a Buddhist monk called Haitong and was completed in AD 713.*

### The Colossi of Memnon

Height: 21 m (70 ft)

*People once travelled to Thebes from all over Egypt to listen to one of the giant Colossi 'sing' each day at sunrise. Both statues were built in 1400 BC. One was damaged in the 1st century AD, and its 'song' may have been the noise of the cracked stone expanding in the heat of the morning sunshine. The Colossus has been silent since the Roman Emperor Severus had it repaired around AD 200.*

### The Great Sphinx

Height: 20 m (66 ft) Length: 73 m (240 ft)

*Hewn from a natural outcrop of rock, the Great Sphinx is the largest of the Egyptian sphinxes, and has guarded the pyramids at Giza for almost 4500 years. For most of that time only the head, a portrait of Pharaoh Khafre, was visible – the rest was buried beneath the shifting desert sands. It was not until the 1920s that the enormous lion's body was again exposed to view.*

# THE STORY OF ART
### *The oldest paintings ever found*

ONCE UPON A TIME, in ancient Greece, two young lovers were about to be parted. Wanting some memento of her beloved before he left on his journey, the girl drew a line on the wall, following the edge of his shadow thrown by the lamplight. The result was the first portrait – a perfect profile of a man.

According to the Roman writer Pliny the Elder, this romantic story actually describes the origin of representational art. Strikingly similar stories have emerged from places as far afield as Tibet and India, but, in fact, none are likely to be true. So why and when and where did representational art actually begin?

The very first paintings known to archaeologists are those found on the walls of the caves of Palaeolithic man in France and Spain. They are believed to be over 20 000 years old. Most of the paintings depict animals and this has given experts a clue to their meaning.

**Magic image** *The oldest known pictures of real-life objects are bison painted by our cave-dwelling ancestors – this example, from the Grotte de Niaux in the French Pyrenees, is over 20 000 years old. These images were probably the focus for magic ceremonies to ensure success in hunting.*

It is now generally accepted that these images had symbolic or magical functions. It is thought Palaeolithic man believed that by painting a picture of a bison pierced with arrows he would ensure a successful hunt.

These images were usually painted in red, brown, yellow and black with brushes or fingers. The pigments were made from natural materials – such as rust and soot – ground into powders and mixed with water. They were stored in bones and skulls.

As the tradition of art developed, its function gradually changed and belief in an image's magical qualities declined. But, even in this century, remnants of this prehistoric belief in the magical power of images still persist in, for instance, the practise of witchcraft and the widespread use of lucky charms.

## THE VENUS OF THE CAVES

TOWARDS THE END of the last century, several miniature carvings were found buried inside a cave in the French Pyrenees. As they represent women, they have been christened 'Venuses', although they are far from beautiful to modern eyes. The figures are highly stylised, with large, lumpy bodies, and featureless faces. The one exception is a small, delicate head of a girl with long hair, which is far nearer the modern-day idea of a conventional beauty.

So who were these women? And what were these tiny sculptures for? It was soon established that the figures had been carved in ivory from the tusks of mammoths, and that the primitive sculptors must have been our cave-dwelling ancestors from the Palaeolithic period. Many similar figures have been found in caves throughout Europe. They are thought to represent Mother Nature, and may have been endowed with magical powers and used in religious ceremonies to encourage abundance and fertility.

Experts believe the Venuses were made over 30 000 years ago, which makes them some of the oldest sculptures in existence.

**Earth mother** *Like all the prehistoric Venuses, this ivory carving from Lespugue in southwest France is very small – it is reproduced here at approximately half its real size.*

# RAGS AND RICHES

### *How true is the popular image of the 'struggling artist'?*

**W**HEN the Baroque sculptor and architect Giovanni Bernini journeyed from Rome to Paris in 1664, he travelled in style. Accompanied by one of his sons, four servants, two assistants and a cook, he made an almost regal progress from town to town, greeted everywhere by local dignitaries and invited to the homes of princes. When the artist approached Paris, King Louis XIV's first minister sent his brother's best carriage to transport

***Gentleman artist*** *When the wealthy Flemish artist Rubens painted this self-portrait in 1609, he proudly depicted himself as a man of taste, with a wife richly dressed in the height of fashion.*

***Bohemian life*** *This picture of an artist huddled by his meagre fire was painted by Octave Tassaert in 1845. In the 19th century, it was commonly held that artistic genius and worldly success were incompatible.*

him into the city, where the king received him with every mark of respect. Bernini's artistic genius had earned him both fame and fortune.

Any successful artist in Bernini's day could expect to live the good life. The wealthiest of all was probably the painter Peter Paul Rubens, who combined an immensely busy artistic career with a lucrative secondary role as a diplomat. By the end of his life he owned a spectacular town house in Antwerp, Belgium, and a castle in the country, and was still able to leave his heirs the large sum of 400 000 guilders – enough money to buy four manor houses. As well as being rich, Rubens was a perfect gentleman. He could not have been farther from today's stereotype of the artist as a poverty-stricken rebel against society.

But there is some truth in this stereotype. Many artists have suffered a near lifetime of destitution before attaining success, which sometimes arrives only posthumously. Vincent van Gogh was such an artist. During the last years of his life, when he painted many of his greatest works, he would have had no money for oils and canvas had he not been helped by his brother Theo. In Vincent's whole life he sold only a few paintings, and he died – by committing suicide – in total obscurity in 1890. He surely could never have imagined that on November 11, 1987, his painting *Irises* would sell for US $53 900 000.

## *Years of rejection*

It is not only individual painters who have had to struggle for recognition. Whole artistic movements, which are now admired, were once reviled. When, in 1874, a group of painters which included Pierre Auguste Renoir exhibited their work for the first time, their style was jeered at by the art world. It took years of rejection before their style was appreciated and they found acclaim as the impressionists.

For some artists, success brings extraordinary wealth. It is said that if Pablo Picasso wanted a house, he need only draw a picture of it – the drawing would be worth more than the building.

# RIVALS IN ART

## *The great artistic collaboration that ended in disaster*

IN 1503, two of the greatest artists who ever lived, Leonardo da Vinci and Michelangelo Buonarroti, were asked to produce paintings of war scenes to decorate the walls of a room in the Palazzo Vecchio in the Italian city of Florence. This might have been a golden opportunity for artistic co-operation – but it was not. Leonardo and Michelangelo loathed one another.

### Clash of the titans

Leonardo was already in his fifties, wealthy and famous. Used to the company of princes, he kept servants, wore the finest clothes to adorn his tall, handsome figure, and was renowned for his charm. Michelangelo, only 29 years old, was very different – bad mannered, ill-kempt, aggressive and solitary. With his broken nose and muscular body, he looked more like a fighter than an artist.

The two men found it impossible to work in harmony. Leonardo was a slow, methodical worker, who conducted himself elegantly at all times. In contrast, Michelangelo threw himself into both painting and tantrums with equal intensity. Leonardo's airs and graces infuriated him. Their professional animosity spilled out onto the streets of Florence where these two great men were seen exchanging insults.

One time Michelangelo taunted Leonardo for failing to complete the most famous project he had ever undertaken – an equestrian statue for the Duke of Milan. It is true that Leonardo tended to leave works unfinished. His astonishingly fertile mind, for ever exploring new ground, would jump from one project to another – from sculpture to architecture to invention – often without seeing them through to

completion. But his finished works, such as his portrait, *Mona Lisa*, are among the finest paintings in art history.

### Renaissance men

Like Leonardo, Michelangelo was a true 'Renaissance man', excelling in numerous disciplines, including architecture, poetry, painting and sculpture. But unlike Leonardo, Michelangelo left behind numerous masterpieces, from the huge statue of *David* in Florence to the magnificent ceiling of the Sistine Chapel in the Vatican.

And what happened to the paintings in the Palazzo Vecchio? Michelangelo's never got beyond the initial drawing (or 'cartoon'). Leonardo's was completed – but the technique he used proved a disastrous failure. The colours started to fade almost as soon as the painting was finished and it disappeared long ago.

***Anatomy lesson*** *Both Michelangelo and Leonardo were fascinated by the human body, but in different ways. Leonardo dissected corpses in his pursuit of exact scientific knowledge, producing anatomical drawings famed for their accuracy (left). Michelangelo exaggerated his powerful, muscular figures for artistic effect, as in his painting of the Holy Family (below).*

## THE ART OF DECEPTION

**T**ROMPE L'OEIL (French for 'deceiving the eye') is a type of painting in which the artist uses all his skill to give a perfect illusion of reality – so that an innocent onlooker might actually mistake the painted object for the real thing. Perhaps the greatest example of trompe l'oeil ever painted is the *Camera degli Sposi* (Bridal Chamber) in the ducal palace of Mantua, in northern Italy.

In about 1465, the artist Andrea Mantegna was asked to decorate this square room – each wall about 8 m (26 ft) long – in a tower of the palace. For the next ten years he worked to transform the enclosed bedroom into an illusory open-air pavilion.

Along the walls he painted rails carrying what appear to be blue-and-gold leather curtains. Where these are pulled back, the room seems to look out onto a sunlit terrace and a broad landscape with mountains and citrus trees, peopled with members of the palace household and the ducal family. Overhead, the ceiling was transformed into a dome open to the sky. Women peer down over a balustrade, while winged cherubs gambol around them.

***Bridal chamber*** *Mantegna's painting in the* Camera degli Sposi *in Mantua is a masterpiece of illusion, if not of realism – the Duke of Mantua appears on two panels, to the right and left of the window.*

# THE POISONED PALETTE
### *How some painters suffered for their art*

**P**IERRE AUGUSTE RENOIR became one of the best loved of all artists through his exceptionally vivid use of colour. His canvases vibrate with thrilling reds, yellows and blues that are a feast for the eye. But two Danish scientists, Lisbet Pedersen and Henrik Permin, now believe the same bright pigments that fill Renoir's art with life gradually crippled the artist's body.

All the most brilliant colours on the artist's palette contained poisonous metals – including cadmium, mercury, lead, cobalt and arsenic. Renoir was in the habit of rolling his own cigarettes while working, a sure way to transfer traces of these metals from his paint-stained hands to his mouth and tongue, where they would be absorbed into the body.

As a consequence of this metal poisoning, Renoir developed chronic rheumatoid arthritis. In his old age, his hands became as rigid as claws and he could paint only by having a paintbrush tied to his arm. In the last few years of his life his illness was so severe that he employed a young assistant to execute his work.

According to the Danish scientists, at least three other artists who are famous for their use of bright colours – Peter Paul Rubens, Raoul Dufy and Paul Klee – suffered from rheumatic disease. Further research may uncover many more martyrs to the pursuit of beauty.

***Crippling colours*** *The brightest oil paints on an artist's palette can be rich in poisonous metals - mercury in reds, arsenic and cadmium in yellows, cobalt and manganese in blues and violet.*

# A COVER-UP JOB

*When islands wrapped in pink plastic are a work of art*

WHEN the Bulgarian-born artist Christo Javacheff put the finishing touches to his work of art *Pont Neuf*, in September 1985, he did not use a paintbrush, a palette knife, or a sculptor's chisel. Christo's masterpiece was the famous Parisian bridge. The artist had completely covered it with nearly 41 000 sq m (440 000 sq ft) of sandstone-coloured plastic sheeting. Christo had spent ten years persuading the French government to agree to his scheme – and he had invested US $3 million of his own money raised by the sale of scaled down models of his work.

*Pont Neuf* was neither the first nor the last of Christo's outlandish schemes. He started wrapping on a small scale – wrapping himself, chairs, naked women – but he soon moved on to bigger things.

He has wrapped buildings, cliffs and mountains. In 1982, he even encircled 11 islands off the coast of Miami, Florida, with 1 660 000 sq km (640 000 sq miles) of pink plastic.

Christo has also built some spectacular 'fences'. His *Running Fence*, made in 1979, consisted of 40 km (25 miles) of white nylon ribbon unravelled across part of northern California.

All of Christo's projects are devised so that they can be dismantled without leaving any permanent damage to the environment. He also ensures that the materials used are recycled.

**Thinking big** *Christo supervises the 300 workers constructing his* Running Fence *(right). In 1970, he wrapped the cliffs at Little Bay, north of Sydney, Australia, in 90 000 sq m (1 million sq ft) of polypropylene secured with orange rope (below).*

## DID YOU KNOW..?

*THE LARGEST painting ever to come up for auction is believed to be* Winter Solstice *by the Swedish artist Carl Larsson. It depicts a scene from Scandinavian mythology and measures 6.4 m by 13.5 m (21 ft by 44 ft 6 in). It was sold at Sotheby's in 1987 to a Japanese buyer for £880 000 (over US $1.5 million). Ironically, when Larsson completed the painting, in 1915, it was rejected by the National Museum of Stockholm as unhistorical.*

# ART ON TRIAL

*The bad review that led to a court case*

ON A VISIT to London's Grosvenor Gallery in 1877, John Ruskin, the most influential art critic in Victorian Britain, was infuriated by the impressionistic works of the American-born artist James McNeill Whistler. One painting in particular excited his anger – *The Falling Rocket.* Purporting to represent a firework display at night by the Thames, it consisted simply of a spattering of gold-coloured paint on a dark blue background.

What annoyed Ruskin was the high price being asked for a picture that could have taken only a very short time to paint. To relieve his outraged feelings, he dashed off a blistering review denouncing the artist for having the impudence to 'ask 200 guineas for flinging a pot of paint in the public's face'.

### Willing contestant

Whistler was a flamboyant dandy, a witty aesthete and a friend of Oscar Wilde. Leaping at the chance of public controversy, he sued Ruskin for libel, demanding £1000 (nearly US $5000 at that time) in damages. However,

***Damaging costs*** *The judge awards Whistler (left) a nominal one farthing in damages against the critic Ruskin (right). Whistler was bankrupted by the costs of the court action.*

when the case came to trial in November 1878, Whistler's fellow artists failed to rally to his defence. Instead he had to rely on his own wit to carry the case before a hostile judge and jury who were sceptical of the value of this strange piece of 'modern' art. When Ruskin's counsel accused Whistler of asking 200 guineas (over $1000 – then a considerable sum) for the mere two days' work it took to complete one of his canvases, the artist replied: 'No, I ask it for the knowledge of a lifetime.'

Leading artists of the time attended the trial as witnesses for both sides, including the Pre-Raphaelite painter, Edward Coley Burne-Jones, who supported Ruskin. Although Whistler won his case, Ruskin had the last laugh.

Whistler was awarded only a farthing (1/2 cent) in damages. The considerable legal costs were shared between the two men – £385 ($1975) each – and both opened subscription lists, inviting the public to contribute. Ruskin's list was fully subscribed, so the case cost him nothing. But no one came forward to pay Whistler's costs and, since he had little money himself, the expense of the trial bankrupted him.

---

## PRETTY AS A PICTURE

EVERY SUMMER, make-up artists, costumiers, lighting technicians, set designers and scene painters gather at Laguna Beach in California to perform artistic magic. Their goal is to recreate the works of the Great Masters – using live models.

The Laguna Festival of Arts has been mounting its annual Pageant of the Masters since 1933 and now attracts some 140 000 visitors a year. They flock to witness the incredibly accurate imitation of works as diverse as Leonardo da Vinci's *Last Supper*

or a Japanese print, an Art Deco sculpture or an ancient Etruscan frieze.

Men, women and children pose, suitably costumed, to look exactly like the figures in the original work. Every detail of scenery, make-up, costume and lighting is precisely calculated to create a powerful illusion of two dimensions. It is so successful that many people in the audience find it almost impossible to believe they are looking at a living, breathing spectacle. The Laguna pageant really brings art to life.

***Art lives*** *Actors at the Laguna Festival of Arts here recreate Winslow Homer's* Snap the Whip, *using make-up, a backdrop and special lighting.*

# A ROOM OF ONE'S OWN

## *The American president who designed his house and furniture*

**W**HEN the British ambassador to the United States was presented to Thomas Jefferson, the third American president, he was shocked by his host's casual attire and disregard for some of the niceties of contemporary manners. Jefferson, the principal author of the Declaration of Independence, expressed his belief in equality and informality by installing a circular table in the President's House, later known as the White House, to avoid seating by social rank at his dinner parties.

His interest in furniture and architecture stretched to designing his own home – Monticello in Virginia – inside and out. It contained many examples of his practical innovations. He installed a small shelved elevator called a dumbwaiter to carry wine from the wine cellar to the dining room. He also designed portable serving tables so that guests could help themselves without the dinner conversation being interrupted by servants. For his study, Jefferson designed a revolving chair that enabled him to reach both a desk and reading stand.

**Presidential practicality** *Thomas Jefferson's Monticello home boasts many practical features. The chaise longue, for example, is fitted with candlestick holders on both arms to provide light for reading.*

He commissioned a calendar clock, which marked the days of the week, and even created a four-sided music stand. This enabled up to five musicians to play from the same stand, and folded up into a compact box when not in use. Perhaps the most advanced of all his furnishings, although not his own invention, was the polygraph. This writing device had two quill pens, connected by rods. As Jefferson wrote with one pen, the other moved as well, making a file copy of his letter.

In 1792, Jefferson anonymously submitted a design for the building of the President's House, but it was not accepted. The building would certainly have been less grandiose had the egalitarian Jefferson had his way. He described the presidential residence derisively as 'big enough for two emperors, one pope and the grand lama'.

**Own design** *Under the dome of his home, which overlooks Charlottesville, Virginia, Jefferson designed a ballroom in which he could indulge his great love of music.*

## AN ACROBAT'S PASSION

IN THE LAST years of the 19th century, Albert Schafer – an English acrobat, clown, inventor and composer – took up an unusual hobby: he began to decorate objects with postage stamps.

Schafer started with small objects such as cups and saucers, and quickly moved on to bigger things. A dining table and chairs, a piano, even a fireplace and over-mantel were completely covered in used stamps. These were not applied at random. He carefully chose stamps for their size and colour, deciding, for example, that George V stamps, stuck on sideways, made perfect fish scales for a stuffed pike.

The hobby proved an ideal way for Schafer to occupy himself during a long convalescence from a high-wire accident. He began to create portraits and land-scapes using stamps, sometimes cutting or crumpling them as needed to make the image more convincing. Fellow circus per-formers sent him stamps from all over the world. The collection – an entire room stuffed with objects covered in stamps – became a tourist attraction, and it was exhibited in the 1951 Festival of Britain.

In the early 1980s, some 30 years after Schafer's death, the collection suffered two disasters: while being moved to a new location, many stamps came loose and blew away in the wind. And, a few years later, water from a burst pipe ruined several exhibits. Schafer, however, had even glued stamps underneath and inside his objects, and restorers used these to replace the lost and damaged stamps.

The remarkable stamp room is now housed in the David Howkins Museum in Great Yarmouth, Norfolk. Philatelists may wince when they see the now rare stamps that Schafer used in his hobby, worth a fortune in good condition. Covered with glue and varnish, they are a stamp-collector's nightmare.

# PLAIN GOOD LOOKING
### *Shaker furniture makes a virtue of simplicity*

THE SHAKER religious sect, which flourished in America in the 19th century, is renowned today for the simple beauty of the furniture its com-munities produced. Yet, paradoxically, it was never the Shakers' intention to make beautiful objects – one of their leaders, Elder Frederick Evans, once declared: 'The beautiful is absurd and abnormal.' Their faith forbade 'fancy objects' of any kind, and all their designs, whether for chairs, tables or clocks, were meant to be plain, durable and strictly functional.

Originating in England as an offshoot of the Quakers, the first Shaker colony in America was founded in the 1770s by Mother Ann Lee, who was believed by her followers to embody the second appearance on Earth of the spirit of Christ. At its peak in around 1845, the movement comprised some 4000 be-lievers living in isolated communities scattered from Maine to Kentucky.

### *Sense of purpose*
The Shakers believed very strongly that their mission was to establish the king-dom of God on Earth and that every-thing therefore had to be perfect. Every detail of their lives was regulated by these beliefs – from which shoe to put on first in the morning (the right one) to the material to be used for doorknobs (wood, not brass). Cleanliness and effi-ciency were highly valued. The Shakers'

scrupulously tidy homes had rows of pegs high on the walls so that chairs could be hung up by their slatted backs when the floors were regularly swept.

The simple, unadorned look of Shaker furniture, which their principles dictat-ed, was offensive to the public taste of their own period, which valued elabo-rate decorative detail. The 19th-century writer Nathaniel Hawthorne, for exam-ple, found their furniture 'a pain and constraint to look at'.

Ironically, in the late 20th century, when only a dozen believers still follow the Shaker life, Shaker furniture has become the height of fashion, selling for thousands of dollars a piece at antique auctions. To the modern eye, every chair the Shakers made exhibits a remarkable grace and harmony, as if created by someone, in the words of the great American monastic writer Thomas Merton, 'capable of believing that an angel might come and sit on it'.

*Pure living* Order, simplicity and cleanliness are the charms of a typical Shaker room. The solid craftsmanship of Shaker furniture-making was a direct expression of their strict religious principles.

# WHAT'S IN A NAME?
## *Thomas Sheraton and 'Sheraton' furniture*

NEXT TO Chippendale, Sheraton is probably the most famous name in late 18th-century English furniture, and many 'Sheraton' pieces are for sale at high prices in the world's antique emporiums today. Yet not a single piece of furniture made by Thomas Sheraton himself has ever been discovered. Indeed, there is no evidence that he ever had a workshop of his own.

Sheraton's enormous influence on English furniture derived from his many design books, but especially from *The Cabinet-Maker and Upholsterer's Drawing-Book*, published between 1791 and 1794. In it he drew together numerous furniture designs in what he called 'the newest and most elegant style'. No one knows how many of these were his own ideas, but they certainly set the design trend for the period.

### *Useful and elegant*

Sheraton's hallmarks were a fragile elegance – elaborate inlaid decoration and slender tapering legs – and adaptability, with many of his designs called upon to serve more than one purpose. At a time when a rapid increase in population led to a shortage of living space – particularly in the cities – affecting rich and poor alike, there was a ready market for tables that converted into library steps or doubled up as writing desks, cleverly revealing hidden shelves, drawers and pigeonholes at the turn of a key.

Some of Sheraton's designs were considered over-refined and effeminate by his contemporaries, however, and few existing pieces of furniture follow his designs exactly. The label 'Sheraton' in an antique auction merely designates an approximate style and period. Sheraton himself died in poverty in 1806 and would no doubt have been astonished by his posthumous fame.

**Ingenious space saver**
*This 18th-century 'Sheraton' lady's writing table is elegant yet practical.*

## THE LANGUAGE OF MAGIC CARPETS

THERE IS OFTEN a secret language in the strange and exotic patterns of Oriental carpets. The designs of Chinese rugs are particularly rich in meaning. Many of them derive from Chinese homonyms – words which sound alike but are written differently. For example, the Chinese word for bat (*fu*) sounds identical to the word for happiness. So a stylised bat is often depicted on carpets to represent happiness. Some numbers are traditionally thought to be lucky, as are some colours. Thus five red bats on a carpet indicate the five forms of supreme happiness: health, wealth, longevity, a natural death and a love of virtue.

Sometimes symbols are combined to convey a special message to the rug's owner. A deer (symbol of prosperity) and a stork (symbol of longevity) might be interwoven to express the wish for a long and prosperous life. Dragons, which often feature in Chinese rug designs, also have a specific meaning: the number of their claws indicates the owner's social rank.

Many of the designs in Persian carpets are drawn from the Muslim religion. Prayer rugs feature the mihrab, or prayer arch, often with a sacred lamp as well. Two trees intertwined symbolise marriage – and if one of the trees has a branch lopped off, it is the second marriage for one of the partners. Cypresses in the corners of a carpet, symbols of renewal and eternal life, denote that it was woven to cover a coffin on the day of a funeral.

Nowadays, however, many of the traditional meanings of designs have been lost. Modern weavers often use age-old symbols for purely decorative effect, ignoring their hidden language.

**Prestigious claws** *A dragon's five claws on a Chinese rug traditionally show that it was designed exclusively for an emperor. Junior royalty were entitled to four-clawed dragons, while commoners had to be satisfied with three.*

# THE ROOM THAT VANISHED

*The priceless amber panels that passed between a king, a tsar and a dictator*

THE MAGNIFICENT Amber Room in the Summer Palace outside St Petersburg was one of the jewels in the crown of tsarist Russia. A British ambassador once described it as 'the eighth wonder of the world'. Twelve tonnes of rare amber went into the priceless panels that clothed its walls.

## DID YOU KNOW..?

*THE SMALL elongated cross that appears in the designs of many Oriental rugs is meant to represent a tarantula. For the Turkoman carpet makers in central Asia, the image of the venomous spider was a lucky charm. It was believed that if you stepped on the woven tarantula you were less likely to tread on a real one.*

Incredibly, this decorative marvel disappeared in the chaos of war in 1945 – and has never been found.

The Amber Room was originally commissioned by Frederick William I, King of Prussia, for his palace at Königsberg in 1701. In 1716, the king presented this extraordinary chamber to Peter the Great of Russia as a gift to seal a military alliance between the two powers, and it was moved to the Winter Palace before being transferred to the Summer Palace by Peter's daughter Elizabeth in 1755.

The room survived the upheaval of the Russian Revolution undamaged, but when the invading Nazi forces captured the Summer Palace during the Second World War, the room was transported back to Königsberg and reassembled there, apparently on the direct orders of

*Resurrected splendours A team of skilled amber carvers are attempting to recreate the glories of the Amber Room, working from photographs, drawings and water colours.*

Adolf Hitler. By the time Germany was overrun by the Allies in 1945, however, it had vanished.

The Soviet authorities, determined to reclaim their national treasure, have been looking for the room ever since. So have a number of bounty hunters and art historians. At different times, clues have led investigators to a castle in Saxony, a Polish salt mine and a Baltic shipwreck. Even the US 9th Army has been suspected of the theft. But in every case, the trail has gone cold. Now craftsmen in the former Soviet Union have embarked on the heroic task of reconstructing the room exactly as it was.

# INDEX

374

# ACKNOWLEDGEMENTS

DORLING KINDERSLEY would like to thank the following illustrators: **Andrew Aloof, Stephen Conlin, Luciano Corbella, Andy Farmer, Giuliano Fornari,Will Giles, Nicholas Hall, Mark Iley, Janos Marfy, Richard Orr, Sandra Pond, Steve Spinks, Mark Thomas, Stephen Thomas.**

DORLING KINDERSLEY would like to thank the following writers: **Diana Barker, Nicholas Best, Stephen Butt, Sue Dyson, Maurice Geller, Adrian Gilbert, Bill Gunston, Paul Hallam, Tony Hare, Hildi Hawkins, Rosanna Hibbert, Charles Hills, Stephen Hoare, Dan Lees, Geoffrey Macnab, Margaret McGowan, Shelagh Meyer, Norman Miller, Paul Murphy, Steve Parker, Chris Riley, Nigel Rodgers, Andi Spicer, Elizabeth Thornton, Deborah Trenerry, Anne Wilkinson, Neil Wenborn, Carola Zentner.**

DORLING KINDERSLEY would like to thank the following researchers: **Colleen Baldwin, Nicholas Booth, Andrew Duncan, Ellen Dupont, Julie Gottlieb, Martin Greenwood, Jen Harvey, Fiona Keating, Celie Parker, Sarah Roseblade, Catherine Treasure, Julie Whitaker, Patricia Wright, Ariana Yakas.**

DORLING KINDERSLEY would also like to thank **Simon Adams, Joanna Chisholm**, and **Uma Ram Nath** for their editorial assistance; **Amanda Lunn, Kevin Ryan** and **Frances de Rees** for their help with the design of the book; **Peter Cooling** for his assistance with the typesetting and **Kate Grant** for her help with the manuscript. The index was compiled by **Hilary Bird**.

PHOTO CREDITS Abbreviations: l = left; r = right; t = top; b = bottom; AAA = Ancient Art and Architecture Collection; BAL = Bridgeman Art Library; BC = Bruce Coleman Ltd.; BL = British Library; BPK = Bildarchiv Preussischer Kulturbesitz; FSP = Frank Spooner Pictures; HD = Hulton-Deutsch; HL = The Hutchison Library; KC = The Kobal Collection; MC = The Mansell Collection; MEPL = Mary Evans Picture Library; NHPA = Natural History Photographic Agency; OSF = Oxford Scientific Films; P = Popperfoto; PEP = Planet Earth Pictures; PNP = Peter Newark's Pictures; RHPL = Robert Harding Picture Library; SPL = Science Photo Library; Z = Zefa.

**Cover** (t row, l to r) HD; Z/H. Sochurek; HD/Bettmann Archive; Z/Dick Hanley; (b row, l to r) P; BC/O. Langrand; MEPL **2** PEP/Herwarth Voigtmann; **10**(t) MEPL, (b) Jean-Loup Charmet; **11** Victoria and Albert Museum; **12** P; **14** MEPL; **15**(t) The Image Bank/Eddie Hironaka, (b) BC/Alfred Pasieka; **16**(t) BC/O. Langrand, (b) SPL/Dr. Tony Brain, David Parker; **18**(t) SPL/David Parker, (b) BC/Dr. Frieder Sauer; **19** Bodleian Library, MS Douce 72 f.15v; **20**(t) BC/Hans Reinhard; **21**(t) NHPA/Haroldo Palo, (b) FSP/Gamma; **22**(l) Frank Lane Picture Agency; **24** Ann Ronan Picture Library; **25**(t) Z/A. and J. Verkaik; **28**(t) Spectrum Colour Library; **28**(b) Camera Press/Cecil Beaton; **29** NHPA/Ivan Polunin; **30**(b) AAA; **31** J-L Charmet; **33**(l) BC/Michael Freeman, (r) Science Museum; **34** SPL/David Parker; **35**(t) SPL/NASA, (b) SPL/Adam Hart-Davis; **36**(r) SPL/Doug Allen; **37**(b) SPL/Dr. Gary Settles; **38** OSF/Stephen Dalton; **39**(b) The Image Bank/Pete Turner; **40** SPL/Cern, P. Loiez; **42** FSP/Gamma; **44** FSP/Gamma; **45** SPL/NASA; **46** FSP/Gamma; **47** SPL/U. S. Geological Survey; **48** SPL/Ronald Royer; **49** SPL/NASA; **51**(b) SPL/NASA; **56** MEPL; **57**(t) SPL/Ronald Royer, (b) David Hardy; **58** SPL/Dr. J. Bloemen; **59**(t) SPL/NOAO, (b) Ian Robson, Phil Appleton; **60** Prof. Lars Hernquist; **61**(t) SPL/NOAD, (b) SPL/David Parker; **62** Telegraph Colour Library; **64**(t) Tony Stone Picture Library/Don and Pat Valenti, (b) RHPL/Geoff Renner; **65** SPL/Stephen Krasemann; **66**(t) RHPL/Photri, (b) BC/M. P. Price; **67** Tony Stone Picture Library; **68**(l) SPL/Simon Fraser; **69** BC/Bob and Clara Calhoun; **71** Spectrum Colour Library; **72** MC; **73**(t) SPL/NASA, (b) SPL/Dr. Ken Macdonald; **74** Heather Angel; **75**(t) PEP/Peter Scoones, (b) BC/Keith Gunnar; **76**(t) RHPL/Ian Griffiths; **77** SPL/Dr. Jeremy Burgess; **81** BC/C. B. Frith; **82**(t) BC/O. Langrand, (b) BC/Anthony Healy; **83**(t) BC/Jane Burton, (b) Heather Angel; **84**(t) P, (b) Jeff Foott; **85** Richard Revels; **86**(t) OSF/Nick Woods, (b) OSF/David Thompson; **87** Heather Angel; **88** NHPA/John Shaw; **89**(t) BC/Kim Taylor, (b) OSF/Donald Specker; **90** BC/Gerald Cubitt; **91**(t) BC/Michel Viard, (b) OSF/Deni Brown; **94**(r) FSP/Gamma; **96**(t) Martin Lockley, (b) FSP/Gamma; **98**(t) OSF/David Macdonald; **101**(t) NHPA/ANT, (b) BC/Des Bartlett; **102**(t) Heather Angel; **103** MEPL; **104**(t) OSF/Ronald Toms; **105**(b) Heather Angel; **108**(t) BC/Brian Coates, (b) BC/Frances Furlong; **110**(t) BC/Gerald Cubitt; **111**(t) BC/John Visser, (b) PEP/Herwarth Voigtmann; **112**(t) BC/Peter Davey, (b) BC/Alan Root; **113**(t) NHPA/K. H. Switak, (b) OSF/G. Bernard; **114**(t) NHPA/Stephen Dalton, (b) NHPA/Haroldo Palo; **115**(t) BC/Jeff Foott, (b) BC/Jen and Des Bartlett; **117** PEP/Chris Prior; **118** PEP/Herwarth Voigtmann; **120**(t) Professors Beatrix and Allen Gardner; **121** BC/Konrad Wothe; **125** NHPA/Stephen Dalton; **126** PEP/Herwarth Voigtmann; **127** BC/Jen and Des Bartlett; **129**(t) NHPA/ANT, (b) BC/Hans Reinhard; **130** BC/Masood Qureshi; **133** Spectrum Colour Library; **134** Marc Henrie; **136** BC/David Hughes; **138**(t) SPL/Dr. Tony Brain, (b) SPL/Dr. Jeremy Burgess; **139**(b) J-L Charmet; **140** HD; **142** MEPL; **143** MEPL; **144** BC/Gary Retherford; **145**(b) SPL/Argentum; **149** MEPL; **150**(t) Z/H. Sochurek, (b) SPL/Astrid and Hans Frieder Michler; **152** KC; **153**(l) Stephen Hyde, (r) P; **154**(t) SPL/CNRI, (b) SPL/Eric Grave; **155**(t) The Image Bank/Robin Forbes, (b) MEPL; **157**(t) Z/Teasy, (b) Z/H. Sochurek; **158**(t) SPL/CEA-ORSAY, CNRI, (b) Ann Ronan Picture Library; **159**(t) FSP/Gamma, (b) SPL/Alexander Tsiaras; **160** MEPL; **164** SPL/Alexander Tsiaras; **166** The Image Bank/Pete Turner; **167** HD; **169** HL/Andre Singer; **170** Rotherham Borough Council; **171** J-L Charmet; **172** Topham Picture Source; **174** BAL; **175**(l) Lowie Museum of Anthropology, University of California at Berkeley, (r) P; **177** KC; **180**(b) Michael Holford; **181** FSP/Hutt; **182**(t) MEPL; **183**(t) MEPL, (r) E. T. Archive; **184** BL; **185**(t) MEPL, (b) J-L Charmet; **186** HD; **187**(t) FSP/Gamma, (b) KC; **188** HL/A. Tully; **189**(t) PNP, (b) HL/Christine Pemserton; **190**(t) BC/Frans Lanting; **192**(t) RHPL/Ian Griffiths; **194**(t) MEPL, (b) HD/Bettmann Archive; **197** Iowa State University Photo Service; **199**(t) PNP, (c) HD, (b) MEPL; **200** Musee d'Art et d'Histoire, Neuchatel, Switzerland; **201** Rex Features/SIPA; **202**(t) SPL/Labat, Lanceau, Jerrican, (b) TRH Pictures/U. S. Army; **203**(t) Photri; **206** MEPL; **208** Aixam Automobiles; **211**(t) SPL/David Parker, (b) Michael Holford; **212** FSP/Gamma; **214**(t) SPL/Hank Morgan, (b) SPL/Philippe Plailly; **218** Z/Paolo Koch; **219**(t) Sonia Halliday, (b) BAL; **220** American School of Classical Studies at Athens; **221** BPK; **224** Japan Information Centre, London; **225**(t) Reuters/Bettmann Newsphotos, (b) Z/R. Halin; **226** P; **227**(b) Z/D. Cattani; **228** MEPL; **229** Courtesy Frank Lloyd Wright Archives; **230** South American Pictures; **233**(t) E. T. Archive, (b) Z; **234** Polish Cultural Institute; **235** Photoresources; **236** Fortean Picture Library; **237**(t) Scala, (r) Photographie Giraudon; **238** Werner Forman Archive; **239** BC/Nadine Zuber; **240** Dominique Darbois; **241** Musee de Grand Orient de France/J-L Charmet; **242** Fine Art Photographic Library Ltd.; **244** MEPL; **245** HL/J. G. Fuller; **246** MEPL; **247**(t) J-L Charmet, (b) RHPL/F. Jackson; **249** P; **251** Peter Newark's Pictures; **252** FSP/Gamma; **253** Department of the Environment; **254**(t) MC; **255**(t) MEPL; **257** John Robert Young; **258**(t) Photographie Giraudon, (b) MC; **259** MEPL; **260** MC; **261**(t) Sheffield City Art Galleries, (b) PNP; **262** MEPL; **263** Michael Holford; **264** (tl, tr) Michael Freeman, (b) HL; **265** BC/Brian Coates; **266** Bryan and Cherry Alexander; **267** J-L Charmet; **268** Z; **270**(l) HL/David Simpson, (r) Photosources, (b) P; **271** MC; **272** Intercol London: Yasha Beresiner/Derrick Witty; **274**(t) The Mariners' Museum, Newport News, Virginia, (b) P; **275** Walker Art Gallery; **276** Walker Wingsail Systems; **277**(b) PNP, (b) Fotoarchief Drents Museum, Assen; **278**(t) Ben Line Group, (b) P; **279** Trireme Trust/Paul Lipke; **280** BL; **283** BL; **284** BL; **285**(t) HL/Christina Dedwell, (b) Somerset Levels Project; **286** Z/Jan Oud; **287**(t) Fortean Picture Library, (b) Spectrum Colour Library; **288** Scala; **289**(t) MEPL, (b) PNP; **290**(t) BAL, (b) PNP; **291** PNP; **292**(t) Z, (b) BC/Jaroslav Poncar; **293**(t) Axel Poignant Archive; **294** PNP; **295** PNP; **296** National Maritime Museum; **297** Bodleian Library; **298** MEPL; **299** MC; **301**(t) MEPL, (b) MC; **302** Z/Hugh Ballantyne; **303** FSP; **304** Z; **305** MEPL; **306** Z; **307** BAL; **310** MEPL; **311** Operation Raleigh; **312** PNP; **313**(t) Associated Press, (b) Frank Lane Picture Agency/K. Ghani; **314**(t) MEPL; **315** FSP; **317** MEPL; **318**(b) Don Emmick; **319** FSP; **320** FSP/Gamma; **321**(t) Camera Press, (b) Z/Dick Hanley; **322** FSP/Gamma; **323** National Motor Museum, Beaulieu/Nick Wright; **324** Rolls-Royce Motor Cars; **325** P; **326**(t) Vauxhall Motors, Luton, (b) General Motors Corporation; **327** TRH Pictures; **330**(t) MEPL, (b) Reg Wilson; **331** MEPL; **332**(l) KC, (r) MEPL; **333** International Shakespeare Globe Centre; **334**(t) The Image Bank/George Obremski, (b) Japan Information Centre, London; **335** Sir Peter Saunders; **336–340** KC; **342** MEPL; **343**(t) All-Sport/Tony Duffy, (b) P; **344**(t) National Baseball Hall of Fame and Museum, (b) BPK; **345** FSP/Gamma; **346**(t) Z, (b) MEPL; **347** MEPL; **348** HD/Bettmann Archive; **349**(t) Simon Fraser University, (b) All-Sport; **350** Photri; **351** MC; **353** MEPL; **355** BAL; **356** The Bowes Museum; **357**(t) Pack Memorial Library, (b) National Portrait Gallery, London; **358** Camera Press; **359** MC; **360**(t) BAL, (b) MEPL; **361** Irish Tourist Board, Dublin; **364**(t) Photoresources, (b) AAA; **365**(l) Photographie Giraudon, (r) MEPL; **366**(l) By Gracious Permission of Her Majesty the Queen, Royal Library, Windsor, (r) Scala; **367**(t) Scala, (b) Service Photographique de la Reunion des Musees Nationaux; **368**(t) FSP/Gamma, (b) Camera Press/Roger Whitaker; **369**(t) MEPL, (b) Laguna Beach Festival of Arts; **370**(t) BAL, (b) HL/Dr. Nigel Smith; **371** American Museum in Britain, Bath; **372** (t) BAL; **373** FSP/Gamma.